THE SOCIOLOGY
OF ECONOMIC
DEVELOPMENT

THE SOCIOLOGY OF ECONOMIC DEVELOPMENT

A READER

Gayl D. Ness
UNIVERSITY OF MICHIGAN

HARPER & ROW, PUBLISHERS
New York, Evanston, and London

THE SOCIOLOGY OF ECONOMIC DEVELOPMENT: A READER
Copyright © 1970 by *Gayl D. Ness*

LIBRARY OF CONGRESS CATALOG CARD NUMBER: 70–103919

CONTENTS

Part II ECONOMIC DEVELOPMENT IN THE MID-TWENTIETH
CENTURY: DEVELOPMENT IN BACKWARD ECONOMIES

PREFACE

Modern economic growth poses important challenges and opportunities for sociological analysis At least three sets of reasons can be described for attempting to meet some of the challenges and identify some of the opportunities. These will be dealt with in greater detail in introductory essays to the various sections, but a brief summary of the argument is useful here.

In the first place, the process of economic development represents a major transformation in social life. Whether development is seen as cause, effect, or simple correlate of change in social organization, it is obviously a change that takes place in aspects of human life that go beyond what we more narrowly define as the economic sector. It is useful, therefore, for the sociologist to turn his analytical perspective to this change. We can profit by raising questions of the relationship between changes in human productivity and changes in social institutions, those larger patterns of human relationships that give some appearance of stability and are to some degree infused with value.

Second, economic development represents a process of change marked by a single underlying quantitative dimension. As we shall point out later, development is operationally defined as an increase in human productivity. This means it is a pattern of social change in which we can identify direction and speed. In this area, almost exclusively, we can speak of progressive change, from lower to higher levels, and we can measure, however imprecisely, the rate of this change. In the social sciences this condition is unique and thus highly important. Using a measure of human productivity we can easily speak of backwardness, progress, growth, advance, stagnation, and retardation.[1] One need only observe the difficulties and arguments raised in the attempt to speak of social, cultural, or political development to recognize the importance of the underlying quantitative nature of economic change. It is not accidental that one of the early journals focusing attention on the non-economic aspects of economic progress was named *Economic Development and Cultural Change*. Sociology, political science, and anthropology are much more conservative in their use of any term that implies progressive change. The recent attempts of political scientists to conceptualize a process of progressive change, and to speak of political development only dramatize the difficulties. Without adequate quantitative measures of behavior patterns that are theoretically meaningful, the conceptualization is at best insightful and suggestive but not testable, or at worst a presumptuous identification of speculation with theory-building.

This is not to argue that only that which is measurable is worthy of study. This argument must be rejected along with its opposite, the only things that are measurable are trivial. It is more rational and useful to adopt a course between these extremes and to recognize that many aspects of human life are worthy of study, whether they are precisely measurable or not. But it is also central to the scientific process to move as much as possible in the direction of systematic, and precise measurement. And this should apply to the study of social change as much as to any other subject.

In economic development we have the advantage of working with a major social change and some rather solid empirical evidence (potential if not always actual) on the rate and direction of change. Much of this advantage derives from the recent development of national income accounting, which provides aggregate measures of human productivity. Whatever its deficiencies, the national income account has the advantage of providing standard units for the unidimensional measurement of a highly diverse set of behaviors. And there is great utility for the student of social change in using these measures to bring greater rigor to his own analysis.

Finally, the study of economic development provides a fruitful arena in which to develop a dialogue between the various social science disciplines. Although the earlier emergence of distinct disciplines has been useful in developing specialized concepts and methods of analysis, it is clear that the proper analysis of such a pervasive change in human organization as economic development requires the concerted analysis of a number of disciplines. This is not to argue that economic development is too important a

---

[1] We can, of course, measure the size and rate of growth in populations, and we can therefore speak of the growth, stagnation or decline in population just as we can in human productivity. This also gives to demography a somewhat greater theoretical and methodological sophistication than we find in sociology in general. At the same time it is quite obvious that for the concerns of this volume the size of a population says less about that population than does the measure of its level of productivity.

subject to be left to the economists, but rather to say that the proper study of change in the organization of human life is the organization of human life itself. We shall do better to see this organization as a many-faceted thing whose full understanding will be advanced by the interchange of the various disciplines competent to analyze the various facets.

The plan of this set of readings, and the selection of the individual pieces represents a specific orientation, or bias, which should be exposed as completely as possible.

In Part I we deal with issues of a general and conceptual nature, which can apply quite broadly to the study of sociology of economic development in many places and in many epochs. We begin with the problem of measurement of human productivity and the correlates in social organization. Next we turn to a selection of theories that have attempted to deal with the social organizational determinants of capital formation, which in one way or another is conceived as a crucial mechanism in increasing human productivity. We then turn to a consideration of population, the denominator in our measure of economic development.

The issues raised in Part I would be as relevant to the study of economic development in the Western world in the nineteenth century as they are to the study of the non-Western world in the mid-twentieth century. But in Part II we turn our attention to a set of issues that appear more critical today than they were when the West embarked on modern economic development two centuries ago. We make the introductory argument that the current process of economic development especially in the new states of the twentieth century is in some critical aspects different from the patterns of growth in the nineteenth century. The important difference arises from the fact of the colonial experience, which produced rather well-developed bureaucratic structures for government and also produced unbalanced economies with highly developed sectors, largely for export products, and relatively backward and untouched indigenous sectors. Further, independence in the new states was accompanied by political nationalist movements with specific economic orientations. All of this implies that the specific character and orientation of the political and bureaucratic structures is a major determinant of the patterns of economic development we currently witness in the new states. This leads us to deal with the broad issue of the political forces that affect the formation of public policies relevant to economic development. Central to the political issues in backward economies is the conflicting demands of discipline and flexibility in public policy. In the first section we turn attention more specifically to the issue of implementing development policies, the bureaucratic aspects of economic development.

The focus of the second part precludes consideration of a series of issues that have often been central to the study of the sociology of economic development. We have not treated the impact of family structure, community, or religion on economic development. These are, to be sure, important concerns, but in the context of the argument developed in Part II, they emerge as less important than the political and bureaucratic variables upon which we focus attention.

This attempt to put together a set of readings relevant to the sociology of economic development owes its genesis to two different, but equally humiliating experiences. The first was my own field research in Southeast Asia, which forced me to come to grips with the recalcitrant facts of modern attempts by new states to deal with the many-faceted problems of organizing a new nation and producing some significant economic change. That these often did not fit neatly into the intellectual molds that I carried to the region, and whose mastering had earned me the exalted title of Doctor of Philosophy, was indeed humiliating. I came away from that experience with a greater respect for the complexity of the underdeveloped world and a greater skepticism for the more or less simple solutions and analyses that had been a part of my earlier intellectual baggage. The second experience has been provided by a number of students at the University of Michigan who did me the great service of constantly pointing out to me how much I did not know, even about those things I had studied for so long. I hope that the pain of these humiliating experiences has been of some benefit and that its impact may be seen in some small way in this collection.

Gayl D. Ness

Part I
GENERAL CONCEPTUAL AND METHODOLOGICAL ISSUES

Section 1
THE MEASUREMENT
AND SOCIAL MEANING
OF ECONOMIC
DEVELOPMENT

Introduction: *Aggregate Measures and Social Organization*

Economic development is defined as a long term, sustained increase in real output per capita.[1] This is essentially a carefully operationalized definition of the more general concept human productivity. For a given group of people we must see an increase in the real output of their labor. The increase must be sustained over a considerable period, measured in decades or generations rather than in single years.

The measurement of human productivity relies almost exclusively on national income accounting; the most common measure is Gross National Product per Capita. The technique itself as well as its advantages and weaknesses is the subject of an extensive literature,[2] but we might call attention to three implications of this technique here. In the first place we are dealing with aggregate measures, which tell us very little about the range and distribution of the various output measures that make up the aggregate. It is, therefore, useful to keep in mind the fact that low levels of human productivity can still encompass sectors of

---

[1] Simon Kuznets, *Six Lectures on Economic Growth*, Glencoe, 1959, p. 3. Or also see his more recent and more detailed, *Modern Economic Growth* (New Haven, 1966).

[2] See for example, Paul Studenski, *The Income of Nations* (New York, 1958), *passim*, for an extensive historical, methodological and empirical treatment of national income accounting. On the weaknesses see especially Oskar Morgenstern, *On the Accuracy of Economic Measurement*, (Princeton, 1963) *passim*.

very high productivity; and that high levels of human productivity can encompass sectors of very low productivity.

Second, we must recognize that the national income account is an accounting *attempt* to measure the value of all the goods and services produced in an economy in a given period. Value, of course, is defined normally as market value. This introduces a wellknown commercial bias into the account, producing a tendency to understate the level of human productivity of the more subsistence, less commercialized economies. There are attempts to correct for this bias by imputing value to subsistence production,[3] but there is also counterargument that the types of price weights used in accounting may actually understate the level of human productivity in the more commercialized economies and overstate it in the less commercialized economies.[4] The resolution of this set of issues has not come through rigorous attempts to estimate biases. Rather it is generally conceded that although the intervals and absolute levels may not be meaningful, we do obtain an accurate measure of relative ranking of various observations from the measurement of output per capita.

Finally, we can relate the issue of the proper period of analysis to an important measurement weakness. Morgenstern has pointed out that the most accurate and reliable national income data are those for the United States, and even here much of the data must necessarily come from estimates that can produce considerable error.[5] The range of error for U.S. data might be as low as ±5%, but it might also be as high as ±20%.[6] Morgenstern has also shown in a simple but penetrating calculation the impact of the period of analysis on the magnitude of error in rates of change, for given error ranges at the terminal points. We can show this in a simple table constructed from Morgenstern's data.

If we assume that the true growth rate is 1.8% annually, and we assume the very modest level of 5% error in estimating total or per capita output, over a one year period the apparent rate is 8.7 percentage points greater than the true rate. The difference declines remarkably to

---

[3] For one example see Charles Kindleberger, *Economic Development* (New York, 1958), pp. 2–3.

[4] Kuznets, *Six Lectures on Economic Growth, op. cit.*, pp. 17–18.

[5] It should also be remembered that national income accounting is only an *attempt* to measure the value of output. It requires extensive estimation and is subject to considerable error, often of unknown magnitude and direction. For example, of the 122 countries on which Russett *et al.* provide data on Gross National Product only 11 are in the category with probable margins of error of ±5%, another 11 have probable margins of error of ±10%; 71 have margins of error of ±20%; and for 29 countries "the error of margin should be under ±50%, but it is impossible to say how much under." B. M. Russett *et al.*, *World Handbook of Political and Social Indicators* (New Haven, 1964), p. 199.

[6] Morgenstern, *op. cit.*, p. 255, n. 15.

*Table 1.   The Influence of the Length of the Period of
Measurement on the Apparent Compound Growth Rate*

Assumed error at terminal points		Period of measurements	Growth rate (compound)	
			assumed true	apparent
t_1	t_2			
—5%	+5%	1 year	1.8%	10.5%[a]
—5%	+5%	5 years	1.8%	3.9%
—5%	+5%	10 years	1.8%	2.8%

Source: Oskar Morgenstern, *On the Accuracy of Economic Measurement*, second edition (Princeton, 1963), pp. 290, 292.

[a] Estimated from the chart provided in figure 11, p. 292.

2.1 points for five years and 1.0 points for measurement over a ten-year period.

Morgenstern also makes an extremely important and often neglected point on the question of accuracy. Since growth rates are based on accounting techniques that use extensive estimating procedures and are subject to wide and unknown margins of error, they must be used with considerable caution. He probably does not overstate the case by arguing that "they are worthless *in view of the exacting uses to which they are being put.*"[7] The emphasis is important. Output figures and growth rates can give us some notion of relative magnitudes, but cannot be used as precise indicators of differences.

This should clearly demonstrate that we must witness rather dramatic increases in human productivity over relatively long periods—decades or generations rather than years—to be sure that we are witnessing real changes in the organization of productive life and not simply errors of estimates or fluctuations caused by such exogenous forces as droughts, floods, or good rains.

We have, of course, witnessed such long-term increases in human productivity over roughly the past two centuries in the limited number of countries that we now call industrialized.[8] For those countries that have experienced this process of modern economic development, two common and distinctive features are easily identified. In the first place, the development was also accompanied by a period of rapid population growth, an issue to which we shall return in Section 3 of Part I. Second, this increase in both population and productivity was associated with

---

[7] Morgenstern, *op. cit.*, p. 300.

[8] We can also probably identify such long term changes in the more distant past. Although we can be less certain about the rates of change, we can often distinguish major social changes that were associated with changes in productivity. We shall not, however, attempt to deal with this more distant historical experience here.

vast changes in the organization of human life. Where people lived, how they lived, where and how they worked, and with whom they interacted all underwent vast changes in the process of modern economic development.

The observation of this change in human organization is essentially at the origins of sociology itself as a distinct intellectual discipline. There is, in fact, a striking similarity in the concepts emerging from a wide range of students of society, which reflects their common attention to and perception of the vast social changes associated with economic development. We can translate Durkheim's *mechanical* and *organic* bases of social solidarity, Toennies' *Gemeinschaft* and *Geselleschaft* characteristics of human communities, Weber's *traditional* and *legal-rational* bases of legitimate authority and even Parson's patterned variables into the dichotomy marked by modern economic development. These are explicitly developed in the following article by Hoselitz with the argument that economic development in some sense *requires* the social transformations that have historically accompanied the process of economic development in the West. All of these observers are talking about some aspect of the new way of life as contrasted with an aspect of the old way of life.

The terms *traditional* and *modern* have become attached to this social dichotomy.[9] The attachment is naturally not without its detractors, who rightly point out that there were often very modern features of ancient forms of organization (Mogul administration is a good example), and there are often traditional elements in modern organization (as indeed are most constitutional monarchs). Although we might prefer a more neutral or a more accurate set of terms, the traditional-modern set appears too well entrenched to move without more effort than may be beneficial at this time. It is useful, however, to try to be somewhat more precise about the characteristics of the social organization we find on both sides of this dichotomy.

By traditional we normally mean that most people in a given population are organized into relatively small and isolated groups in rural areas; they consume most of what they produce and produce most of what they consume in essentially subsistence economies; their work is largely agricultural with a related set of activities essentially derived from their agricultural production; they are connected with one another as specific persons with a highly diffuse set of obligations and claims upon one another; and by and large they experience a low level of welfare, marked by high morbidity and mortality. By modern, on the

---

[9] See the *Journal of Social Issues*, Vol. IV, No. 4 (October, 1968), for a series of articles under the editorship of Joseph Gusfield treating *Tradition and Modernity: Conflict and Convergence*.

other hand, we mean something like the opposite of each of the above. Most people in a given population are organized in larger collectivities with a great deal of literate communication and interaction with a large and ever growing community, and they live more in urban areas than in rural areas; they sell most of what they produce and buy most of what they consume in highly complex and extensively commercialized economies; they work in factories with machines, and in a wide range of highly specified services; they are related with one another largely on the basis of limited interchanges in which obligations and claims are tied to specific performances or roles rather than to specific persons; and by and large they have high levels of welfare, marked by low morbidity and mortality.

The terms traditional and modern give us a useful shorthand way of expressing this variety of characteristics and changes, but we should not lose sight of the fact that the change from traditional to modern is a many-faceted change. As we have laid out the characteristics above (and one could expand on them at some length), we have a set of variables. Though more complex, this set is more powerful analytically than the simple dichotomy, for it allows us to raise the question of the amount of change required in any variable to produce changes in human productivity. Or we can ask how specific changes in any of these variables affect either the rate or the direction of economic change.

The following articles by Hauser and Patel provide measures of some of these social changes associated with economic development. Hauser draws attention to the demographic changes associated with development. Patel illustrates the close association of industrialization with economic development, and exposes some important long-term variations in the rate and character of industrialization as well.

We can also see some of these changes in Table 2. Here we present a set of correlation coefficients, showing the extent to which a wide variety of variables is associated with Gross National Product per Capita, our single measure of economic development. Since this table provides an excellent example of both the advantages and problems of analysing social change and economic development, it will be useful to consider it at greater length. For convenience, the variables have been arranged in descending order of their correlation with Gross National Product per Capita, without regard to the direction of the association.

In the first place we should note that these data were collected for a large number of countries (for as many as 122 depending on the variable in question) at approximately one point in time, about the mid–1950s. That is, these are cross-sectional data. Ideally, we should use historical or time series data for the study of social change and economic development, because we are really interested in how a given

*Table 2.   Pearsonian Correlation Coefficients between GNP
per capita (1957 US$) and Given Variables*

I High (±0.70 or higher)

1. Items domestic mail per capita	.89	(75)
2. Female life expectancy at age zero	.86	(67)
3. Percent of labor force employed in agriculture	—.86	(95)
4. Radios per million	.85	(107)
5. Nonagricultural employment as % of working age population	.84	(76)
6. Govt. employees as % of working age population	.83	(18)
7. Percent of GNP originating in agriculture	—.81	(75)
8. Inhabitants per physician	—.81	(114)
9. Newspaper circulation per mil	.80	(111)
10. Primary and secondary school pupils as % population 15–64	.80	(111)
11. Percentage literate of population 15 plus	.80	(117)
12. Industrial employment as % of working age population	.79	(77)
13. Inhabitants per hospital beds	—.77	(117)
14. Wage and salary earners as % of working age population	.76	(115)
15. Crude birth rate	—.76	(79)
16. Infant death rate	—.76	(50)
17. Television sets per million	.75	(69)
18. Percent of population in localities 20,000 plus	.71	(110)

II Medium (±0.40 to ±0.68)

19. All Christians as % of population	.68	(88)
20. Cinema attendance per capita	.65	(100)
21. Radios per million, average annual increase	.63	(96)
22. Items of foreign mail sent per capita	.61	(73)
23. Annual rate of natural increase of population	—.59	(60)
24. Students in higher education per 100,000 population	.58	(102)
25. General govt. revenue as % of GNP	.58	(29)
26. General govt. expenditure as % of GNP	.53	(28)
27. GNP	.53	(122)
28. Percentage of population working age (15–64)	.48	(115)
29. Central govt. revenue as % of GNP	.47	(41)
30. Speakers of dominant language as % of population	.47	(58)
31. Votes in national election as % of voting age population	.46	(87)
32. GDCF as % of GNP	.45	(77)
33. Immigrants per million	.45	(41)
34. Private consumption as % of GNP	—.44	(62)
35. Moslems as % of population	—.44	(88)
36. Deaths from domestic group violence per million population	—.43	(74)
37. Marriages per million	.41	(50)
38. Crude death rate	—.41	(56)
39. Gini index, income distribution inequality before taxes	—.40	(20) (5% sig)
40. Central govt. expenditure as % of GNP	.37	(41)

III Low (±0.22 to ±0.37)

41. Expenditure of central government as % of GNP	.37	(41)
42. Emigrants per million	.36	(40)

43. Roman Catholics as % of population	.31 (117)
44. Female wage & salary earners as % of all employees	.31 (69)
45. Gini index, income distribution inequality after taxes	−.30 (12)
	(33% sig)
46. Unemployed as % of working age population	.29 (49)
47. Inhabitants per hospital bed, annual % rate of change	.29 (89)
48. Foreign items sent/foreign items received (ratio)	.28 (73)
49. Annual growth rate of GNP per capita	.28 (68)
50. Gini index of inequality of agricultural land distribution	−.26 (40)
51. Average annual increase in % literate of population over 15	−.25 (43)
52. Votes for Socialist parties as % of total vote	.24 (58)
53. Population per square kilometer	.22 (117)

IV No correlation (Below ±0.20)

54. Total population
55. Annual % rate of increase in population
56. Percent population in places 20,000 plus, annual average increase
57. Military personnel as % of population 15–64
58. Defense expenditure as % of GNP
59. Votes for Communist Party as % of total vote
60. Votes for religious parties as % of total vote
61. Votes for non-Communist secular parties as % of total vote
62. Executive stability (no. yrs. independent/no. chief executives)
63. Area, square kilometers
64. Foreign trade as % of GNP (exports plus imports)
65. Annual average change in % of LF employed in agriculture
66. Unemployed as % of wage and salary earners
67. Index of achievement motivation—children's readers
68. Farms on rented land as % of all farms

Source: Constructed from B. M. Russett, *et al.*, *World Handbook of Political and Social Indicators* (New Haven: Yale University Press, 1964), p. 277.

society or economy changes over time as it grows, remains stable, or declines. The cross-sectional data only tell us something about the difference between wealthier and poorer countries. We commonly use the cross-sectional data because they are more available and more accurate. Historical data are available at best for only a few countries, and generally the further back we go in time the less confidence we can place in data.

This use of cross-sectional data means that we can only make *inferences* about the actual process of change from these correlations. There is, of course, considerable variation in the amount of confidence we can place in these inferences, a point that will become clear as we examine some of the variables. Nonetheless it is extremely useful to have such an extensive set of measures that can be related to the measure of human productivity.

In the first place, we can find a number of measures relating directly to the set of variables we described above on the traditional-modern dichotomy. Let us consider first only those measures with a quite high correlation (above 0.70). A number of variables (numbers 1, 4, 9, 10, 11, and 17) give us some measure of communication, indicating the extent to which people or groups in the society are isolated or connected with one another. Quite consistently the wealthier countries have larger internal mail volumes, more radios, more newspaper circulation, more children in school, more literacy, and more television sets than poorer countries. The rural versus urban living places is indicated by variable 18, the proportion of the population living in places of 20,000 or more: wealthier countries are more urbanized than poorer countries. Variables 3, 5, 7, and 12 all indicate the extent of industrialization as against the dominance of agriculture. Wealthier countries have smaller proportions of the labor force in agriculture, larger proportions in nonagriculture,[10] smaller proportions of gross domestic product coming from agriculture and larger proportions of the working age population engaged in industrial employment than do poorer countries. These are also indirect measures of subsistence versus commercialized economies. We need not belabor the point that people working in factories require others working in agriculture and related activities to feed them.

We get a significant though indirect measure of interpersonal relations, claims, and obligations from variable 14, which shows that wealthier countries have larger proportions of the working age population as wage and salary earners than do poorer countries. In poorer countries we should find the converse, higher proportions as self-employed, unpaid family labor, or involved in some form of payment in kind, as share tenancy. Wage and salary employment is taken here to indicate highly specified and limited relationships, with claims and obligations based upon specified and limited performance. This is another way of saying that people are related not as complete persons, but in a diverse number of limited *roles*.

Finally we have a number of variables (2, 8, 13, and 16) indicating that wealthier countries have higher levels of welfare than poorer countries. Wealthier countries have longer life expectancy for women, lower infant death rates, and more doctors and hospitals beds per person than do poorer countries. The first two variables are the more direct measures of welfare, while the latter two indicate some of the mechanisms by which the higher levels of welfare are achieved. This is, of course, welfare in its most basic aspect, the capacity of a population to keep its members alive. We should expect that nutritional measures would show the same relationship, and we can also consider education

---

[10] Note that these two measures are not exactly the same. One uses the working age population as a base, the other uses the labor force as a base.

as a different form of welfare, which is also closely related to human productivity.

We have explicit time series data as well as precise impressions that the variables considered above are rather directly related to the process of economic development in individual societies. Urbanization, industrialization, increasing levels of welfare and a more extended communications network are historically related to the long-term increase in human productivity in those countries we now call industrialized, wealthy nations. That is, we can have considerable confidence in the inferences about process that we can make from these cross-sectional data, because we also have historical observations that support the inferences.

The thrust of this analysis is questioned in part in the following articles by Bauer and Yamey, and Polly Hill. The former argues that the industrial classifications for the labor force distribution or for the sectoral origins of product are applicable only to the industrialized nations and are meaningless when applied to the more backward economies. They point out that agriculturalists in West Africa for example are engaged in a wide range of activities including transportation, marketing, and small-scale manufacturing as well as the growing of products from the land. Thus it is meaningless to classify them simply as agriculturalists and to neglect their other activities. Hill maintains that the economic classifications for production or welfare are similarly inapplicable to the backward economy. While these arguments contain much truth, they do not constitute a refutation of the general argument that long-term increases in human productivity bring substantially the type of social changes we have been illustrating.

The resolution of this argument in fact brings us to a clearer understanding of the processes of social change that are associated with economic development. What we are witnessing is the increasing differentiation of functions, which constitutes the basic process of social change associated with economic development. It is quite true that agriculturalists in a backward economy perform a wide range of functions, but this is also one of the reasons that their labor is so low in productivity. Increases in human productivity appear to require an increasing division of labor and specialization of function. And this is a process that is quite pervasive in a society, not simply a matter of work alone. At the higher levels of human productivity, then, we find societies in which individuals carry out a limited number of more specialized tasks. This makes them more dependent upon one another and requires that they be brought more into contact with one another through a wide range of social mechanisms. This also means that they will be interacting with one another in quite limited aspects of their broader lives as individuals.

Returning to the table of correlations, we can also consider a range of measures for which our historical inferences must be more problematic. Here we can identify at least two types of variations in the process; one concerns timing, the other concerns individual or regional variation. The demographic measures illustrate the variation in timing. We note that there is a strong negative relationship between human productivity and fertility (-0.76). Poorer countries have higher fertility than wealthier countries. At the same time, the relation between crude death rates and human productivity is much weaker (-0.41). Wealthier countries have lower death rates than poorer countries, but there are also apparently a number of poorer countries with lower levels of mortality than we might expect given their level of human productivity. Taken together these measures illustrate the problem of variable timing, which in this case has produced what we call the population explosion. To anticipate the argument to be made in Section 3 of Part I, we know that the recent development of medical and public health technology has brought dramatically rapid reductions in mortality to the poorer nations. Many are experiencing the same amount of death rate reduction in one generation that required as much as three generations in the process of economic development in the Western world. This clearly illustrates that for a large number of changes there is no reason to expect that the timing will be the same in the currently developing countries as it was in the western world in the nineteenth century.

The measures relating government revenues and expenditures (variables 25, 26, 29, and 40) to human productivity are also positive, but of only moderate strength (from 0.37 to 0.58). The positive association allows us to infer that as societies become more productive, larger and more complex, they require more extensive governmental functions to integrate and coordinate the interdependent parts. The fact that the correlations are only of moderate strength may indicate some variability in the timing of changes, or it may represent individual or regional differences as well. Apart from the difficulties of measurement, we have observed the recent emergence of a series of socialist states, where government involvement in economic activities is a matter of political choice rather than an historic association with human productivity. The recognition of these individual or regional variations introduces an important stricture against the too facile drawing of universal inferences from these cross-sectional data.

This caveat is especially important in the attempts to relate economic development to political characteristics. Variable 31 suggests that at least for the 87 countries included in the analysis, there is some direct association between voting turnout and human productivity. Of the many other attempts to illuminate this relationship, that by Phillips

Cutwright, included in this section, is one of the more careful and sophisticated, at least methodologically. Cutwright argues that political development must mean an increase in complexity, measured by the extension of the franchise. Drawing a larger proportion of the population into the decision-making process requires a more complex political system. Development also means an increasing specialization of function, measured by the extent of operation of political parties. Parties are here seen as highly specialized mechanisms for articulating interests in the political arena. Cutwright constructs an ingenious index to quantify this concept of development and then measures the correlation of this index with measures of communication, human productivity, urbanization, and industrial distribution of the labor force (the proportion in agriculture). His correlations are all high and he emerges with much the same picture we have found for economic development and social change.

Although this specific methodological strategy is quite appropriate, the results can still be questioned, especially in the extent to which we can make historical inferences from these cross-sectional data. The scattergram Cutwright provides shows clearly one of the important qualifications in the striking regional clusters. The Western democracies are clustered closely about the upper end of the regression line. The Latin American countries, and significantly the Philippines, are clustered in the middle of the distribution and quite above the regression line. That is, they show more political development than communications development. The Communist bloc countries are clustered also at the middle of the distribution, and *below* the regression line, though not so much below as our stereotypes might lead us to predict. Given the close relationship between communications and economic development, we might expect roughly the same type of distribution in the scattergram of political development and economic development. These clusters clearly indicate a considerable degree of independence in historical development between changes in human productivity and political changes. The data and their analyses are provocative and suggestive, but it is difficult to have much confidence in the historical or universal inferences that we can draw at this time.[11]

A final issue to be explored at this time is that of the units of analysis. The data presented above and those in the following articles use nations as units of analysis. This is almost universally the case in

[11] See Brian L. J. Berry, "By What Categories May a State Be Characterized," *Economic Development and Cultural Change* (October 1966), pp. 91–93, for a general review of the Russett *et al.* data presented in our Table 2. Berry gives especial attention to the tenuousness of the inferences that can be made from these cross-sectional data. He shows, as we have suggested above, that some measures appear to have universal significance, while others appear to have only regional significance.

the analysis of social change and economic development. There are a few attempts to study regions within individual nations, and some concerned with multinational regions, though even these latter are in most cases simply analyses of nations in a given region. For the most part, however, analyses of economic development are analyses of nation states. There is, to be sure, some arbitrariness in this selection of units, and a good part of the selection is based on the simple fact that it is nations that collect data. We are often forced to use the nation state as the unit of analysis simply because it is only in this form that data are available.

There is, however, more justification than the accident of data collection for using the nation as the unit of analysis. The nation state is, after all, a collectivity with boundaries that encompass significant social forces. National boundaries establish systems of distinctive rules, organizational procedures and values that control human activities fundamental to the processes of production and distribution. Nations control their boundaries, limiting or facilitating the flow of goods and people through such devices as tariffs and immigration laws, thus varying their interaction with other nations. The very fact of nationhood assumes both the prerogative of controlling such boundary flows, and of preventing the emergence of boundary controls within the nation.

The common exclusion of deviant cases from this rule in the analysis of economic development only serves to remind us of the importance of national boundary control. Although Kuwait is the wealthiest country in the world as measured by its gross national product per capita, it is almost never included in analyses of the historical process of economic development. Kuwait is in many respects simply a factory extension of an international petroleum organization. For all practical purposes it does not control flows across its boundaries. At the other end of the scale would be Laos, also seldom included in analyses of socioeconomic development. This is only partly because of the lack of data. In many respects it cannot seriously be regarded as a nation, since the accident of its position in a larger world of conflict allows it to have little if any real control over its boundaries. Both countries do, of course, have some control over their boundaries, but it is so limited as to make these unsuitable units of analysis.

It is impossible to be precise about how much boundary control a group needs to qualify for nationhood in this sense, especially since we see considerable variation in the amount of control individual nations do exercise. Nonetheless, without attempting to be too precise, we gain a sense of a threshold, below which a unit ceases to be useful for analysis. Kuwait and Laos clearly lie below that threshold at least at this time in history.

In addition to controlling flows over the boundary, nations constitute significant units for mobilizing human resources and articulating diverse interests within their boundaries. We can see this in the impact of specific national policies on economic development. As recent and dramatic examples we can cite the post-independence economic policies of a number of Southeast Asian countries. Burma and Indonesia have engaged in policies that, whatever their aims or motivations, have had the effect of reducing human productivity. Singapore and Malaysia, on the other hand, have engaged in distinctive national policies that have increased human productivity. Both sets of movements have been clearly independent of natural resource bases and can be quite explicitly tied to mobilizing and articulating policies that have been distinctly national policies. Japan's earlier reaction to Western incursion, which led it to rapid economic growth, was also clearly a national reaction. It was composed of a series of actions that the nation, as such, was capable of performing and controlling. This only serves to illustrate the point that the nation constitutes a unit whose actions have some independence and also have a significant impact on the process of economic development. That we can observe considerable variance in the national characteristics that are related to the speed and direction of economic change only enhances the argument that the nation is a useful unit of analysis for the study of socioeconomic change.

On the other hand, this is not to argue that nations operate in a vacuum or that observed patterns of socioeconomic change are the result only of intranational characteristics. It is quite consistent with the use of nations as units of analysis to accept the fact that they exist in an environment of nations and that their interactions with that environment affect their patterns of socioeconomic change quite significantly. The extent to which they are willing and capable of interacting with other nations, and the extent to which they are allowed by other nations to control their own boundaries are certainly important considerations for the individual national processes of socioeconomic change. Further, the store of knowledge or the level of technology available in the world as a whole will affect such development quite independently of the internal characteristics of a given nation. This does, in effect, raise important qualifications in the use of nations as units of analysis, but it still does not negate the utility of these units.

In summary, then, although we are somewhat constrained to use nations as units of analysis by the organization of data gathering, the units are not totally arbitrary and useless. We still have in nations very useful units of analysis.

MAIN CONCEPTS
IN THE ANALYSIS
OF THE SOCIAL IMPLICATIONS
OF TECHNICAL CHANGE

Bert F. Hoselitz

The growing maturity and sophistication of the social sciences in the last quarter-century have brought about a great proliferation of technical terms and a multitude of new definitions and conceptualizations. Though a large number of these technical terms have chiefly specialized uses, several of them have come to be applied to quite usual phenomena in the study of social change; and many students of the process of economic and technological change and its social implications have found it useful to codify and inventory not merely the theories, but also the concepts commonly in use, to describe the generalized phenomena of social and cultural change. A recent publication produced under the guidance of the International Research Office on the Social Implications of Technological Progress constitutes one such attempt;[1] and the proposed "Dictionary of Social Sciences Terms," which is planned by UNESCO and will doubtless appear shortly, is another effort in the same vein. It cannot be the purpose of this paper either to repeat the performance of the International Research Office or to offer a selection from the forthcoming

From Bert F. Hoselitz, "Main Concepts in the Analysis of the Social Implications of Technical Change," Bert F. Hoselitz and W. E. Moore (eds.), *Industrialization and Society* (New York: Humanities Press, 1963), pp. 11–31. Copyright 1963 by UNESCO. Reprinted by permission of Humanities Press and UNESCO.

[1] See *Social Economic and Technological Change: A Theoretical Approach* (Paris: Bureau International de Recherche sur les Implications Sociales du Progrès Technique, 1958).

"Dictionary"; nor would this essay be a suitable vehicle for propounding an elaborate theory of social and economic concomitants of industrialization.

It appears that, perhaps, the best path to follow is to present first some aspects of the basic contrast, in social structure and cultural relations, between a society which has not yet entered the process of industrial development and a society which has passed through this process; and, after discussing some of their contrasting features, to draw attention to the principal factors which seem to be most crucial in this process of change.[2]

One may conveniently begin this task by referring to well-known contrasts in social and cultural features of differing types of society—e.g., the dichotomy between folk and urban cultures; or between "community" and "society" (Gemeinschaft and Gesellschaft); or between tradition-oriented patterns of social action and those conforming to the canons of purposive and substantive rationality.[3] We need not dwell long on the dichotomies originally proposed by Robert Redfield or Ferdinand Toennies, since, whatever their merits for the comparative study of culture, reference to them has been infrequent in studies of technical and economic change. The distinction between traditional and rational action, ultimately going back to Max Weber, is much more important. We find often that action and behavior patterns in technologically and economically little developed societies are described as "traditional," and that this concept implies that these action patterns are inefficient, technologically non-complex, and strongly resistant to innovation.

Before we enter into a more detailed analysis of the concept of tradition-oriented behavior, it would be useful, however, to draw attention to two features of nonindustrialized societies that have received extensive treatment in the works of Redfield and Toennies and their followers. Redfield frequently reiterated the point that social acts in a folk or folk-like society typically are not "single-interest" but "multiple-interest" actions. This means that productive activity, for example, has not only an economic purpose; it also is conceived, by the members of folk societies, as containing ritual elements, elements pertaining to social cohesion or structure, "political goals," and others. This very "multidimensionality" of all social behavior in folk societies is at the bottom of some of the difficulties of bringing about changes in behavior.

---

[2] This approach has also been used in a recent essay by Charles P. Loomis, "Toward a Theory of Systematic Social Change," Interprofessional Training Goals for Technical Assistance of Personnel Abroad (New York: Council on Social Work Education, 1959), pp. 165–98.

[3] Several other dichotomies of this nature are mentioned in the essay by Loomis. On the original statements of the folk-urban dichotomy, see Robert Redfield, "The Folk Society," American Journal of Sociology, LII (January, 1947), 293–308; on the Gemeinschaft-Gesellschaft dichotomy, see Ferdinand Toennies, Community and Society— Gemeinschaft und Gesellschaft (East Lansing, Michigan, 1957); on the rationalism-traditionalism dichotomy, see Max Weber, The Theory of Social and Economic Organization (New York, 1947), pp. 115 ff.

If social behavior were uni-dimensional, change would be relatively easy. However, a given action is considered—in addition to meeting one specific objective—as simultaneously meeting other objectives. Thus, change is possible only if the new way of acting can be interpreted as comprising all these associated objectives also. In brief, behavior such as planting, or harvesting, or engaging in exchange, is conceived of not merely as productive activity, but, at the same time, as behavior maintaining the stability and relational adequacy of a person's position in his culture. Hence, if different forms of productive activity are proposed, they will prove acceptable (without strong external compulsion) only if they also fulfil in one form or another, all or most of the other objectives fulfilled by the activity to be replaced. The prevalence of many folk-like elements in the productive relations of nonindustrialized societies accounts for some of the serious obstacles to economic and technical change that have been experienced there.[4]

The emphasis that Toennies and his disciples have placed on the significance of community has also played an important role in the study of conditions surrounding technological change and economic innovation. In this context, the significant point is that, for many nonindustrialized societies, the small group is the relevant unit of social cohesion. This small community often has its origin in tribal or kinship groups. Its importance lies in the fact that its membership is usually strictly circumscribed—limited to persons who have either long-standing face-to-face relationships or, where these are rarer, some other kind of close common identification with one another. All outsiders—i.e., all persons who do not belong to the small community—are strangers and are often regarded with suspicion. The small group, and the area within which it resides and maintains mutual contacts, form a world of their own which is regarded as opposed to the world beyond. One's loyalty is confined to the members of one's group, and everyone outside it is a stranger—regardless of whether or not he shares in a similar or closely related culture.

In many underdeveloped countries, these highly particularistic groups still exist; and in some instances, they have considerable strength. They are frequently tribal groups; but they may also constitute village communities or castes and other associations based on kinship or quasikinship ties, or on joint occupancy of a small area. Usually, the group lives in a regionally compact area, and its members are related by blood or marriage ties. Geography and familiarity thus reinforce one another; and the small community appears, in certain cultural contexts, as a hard-shelled unit whose main forms

[4] Numerous actual examples might be cited from the literature on economic relations among non-industrial peoples. See, for example, F. G. Bailey, *Caste and the Economic Frontier* (Manchester, 1957); Cyril S. Belshaw, "In Search of Wealth," *American Anthropologist*, LVII (February, 1955), Part II ("Memoirs of the American Anthropological Association," No. 80); Manning Nash, *The Machine Age Maya* (Glencoe, Ill., 1958).

of social interaction occur only within the group, and whose relations to the outside are tenuous and often associated with suspicions and fears. In the development process, strong tendencies are set in motion to break up this isolation of the community and to enmesh its members in manifold social relations with the outside. Moreover, frequently those persons who have low status within the community are the ones who penetrate most easily the wall built around it and who tend to interact most with the remainder of the society. This disrupts the internal structure of the small community, and often leads its high-status members to reinforce their isolation against the outside.

Thus the small community is significant (1) in its resistance against absorption into the "great society"; and (2) as a source of conflicts which arise, on the social and personal levels, in the process in which primary loyalties to the small group gradually tend to be replaced by loyalties to the larger society. Moreover, many of the institutions which have meaning within the context of the small community lose this meaning in the framework of the larger society. The family loses its place as a productive and economic security-yielding unit in a society in which industrialization has taken place, and where economic ties are with persons outside the kinship group, and economic security is obtained through governmental or other insurance schemes. Similarly, the intimate relation with tribal or village deities loses its full import for those who enter the larger society; and the patterns of deference and authority within the small community have no force outside it. All this tends to produce conflicts within and beyond the small community, as in India, where they manifest themselves in conflicts within and between castes; in Africa, where they appear as struggles between centralized authorities and tribal chieftains; and elsewhere, where they assume still different forms.

The strong nationalism which permeates many industrializing countries is the chief ideological underpinning for a process of social change that leads from the ubiquity of small particularistic communities to a more uniform, structurally diversified, but more highly interdependent society. Other processes, associated with industrial development and less subject to manipulation by agitators and intellectuals, support this trend. Among them are urbanization and bureaucratization of governmental and productive procedures. The onslaught on the small community thus comes from all sides; and it is not likely that it can withstand the combined impact of these forces.

From the description of the small community and of the folk society, with its multifaceted features of social interaction, we can see that these two concepts are chiefly different designations of the same social type.[5] A third and, on the whole, more popular, way of describing it is to point to its traditionalism—or, perhaps more correctly, to represent it as a society in which tra-

[5] The combined features of the folk society and the small community have been given a perhaps classic expression in the work of Robert Redfield, *The Little Community* (Chicago, 1955).

ditional forms of action predominate. In fact, the most common way to delineate societies with little industrialization and a limited application of scientific technology to production processes is simply to call them—as is done, for example, by W. W. Rostow—"traditional societies."[6] As we have seen, the concept of traditional social action ultimately goes back to Max Weber, who contrasted it with different forms of rational action. Since the concept of traditional or tradition-oriented action has gained such wide popularity, it might be considered a worth-while task to explore it somewhat more in detail. It is not my purpose to undertake an exhaustive analysis of the concept of tradition and traditional action, especially since I have presented my views on this problem in a recent publication elsewhere.[7]

The main point of this discussion relates to the definition of the concept of traditional action and its distinction from traditionalistic action. Though Max Weber did not make this distinction explicitly, it is implicit in his work. Traditional or tradition-oriented social action is found in all societies. Weber described it as action based upon "the psychic attitude set for the habitual workaday and . . . the belief in the everyday routine as an inviolable norm of conduct."[8] But beyond this, the concept of traditional action may be widened by also including forms of social behavior which have been taken over from ancestors and forebearers, because all populations have a sense of their historical past and a need for continuity of behavioral norms, and because these forms of social action can appropriately be fitted into the action scheme of a society. This does not mean that traditional action excludes change. Tradition does not consist in a stereotype in external aspects of behavior; on the contrary, it is based on a continuity of attitudes and states of mind. Many practices in modern, highly industrial societies are based on tradition and traditional norms. This is true of such everyday behavior patterns as forms of greetings and rules of personal conduct; and it is also true of more complex behavior in the political and economic spheres. It would be difficult to differentiate societies at different levels of economic performance by the relative "quantity" of tradition-oriented behavior that their members exercise.

Traditionalism, on the other hand, may be defined as action based on the "self-conscious deliberate affirmation of traditional norms in full awareness of their traditional nature and alleging that their merit derives from that traditional transmission from a sacred orientation."[9] In other words, tra-

6 See W. W. Rostow, *The Stages of Economic Growth* (Cambridge, 1960), pp. 4–6.

7 See Bert F. Hoselitz, "Tradition and Economic Growth," in Ralph Braibanti and Joseph J. Spengler (eds.), *Tradition, Values, and Socio-Economic Development* (Durham, N.C., 1961), pp. 83–113.

8 See Max Weber, "The Social Psychology of the World Religions," in H. H. Gerth and C. W. Mills (eds.), *From Max Weber: Essays in Sociology* (New York, 1946), p. 296.

9 See Edward A. Shils, "Tradition and Liberty: Antinomy and Interdependence," *Ethics*, LXVIII (April, 1958), 160–61.

ditionalistic action is a conscious revival of things past—a conscious return to a past glorious age or a past sacred lore, an ideology which looks to the great achievements of a past golden age as providing a set of norms whose revival would again lead to splendor and greatness. In the nationalisms of many industrializing countries—especially those whose roots go deeply into a great past—like the civilizations of India or the Islamic countries—we can find strong traditionalistic admixtures. Their ideologies go deeper than the mere rejection of Western values: the revival and revitalization of old values, often long dead, are demanded; and external behavior is approved that is considered to be in conformance with these norms.

Though traditional behavior may sometimes conflict with the demands of modernization and technological change, usually it is an important reinforcing element in the maintenance or support of stability in a period of rapid change. On the whole, the persistence of traditions in social behavior may be an important factor mitigating the many dislocations and disorganizations which tend to accompany rapid industrialization and technical change. Since traditionalistic action, on the other hand, tries to elevate outdated practices and values to the level of current behavioral norms, it usually has strong reactionary ingredients, and hence is a factor acting to retard economic change.

In brief, we need examination and study of the traits contributing to what is commonly described as traditional or tradition-oriented action. Weber himself was preoccupied with the analysis of rational action, which he regarded as the mainspring of economically and politically progressive societies. Hence tradition, the opposite of rationalism, became regarded as a characteristic of all that was static, stagnant, and retarded. But, as we have seen, traditions may have positive as well as negative effects; and, rather than leaving the whole body of ideas surrounding the analysis of tradition unsurveyed, we must make a more careful and precise study of the aspects of tradition that conduce to economic and technological progress, and of the aspects that may impede such progress.

One attempt to elaborate further the characteristics of tradition-oriented societies, and, in fact, to breaking the rationalism-tradition dichotomy into its components, is the description of societies at different levels of economic performance by means of the pattern variables proposed by Talcott Parsons.[10] Though the entire apparatus developed by Parsons is not often applied to the analysis of the social implication of industrialization, many of the chief pattern alternatives he describes—e.g., ascription or particularism—are fre-

[10] See Talcott Parsons, *The Social System* (Glencoe, Ill., 1951), pp. 58 ff. Applications of Parsons' theory to situations of social change have been attempted by William L. Kolb, "The Social Structure and Functions of Cities," *Economic Development and Cultural Change*, III (October, 1954), 30–46; and Bert F. Hoselitz, *Sociological Aspects of Economic Growth* (Glencoe, Ill., 1960), esp. chap. II.

quently found in the literature. It may, therefore, be useful to present the pertinent parts of Parsons' theory and to apply it, in particular, to the problem under investigation.

Three of the five pairs of pattern alternatives stated by Parsons are more immediately applicable to our problem. These are the choice between modalities of the social object (achievement *vs.* ascription) ; the choice between types of value orientation standard (universalism *vs.* particularism) ; and the definition of scope of interest in the object (specifity *vs.* diffuseness). In applying these three pattern variables to the distinctions between industrialized and predominantly nonindustrial societies, we find that the former are characterized by the preponderance of achievement standards in the distribution of economic roles and objects; that they also employ universalistic criteria in this distribution process; and that economic roles in these societies are typically functionally specific. Primitive and other nonindustrial societies, on the other hand, exhibit predominantly features of ascription, particularism, and functional diffuseness in the corresponding fields of social action. Let us now consider each pair of variables in somewhat more detail.

We should begin by pointing out that we are concerned with norms of social behavior. It is true, of course, that actual social behavior often does not conform to these norms; and there may even be cases in which it would be appropriate to say that the norms are honored in their breach. In other words, the complex of pattern variables alleged to describe economic activity in a society constitutes an ideal type; and, as in other cases when ideal types are applied to the analysis of actual societies, we find that the reality presents features which are more or less deviant from the ideal-type construct.[11] But pattern variables may be used, to help discover elements of social change, for estimating the degree to which actual practice in any given society deviates from the "pure" state which a social system would have if the norms corresponding to the complex pattern variables were actually enforced. For example: in a given society, ascription is regarded as the norm for distributing economic roles. However, we find that actually a number of these roles are assigned on the basis of achievement or performance. In such a case, we may discern an incipient process of social change, whose further ramifications may be traced by empirical inquiry.

Let us now return to the pattern variables. The achievement-ascription dichotomy is closely related to, though not identical with, the contrast between status-oriented and contract-oriented societies.[12] If we apply this dichotomy to economic objects, we find that, in a society in which ascription is the norm, economic roles are distributed ideally on the basis of who a person is rather

[11] On the concept and use of the ideal type, see Max Weber, *On the Methodology of the Social Sciences* (Glencoe, Ill., 1949), pp. 90 ff.

[12] On the status-contract dichotomy, see Sir Henry Sumner Maine, *Ancient Law*, ed. Sir. Frederik Pollock (New York, 1906), pp. 163–65.

than of what he can do. A practical example of a society based on ascription would be an "ideal" caste system, in which each caste is in full control of a certain occupation—that is, where only members of a specific caste are admitted to that occupation. Now the caste system—though it may have come close to this ideal in some localities, at certain times—has never, as a whole, exhibited fully ascriptive features. But it is quite clear, from the example given, that, in a society in which economic roles are assigned on the basis of status or ascription, social mobility is made difficult, and social change, to the extent to which it depends upon mobility, is severely impeded.

In contrast, if an achievement norm predominates with respect to the distribution of economic roles, then the primary criterion for attaining a certain occupation is based on a person's capacity to perform the required tasks for this occupation. In practice, an actual test may be involved in the process of allocating economic roles; in the absence of such a test, certain objective criteria—such as successfully passing through a certain number of school years, the obtaining of a degree, etc.—may be prescribed. Again, it is well known that pure performance criteria are not applied everywhere in industrialized countries—economic roles are sometimes allocated there on the basis of strong ascriptive criteria. Inheritance of property, the preponderance of extended kinship groups—especially among the upper social classes—and general impediments against social mobility, are some factors which inhibit the full application of achievement norms. But the ideal of an achievement norm is strong enough so that, even where economic roles are actually allocated on the basis of ascription, the pretense is made that the performance requirement has been met. An illustration of this is provided by the fact that, in quite a few American companies, the son of the boss must work his way to the top in the firm—though it is perhaps not doubtful from the beginning that he will succeed in this endeavor.

The next pair of pattern alternatives, particularism and universalism, are related to the first pair. They do not prescribe norms designating who is to perform a given role, but are concerned with whether the same rules of recruitment for economic roles apply to everyone. Medieval European society illustrates the application of particularistic norms to economic action—in that society, specific rules applied to peasants and burghers, to nobles and commoners. Certain markets and certain transactions were reserved to certain groups; and only an outsider's admission to an otherwise closed group could permit him to perform the functions reserved for that group. The principle of universalism, on the contrary, makes no such distinctions. The same rules apply to all; the principle of formal equality is elevated to a general norm of social behavior.

It almost follows logically that, in a society in which economic roles are distributed on the basis of universalistic performance criteria, the roles themselves are functionally highly specific. This requirement issues from the rigorous application of the principle of achievement, for the latter would be of little value unless a role could be clearly defined and circumscribed. Moreover, functional specificity flows from the increasing division of labor. Adam Smith, in his famous example of the manufacture of pins, has clearly demonstrated its economic advantages. For, as he points out:

> The improvement of the dexterity of the workman necessarily increases the quantity of work he can perform; and the division of labour by reducing every man's business to some one simple operation; and by making this operation the sole employment of his life, necessarily increases very much the dexterity of the workman.[13]

Smith sees that there are other advantages that accrue from the division of labor; but he quite accurately places the development of a high degree of functional specificity first.

Functional diffuseness stands in direct contrast to specificity. The simple peasant in a nonindustrial society is a characteristic representative of this type of work norms. He not only performs all work connected with producing a crop, but he also builds his house, makes his implements, and often produces his own clothes and other final consumption goods. As in cases of the ascription-achievement duality and the particularism-universalism duality, we find noncharacteristic instances which seem to contradict the generalization that diffuseness is normally associated with non-industrial societies. In India, for example, the system of social division of labor under the predominance of caste has led, even in a nonindustrial society, to a high degree of functional specificity. On the other hand, certain occupations, especially on the highest managerial level, are functionally diffuse, even in highly industrialized societies. In general, functional specificity has been instituted more widely for the simpler and less complex tasks; but the progressive specialization in business management, and even in scientific pursuits, indicates that this process of occupational differentiation is ubiquitous and strong in modernizing societies.

The use of pattern variables has had the advantage of putting some of the strategic mechanisms of social change associated with industrialization and technical progress into sharper focus. Universalistic norms need not generally replace particularistic ones. However, the transitions from allocating economic roles according to a system of ascription to assigning them on a basis of achievement, and the replacement of functionally diffuse by functionally specific norms for the definition of economic tasks, appear to have occurred in all cases of successful modernization. Before we examine the institutional changes associated with these two processes of transition, it may be useful to relate the description of industrial and nonindustrial social

[13] Adam Smith, *An Inquiry into the Nature and Causes of the Wealth of Nations,* ed. Edwin Cannan (New York, 1937), p. 7.

types, made in terms of the pattern variables, to the earlier description, made by means of the folk-urban continuum and the community-society dichotomy.

We have already seen that the folk society is characterized by the fact that economic acts have a multidimensional meaning—i.e., they have relevance not merely as acts of production or exchange, but also as acts of ritual, assertion of associative values, etc. Alternatively, this characteristic can be described by indicating the high degree of functional diffuseness of economic acts in the folk society. If a particular form of social behavior has meaning in several segments of social action—if it is not clearly confined to the set of adaptive, or integrative, or any other subsystem of social action—it must necessarily be diffuse. It has many meanings; and, though the actual manipulations demanded in its performance may be rigidly prescribed, its multidimensionality gives it the character of functional diffuseness—which, incidentally, also makes it so resistant to change.

Similarly, we may conceive of the little community as a set of institutionalized relationships, among persons, based primarily on ascriptive characteristics. The cohesion and compactness of the small community are enhanced because economic roles are tied to ascriptive status, and because, even where there is a considerable degree of specificity in different economic roles (as, for example, in the Indian village), ascriptive norms provide a stability and internal rigidity that render change from within exceedingly difficult. Only the breakup of the small community, or its infiltration from the outside, tends to reduce the significance of ascription in the distribution of economic (and other, e.g., political or deference) roles. Sometimes ascriptive norms are transferred into the wider society, but there, because of the absence of well-circumscribed boundaries for the group, they have primarily symbolic, rather than real, meaning.

The gradual destruction of the "traditional" folk-like small community thus is accompanied, in the economic and technological spheres, by a process of differentiation of economic roles and by a relaxation of the rules assigning these roles to particular actors. But the process is not a smooth one; it proceeds in spurts and jolts. During it, new institutions develop; and, as each new institution becomes established, it provides a pivotal point around which further changes gather momentum. If the juxtaposition of societies on different levels of economic modernization provided a classic case of the comparative analysis of social institutions, the analysis of the transition from one to the next level of economic performance may be regarded as a study of institutional change.

We shall now turn briefly to an examination of some of the principal concepts which have been developed in examining this process of institutional change. It must be repeated that we are not dealing here with a theory of social or cultural change, and hence it is not maintained that the concepts which will be discussed necessarily fit into a neat theoretical scheme. Nevertheless, we shall attempt to provide some indication of the relation between the various major concepts which have been employed in the description of the social implications of technical progress.

Let us begin by considering more carefully the process of institutional change and associated phenomena of social transformation. Industrial development may be regarded as requiring that two preconditions be fulfilled without which it is unlikely to start on any relatively large scale. One is the buildup of certain forms of physical overhead capital—such as communications and transport facilities; some warehouses and similar installations, especially favoring international trade; educational facilities and other public buildings. The other is the development of an institutional framework in the legal, familial, and motivational orders. Once these new institutions have been created, they provide an impetus of their own to further economic development and growth. Thus we may consider that this change in the institutional order is an important feature of social change in a pre-industrial or little-industrialized society—especially in areas which transform a society, from one in which capital formation and the introduction of modern technical devices in production are difficult, to one in which the accumulation of capital and the acceptance of innovations in production technique and economic organization appear as "natural" and unquestioned concomitants of general social progress.

Among the basic bottlenecks which have been identified in the process of modernization are shortages of capital, of skilled workers, and of entrepreneurs. Hence, from the viewpoint of industrialization, institutional arrangements which will contribute to the breakdown of any obstacles to larger supplies of these productive factors are of primary importance.

It was early recognized that the supplies of savings, of skilled labor, and of entrepreneurial talent are, in part, functions of the psychological makeup of a population. We may regard the willingness or propensity to save, as well as the propensity to run enterprises, as stemming from attitudes endemic to technically advanced societies. Some writers have been so impressed with these attitudes that they have regarded them as the chief psychological ingredients of capitalist society. For example, the main substance of Sombart's *Quintessence of Capitalism* is based upon his description of the capitalist spirit as a tension between rationalism and irrationalism, between calculation and speculation, between the bourgeois spirit and the robber spirit, between prudence and venturesomeness.[14] It is quite clear that Sombart describes, in these terms, two personality types: the first type is recognizable as the embodiment of the Puritan virtues of thrift and hard work; and the other, as the visionary entrepreneur whose role in economic development has been stressed by Schumpeter. Now, it may be argued that the motivational dispositions to save and work hard and innovate are preconditions of eco-

[14] See Werner Sombart, *The Quintessence of Capitalism* (London, 1915), *passim;* especially pp. 63–129.

nomic and technical progress; but the impact of these traits on a society is greatly enhanced by the presence of institutions within whose framework they can be exercised. Among the chief institutions which supported these attitudes in the Western world were the legitimation of interest and the social approval of profit maximization as a goal of economic activity. Both had been present in Western societies before these societies had entered a full process of industrialization; and it is in this sense that industrialization and the exploitation of technical innovations for economic ends were given an important impetus.

In societies in which these institutions are not present or only weakly developed, others may have to take their place. One of the reasons for the predominance of governmental planning in the economic development process of the countries of Asia and Africa is the weakness or absence of these institutions and the need to find a different institutional framework—in this case, the expansion of the role of government as the custodian of economic advancement. But in some "mixed economies," for example in India, the taking of interest and profit maximization as institutionalized norms have gained a sufficient foothold to justify placing reliance on them as focal points for the mobilization of private savings and their channeling into productive investment. Given a favorable environment, these features of the social system have been observed to produce decided results in the realm of industrialization—although other institutions, e.g., the pooling of resources within the context of the extended family, have also played an important role. In India, certain communities—for example, the Marwaris, or Bhatias, or Parsees —have played a particularly strategic role in the industrialization process. This fact appears to indicate that the institutionalization of norms furthering the economic exploitation of technical innovations is distributed unevenly in the society and has stronger roots in certain communities than in others.[15]

This consideration of the conditions leading to the positive grasping of opportunities, in the economic field, provided by technical innovations brings us near to the study of entrepreneurship—a factor which has played, and continues to play, a considerable role in discussions of economic development and technological modernization. But, although entrepreneurship has often been examined, and although sometimes exaggerated claims have been made for the function of entreprenuers in the industrialization process, there is still confusion about the exact meaning of "entrepreneurship" and there is still a good deal of ignorance about its social and psychological components. Concerning the role of entrepreneurship in economic development, the meaning which

[15] On the Indian communities specially attracted to entrepreneurship, see Helen Lamb, "The Indian Business Communities and the Evolution of an Industrial Class," *Pacific Affairs*, XXVIII (June, 1955), 101–16; on the role of the extended family as a source of industrial capital, see James J. Berna, "Patterns of Entrepreneurship in South India," *Economic Development and Cultural Change*, VII (April, 1959), 343–62.

Joseph Schumpeter attributed to it is usually paramount. In a now famous passage, Schumpeter defined the entrepreneur in the following words:

> We now come to the third of the elements with which our analysis works, namely the "new combinations of means of production," and credit. Although all three elements form a whole, the third may be described as *the fundamental phenomenon* of economic development. The carrying out of new combinations we call "enterprise"; the individuals whose function it is to carry them out we call "entrepreneurs." . . . The ordinary characterisation of the entrepreneur type by such expressions as "initiative," "authority," or "foresight" points entirely in our direction.[16]

In this passage, Schumpeter makes it clear that he regards the entrepreneur as an innovator, and that he considers the introduction of "new combinations of means of production" as the crucial element in giving an economic system the impetus to rise toward higher levels of productivity. In his work, Schumpeter lists in greater detail what he means by "new combinations." Among these he distinguishes: (*1*) the introduction of a new good; (*2*) the introduction of a new method of production; (*3*) the opening of a new market; (*4*) the conquest of a new source of supply of raw materials; and (*5*) the carrying out of the new organization of any industry.[17] As this list indicates, the first, third, and fourth alternatives apply primarily to commercial enterprises, whereas the second applies mainly to industrial enterprises. The fifth applies to all kinds of enterprises in industry, commerce, and finance. As a consequence, the exercise of entrepreneurship, in Schumpeter's sense, extends over the whole range of economic activity and is not confined to industrial entrepreneurship alone.

In much of the literature on the role of entrepreneurship in economic development, little or no distinction has been made about whether this activity was exercised in the commercial, the financial, or the industrial field. Yet even a superficial study of business leaders in many underdeveloped countries shows that industrial entrepreneurship is not exercised in some countries in which commercial and financial entrepreneurship flourishes. Why do we find, in so many underdeveloped countries, native moneylenders and traders, and so few native industrialists? Various arguments have been devised to explain this phenomenon; and, since we are interested in industrialization in particular, these arguments may be relevant.

The first of these arguments is the statement that native industrialists, especially in former colonial areas, were unable to compete with the powerful industrial enterprises set up by foreigners. This is hardly convincing, for the same competition was equally severe in commerce and banking. And, if we

---

[16] Joseph Schumpeter, *The Theory of Economic Development* (Cambridge, Mass., 1934), pp. 74–75. (Italics not in original.)

[17] *Ibid.*, p. 66.

examine the kinds of enterprises that native entrepreneurs did establish in the trading and moneylending fields, we find that they were supplementary to similar activities exercised by large European firms. Native traders and moneylenders found a place in the interstices of the economic system left unoccupied by larger foreign firms. They mediated between the larger urban centers and the countryside; they provisioned small and minute retailers; they serviced the needs for loans of that part of the rural population which was without capacity to offer bankable securities.

Why is no parallel phenomenon discernible in the industrial field? Clearly, small native entrepreneurs could not be expected to have entered into competition with the large foreign mining and transportation companies. But there were, and are, numerous industrial branches in which there appears to be ample opportunity for the establishment of small- and medium-scale plants, which could play a role, with respect to the larger foreign-financed enterprises, similar to that of the native trader and moneylender to the foreign wholesaler and banker.

One of the reasons for the sluggish evolution of industrial entrepreneurship may be the fact that the talents required to guide an industrial enterprise differ from those needed for successful commercial or financial entrepreneurship. The small trader or moneylender can operate with few, and often without any, permanently employed assistants; whereas the industrial entrepreneur (provided he is more than a craftsman) typically must hire a group of men whose labor he must organize and direct. In addition to being motivated by the expectation of profit, and his capacity for applying innovations, he must have managerial abilities and, above all, the ability to command and organize. The chief characteristics of a small industrial entrepreneur are not so much his venturesomeness, nor his motivation to make profits, but his capacity to lead other men in a common undertaking, and his inclination to introduce technical innovations; and, in the early stages of industrialization, the vast bulk of these innovations are of a technological nature requiring the direct and immediate participation of the entrepreneur.

Finally, the capital employed by a trader or moneylender turns over much faster than that used in industrial establishments. A trader may carry on his business without ever attaining property rights in the objects he deals with. If he is a broker or commission agent, he may merely lose his earnings from a transaction, but not the capital invested in it. Moreover, a moneylender or banker deals in that commodity that has the widest currency, that is accepted by anyone, that can easily be transported or hidden, and that can be directly used to bribe officials or persons in power, if the need should arise. An industrial entrepreneur usually has more property tied up in his plant for a longer time than either the merchant or banker; he depends upon an often imperfect market to sell his output; his property is exposed to a series of dangers—destruction by fire or other accidents—which the others may escape.

Other things being equal, the risks and uncertainties of putting a given amount of capital into industrial assets are much greater than those involved in trading and moneylending.

Hence, in speaking of a "favorable climate" for entrepreneurship, one must distinguish carefully whether the entrepreneurs who do flourish in this climate belong to the commerical and financial groups or are industrialists. Apparently, for industrialization to take hold and for industrial business leaders to come forward, a favorable climate for entrepreneurship by itself is not sufficient. I am not aware that the additional conditions which must be present to convert a commercial upsurge into an industrial upsurge have been investigated carefully enough to provide us with sufficient empirical data to distinguish more precisely the role which entrepreneurship actually does play in the process of industrialization. Doubtless, it plays an important role; but how this is to be fitted in with other alterations in social structure, and with changes in the institutional order and the normative prescription of a society, is as yet little explored.[18]

One additional characteristic of industrial entrepreneurs should be mentioned—i.e., that they have quite universally been regarded as "new men." Marx already talked of the accumulating capitalist in these terms; and much of the recent work on entrepreneurship has seen, in entrepreneurial activity —especially as opposed to governmental disposition over resources—a new form of economic behavior.[19] In part, the conflict about whether entrepreneurs are "new men" and whether entrepreneurial activity is a new form of social behavior depends upon what is meant by "entrepreneurship." If we adopt Schumpeter's definition and identify entrepreneurship with the introduction of innovations, we find that entrepreneurs have always existed—from the prehistorical past, when man first applied the wheel and introduced sedentary agriculture and cattle herding, to the most recent period. If we consider entrepreneurship to be exercised primarily within a context of formal organizations, called "business enterprise"—which is itself again a unit in a group of social institutions—as does Arthur H. Cole, we come to stress the personal psychological connotations of the entrepreneurial personality less than the social setting in which entrepreneurial activity is exercised; and here we find that the social setting grows progressively more hospitable to entrepreneurship as we move to the modern period.

But if we interpret entrepreneurship in the second sense and regard it

[18] Perhaps the most extensive and most systematic inquiry into the problem of entrepreneurship and its role in the industrialization process has recently been published by Arthur H. Cole, *Business Enterprise in its Social Setting* (Cambridge, Mass., 1959). Though its author does not claim that this is a definitive study, he discusses, with profound insight and great wisdom, many of the points which have been raised in the postwar period among students concerned with entrepreneurship and its social and historical dimensions.

[19] See, for example, *ibid.*, pp. 99–100.

as largely coincident with business leadership, then we may trace through its gradual development in an institutionalized setting. Then the application of certain sociological categories—such as deviance and social or cultural marginality—to the analysis of the gradual evolution of entrepreneurship makes sense. Of course, the concepts of social deviance and social marginality have usefulness in other areas also. They may be applied to such phenomena as the growth of scientific and technological inquiry, the development of more secular attitudes in a society, and a host of other problems—many of which may be only slightly related to the process of industrialization and technological change.

Let us consider social deviance briefly. As already stated, we are concerned primarily with those forms of deviant behavior which are relevant for economic activity and organization. Now if the concept of deviance is to have operational meaning, it cannot be interpreted as signifying simply behavior which is new; it must also imply that a set of innovating acts is opposed, in some way, to existing social norms or approved forms of behavior. In other words, a deviant always engages in behavior which constitutes a breach of the existing order and is either contrary to, or at least not positively weighted in, the hierarchy of existing social values. Applying this concept to the behavior of businessmen and merchants during the course of the economic history of Western Europe, we find that we can speak of genuine deviance in those periods and societies in which entrepreneurial behavior did not belong to the category of social actions which were considered as constituting the "good life." As late as the fifteenth century, this was true of certain kinds of financial entrepreneurship, which was always tainted by the Church's official opposition to usury. And later, when financial entrepreneurship became fully respectable, industrial entrepreneurship became regarded with some disdain because it often dirtied one's hands. These sentiments toward business or industrial activity as not quite proper for a gentleman to carry out are familiar in many underdeveloped countries today. This interpretation also provides an additional explanation for the differential response made by members of different castes in business. Since caste membership is associated with ritual status, the exercise of deviant behavior provokes different sanctions in different castes; and, most importantly, the meaning and interpretation of deviance vary between castes.

If "deviance" implies a breach with existing social norms, it is interesting to investigate further the social classes or groups from which persons come who engage in various forms of deviant behavior. Clearly, the expected rewards of their deviance must be attractive; and persons engaged in it are likely to feel a strong urge to rise in the social scale (perhaps a strong motivation for achievement), or must have resentments against some aspects of the existing order. In brief, it is quite possible to reconcile the theory of deviance with various alternative, social-psychological hypotheses—e.g., the theories of David C. McClelland or Everett E. Hagen—which have been proposed in explanation of the rise to prominence of business leaders.[20]

However, an alternative hypothesis is that persons engaging in deviant behavior are at the margin of a given culture or are in a social or cultural position in which they straddle more than one culture. In short, we may identify cases in which deviance coincides with social marginality. For example, in medieval Europe the earliest moneylenders were often foreigners. In Italy, at the time of Gothic and Lombard rule, they were Syrians, Byzantines, and Jews. Later, when Italians turned to financial entrepreneurship on a large scale, the Genoese and Pisans, Sienese and Florentines—who were all lumped together under the name of "Lombards"—became the financial entrepreneurs north of the Alps.

The role of marginal individuals in diverse economic pursuits in many economically little advanced countries is eminently manifest today. One can cite the Chinese in various South-East Asian countries, the Indians in East Africa, and the widely scattered Lebanese and Syrians who make their appearance as businessmen in West Africa, Latin America, and elsewhere in less advanced countries.

What is the mechanism which allows marginal individuals to perform the roles they apparently have so widely accepted? As Robert E. Park, the inventor of the concept and the discoverer of the significance of social marginality, has stressed, marginal men are—precisely because of their ambiguous position from a cultural, ethnic, linguistic, or socio-structural standpoint—strongly motivated to make creative adjustments in situations of change, and, in the course of this adjustment process, to develop innovations in social behavior.[21] Although many of Park's very general propositions have been refined by subsequent researchers, the theory of social marginality has not advanced sufficiently to supply convincing evidence for the role that marginal individuals may play in all episodes of social change. Even if it is admitted that marginal persons are inclined more often to make creative adjustments than to relapse into old orthodoxies or to embrace new ones, the record is not at all clear; and there are some students who warn us that marginal individuals may be more prone than others to succumb to *anomie* and thus to become carriers of trends leading toward social disorganization rather than toward creative innovations.

In circumstances in which a certain amount of deviant behavior has been displayed, the anchoring of this behavior in a new institution is of strategic

[20] See David C. McClelland, "Some Social Consequences of Achievement Motivation," in Marshall Jones (ed.), *Nebraska Symposium on Motivation,* III (Lincoln, 1956), pp. 41–72; and Everett E. Hagen, "The Process of Economic Development," *Economic Development and Cultural Change,* V (April, 1957), pp. 208–15.

[21] Robert E. Park, *Race and Culture* (Glencoe, Ill., 1950), pp. 345 ff., especially 375–76.

significance. Once a form of deviant behavior has been able to find the shelter of an institution, it ceases to be deviant, it becomes routinized, and it may display all the characteristics of highly approved forms of social behavior. Thus, institutions in which deviant action is anchored form an advance post from which additional deviance becomes possible. For example, the institutions which arose in Western Europe before the industrial revolution, and in Japan before the Meiji period, were already the end products of a process of social change that had begun with deviant behavior; but by their very existence, these institutions, in turn, made possible further economic and technological change.

Whether or not any given form of deviance will lead to the elaboration of new social institutions and to the ultimate routinization of this hitherto deviant pattern of social action is contingent on several factors. Among these, the system of sanctions existing in the society may be the most important. These sanctions may be internalized, i.e., they may reside in the values and beliefs of a population; or they may be externalized, i.e., they may be imposed by persons in power, by the elite, against actual or would-be deviants. In some societies, e.g., imperial China, both types of sanctions seem to have been very strong. In pre-Meiji Japan, internal sanctions had partially broken down, and the power of the shogunate had become increasingly weak; so external sanctions had been softened to the point where they were inadequate to prevent the formation of new institutions, or at least the beginnings of these innovations.

Thus the analysis of social change may be conducted largely through considering the impact of deviance—whether exercised by marginal men or not—the gradual institutionalization and routinization of deviant behavior and the range of sanctions opposed to it. This analysis may be carried out, in first approximation, on the "aggregate level"—i.e., it may take into account an entire complex society at once. But our insights on social change are sharpened if we disaggregate the variables in our analysis—in other words, if, in a complex society, we take account, not of changes affecting the society as a whole, but of those affecting specialized sections or classes in the society. For deviance, sanctions, and the process of institutionalization have a different place and impact among different groups. Let us use sanctions to illustrate this point. Clearly, in a society in which ascriptive norms are strong, different individuals will, according to their respective status positions, be subject to different internalized sanctions; and in a society with extensive particularisms, even external sanctions will be imposed and enforced to very different degrees on persons belonging to different special groups or classes.

This means that we are likely to discover, in any society, certain strategic groups which become the carriers of innovations. In many instances, these groups are composed of marginal men—especially if the innovations are transmitted from the outside. The role of marginal individuals in the acculturation or culture-contact process has as yet been insufficiently explored; but their prominent participation in it follows almost as a matter of definition. Another group which may, and often actually does, play a strategic role is the elite of a society. Though considerable attention has been given to the part of the elite in preserving a status quo, its impact on the introduction of organizational and technological innovations has, perhaps, been underestimated. In general, social change has been perceived as accompanied by a "circulation of elites," rather than as a process in which existing elites were capable of reorienting an entire society's goals and attempting to implement them. Yet in the present economically little advanced countries, where so much economic change is managed by the leaders of political power, the role of the elites as innovators must be acknowledged. The entrepreneurial functions— which, in Western countries, were performed predominantly by independent businessmen who often belong to a not fully enfranchised and politically impotent bourgeoisie—have been taken over by bureaucrats who operate with the blessing, and under the protection, of the political power apparatus.

In part, the intervention of the state in the industrialization process is certainly a consequence of the greater pressures, of the greater distance between reality and aspirations, that exist in the present. In a perceptive essay, Alexander Eckstein has presented several factors which tend to enhance the role of the state in the process of economic growth. He lists the following factors: The urge for massive state intervention in the process of economic and industrial growth will be the stronger (1) the greater the range of ends and the higher the level of attainment sought; (2) the shorter the time horizon within which the ends are to be attained—that is, the more rapid the rate of economic growth desired; (3) the more unfavorable the factor and resource endowments; (4) the greater the institutional barriers to economic change and industrialization; and (5) the more backward the economy in relative terms.[22] Now, as time goes on, the fifth condition is bound to obtain—simply because the more the onset of industrialization is delayed in a country, the more backward it will be in relative terms. But if this condition holds, it is likely that the first, second, and fourth conditions will also obtain. We may conclude, from this empirically derived set of conditions, that, in the course of time, incentives and urges for state intervention in the industrialization process have constantly increased. As corollaries of this conclusion, we must assume that industrialization, as a goal, has progressively become an objective of over-all social policy; and that existing elites, whatever their primary ends may have been in the past, have reoriented the hierarchy of the systematic goals they try to implement by assigning an increasingly important place to economic development. However, the increased interest of governments in economic growth and industrialization means more than merely that they

[22] Alexander Eckstein, "Individualism and the Role of the State in Economic Growth," *Economic Development and Cultural Change*, VI (January, 1958), p. 83.

are capable of exercising control over the total resources of a society to be applied to its economic buildup. It also means that a government, more effectively than any other agency, can influence the forms of social behavior by altering patterns of rewards and sanctions, by reallocating responsibility and authority, and by intervening in other ways in the social structure. But if a government is to exercise this influence successfully and beneficially, and is to avoid, as much as possible, unanticipated detrimental secondary consequences, it is necessary that the interaction between social and cultural change, on the one hand, and between economic and technical progress, on the other, be better understood. . . .

DEMOGRAPHIC INDICATORS OF ECONOMIC DEVELOPMENT

Philip M. Hauser

The levels of economic activity and growth, despite complex conceptions and technical problems, are reasonably well measured in the economically more advanced nations of the world. In such countries statistics relating to economic activity are generally available, including data on national income, industrial production, agricultural production, employment, size and composition of the labor force, nonhuman energy utilized, transport and communication facilities, and the like. Where such direct measurements are available, population statistics need not be resorted to as "indicators of economic development". On the contrary, the economic data are often used as independent variables to help explain the significant demographic changes that have occurred as concomitants of economic development.

In the economically less developed nations of the world, in contrast, information about economic activity and growth is usually quite deficient or entirely absent. Moreover, population data are also scanty and inadequate, although they are more likely to be available than economic data. In fact, the absence both of adequate economic and demographic statistics may itself be regarded as one of the indicators of economic "underdevelopment".[1] In

From Philip M. Hauser, "Demographic Indicators of Economic Development," *Economic Development and Cultural Change*, 3:2:98–116 (January 1959). Reprinted by permission of The University of Chicago Press.

[1] P. M. Hauser, "Population Statistics and Research in Planning Economic Development", in United Nations, *World Population Conference*. Vol. V (New York, 1955), pp. 927 ff.

such areas the inadequacy or absence of direct measurements of economic performance and change impel the use of various indirect indices. Among these indices are the various population statistics which are becoming increasingly available. Researches of both economists and demographers have demonstrated a high degree of relationship between economic and demographic variables tending to justify the use of demographic data as indicators of economic level.[2] This paper outlines some of the demographic measurements which may have utility as indicators of economic development and essays a brief discussion of their value and limitations.

GENERAL CONSIDERATIONS

Since the purpose of using the population statistics described below is to obtain some indication both of levels of economic activity and economic growth or change in levels, measurements of population change, as well as cross-section characteristics, must be considered. The date 1950 is suggested as the "current" date for cross-section analysis because under the statistical programs of the United Nations, the Specialized Agencies, and other bodies such as the International Statistical Institute and the Inter American Statistical Institute, a special effort was made to maximize the number of countries for which demographic and other statistics would be available on or near this date. Between 1945 and 1954, in consequence, about 80 percent of the world's population was enumerated in some kind of census. This undoubtedly is a higher proportion of the world's population than that ever before subjected to measurement. It may be anticipated that this proportion will be even further increased under the United Nations World Census Program for census undertakings to be conducted in and around 1960.[3]

While the cross-section data on or near 1950 will undoubtedly, for the time being, constitute the major body of demographic data available as indicators of economic development, efforts should be made to place these cross-section measurements in the context of population trends. For this purpose, even relatively rough analyses of patterns of change between 1900 and 1950 would be highly desirable. Data for such analyses have become increasingly

[2] For discussion and bibliography, see United Nations, *Determinants and Consequences of Population Trends* (New York, 1953), Part Two. See also Simon Kuznets, "Quantitative Aspects of the Economic Growth of Nations. I. Levels and Variability of Rates of Growth; II. Industrial Distribution of National Product and Labor Force; and III. Industrial Distribution of Income and Labor Force by States, United States, 1919 to 1955", in *Economic Development and Cultural Change*, Vol. V, No. 1 (October 1956); Supplement to Vol. V, No. 4 (July 1957); and Vol. VI, No. 4, Part II (July 1958).

[3] United Nations, *Principles and Recommendations for National Population Censuses*, Statistical Papers, Series M. No. 27 (New York, 1958).

available, largely as a result of the efforts of the United Nations.[4] Even rough analyses of direction of change, magnitude of change, and measurement of central tendency and dispersion in change would enhance the value of the demographic data as indicators of differences in level of economic activity and change therein between the more, and the less, economically advanced nations.[5]

In analyzing patterns of change in population size, composition, and distribution in the components of change itself, it will be important to attempt some control of factors distorting secular trend. That is, it would be desirable to take into account the impact of such factors as war and fluctuations in the business cycle on demographic trends. Here again only rough controls may be possible, because of the limitations of the data, but even rough controls to obtain "normal" or trend benchmark points would undoubtedly be useful.[6]

With this injunction in respect of the importance of obtaining dynamic as well as static population measurements, the discussion which follows will focus on the population statistics of greatest utility without repetitive references to the desirability of obtaining indices of change as well as cross-section measurements.

PROPOSED DEMOGRAPHIC INDICATORS

The population statistics which are proposed as indicators of economic development are presented under the following headings: (1) population growth, (2) components of population change, (3) population composition, (4) population distribution, and (4) interrelated indices.

Population Growth

The rate of population growth is without question the most significant demographic measurement for consideration in relation to economic development. Even though rate of population growth is not unambiguously an indicator either of economic level or economic change (see Table 1), it is nevertheless a strategic statistic in relation to components of population change, namely, natality, mortality, and migration; and a basic datum to which to relate any direct measurements of economic activity which may be available. Unfortunately, estimates of population changes for post-censal periods are, in the absence of adequate vital registration systems and migration statistics, subject to great

[4] See United Nations, *Demographic Yearbook* and *Statistical Yearbook* (New York, 1948 to 1957).

[5] Kuznets, Vol. V, No. 1, *op. cit.*

[6] *Ibid.*, pp. 11 ff.

error. It is necessary, therefore, to use measurements of inter-censal change. Decadal or annualized percentages of change in total population for the nations of the world would constitute a starting point for the preparation of demographic indicators of economic development. Kuznets' utilization of rates of population growth in relation to economic development sets a pattern which may well be followed and elaborated upon. While his consideration of rates of population growth for the first half of the century embraces over 50 countries, the number of areas could be increased somewhat if change for the last inter-censal decade only were utilized.[7] Further reference to the use of population change as an indicator of economic development will be made in the consideration of components of population change and the demographic typology below.

Components of Population Change

Mortality.   Mortality data, in various forms, afford not only a measurement of one of the components of total population change, but also constitute, in themselves, one of the best indicators of level of economic development and growth. The crude (or general) death rate, despite the fact that it is in part a function of the age structure of population and therefore raises questions of comparability, has been historically sensitive to economic development. In the experience of the more developed nations, decreases in the crude death rate were highly correlated with increased levels of economic activity. In fact, it was the relatively great decline in mortality reflected in the decrease in the crude death rate which was largely responsible for the "demographic revolution"—the great increase in the rate of population growth experienced by the nations first to achieve relatively high economic development.[8] The utility of the crude death rate as a correlate of economic advance is enhanced by using it in relation to general fertility rates as a basis for the demographic typology discussed below. (See Table 1.)

Mortality data, quite apart from their role as a component of population change, may also be interpreted *sui generis* as a measurement of the extent to which a nation provides a milieu in which life itself can be sustained. In this sense, differences in death rates represent measurements of differences among nations not only in level of economic development, but also in social and political organization as they may affect life itself. But despite this admixture of forces, it is clear that level of economic development has played a major role in the past in accounting for differential mortality conditions. For the analysis of differences in mortality conditions, a number of

[7] Kuznets, Vol. V, No. 1, *op. cit.*, pp. 10 ff.

[8] United Nations, *Determinants and Consequences of Population Trends* (New York, 1953), Ch. 14; George Stolnitz, "A Century of International Mortality Trends", *Population Studies* (July 1955).

measurements superior to the crude death rate are available.[9] These include the infant mortality rate, the "late infant mortality rate", various mortality ratios, life expectancy, cause of death analyses, and various composite indices derived largely from a life table. In general, in these types of measurements, national differences may be interpreted as reflecting differences in conditions conducive to mortality, relatively free of the distorting influences of differences in age structure.

The infant mortality rate is a relatively sensitive indicator of differences in level of economic development. Historically, among the economically advanced nations, the earliest and greatest gains in improved mortality conditions were manifest in the relatively great reductions in deaths to persons under one year of age; and a similar pattern is discernible in the improving mortality conditions in the less developed areas of the world today. Even more sensitive than the infant mortality rate, however, is the "late infant mortality rate"—that is, infant mortality (deaths during the first year of life) minus neo-natal mortality (deaths during the first month of life). Late infant mortality is the more sensitive indicator because deaths occurring during the first months of life are more attributable to biological and congenital forces than to economic and social factors. Deaths to infants during the last 11 months of their first year of life reflect more than deaths during the first month of life, the impact of economic and social conditions.

Various forms of death ratios tend also to be highly correlated with level of economic development. Among the more important of these are: infant mortality as a percent of total mortality; deaths of children under five as a percent of total death; deaths of persons 50 years of age and over as a percent of the total deaths. The first two of these ratios are inversely related with economic level; the latter, directly related.

A particularly elegant measurement of differences in mortality conditions is afforded by the life table function, "expectation of life". The expectation of life of the population at birth summarizes the effects of death rates at all ages and provides a single numerical expression of mortality conditions in a nation. This index may be computed for ages other than the beginning of life for varying analytical purposes.

Also sensitive to differences in economic level is the analysis of mortality by cause. In general, in the less developed nations of the world, deaths from the parasitic and infectious diseases constitute a relatively high proportion of all mortality; in the more developed nations of the world, a high proportion of all deaths is attributable to degenerative causes—coronary and circulatory diseases, cancer, and the like. These differences in cause of death

[9] L. I. Dublin, Alfred J. Lotka, and Mortimer Spiegelman, *Length of Life* (New York, 1949), Ch. 1 and 15; D. J. Bogue and E. M. Kitagawa, *Techniques of Demographic Research*, Population Research and Training Center, University of Chicago (preliminary draft, hectographed).

Table 1. Indices of Economic Development and Specified Demographic Indices for Selected Countries, circa 1950 to 1956

	United States	Belgium	United Kingdom	Nether-lands
1. National income per capita: 1952–54 average (U.S. dollars)	1,870	800	780	500
2. Percent of gross national product from agriculture *circa* 1956	5	8	4	11
3. Percent of labor force in agriculture	12.2	12.1	4.9	19.5
4. Steel consumption per capita	1,323	653	838	522
5. Rate of population increase, 1953–56	1.8	0.6	0.4	1.2
6. Crude birth rate	24.9	16.8	16.1	21.2
7. Crude death rate	9.4	12.1	11.7	7.8
8. Infant mortality rate	26.0	45.7	24.5	19.0
9. Expectation of life at birth, male	67.3[e]	62.0	67.5	71.0
10. Percent of population 65 years and older, *circa* 1950	8.2	11.1	10.8	7.9
11. Dependency ratio	62.9	49.2	51.6	62.1
12. Percent urban 20,000 and over	46.4[d]	32.0	70.8	49.7
13. Demographic type	5	5	5	5
14. Index of child wastage	4.1	7.6	3.3	3.1
15. Index of human wastage in reproduction	7.6	9.1	5.0	4.4
16. Index of human wastage in production	35.4	35.8	29.6	21.6
17. Index of relative development[c]	+320.2	+79.8	+75.3	+12.4

[a] Data are for former "Banovina of Drava" (part of present Slovenia) and are for 1931–33.
[b] Data are for 1936–38.
[c] Index based on 55 country total.
[d] Linear interpolation of age or size group.
[e] Data are for white population only. For nonwhite males 1955, 61.2 years.

Source: ITEMS 1 and 17. United Nations, *Per Capita National Product of 55 Countries: 1952–1954*, Statistical Papers, Series E, No. 4, Table 2.
ITEM 2. *Statistical Abstract of the United States, 1958*, Table 1186.

indicate the differential ability of nations to keep their populations alive for major portions of the span of life. The cause of death measurements may be expressed either as cause-specific rates or as mortality ratios.

Finally, even though data for the purpose are relatively limited, reference should be made to the prospect of utilizing various composite indices which are undoubtedly highly correlated with differences in economic development and are subject to interpretations with special import for economic development. Three such indices, which may be readily calculated for nations for which life tables are available, are proposed: the "index of human wastage in reproduction";[10] the "index of child wastage"; and the "index

[10] Philip M. Hauser, "Differential Fertility, Mortality and Net Reproduction", unpublished Ph.D. dissertation, Department of Sociology (University of Chicago, 1938), pp. 58 ff.

Argentina	Mexico	Portugal	Japan	Philip-pines	Paraguay	Egypt	India	Yugoslavia
460	220	200	190	150	140	120	60	—
18	—	28	20	40	51	35	44	30
25.2	57.8	47.7	48.3	65.7	53.8	53.6	70.6	66.8
161	95	77	245	32	—	22	21	101
1.9	2.9	0.8	1.3	1.9	2.9	2.1	1.3	1.6
23.8	46.4	22.9	18.5	24.4	49.0	40.0	27.0	25.8
8.2	13.7	12.1	8.0	9.2	10.6	18.4	11.7	11.2
58.5	83.3	87.8	40.7	110.9	81.4	148.5	99.9	98.0
56.9	37.9	58.8	63.9	48.8	—	35.7[b]	32.5	50.1
3.9	3.4	7.0	4.9	3.2	3.7	3.1	3.6	5.7
55.7[d]	82.3	56.1	64.1	89.8	90.4	70.0	69.6	61.0
48.3	—	16.5	42.4	55.6	15.2	29.1	12.0	12.3
4	3	4	4	2	3	2	2	4
12.0	33.4	13.4	6.4	—	—	39.1[b]	40.0	20.0[a]
13.0	31.4	7.4	9.6	—	—	21.6[b]	47.1	17.5[a]
42.8	61.2	33.4	33.4	—	—	55.0[b]	74.2	43.7[a]
+3.4	−50.6	−55.1	−57.3	−66.3	−68.5	−73.0	−86.5	—

ITEM 3. United Nations, *Demographic Yearbook, 1956*, Table 12.
ITEM 4. *Statistical Abstract of the United States, 1958*, Table 1189.
ITEM 5. United Nations, *Statistical Yearbook, 1957*, Table 1.
ITEMS 6, 7, 8, and 9. *Statistical Abstract of the United States, 1958*, Table 1184.
ITEM 10. Table 3.
ITEM 11. United Nations, *Demographic Yearbook, 1956*, Table 4; *Demographic Yearbook, 1955*, Table 10, Part A.
ITEM 12. United Nations, *Demographic Yearbook, 1955*, Table 8.
ITEMS 14, 15, and 16. Computed from data in United Nations, *Demographic Yearbook, 1957*, Table 26.

of human wastage in production". The first of these indices is a measurement of the proportion of females who fail to survive during their child-bearing period ($100 - M_{sf}$, where M_{sf} is the percentage of female survivors between ages of 15 and 45). The second index is a measurement of the proportion of a population which fails to survive to productive age ($100 - S_{15}$, where S_{15} is the percentage of survivors of both sexes to age 15). The third index, of special economic import, is a measurement of the proportion of males who fail to survive during their productive age ($100 - M_{sm}$, where M_{sm} is the percentage of male survivors between the ages of 15 and 65).

The index of human wastage in reproduction is a measurement of differentials in the ability of nations to enable women to survive for the reproduction of the subsequent generation. The index of child wastage is the measurement of differentials among nations in their ability to rear their populations to productive age. The index of human wastage in production may be interpreted as an indication of the differential ability of nations to achieve a productive return on investment in the rearing of their populations.

More elaborate measurements of the same type are possible in estimating the number of man-years of labor force activity which are lost as the result of mortality or other causes preventing the population from labor force participation. But such indices require reasonably good age specific labor force participation rates as well as life tables, and such data are not widely available for the less developed nations of the world. Composite indices derivable from life tables alone may provide more comprehensive world coverage, especially because life tables may be calculated with reasonably good results from census returns of population classified by age. In general, the simpler the rate to which reference has been made above, the more generally available it is likely to be. A Committee of Experts, convened by the Secretary General of the United Nations jointly with the International Labour Office and the United Nations Educational, Scientific and Cultural Organization, has particularly recommended the use of expectation of life at birth, the infant mortality rate, and the crude annual death rate as indicators of a proposed "health component" of the level of living.[11] More recently an Expert Committee on Health Statistics of the World Health Organization proposed the utilization of "the percentage of deaths at ages 50 and over to total deaths" as a "comprehensive health indicator".[12] Each of the indices discussed is worth consideration in efforts to relate demographic phenomena to economic development.

Although decline in mortality has been highly associated with economic development in the experience of the more advanced nations, recent developments indicate that this relationship may, for the time being at least, be breaking down. Among the more advanced nations, reductions in the death rate were achieved over relatively long periods of time during which product per head and levels of living rose. For example, in rough summary, it may be stated that general improvement in food supply reduced the death rate by about ten points from a level of about 40 (deaths per 1,000 total population per year); that an additional ten points of improvement were gained through environmental sanitation and other public health measures; and that a further reduction of ten points was achieved by improvements in medical practice to bring about a crude death rate of about 10. These successive developments in the experience of the more advanced nations were spread out over several centuries.

In contrast, under various economic development programs in the less

---

[11] United Nations, *Report on International Definition and Measurement of Standards and Levels of Living* (New York, 1954), pp. 28 ff.

[12] World Health Organization, Expert Committee on Health Statistics, *Fifth Report*, WHO Technical Report Series No. 133 (Geneva, 1957), pp. 20–21.

advanced areas of the world conducted with the technical assistance of the more advanced nations through the United Nations, the Specialized Agencies, and various unilateral programs, great reductions in mortality are being effected in relatively short periods of time during which relatively little, if any, increase in product per head or level of living is being achieved. A dramatic instance of this development is afforded by the experience of a relatively small underdeveloped area, Ceylon, in which, as a result of a combination of anti-malarial activities and the widespread administration of antibiotics and other modern medical practices, the death rate was halved in considerably less than 10 years. To the extent that great improvements may be achieved in health and longevity as a result of modern medicine, without the benefit of increased product per head or levels of living, the usefulness of measurements of mortality as indicators of economic development will be impaired (see Table 1).

Such impairment, however, is more likely to affect post-World War II and future developments, than the relationships between mortality and economic development prior to World War II. It may turn out, of course, that in the long run the relationship between death rates and economic development may again emerge. For it is unlikely that such improvement in level of mortality can be maintained for any length of time in the absence of economic growth.

Fertility. Fertility, like mortality, may be utilized as an indicator of economic development, both as a component of population growth, and, *sui generis*, as a reflection of national differences in economic, social, and political organization. The experience of the more economically advanced nations of the world reveals a high inverse correlation between birth rates and level of economic development in both senses. That is, the economically advanced nations have, with some lag, manifested declines in fertility as well as declines in mortality.

The general or crude birth rate, like the crude death rate, reflects not only fertility conditions but also differences in the age and sex structure of the population. In addition to crude rates, therefore, it is desirable, in order to improve comparability, to use birth rates which control population composition, such as fertility rates (rates related to females of reproductive age) and age standardized rates. One simple form of the standardized fertility rate is the measurement of "total fertility" (the summation of age specific fertility rates); or the gross reproduction rate (like the total fertility rate, except that it is restricted to female births). Net reproduction rates (like gross reproduction rates, but with allowance for mortality of women) which indicate the replacement implications of current fertility and mortality may also be useful as indicators but are likely not to be unambiguous indicators of economic development.

Again the simpler rates are likely to be more widely available and provide the more comprehensive world coverage. Of considerable usefulness in this regard may be the "effective fertility ratio", an indirect measurement of the birth rate which, in the absence of vital registration statistics, may be calculated from an age distribution afforded by a population census (number of children under 5 per 1,000 women of reproductive age). Since the fertility ratio is affected by child mortality, national cross comparisons are possible only among nations of approximately the same mortality levels. Differences between the more developed and the less developed nations, however, are large enough so as to make the fertility ratio a useful indicator. In fact, because of the higher mortality levels in the less developed nations, the differences tend to be understated.

Birth rates as indicators of economic development may, like death rates, be more useful for pre-World War II than post-World War II conditions. Postwar booms in marriages and births, particularly in many of the economically advanced nations, tend to impair the utility of birth rates as an indicator of economic level (see Table 1).

In view of these limitations, it may be that the most effective use of birth rates as indicators of economic development lie in their relationships to death rates. Variations in interrelations of birth and death rates make possible the construction of a demographic typology which merits consideration as an indicator of economic development.

Demographic Type. Efforts on the part of demographers to explain the "demographic revolution" have produced the "theory of the demographic transition".[13] In brief, this theory is a generalization holding that the industrial revolution and related changes effected modification of fertility-mortality relationships so as to produce "stages" of demographic change. Patterns of mortality-fertility relationships have been variously described in the literature. Particularly useful for the purpose at hand is the scheme adopted by the United Nations as a basis for its world, regional, and national population projections in 1954.[14] The United Nations typology differentiates five patterns of birth-death rate relationships in addition to an "undefined" one. This typology, with the allocation of the areas of the world, the population, and the percentage of the world's population which fall into each category, is reproduced in Table 2.

An examination of the areas of the world by demographic type indicates the general association between fertility-mortality patterns and levels of economic development. A cross-section analysis of this kind is undoubtedly useful, but it must be emphasized that the assumption that the less developed

[13] United Nations, *Determinants and Consequences of Population Trends*, pp. 44 ff.
[14] United Nations Population Division, "Framework for Future Population Estimates 1950–1980, by World Regions", *World Population Conference* (New York, 1955), Vol. III, pp. 285 ff.

Table 2. *World Regions Classified by United Nations Demographic Typology, by Population and Percent of World Population in Each Class,* circa 1950

Birth rate	Death rate	Area	Population (in millions)	Percent of world population
1. High	High	Middle Africa	141	6
2. High	Declining but still high	North Africa Asia (except Japan)	1,280	52
3. High	Declining but fairly low	Southern Africa Middle America Tropical South America	149	6
4. Declining	Fairly low	Temperate South America Japan USSR Balkan Peninsula	359	15
5. Low or fluctuating	Low	North America Most of Europe Australia and New Zealand	523	21
6. Undefined		Pacific Islands	2.8	

Source: United Nations, *World Population Conference, 1954,* New York, 1955, Vol. III, pp. 288 ff.

areas will necessarily undergo the same stages of demographic transition that the more developed nations experienced is a tenuous one.[15] In consequence, it may be that the demographic type may in the future cease to be as useful an indicator of economic development as it appears to be at the present time.

Population Composition

Changes in fertility and mortality produce changes in the age structure of a population. Thus, even where adequate vital registration systems do not exist to provide measurements of birth and death rates, a census tabulation of population by age shows the effects of previous natality and mortality behavior. Differences in the age composition of populations, in consequence, are also indicators of differences in level of economic development.

The simplest of the measurements of differences in age structure is

[15] United Nations, *Determinants and Consequences of Population Trends,* Ch. XV; S. Kuznets, *Towards a Theory of Economic Growth* (Columbia University, 1955), mimeographed.

afforded by the proportion of the population that is under 15 years of age, or 65 years of age and over. The former is inversely, and the latter directly, related to level of economic development. Table 3, listing 72 countries ar-

Table 3. Population 65 and Over for 72 Countries circa 1950

Country	Percent of population 65 and over	Country	Percent of population 65 and over
France	11.79	Jamaica	3.92
Belgium	11.05	Argentina	3.92
Great Britain	10.83	Puerto Rico	3.80
Ireland	10.69	Paraguay	3.72
Sweden	10.32	South Korea	3.70
Austria	10.13	Alaska	3.69
West Germany	9.98	Union of South Africa	
Norway	9.64	(non-European)	3.64
New Zealand (except Maoris)	9.58	India	3.58
Switzerland	9.57	Ecuador	3.54
East Germany	9.28	Chile	3.50
Denmark	9.11	Ceylon	3.48
United States	8.18	Turkey	3.41
Italy	8.06	Mexico	3.36
Australia	8.02	Cuba	3.34
Netherlands	7.86	Panama	3.33
Canada	7.75	Malaya	3.21
Czechoslovakia	7.58	Philippines	3.15
Iceland	7.52	Egypt	3.10
Spain	7.23	El Salvador	2.96
Portugal	6.98	Angola	2.93
Hungary	6.97	Colombia	2.90
Soviet Union	6.90	Costa Rica	2.89
Finland	6.62	Dominican Republic	2.86
Greece	6.31	Nicaragua	2.85
Basutoland	6.24	Burma	2.83
Union of South Africa		Algeria (Moslems)	2.70
(European)	6.18	Venezuela	2.66
Yugoslavia	5.67	Guatemala	2.61
Poland	5.08	Thailand	2.58
Japan	4.94	New Zealand (Maoris)	2.54
Peru	4.32	Formosa	2.50
Trinidad and Tobago	4.11	Brazil	2.45
Haiti	4.00	Mozambique	2.24
Israel	4.00	Greenland	2.17
British Guiana	3.99	Gold Coast	1.52
Honduras	3.97	Togoland	1.46

Source: Compiled from United Nations, *The Aging of Populations and Its Economic and Social Implications* (New York, 1956); and United Nations, *Demographic Yearbooks* since 1950.

rayed in order of percentage of population 65 years of age and over, suggests the utility of age structure as an indicator of level of economic development.

The United Nations has classified the nations of the world into three categories, the "aged", the "mature", and the "young".[16] The "aged" nations, those with over 7 percent of their populations 65 years of age and over, are on the whole the more economically developed nations of the world. The aged countries are entirely in Europe or areas mainly settled by Europeans, in North America and Oceania. The "mature" countries, that is, countries with 4 to 7 percent of their population 65 years of age and over, are primarily countries undergoing industrial transition or nations with income per head intermediate between the aged and young nations. The "young" nations, those with less than 4 percent of their population 65 years of age and over, are without exception the economically less developed countries of the world. They are located largely in Asia, South America, and Africa.

Another index based on age structure of the population with direct economic significance is afforded by the "dependency ratio" and its components. The dependency ratio is a measurement, based on age structure alone, of the number of persons of "dependent" age per 100 persons of "productive" age. Conventionally, population of dependent age is regarded as that under 15 or 65 and over; population of productive age is that 15 to 64 years old. This index may be broken into two components, namely, one which gives younger dependents, and the second, older dependents per 100 persons of productive age. The dependency ratio has direct economic significance in that, all other things being equal, decreases in the dependency ratio tend to result in increases in product per head.

Other statistics relating to population composition may also be useful as indicators of economic development. Without question, the most significant would be the proportion of the working population engaged in agriculture and other labor force statistics. The labor force data, however, are not elaborated upon here. Also useful would be such statistics as those relating to literacy or years of schooling. Detailed statistics on population composition, however, are not likely to be available in adequate form for many of the less developed nations of the world.

Population Distribution

Economic development based on industrialization has, in the experience of the more advanced nations, been accompanied by increased urbanization—that is, by increasing proportions of population resident in cities. The urbanization of a population is, therefore, positively correlated with level of economic development.

[16] United Nations, *The Aging of Populations and Its Economic and Social Implications* (New York, 1956), pp. 7 ff.

National practices differ considerably in the definition of "urban" population.[17] To obtain comparable indices of urbanization, therefore, it is desirable to follow the proposal of the United Nations that size of population agglomeration be used for purposes of international comparability. It is suggested that the proportion of population resident in places of 20,000 population and over be taken as a suitable indicator of economic development. The choice of this size classification would tend to avoid problems arising from differences in practices in incorporation and in designation of smaller agglomerations as "cities"; and tend also to minimize the inclusion of populations as "urban" which are essentially agricultural and rural in character.

Refinements of an index of urbanization are possible, of course, by introducing various city-size categories. Among the significant breaking points would be cities of 100,000 and over and cities of 1,000,000 and over. Improved collection of data promises to make urbanization data more useful in the coming years as indicators of economic development.[18]

Interrelated Indices

Population statistics, in the absence of direct measurements of economic activity and growth, may serve, as suggested above, as indicators of economic development. Used in conjunction with direct measurements of economic activity, however, population data may increase their significance and provide better indices of changes. The use of population statistics in relation to economic data in the calculation of per capita indices, and various ways of relating changes in economic activity to changes in population, are considered in the section which follows.

Despite patent limitations for purposes of international comparability of an index expressed in monetary terms, perhaps the best single measurement of economic level and economic growth is the measurement of per capita national income. Per capita national income would presumably be a direct measurement of level of economic development and, for different periods of time, of changes in level. This index may be further refined by obtaining various per capita expressions of components of national income, as for example, savings, consumer expenditures, disposable income, investment (of various categories), output of food (in calories), industrial production, utilization of non-human energy, output and consumption of steel, and the like.

Measurements would be desirable also relating rate of economic growth to rate of population growth. Indices of this type can be calculated by relat-

17 United Nations, *Demographic Yearbook, 1955* (New York, 1955), p. 16.

18 Kingsley Davis and Hilda Hertz, *The Pattern of World Urbanization*, forthcoming; Philip M. Hauser, "World and Asian Urbanization in Relation to Economic Development and Social Changes", in Philip M. Hauser, ed., *Urbanization in Asia and the Far East* (Calcutta, 1957), pp. 53–95.

ing the rate of increase in national income to the rate of population increase expressed either as a ratio or as a difference. This index may be difficult to use on a current basis because of relatively large errors in statistics on year to year changes both in national income and in population.

Also worthy of consideration as a measurement of the relative position of a nation in the scale of economic development is an index relating the nation's proportion of total world product (as measured by national income, industrial output, agricultural output, etc.) to its proportion of total world population.[19] The "index of relative development" obtained in this manner would be an expression of the extent, in percentage terms, to which a nation has more than its share, or less than its share, of world income, in relation to its share of world population.

The index is given by the following expression:

$$R = \left[\frac{\dfrac{Y_i}{\sum\limits_{i=1}^{n} (Y)}}{\dfrac{P_i}{\sum\limits_{i=1}^{n} (P)}} \right] 100 - 100 \tag{1}$$

where

R = index of relative development

Y_i = income of ith nation

$\sum\limits_{i=1}^{n} (Y)$ = income of all nations of world, or of all for which there are data

P_i = population of ith nation

$\sum\limits_{i=1}^{n} (P)$ = population of all nations of world, or of all for which there are data

The calculation of the index can, of course, be simplified by multiplying the per capita income of each nation by a constant, the reciprocal of the per capita income of the world. That is, R is also given by:

$$R = \frac{Y_i}{P_i} \left[\frac{\sum\limits_{i=1}^{n} (P)}{\sum\limits_{i=1}^{n} (Y)} \right] 100 - 100 \tag{2}$$

[19] For examples of other uses of this index see: Philip M. Hauser, "Workers on the Unemployment Relief Rolls in the United States, March, 1935", *Monthly Report of the Federal Emergency Relief Administration* (Washington, April 1936), pp. 1–29; Simon Kuznets, *ibid.*, p. 17; see also the use of P. Sargant Florence, W. G. Fritz, and R. C. Gilles, "Measures of Industrial Distribution", National Resources Planning Board, *Industrial Location and National Resources* (Washington, 1943), Chapter 5.

The index is, in fact, also interpretable as the extent to which, in percentage terms, the per capita income of a nation is above or below world per capita income.

Parallel to this index would be the analogous dynamic one relating change in national income to change in population. Thus, a nation's proportion of the world's total change in income for a specified period could be related to its proportion of total change in world population.

The index is given by the expression:

$$R_c = \left[\frac{\dfrac{\Delta Y_i}{\Delta \sum\limits_{i=1}^{n} (Y)}}{\dfrac{\Delta P_i}{\Delta \sum\limits_{i=1}^{n} (P)}} \right] 100 - 100 \qquad (3)$$

where

R_c = index of change in relative development

ΔY_i = increase in income of ith nation over specified period

$\Delta \sum\limits_{i=1}^{n} (Y)$ = increase in income of all nations in world, or all available nations, over specified period

ΔP_i = increase in population of ith nation over specified period

$\Delta \sum\limits_{i=1}^{n} (P)$ = increase in population of all nations in world, or all available nations, over specified period

The same short cut in calculation is possible, as was indicated above for the "index of relative development" (equation 2), and the same alternative interpretation is also possible, namely as an index of the extent to which national change in per capita income was above or below world change.

These indices can, of course, be employed for any item in relation to any base, provided that the items in both the numerator and denominator are aggregative for the world, or for a large enough part of the world to make the index meaningful.

CONCLUDING OBSERVATIONS

With increasing interest in the relative economic position of the nations of the world, it may be anticipated that continuing efforts will be made to measure differences and changes in differences in national economic activity and levels of living.[20] Without doubt both

[20] E.g., United Nations, *Report on the World Social Situation* (New York, 1957); United Nations, *Report on International Definition and Measurement of Standards and Levels of Living.*

economic and demographic data will improve in the less economically developed, as well as in the more economically advanced, nations of the world. For some time to come, however, basic economic and demographic data will be subject to much error and will continue to be unavailable for many of the less developed areas. It is likely, however, that demographic data may become available for many of the less advanced nations before direct measurements of economic activity are obtained. In consequence, demographic data will undoubtedly be used as indices of economic level, in the same manner as proposed in the research program, "Regionalization of Underdevelopment", undertaken by the Department of Geography and the Research Center in Economic Development and Cultural Change at the University of Chicago, in response to which this paper was prepared.

The various indices prepared, described, and discussed above are obviously no adequate substitute for direct measurement of economic activity. On the other hand, a number of the demographic indices seem highly related to level of economic development. The data for selected countries in Table 1 point both to the usefulness of demographic indices as indications of economic development and to their limitations. For the data in Table 1 fall far short of perfect correlation and point to the ambiguous character of a number of the indices (see Table 4).

It has not been possible within the limits of this assignment actually to attempt a rigorous quantitative evaluation of demographic rates as indices of economic development. A cursory analysis of the data in Table 1 based on rankings of the arbitrarily selected countries for the data presented in Table 4 does permit a number of at least tentative conclusions.[21]

First, the direct measures of economic activity used in Table 1, items 1 to 4, are reasonably consistent in ranking the arbitrarily selected nations by what may be presumed to be level of economic development. Second, some of the demographic rates are poor predictors of the economic measurements used. These include the rate of population increase, the crude birth rate, the crude death rate, the dependency ratio, and the percentage of population urban. Third, some of the demographic rates do appear to have a high order of relationship to the indices of economic activity. Among these are the infant mortality rate, expectation of life at birth, percentage of population 65 years old and over, and the three "wastage" indices, based on mortality. "Demographic type" seems to have discriminating power, but of a broad character that would admit only of very gross differentiation. The "index of relative

---

[21] No more rigorous analysis such as a rank correlation analysis is undertaken because of the limited number and arbitrary character of the selection of the countries considered. The study under way by the Department of Geography and the Research Center in Economic Development and Cultural Change will collate the data for as many countries as possible and permit both a more comprehensive and more intensive analysis of the interrelationships of the economic and demographic indices.

*Table 4. Rank Order of Nations by Indices of
Economic Development and Specified Demographic Indices,
for Selected Countries, circa 1950 to 1956*

	United States	United Kingdom	Belgium	Nether-lands
1. National income per capita: 1952–54 average (U.S. dollars)	1	3	2	4
2. Percent of gross national product from agriculture *circa* 1956 (inverse)	2	1	3	4
3. Percent of labor force in agriculture (inverse)	3	1	2	4
4. Steel consumption per capita	1	2	3	4
Average rank[a]	1	1	3	4
5. Rate of population increase, 1953–56	8	1	2	4
6. Crude birth rate	8	1	2	4
7. Crude death rate	5	8	10	1
8. Infant mortality rate	3	2	5	1
9. Expectation of life at birth, male	3	2	5	1
10. Percent of population 65 years and older, *circa* 1950	3	2	1	4
11. Dependency ratio	7	2	1	6
12. Percent urban 20,000 and over	5	1	7	3
13. Demographic type	1	1	1	1
14. Index of child wastage	3	2	5	1
15. Index of human wastage in reproduction	4	2	5	1
16. Index of human wastage in production	5	2	6	1
17. Index of representation income	1	3	2	4

Source: Based on Table 1.

[a] Ranked on the basis of an average rank for the four variables.

development" produces, of course, the same ranking as per capita income and may be, despite its many limitations, the best single measure of relative economic development.

Additional research and analysis would, without question, improve the possibility of using demographic data as economic indicators. Such additional research is needed, in any case, both to illuminate economic development and demographic phenomena; and especially to improve our knowledge on the interrelations of demographic and economic variables, particularly in the underdeveloped areas.

Argentina	Japan	Portugal	Mexico	Yugoslavia	Egypt	Philippines	Paraguay	India
5	8	7	6	—	11	9	10	12
5	6	7	—	8	9	10	12	11
5	7	6	10	12	8	11	9	13
6	5	9	8	7	11	10	—	12
5	6	7	8	9	10	11	12	13
9	5	3	12	7	11	9	12	5
6	3	5	12	9	11	7	13	10
3	2	10	12	7	13	4	6	8
6	4	9	8	10	13	12	7	11
7	4	6	10	8	11	9	—	12
8	7	5	11	6	13	12	9	10
3	8	4	11	5	10	12	13	9
4	6	9	—	11	8	2	10	12
5	5	5	9	5	11	11	9	11
6	4	7	9	8	10	—	—	11
7	6	3	10	8	9	—	—	11
7	3	3	10	8	9	—	—	11
5	8	7	6	—	11	9	10	12

RATES
OF INDUSTRIAL GROWTH
IN THE LAST CENTURY,
1860-1958

*Surendra J. Patel**

Nearly two centuries have elapsed since the start of the industrial revolution. But in the first of these two centuries the revolution was essentially an experimental and small-scale affair. Although many inventions had been made by the middle of the nineteenth century, the adoption of advanced technique was limited to Great Britain and even there, except for the textile industry, only on a small scale. The world of the first quarter of the nineteenth century had little experience with the steam locomotive and the railways which were to revolutionize transportation; even by 1850, the total length of the railway network in the three most developed countries—the United Kingdom, France and Germany—was not quite 20,000 kilometers, i.e. less than a sixth of the network that these countries had by the end of the century. The output of pig iron in the whole world was only 4.6 million tons in 1850, half of which was in Great Britain. The technique of producing steel had hardly gone beyond the handicraft stage. Even the most advanced countries in the world were still in the last days of the iron age. Cast iron could be used in rails, pillars, bridges, engine cylinders and even wheels, but it had its limits; it was not suited for the working parts of engines and machines. The steel age was about

From Surendra J. Patel, "Rates of Industrial Growth in the Last Century, 1860–1958," *Economic Development and Cultural Change*, 9:3:316–330 (April 1961). Reprinted by permission of The University of Chicago Press.

* The author is a member of the Secretariat of the United Nations Economic Commission for Europe at Geneva. The views expressed herein, however, are his personal views and should not be interpreted as those of the Organization.

to begin. The Bessemer converter was invented in 1856 and even with the advance made by the Martin-Siemens process (1864–67) the total output of steel in the world was no more than 700,000 tons in 1870, or less than one-half of India's output in 1958.

Hence only the last hundred years can be regarded as a century of the machine age and industrial expansion. This study attempts to measure the scale and the speed of this growth and the relationship between the major sectors of industrial output in various countries; it also sets out to indicate the rates of growth at which the gaps in the volume of industrial output among the major industrial countries were closed in the past in order to suggest the rates of growth that may be necessary to close the present gap between the industrial and the pre-industrial countries.

The limitations of index number series stretching over a hundred years should not be overlooked. The availability and accuracy of the figures cannot be expected to be uniform over so long a period of such rapid change. More-over, since they were prepared in part by different individuals or institutions, linking the various series introduces a number of distortions in the continuity. In consequence, and in order to avoid repeating words of caution every time these figures are mentioned, it should be emphasized right at the beginning that they represent no more than an order of magnitude—adequate for in-dicating the broad sweep of movement over the century, but not precise enough to measure accurately each succeeding stage.

I. THE RATES OF GROWTH OF INDUSTRIAL OUTPUT

Over the last century industrial output[1] in the world as a whole rose some thirty- to fortyfold (see Table 1). World population, on the other hand, slightly more than doubled. Hence industrial output per capita is now some 15 to 20 times higher than a hundred years ago. The absolute growth in per capita industrial output in the last 100 years was thus a number of times higher than that attained in the entire preceding period of man's existence; and the per capita rate of growth (2.6 percent per year in contrast to less than 0.1 percent in preceding centuries) was much higher still.[2]

Considerable interest attaches to an analysis of the rates of growth of industrial output for the world as a whole and for the major industrial coun-tries. As can be seen from Table 2, world industrial output has expanded by about 3.6 percent per year over these hundred years. Whatever the period chosen, the rate has varied little, except during the inter-war period (1918–1938) of stagnation and the great depression, when the rate fell to 2.4 percent

---

[1] Throughout the study, industrial output refers to the production in factories and excludes that of the handicraft and cottage industries sector.

[2] See J. M. Keynes, *Essays in Persuasion* (London, 1931), p. 360.

*Table 1. Growth of Industrial Output and Population in
World and Selected Countries, 1860–1958*

Period	World[a]	United Kingdom	France	Ger-many[b]	United States	Italy	Sweden	Japan	USSR
				(Index numbers of industrial output, 1953 = 100)					
1860	4	15	15	6	2	—	—	—	—
1870	5	19	20	8	3	5	2	—	(1)
1880	8	23	24	10	5	7	3	—	(1)
1890	12	28	31	18	8	12	7	—	1
1900	16	33	40	29	12	17	16	10[c]	3
1910	24	36	56	42	20	30	23	12	4
1913	28	43	66	51	23	35	26	16	5
1920	26	43	45	30	30	32	25	28	1
1925–29	38	45	80	53	39	50	33	44	5
1932	30	45	67	35	24	41	34	49	12
1938	51	64	74	77	36	61	59	88	31
1950	—	94	87	72	84	79	97	55	69
1953	100	100	100	100	100	100	100	100	100
1958	133	114	150	151	102	142	118	168	172
1959	—	120	159	162	115	158	121	208	191
				Population in millions					
1850	1,200	28	36	36	23	24	3.5	—	60
1900	1,600	42	39	56	76	33	5.1	47	111
1950	2,400	51	42	(50)	152	47	7.0	83	—
1958	2,800	52	45	(54)	174	49	7.4	92	(206)

Sources: Industrial output: 1860 from Rolf Wagenführ, *Die Industriewirtschaft, Ent-wicklungstendenzen der deutschen und internationalen Industrieproduktion, 1860 bis 1932,* Institut für Konjunkturforschung (Berlin, 1932); 1870–1900 from League of Nations, *Industrialization and Foreign Trade* (Geneva, 1945), except for Sweden and Russia up to 1910, Japan up to 1932 and the world up to 1938; 1910 to recent years from O.E.E.C., *Industrial Statistics 1900–1957* (Paris, 1958), and United Nations, *Statistical Yearbook and Monthly Bulletin of Statistics*; also United States, *Historical Statistics: 1789–1945,* U.S.S.R., *Narodnoye Khozyaistvo* (Moscow, 1956); I. Svennilson, *Growth and Stagnation in the European Economy* (Geneva, 1954) and Y. Kotkovsky, *International Affairs,* No. 2 (1959). For population, W. S. Woytinsky and E. S. Woytinsky, *World Population and Production* (New York, 1953).

Note on Methods: World index of industrial output (excluding mining up to 1938 and handicraft production throughout the period) based on League of Nations up to 1938; figures based on the "net value added" concept, except for the U.S.S.R. where they refer to the gross value of output and may overestimate the trend between 1925–29 and 1938; for postwar years, United Nations index linked to these and adjusted, in a very rough and ready way, for the inclusion of the output in the U.S.S.R., eastern Europe and China, thus: 1953 adjusted world-weights were derived by taking U.S.S.R. output as one-third of that of the United States, eastern European as one-half of U.S.S.R. and Chinese output as one and a half to two times that of India; 1925–29 index (base period of League of Nations index) linked with 1953 index by deflating the weights of U.S. industrial output in the world total for 1925–29 and 1953 by the movement of the U.S. index in this period.
[a] Incl. U.S.S.R., eastern Europe and China. [b] Western Germany only for postwar years.
[c] 1905.

per annum. But these years of inhibited growth seem to have piled up such a vast backlog of demand for capital and consumer goods that under its pressure the recent postwar decade was a period of very rapid industrial growth. Consequently, if the whole period from 1913 to 1958 is considered, the rate of 3.5 percent per year is not substantially different from the rate of 3.6 percent per year for the century as a whole.

The relative constancy of the rate of growth of industrial output for the world as a whole does not imply that all countries expanded their output at the same rate. The factors responsible for different rates of economic growth are complex and beyond the scope of this study. Broadly speaking, industrial output grew rather slowly in the countries where industrialization started earlier. Thus, for instance, the lowest growth rates are found in the United Kingdom and France. On the other hand, the rate of growth of industrial output attained by each new entrant in the field of industrialization has tended to be successively higher. As can be seen in Table 2, where the countries are arranged from left to right in the approximate chronological order in which they began industrializing, this trend is maintained in the period before as well as after the first world war.

For the period of 33 years (1880 to 1913) the rate of growth of industrial output rises from about 2 percent per year in the United Kingdom, to 3 percent for France, 5 percent for Germany, the United States and Italy, and to about 6 percent for Sweden and Russia. For the 45-year period from 1913 to 1958 the rates rise from about 2 percent for the United Kingdom and France to 2.4 percent for Germany, over 3 percent for the United States, Italy and Sweden, 5.4 percent for Japan and over 8 percent for the U.S.S.R.—and in these crowded 45 years there were two world wars and an international depression! The list of countries is not, of course, complete; but it does include nearly all the major countries, which accounted throughout the period for eighty to ninety percent of the world's industrial output.

One explanation for this rise in the rate of industrial growth for each successive new entrant into the industrial field might be the fact that the volume of its industrial output in the initial stage was so small that relatively limited additions to it would appear large in percentage terms. But this seems an inadequate explanation, for two reasons. First, the high rates would continue for the initial years only; they would not be almost consistently maintained, as they were, for a rather long period. Second, it would then be reasonable to expect that in some early phase of industrial development in the advanced industrial countries the rate of growth was also very high and that it declined subsequently as the volume of their industrial output rose. But the available evidence does not seem to support this. In the early stage of industrial expansion in Great Britain—the forty years (1820 to 1860) following the Napoleonic wars—the rate of growth of industrial output was a little over 3 percent per year, which was very close to the rate of 3 percent

Table 2. *Annual Rates of Growth in Industrial Output in Selected Countries, 1860–1958, Percent (Compounded)*

Period	World[a]	United King-dom	France	Ger-many[b]	United States	Italy	Sweden	Japan	USSR
1860 to 1880	3.2	2.4	2.4	2.7	4.3	—	—	—	—
1880 to 1900	4.0	1.7	2.4	5.3	4.5	4.5	8.1	—	6.4
1900 to 1913	4.2	2.2	3.7	4.4	5.2	5.6	3.5	3.8[c]	4.8
1913 to 1925–29	2.2	0.3	1.4	0.3	3.7	2.6	1.6	7.5	1.1
1925–29 to 1938	2.8	3.1	−0.7	3.5	−0.9	1.7	5.4	6.5	17.2
1913 to 1938	2.4	1.4	0.4	1.7	1.7	2.2	3.3	7.1	7.8
1938 to 1958	4.9	2.9	3.6	3.5	5.3	4.3	3.5	3.4	8.9
1860–1913	3.7	2.1	2.8	4.1	4.6	—	—	—	—
1880 to 1913	4.1	1.9	3.1	4.9	4.8	4.9	6.3	—	5.7
1880 to 1958	3.8	2.1	2.3	3.5	3.9	3.9	4.6	—	7.2
1900 to 1958	3.7	2.2	2.3	2.9	3.7	3.7	3.5	5.0[c]	7.5
1913 to 1958	3.5	2.2	1.9	2.4	3.3	3.1	3.4	5.4[d]	8.3
1925–29 to 1958	4.1	3.0	2.1	3.5	3.1	3.4	4.2	4.4	11.8

Sources: Same as Table 1.
[a] Including U.S.S.R., eastern Europe and China.
[b] Western Germany only for post–World War II years.
[c] 1905–58.
[d] 1938 level reached only in 1952. If these 14 years are excluded, the rate would be 8.2 percent.

for the 31 years (1925–29 to 1958) following the first World War. Examination of the long-term development suggests that there was a fair amount of almost monotonous continuation of nearly the same per capita rate of growth in the United Kingdom, France, Germany and the United States; disregarding a few years of slow growth—due to either a war or a depression—even the older industrial countries do not seem to have suffered from what Keynes called "the rheumatics of old age." Although rates of growth after the first World War were in most countries somewhat lower than those before it, with the notable exception of Japan and the U.S.S.R., this is—as shown above—almost entirely explained by changes in the rate of population growth—not to speak of the influence of the years spent in war and the depression.

Perhaps a more valid explanation of the progressively higher rates of growth of industrial output for each new entrant to the process of industrialization lies in the opportunity of benefiting from accumulated technological advance—a factor which was so emphatically stressed by Veblen. It is reasonable to suppose that the rate of growth in the United Kingdom and France was determined in the main by the pace of technological advance. These countries could only apply new techniques as they evolved; whereas for each new entrant there was already an accumulated body of technological progress to assimilate. The newly industrializing countries did not have to follow religiously the slow and necessarily step-by-step developments in techniques common to the countries which set out early on the road to industrialization. Nor did they have to bear the costs and delays of evolving and industrially trying out the new techniques; the countries which were ahead continued doing most of this. The later a country entered the field of industrialization, the larger was the fund of technological advance upon which it could draw, and hence the faster its possible rate of growth. So long as the technological gap between the pioneering countries and the newcomers was not bridged, the high rate of growth in the latter could be maintained.

It would follow that, in technological terms, the rates of industrial growth could not have been much higher in the pioneering countries. For the same reason—and again technologically speaking—the rates of growth in the countries just starting industrialization in the second half of the twentieth century can be higher (depending upon the ability to assimilate and spread advanced technology) than the rates attained by the countries industrializing in the first half of the twentieth century, and substantially higher than the rate of growth attained by countries which began industrializing earlier.

As to growth in per capita output—during the last century, population increased by less than 1 percent per year in the older industrial countries (and much less in France) or at about the same rate as the population of the world as a whole. The increase was in general faster in the first half than in the second half of the century. Only in the United States, where Europeans migrated in large numbers in this period, was the rate of growth of population for the century as a whole as high as about 2 percent per year. As in the other countries, in the United States the rate of growth during the first half of this period—nearly 3 percent per year—was more than twice as high as that during the second period.

As shown in Table 2, the rate of growth of industrial output in the older industrial countries in the period 1913 to 1958 was somewhat lower than in the period 1860 to 1913. This decline has often been attributed to two causes: the expectation of a slowing down in the rate of growth as the industrial base became larger; and the disturbances caused by the two wars and the great depression. However, when the rate of growth of industrial output is deflated by changes in the rate of population growth, there is relatively little difference in the per capita annual rate of growth for both the periods, before and after the first World War. This is strikingly borne out by the experience in the United States, where the growth of industrial output was 4.6 percent in the period of 1860–1913 and 3.3 percent in the period 1913 to 1958; but the rate of growth of population was about 3 percent a year in the first period and 1.3 percent in the second period. Per capita industrial output thus grew at roughly the same rate—in fact slightly faster in the second period—despite the fact that the volume of output in the period after 1913 was substantially higher than in 1860 and that there was a decade of depression.[3] Analysis of per capita rates of growth of industrial output in the United Kingdom, Germany and France shows that in each country the rate was not significantly different in either of the two periods.

Viewed over this long period, the differences in the rates of growth of population and industrial output bring out forcibly the immense power of compound growth at higher rates. The differences in rates of growth of 1 to 2 percent (population) and 3 to 7 or more percent (industrial output) are indeed large. But they may not appear spectacular. Only when these rates are compounded over a long period—say a century—can one see the full impact of the staggering force of compound growth at higher rates. Over a century, a given quantity (population or output) will increase 2.7 times at 1 percent, 7.2 times at 2 percent, 19 times at 3 percent, 50 times at 4 percent, and 130 times at 5 percent. The extent of the growth during a hundred years at still higher rates is almost incredible: 340 times at 6 percent, 870 times at 7 percent, and—just to underline the spectacular effect of high compound rates— nearly 14,000 times at 10 percent in a century. If the rate of growth of industrial output is some 2 to 4 percent higher than population growth, the rise in per capita output over a century would be much higher than might be suggested by the rather modest difference in the rates of growth.

II. THE PATTERN OF INDUSTRIAL GROWTH

In recent years a number of countries have initiated programmes and plans of economic development in which special attention is paid to industrial growth. For them, decisions concerning the patterns of industrial development have assumed great practical importance. In view of the wide difference in the endowment of natural resources in various coun-

---

[3] A similar conclusion for the growth of total per capita output for the last 120 years in the United States was advanced by Raymond Goldsmith. See United States Congress, Joint Economic Committee, *Employment, Growth, and Price Levels, Hearings* (86th Congress, 1st Session), Part II (Washington, April 7–10, 1959), pp. 230 ff.

tries, a study of the development of specific industries in the industrial countries is not likely to furnish a useful guide to determining investment priorities in the preindustrial countries at the present time. But a study of the historic evolution of the over-all sectoral pattern—the relationship between producer goods and the consumer goods—in the major industrial countries may be more relevant. Consumer goods, as defined here, include all those finished goods and also semifinished goods (e.g. yarn) which, although often used in industry, are largely bought by the public in a finished form—primarily for consumption in the home. Producer goods include raw materials, semimanufactured articles and capital goods which are used by manufacturers.[4]

It is indeed striking that in all the major industrial countries for which data are shown in Table 3 there was a continuous decline over time in the share of consumer goods in total industrial output. At the beginning of industrialization in these countries, consumer goods accounted for two-thirds or more of total industrial output, and producer goods for the remainder. In the course of industrial development, however, the relative position of these two sectors was almost completely reversed—the share of consumer goods falling to around one-third of total industrial output and that of producer goods rising correspondingly. The rate of growth of the producer goods sector was thus throughout this period higher than that of the consumer goods sector.

In the early phase of industrialization—stretching from a few decades to half a century in the United Kingdom, France, Germany, the United States, Italy, Japan,[5] and the U.S.S.R.—the producer goods sector grew one and a half to more than two times as fast as the consumer goods sector (see Table 4). Once industrialization had reached a fairly high level and the proportion of consumer goods in total industrial output had fallen to around one-third, the differences in the rates of growth of both these sectors narrowed down

---

[4] The definition, and part of the data used in this section, are from Dr. W. Hoffmann's two studies, *British Industry, 1700–1950* (Oxford, 1955), and *Stadien und Typen der Industrialisierung* (Jena, 1931). The latter book has recently been published, in a somewhat revised and expanded version, in English translation under the title, *The Growth of Industrial Economies* (Manchester, 1958). The consumer and producer goods industries are defined to include four broad groups of industries under each—the consumer goods sector includes food, drink and tobacco, clothing (including footwear), leather goods and furniture (excluding other wood-working industries); the producer goods sector includes ferrous and non-ferrous metals, machinery, vehicle building and chemicals. These groups account for "two-thirds of the net output of all industry." For details, see *The Growth of Industrial Economies*, pp. 8–17.

[5] Owing to statistical limitations, the data for Japan are not shown in Table 4; but the developments there were essentially similar to those elsewhere. See W. W. Lockwood, "The Scale of Economic Growth in Japan, 1868–1938," in Simon Kuznets, W. E. Moore, and J. J. Spengler, editors, *Economic Growth: Brazil, India, Japan* (Durham, 1955), pp. 153–154.

Table 3. Decline in the Share of Consumer Goods in
Industrial Output in Selected Countries

Country	Year and share in percentages				
Great Britain	1871	1901	1924	—	1946
	52	41	40		31
France	1861–65	1896	1921	—	1952
	65	44	35		34
Germany	—	1895	1925	1936	1951
		45	37	25	23
United States	1880	1900	1927	—	1947
	44	34	32		30
Belgium	1846	1896	1926	1936–38	—
	80	49	37	36	
Switzerland	1882	1895	1923	—	1945
	62	45	38		34
Italy	—	1896	1913	1938	—
		72	53	37	
Japan	—	—	1925	—	1950
			59		40
USSR	—	1913	1928	1940	1955
		67	61	39	29

Sources: Data for Great Britain, France, Germany, the United States, Belgium, Switzerland and Japan from W. Hoffmann, *The Growth of Industrial Economies*, Statistical Appendix; for Italy, from A. Gerschenkron, "Rate of Industrial Growth in Italy, 1881–1913," in *Journal of Economic History*, XV, No. 4 (December, 1955), 365; data for Japan (1950) from United Nations, *Supplement to the Monthly Bulletin of Statistics* (1954) and for France (1952) from OEEC, *Statistical Bulletin, Definitions and Methods: Indices of Industrial Production* (Paris, 1957) ; and for the U.S.S.R. from *Narodnoye Khozyaistvo* (Moscow, 1956), p. 52.
Note: Owing to the limitations of statistical comparability, the figures are to be treated as crude indicators only. The data are based on "net value added" in manufacturing industries (excluding mining and building) for all countries except the U.S.S.R. where they refer to the gross value of output and include mining. For definitions, see the opening paragraph of this section and the footnote to it.

significantly, with the producer goods sector expanding only a little faster than the consumer goods sector. This general pattern of industrial growth— producer goods expanding nearly twice as fast as consumer goods in the early phase of industrialization and the gap between the rates of growth for the two sectors narrowing down later on—appears to have been a characteristic feature of economic development in all the major industrial coun-

Table 4.   Rates of Growth of Consumer and Producer Goods and
Their Ratio in Selected Countries

Country and period	Total industrial output (a)	Consumer goods output (b)	Producer goods output (c)	Ratio of producer goods output to consumer goods output col. c / b
		Percent per year		
Great Britain				
1812 to 1851	3.4	3.1	4.0	1.3
1851 to 1881	2.7	2.0	3.8	1.9
1881 to 1907	1.8	1.5	2.0	1.3
1907 to 1935	1.0	0.8	1.2	1.5
France				
1861–65 to 1896	2.4	1.2	3.3	2.7
1896 to 1921	0.5	—	1.1	—
Germany				
1860 to 1880	2.9	1.8	3.9	2.2
1880 to 1900	5.0	3.7	5.4	1.5
1900 to 1913	3.4	2.5	3.7	1.5
United States				
1880 to 1900	4.5	3.2	5.1	1.6
1900 to 1927	4.2	3.9	5.5	1.4
Italy				
1896 to 1913	5.4	3.5	8.7	2.5
USSR				
1928 to 1940	17.0	12.0	21.2	1.8
1940 to 1955	8.1	6.1	9.1	1.5
1958 to 1965 (Plan)	8.8	7.3	9.3	1.3

Sources and Methods: W. Hoffmann, *British Industry 1700–1950* (Oxford, 1955); Rolf Wagenführ, *Die Industriewirtschaft* (Berlin, 1932); for Italy and the U.S.S.R., the same as in Table 3; also N. S. Khrushchev's *Report to the XXI Congress of CPSU* (Moscow, 1957). The rates of growth for France and the United States derived by applying the proportions for each of the sectors given in the Statistical Appendix to Hoffmann's study, *The Growth of Industrial Economies*, to the movement of the index of manufacturing production for the periods concerned.
Note: See Note to Table 3.

tries.[6] Among these countries, there were very real differences in their natural resources endowment, in the accumulation of technical skills, in the period

[6] This pattern of growth, however, is not restricted to the major industrial countries only. As Hoffmann has shown by an analysis of changes in industrial structure over time, it applies to small industrial countries also. He has defined three basic stages in industrial growth in accordance with the changes in the ratio of the volume of consumer goods output to that of producer goods output; in the first stage, the ratio is $5(\pm 1):1$, in the

when they began industrialization, in the speed of their growth, in their at-titude and actual experience regarding international trade and capital movements, in the proportion of capital goods output devoted to exports, in the fiscal and other forms of economic policies pursued, and in how industrial growth was promoted—through private enterprise (and therefore without a strict pre-determination of sectoral priorities) or through state encouragement and central planning. Despite these differences there was nevertheless a striking uniformity in the evolution of the sectoral pattern of their industrial growth.

In a broad historical sense, there is nothing surprising in such a development. It is only a common sense proposition that since output of producer goods is the least developed segment in the early phase of industralization, it should expand much faster than the consumer goods sector. Moreover, the share of investment (and hence producer goods) in national output and expenditure usually rises in the process of economic growth and calls for a more rapid expansion of the supplies of producer goods than of consumer goods. This process is generally reinforced by an increasing substitution of imported producer goods by domestic output.[7] The relatively faster expansion of producer goods often continues even at a later stage of economic growth when the share of investment in national expenditure becomes more or less stable largely due to a rise in the actual machinery and equipment content per unit of fixed asset formation and in the share of producer goods in exports.[8] Many economic historians have regarded such a development as an essential feature of industrial growth,[9] although other economists, perhaps owing to their limited acquaintance with long-term experience and their preoccupation with contemporary concerns, have been less than clear on this point.

III. CHANGING SHARES IN THE WORLD'S INDUSTRIAL OUTPUT

Differences in the rates of growth of industrial output, described above, have led to important changes in the relative position of various countries and areas in total world industrial output. An

second 2.5($\pm$1):1 and in the third it is 1($\pm$0.5):1. The fourth stage has a still lower ratio. See Hoffmann, *The Growth of Industrial Economies*, op. cit., pp. 2–3, also Chapter IV.

[7] For elucidation of a similar conclusion reached by a discussion of export prospects, see Surendra J. Patel, "Export Prospects and Economic Growth: India," in the *Economic Journal*, LXIX, No. 275 (September, 1959), 490 ff.

[8] This may also be explained to some extent by the fact that a part of the final output of the metal, vehicle and chemical industries is destined for consumers.

[9] See W. Hoffmann, *British Industry, 1700–1950*, op. cit., p. 73; and *idem, The Growth of Industrial Economies*, op. cit., p. 2. Also see A. Gerschenkron, "Rate of Industrial Growth in Italy, 1881–1931," in the *Journal of Economic History*, XV, No. 4 (December, 1955), 365.

analysis of these changes is of great interest in elucidating the conditions under which the gap between the most advanced industrial nations and the late-comers was closed. Its relevance to the contemporary problem of closing the gap between rich industrial countries and poor pre-industrial areas needs no emphasis.

Great Britain was the seed-bed for the early phase of the industrial revolution. Although it had only about 2 percent of the world's population, more than one-half of the world's industrial output was concentrated in these islands throughout the first half of the nineteenth century. In a world in which the growth of output in relation to population was almost stagnant, Great Britain attained a decisive superiority by realizing rates of growth of 2 to 3 percent per year. Although these rates appear very modest in comparison with those current in many parts of the world in the last few decades, they were a powerful engine of massive expansion—particularly when cumulated over a long period—in a more or less stagnant world. The benefits they yielded in the nineteenth century to Great Britain in terms of wealth and power are now a matter of common knowledge. This was the period of which it is rightly said that England was the workshop of the world.

The growth of industrial output in other countries in Europe and in the United States at rates twice as high as in Great Britain had started making inroads into British industrial supremacy during the second half of the nineteenth century. To the contemporary Europeans, the economic race between Great Britain and Germany was not just a subject of idle curiosity; it was intimately bound up with the realities of power and influence over the rest of mankind. While this contest constituted a center of attention for the historians of the late nineteenth century, the rapid emergence of the United States as a world industrial power was of far greater significance.[10] Already by the close of the nineteenth century the United States had surpassed Great Britain in total volume of industrial output (see Table 5), which by the end of the century was one and a half times higher than in Great Britain, and total German output was not far behind the British. Since the First World War the United States has remained the center of the industrial world, accounting for nearly 40 percent of its output.[11] Less than half a century was needed to accomplish this change.

[10] To the historians who study the present economic competition between the United States and the U.S.S.R., it may be suggested that the economic developments in contemporary China may not have an altogether dissimilar significance for the twenty-first century.

[11] Whatever the shift in the relative position of Great Britain and the United States, the total industrial output in these two English-speaking countries has continued to account for one-half or more of the world's industrial output throughout the nineteenth century and the first half of the twentieth century. Economics—the whole body of theoretical premises, the neat schemes of internal balances and disturbing elements, the bundle of logical deductions and policy conclusions—is in no small measure associated with this; for

*Table 5. Relative Position of Selected Countries in World Industrial Output,
Percentage Share in World Industrial Output*

	Private enterprise economies							Centrally planned economies		
Period	Total	US	United King-dom	Ger-many[a]	Total Western Europe	Japan	Others	Total	USSR	Eastern Europe	China
1870	97	23	32	13	62	—	12	3	—	—	—
1896–1900	96	30	20	17	53	—	13	4	—	—	—
1913	95	36	14	16	44	1	14	5	—	—	—
1926–1929	95	42	9	12	35	2	16	5	(2)	—	—
1953	77	41	6	6	25	2	9	23	14	(7)	(2)
1958	69	31	5	7	25	3	10	31	18	—	—

Sources: Same as Table 1. Data for 1870 to 1926–1929 from League of Nations, *Industrialization and Foreign Trade* (Geneva, 1945), p. 13, and for 1953, as indicated in the general note to Table 1; those for 1958 derived by deflating the relative weights by the movement of the index of industrial output; the weight assigned in the League of Nations' study to the industrial output in the U.S.S.R. in 1926–29 adjusted to agree with the movement of the index for the U.S.S.R. in Table 1.
Note: The relative shares of countries are based on very crude data and any intercountry comparisons should be limited to broad order of magnitude rather than precise statistical measurement.
[a] All of Germany up to 1926–29 and only western Germany thereafter.

During the first half of the twentieth century, other countries—Italy, Japan and the U.S.S.R.—began industrializing. Their pace of growth was still higher, but their share in world output in the initial period was so low that until the middle of this century their growth had little effect on the relative positions of other countries. This, however, was no longer the case by the end of the fifties. By then, the division of the world into two zones or regions was a fairly settled affair: the private enterprise economies, which basically maintained—although with considerable modifications in recent years—private ownership of means of production and depended on private enterprise for economic growth; the other, the centrally planned economies, where the resourcefulness and the financial ability of the individual daring entrepreneur of the Schumpeterian type was replaced by the leadership of the state in planning and promoting industrial growth. The precise measurement of the rates of growth which the latter group has attained remains a

economics is for the most part a product of the English-speaking countries with occasional contributions from the outside.

subject of considerable controversy among western scholars, but there is general agreement that these rates have been high—they are usually placed in the range of 8 to 10 percent per year,[12] or more than twice as high as in the United States and nearly four times the rate common in the older industrial countries.

The relative position of the two groupings shown in Table 5 is very approximate, in fact only illustrative, and no attempt should be made to read into it any statistical precision. For the purpose of a broad survey of this type, it is not very important whether a few percentage points are added to or subtracted from either region. What is of decisive importance is the present relationship between their respective rates of growth. Given this relationship and given its continuation over the next decade or two, little arithmetical skill is needed to indicate that the industrial output of the centrally planned economies could approximate that of the rest of the world 15 to 25 years hence. Whether the level of industrial output in the centrally planned economies in recent years is taken as one-half, one-third or one-fourth (and these relative positions have been suggested by various scholars) of that in the private enterprise economies makes a difference of only a decade to the period—15 years or 25 years—in which the industrial output in both groupings could become approximately equal.

Whether the present differential in the rates of growth in these two areas will continue or will narrow is not the main concern of this paper. The important point is this: once the continuation of the differential in the rates is assumed, the closing of the gap in a relatively short period is an arithmetically inevitable consequence. It would merely be a repetition of what Great Britain attained in the first half and the United States and Germany in the second half of the nineteenth century. In all these countries the underlying conditions were also the same, that is, the rate of growth of the newcomer was twice (or more) as high as that of the old-timer; and the period needed for closing the gap was less than half a century—the lifetime of a man in his twenties.

One further observation of some relevance may be made in this connection. Although a number of countries have become industrially strong over the last century, over 90 percent of the world's industrial output has con-

[12] For details regarding rates of growth in the Soviet Union, see Donald R. Hodgman, *Soviet Industrial Production, 1928–51* (Cambridge, Mass., 1954), pp. 89, 134; Naum Jasny, *The Soviet Economy During the Plan Era* (Stanford, 1951), p. 23; Colin Clark, *The Conditions of Economic Progress*, second edition (London, 1951), p. 186, and F. Seton, "The Tempo of Soviet Industrial Expansion" in *Bulletin of the Oxford University Institute of Statistics* (February, 1958), 18. The rates of growth of industrial output in the U.S.S.R., estimated by western scholars for the period 1928 to 1940, are lower than official estimates, although the difference between these has continued to narrow with the passage of time. The annual rate of growth was 11 percent according to Jasny and Clark, 13 percent according to Hodgman and about 13 to 14 percent according to Seton; the official estimate was 16 to 17 percent.

tinued to be concentrated in areas (including eastern Europe and the U.S.S.R.) inhabited by peoples of European origin—peoples now accounting for rather less than one-third of the population of the world. There have been varying degrees of industrialization in other countries (Japan, India, and China) but the share of these countries in world output was very small until recent years. An unfortunate consequence of observing such a concentration was the cultivation of a belief in some quarters that industrial growth was somehow an exclusively European plant which might be grown with great care in a few and specially selected gardens in the rest of the world but could hardly be expected to become a matter of mass cultivation.

It is true that all new technical developments require attaining adequate training and in many instances adaptation of habits of thought and behavior.[13] But in a wide historical perspective, industrial growth, or more precisely the application of machinery to productive use, would seem to be no more the exclusive hall-mark of a particular geographic (and hence ethnic) region than were all the past landmarks in mankind's long development—early use of fire and later the taming of it, domestication of animals, agriculture and irrigation, smelting of ores and use of metals, invention of scripts, paper and the art of printing, ship's sternpost rudder and marine-compass, gunpowder, Indian numerals and the methods of calculation, and many others. Many areas of the world would recognize in such a list their own contribution—which was carried forward, enriched and brought to fruition in some other parts at another time. The experience of industrial growth in Japan, and in more recent years in India and China, should indicate that the idea of industrialization as an exclusive possession of the peoples of European origin is based on an arrogant ignorance of history rather than on facts.

IV. PERSPECTIVES FOR THE PRE-INDUSTRIAL COUNTRIES

While looking back over the broad sweep of industrial growth over the last century, it is indeed tempting to peer into the years to come. In any such crystal-gazing, the dominating theme is bound to be the spread of the machine age and industrial growth to the countries which have so far remained almost wholly untouched by it. The increasing attention being devoted to the problem of narrowing international disparities in incomes and levels of living is evidence of the growing importance of the problem.

If, in a map of the world, the oceans are removed and the continental land masses huddled together, the resulting conglomeration of countries looks like an inverted flower-bud, with Great Britain forming the stem, France,

[13] A. Gerschenkron has drawn pointed attention to this. See his paper, "Economic Backwardness in Historical Perspective," in Bert F. Hoselitz, editor, *The Progress of Underdeveloped Areas* (Chicago, 1952), p. 23.

Germany and central Europe the heart, Canada, the United States, Australia and New Zealand one calyx, and the Scandinavian countries, eastern Europe, the U.S.S.R. and Japan the other; and the large continents of Asia, Africa and Latin America lie together like the closed petals of this flower-bud. After thousands of years of cold and dreary winter, the arrival of spring-time of mankind—a century of the machine age—has just barely seen the invigorating sap pass through the stem, heart and calyx of the bud. The dominant process in the century to come will no doubt be its full blossoming.

A number of factors will have great relevance in determining the time, and the extent of the growth of industrialization in these continents. Foremost among them will no doubt be natural resources—not in any static form as something given once and for all, but as a dynamic function of man's ever-growing technological ability to use these more fruitfully than before—and the social structure with its internal drive and stresses and the ability to grow without overstraining. Many new problems will arise; and many of the older problems will probably be approached and solved differently in the light of changed circumstances and possibilities. Furthermore, adequate development of agriculture and other sectors besides modern manufacturing industries is needed for an economy's overall growth. Consideration of all these important points is beyond the scope of this study.

The arithmetical pre-condition for narrowing and finally closing the gap in standards of living between the industrial and pre-industrial countries is that the rate of economic growth in the nonindustrial countries should be higher than in the industrial ones. Overall economic growth and levels of living include of course, as mentioned above, the development of many sectors—agriculture, health, education, housing, etc.—besides industries. In such all-round development, it is now generally accepted that industrialization plays a crucial role. One of the findings of this study is that the rate at which industrial growth has taken place in each of the newly industrializing countries over the last century has progressively continued to rise—from some 2 to 3 percent in early nineteenth century to 4 to 5 percent up to the first World War and some 8 to 10 percent in the last few decades. Moreover, growth at such rates has continued for a number of decades.

Thus, if a newly industrializing country can attain an annual increment of 8–10 percent in its industrial output, and can maintain this for 3 to 5 decades, the task of narrowing substantially and even closing the gap in output between the older industrial countries and the newcomers is not formidable at all. This is because of the relentless force of growth at compound rates over a period of time—particularly towards the end of the period.[14] The

---

[14] Drawing attention to the staggering increase involved in compound rates of growth, Keynes once illustrated this by the probable growth of the treasure of £40,000—the prodigious spoils of the *Golden Hind*—with which Captain Drake returned to England in 1580. See Keynes, *op. cit.*, p. 362.

expansion in 50 years at 2 percent will be 2.7-fold, and at 4 percent 7-fold; but at 8 percent it will be 47-fold and at 10 percent 120-fold. A few more decades and it assumes staggering proportions. By estimating the present differences in per capita output between some of the preindustrial countries and the industrial ones, it is not difficult to estimate that once a rate of 8 to 10 percent annual growth is maintained, it is only a matter of half a century or a little more—just a lifetime—to close even the widest gap.

Although the desirability of high rates of industrial growth for the pre-industrial countries has been stressed in the preceding pages, it is not meant to suggest that these countries should somehow be permanently obsessed with faster growth for its own sake. Such folly would have few lasting rewards. At the same time, there is little ground for pathetic patience with postponing the possible—a very rapid elimination of want and poverty. Once this is done, different nations may decide differently the length of time during which they may wish to pursue the race for conspicuous consumption. A more appropriate strategy of growth for these countries would be to attain very high rates of growth in the earlier phase and cumulate the enlarged mass of output at somewhat lower rates.

While the importance of a high rate of growth in alleviating rapidly mankind's age-old afflictions of poverty and squalor is obvious, the difficulties involved in maintaining it need not be overlooked. Many countries, both in the private enterprise economies and in the centrally planned economies, have for fairly long periods maintained rather high rates of industrial growth. An adequate analysis of their experience, without necessarily accepting in John Stuart Mill's words "the slavery of antecedent circumstances," should be of great relevance in throwing light on the prerequisites for attaining similar or higher rates of growth in the nonindustrial countries of today and on the nature and extent of the avoidable and the unavoidable difficulties involved. Moreover, such difficulties will have to be adequately balanced, as has rarely been done so far in the discussion on economic development, against the very real costs of stagnation or slow growth and the persistence of economic poverty. If narrowing the gap between the rich industrial and the poor nonindustrial countries is to be the dominant theme for the century to come, the central task of economic theory and analysis would then seem to be the elucidation of the preconditions for attaining—and maintaining for a few decades—higher rates of economic growth in the nonindustrial countries.

ECONOMIC PROGRESS AND OCCUPATIONAL DISTRIBUTION

P. T. Bauer and B. S. Yamey

1. The principal purpose of this article is to examine the validity and significance of the widely held view that economic progress is generally associated with certain distinct, necessary and predictable changes in occupational distribution, in particular with a relative increase in the numbers engaged in tertiary activities.[1] Our method is largely analytical; but since a strong empirical basis is claimed for the generalisation we are examining, we have found it necessary to make frequent descriptive reference to the composition of economic activity in economies at different stages of development. Most of the description is concentrated in the first section of the article, which describes and analyses the volume and significance of trading activity in British West Africa. The remaining sections of the article examine

From P. T. Bauer and B. S. Yamey, "Economic Progress and Occupational Distribution," *The Economic Journal*, 61:244:741–755 (December 1951). Reprinted by permission of *The Economic Journal* and the authors.

[1] "For convenience in international comparisons production may be defined as primary, secondary and tertiary. Under the former we include agricultural and pastoral production, fishing, forestry and hunting. Mining is more properly included with secondary production, covering manufacture, building construction and public works, gas and electricity supply. Tertiary production is defined by difference as consisting of all other economic activities, the principal of which are distribution, transport, public administration, domestic service and all other activities producing a nonmaterial output." Colin Clark, *The Conditions of Economic Progress*, 1st edition, p. 182.

See also, Professor A. G. B. Fisher, *Economic Progress and Social Security*, pp. 5 and 6.

the analytical and statistical foundations of the generalisation and suggest that these are defective.

I

2. The few available occupational statistics of backward economies, especially in the colonies, purport to show that the great bulk of the population is occupied in agriculture. This impression is also conveyed in official statements on economic activity in these territories. An example may be taken from *An African Survey:*

> In the Northern Province of Nigeria, at the census of 1931, about 84% of occupied males whose returns permitted them to be classified were shown as engaged in agriculture and fishing, about 9% in manufacture, and under 3% in commerce and finance. . . . For Southern Nigeria less detailed information is available. The returns, which are less reliable than those for Northern Nigeria, would suggest that the proportion of males engaged in agriculture is about 82% and that concerned with handicrafts about 4.7%.[2]

Trade and transport are not mentioned. No attempt is made to reconcile this with another statement (on the same page) that almost 30% of the population of Nigeria lived in towns of over 5,000 inhabitants. In the same vein the official *Annual Report on Nigeria* states year after year that the great majority of the population is occupied in agriculture: trade is not among the other occupations listed.

In contrast to these statements and statistics a remarkable multitude of traders, especially of small-scale sellers of both local produce and of imported merchandise, is a most conspicuous feature of West Africa. This is so apparent that it has not escaped attention. It is freely said by responsible administrators that in the southern parts of Nigeria and the Gold Coast everybody is engaged in trade, and this is hardly an exaggeration.

3. For reasons to be explained it is not possible to give specific quantitative information about the volume of trade or of the numbers engaged in it. Certain sporadic but conservative data, relating, for example, to numbers of market stallholders and hawkers' licences, indicate that the number of selling points, including children hawking very small quantities of goods, is very large in the principal markets. But the figures give an imperfect idea of the multitude of people engaged either part-time or whole-time in selling small quantities of goods or conveying them to dispersed points of sale. In the aggregate there is an enormous amount of activity the quantitative significance of which is obvious to the observer.

4. The seriously misleading impression created by official statistics and statements derives from the inappropriateness of classification by distinct occupational categories in an economy in which occupational specialisation

2 *An African Survey*, 2nd edition, pp. 1425–6.

is imperfect. The economic activity of a large proportion of the population of West Africa is better described as the performance of a number of different things rather than as the pursuit of a definite occupation. In many of the so-called agricultural households the head of the household trades part-time even during the normally short farming season, and more actively outside the season, whilst members of the family trade intermittently throughout the year. Even if only main activities are considered, it is doubtful whether five-sixths of the population is engaged in agriculture; when it is realised that even the head of the family is likely to have part-time economic activities and that many of his dependents (including children) are engaged at least periodically in trade, it becomes clear that the official statistics in their present form are apt to mislead.

The imperfect specialisation of economic activity is not confined to the agricultural community. Many African doctors and lawyers and almost all the leading chiefs have extensive trading interests. Government employees and servants of the European population trade part-time, either importing merchandise or dealing in merchandise and foodstuffs bought locally. The fluidity of activity extends to personal relations where they bear closely on economic life. A prominent African trader in Lagos whose children are being educated at expensive universities and schools in England includes his wife among his principal retailer customers. Similar commercial relations exist between other prominent Africans and their wives and children.

Even where the conceptual and statistical difficulties arising from imperfect occupational specialisation are fully appreciated[3] it is difficult to collect the required information on subsidiary activities of individuals, particularly on part-time trade. Africans frequently do not regard trade as an occupation, especially when carried on by dependents, and would not refer to it as such when questioned, because they regard it as part of existence and not as a distinct occupation. In many cases it may not be possible to draw the line between the social and commercial activities of, say, a group of women traders in the market. There is, however, no doubt that the commercial element is generally substantial.

5. Once the level of economic activity has risen from that of a subsistence economy to that of an emerging exchange economy—a process which is encouraged and promoted by the activities of traders—the task of distribution may require a substantial volume of resources. Much depends upon physical and climatic conditions. But the circumstances of West Africa are certainly not exceptional in requiring a large volume of distributive activity. The large number of dispersed farmers and holdings, poor natural communications and long distances and the difficulties of prolonged storage in the open, together postulate a substantial volume of resources in distribution and

---

[3] It is not suggested that those responsible for census work in the colonies are unaware of these difficulties. But they are not appreciated by many of those who publish and use the results of their work.

transport for raising and maintaining the economy above the subsistence level even at an early stage in economic development. In this type of economy the indispensable tasks of assembly, bulking, transport, breaking of bulk and dispersal may require a large proportion of available resources. Moreover, in an economy which has recently emerged from the subsistence level, sòme transactions are still likely to be on a barter basis. Barter tends to use more resources, especially labour, than a fully developed money economy to transact a given volume of trade.

6. There is in West Africa widespread involuntary idleness of unskilled labour, resulting from lack of other co-operant resources, especially capital, to set it to work. This lack of employment is a major feature of comparatively undeveloped economies which in the aggregate comprise probably over half of the population of the world, including India, China, Java, large parts of Eastern and Southern Europe and much of Africa. The dependence of the volume of employment on the amount of the stock of capital used to be a major topic of political economy. The subject gradually receded from economic discussion as economists became preoccupied mainly with unemployment in advanced industrial economies, resulting not so much from lack of cooperant resources as from fluctuations in aggregate demand or various other influences discouraging investment and enterprise. Interest in the subject has revived with the growing realisation of its importance. Very recently unemployment in the "empty economy"[4] has brought the problem nearer home.

The missing cooperant factor (or factors) of production can be capital, land or technical and administrative skill. The type of scarcity or its incidence varies greatly in different regions and even districts in West Africa as elsewhere. But in many regions the low level of capital and of suitable administrative and technical skills constitutes the principal shortage.

7. Entry into small-scale trade is easy, as at this level no technical or administrative skill is required and only very little capital. Trade is attractive even for very low rewards in view of the absence of more profitable alternatives.[5] Women and children are also available for trade, partly for social reasons; for example, in some areas the wife is expected to make a contribution to the family's income; also there is little for women to do in the house and there are few schools for children.[6]

[4] J. R. Hicks, "The Empty Economy," *Lloyds Bank Review* (July 1947).

[5] The relative increase in the numbers engaged in retail distribution in Great Britain and elsewhere during the depression of the early 1930s is a more familiar example which can be largely explained in terms of reduced supply price arising from the absence of suitable alternatives.

[6] It is possible that the numbers attracted into trade in West Africa are increased because of a largely institutional rigidity in money wages. But even if money wages were to fall to the equilibrium level the number who would find trade attractive would still be very large as long as the underlying economic factors remained broadly unchanged.

8. The type of resources to be found in trade and transport depends, given the state of technique, upon the relative terms at which different productive resources are available. In an economy such as West Africa, where capital is scarce and expensive and unskilled labour abundant and cheap, the large volume of resources in distribution and transport consists very largely of labour. As compared with more advanced economies there is a mass emphasis on labour rather than on capital. This tendency, which may proceed very far and reveal unsuspected possibilities, permeates West African trading arrangements; a few examples will illustrate it.

9. In West Africa there is an extensive trade in empty containers such as kerosene, cigarette and soup tins, flour, salt, sugar and cement bags and beer bottles. Some types of container are turned into household articles or other commodities. Small oil-lamps are made from cigarette and soup tins, whilst salt bags are made into shirts or tunics. But more usually the containers are used again in the storage and movement of goods. Those who seek out, purchase, carry and distribute second-hand containers maintain the stock of capital. They prevent the destruction of the containers, usually improve their condition, distribute them to where they can best be used, and so extend their usefulness, the intensity of their use and their effective life. The activities of the traders represent a substitution of labour for capital. Most of the entrepreneurs in the container trade are women or children. The substitution is economic as long as six or eight hours of their time are less valuable (in view of the lack of alternatives) than the small profit to be made from the sale of a few empty containers. So far from the system being wasteful it is highly economic in substituting superabundant for scarce resources; within the limits of available technical skill nothing is wasted in West Africa.

For various reasons, of which the low level of capital is one, the individual agriculturalist produces on a very small scale. Moreover, the same lack of capital is reflected in the absence of suitable storage facilities and of cash reserves. As a result each producer has to dispose of small quantities of produce at frequent intervals as they become available during and immediately after the harvesting season. This postulates a large number of intermediaries, who, because of the high cost of capital, employ methods of transportation using relatively little capital and much labour. Donkey and bicycle transport are examples, while in some cases there is still head loading and human porterage, especially in the short-distance movement of local crops. The available transport equipment is used continuously with the assistance of large quantities of labour (subject to frequent breakdowns owing to poor roads and low technical skill).

The same phenomenon of the more intensive use of capital, that is its more rapid turnover, can be observed in the breaking of bulk into the minute quantities in which imported merchandise is bought by the ultimate consumer. The purchase of a box of matches is often still a wholesale transaction as the buyer frequently breaks bulk and resells the contents to the final consumer in small bundles of ten to fifteen matches. Similarly, at the petty retail stage sugar is sold in lots of three cubes, trade perfume by the drop, salt by the cigarette tin and cheap biscuits by the small heap of three or six. The small purchases are the result of low incomes and low capital, and the activities of the numerous petty retailers represent a substitution of labour for capital.

In Nigeria the small number of telephones and the low rate of literacy render it necessary for the importing firms and the larger distributors to use the services of numerous intermediaries to keep contact with smaller traders and to distribute their goods to them at an economic rate of turnover. The intermediaries reduce the size of stocks which need to be held. This is of particular importance, since the low level of fixed capital tends to enhance the economy's requirements of working capital. The large accumulation of unrailed groundnuts in the producing region of Nigeria is a familiar instance of a general problem.

The narrowness of markets and the backwardness of communications are reflected in interregional price differences which provide profitable opportunities for successful arbitrage (particularly in locally produced goods), from region to region. This attracts traders and intermediaries, and also makes it profitable for non-trading travellers to take part in trade, which they frequently do on a casual basis.

10. The foregoing may be summarised as follows: in West Africa, as in other emerging economies, the indispensable task of commodity distribution is expensive relatively to available resources; of the available resources, capital is scarce and unskilled labour is abundant; the multiplicity of traders is the result of the mass use of unskilled labour instead of capital in the performance of the task of distribution. There is an extensive demand for the services of intermediaries, and there is a large section of the population available to perform these services at a low supply price in terms of daily earnings.

II

11. The description and analysis of Section I show that there are severe limitations and qualifications to the view that a high proportion of labour in tertiary production is both a consequence of and a pointer to a high standard of living. As is well known, this generally held view derives from the statistical investigations and analysis of Mr. Colin Clark and Professor A. G. B. Fisher. Thus according to Mr. Colin Clark:

> Studying economic progress in relation to the economic structure of different countries, we find a very firmly established generalisation that a high average level of real income per head is always associated with a high proportion of the working population engaged in tertiary industries. . . . Low real income per head is always associated with a low proportion of the working population engaged in tertiary production and a high percentage

in primary production, culminating in China, where 75–80 per cent of the population are primary producers. High average real income per head compels a large proportion of producers to engage in tertiary production.[7]

Professor Fisher writes:

> We may say that in every progressive economy there has been a steady shift of employment and investment from the essential "primary" activities, without whose products life in even its most primitive forms would be impossible, to secondary activities of all kinds, and to a still greater extent into tertiary production. . . .
>
> The shifts of employment towards secondary and tertiary production revealed by the census are the inescapable reflection of economic progress.[7]

12. It would appear that the general proposition of Mr. Clark and Professor Fisher is based partly on analytical reasoning and partly on statistical evidence. Both types of verification appear to be defective.

The analytical reasoning purporting to sustain the generalisation seems to be based on the view that tertiary production is less essential than primary or secondary production; and that its products are in the nature of luxuries which cannot be afforded in economies with low real incomes. In essence the argument is that the income elasticity of demand for tertiary products is higher than that for the products of primary and secondary activities; and that therefore the demand for tertiary products increases relatively more rapidly with economic progress. Moreover, it is argued that technical progress is relatively slower in tertiary production. For both reasons taken together the proportion of occupied labour in tertiary production is supposed to rise with economic progress. The next section calls into question the validity of this reasoning; in Section IV it is suggested that the statistical verification claimed for the generalisation is inconclusive.

III

13. The analytical basis of the generalisation of Mr. Clark and Professor Fisher is open to criticism on several independent grounds of which the following are the most important. First, a substantial proportion of tertiary products are not luxuries with a relatively high income elasticity of demand; conversely, some products of primary and secondary production, possibly on a large scale in their aggregate, are such luxuries. Secondly, there may be large-scale substitution of capital for labour in tertiary production in the course of economic progress. Thirdly, the concept of the income elasticity of demand applied to a whole economy raises problems of aggregation which render doubtful any universal proposition about changes in its average value in conditions of change and economic growth; and this is particularly doubtful when relative factor prices and the distribution of incomes change.

[7] *Op. cit.*, pp. 6–7.

14. For reasons already mentioned in Section I the distributive task in the early stages of economic development is likely to be expensive in terms of *all* resources. A considerable volume of trading and transport is necessary to develop and sustain an exchange economy at an early stage of its development; it is an essential prerequisite for the development of specialisation and thus to the raising of productivity in primary production. Thus the proportion of resources engaged in tertiary production, notably in trade and transport, is likely to be high. It is possible that this proportion may fall at certain stages because the distributive task becomes relatively easier and less expensive in resources as the economy develops. The task may become lighter with the growth of internal security, the development and improvement of communications and the growth and stabilisation of markets, all of which contribute towards more regular and continuous commercial contacts, more intensive use of available resources in distribution and an increase in the size of trading units. These improvements are likely to have differential effects on productivity in various types of economic activity. It is not unlikely that trade and transport may be particularly favourably affected, and thus that the proportion of resources engaged in them may decline. This decline may continue until the fall is arrested by the possibly increasing volume of other kinds of tertiary products (including more elaborate distributive services) which may be called for at higher levels of real income.

Tertiary production, as it is usually understood, comprises a heterogeneous collection of different services. Some of these are qualitatively indispensable throughout economic development and quantitatively important at an early stage; others are not indispensable at all stages and are quantitatively important only in more advanced economies. The term "tertiary" carries the misleading suggestion that all these services belong to the latter category of luxuries.

15. There is no *a priori* reason to believe that as wealth increases a greater proportion of the luxuries consumed must be products of tertiary activities. The durable consumer goods of the North American economies provide numerous examples on a large scale of heavy expenditure on the products of secondary activities with growing wealth. Expensive motor cars, jewellery, works of art, mass produced but high-grade textiles and handmade bespoke clothes and shoes are products of secondary activities.[8]

16. The proportion of all resources in tertiary production will not provide an index of economic progress. Moreover, even if it did it would not follow that the proportion of occupied labour engaged in tertiary production must rise with economic progress. This proposition would be valid only if additionally it were legitimate to assume that labour and other productive

[8] Perhaps more fancifully purchases of fur coats, oysters, caviare, lobsters, pheasants and orchids sustain hunting, fishing and farming which are primary activities.

resources were employed in tertiary production in fixed proportions. This would be true only if substitution were not possible in the whole range of tertiary production, or if the relative terms upon which labour and other factors of production could be obtained remained unchanged throughout the whole course of economic progress. These assumptions are inadmissible. Technical possibilities of substitution between productive resources are obviously possible in tertiary production; and clearly the terms on which labour and capital are available are certain to change in a growing economy.

In Section I examples have been given to show the emphasis in the use of labour rather than capital in tertiary production in an under-developed economy. An example has also been given (the trade in used containers) to show how a tertiary activity expands with a lavish use of labour to make good a shortage in the products of secondary production. Conversely, examples abound in more advanced industrialised economies where capital replaces labour in tertiary activities and where secondary production expands to economise on labour-intensive tertiary activities. There are familiar examples on a large scale in domestic services, laundry and repair services, and restaurant and retailing services, where capital equipment is now used instead of labour. The purchase of precooked or prepared canned or processed food, or of paper cups and plates intended for one use only, represents an extension of secondary production to replace the tertiary activities in the kitchen. The mass substitution of capital for labour in tertiary activity in North America is as striking as the reverse substitution in West Africa.[9]

17. The neglect of the "substitution effect" destroys the general validity of the quantitative law connecting society's real income and the proportion of occupied population in tertiary production. Technical progress may greatly affect the demand for labour in primary, secondary and tertiary production, the possibilities of substitution between labour and other resources and the relative supply prices of productive resources.

Changes in relative factor prices and differential rates of technical progress in different branches of production will also affect the relative prices at which different luxuries (that is, goods or services with relatively high income elasticities of demand whether the products of primary, secondary or tertiary production) are available to consumers. This need not necessarily favour the luxuries which are the products of tertiary activities. If it were true, as is sometimes assumed, that productivity increases faster in secondary than in tertiary production, there would be a tendency for consumers to substitute luxuries which are produced by secondary production to those produced by tertiary production.[10]

[9] Of course even in West Africa the time may come when eight hours of a woman's time may be more valuable than the profit margin on the sale of three beer bottles.

[10] There is no *a priori* reason why technical progress should always be relatively more rapid in primary and secondary production than in tertiary production. But even if

18. In any society it is unlikely that all members spend the same proportion of their incomes on tertiary products. Differences may arise either because of differences in incomes or because of differences in tastes and individual circumstances. The share of the total national expenditure on tertiary products is obviously an average for the population as a whole. There is no ground for assuming a unique relationship between changes in this average and changes in national income. Indeed, this average may well fall if the bulk of any increase in the national income accrues to members whose relative expenditure on tertiary products is below the average. In these circumstances the average can be pulled down, even though the income elasticity of demand of each member for tertiary products exceeds unity (which, of course, is by no means necessary). This is a very likely contingency in societies such as India and China, where a large proportion of the population live near starvation levels and where there are great differences in the proportion of individual incomes spent on tertiary products. If in such communities there is a general increase in productivity the proportion of the total national expenditure devoted to the products of primary and secondary activity is almost certain to increase. The same increase in productivity is likely to reduce the superfluity of very cheap labour formerly available for employment in certain types of tertiary activity, notably domestic service, petty trade and menial tasks generally, and may thus accentuate the relative decline in tertiary activity.

A reduction in the national average expenditure on tertiary products may also be brought about as a result of other causes not necessarily connected with increasing productivity. Thus graduated taxation and social-security payments may reduce the share of national expenditure on tertiary products through their effects on the pattern of demand and on the supply price of labour.

19. An important practical conclusion follows from the possibility that there may be a fall in the average proportion of expenditure on products of a relatively high income elasticity of demand with an increase in income if this proposition is extended internationally. If a large proportion of an increase in world income accrues to countries or to individuals who spend a smaller proportion than the world average on products of a luxury type it follows that the demand for luxuries would suffer a relative decline. This would tend to turn the terms of trade in favour of the producers of relative necessities and against the producers of relative luxuries. On an international scale the luxuries would be mainly the products of industrialised countries. There is implicit in this possibility a threat to the standard of living of some of these countries. It reinforces the more familiar argument based on population increase, especially in the primary producing countries. The relative demand

_____

it were, it would support Mr. Clark's generalisation only if the possibility of substitution mentioned in the text is disregarded.

for the essentials of life can clearly increase either because there are more mouths to feed or because an increase in incomes accrues largely to the relatively poor.[11]

20. The foregoing analysis may now be summarised. Even if acceptable statistics were found which should show that the proportion of tertiary activities has increased in particular countries with economic progress the findings would not be evidence of any necessary or predictable tendency. Tertiary production is an aggregation of many dissimilar activities, including domestic service, government service, transport, retail and wholesale distribution, entertainment, education and others. There is no reason why the demand for every one of these should follow a common trend. The only feature common to all tertiary production is that the output is nonmaterial. This does not appear to provide a logical category of significance in the analysis of demand or of economic progress. Moreover, on the supply side the proportion of the labour force in tertiary production depends upon a number of different forces, the individual and total effect of which is in no way unambiguously determined by secular changes in the national income. Thus any observed correlation between economic progress and occupational distribution should be regarded as more in the nature of a statistical accident than as an indication or proof of a significant economic law.

IV

21. The empirical verification seems to be based upon occupational statistics which generally show both a high proportion of the occupied population in tertiary industries in advanced countries compared with underdeveloped countries and also an increasing proportion in time series for individual developing countries. These types of comparison seem to be vitiated principally on two counts. First, occupational statistics cannot take into account important difficulties arising out of imperfect economic specialisation. Secondly, the comparability of these statistics is affected by shifts of labour between unpaid and paid activities.

22. Clear-cut occupational classifications are inappropriate in underdeveloped countries where specialisation is imperfect. We are not concerned with possible inadequacies in the coverage and the arithmetical accuracy of the statistics but with their significance as a picture of economic activities. As has already been stated in Section I above, in these economies statistics convey a false impression of activities by concentrating on one activity of the

---

[11] The two cases differ in their effects. Thus where there is a mere increase in numbers average income per head must fall, and those whose terms of trade are adversely affected are necessarily worse off absolutely. In the other case average income per head must rise, and those whose terms of trade are adversely affected need not necessarily be worse off absolutely.

head of the household to the exclusion of his other activities and of those of the other members of his household.[12] Over a considerable period of development many activities, especially trading, porterage and domestic service, would not be regarded as separate occupations either by official enumerators or by the subjects themselves. This applies particularly where occupations are carried on by part-time workers or dependents. As specialisation becomes more definite and pronounced and as these activities are carried out by specialists, the performers and their performance are more easily identified and recognised and their quantitative extent looms larger, possibly much larger, in occupational statistics, even though in total the volume of these activities may be unchanged or even reduced.

23. It would seem that the classification of economic activities into three types, while superficially convenient and clear, conceals large arbitrary elements which greatly reduce its value. The activities of the agricultural producer selling his crops can be regarded partly as primary and partly as tertiary; this is particularly evident where he sells to the final consumer. Yet until they are taken over by an intermediary his activities will be regarded as primary. Where the intermediary is a member of the family the activity may continue to be classed as primary. Its tertiary character is likely to be recognised only when the intermediary is an independent middleman. Since the emergence of an intermediary is likely to reduce the total effort in marketing a given volume of produce, tertiary activity may appear to be increasing at a time when it is actually decreasing.

It should not be thought that these difficulties of classification disappear entirely in more advanced economies. On a smaller scale similar difficulties appear in the classification of the activities of different departments of a manufacturing firm or of most forms of large-scale enterprise. Again, the activities of the cobbler and the milliner are likely to be classified as tertiary when these are carried out in establishments (shops) dealing with the public. Yet under factory conditions the activities would be treated as secondary production. A classification of economic activity which is tacitly based on a particular assumed but undefined degree of specialisation and disintegration of functions appears to have little value for economic analysis or statistics. When census material is used it is more than likely that the assumed degree of specialisation differs between countries and periods.

24. The difficulty of classifying and comparing economic activity where there are differences in the degree of occupational specialisation largely undermines the statistical approach to the study of the relationship between occupational distribution and economic progress. There is much scattered evidence of the importance of some of the main tertiary activities in under-

12 It is not even certain on what criteria the principal activity of the head of the household is chosen for statistical purposes.

developed societies today,[13] as well as in earlier periods in the history of Great Britain and Western Europe, especially when the services of part-time workers and dependents are also considered.[14] However, because of the inherent statistical difficulty meaningful quantification seems to be impossible either in support or in refutation of Mr. Clark's generalisation, both with reference to a time series for one country and with reference to international comparisons.

25. The substitution of unpaid labour, with or without capital, for paid labour (or vice versa) is a form of substitution which affects the proportion of occupied labour in tertiary production and which illustrates and emphasises a conceptual difficulty present in a wide range of problems of economic statistics, particularly of indices of economic welfare. Such substitution takes place at all levels of economic progress, and not necessarily in the same direction at any given level. An obvious example in an advanced economy is the substitution of the activities of the household for those of the paid domestic servant; conversely, the household may frequently purchase the services of restaurants, laundries and repair agencies. Economic progress provides no general indication of the direction in which the shift between paid and unpaid labour will take place. Retail trade provides examples. In a poor economy the poverty of consumers does not allow them to buy in advance of requirements and to store their purchases. The tasks of holding stocks and of breaking bulk into the small quantities required for almost daily consumption devolve upon the paid intermediary. In these instances the activities of middlemen arise in response to the needs of poor consumers, to whom they secure access to commodities which would otherwise be outside their reach. By contrast, in advanced economies today housewives may store substantial quantities of consumer goods, especially of food, and may actually break bulk themselves. This development has gone far in North America. The tertiary activity remains, but unpaid labour of consumers and their own capital are being substituted for the services of the intermediary.

The examples in the preceding paragraph underline the arbitrariness of certain distinctions which are fundamental to national income and employment statistics. The shifting lines of demarcation suggest the advisability of caution in the use of such statistics as indices of economic welfare or as the basis of extrapolation.

---

[13] In this respect conditions in West Africa are not exceptional. The large number of full-time or part-time domestic and menial servants in India and the Middle East is another obvious example.

[14] Thus there may have been a declining proportion of labour in tertiary activity in the early part of the industrial revolution with a rapid growth in factory production, particularly when allowance is made for paid domestic service performed by dependent members of agricultural households.

A PLEA
FOR INDIGENOUS
ECONOMICS:
THE WEST AFRICAN
EXAMPLE

*Polly Hill**

This article is concerned with the need, in underdeveloped regions such as West Africa, to pursue a subject which, for want of a better term, I call "indigenous economics"—or the study of indigenous economies. I shall start by outlining the general nature of the subject and by discussing the reasons for its neglect, both during the colonial period and today. Although the whole of my discussion relates to West Africa, it has some relevance to certain other newly developing tropical regions.

Indigenous economics is concerned with the *basic fabric* of existent economic life, with such economic activities as the production of export or other cash crops, subsistence farming, cattle raising, fishing (for cash or subsistence), internal trading in foodstuffs, transportation, economically motivated migration (to cities, industries, and farms), indigenous credit-granting systems, and so forth. Far from being identified with either premonetary or subsistence economics, our subject is more concerned with "cash activities," not because of their greater importance, for here there is much variation, but

From Polly Hill, "A Plea for Indigenous Economics: The West African Example," *Economic Development and Cultural Change*, 15:1:10–20 (October 1966). Reprinted by permission of The University of Chicago Press.

* The author is Research Associate, Center for Research on Economic Development, The University of Michigan, and Visiting Senior Research Fellow, NISER, University of Ibadan, Nigeria. I am very grateful to Prof. Meyer Fortes for his constructive criticisms of an earlier draft of this polemical article, but he must certainly not be assumed to agree with any of the views expressed.

for the practical reason that the cash sector is easier to study. Nor are we particularly interested in the old-fashioned evolutionary ideas which would identify "progress" with a shift from subsistence to cash agriculture, for we know that most West African farmers produce both for subsistence ("own consumption") and for cash, and that an increase in the one type of activity may actually enhance a growth in the other; it is the structure of the relationship between the two types of activity which is interesting and important.

If the scope of indigenous economics is so wide, what, then, distinguishes it from conventional economics? As I hope that the general nature of this distinction will emerge from the later discussion, I make only a few preliminary points. Firstly, although it is true that the indigenous economist stands in some ways opposed to the "development economist," he is much interested in processes of change and modernization; but he does tend to regard these processes from a nongovernmental standpoint. Secondly, the distinction between the two types of economics is not hard and fast, but is mainly a matter of approach: while an indigenous economist might find himself very interested in problems of recruiting labor for a new factory, it could happen that he was unconcerned with whether that factory produced textiles or cement. Thirdly, the indigenous economist tends to take the broad lines of government economic policy for granted, in that he is not concerned with their formulation, though he may indeed hold strong views on the effects of introducing new measures! Fourthly, the indigenous economist holds that, while his subject is similar, in a general way, to conventional (or Western) economics,[1] the factors which require emphasis in any situation may be unexpected, so that those who guess on the basis of Western experience are apt to go wrong even on fundamentals; he insists that the economic behavior of individual West Africans is basically "rational" and responsive, but that the structure of this rationality requires studying in the field.

The study of indigenous economics was neglected during the colonial period and is contemptuously regarded by nearly all economists today. (Those same intellectual, political, and emotional processes associated with the collapse of colonialism, which provided African historians with such glorious new opportunities,[2] hardened the arteries of economists in relation to indigenous studies—and the new history is seldom economic history.[3])

---

[1] Some writers assume quite the contrary. Thus, W. C. Neale, in his chapter, "The Market in Theory and History," in Karl Polanyi et al., eds., Trade and Market in the Early Empires (1957), states on p. 371 that "the social scientists writing this volume are at least tentatively committed to the view that self-regulating markets [as distinct from fixed-price markets] are the exception rather than the rule—even to the view that they are unique to the nineteenth and twentieth centuries." A similar ideology is evident in the Introduction to P. Bohannan and G. Dalton, eds., Markets in Africa (1962).

[2] See I. Wallerstein, "The Search for National Identity in West Africa," Presence Africaine [Engl. ed.], VI/VII (1961).

[3] This is especially true of modern history.

Traditionally, during the brief colonial period, economists were concerned with the point of contact between West African and European economies, with the economic relationship between the metropolitan country and the Colony. This led them to concentrate nearly all their attention on external trade, on the acts of exportation and importation as such, rather than on export crop production or indigenous systems of internal distribution. Faced with the question of *how* export production was organized (by whom, on what sort of scale, under what conditions of land tenure, with what capital and labor, etc.), economists were usually obliged to guess. Quite often, as present evidence is beginning to show, they happened to guess wrong, and a formidable body of "economic folklore," which took strength from its re-iteration in books and official publications, established itself during half a century. One of the incidental concerns of the indigenous economist is the destruction of these economic myths, both by means of providing an alternative analysis and by the mere process of calling them into question. Even though he so often lacks the material which would enable him to set up a solid structure in place of any myth, he is encouraged to note that, as his work proceeds, he begins to be able to make judgments, in certain contexts, of the kinds of economic happenings which are likely to make good sense, so that he may be quite an effective critic.

In insisting on the narrow scope of conventional economics in regions such as West Africa, I am not exaggerating. We are all far more ignorant than we are knowledgeable. From Dakar to Cameroon, there is very little systematized knowledge relating to the economic organization of internal trade in West African foodstuffs and raw materials—there is scarcely any literature on this subject fit to be thrust into the hands of the visiting expert. Of course, some anthropologists have ventured into economic fields, but they have seldom been concerned with the kinds of generalization which typify economists. Their example is of profound importance to the indigenous economist—but they have not done his fieldwork for him.

Most British, unlike American, economists are wholly ignorant of agricultural economics, which they regard as a separate discipline. The findings of those few agricultural economists who have worked in the field in Nigeria and Ghana, for instance, have had little influence. Besides, agricultural economists have "neglected traditional agriculture, leaving it to anthropologists, who have made some useful studies."[4] Present-day economists are far more ignorant of the rural economies of certain poorer regions, including West Africa, than were their nineteenth century counterparts of the rural economies of Europe. There has been a retrogression of knowledge:

> While agriculture is the oldest production activity of a settled community, surprisingly little is known about the incentives to save and invest where

[4] See T. W. Schultz, *Transforming Traditional Agriculture* (1964).

farmers are bound by traditional agriculture. Oddly enough, economics has retrogressed in analysing the savings, investment and production behaviour of farmers in poor countries. The older economist had a better conception than economists now have of the particular type of economic equilibrium relevant under these circumstances.[5]

. . . Growth economists have been producing an abundant crop of macro-models that are, with few exceptions, neither relevant in theorizing about the growth potentials of agriculture nor useful in examining the empirical behaviour of agriculture as a source of growth.[6]

Agricultural economists are themselves, occasionally, very frank about their ignorance:

We hear a lot about this gap between the scientific agriculturalist and the native peasant farmer in the tropics. . . . But I don't think there is a gap. You see, neither of them knows how to improve agriculture. . . . What do we really know about the effect of the organic matter as compared with the minerals in the dung of cattle on particular savannah soils in Africa? What do we know about the probable results of attempts to integrate livestock and crop production to get more modern farming systems, not only in savannah Africa but in very many other areas?[7]

A great deal of trouble is caused for us and for the natural scientists themselves because, individually and in subject groups, they assume that their pet ideas and results are more fully finished and marketable than in fact they are. They therefore proclaim that much of their knowledge lies unused.[8]

When West African governments announce that the time is ripe for the introduction of large-scale mechanization programs in agriculture, agricultural scientists lack either the courage or inclination to raise their voices protesting their ignorance of the consequences—but rather offer their services, usually through international specialized agencies,[9] as technical experts. When West African politicians deplore, as they so often do, the backwardness of farm people, they are unaware of the extent to which they are echoing the conventional ignorance of economists. In West Africa, nowadays, the educated urban classes, notably the politicians, increasingly refer to farmers

---

[5] *Ibid.*, p. vii.

[6] *Ibid.*, p. 6.

[7] From an article by J. R. Raeburn in *Proceedings of the Ninth International Conference of Agricultural Economists* (1956), p. 483.

[8] *Ibid.*, p. 484.

[9] Many technical experts are quite deficient in relevant expertise, compared with certain old-style colonial servants. This is especially true of agriculturalists, who seldom remain in any post for more than a couple of years. (Outside technological fields proper, the whole notion of the "technical expert," whose expertise is applicable anywhere, is apt to be sham.)

as "peasants;" this is condescending and misleading, for

> The word "peasant" denotes, among other things, a degree of rusticity, in comparison with his betters, which we do not feel justified in attributing to the African villager. . . . African villagers do not seem to feel the same degree of ambivalence toward the political superstructure that European, Asian and Latin American peasants do . . . they do not to the same extent feel judged from above by a set of standards which they cannot attain.[10]

The Beatrice Webb tradition of qualitative field observation and experiment[11] has been out of fashion for some half a century, so it is no wonder that field enquiries were neglected in the colonies. But even had this spirit of scientific enquiry not fallen into desuetude, it is likely that conventional British assumptions about West African economic behavior would have inhibited field investigation. Typical implicit assumptions were:

(a) That it was the expatriate trader who taught the West African, if only by example, the elementary facts of economic life. (It followed that the economic response of indigenes was essentially western and familiar and required no study: if it was not familiar it was not economics.)

(b) That the basic fabric of economic life was so simple as to be devoid of interest to economists. (Only by assuming that indigenous economics and Western economics were identical did the former become worthy of study—but then assumption (a) came to the rescue.)

(c) That, given the complexities associated with "tribalism" (local land tenure, kinship and inheritance, communal work systems, and so forth), indigenous economics operate on too small a scale, or on too local a basis, to be of interest to economists—and are anyway incomprehensible. (Not until social and political systems have been "modernized" will economic processes become intelligible. By hastening the collapse of "tribalism," economists hope to move rapidly towards the day when they will understand events.)

Why is each of these implicit beliefs likely to be misleading?

(a) *The Western trading example.* Of course this was important: West Africans, like everyone else, are apt to be imitative in their economic behavior. But there were many reasons why the *Western* example was much less important than is commonly assumed, and I select three of these for emphasis.

(1) Other examples were often more important. Thus, it was the North African, or Arabian, example, as demonstrated in the ancient trans-Saharan trade in gold, ivory, slaves, kola nuts, cloth, etc., which set the pattern for long-distance trade within much of West Africa. If we define West Africa, for present purposes, as bounded by a line of the latitude of the northern boundaries of Ghana and Nigeria, then this trading system may be denoted

---

[10] From L. A. Fallers, "Are African Cultivators to Be Called 'Peasants'?" *Current Anthropology* (April 1961), 110.

[11] See Beatrice Webb, *My Apprenticeship.*

as the Northern Muslim example. The principal long-distance traders who linked the northern Savannah with the southern forests were the Dioula (who operated mainly in francophone territory) and the Hausa of northern Nigeria, all of them Muslim. Their example was profound, and many non-Hausa speaking people in the South employ Hausa trading terms.

(2) In the field of agricultural production, no Western example existed, there being no common basis of agricultural experience and no contact between the farmer and the expatriate trader, who dealt always with African middlemen. Agriculture, unlike trade, was seldom supported or organized by indigenous political authorities, who drew little (if any) revenue from it. This is not to say that agriculture was, in any useful sense, "inefficient," but rather that it was mainly based on local experimentation and local tradition, adapted to soil, climate, crops, and levels of technology. Recent developments, such as the increased migration of farmers[12] and laborers, which followed the introduction of new export crops, have tended to create more geographical uniformity than existed hitherto—but this should not be exaggerated.

(3) The expatriate trading firms' strength lay in their ability to adapt themselves to indigenous trading methods—rather than *vice versa*. The firms were sophisticated: they learned how to insinuate themselves into the existing trading structure, and they were not afraid of credit. But as buyers of export produce, they scarcely ventured inland until after 1900. Thus, the firms which exported Gold Coast cocoa before 1914 knew scarcely anything of the organization of cocoa farming or of methods of bush buying, which increasingly fell into the hands of Nigerian middlemen. Of course, the actual exporting function of the expatriate firms was indispensable; of course, in the end, they established networks of buying stations throughout the cocoa area—though they continued to rely on the Nigerian middlemen for much "detailed buying." Indigenous methods of marketing the kola nut (a crop which, in several ways, closely resembles cocoa) owe nothing to the Western expatriate example—they are far more ancient, being based on the northern trading influence.[13]

(b) *The belief that indigenous economics is too simple for economists.* An alternative version of this doctrine is that it is quite permissible for economists to derive conclusions from generalized data, which has a greater validity than more localized material, despite the admitted variations in basic background circumstances. An awful and famous example is provided by Prof. P. T. Bauer, who insisted, in the early nineteen fifties,[14] that the various West

---

[12] Certain farmers, as well as laborers, are much inclined to migrate. See, for instance, this writer's *The Migrant Cocoa Farmers of Southern Ghana* (1963), and Marguerite Dupire, "Planteur Autochtones et Etrangers et Basse-Côte d'Ivoire Oriental," *Études Éburnéennes* (Abidjan), VIII (1960).

[13] See Abner Cohen, "Politics of the Kola Trade," *Africa* (January 1966).

[14] See P. T. Bauer, *West African Trade* (1955).

African cocoa marketing boards had fixed the price to the farmer so far below the world cocoa price that cocoa output was bound to fall catastrophically— although, as the whole world knows, it has since risen, as one might say, catastrophically. Prof. Bauer's difficulty resulted not so much from his *laissez-faire* outlook (which has, as a matter of fact, a considerable relevance in West Africa), as from his implicit assumption that the basic socioeconomic organization of cocoa farming was irrelevant. When one began to study this organization, in all its diversity, one was struck by the fact, then recorded in none of the books, that rapid cocoa development usually involves migration of farmers, and by the remarkable long-sightedness of the migrant cocoa-farmers, who would not stop planting existing lands, or making future plans for the planting of newly acquired lands, just because the cocoa price seemed low during a run of years—which, in any case, in the early nineteen fifties it did not. A decade is to a cocoa-farmer what a year is to Prof. Bauer, and this made nonsense of his generalized statistics, which were somewhat shaky anyway. Furthermore, Prof. Bauer altogether failed to appreciate the strength of the appeal of the marketing board system of fixed prices for producers which, though introduced by the British at the beginning of the war, was exceedingly acceptable to West Africans, even though prices fell as a result. The notion of a "right price"—a price which, ideally, should remain stable indefinitely—is very common in West Africa, where economic life is riddled with (largely unsuccessful) attempts to fix prices on a local (or even wider) basis, usually by implicit agreement, for even among well-organized traders, such as butchers, machinery for centralized price-fixing is nonexistent. While very short-term price-fixing is sometimes effectively achieved, prices are never stable in the longer run (they *are* determined by supply and demand), and institutions which actually lead to the attainment of this ideal are, therefore, usually welcomed with open arms.

Many economists have visited West Africa in advisory capacities since the war, and much of their advice has been very valuable to governments. But convinced as they have been of the simplicity of indigenous economic organization, few of them, or, indeed, of the growing band of prominent West African economists (most of them Nigerians), have used their influence to urge the need for more "grass roots research."[15] Also, some of the expatriate advisers, especially a few who have visited Ghana, have ventured into pastures much wider than those in which they are accustomed to graze—with somewhat unexpected results. It may be that when Prof. W. A. Lewis asserted, in a much-read report on industrialization of the Gold Coast,[16] that agriculture was stagnant, he had an over-simplified image of agricultural organiza-

[15] Prof. W. F. Stopler is exceptional, his forthcoming book on Nigerian economic planning being entitled *Planning without Facts*.

[16] *Report on Industrialisation and the Gold Coast* (Accra: Government Printer, 1953).

tion based on the presumptions that a simple technology necessarily implies simple socioeconomic organization, "inefficiency" (in some absolute, though undefined, sense), and small-scale production—though none of these notions are necessarily true or meaningful.

In questioning these assumptions, as necessary assumptions, I am making no statement at all about the efficiency of West African agricultural systems, though I would observe that economists are much too prone to make "efficiency judgments" before they have examined existing mechanisms and alternatives. But I am insistent that an apparently common-sense corollary to the stagnation thesis, to the effect that industrialization cannot proceed until labor is "released" from the farms, as a result of improved agricultural efficiency imposed from outside happens not to be a corollary. This piece of folklore ignores the special factors, which are summed up in the statement that the supply of labor (mostly of savannah origin) is often best regarded as unlimited in quantity. I am not here referring merely to the magnetic attractive power of industrial employment, but also to the willingness and ability of many West Africans to migrate to rural areas—perhaps sometimes happening to fill the jobs vacated by those who have migrated to the cities. It may well be[17] that, up to the present, food farmers have generally organized themselves so as to keep pace with the vastly expanding demand for marketed food which has resulted from the spectacular increase in West African urbanization. So we see how it may come about that economic policies based on apparent economic common sense are more damaging than no policy.

(c) *The belief that indigenous economics is too complex for economists.* It is here that the economists are deserving of everyone's sympathy. Where is the social anthropologist, let alone the economist, who has not heaved a sigh at the appearance of yet another detailed study of "all aspects" of a small society? And yet, lamentably, there is hardly any nonanthropological, nonstatistical material fit for the consumption of economists desirous of acquiring local background. My point is that such material might be useful, as well as comprehensible. I am insisting that if economists would persist with detailed studies in the field, they would soon learn to discern a variety of forms of standard economic behavior amid the diversity—that economic behavior is often more standardized in West Africa than it is in the West. The difficulty is that the diversity *and* the uniformity require simultaneous emphasis. Thus, taking an actual example, we are the more inclined to insist that *most larger cocoa farmers* (defined, say, as those with 10 acres of cocoa or more) *employ laborers,* because we know that there are some such farmers who rely solely

---

[17] Those who draw up development plans often *assume* the contrary. Thus, on p. 85 of Ghana's *Seven-Year Development Plan* (Accra, 1964), it is asserted that the farmers had failed to keep up with the growing demand for food, though the official published statistical time series relating to prices and quantities of Ghanian foodstuffs rather indicated the contrary—insofar as one cared to regard them as reliable indicators.

on family labor and can partially understand why their circumstances are "different." As we gain experience, we come to see what "kinds" of cocoa farmers employ laborers and to associate various types of work with various systems of employment. Nor do we need to travel everywhere in the cocoa-growing zone before attempting such generalizations, as has been shown by the work of Dr. Marguerite Dupire[18] among the cocoa farmers of the south-eastern Ivory Coast.

These, and other, implicit assumptions have partially accounted for the unwillingness of economists to study the basic fabric of economic life in tropical regions such as West Africa. But there are also many practical diffi-culties, one of the most troublesome being the *compartmentalism* of indig-enous life, which necessitates studying it in terms of individual industries, occupations, sectors, etc., as well as, all too often, in terms of ethnic groups[19] within these classifications. It is this latter point which tends to break the back of the conventional economist, observing, as he must, the obsessional interest of the "ethno-economist" in such matters as occupational specializa-tion in relation to ethnic group: how can he learn to think in terms of seven-teen (or more) separate (ethnic) labor forces, or fail to be dismayed by the pursuit of ethnic classificatory questions as ends in themselves?

It is this compartmentalism of economic life which partly explains the widespread belief among economists that saving and investment are rare, even as concepts, in indigenous economic life; the economist is so unfamiliar with the forms such saving and investment are apt to take that he does not know where to look for evidence of their existence. (I have heard UN financial experts seriously argue that the admitted unwillingness of individual Ghanaians to buy government securities is evidence of their inability to "save" in any sense of that word.) The failure of capital to flow between sectors, as in more developed economies, is partly because many farmers, traders, and other business people have such well developed, even strict, no-tions of the distinction between capital and spending money and of the proper usages of the former. Though the migrant cocoa farmers of southern Ghana traditionally invested their savings from cocoa-growing in land-pur-chase, in the building of houses in the homeland, and in the purchase of lorries (connected with cocoa and food transport), they were usually uncon-cerned with investing capital in other forms of economic activity. It is only by studying indigenous capital formation sector by sector that the pos-sibilities of intersectoral flow may come to be properly appreciated. At pres-

[18] Dupire, *op. cit.*

[19] Ethnic occupational specialization is apt to be very rigid in West Africa, both in cities where there are many strangers and among rural immigrants. This matter of ethnicity is bound to seem of distracting complexity to the newcomer, though two simplifying factors are the large size of some ethnic groups (e.g., Hausa, Yoruba, and Ibo), and the inter-national character of much of the occupational specialization.

ent, many of the most important forms of fixed capital, such as cocoa farms, are omitted from all official national accounts, mainly because this reflects traditional accounting in developed countries, but also because such farms are wrongly presumed to have come into existence almost accidentally—to be acts of God, rather than man-made capital assets, the creation of which often involved much effort, abstention, and planning.

Given this need to study economic life compartmentally (and, alas, plod-dingly), should the methods of economists and social anthropologists be distinguished? If the investigator is a social anthropologist, then he must understand the necessity of isolating economic factors; he must also be prepared to use every opportunity of hinging the material he collects either to already existing statistics (or to other broadly based, administratively organized data, such as farm maps, nominal rolls, etc.), or in the last resort (in the absence of existing material) to collect a minimum of simple figures himself. If, however, the investigator is an economist, he should usually dis-card his traditional procedure of collecting most of his material through field assistants, using questionnaires, in favor of a method, learned from anthro-pologists, which mainly relies on questioning and observing individuals while they are at work. Market women should be interviewed in markets, lorry drivers in lorry parks, farmers on their farms (or at their houses), fishermen on the beach. The procedure should be semi-statistical, in the sense that similar, even identical, questions should be put to many informants in-dependently, with a view to comparing, or even totaling, their replies.

The investigator must adopt an economic point of view. When studying the economic organization of companies of beach-seine fishermen, he may not need to go to sea in the canoe, but it will be essential to witness the selling of fish to women on the beach and to appreciate that the division of labor between men and women is based on economic good sense—not on mys-terious traditional sex roles. It is because he has a point of view that the investigator is able to use his judgment as to what is relevant.

Questionnaires, as I have said, must be discarded by the investigator, for the simple reason that it is impossible to draw up a satisfactory form until after the research has been completed. The indigenous economist studies the *quality* of economic life, a statement which may be made respectable to statisticians by adding that he is concerned rather more with identifying the important variables than with measuring their movements. The conventional type of pilot survey is useless, involved as it is with procedural details, rather than with fundamentals. As for the use by the economist of the full-blown questionnaire, this in West African conditions is a far more dangerous im-plement than is commonly realized—one which should only be handled by the surgeon himself. Not only are the wielders of questionnaires often in-dulging in a kind of anti-intellectual activity (setting out on a voyage of discovery enclosed in blinkers), but there is also the fact that field assistants have a remarkable capacity to classify recalcitrant material so that it appears to fit neatly into inappropriate boxes, which results in the hardening of prejudices that rather require demolition.

I hasten to insist that I am not denigrating economic statistics as such: of course they are the life-blood of economics, though our dismal science should scarcely be *identified* with statistics, as is happening increasingly in some poorer regions. But I am making four assertions about them. Firstly, large-scale statistical enquiries, or even enquiries which are basically much dependent on the collection of statistics, are usually best undertaken by government or other official agencies, which alone command the resources required. Secondly, such "large-scale statistics" seldom expose the fundamental variables that lie at the "grass roots" level. Thirdly, it is the duty of social scientists to use such statistics with great discretion in underdeveloped countries, as they are liable to be very misleading. (Official statistics are often assumed to be reliable, just because they are official. Specialized UN agencies, such as FAO and the Economic Commission for Africa are so dependent on these statistics that they feel they must either accept them entirely, or pack up.) Fourthly, statisticians generally, not only expatriate technical experts, usually fail to appreciate the degree of "geographical diversity" (ecological, economic, and social) which typifies many new underdeveloped countries, including those of the smaller ones which extend from the Coast to the northern savannah. The statistical technique of the UN experts responsible for organizing agricultural censuses in West African countries may be impeccable, so far as concerns the choice of the individuals, or farms, to be counted in any locality; but the whole operation is apt to be invalidated by the failure to select sufficient localities for study, given this great degree of "geographical diversity." Such agricultural censuses are wished on the poorer countries by the UN and are a monstrous waste of their financial and manpower resources.

The official statistics of the poorer countries are apt to become in some respects less accurate as, partly in response to outside pressure, they become more detailed. The many published reports on the 1960 Ghana population census are monumentally fascinating sources of huge scope—real landmarks of organization and scholarship. Yet, *some* of the statistics are of much worse quality than those collected in previous censuses, and one needs to be an indigenous economist properly to understand this. Certain of the occupational statistics, which appear so accurate because they are so detailed, are very misleading. The traditional prejudices with regard to the relationship between cocoa-farmers and their laborers (the latter usually being presumed to do most of the work, in the absence of the former) led to a failure to distinguish laborers from farmers, though they are quite distinct categories.

Then, most of the wholesalers of Ghanaian foodstuffs in southern Ghana are women[20]—but the census statistics show them to be nearly all men.[21] In general, the process of demolishing the statistical myths, with the aid of field research, will be a slow one: there is a mystique about official statistics which withstands much battering.

I have suggested a number of reasons why, as it were, traditionally, economists have neglected the study of indigenous economics in West Africa. Nowadays, there is another general and most powerful resistance at work— the whole ideology of those who count themselves underdevelopment specialists is nearly always actively opposed to indigenous studies. Theoreticians, econometricians, and planners all share a common philosophy of ideological optimism, based on the past success in solving certain economic problems, particularly that of mass unemployment in some industrial countries. The uncritical acceptance of conventional types of official statistics is one consequence of this optimism; while economists know in their hearts that most West African food production figures are guesses (even wild guesses), they hardly ever admit this when quoting and comparing the figures,[22] the idea being, presumably, that some figures are always better than no figures. The theoreticians do not seek to revolutionize their model-building by drawing new ideas from anthropologically oriented material; the econometricians are so much concerned with manipulating their series that they hardly consider the reliability of the statistical data in terms of the humdrum problems of its basic collection in the field,[23] the planners, and advisors, regard themselves as economic doctors with the duty of making quick diagnoses and judgments on the basis of inadequate knowledge.

This philosophy of optimism would be more justifiable were there more evidence that the economists had met with marked success in solving the economic problems of the poorer countries. Now they are in a hurry, because they had given no thought to such problems (was not the very word "underdevelopment" coined little more than twenty years ago?) until the under-

---

[20] This statement is based on material collected by the present writer which is, as yet, unpublished.

[21] Perhaps the category "wholesaler," which went undefined in the census, related only to those who handled imported goods or who had office premises. Certainly, in West African conditions, the category is too difficult to define to be suitable for handling by census enumerators.

[22] See Helen C. Farnsworth, "Defects, Uses and Abuses of National Consumption Data," *Food Research Institute Studies* [Stanford University], II, No. 3 (November 1961). "To call such guesses [involving subsistence crops] 'production estimates' is at best semantic fiction, at worst actual falsehood; to derive residual 'consumption' estimates from them is farcical . . ." (p. 192).

[23] These problems are apt to be much more pronounced in poorer than in richer countries, both for the general reasons already discussed, and because of such practical difficulties as that of quantifying foodstuffs which are never weighed for trading purposes.

privileged, expressing themselves politically, left them no choice. It is the politicians and people of the poorer countries who see their salvation in development, who demand assistance from the richer and the better educated. Although economists do their best to keep up with this demand, and although their advice is often ignored, part of the responsibility for the ever-widening gap between the living standards of rich and poor countries is surely theirs. And is there not a sense in which development proceeds, despite the economists?

The future role of the indigenous economist will be a modest one. He will pursue his subject partly for its own sake and partly in the hopes that in the longer run he may help to create a more realistic climate of economic thought, especially about rural activities, which will continue to engage most West Africans for many years to come. The present-day planner has no time to read our obscure sources, and we may even sympathize with him when he regards our material as obsolescent, or as an impediment to the ideal with which he is playing. Someone (and I do not know who this should be) should set about digesting our material in a way which would give it some comprehensibility and appeal to those who do not sympathize with our methods and aims.

The situation is educationally urgent. On the one hand, there are no respectable textbooks of applied economics appropriate to West African conditions; one certainly need not beg the question of whether basically rural societies, lacking a capitalist land-owning class, may become fully socialist without first passing through an industrial stage, before insisting that Marxist textbooks are no more relevant than the capitalist variety. On the other hand, sufficient generalized nonsense is written about African economic conditions, especially by British and American academics, to ensure the hardening of prevailing economic myths.

One of the most fashionable myths is that *shifting cultivation is bad.* Without defining terms, and without considering the possible efficiency of alternative cultivation systems, economists both condemn shifting cultivation out of hand and regard it as usual in sub-Saharan Africa. In point of fact, in West Africa shifting cultivation, properly regarded,[24] is far less common than are systems of "recurrent cultivation,"[25] which commonly involve individual farmers returning to cultivate their portions of land after the restoration of fertility through fallow. Whereas the term shifting cultivation implies a ramshackle, wasteful, obsolete state of affairs, systems of recurrent cultiva-

---

[24] W. Allan, *The African Husbandman* (1965), restricts the use of the term "shifting cultivation" to circumstances "in which the whole community of cultivators moves" (p. 6). A typically sophisticated anthropological discussion is to be found in P. C. Lloyd, *Yoruba Land Law* (1962), p. 73.

[25] Allan's book (*ibid.*) is a most valuable new work by an agriculturalist, a former colonial servant.

tion, if understood, could often be represented as respectable, even scientific
—they usually, of course, involve crop rotation.

Even with systems of continuous cultivation, which are much commoner
in West Africa than is generally realized,[26] it is unjustifiable to assume, as
most economists do, that the Malthusian brink is necessarily nearby, if only
because such systems are compatible with the simultaneous existence of unused, or partially cultivated, land.[27] However, if the degree of pressure on
the land does happen to justify Malthusian despair, the means by which the
local population attempts to alleviate the situation (refusing to die off) are
often well worthy of study, especially as many population density maps are
surprisingly patchy, so that short-distance migration of farmers often presents
possibilities.

Tied up with Malthusianism are the presumed dangers of *fragmentation*.
(So conflicting are the various definitions of this emotive term that it certainly should be discarded, though it serves well enough for present polemical
purposes.) The economists, who are apt to be so much less sophisticated than
their subjects, the farmers, presume the latter to be unaware of the dangers
of farms becoming smaller and smaller over time—although the fact is that
in many instances their socioeconomic systems have built-in safeguards
against such a process. In many societies, a man has a sole heir who inherits
all his rights over land; in others, the much-abused "family system"[28] en-
sures that, for instance, self-acquired land is divided only between sons and
not between grandsons, who are obliged to share their fathers' portions. It
is true that fragmentation *may* be a problem; but then so may be the over-
consolidation of land in the hands of a sole inheritor.

Most West African farmers in the forest zone (and perhaps also in the
savannah) produce much of the food they require for their own consumption—they are *subsistence producers*. But subsistence does not necessarily
imply inefficiency, as economists usually assume. There are many reasons
why this may be so, and I select the following for mention: (a) multicrop-
ping (the growing of two or more crops simultaneously on the same land)
makes such good agronomic sense in West Africa that specialization on one
crop is seldom desirable; (b) cocoyam and plantain are necessary cover
crops for young cocoa seedlings, so that cocoa farmers with new farms can-

---

[26] Notably in certain densely populated districts of Northern Nigeria. For a general
discussion, see *ibid*.

[27] Such land may be less conveniently situated than that under continuous cultivation.

[28] One of the most dangerous, crude, and fashionable beliefs of economists is that
the "family system" (whatever may be meant by this) is necessarily *bad* from the angle
of economic enterprise; see *Migrant Cocoa Farmers, op. cit.*, for a brief discussion of this
point. (It is sad that in expressing these beliefs some economists are hoping to indicate
the width of their sociological approach.)

not avoid producing these foodstuffs; (c) labor, rather than land, is often the scarce factor, so that to get the maximum output farmers must distribute the available manpower between crops with different growing cycles; (d) it is sometimes cheaper to grow food, if need be with hired labor, rather than to buy it, considering the great bulkiness of certain staple West African foodstuffs, especially cassava and plaintain; (e) it is often economic for laborers who are primarily employed in connection with the production of a cash crop to produce subsistence crops, both for themselves and their masters; (f) given existing technology, there are few obvious advantages in really large-scale production of any crop—nor need there be with mechanization, were tractor-hiring services more often available to the private farmer.

So the problem for economists is that of the right balance, in different circumstances, between subsistence and cash production—the general responsiveness of farmers to the growing demand for marketed food not being in doubt.

Of course, there are many economists who are well aware that economic circumstances in underdeveloped countries are "different," one of them being Mr. W. B. Reddaway, whose experience in India led him to emphasize the need for economists to adopt new sets of instinctive assumptions in underdeveloped countries.[29] But how should the advisory economist set about acquiring such assumptions, given that the civil servants (on whom, presumably, he mainly depends for information) are those most proficient in soaking up, and relaying, prevailing economic folklore, much of it Western in origin? Might not the indigenous economist help?

The indigenous economist is bound to remain a laughing stock, with governments and main-stream economists alike. As he is not primarily interested in modernization, he will appear to be an intellectual, if not a political, conservative—and perhaps it *is* impossible to study existing institutions unless, with a part of one's mind, one wishes to preserve them, at least for the length of time required for their study. So division of labor must continue to be the rule among economists. But we do ask the planner with whom (so far as we are concerned) all power lies, to agree that a partial return to the Webb tradition of socioeconomic observation on crying issues would be a forward, not a backward, step.

[29] "The Economics of Under-Developed Countries," *Economic Journal* (March 1963).

NATIONAL
POLITICAL
DEVELOPMENT

Phillips Cutright

Large-scale comparative studies of national political systems offer the social scientist a method of great power if only proper use can be made of the material at hand. It is the purpose of this article to examine in some detail a single sociological effort to apply the comparative method to national political systems and, following this discussion, to offer a number of solutions to the problems which seem to block further progress. Perhaps the best known and most articulate effort by a sociologist to deal empirically with a large number of contemporary national political systems is that of Seymour M. Lipset.[1]

Lipset identifies two groupings of national political systems, stable democracies on one hand and, on the other, unstable democracies, popular dictatorships, and elite-based dictatorships. He then poses the question: What differences in national economic development might explain why a nation

From Phillips Cutright, "National Political Development," in Nelson W. Polsby, *et al.* (eds.), *Politics and Social Life* (Boston: Houghton Mifflin, 1964). Reprinted by permission of Houghton Mifflin.

[1] See Seymour M. Lipset, "Some Social Requisites of Democracy: Economic Development and Political Legitimacy," . . . See also Lyle W. Shannon, "Is Level of Development Related to Capacity for Self-Government?" *American Journal of Economics and Sociology*, Vol. 17 (July, 1958), pp. 367–82, and a follow-up study also by Shannon, "Socio-economic Development and Demographic Variables as Predictors of Political Change," *Sociological Quarterly*, 1962. Leo F. Schnore's "The Statistical Measurement of Urbanization and Economic Development," *Land Economics*, Vol. XXXVII (August, 1961), pp. 229–45, contains an assessment of the relationship among a number of different indicators of national development we will use in this paper.

would be in one group and not in the other?[2] To answer this question he offers a number of indicators of wealth, industrialization, education, and urbanization. (He does not combine indicators to form a scale of wealth, industrialization, or economic development, although development forms one half of the central theme of the paper. The other half, "democracy," is not scaled either.) Lipset presents statistical averages for the nations in each of the two political groups (stable democratic as opposed to all other forms of government) in two areas of the world, an English-speaking and European area, and the Latin American area. A sample of his analysis of these averages is instructive. Among the English-speaking and European stable democracies the mean number of telephones per 1000 persons (a "wealth" indicator) is 205 compared to only 58 per 1000 in "European and English-speaking unstable democracies and dictatorships."[3] Similar differences favoring democratic nations are revealed by all the indicators of wealth, industrialization, urbanization, and education among the English-speaking and European groups and, also, among Latin American nations.

Lipset seeks to show the effect of economic development on national political systems. The statistics are offered as proof that a strong relationship exists. However, a comparison of mean averages may show that differences exist between two groups without telling us the strength of the association between the independent variables that are presumably responsible for these observed differences. Thus, when Lipset notes that stable democracies have 205 telephones per 1000 persons compared to only 58 per 1000 in nondemocratic nations, he implies that there is a "strong" relationship or association

---

[2] Ratings by a single expert—or by panels of experts whose opinions on such matters as the condition of the press, political freedom, and so on, are averaged together —are of less value than a more objective indicator of political development. Careful examination of Russell H. Fitzgibbons, "A Statistical Evaluation of Latin American Democracy," *Western Political Quarterly*, Vol. 9 (1956), pp. 607–19, as well as Lipset's attempt to place nations in "democratic" or what amounts to "undemocratic" clusters, reveals the problems of this method of subjective evaluation. The shift in the rank order in which experts place the Latin American nations at different times allows the person using an index based on their ratings to take his pick of the democratic and undemocratic nations. Furthermore, raters disagree on the rank order in which groups of nations should be placed, and, when the number of nations is large, subjective evaluations have to be abandoned in favor of objective indicators—what expert can be in intimate contact with the political histories of all the nations of the world and also be willing or able to order them on simple scales, let alone multiple dimensions? We can devise statistical and objective methods of measuring political development, just as the economist does when he asks about energy consumption per capita, and not have to rely on what an expert believes the whole economy of a nation has been doing over the past year. This implies that we can also remove ourselves from the world of ethnocentric judgments about the goodness or evil of political systems and turn to other aspects of political systems in order to understand them.

[3] Since there were no English-speaking dictatorships, this seems to be an oversight in tabular presentation.

between this indicator of national wealth and the type of political system observed.

To give a little depth to his claims, Lipset presents the ranges for each indicator. Here some curious findings appear. The first and most obvious is that, even though the mean averages for the two types of national governments differ, the spread in the values on almost every indicator is so extreme that it would be very difficult to place a single nation in either the democratic or nondemocratic category knowing, for example, only its score on the number of telephones. In the European and English-speaking stable democracies a nation may have from 4 to 400 telephones per 1000 population while a European dictatorship may have as few as 7 or as many as 196 per thousand. One wonders about the stable European democracies that have only 43, 60, 90, 130, 150 or even 195 telephones. How do they manage, while "dictatorial" European nations can at the same time have as many as 196 telephones per 1000? More striking is the case of Latin American *democracies,* in which the average number of telephones is 25 and the range is from 12 to 58. The number of telephones in Latin American democracies seems paltry when compared to the number of telephones in European dictatorships. European dictatorships, on the average, score twice as high on the number of telephones (and "wealth" and "economic development") as Latin American democracies.

Such a peculiarity can exist for a number of reasons. The first may be a failure to develop a scale of "democracy" that has as many gradations as the scale on which all the independent variables are defined. A nation is either democratic or it is not according to the Lipset scoring system. It makes little difference that in discussing national political systems one talks about shades of democracy if, in the statistical assessment, one cannot distinguish among nations. However, one cannot differentiate national political systems without a scoring system that assigns values to different nations according to some stated criteria. Although Lipset states his criteria, he does not discriminate between France and Albania, Brazil or Chile. We would be better able to assess his descriptive statistics if the dependent variable—the national political system had been indexed or scaled.

A second reason for the peculiar findings reported above is a lack of a theoretical focus specifying what variables matter in determining whether a political system is democratic or not. A theoretical focus means one has a hypothesis to test, using a set of predicting variables that are "given" by the theoretical scheme. Lipset seeks to test the hypothesis that democracy will flourish in nations where wealth is distributed rather equally and in which large masses of starving or near-starving farmers and workers are not dominated by an elite of wealth and aristocracy. Do populations with a relatively high standard of living possess the "self-restraint" necessary to sustain "democratic institutions?" Lipset makes no distinction between the varieties of "democratic" or non-democratic political systems. His working hypothesis asks only whether or not a significant difference on each economic indicator exists between nations with two types of political characteristics. When the hypothesis is confirmed he explains the finding through discussion of what people want or what the effects of education might be on self-restraint.

The concept of social change does not appear in Lipset's analysis of his data but he refers to studies by Schnore and Lerner in which the statistical interdependence of many of the same indicators he uses is demonstrated; and, in the case of Lerner, some links between education, communication, urbanization, economic development, and individual political participation are tentatively established.[4] Lerner's analysis is, however, restricted to the Middle East.

RESEARCH OBJECTIVES AND HYPOTHESES

Let us move, then, to an attempt to build on the beginning furnished by Lipset, by developing an index of political development. The degree of political development of a nation can be defined by the degree of complexity and specialization of its national political institutions. Each nation can be placed on a continuum of political development which will allow it to be compared with any other nation in the world. We will bank heavily on the role played by political parties in national political life in measuring political development.

The principal hypothesis tested is that political institutions are interdependent with educational systems, economic institutions, communications systems, degree of urbanization, and the distribution of the labor force. A nation's economic system can develop only if its educational system keeps pace, if people concentrate in urban areas, if communications and transportation systems emerge, and if changes occur in family and social life that induce people to fit into the occupational demands of the unfolding system. Leo Schnore has measured the interdependence among certain of these factors.[5]

[4] See Daniel Lerner, *The Passing of Traditional Society* (Glencoe, The Free Press, 1958).

[5] For a matrix of rank-order correlations of a number of indicators of these variables, see Schnore, *op. cit.*, p. 236. Schnore's correlations tend to be slightly higher than product-moment correlations using the T-scoring method, but slight differences in the number of nations included may account for such differences.

See also Alex Inkeles, "National Character and Modern Political Systems," in *Psychological Anthropology* (ed.) Francis L. K. Hsu (Homewood, Illinois, The Dorsey Press, 1961), pp. 172–208. . . . He reviews various approaches to this topic and cites studies which suggest connections between national character and modern political systems. However, no conclusions can be drawn from this body of work in part because it lacks a standard measure of political systems with which different national characters might be associated. For a definite point of view on the subject of the importance of personality to social change generally and economic and political change in particular,

But to test the hypothesis that political institutions are not set apart from the rest of a society's institutions we must construct an index of political development and then test the hypothesis by assessing the association between political development and other measures of national systems.

Constructing an Index of Political Development

The following items were selected and given the weights indicated. The time period covered by the data is 1940 through 1961.[6] The score each nation received for the first year was added to the score it received the following year to get a cumulative total score.

This scheme for scoring the nations, in which high scores mean high development, should penalize each nation for political instability which represents "backsliding" and reward it for achieving or retaining more complex political forms of organization. Points for any one year were awarded in the following manner.

1. Legislative Branch of Government

Two points for each year in which a parliament existed in which the lower or the only chamber contained representatives of two or more political parties and the minority party or parties had at least 30 per cent of all seats.

One point for each year in which a parliament existed whose members were the representatives of one or more political parties, but where the "30 per cent rule" was violated.

No points for each year no parliament existed or for years when either of the above types of parliaments was abolished or discarded by executive power. Parliaments whose members are not members of political parties are

---

see Everett E. Hagen, *On the Theory of Social Change* (Homewood, Illinois, The Dorsey Press, 1962). Hagen's theory has the virtue of being testable, but he presents little supporting evidence himself—again in part, because the evidence simply does not exist. In rejecting economic theories of social change, Hagen swings to psychological explanations, and in the process by-passes sociological perspectives.

[6] The primary source for the materials used in this study was the *Political Handbook of the World: Parliaments, Parties and Press,* published annually for the council on Foreign Relations (New York, Harper and Brothers from 1940 through 1961). Needed supplementary checks were secured by reference to the *Encyclopaedia Britannica* and other reference works. Nations included for study are listed in Table 2. All independent nations are included on all continents except Africa. These were excluded because inclusion would have inflated correlation coefficients artificially—their political development scores lump together in one corner of the scattergram. A more refined index of political development might distinguish variation in development. A total of 76 independent nations are included.

given a zero. Parliaments that are not self-governing bodies (e.g., the mock parliaments of colonial governments that have no powers to override an executive veto or to force a government out of office by voting no confidence) are given a zero.

2. Executive Branch of Government

One point for each year the nation was ruled by a chief executive who was in office by virtue of direct vote in an open election where he faced competition or was selected by a political party in a two or more party system as defined by the conditions necessary to get 2 points on the legislative branch indicator above. If the parliament ceased being a multi-party parliament, the chief executive stopped getting points.

No points for each year the nation was ruled by a chief executive selected by criteria other than those necessary to attain 1 point as given above. Colonial governments received a zero.

It is possible for a nation to acquire zero, one, two or three points per year. Over the 22-year period of our study it would be possible for a nation to accumulate a total of 66 points. This scoring system converts attributes into one continuous variable, just as the attribute "male" or "female" can be converted into a continuous variable by measuring the proportion of males in a group.

RELATIONSHIP OF POLITICAL TO OTHER MEASURES OF NATIONAL DEVELOPMENT

This study began with the aim of measuring the degree of association between political development and other types of social-economic development. The objective was a statistical assessment of the degree of association between educational development, urbanization, communication development, economic growth and labor force characteristics and the measure of political development.[7] A statistical statement of the proportion of the variation around the mean of the political development index that could be accounted for by covariation with selected independent variables

[7] Social-economic statistics used in this report were drawn from the last reporting year from the following United Nations sourcebooks: Demographic Yearbook, 1960, Statistical Yearbook, 1960, and Report on the World Social Situation, 1957. The Yearbook of Labor Statistics, 1960, was the source for labor force statistics. Statistical assessment followed T scoring of the data. A simple technique for computing the T score is given in Allen E. Edwards, Statistical Methods for the Behavioral Sciences (New York, Holt, Rinehart and Winston, 1954). For a single item, T scoring of the raw data will yield a mean of 50 and a standard deviation of 10. If we add items together to form an index, a four-part item with a sum of 200 represents a subject (or nation) with an average index score. All single item indicators and combined indices in this paper have been T scored.

was also sought. Finally, if the association was reasonably close, one might build a prediction equation which would describe for each nation whether its level of political development was commensurate with the values it received on the independent variables in the prediction equation.

Of the several independent variables considered, the communications development index[8] had a Pearson zero-order association with political development of .80.[9] The communications development index is tightly related to an index of economic development (.95) but is a better predictor of political development than is economic development.[10] The communications index reflects the ability and the needs of national systems to maintain differing types of communication systems depending on the varying degrees of literacy of their population and varying levels of integration of the economic and social order.

The relationship between national communications development and political development may be seen in graphic form in Figure 1. This scattergram makes the correlation coefficient more meaningful. The communications development scores on the horizontal axis increase from left to right; the political development scores on the vertical axis increase from bottom to top.

The most striking thing about the Figure 1 is the steady increase in the level of political development as the level of communication development increases. The main diagonal is the *regression line*. If every nation's scores were such as to put it exactly on that line, the correlation coefficient would be 1.00. We see, however, that some nations are above the line and some are below. What is the difference? A nation below the line is politically underdeveloped in relation to its given level of communications development.[11] To find the

---

[8] The communications development index is formed by summing the T scores a given nation received on newspaper consumption, newsprint consumption, telephones, and the number of pieces of domestic mail per capita. If one or two indicators were missing we took the average of the two or three available indicators and added their scores to estimate the total index score. Five of the 76 nations had less than two communications indicators and their scores were estimated and used in the prediction equation developed later in the paper. They are omitted from Figure 1.

[9] Variables considered but not included in the matrix because of high intercorrelations with variables already in the matrix were the economic development index and industrial labor force index. Economic development was measured by combining the T scores for a given nation of per capita measures of energy consumption, steel consumption, income in U.S. dollars, and the number of motor vehicles. These items are all highly intercorrelated. (See Schnore, *op. cit.*, p. 236.)

[10] The product-moment correlation of communications development with political development was .80 compared to .68 for economic development with political development.

[11] Our use of the terms politically over- or underdeveloped should not be understood as a moral or ethical judgment of where the nation ought to be. A politically underdeveloped nation lacks sufficient points which it could obtain only if it met the criteria set by our political development index. In severe cases it may lack any political party or even a parliament. Our statements of whether or not a nation is under- or overdeveloped are not made with sole reference to its score on the political development index—a nation

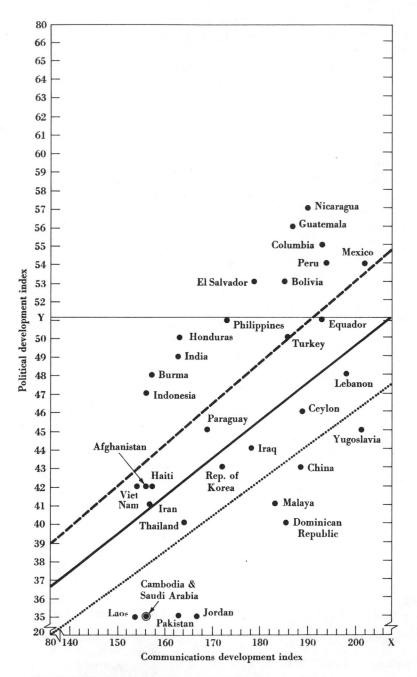

*Figure 1.   Relationship of political development to
communications development: 71 nations*

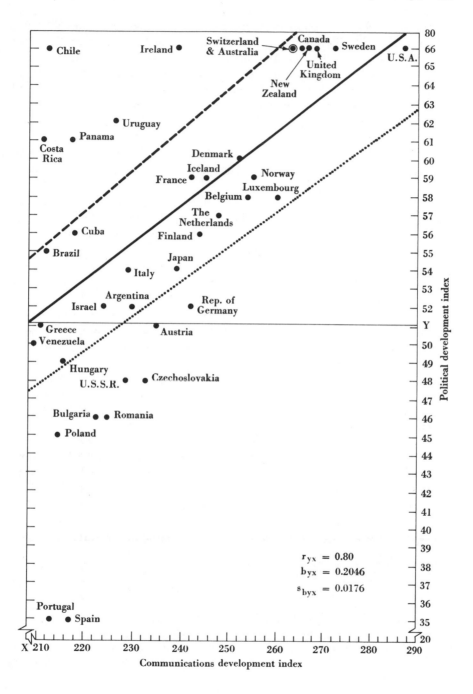

political development score that any nation below the line "should" have, draw a line vertically up until it meets the regression line. Then draw a right angle or horizontal line until it intercepts the political development axis. (Then compare this "expected" development score with the actual development score.) Nations below the line may be defined as politically "backward" relative to their level of communications. Just the opposite is true for the nations above the line. They are politically overdeveloped. The difference between the communication index scores that the politically overdeveloped nations (above the line) really have and what they should have if they were on the regression line represents the extent of possible imbalance in the social system of the nation.

If the sociological conception of an interdependent social system in equilibrium is valid, we can apply that theory to this statistical model, taking the regression line as that set of points toward which the nations "should" be moving if they are not already on it. Nations above the line (politically overdeveloped) can reach the line by increasing their communication development (and maintaining their political development) or by "backsliding" on political development while maintaining the same score on communications.

Nations below the line face similar alternative routes to the equilibrium point. They can increase their level of political development and rise vertically to the line or they can decrease their communications and move to the left until they meet the line—maintaining or perhaps decreasing their level of political development. Such movements as this may seem unlikely to people living in a society in which communication systems are believed to increase steadily in complexity, but alternative (even "impossible") movements can occur during revolutions, civil wars, and territorial occupation by a foreign power, or through economic disasters. Internal social change may be violent or not, but in any case should result in movement in the predicted direction.

Mathematical models have been considered[12] which might be applied to data like these to test the notion that there will be movement toward the line. Empirical testing would be the only way to state whether nations do in fact increase or decrease either variable in order to come into equilibrium. However, if measurements are made each year for a period of years, the movement of nations can be precisely plotted. If empirical tests do not show nations moving toward their equilibrium point, then it is also possible that the same test will reveal different equilibrium points for nations in different social and

---

is either high or low or in between on the index. The judgment is being made only with reference to the political development score the nation should have *relative* to its level of communications development. Thus, a nation with a one-party system may actually be overdeveloped politically in relation to its communications system or its level of urbanization and other measures of national growth.

[12] See James S. Coleman, "The Mathematical Study of Small Groups," in Herbert Solomon (ed.) *Mathematical Thinking in the Measurement of Behavior* (Glencoe, The Free Press, 1960), pp. 26–30.

economic circumstances. We have conveniently assumed a common set of equilibrium points rather than several (one could have several equilibrium points simply if different clusters of nations had different regression lines, a possibility to be explored in later research).

In Figure 1 we have drawn broken lines on either side of the regression line we actually observed for the 71 nations on which we had communication index scores. For these data the sample estimate of the standard error of the regression coefficient can be applied to describe what is a "small" and what is a "large" departure from the regression line. The broken lines represent alternative regression lines that would be likely to occur if we were drawing a sample of 71 from a larger population. Although these conditions are not met in this case, the use of a high and a low estimate of alternative regression coefficients establishes hypothetical confidence bands which may help us sort out errors of measurement and other types of error that may result in moving a nation several points away from the line when actually it should be closer to it. Measurement errors may also place a nation on the line when it ought not to be there, but this is less likely than the former movement which decreases correlations. The inability of either one of our indices actually to distinguish for every nation the refinements of political development; missing data and substitution of estimates for communication scores; the mis-reporting of political information—all of these types of error exist and should be considered before refined explanations of minor deviations from the line are attempted. For the benefit of students who may wish to consider these possibilities, the nations that lie between the two bands of broken lines may be considered as being off the regression line because of measurement and other errors; hence attention may be devoted to nations that are outside the bands for deviant-case analysis or comparison of extreme cases on either side of the line.

ACCOUNTING FOR NATIONAL POLITICAL DEVELOPMENT

Inspection of the matrix of correlations in Table 1 reveals a high degree of association between each predicting variable and political development. But the variable most closely associated is the communications development index. If taken alone it accounts for 64 per cent of the variation of the political development scores around the mean. It is appropriate to ask whether or not the additional variables add to an over-all explanation of the variation and, if so, how much?

Computation of a multiple correlation coefficient using all four independent variables simultaneously yields a multiple R of .85. Thus, a total of 72 per cent (R^2) of the observed variation around the mean of the dependent variable is associated with covariation in the independent variables. This compares with the 64 per cent of variation that could be accounted for by using communications as a single predictor. By way of further comparison, only 38 per cent—$(.62)^2$—of the variation around the mean could have been accounted for by variation in the scores on the education index had we used that as a single predictor.

The intercorrelations suggest that we should not be too hasty in abandoning the use of multiple criteria. The fact that the communication index is highly correlated with the education index and its .95 correlation with economic development reveal the highly interdependent nature of national social organization. The statistical meaning of the zero-order correlation coefficient of education and communication is the same as that of the multiple correlation coefficient, which happened also to be .85. Both mean that 72 per cent of variation around the mean of a "dependent" variable was "explained" by covariation with the other variable(s). Thus, the score a nation receives on communications development is itself highly dependent on the national level of educational development, urbanization, movement of the labor force out of agricultural employment, and economic development. That communications and not economic development, urbanization, or education best accounts for the political development of a nation is significant. It should not obscure, however, the essential interdependence of this matrix of characteristics, which collectively give a distinctive profile to any given nation and collectively interact to yield political outcomes which in turn yield further changes in the independent variables themselves.[13]

USING THE PREDICTION EQUATION TO FULL ADVANTAGE

Political development scores can be used in several ways. We can make a simple statement about the relative position of any nation regarding its political development by comparing the index score of one country with scores of other nations. We can extend the power of such comparison considerably, however, if we use the prediction equation (a by-product of our computation of R) and, on the basis of the existing interrelationships among the variables in the matrix in Table 1, predict what the score of any nation on political

[13] It is of interest to note that when intercorrelations are high it becomes impossible to give any meaning to the size or sign of the beta weights in the prediction equation. This is a favorite pastime of some sociologists, but inspection of the correlations and beta weights in Table 1 should make them hesitate to partial out variation to any specific independent variable in a multiple regression analysis. Since I have indulged in this statistical fantasy myself, I feel well qualified to bring it to the attention of my colleagues. The use of partial correlations to produce meaningful correlations when intercorrelations are high is also of doubtful usefulness. Removing the effect of "communication" and then seeing what the partial is between education and political development would reveal a coefficient of near zero, but this certainly would not mean that education was not a vital factor. Partial correlation is a way of finding out what added gain one may expect by including certain variables in a multiple regression equation, but it tends to oversimplify our conception of the world under some conditions. It is what might be called an "anti-systems" statistic, albeit an occasionally useful one.

Table 1. *Matrix of Correlations of National Measures of*
Political Development, and Levels of Education, Communication,
Urbanization, and Employment in Agriculture

	1	2	3	4	5	Means	S.D.
1) Communication		71	85	−79	80	207.6	35.8
2) Urbanization	[69]		75	−72	64	49.7	8.8
3) Education	[69]	[70]		−72	62	107.1	16.4
4) Agriculture	[57]	[56]	[58]		−56	50.5	10.5
5) Political Development	[71]	[74]	[72]	[58]		50.0	9.5

$$\hat{Y} = (-21.46) + (.300X_1) + (.376X_2) + (-.221X_3) + (.282X_4)$$
$$R_{y.1234} = .85$$

Numbers above the diagonal are product-moment correlations. Numbers below the diagonal give the number of cases on which the appropriate correlation was based.

The communications index summed the T scores of newspaper readers per capita, newsprint consumption per capita, the volume of domestic mail per capita, and the number of telephones per capita.

The urbanization index is the T score of the proportion of the population of the nation living in cities over 100,000. The proportion of the economically active labor force employed in agriculture was T scored. The education index was formed by combining T scores of literacy with T scores of the number of students per 100,000 enrolled in institutions of higher education.

Political development scores are computed by T scoring the 76 nations' raw political development scores.

Means and standard deviations of independent variables are based on the largest reported N in row 5. N for the political development mean and standard deviation was 74.

development "should be" on the basis of its "complete" profile of national development. Knowing its scores on communications development, urbanization, educational attainment, and agricultural labor force, we can calculate an estimated or predicted political development score.

When this is done the predicted value of political development can be compared to the actual value of any nation. If we subtract the predicted value from the actual value we get a positive or a negative number that represents error of prediction. If the error is positive, the nation has a higher than expected political development score. If the error (or the "residual") is negative, the nation has a lower than predicted score for its political development.

For example, the actual political development score for Canada was 66 and its predicted value, 61.3. The difference is +4.7. Canada has a larger than predicted political development score. On the other hand, Venezuela had an actual political development value of 50, but a predicted value of 56.1, with a negative residual of −6.1. Venezuela's actual political development was less than expected on the basis of its social characteristics.

These errors may tell us much about some of the factors that influence political development. One such factor is revealed in Table 2, which groups nations according to their geographic location. The size of the average net residual error for the 12 nations in North America was a positive 4.3. The

Table 2. Residual Error of Prediction of Political Development:
By Continent and Nation

North America		South America		Asia		Europe	
Canada	4.7	Argentina	−2.3	Afghanistan	−0.3	Albania	0.8
Costa Rica	7.5	Bolivia	5.9	Burma	10.1	Austria	−2.6
Cuba	3.2	Brazil	−0.9	Cambodia	−6.2	Belgium	2.3
Dom. Repub-		Chile	12.5	Ceylon	1.6	Bulgaria	−7.1
lic	−5.7	Colombia	3.3	China	−3.1	Czechoslova-	
El Salvador	9.1	Ecuador	2.0	Fed. of Ma-		kia	−3.0
Guatemala	7.2	Paraguay	3.8	laya	−6.7	Denmark	−0.5
Haiti	2.7	Peru	4.9	India	11.1	Finland	−2.9
Honduras	10.4	Uruguay	8.3	Indonesia	7.3	France	4.4
Mexico	1.3	Venezuela	−6.1	Iran	−3.5	W. Germany	−2.8
Nicaragua	7.1			Iraq	−1.7	Greece	1.1
Panama	6.5			Israel	−1.3	Hungary	1.3
United				Japan	−3.8	Iceland	0.5
States	−2.6			Jordan	−6.3	Ireland	9.7
				Rep. of		Italy	−1.0
				Korea	−0.4	Luxem-	
				Laos	−4.5	bourg	−4.1
				Lebanon	−1.8	Netherlands	1.3
				Mongolia	−6.0	Norway	−1.7
				Muscat	−3.6	Poland	−6.4
				Nepal	−3.5	Portugal	−17.2
				Pakistan	−5.3	Romania	−9.9
				Philippines	10.7	Spain	−20.3
				Thailand	−2.0	Sweden	0.9
				S. Arabia	−7.3	Switzerland	4.3
				Turkey	−1.6	United King-	
				Viet Nam	0.3	dom	1.3
				Yemen	−3.6	Yugoslavia	−2.1
				Australia	−0.1	U.S.S.R.	−0.7
				N. Zealand	2.3		
Mean of Net Residual Errors of Prediction +4.3		+3.5		−1.4		−2.1	
N = [12]		[10]		[28]		[26]	

Standard Deviation of residuals:*
$s_{y \cdot x} = \pm 5.05$

* Adapted from Edwards, op. cit., p. 162.

table also shows that of the 12 nations in North America, ten had positive residuals. The situation is similar for South America. There, average net residuals reveal greater than predicted political development—an average error of more than three T-score values. Looking over the table as a whole, it is clear that nations located in the Western Hemisphere enjoy a considerable advantage in their political development over nations located in Asia or Europe.[14]

We might speculate that the absence of international conflict over the long history of North and South America has resulted in far greater benefits for their political development than we anticipated. Our common stereotype of Latin American political instability is subject to some re-evaluation when seen from the world perspective. Far from being unstable, the prediction equation suggests that they are not only relatively stable but relatively more developed than comparable nations around the world. The absence of international conflict may well be one of the crucial variables to consider as a background to understanding the political development of nations. Of course, without an international conflict within the Western Hemisphere it is impossible to differentiate nations within the hemisphere. Little can be said about the relation of war to political development in the Western Hemisphere because such conflicts do not exist. In these circumstances, what does not exist in the Western Hemisphere but does exist in other areas of the world can be invoked as an "explanation" of the direction of the residual values!

We are, however, in the fortunate position of being able to compare societies that have not experienced international conflict with societies that have, to see if the pattern of differences observed sustains our suggested explanation for the pattern of positive residuals in North and South America. When we combine Europe with the Western Hemisphere (Table 3) we have a total of 48 nations. Of these, 19 were penetrated by land armies in World War II, and 29 were not.[15] Of the 19 nations so directly affected by the War only 31 per cent show positive political development residuals while 76 per cent of the 29 nations not affected reveal political development gains.[16]

[14] The U.S.S.R. is considered to be in Europe and New Zealand and Australia in Asia for the convenience of presentation.

[15] We use World War II alone because it occurred during the period covered by our study. Had we gone back to the era of the First World War, roughly the same nations would have again been involved. The effect observed in Table 3 may not be attributable to World War II but to longer-run effects of war on the political development of nations.

[16] The reader may argue that I have "stacked the deck" in favor of this outcome by starting my time series in the year 1940, a time at which Europe was engaged in a war which resulted in the loss of national autonomy for a number of nations—hence an inability to collect political development points. This criticism applies to very few nations. Only a few European nations had multi-party political systems before 1940 and about half of these avoided conquest by staying neutral or by physical location. In fact, France

While the implication of disruption of a complex social system by such phenomena as war may seem obvious to some readers, war should not be viewed as the sole source of disruption or even as a disruptive force in some areas. What of the pattern of political underdevelopment in Asia? Does it not refute the data in Table 3?

Table 3. Territorial Involvement in World War II and
National Development: Western Hemisphere versus Europe

	Territory invaded during the war	Territory not reached by war
Per cent of nations revealing political development gains	31%	76%
100% =	19	29

$$\chi^2 = 7.46; \ df = 1; \ p < .01$$

If one relies solely on a few statistics, without some other types of distinctions among different types of nations, his analysis may falter. We omitted Asia from Table 3 because it obscures the relationship, but we learn something by so doing. We learn that war is disruptive to complex social systems and that this fact is revealed by Table 3, which is composed of nations that are, for the most part, in a stage of advanced political and economic-social development. Asian nations, with a few exceptions, are not yet at the stage where the effects of war will be reflected on the political development index. In fact, a number of Asian nations received their independence largely through the indirect effects of World War II and were thus able to join the ranks of independent nations. The Asian nations that have more complex political organization than predicted are India, Indonesia, Burma, and the Philippines. These achieved independence *after* the war was over. But most of those Asian nations which have been independent for a long period have *lower* than predicted political development. There are, in short, no single factor explanations

and Belgium, both of which were occupied and both of which had multi-party systems in the prewar period, reveal positive residual values while across the Pyrenees, Spain and Portugal both show gross political underdevelopment. Neither Spain nor Portugal had complex political institutions before, during, or after the war. The over-all effect is best summarized in Table 3.

Greater depth of analysis of the variation among nations with continents can be achieved by subtracting out the "bias" effect that being located on a particular continent gives to a nation, and each nation can then start out on equal terms for further analysis. For example, we could subtract 4.26 from each *actual* score of the North American nations and 3.47 from each South American nation. In similar vein, we could add 1.38 to each Asian nation and 2.14 to each European nation.

of political under- or overdevelopment. The presence or absence of international conflict on the territory of a nation, and other violent conflict may, if protracted, influence the development of nations; and complex social systems are especially vulnerable to such changes. Changes that disrupt socio-economic life may be expected to disrupt other aspects of the national system. We might hypothesize that the amount of disruption would be related to the degree of complexity of organization and interdependency within a given nation.

THE USE OF ERRORS OF PREDICTION IN TESTING THEORIES OF POLITICAL CHANGE

Under the assumption that the institutions of a society form an interdependent system in equilibrium nations should tend to move to the regression line so that their communications development equilibrates with their political development. This should hold for politically overdeveloped nations and for politically backward nations. To reach the line, a nation must change its score on political development or communications development or on both.

In multiple regression analysis, the predicted values may be treated as the regression line. They represent the set of points toward which any one nation should move regarding political development and the scores the nation has on the four predictor variables. When we compare the predicted with the actual score and find that a nation has departed from its predicted values, we can view it as being out of equilibrium. Hypothetically, it should be under some pressure to move toward the predicted score on political development. The student interested in mass movements, political change, or revolution may have seen in the preceding discussions a means of locating nations that should be experiencing deep strains in their socio-political system.

For example, theories of political change which view mass movements as the carriers of political change usually portray such action as taking place when the political institutions are not "adequate" in form or function and are sufficiently out of phase with other areas of national development to set up the conditions that allow traditional bonds of allegiance of the masses to the elites and to existing political institutions to be broken in a mass upheaval. The meaning of the deviation from the "multiple" regression line formed by a set of predicted political scores may be translated in terms of its possible measurement of pressures on certain social classes, or economic or power elites. Kornhauser regards the historic development of national social systems in terms of their *rate* of development (i.e., rate of urbanization, industrialization, transformation of the educational institutions, and the complexity of the economy and communications systems) in relation to political behavior of certain segments of the population that are affected by rapid change.[17] Other theorists focus on the importance of changes in national character before the economic transformations which led to political disequilibrium can occur.[18]

The method presented in this paper makes a *prediction* about which nations should experience political movements of a specific type (either toward increasing complexity or decreasing complexity). Theories of change can then be tested against what actually happens. This frees us from the primary and very legitimate criticism leveled against most theorists of political change: that they are always talking about something that is past and done with.

Taking Asia as an example, we have already noted the politically overdeveloped character of India (11.1), the Philippines (10.7), Burma (10.1), and Indonesia (7.3). These are the only Asian nations whose positive errors of prediction are larger than one standard deviation ($s_{y \cdot x} = \pm 5.05$) of the residuals. Changes have been occurring in these nations, and the more dramatic of these changes are political. Burma and Indonesia have turned away from complex political organization and have abandoned multi-party politics. They will move toward the regression line not only by increasing their socio-economic development scores (a problematic event) but by decreasing their level of political development to the point where equilibrium is reached. When they reach the line, the strain to re-establish more complex political forms ought to resume, providing socio-economic development continues.

The pressures in India and the Philippines toward similar political "backsliding" may also be strong and whether they will follow the path taken by Burma and Indonesia is problematic. If rapid economic and social development can occur they may achieve equilibrium.[19]

For the student of social change who is oriented to case studies, this technique supplies a basis on which to pick cases on more than "expert" testi-

[17] William Kornhauser, *The Politics of Mass Society* (Glencoe, The Free Press, 1959). See also the discussion by Joseph R. Gusfield, "Mass Society and Extremist Politics," *American Sociological Review*, Vol. 27 (February, 1962), pp. 19–30.

[18] Hagen, *op. cit.*, and Inkeles, *op. cit.*

[19] Philippine deviation may be partially explained by this observation. "While Washington officials and Ambassador Spruance took great pains to maintain neutrality between the candidates, they made it clear to the Philippine government that the conduct of the election was of vital concern to the United States. Had the Liberal Administration been returned to power by means of fraud and violence, it would have been in no position to bargain successfully for badly needed economic assistance and for the much desired revision of the Bell Act!" *Internal pressures* for an honest election, however, are also cited. Willard H. Elsbree, "The 1953 Philippine Presidential Elections," *Pacific Affairs*, Vol. XXVII (March, 1954), p. 13. It is interesting to note that representation in the Philippine lower House conformed to our definition of multi-party representation only during the first decade of independence, and has violated the "30 per cent rule" of minority party representation since 1957. In India, the Congress party's majorities also override the 30 per cent rule.

mony. Here is a tool for locating deviant cases if one wishes to compare different types of nations in detail to see the institutional mechanisms or other national characteristics that allow a nation to wander far from the regression line and stay out of equilibrium for many years. He might wish to contrast, for example, Ireland (9.7) with Spain (−20.3), or Uruguay (8.3) with Venezuela (−6.1).

In tracing out the social correlates of the political development of nations, one need not wait for the future. The design used here could be taken back to 1930. One might calculate the residual values at five-year intervals and re-calculate the deviations, observing the differences among different types of nations. Continued up to 1960, the sample of points and deviations would look approximately like our own.[20] Such an analysis might reveal cut-off points in social-economic development beyond which change in the political system is apparently unavoidable. It could reveal a cut-off point further down the scale where complex political institutions cannot stand for long. Such a longitudinal study could get at the interaction between political and other institutions in the society. It could measure some of the non-economic aspects of economic growth that so trouble students of underdeveloped nations. Does the existence of complex (given their level of socio-economic development) political or-ganization in Latin American States give them an advantage over their politi-cally backward counterparts in Europe and Asia? What are the effects of sustained political overdevelopment on other systems within the nation that will allow it to "take off" to new heights of social growth or plunge it into revolution and political traditionalism? What differences in national character sustain political change, economic change or traditionalism, and how is national character affected by increasing levels of organizational complexity in nations?[21]

SUMMARY

This report developed some of the possible applications of an index of political develop-ment for 76 independent nations in all continents except Africa. (Africa was

[20] Space restrictions prohibit more than mention of the statistical problems of treat-ing change over time: for example, one would need measures of both political and non-political values. It is possible to study development without reference to a nation's relative position in the world. This is the approach usually followed by the case-study worker. Both approaches have limitations and advantages.

[21] For one example of changes induced by the onslaught of industrialization see Alex Inkeles and Peter H. Rossi, "National Comparisons of Occupational Prestige," *American Journal of Sociology*, Vol. LXI (January, 1956), pp. 329–39, for a study of ranking of occupations by inhabitants of six nations. Rankings are highly correlated. The authors interpret this as an outcome of the industrial occupational system and the cen-tralized national state.

omitted for statistical reasons, in order not to inflate the persuasiveness of our results.) Knowledge of the level of the development of the communications system of a nation accounts for 64 per cent of the variation in scores around the mean of the political development index. A multiple regression equation which added educational development, agriculture labor force, and degree of urbanization to the communication index as predictors of political development raised the level of explained variation to 72 per cent.

The matrix of intercorrelations among a variety of indicators of the specialization and level of development of different aspects of national, social, economic, and political life supported the idea that social systems are indeed systems—that is their parts are interdependent. The concept of interdependence and the statistical method of this study led us to consider the existence of hypothetical equilibrium points toward which each nation is moving. It is possible for a nation to be politically overdeveloped or underdeveloped, and we suggest that either political or non-political changes will occur to put the nation into equilibrium.

The extent to which a nation diverges from its predicted level of political development was considered and possible ways to utilize these errors of prediction were discussed. Finally, the ability of social scientists to test theories concerning revolution, mass movements and political change was discussed.

Section 2
THEORIES
OF DEVELOPMENT

Introduction: *Technological Progress, Capital Formation and Institutional Change*

Economic development requires technological progress; and technological progress requires capital formation. This statement would be common to the vast majority of economic theories of economic development. It is worth examining in some detail.

The first part of the statement is a proposition. For any given system of production a new technology is required to produce sustained increases in human productivity. This calls to mind images of new machines and new forms of energy production, steam to replace streams, oil to replace coal to be replaced by hydroelectricity to be replaced by nuclear power. In agriculture it calls up images of new equipment, large-scale water control, scientifically selected high-yielding seeds and breeds, and chemical fertilizers and feeds. New techniques are needed if men are to produce more goods.[1]

The second part of the statement is part definition (or tautology) and part proposition. If capital formation is simply the accounting term applied to acts of replacing old equipment or creating new productive equipment, then almost by definition technological progress is capital

---

[1] There is, of course, some disagreement on just what is meant by technology. Some would restrict the meaning to tools and a few procedures. Others would include a wide range of organizational characteristics.

formation. The former refers to the act, the latter refers to the classification of the act in some accounting scheme. In another sense, however, capital formation implies a proposition. Wealth must be diverted from immediate consumption to pay for the productive facilities to be used in the future. Further, substantial amounts of wealth must be diverted if the productive facilities of the future are to allow men to produce more than they produced yesterday. Thus capital formation, which is necessary for economic development, implies pressures to hold down or even to depress consumption.

Economic theories, from those of Adam Smith and Karl Marx to the modern Keynesians and the modern Marxists, appear to agree on this point. Whether the focus is on the individual firm, with businessmen's profits as the mechanism of capital formation (the Classicists), or on the aggregate activity of the economy, with the more complex and impersonal credit mobilizing and transferring arrangements as the mechanisms (the Keynesians), capital formation is viewed as necessary for technological progress. Whether the surplus of production is wrenched from the producers by political arrangements based on private property, is forcefully drawn from the producers by a socialist government unfortunate enough to come to power under conditions of economic backwardness, or is agreed upon by a mass supporting a socialist government fortunate enough to come to power under conditions of high productivity, technological progress requires the diversion of an economic surplus from immediate consumption to paying for future productive facilities.

For the most part, these theories exclude from the analysis the institutional arrangements under which production and distribution take place. Adam Smith, for example, assumed a constant flow of innovations, with technological progress simply adjusted to the availability of capital to pay for the utilization of the innovations. Further, the availability of capital was largely a function of the level of businessmen's profits. The individual firm was the unit of analysis and the businessman or entrepreneur was the instrument by which technological progress was directed to production to provide the motor of increasing human productivity. The larger institutional setting, including the organization and control of labor and entrepreneurship, were assumed constant or exogenous in the analysis.

Even when Keynes shifted the focus to the total economy, a whole set of institutional arrangements, including values, tastes, and again the organization of labor, were assumed to be constant. For Keynes the major determinant of capital formation was the marginal efficiency of capital, which is determined by the businessman's view of the future. Since the view of the future can be assumed to be the same as the view of the present, interest rates can provide an accurate reflection of the present state. Now, since the interest rate is a function of the stock of money and of liquidity preferences, and can to a certain extent be legally regulated (given the present institutional structure), capital formation becomes amenable to manipulation by the political structure through institutions and arrangements such as banks, taxation, and transfer mechanisms. Although this provides a recipe for institutional manipulation of the process of economic development, it still does not make the institutional structure a central variable in explaining the process of development.

The Keynesian focus on the aggregate economy has more recently produced a general set of theories concerning development in backward economies.[2] Associated with the names R. F. Herrod and E. D. Domar, these theories continue to exclude institutional arrangements from a central position in the analysis, but nonetheless make important assumptions concerning the character of institutions in backward economies. It is, for example, common in Herrod-Domar models to assume that backward economies have low levels of both technology and technological growth, and that they have little if any unused productive capacity. Thus backward economies are poor because they are poor. With very low levels of technology and thus of output, they have no real capacity to reduce consumption to provide for the capital formation that alone can provide for technological progress. Further, with little unused capacity, they cannot be assisted from the outside or from deficit financing, since this increase of available income would only result in inflationary pressures that would dissipate any possible growth stimulation.

The assumptions of a constant or exogenous institutional structure have given considerable power to analytical economics in theorizing about development. This is especially evident in the analysis of capital formation, its measurement, and its relation to increases in output. At the same time, this power has been purchased at the expense of the consideration of a wide range of variables that, at least on the surface, appear to have considerable significance for the historical process of increasing human productivity. This is at least partly responsible for one very common criticism of economic theory in relation to backward economies: that these theories are developed in the West, apply only to western institutional settings, and are inapplicable to the situations of backward economies, especially those in Asia and Africa.

Hla Myint's selection, which opens this section, addresses itself

[2] For an excellent review of the modern set of "capital stock adjustment" theories see Henry J. Bruton, "Contemporary Theorizing on Economic Growth," in B. F. Hoselitz, ed., *Theories of Economic Growth* (New York, 1960), pp. 239–298.

to this criticism. He argues that much of the criticism is misplaced, that there is a good deal of utility in western economic theory, especially in the theory of optimal allocation of resources, and proposes a more detailed and intensive empirical study of the market conditions in the backward economies. Market imperfection produces distorted allocations, and market forces tend to reinforce and fossilize these distortions. While this may be generally agreed upon, Myint argues that greater attention needs to be directed to the character of market imperfections that do exist, how markets work, and what impact government policy has upon the private, and especially the subsistence, sector.

Beyond Hla Myint's proposal to use certain aspects of current economic theory carefully and empirically, it is useful to raise other issues of the relation of the institutional structure to the process of development. We have included a series of articles selected to focus attention on these institutional structures that appear most relevant to the process.

Max Weber takes perhaps the largest historical and geographic view of the process of economic development. Weber was primarily interested in understanding why it was that modern economic development, and its institutional referent industrial capitalism, appear first in the Western world. He considers this emergence to be of universal significance, largely because the underlying relationships in this type of system have gained pervasive significance throughout the world.[3]

For Weber the key to modern development is the *rational* organization of *free* labor. But even more fundamental than this is the *pervasiveness* of rational organization. His central concern was with this type of organization in economic activity, but he saw similar elements of rationality in science, architecture, music, law, and mathematics in the Western world. Further, Weber traced the roots of this rationality to early Christianity, through the development of an urban community in medieval Europe, and finally to the Protestant revolt and the subsequent emergence of industrial capitalism by the middle of the 19th century. The march of economic rationality is accomplished by institutional developments that progressively free man from relationships that preclude an independent and calculated approach to specific goals. Against this long historical view, Weber contrasted a view of ancient India, China, and Judaism exposing in each case what he considered the critical relation between values, social organization, and economic activity.

Weber's protestant ethic thesis has been one of the most influential institutional theories of modern development. Originally it was a polemic against the Marxists, attempting to show that ideas are not mere reflec-

[3] For a more recent historical analysis with the same point of view, see William H. McNeill, *The Rise of the West* (Chicago, 1963), especially Chapters XI, XII, and XIII.

tions of economic structure, rather that they have some independent determining power of their own.

Weber's theory has given rise to considerable criticism,[4] but it has also influenced a generation of social scientists who have focused attention upon the entrepreneur as the critical actor in the process of growth.[5] While this brings a useful correction to the economic theories, much of it has misplaced Weber's emphasis by focusing on the psychological aspects of the entrepreneur rather than upon the institutional obstacles to rational calculation. This is well illustrated by the provocative studies of McClelland and Hagen, whose articles on entrepreneurship are included in this section.

It has been widely observed that merchant and entrepreneurial groups have often occupied outcaste positions in society. The Jews of medieval Europe, the Parsis and Marwaris in India, and the Chinese in Southeast Asia are all excellent examples. Hagen attempts to show how such status-deprived groups might transform themselves into economic achievers in an attempt to regain their lost status. Similarly, McClelland focuses upon what he considers one of a basic set of needs, the need for achievement, as the dominant characteristic of the entrepreneurial personality character. Persons and groups with high need achievement are those that provide the real human engines of economic growth. And when (some unspecified) social forces make the need to achieve rather pervasive in a society, economic development ensues.

A major unanswered question in these analyses is that of timing. Quite apart from the difficult problem of ascertaining the extent of status deprivation or need achievement, neither Hagen nor McClelland attempts to deal systematically with the time lag between the generation of the needed psychological attribute and the onset of rapid economic development.

This psychological interpretation versus the institutional interpretation of Weber is joined in issue by Robert Bellah. In effect, we can assume that the psychological attributes of entrepreneurship are randomly distributed through space and time. We can find them in virtually all societies at all times. What is crucial, then, is the set of organized constraints and incentives that determines the specific type of activities into which the entrepreneur-types will be led to proceed. It is the institutional setting that determines whether innovative, achieving personalities will become reactionary landlords or merchants, industrialists, bureaucrats and politicians whose impact on the organization of production will be revolutionary.

[4] See especially Kurt Samuelsson, *Religion and Economic Action* (London, 1961).

[5] See for example, the long series of studies in *Explorations in Entrepreneurial History* (Cambridge, Mass.), Series 1 from 1949–1958, Series 2 from 1963.

Another provocative attempt to introduce institutional variation into the analysis of development is represented by W. W. Rostow's article on the stages of economic growth. Like Weber's protestant ethic theory, Rostow's stage theory enjoys wide influence and equally powerful criticism. The concept of the take-off could hardly be more popular in current discussion even though the theory has been subject to a thoroughly devastating critique by economists. In the selection included here Rostow proposes three major stages in modern economic growth, moving through an economically backward traditional stage, to the transitional stage in which the preconditions for development are laid down. Finally, during the take-off stage, capital formation enters once again as the critical variable, with rates suddenly jumping from about 5 percent of total output or less to 10 percent or more. In later developments of the theory two other stages are added. The take-off is followed by the drive to maturity in which the successful economy demonstrates that growth leadership can be transferred from one (declining) sector to another (growing) sector or industry. Finally the mature economy is capable of engaging in high mass consumption.

The criticisms of Rostow's theory have been so pervasive that it will be useful to review them briefly here.[6] Much of the criticism focuses on three issues. One is the motor of the stages, which for Rostow is provided by a theory of cycles. Industries or sectors tend to experience cycles of growth, maturity and decline. Thus, for example, the take-off will find one industrial sector in the vanguard, providing the major impetus for growth. But by the nature of cyclical processes, the leading industry must lose its vigor. If the society is successful in its take-off, it will be because another industry or sector emerges to take over the leadership from the declining sector.

The cycles also have their reflection in human family cycles, which are purported to show a shirt-sleeves to shirt-sleeves transition in three generations. Rostow gives this phenomenon the title of the "Buddenbrooks" complex, after the novel by Thomas Mann. The critics point out that it is difficult, if not impossible, to demonstrate that such cycles do in fact exist. Without a theory of cycles, a major part of the motor goes out of stage theory.

There is also the logical question of the relation of the stages to one another. Rostow gives no clear idea how a society moves organically from one stage to another. There is nothing in any of the stages that logically determines how or whether the onset of the next stage will be achieved. Related to this is the question of the empirical evidence of stages. Kuznets questions whether it is possible to see historical periods

[6] There is a useful selection of criticisms in G. M. Meier, *Leading Issues in Development Economics* (New York, 1964), pp. 25 ff.

in which there is a sudden rise in capital formation proportions to the 10 percent levels Rostow argues indicate the take-off. Nor is there any systematic attention given to the general historical conditions under which the stages operate. Clearly not all economies have passed through these stages; some are arrested, while others appear to have been able to skip stages. Gerschenkron suggests a spurt to development from greater economic backwardness assumes more control over the economy to establish the spurt.[7]

It must be admitted that the theory of stages of economic growth has not been sufficiently developed to provide much analytical power. Nonetheless, there is a great common-sense appeal to the general thrust of the argument if not to its many propositions.[8] It is easy to accept the notion that India is at a stage of development different from that of the countries of West Africa. This implies that India has had certain experiences that have had a cumulative effect and that it now has requirements for sustained growth different from those of West Africa. In this sense, the idea of stages has considerable attraction, but we must wait further specifications of the conditions to obtain the analytical power of a really useful theory.

A final criticism of stage theory is that it tends to see nations developing almost in a vacuum. This is, to be sure, a more general danger of using nations as units of analysis, and certainly most economic theory has tended to view the problem of international interaction as almost incidental to that of national economic development. Among other things, the Marxists provide a useful correction to this view. Included in this section is Paul Baran's article on the political economy of growth, which was later developed in greater detail in book length.[9] While this analysis does not fully treat institutional arrangements as the central variables in explaining growth, it does use a different set of institutional assumptions and raises another set of institutional issues.

The common Marxist focus on stratification and its inherent conflict turns attention to the relations among nations that are arranged hierarchically in respect of their power and wealth. The process of economic development is determined not only by a nation's internal characteristics, its particular stage in the longer historical process of change, but by its place in this international environment. Further, this environment is

---

[7] Alexander Gerschenkron, "Reflections on the Concept of Prerequisites," in Alexander Gerschenkron, ed., *Economic Backwardness in Historical Perspective* (Cambridge, 1962), pp. 31–51.

[8] Hla Myint, above, uses the idiom of stages, if not the details of stage theory in his discussion.

[9] See his *Political Economy of Growth*, 1962 edition (New York, 1962), especially his "Foreword to the 1962 Printing," pp. xi–xli.

inherently charged with conflict and oppression. In the individual firm, employers and workers are inherently in conflict because technological progress is constantly capital absorbing and labor saving. To stay alive in the environment of firms, each firm must constantly improve its productivity and this can only be done by depressing wages, since it is assumed that wages and profits cannot rise together, and it is profits that pay for the technological progress. Similarly, in the competition among nations, the advance of one must be at the expense of another, with the wealthier nations using international political and military power to reinforce their economic advantages. The terms of trade must necessarily run against the primary producing nations that supply the raw materials to the industrial nations. And where a nation attempts to break out of its political and economic encirclement, international economic and military force will be used to keep it in place.[10]

In Marxist theory this oppression occurs primarily because the organization of production is based on private property, from which emerge political and coercive forces that take wealth from the truly productive members and transfer it to the nonproductive members of the national or international system. When a nation does succeed in breaking out of this mold, through the great power of its revolutionary forces, it may be faced with extremely demanding external conditions, depending in part upon its particular stage of development. In all cases, economic development requires technological progress, which in turn requires capital formation. If a nation experiences a socialist revolution while it is still economically backward, just as any other backward economy, it will have to curtail consumption to pay for its development and this may require considerable repression. The hostility of the rest of the capitalist world will increase the pressures to hold down or even depress consumption since allocations will have to be made to nonproductive defense activities. Thus the repression that is common to the socialist economies, is not an inherent condition of those economic systems, but results from the requirements of economic development in conditions of economic backwardness in a hostile world.

As with the earlier Marxian analysis of the relation between economic and social structure, this line of thought is probably more important for the questions it raises than for the answers it provides. It is quite clear on an impressionistic level that the relations between nations is of considerable importance in determining the rate and direction of social and economic change. These issues have received useful treatment in the field of international relations, but more systematic analysis is

---

[10] For one attempt to deal with this process, see Irving Horowitz, *Three Worlds of Development* (New York, 1966). Unfortunately the significant issues this raises and the occasional insight are marred by the tendentious and unsystematic nature of the work.

required in the relation between social and economic processes of change. For example, Kuznets points out that the pattern of foreign investment has changed considerably over the past half century.[11] Up to World War II the largest proportion of net capital flows moved among the developed nations and were generated largely in the private sector. Since World War II, much larger proportions of net capital flow have moved to the underdeveloped nations and in the form of public sector grants and loans. This implies that there is considerable difference between, for example, the Latin American countries, who achieved independence in the 19th century and sometimes, like Mexico, also experienced major political transformations early in the 20th century, and the countries of Asia and Africa, which achieved independence and embarked on new economic development policies in the mid-twentieth century. We shall touch on this issue later, but we can observe here that it is clearly an issue that deserves rigorous and systematic treatment both empirically and theoretically.

[11] Simon Kuznets, *Modern Economic Growth* (New Haven, 1966), Chapter 6.

ECONOMIC THEORY AND THE UNDERDEVELOPED COUNTRIES

Hla Myint

How far is the economic theory of the industrially advanced countries applicable to the underdeveloped countries? This question has been raised, at one time or other by a variety of people. Some of the sociological writers have questioned the applicability of the concept of the "economic man" to the underdeveloped countries where traditional values and attitudes still prevail. The Historical and Institutional economists have argued that the generalizations of economic theory are based on the particular circumstances of the advanced countries and are therefore not "universally valid". Finally, there has been a long line of critics from the underdeveloped countries. In the nineteenth century, Hamilton, Carey and List questioned the applicability of the English classical free trade theory to the underdeveloped countries of that period, viz. the United States and Germany. They have been followed, amongst others, by Manoilesco from Southeast Europe and Prebisch from Latin America. With the emergence of the underdeveloped countries of Asia and Africa, the questioning of the usefulness of the "western" economic theory to these countries has become widespread. Now, many Western economists, not normally regarded as Historical or Institutional economists, have joined the ranks of the critics.

There are two main lines of criticism currently adopted against economic

From Hla Myint, "Economic Theory and Underdeveloped Countries," in Kurt Martin and John Knapp (eds.), *The Teaching of Development Economics* (Chicago: Aldine Press, 1967), pp. 33–52. Reprinted by permission of Frank Cass & Co., Ltd.

theory. The first is to elaborate the older line of criticism, stressing the differences in the social and institutional settings and stages of development between the advanced and the underdeveloped countries. This may be described as attacking the "realism" of economic theory. The second and newer line of attack is to question the "relevance" of economic theory to the underdeveloped countries. It is argued that "Western" economic theory is geared to the preoccupations of the advanced countries which, having already achieved sustained economic growth, are concerned with other problems, such as the optimum allocation of resources, the maintenance of full employment and perhaps the prevention of "secular stagnation". Thus the conventional economic theory is likely to be out of focus, if not largely irrelevant, for the central problem of the underdeveloped countries which is to initiate and accelerate the "take-off" into sustained growth.

Critics vary considerably in the emphasis they attach to these two different lines of attack.[1] But they share a common viewpoint on other issues. First, their attack on the applicability of economic theory to the underdeveloped countries is closely linked up with their attack on the applicability of free trade and laissez-faire policies to these countries. Thus, their sharpest attack on "Western" economic theory is reserved for the "orthodox" classical and neo-classical theory associated with the laissez-faire approach. The "modern" Keynesian economics is accepted less critically and is frequently used in support of deficit financing for economic development or as a basis for overall economic planning in terms of aggregate capital requirements to achieve a target rate of increase in national income, assuming a fixed capital output-ratio. Other modern developments of the neo-classical General Equilibrium theory, such as welfare economics, input-output analysis, linear programming, etc., are also acceptable provided they are used not as techniques for studying the performance of the market economy but as techniques of planning.

Further, all the critics share a common suspicion of the dispassionate "positivist" approach advocated by some of the orthodox economists.[2] The critics feel strongly that something should be done very urgently to relieve the poverty in the underdeveloped countries. They are also sceptical of the possibility of maintaining strict ethical neutrality in economics, and regard "positivism" merely as a cloak for inertia and an underdeveloped social conscience. Thus they feel that economists should give up the pretence of traditional academic detachment and become the champions and spokesmen for the underdeveloped countries. Some of them have come to look upon the eco-

[1] D. Seers, "The Limitations of the Special Case", *The Bulletin of Oxford Institute of Economics and Statistics* (May 1963), stresses the "realism" aspect, while G. Myrdal, *Economic Theory and the Underdeveloped Regions* (London, 1957), stresses the "relevance" aspect.

[2] E.g. G. Myrdal, *op. cit.*, chapter 12; Seers, *loc. cit.*, p. 83.

nomics of the underdeveloped countries not as a subject of impartial study but as an exercise in making out a persuasive case for increasing international economic aid to these countries.

The aim of this paper is to clarify and appraise some of the issues which have arisen at the present stage of the discussion on the question of the applicability, particularly the "relevance" of economic theory to the underdeveloped countries. Since this is closely bound up with the further question of the applicability of the laissez-faire policy to these countries, we shall make use of the arguments directed against the market mechanism to illustrate the arguments directed against economic theory. To clear the air, the underlying standpoint adopted in this paper towards planning and private enterprise in the underdeveloped countries may be stated as follows. There is no reason to suppose that economic policies considered appropriate for the advanced countries will prove to be equally appropriate to the underdeveloped countries. But this "realistic" objection to generalizations should apply not only to the laissez-faire but also to the planning policies in the underdeveloped countries. Further, given the wide differences which exist among the under-developed countries themselves with respect, say, to the degree of population pressure, the overall size of the economy, the general level of administrative efficiency and the coherence of the institutional framework, etc., it is highly unlikely that any single standard model of development planning will be appropriate for all of them.[3]

The plan of the paper is as follows. In section I we shall examine the various arguments directed against the market mechanism in the under-developed countries and use them to illustrate and clarify the various arguments directed against the applicability of economic theory to these countries. In section II we shall argue that while the need for a greater "realism" is fully conceded, the arguments directed against the "relevance" of the "Western" economic theory to the underdeveloped countries are more debatable. In particular, we shall argue that the orthodox static theory of the optimum al-location of resources is as relevant as any other part of the existing economic theory. In Section III we shall argue that a realistic approach to the under-developed countries has been hindered not only by the tendency to generalize from the "special case" of the advanced countries (as some critics have main-tained), but also from the tendency to generalize from the "special case" of a particular underdeveloped country, such as India; and that this has been ag-gravated by the popularity of the "take-off" theory and by the tendency of some of the modern writers to treat the subject not as an academic discipline but as an adjunct to making out a persuasive general case for increasing in-ternational economic aid to the underdeveloped countries.

[3] For a fuller development of this argument, see my book *The Economics of the Developing Countries* (London, 1964).

When the sociological writers questioned the applicability of economics to the underdeveloped countries on the ground that people there do not behave like the "economic man", they were questioning the "realism" of economic theory. It is not difficult to meet this type of criticism by showing that, with suitable adaptations to take into account local circumstances, the demand and supply analysis can be made to explain the behavior of individuals in the market and the prices and quantities bought and sold, etc., in the underdeveloped countries as well as in the advanced countries. For instance, the much cited case of the "backward-bending" supply curve of labour in the underdeveloped countries (even if it really exists) can be explained in terms of the demand and supply apparatus, not to speak of refinements such as the "Income Effect" and the "Substitution Effect". Similarly, even the reaction of the "subsistence sector" to the impact of the exchange economy can be dealt with by extending the concept of "retained" demand and supply and the factor-proportions analysis of the international trade theory.[4] But this type of defense does not impress some of the modern critics who are questioning the "relevance" of economic theory to underdeveloped countries. They are not really concerned with the question of whether the basic tools of economic theory, such as the demand and supply analysis, can explain economic behaviour in a wide range of underdeveloped countries. What they are concerned with is whether it is *important* for the underdeveloped countries to give a central place to the study of the market mechanism and how far the theory of the optimum allocation of resources which goes with this approach is relevant for countries seeking rapid economic development.

Now, the discussion would have been much simpler if the critics had simply concentrated on this suggestive line of attack. We could then go on to discuss the usefulness or otherwise of the concept of the static optimum for economic development. But what they usually tend to do is: first to identify the existing "orthodox" theory with the laissez-faire approach; next to argue that the free play of market forces in the underdeveloped countries will not lead to an optimum allocation of resources because the conditions of Perfect Competition, such as perfect mobility and divisibility of resources and perfect knowledge, are lacking; and finally to emerge with the twin conclusion that both the existing economic theory and the laissez-faire policy are inapplicable to the underdeveloped countries. This type of argument tends to obscure a number of issues.

First, take Perfect Competition. It may be taken for granted that the ideal conditions required by it will not be fulfilled in any real life situation, whether in the advanced or the underdeveloped countries. What is more interesting is

[4] Cf. H. Myint, "The 'Classical Theory' of International Trade and the Underdeveloped Countries," *Economic Journal*, 1958.

to find out how far these two types of country suffer from the same types of market imperfections and how far the existing theories of imperfect competition arising out of the problems of the mature industrial economies are relevant to the underdeveloped countries at a much earlier stage of development in market institutions. Further, given the important differences in population pressure, the overall size of the economy, and the general stage of development, etc., among the underdeveloped countries, it would be interesting to find out how far the different types of underdeveloped country suffer from different types of market imperfections. But many critics have been distracted by the easy target offered by the Perfect Competition model from making a "realistic" exploration of how the market mechanism actually works or fails to work in the different types of underdeveloped economic framework.

This has an interesting consequence on current writings on "planning" in the underdeveloped countries. On the one hand, we have the rejection of the Perfect Competition model. On the other hand, it is quite fashionable to formulate "pure" planning models, with given target figures of outputs, given production functions with constant sectoral capital-output ratios, and given supplies of resources, and make a great show of testing the formal consistency of the plan. Such a plan is supposed to cover the economy as a whole, but the fact that most governments of underdeveloped countries control a relatively small part of their G.N.P. (10 to 20 per cent) through taxation is used as evidence that there is a larger scope for the expansion of the state sector rather than as the evidence of a need for a more systematic analysis of how the private (including the subsistence) sector will react to government policy. Although some lip service is paid to the role of the fiscal, monetary and commercial policies of the government, the attention is focused mainly on the "quantifiable" aspects of the plan. Thus much in the same way as the Perfect Competition model fails to tell us how the market mechanism will actually overcome the existing immobility of factors and particularly existing imperfect knowledge, the "pure" planning model fails to tell us how the state mechanism will actually perform these tasks in the given administrative and institutional framework of an underdeveloped country. The substitution of the word "planning agency" for the "market mechanism" merely glosses over the actual problems of the mobilization and allocation of resources according to the plan and above all the problems of co-ordination and flexible readjustments. Thus the failure to study systematically how the economic forces work in the private sector of the underdeveloped countries, which produces the bulk of their G.N.P., has contributed to the failure to develop a satisfactory analysis of the "mixed economy" in the underdeveloped countries.

Next, take the Optimum. Much confusion has been caused by the habit of identifying the laissez-faire approach with the theory of the optimum allocation of resources. Although there is a historical association, there is no necessary logical link between the two. Thus it is possible to accept and work on the basis of an optimum allocation of resources without accepting the laissez-faire policy: for instance, welfare economics is mainly concerned with correcting the market forces to get closer to the optimum. Conversely, it is equally possible to reject the concept of the optimum as being too "static" and yet advocate a laissez-faire policy. The case for laissez-faire can then be made on other economic grounds, such as that it is likely to impart a "dynamism" to the economy by stimulating enterprise, innovation and investment. Thus in criticizing the working of the market mechanism in the underdeveloped countries, it is necessary to distinguish clearly whether we are concerned with its defects as the means of attaining the (accepted) norm of the optimum allocation of resources or whether we are concerned with the inadequacy of the concept of the optimum itself for the purposes of promoting the economic development of these countries.

Few critics have done this. Instead, they tend to bring out further objections against the market mechanism in the underdeveloped countries which are also used as the arguments against the applicability of the existing conventional economic theory to these countries. These various arguments may be grouped under four main lines of attack on the market mechanism.

(1) The first type of criticism runs in purely relative terms.[5] It is argued that the market mechanism works *more* imperfectly in the underdeveloped than in the advanced countries for various reasons, such as, a greater degree of immobility and indivisibility of resources and imperfect knowledge. Thus free market forces will lead to larger deviations from the optimum, requiring a correspondingly greater degree of state interference in the underdeveloped compared with the advanced countries. This type of criticism implies that the market imperfections in the advanced and the underdeveloped countries differ in degree rather than in kind and that the existing theory of the optimum and the deviations from the optimum may be usefully extended and adapted to deal with the problems of the economic development in the latter countries.

(2) The second type of criticism is based on the view that the most important problem facing the overpopulated underdeveloped countries is that they suffer from a surplus of labour and a shortage of other factors, viz. capital and natural resources. It is argued that this fundamental disequilibrium in factor proportions cannot be corrected merely by improving the allocative efficiency of the market mechanism on the basis of *given* resources, techniques and pattern of consumers' demand.[6] So long as these structural determinants of the economy remain unchanged perfect competition, even if it were attain-

---

[5] Most critics have put forward this argument at one time or another. For a clear exposition of this view, see T. Balogh, "Economic Policy and the Price System", *United Nations Economic Bulletin for Latin America* (March 1961).

[6] Cf. .e.g. R. S. Eckaus, "The Factor-Proportions Problem in the Underdeveloped Countries", *American Economic Review* (September 1955).

able, would merely bring out this problem sharply; according to the logic of the optimum theory, since labour is redundant relatively to given wants and technology, it should have zero wages. This type of criticism implies a rejection of the concept of the static optimum. But, unfortunately, in the absence of a thoroughgoing dynamic theory, many exponents of this view revert to the conventional methods of correcting the deviations from the static optimum. This can be best illustrated by the argument that the manufacturing sector of an underdeveloped country should be subsidized or protected because it is having to pay positive wages to labour whose social opportunity cost in agriculture is zero.[7]

In this connection, it may be noted that current writings tend to restrict the market mechanism too narrowly to its role of allocating given resources, neglecting its possible longer-term effect on the supply of factors, particularly capital.[8] Private savings may increase through improvements in the market for finance or through a rise of a capitalist class ploughing back profits. Even if it is decided that savings should increase only through public channels, such as taxation, marketing boards and the issue of government securities, the success of such a policy will still depend considerably on the market factors including the stage of development of the exchange economy and the development of a capital market.

(3) The third type of criticism is based on the view that the underdeveloped countries are trapped in a very stable low-income equilibrium and that they can be jerked out of this only through a "balanced growth" development programme big enough to overcome the smallness of the domestic markets and to take advantage of the economies of scale and complementarities. It is argued that at its best the market mechanism can only make one-at-a-time "marginal" adjustments, whereas an effective development programme requires large "structural" changes introduced by a simultaneous expansion of a wide range of complementary industries.

Without going into all the different versions of the "balanced growth" theory, it is sufficient to point out that we can adopt at least two different attitudes towards the role of the optimum allocation of resources in economic development, depending on the version of the theory we favour.

(*a*) One version emphasizes the overall size of the investment programme which must be large enough to overcome technical indivisibilities and the smallness in the size of domestic markets caused by the low levels of pur-

[7] Cf. e.g. W. A. Lewis, "Economic Development with Unlimited Supplies of Labour", *The Manchester School* (May 1954), p. 185.

[8] In international trade theory, there has been some discussion of how far the expansion of primary exports of the underdeveloped countries tends to aggravate the initial "skewness" of their factor endowments. Cf. C. P. Kindleberger, *Foreign Trade and the National Economy*, chapter 3.

chasing power in the underdeveloped countries.[9] Those who adopt this version tend to attach a greater importance to the problem of the aggregate level of investment and effective demand than to the problem of better allocation of resources at a given level of economic activity. Professor Hirschman has justifiably described this as "a variant of the Keynesian analysis of the slump".[10] Many of the "balanced growth" economists of this school would, for instance, be willing to put up with the possible distortion in the allocation of resources through inflationary methods of financing development rather than cut down the overall size of the investment programme. (b) This may be contrasted with the other version of the "balanced growth" theory which stresses the interrelationships between investment in different sectors of the economy and the need for a government "planning agency" to co-ordinate the investment plans so as to achieve an optimum allocation of resources.[11] Those who adopt this version believe that the market mechanism is ineffective in the underdeveloped countries, not because the people there do not behave like the "economic man" in responding to its signals, but because the market signals themselves are defective and cannot accurately forecast what the future economic situation would be, after a complex of large-scale inter-related projects has been carried out. Thus, far from belittling the importance of the optimum, this second group of "balanced growth" theorists have made important contributions to the theory of the optimum involving complex interrelations between investment in different sectors of the economy over a period of time.

(4) Finally, there is the criticism which is based on the view that the free play of market forces tends to fossilize or exaggerate the existing market imperfections and the inequalities in income and bargaining power which are to be found in many underdeveloped countries.[12] The idea of the cumulative disequalizing forces has been applied both to the international economic relations between the advanced and the underdeveloped countries and to the internal economic relations between the "advanced" and the "backward" sectors or groups of people within each underdeveloped country. This type of criticism attempts to break sharply away from the conventional ideas of a stable equilibrium and the optimum and focus attention on the concept of

[9] The most notable exponent of this version is P. N. Rosenstein-Rodan. Contrast, however, his early paper, "Problems of Industrialisation of Eastern and South-Eastern Europe", *Economic Journal*, 1943, with his *Notes on the Theory of the* "Big Push", 1951.

[10] A. O. Hirschman, *The Strategy of Economic Development* (New Haven, 1958), p. 54.

[11] Cf. e.g. T. Scitovsky, *Two Concepts of External Economies*, *J.P.E.* (April 1954), and H. B. Chenery, "The Interdependence of Investment Decisions", in Abramovitz *et al.*, *The Allocation of Economic Resources* (Stanford, 1959).

[12] Cf. e.g. T. Balogh, *Static Models and Current Problems in International Economics*, O.E.P. (June 1949); also H. Myint, *An Interpretation of Economic Backwardness*, O.E.P. (June 1954); and G. Myrdal, *op. cit.*, chapter 3.

the "dualism" in the economic structure of the underdeveloped countries which underlies most other types of criticism of the working of the market mechanism in these countries.

Although the ideas contained in this line of attack are suggestive, they have not been satisfactorily formulated so far. The concept of "dualism" needs more systematic study and the theoretical mechanism of how the cumulative disequalizing factors work has been sketched out in a rather impressionist manner. For instance, while the fragmentation of an economy into an "advanced" and a "backward" sector will lead to a deviation from the optimum in a static sense, might not "dualism" have certain dynamic advantages enabling the "leading" sector to drag the "lagging" sector in its wake? Following the trend of thought suggested by Professor Hirschman's "unbalanced growth" approach, might not an attempt to impose a dead-pan uniformity and equality between the different sectors of the economy lead to the elimination of "growth points" and dynamic tensions for further economic development? These questions bring us to the difficult problem of choice between economic equality and rapid economic development. Here the critics are not always clear whether they object to the free play of market forces because they want to' prevent economic inequality for its own sake or whether because they think that this inequality will in its turn inhibit the growth of the economy as a whole.

II

The relations between the four main types of criticism of the market mechanism in the underdeveloped countries and the theoretical approaches they suggest for development economics may be summed up schematically as follows:

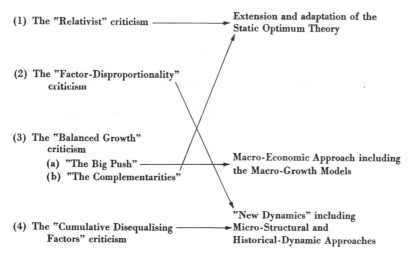

(1) The "Relativist" criticism ——————→ Extension and adaptation of the Static Optimum Theory

(2) The "Factor-Disproportionality" criticism

(3) The "Balanced Growth" criticism
    (a) "The Big Push" ——————
    (b) "The Complementarities"   Macro-Economic Approach including the Macro-Growth Models

(4) The "Cumulative Disequalising ——→ "New Dynamics" including Factors" criticism   Micro-Structural and Historical-Dynamic Approaches

We are now in a position to appraise the criticisms directed against economic theory (as distinct from those directed against the market mechanism) in the context of the underdeveloped countries. There can be no serious quarrel with those critics who stress the need to increase the "realism" of economic theory by taking into account the various social, historical and institutional differences between the advanced and underdeveloped countries. If anything, our analysis has suggested the need also to take into account the differences between the underdeveloped countries themselves with respect to the degree of population pressure, the overall size of the economy, the general level of economic development and institutional framework and various other factors which may be expected to introduce significant differences in the structure and texture of their economic life. In particular, we have suggested that a failure to study systematically how the market forces actually work or fail to work in the different types of underdeveloped framework has contributed to the failure to develop a satisfactory analysis of the "mixed economy" in the underdeveloped countries. A study of the different patterns of market imperfections in different types of underdeveloped country is largely an unexplored subject.[13]

The argument of those critics who question the "relevance" of "Western" economic theory, in particular the relevance of the "orthodox" static theory of the optimum allocation of resources tó the underdeveloped countries, is more debatable. In the light of the criticisms (2) and (4) above, few will question the need for a thorough-going "new" dynamic approach to economic development involving changes in the supplies of factors, techniques of production and the "transformation" of the whole organizational structure of the economy. It may be that such a new approach means widening the scope of conventional economics to take into account the broader sociological factors which made up "Political Economy" in the classical sense. But there is no need to argue about this since orthodox opinion has never imposed a methodological interdict on such a process. As Marshall wrote: "each economist may reasonably decide for himself how far he will extend his labour over that ground".[14]

What is really at stake is how far we should discard the existing static optimum theory before we have time or are clever enough to build up a satisfactory "dynamic" approach to the underdeveloped countries. That is to say how far are we to follow Professor Myrdal's advice to the "young economists in the underdeveloped countries" to "throw away large structures of meaningless, irrelevant and sometimes blatantly inadequate doctrine and theoretical

---

[13] For a pioneer effort in this field, see Morton R. Solomon, "The Structure of the Market in Underdeveloped Economies", *Q.J.E.* (August 1948).

[14] *Principles*, p. 780; see also Robbins, *Nature and Significance of Economics*, 2nd ed., p. 150.

approaches."[15] There are a number of considerations against following this advice, if this means throwing away the static optimum theory.

The first and most powerful is that the underdeveloped countries are too poor to put up with the burden of preventable waste which arises even within the static framework of given wants, techniques and resources. As Professor Galbraith has suggested in his *Affluent Society,* only the richer advanced countries can afford to take an indulgent view towards the misallocation of resources. There is a real danger that in searching for newer approaches and more advanced techniques of analysis, the economist (particularly if he is a visitor) in the underdeveloped countries may easily overlook quite glaring sources of wastage through misallocation, whether due to spontaneous market imperfections or inept state interference.

To give an example of the latter: after her Independence, Burma followed a policy of cutting out all private middlemen from her rice marketing board operations and opening numerous state buying stations all over the country to purchase rice directly from the peasant producers. Until very recently, the government insisted on paying the same fixed price all the year round, to cut out "the speculators". It also insisted on paying the same fixed price to all inland rice cultivators, irrespective of their distance from the main seaports (on grounds of regional justice). The consequences of conducting a marketing board on the basis of zero rate of interest and storing cost and zero transport cost are apparent from elementary optimum theory. As it happened, the rice crop, which normally took about four to six months to be cleared under free market conditions, now had to be cleared almost at once, since no one had any incentive to hold the rice stocks. This would have wrecked a very much more efficient marketing machinery than the government had been able to provide: the wastage and deterioration of the rice through bad storage, e.g. fire, rain, theft, mixing of different grades, etc., was enormous. Further, the remoter regions which used to grow rice for local consumption now sold their crop to the state buying centre, which sent it down to seaports for export, so that consignments of milled rice from the seaports had to be sent back to these remoter regions to prevent food shortages, entailing two useless journeys on the country's limited transport system. Yet many economists visiting Burma during this period characteristically overlooked this "simple" but extremely wasteful misallocation of resources in their preoccupation with the more elaborate development plans, including the expansion of investment in "infrastructure". It is hard to believe that this is an isolated instance.[16]

[15] G. Myrdal, *op. cit.,* p. 101.

[16] See however A. C. Harberger, "Using the Resources at Hand More Effectively", *American Economic Review* (May 1959). Harberger argues that for economies like Chile, Brazil and Argentina, reallocating resources, with existing production functions, "would raise national welfare by no more than 15 per cent". He considers that although substan-

If the underdeveloped countries are too poor to put up with the waste from preventable misallocation of resources, they are presumably also too poor to forgo immediate sources of relief from poverty for the sake of larger benefits promised in the future. Here, the time-preference which the critics have adopted on behalf of the underdeveloped countries shows a curious kink. In arguing for more international aid, they stress the urgent need to do something to give immediate relief to the underdeveloped countries; but in other contexts they tend to adopt a much lower valuation of the present in favour of the future. Thus they generally stress the longer-run social benefits from various forms of development expenditure to justify their immediate cost to the developing countries. Again, as against the orthodox presumption that the underdeveloped countries should choose less capital intensive methods of production with quicker returns, some of the critics would defend capital intensive methods on the ground that these are necessary for a higher rate of economic growth in the future. Thus the critics may be regarded as exercising the same pattern of time-preference in the choice of theoretical techniques when they urge that the existing static theory should be discarded in favour of a new dynamic theory which is rather sketchy at present and which promises to yield results in the somewhat indeterminate future. There are strong reasons to be worried about the future of the underdeveloped countries, but there are equally strong reasons to be worried about their present poverty, and the former should not be stressed almost to the exclusion of the latter. If it is urgent to give immediate relief to the underdeveloped countries by stepping up international aid, it is equally urgent to find out how far they can help themselves by stopping obvious sources of waste through misallocation of resources. The significance of the conventional static theory of the allocation of scarce resources to the underdeveloped countries can be properly appreciated only in this perspective.

So far we have been concerned with criticisms (2) and (4). Let us now turn to criticism (3a) which may be regarded as the Keynesian criticism of the orthodox economics. This tendency to neglect the problem of allocating scarce resources in the writings on the underdeveloped countries has been aggravated by the "backwash" effect of the Keynesian Revolution. In the early post-war years at least, the Keynesian reaction against orthodox economics was automatically extended from its original context in the advanced countries to the underdeveloped countries. The Keynesian approach was enthusiastically adopted both as a basis of economic planning at macro-economic

---

tial, this is relatively small compared with the large potential dynamic gains to be obtained from technical improvements raising labour productivity. One may reply that any source of gain is likely to appear small compared with the gains from technical improvements. But from the point of view of this paper Harberger's article remains an interesting attempt to apply the optimum analysis in a quantitative manner to the underdeveloped countries.

level and also as an argument for the deficit financing of development plans. Since then there has been an increasing realization of the need to probe below the macro-economic approach into the "structural" and "frictional" factors in the underdeveloped countries. Nevertheless, the point raised by criticism (3a), viz. how far we should put up with the possible distorting effect of inflation on the allocation of resources before cutting back the overall size of the investment programme, still remains a live issue dividing the expansionist and the orthodox economists. But even here an important change is noticeable. In the earlier days, the case for deficit financing of economic development was made mainly at the macro-economic level. Thus it was argued that the investment expenditure financed by pure credit creation would expand the money incomes but keep them stabilized at a certain level according to the Multiplier theory. Thus the increase in physical output from the newly created capital goods would have a chance to catch up with the increase in money incomes until at last prices were restored to the initial level and inflation destroyed itself.[17] More recently, however, the structural and allocative factors have been brought into the forefront. It is now argued that a mere negative elimination or ending of the inflationary pressure will not lead automatically to an optimum allocation of resources and that what is really needed is "carefully discriminatory policies" designed to correct the structural imbalance and market imperfections in the underdeveloped countries.[18] One can follow up this point by asking how far the government of an underdeveloped country will in fact be in a position to pursue such discriminatory policies effectively and consistently after the inflationary pressure and balance of payments difficulties have got beyond a certain point.[19] But for our present purpose it is sufficient to point out the shift of emphasis from the Keynesian approach to the optimum approach.

We can now pull together the threads of our argument so far. As shown by our chart, the various criticisms of the working of the market mechanism in the underdeveloped countries have suggested three types of theoretical approach to these countries: viz. (i) the extension and adaptation of the

[17] W. A. Lewis, "Economic Development with Unlimited Supplies of Labour", *Manchester School* (May 1954), p. 165. Lewis himself points out "the usual objections against applying multiplier analysis to inflationary conditions, namely the instability of the prepensity to consume, the effect of secondary investment and the dangers of cost inflation".

[18] T. Balogh, "Economic Policy and the Price System", *U.N. Economic Bulletin for Latin America* (March 1961), p. 53.

[19] For instance, the differential advantages offered by tariff protection to "infant industries" are likely to be swamped under random short-term speculative rises in prices of the non-protected imports when successive rounds of quantitative import restrictions have to be imposed because of a balance of payments crisis. For a fuller treatment see my paper, chapter 7 in *International Trade Theory in a Developing World*, eds. R. Harrod and D. C. Hague, Macmillan (London, 1963).

existing static theory of the optimum allocation of scarce resources; (ii) the extension of the Keynesian macro-economic approach, including the macro-growth models of the Harrod-Domar type; and (iii) the introduction of a new thoroughgoing dynamic approach which is capable of dealing with the changes in the long-run supplies of factors of production and changes in the techniques of production involving the "transformation" of the whole organizational structure of the underdeveloped economies. In the post-war writings on the underdeveloped countries there has been some progress made in the application of the optimum theory to development economics, particularly on the problems of complementary investment and of optimization over a given plan period.[20] But, nevertheless, the optimum approach to the underdeveloped countries has been unduly neglected by the critics of the "orthodox" economics, partly because they identify this with the laissez-faire type of liberal economics, partly because they feel that anything short of a thoroughgoing dynamic approach should be discarded, and partly because of the "backwash" effect of the Keynesian Revolution. While fully admitting the need to develop a new dynamic approach to the underdeveloped countries, we have tried to show: (1) that the orthodox static theory of allocation of scarce resources remains as "relevant" to these countries as any other part of economic theory so long as they suffer from serious misallocations of resources which they can ill afford, and (2) that the optimum approach can be made more fruitful by a "realistic" study of how the market forces actually work or fail to work in the different settings of the different types of underdeveloped country.

III

Some critics have attributed the lack of "realism" in the current writings on the underdeveloped countries to the tendency of the Western economists to generalize from the "special case" of the advanced countries.[21] But this is only half the trouble; the other half of the trouble must be traced to the tendency to generalize about all underdeveloped countries from the "special case" of a particular type of underdeveloped country; and this has been aggravated by the tendency to treat the whole subject as an adjunct to making out a persuasive case for increasing international aid. Thus it is no accident that the theory of economic development of the underdeveloped countries should come to be dominated by a "conventional" model of the under-developed country which most closely resembles India. For the case for in-

---

[20] E.g. H. B. Chenery, *loc. cit.*, in Abramovitz *et al.*, "The Allocation of Resources", and also "Comparative Advantage and Development Policy", *A.E.R. Proceedings* (March 1961), also A. K. Sen, *The Choice of Techniques*, 1961, and O. Eckstein, "Investment Criteria for Economic Development and Intertemporal Welfare Economics", *Q.J.E.* (February 1957).

[21] E.g. Seers, *loc. cit.*, pp. 79–83, and *passim*.

creasing international aid to the underdeveloped countries is strongest when we have a country like India. Given India's acute population pressure on natural resources and material poverty, the case for increasing aid to her on purely humanitarian grounds is obvious. Given her low ratio of foreign trade to national income, she cannot hope to earn enough foreign exchange through the expansion of her exports even if the market prospects for them were brighter, and when she has reached the limits of borrowing on commercial terms, there is little alternative but to rely on aid. One further consequence of a low ratio of foreign trade to national income is that foreign exchange shortage cannot be overcome by increasing domestic saving. Again, given the very large overall size of her economy, it is reasonable to suppose that she will be able to reap the economies of scale from setting up a large and interrelated industrial complex, including a capital goods sector orientated towards the domestic market. Finally, whatever our views about India's chances of ultimate success in achieving economic development through integrated economic planning, it is generally admitted that her general institutional framework and her administrative and planning machinery are well in advance of other developing countries. Thus in India's case both the need to receive material aid and the ability to absorb aid for successful economic development are stronger than in most other underdeveloped countries. Only Mexico and Brazil, at about the same stage of general development as India, but without her population pressure, seem to have a comparable capacity to absorb material aid.

Now there is nothing wrong with concentrating on such a type of underdeveloped country, provided it is clearly recognized as a very "special case". The danger arises from trying to generalize from the Indian case and, in particular, trying to apply the standard Indian model of development planning to other underdeveloped countries. Here are some of the more obvious limitations of this "special case". (i) Although population is growing very rapidly all over the underdeveloped world, there are still many sparsely populated countries, covering most of Latin America, considerable parts of Africa and most of South-east Asia, where the Indian type of extreme pressure of population on natural resources does not apply. The concept of "disguised unemployment" has limited application for these countries and their problem is how to make the best use of the available elbow room of natural resources before plunging into the more heroic measures of development required by the Indian situation. (ii) Even among the overpopulated countries, the overall size of the population and area of India has no peer except for China. Many of the overpopulated countries are much smaller countries which, unlike India, have a high ratio of foreign trade to national income and which because of their smallness cannot hope to imitate the Indian model of industrialization based on a substantial capital goods industry and oriented mainly towards the domestic market. Short of organizing themselves into larger common market units for which they are not politically ready, exports, particularly export of primary products, must continue to play an important role in their economic development. In this respect the position of the small overpopulated countries, some of them overcrowded islands, is harder than that of a big overpopulated country like India with a domestic market potentially large enough to yield the economies of scale. While a few small countries like Hong Kong and Puerto Rico may have found an escape route in the export of "simple manufactures" and/or emigration, this is not likely to be open to the others because of various obstacles, partly of their own creation, and partly created by the advanced countries. (iii) Above all, it should be stressed that the underdeveloped countries are at widely varying stages of general social, political and economic development. At one end of the scale are a few countries, like India, Mexico and Brazil, which have reached a stage of development where they may be considered to be within a reasonable striking distance of the "take-off". The rest of the underdeveloped countries are at different sub-stages of the "pre-take-off" phase, trailing off into a considerable number of countries which are hard put to maintain even the minimum of law and order, political stability and public services and which clearly do not yet possess the necessary institutional framework to carry out elaborate economic development planning.

Given the popularity of the conventional Indian model of economic development, however, most underdeveloped countries have tried to fulfill the first and the second of Professor Rostow's conditions for the take-off: viz. "(a) a rise in the rate of productive investment from (say) 5 per cent or less to 10 per cent of national income (or net national product); (b) the development of one or more substantial manufacturing sectors, with a high rate of growth". But in their preoccupation with quantitative planning and target figures, they have neglected his third elusive condition: "(c) the existence or quick emergence of a political, social and institutional framework which exploits the impulses to expansion in the modern sector and the potential external economy effects of the take-off and gives to growth an ongoing character".[22] It turns out that condition (c) is the most important of the three in the sense that unless it can be fulfilled it is not possible to keep the other two conditions fulfilled for long. It is also the most important factor determining an underdeveloped country's capacity to absorb aid productively.

Yet in spite of the fact that the majority of the underdeveloped countries are either just emerging from the "traditional society" or are somewhere in the "pre-take-off" stage, the discussion of this earlier phase is perhaps even more unsatisfactory than the rest of the take-off theory.[23] The central

[22] W. W. Rostow, "The Take-Off into Self-Sustained Growth", *E.J.* (March 1956), p. 32, and "The Stages of Economic Growth", p. 39.

[23] Cf. S. Kuznets, "Notes on the Take-Off", in Rostow *et al.*, *Economics of Take-Off into Sustained Growth* (Macmillan, 1963).

problem of these countries is not how to plan for an immediate take-off but how to compress the pre-take-off phase into a few decades instead of "a long period up to a century or conceivably more" which the Western countries are said to have taken. Here, one may agree that if these countries are not yet ready for the final "big-push" into take-off, they need not rely solely on the unaided working of the market forces to shorten the preliminary period. In the past, even the so-called laissez-faire colonial governments encouraged the growth of the exchange economy, particularly through the provision of better transport and communications. But beyond this, analysis has not proceeded very far.

For instance, the success of a policy of concentrating on "infra-structure" investment will depend on the various economic factors determining the structure and behaviour of the "subsistence sector" and on the question how far its persistence is due to the limitations on the demand side, i.e. lack of marketing facilities and outlets, and how far it is due to limitations on the supply side, i.e. lack of a marketable surplus. Yet there is little systematic study of the mutual interactions between the "subsistence sector" and the "money economy" (including the government sector) in the different types of under-developed country, taking into account the differences in the degree of population pressure, the nature and extent of the export production and the urban manufacturing sector. In this context, we may also ask how far the more sophisticated monetary policy of deficit financing is really suitable for the earlier stages of the development in the money economy, when we should be concerned with encouraging the people from the subsistence economy to use money not only as a medium of exchange, but also as a unit of account for a rational economic calculus and as a store of value. Recently there has been a shift of interest from investment in material "infra-structure" to "investment in human capital", particularly in education. Yet so far this line of approach has been limited by too much emphasis on what the government should do in the way of a "crash programme" in education combined with too little analysis of the demand and supply factors affecting the market for skilled labour at various stages of economic development.[24]

All this is merely another way of stating our argument at the end of the last section that we need to have a more systematic study of how the market forces actually work or fail to work in the different types of underdeveloped country. Applied to the majority of the underdeveloped countries at the earlier "pre-take-off" stages of economic development, this now assumes a special significance. The degree of effective control which the government of such a country can exercise over the rest of the economy depends more clearly than elsewhere on the growth of suitable monetary, fiscal and market

[24] For further discussion, see my papers, "The Universities of South-east Asia and Economic Development", *Pacific Affairs* (Summer 1962), and "Social Flexibility, Social Discipline and Economic Growth", *International Journal of Social Science* (Paris, 1964).

institutions through which it can extend its control. Thus we may reasonably suggest a more systematic study of the market forces in such an underdeveloped country even to the most planning-minded economist.

To sum up: current writings on the underdeveloped countries have been vitiated not merely by the tendency to generalize from the "special case" of the advanced countries, but also by the tendency to generalize from the "special case" of a particular type of underdeveloped country, notably India. This in its turn has been aggravated by the popularity of the idea of development planning based on the "take-off" theory and by the tendency to treat the subject not as an academic discipline but as an adjunct to making out a persuasive general case for increasing international aid to the underdeveloped countries. The new crusading spirit has rendered a valuable service in getting the idea of giving aid to these countries firmly established in the advanced countries. But now that the general good will towards these countries seems to have outstripped an accurate knowledge of how the economic systems of these countries really function, one may venture to urge the revival of the traditional academic approach to the subject.

THE PROTESTANT ETHIC
AND THE SPIRIT
OF CAPITALISM

Max Weber

AUTHOR'S INTRODUCTION

A product of modern European civilization, studying any problem of universal history, is bound to ask himself to what combination of circumstances the fact should be attributed that in Western civilization, and in Western civilization only, cultural phenomena have appeared which (as we like to think) lie in a line of development having *universal* significance and value.

Only in the West does science exist at a stage of development which we recognize to-day as valid. Empirical knowledge, reflection on problems of the cosmos and of life, philosophical and theological wisdom of the most profound sort, are not confined to it, though in the case of the last the full development of a systematic theology must be credited to Christianity under the influence of Hellenism, since there were only fragments in Islam and in a few Indian sects. In short, knowledge and observation of great refinement have existed elsewhere, above all in India, China, Babylonia, Egypt. But in Babylonia and elsewhere astronomy lacked—which makes its development all the more astounding—the mathematical foundation which it first received from the Greeks. The Indian geometry had no rational proof; that was another product of the Greek intellect, also the creator of mechanics and physics.

From Max Weber (translated by Talcott Parsons), *The Protestant Ethic and the Spirit of Capitalism*, pp. 13–27 (New York: Charles Scribner's Sons, 1930). Reprinted by permission of Charles Scribner's Sons and George Allen & Unwin Ltd.

The Indian natural sciences, though well developed in observation, lacked the method of experiment, which was, apart from beginnings in antiquity, essentially a product of the Renaissance, as was the modern laboratory. Hence medicine, especially in India, though highly developed in empirical technique, lacked a biological and particularly a biochemical foundation. A rational chemistry has been absent from all areas of culture except the West.

The highly developed historical scholarship of China did not have the method of Thucydides, Machiavelli, it is true, had predecessors in India; but all Indian political thought was lacking in a systematic method comparable to that of Aristotle, and, indeed, in the possession of rational concepts. Not all the anticipations in India (School of Mimamsa), nor the extensive codification especially in the Near East, nor all the Indian and other books of law, had the strictly systematic forms of thought, so essential to a rational jurisprudence, of the Roman law and of the Western law under its influence. A structure like the canon law is known only to the West.

A similar statement is true of art. The musical ear of other peoples has probably been even more sensitively developed than our own, certainly not less so. Polyphonic music of various kinds has been widely distributed over the earth. The co-operation of a number of instruments and also the singing of parts have existed elsewhere. All our rational tone intervals have been known and calculated. But rational harmonious music, both counterpoint and harmony, formation of the tone material on the basis of three triads with the harmonic third; our chromatics and enharmonics, not interpreted in terms of space, but, since the Renaissance, of harmony; our orchestra, with its string quartet as a nucleus, and the organization of ensembles of wind instruments; our bass accompaniment; our system of notation, which has made possible the composition and production of modern musical works, and thus their very survival; our sonatas, symphonies, operas; and finally, as means to all these, our fundamental instruments, the organ, piano, violin, etc.; all these things are known only in the Occident, although programme music, tone poetry, alteration of tones and chromatics, have existed in various musical traditions as means of expression.

In architecture, pointed arches have been used elsewhere as a means of decoration, in antiquity and in Asia; presumably the combination of pointed arch and cross-arched vault was not unknown in the Orient. But the rational use of the Gothic vault as a means of distributing pressure and of roofing spaces of all forms, and above all as the constructive principle of great monumental buildings and the foundation of a *style* extending to sculpture and painting, such as that created by our Middle Ages, does not occur elsewhere. The technical basis of our architecture came from the Orient. But the Orient lacked that solution of the problem of the dome and that type of classic rationalization of all art—in painting by the rational utilization of lines and spatial perspective—which the Renaissance created for us. There was printing in China. But a printed literature, designed *only* for print and only possible through it, and, above all, the Press and periodicals, have appeared only in the Occident. Institutions of higher education of all possible types, even some superficially similar to our universities, or at least academies, have existed (China, Islam). But a rational, systematic, and specialized pursuit of science, with trained and specialized personnel, has only existed in the West in a sense at all approaching its present dominant place in our culture. Above all is this true of the trained official, the pillar of both the modern State and of the economic life of the West. He forms a type of which there have heretofore only been suggestions, which have never remotely approached its present importance for the social order. Of course the official, even the specialized official, is a very old constituent of the most various societies. But no country and no age has ever experienced, in the same sense as the modern Occident, the absolute and complete dependence of its whole existence, of the political, technical, and economic conditions of its life, on a specially trained *organization* of officials. The most important functions of the everyday life of society have come to be in the hands of technically, commercially, and above all legally trained government officials.

Organization of political and social groups in feudal classes has been common. But even the feudal[1] state of *rex et regnum* in the Western sense has only been known to our culture. Even more are parliaments of periodically elected representatives, with government by demagogues and party leaders as ministers responsible to the parliaments, peculiar to us, although there have, of course, been parties, in the sense of organizations for exerting influence and gaining control of political power, all over the world. In fact, the State itself, in the sense of a political association with a rational, written constitution, rationally ordained law, and an administration bound to rational rules or laws, administered by trained officials, is known, in this combination of characteristics, only in the Occident, despite all other approaches to it.

And the same is true of the most fateful force in our modern life, capitalism. The impulse to acquisition, pursuit of gain, of money, of the greatest possible amount of money, has in itself nothing to do with capitalism. This impulse exists and has existed among waiters, physicians, coachmen, artists, prostitutes, dishonest officials, soldiers, nobles, crusaders, gamblers, and beggars. One may say that it has been common to all sorts and conditions of men at all times and in all countries of the earth, wherever the objective possibility of it is or has been given. It should be taught in the kindergarten of cultural history that this naïve idea of capitalism must be given up once and for all. Unlimited greed for gain is not in the least identical with capitalism, and is still less its spirit. Capitalism *may* even be

---

[1] *Ständestaat.* The term refers to the late form taken by feudalism in Europe in its transition to absolute monarchy.—*Translator's note.*

identical with the restraint, or at least a rational tempering, of this irrational impulse. But capitalism is identical with the pursuit of profit, and forever *renewed* profit, by means of continuous, rational, capitalistic enterprise. For it must be so: in a wholly capitalistic order of society, an individual capitalistic enterprise which did not take advantage of its opportunities for profit-making would be doomed to extinction.

Let us now define our terms somewhat more carefully than is generally done. We will define a capitalistic economic action as one which rests on the expectation of profit by the utilization of opportunities for exchange, that is on (formally) peaceful chances of profit. Acquisition by force (formally and actually) follows its own particular laws, and it is not expedient, however little one can forbid this, to place it in the same category with action which is, in the last analysis, oriented to profits from exchange.[2] Where capitalistic acquisition is rationally pursued, the corresponding action is adjusted to calculations in terms of capital. This means that the action is adapted to a systematic utilization of goods or personal services as means of acquisition in such a way that, at the close of a business period, the balance of the enterprise in money assets (or, in the case of a continuous enterprise, the periodically estimated money value of assets) exceeds the capital, i.e. the estimated value of the material means of production used for acquisition in exchange. It makes no difference whether it involves a quantity of goods entrusted *in natura* to a travelling merchant, the proceeds of which may consist in other goods *in natura* acquired by trade, or whether it involves a manufacturing enterprise, the assets of which consist of buildings, machinery, cash, raw materials, partly and wholly manufactured goods, which are balanced against liabilities. The important fact is always that a calculation of capital in terms of money is made, whether by modern bookkeeping methods or in any other way, however primitive and crude. Everything is done in terms of balances: at the beginning of the enterprise an initial balance, before every individual decision a calculation to ascertain its probable profitableness, and at the end a final balance to ascertain how much profit has

[2] Here, as on some other points, I differ from our honoured master, Lujo Brentano (in his work to be cited later). Chiefly in regard to terminology, but also on questions of fact. It does not seem to me expedient to bring such different things as acquisition of booty and acquisition by management of a factory together under the same category; still less to designate every tendency to the acquisition of money as the spirit of capitalism as against other types of acquisition. The second sacrifices all precision of concepts, and the first the possibility of clarifying the specific difference between Occidental capitalism and other forms. Also in Simmel's *Philosophie des Geldes* money economy and capitalism are too closely identified, to the detriment of his concrete analysis. In the writings of Werner Sombart, above all in the second edition of his most important work, *Der moderne Kapitalismus*, the *differentia specifica* of Occidental capitalism—at least from the viewpoint of my problem—the rational organization of labour, is strongly overshadowed by genetic factors which have been operative everywhere in the world.

been made. For instance, the initial balance of a *commenda*[3] transaction would determine an agreed money value of the assets put into it (so far as they were not in money form already), and a final balance would form the estimate on which to base the distribution of profit and loss at the end. So far as the transactions are rational, calculation underlies every single action of the partners. That a really accurate calculation or estimate may not exist, that the procedure is pure guess-work, or simply traditional and conventional, happens even to-day in every form of capitalistic enterprise where the circumstances do not demand strict accuracy. But these are points affecting only the *degree* of rationality of capitalistic acquisition.

For the purpose of this conception all that matters is that an actual adaptation of economic action to a comparison of money income with money expenses takes place, no matter how primitive the form. Now in this sense capitalism and capitalistic enterprises, even with a considerable rationalization of capitalistic calculation, have existed in all civilized countries of the earth, so far as economic documents permit us to judge. In China, India, Babylon, Egypt, Mediterranean antiquity, and the Middle Ages, as well as in modern times. These were not merely isolated ventures, but economic enterprises which were entirely dependent on the continual renewal of capitalistic undertakings, and even continuous operations. However, trade especially was for a long time not continuous like our own, but consisted essentially in a series of individual undertakings. Only gradually did the activities of even the large merchants acquire an inner cohesion (with branch organizations, etc.). In any case, the capitalistic enterprise and the capitalistic entrepreneur, not only as occasional but as regular entrepreneurs, are very old and were very widespread.

Now, however, the Occident has developed capitalism both to a quantitative extent, and (carrying this quantitative development) in types, forms, and directions which have never existed elsewhere. All over the world there have been merchants, wholesale and retail, local and engaged in foreign trade. Loans of all kinds have been made, and there have been banks with the most various functions, at least comparable to ours of, say, the sixteenth century. Sea loans,[4] *commenda*, and transactions and associations similar to

[3] *Commenda* was a form of medieval trading association, entered into *ad hoc* for carrying out one sea voyage. A producer or exporter of goods turned them over to another who took them abroad (on a ship provided sometimes by one party, sometimes by the other) and sold them, receiving a share in the profits. The expenses of the voyage were divided between the two in agreed proportion, while the original shipper bore the risk. See Weber, "Handelsgesellschaften im Mittelalter," *Gesammelte Aufsätze zur Sozial- und Wirtschaftsgeschichte*, pp. 323–8.—*Translator's note.*

[4] The sea loan, used in maritime commerce in the Middle Ages, was "a method of insuring against the risks of the sea without violating the prohibitions against usury. . . . When certain risky maritime ventures were to be undertaken, a certain sum . . . was obtained for the cargo belonging to such and such a person or capitalist. If the ship was

the *Kommanditgesellschaft*,[5] have all been widespread, even as continuous businesses. Whenever money finances of public bodies have existed, money-lenders have appeared, as in Babylon, Hellas, India, China, Rome. They have financed wars and piracy, contracts and building operations of all sorts. In overseas policy they have functioned as colonial entrepreneurs, as planters with slaves, or directly or indirectly forced labour, and have farmed domains, offices, and, above all, taxes. They have financed party leaders in elections and *condottieri* in civil wars. And, finally, they have been speculators in chances for pecuniary gain of all kinds. This kind of entrepreneur, the capitalistic adventurer, has existed everywhere. With the exception of trade and credit and banking transactions, their activities were predominantly of an irrational and speculative character, or directed to acquisition by force, above all the acquisition of booty, whether directly in war or in the form of continuous fiscal booty by exploitation of subjects.

The capitalism of promoters, large-scale speculators, concession hunters, and much modern financial capitalism even in peace time, but, above all, the capitalism especially concerned with exploiting wars, bears this stamp even in modern Western countries, and some, but only some, parts of large-scale international trade are closely related to it, today as always.

But in modern times the Occident has developed, in addition to this, a very different form of capitalism which has appeared nowhere else: the rational capitalistic organization of (formally) free labour. Only suggestions of it are found elsewhere. Even the organization of unfree labour reached a considerable degree of rationality only on plantations and to a very limited extent in the *Ergasteria* of antiquity. In the manors, manorial workshops, and domestic industries on estates with serf labour it was probably somewhat less developed. Even real domestic industries with free labour have definitely been proved to have existed in only a few isolated cases outside the Occident. The frequent use of day labourers led in a very few cases—especially State monopolies, which are, however, very different from modern industrial organization—to manufacturing organizations, but never to a rational organization of apprenticeship in the handicrafts like that of our Middle Ages.

Rational industrial organization, attuned to a regular market, and neither to political nor irrationally speculative opportunities for profit, is not, however, the only peculiarity of Western capitalism. The modern rational organization of the capitalistic enterprise would not have been possible without two other important factors in its development: the separation of business from the

---

lost, no repayment was exacted by the lender; if it reached port safely, the borrower paid a considerable premium, sometimes 50 per cent." Henri Sée, *Modern Capitalism*, p. 189.—*Translator's note.*

    [5] A form of company between the partnership and the limited liability corporation. At least one of the participants is made liable without limit, while the others enjoy limitation of liability to the amount of their investment.—*Translator's note.*

household, which completely dominates modern economic life, and closely connected with it, rational bookkeeping. A spatial separation of places of work from those of residence exists elsewhere, as in the Oriental bazaar and in the *Ergasteria* of other cultures. The development of capitalistic associations with their own accounts is also found in the Far East, the Near East, and in antiquity. But compared to the modern independence of business enterprises, those are only small beginnings. The reason for this was particularly that the indispensable requisites for this independence, our rational business bookkeeping and our legal separation of corporate from personal property, were entirely lacking, or had only begun to develop.[6] The tendency everywhere else was for acquisitive enterprises to arise as parts of a royal or manorial *household* (of the *oikos*), which is, as Rodbertus has perceived, with all its superficial similarity, a fundamentally different, even opposite, development.

However, all these peculiarities of Western capitalism have derived their significance in the last analysis only from their association with the capitalistic organization of labour. Even what is generally called commercialization, the development of negotiable securities and the rationalization of speculation, the exchanges, etc., is connected with it. For without the rational capitalistic organization of labour, all this, so far as it was possible at all, would have nothing like the same significance, above all for the social structure and all the specific problems of the modern Occident connected with it. Exact calculation—the basis of everything else—is only possible on a basis of free labour.[7]

And just as, or rather because, the world has known no rational organization of labour outside the modern Occident, it has known no rational

---

[6] Naturally the difference cannot be conceived in absolute terms. The politically oriented capitalism (above all tax-farming) of Mediterranean and Oriental antiquity, and even of China and India, gave rise to rational, continuous enterprises whose bookkeeping —though known to us only in pitiful fragments—probably had a rational character. Furthermore, the politically oriented adventurers' capitalism has been closely associated with rational bourgeois capitalism in the development of modern banks, which, including the Bank of England, have for the most part originated in transactions of a political nature, often connected with war. The difference between the characters of Paterson, for instance—a typical promoter—and of the members of the directorate of the Bank who gave the keynote to its permanent policy, and very soon came to be known as the "Puritan usurers of Grocers' Hall", is characteristic of it. Similarly, we have the aberration of the policy of this most solid bank at the time of the South Sea Bubble. Thus the two naturally shade off into each other. But the difference is there. The great promoters and financiers have no more created the rational organization of labour than—again in general and with individual exceptions—those other typical representatives of financial and political capitalism, the Jews. That was done, typically, by quite a different set of people.

[7] For Weber's discussion of the ineffectiveness of slave labour, especially so far as calculation is concerned, see his essay, "Agrarverhältnisse im Altertum", in the volume *Gesammelte Aufsätze zur Sozial- und Wirtschaftsgeschichte.—Translator's note.*

socialism. Of course, there has been civic economy, a civic food-supply policy, mercantilism and welfare policies of princes, rationing, regulation of economic life, protectionism, and *laissez-faire* theories (as in China). The world has also known socialistic and communistic experiments of various sorts: family, religious, or military communism. State socialism (in Egypt), monopolistic cartels, and consumers' organizations. But although there have everywhere been civic market privileges, companies, guilds, and all sorts of legal differences between town and country, the concept of the citizen has not existed outside the Occident, and that of the bourgeoisie outside the modern Occident. Similarly, the proletariat as a class could not exist, because there was no rational organization of free labour under regular discipline. Class struggles between creditor and debtor classes; landowners and the landless, serfs, or tenants; trading interests and consumers or landlords, have existed everywhere in various combinations. But even the Western medieval struggles between putters-out and their workers exist elsewhere only in beginnings. The modern conflict of the large-scale industrial entrepreneur and free-wage labourers was entirely lacking. And thus there could be no such problems as those of socialism.

Hence in a universal history of culture the central problem for us is not, in the last analysis, even from a purely economic view-point, the development of capitalistic activity as such, differing in different cultures only in form: the adventurer type, or capitalism in trade, war, politics, or administration as sources of gain. It is rather the origin of this sober bourgeois capitalism with its rational organization of free labour. Or in terms of cultural history, the problem is that of the origin of the Western bourgeois class and of its peculiarities, a problem which is certainly closely connected with that of the origin of the capitalistic organization of labour, but is not quite the same thing. For the bourgeois as a class existed prior to the development of the peculiar modern form of capitalism, though, it is true, only in the Western hemisphere.

Now the peculiar modern Western form of capitalism has been, at first sight, strongly influenced by the development of technical possibilities. Its rationality is today essentially dependent on the calculability of the most important technical factors. But this means fundamentally that it is dependent on the peculiarities of modern science, especially the natural sciences based on mathematics and exact and rational experiment. On the other hand, the development of these sciences and of the technique resting upon them now receives important stimulation from these capitalistic interests in its practical economic application. It is true that the origin of Western science cannot be attributed to such interests. Calculation, even with decimals, and algebra have been carried on in India, where the decimal system was invented. But it was only made use of by developing capitalism in the West, while in India it led to no modern arithmetic or bookkeeping. Neither was the origin of mathematics and mechanics determined by capitalistic interests. But the *technical* utilization of scientific knowledge, so important for the living conditions of the mass of people, was certainly encouraged by economic considerations, which were extremely favourable to it in the Occident. But this encouragement was derived from the peculiarities of the social structure of the Occident. We must hence ask, from *what* parts of that structure was it derived, since not all of them have been of equal importance?

Among those of undoubted importance are the rational structures of law and of administration. For modern rational capitalism has need, not only of the technical means of production, but of a calculable legal system and of administration in terms of formal rules. Without it adventurous and speculative trading capitalism and all sorts of politically determined capitalisms are possible, but no rational enterprise under individual initiative, with fixed capital and certainty of calculations. Such a legal system and such administration have been available for economic activity in a comparative state of legal and formalistic perfection only in the Occident. We must hence inquire where that law came from. Among other circumstances, capitalistic interests have in turn undoubtedly also helped, but by no means alone nor even principally, to prepare the way for the predominance in law and administration of a class of jurists specially trained in rational law. But these interests did not themselves create that law. Quite different forces were at work in this development. And why did not the capitalistic interests do the same in China or India? Why did not the scientific, the artistic, the political or the economic development there enter upon that path of rationalization which is peculiar to the Occident?

For in all the above cases it is a question of the specific and peculiar rationalism of Western culture. Now by this term very different things may be understood, as the following discussion will repeatedly show. There is, for example, rationalization of mystical contemplation, that is of an attitude which, viewed from other departments of life, is specifically irrational, just as much as there are rationalizations of economic life, of technique, of scientific research, of military training, of law and administration. Furthermore, each one of these fields may be rationalized in terms of very different ultimate values and ends, and what is rational from one point of view may well be irrational from another. Hence rationalizations of the most varied character have existed in various departments of life and in all areas of culture. To characterize their differences from the viewpoint of cultural history it is necessary to know what departments are rationalized, and in what direction. It is hence our first concern to work out and to explain genetically the special peculiarity of Occidental rationalism, and within this field that of the modern Occidental form. Every such attempt at explanation must, recognizing the fundamental importance of the economic factor, above all take account of the economic conditions. But at the same time the opposite correlation must not be left out of consideration. For though the development of economic rationalism is partly dependent on rational technique and law, it is at the same time determined by the ability and disposition of men to adopt certain types of practical rational conduct. When these types have been obstructed by spiritual obstacles, the development of rational economic conduct has also met serious inner resistance. The magical and religious forces, and the ethical ideas of duty based upon them, have in the past always been among the most important formative influences on conduct. In the studies collected here we shall be concerned with these forces.[8] . . .

---

[8] That is, in the whole series of *Aufsätze zur Religionssoziologie*, not only in the essay here translated. See translator's preface.—*Translator's note.*

HOW ECONOMIC
GROWTH BEGINS:
A THEORY OF SOCIAL CHANGE

Everett E. Hagen

This paper proposes a theory of how a "traditional" society becomes one in which continuing technical progress (hence continuing rise in per capita production and income) is occurring. I shall define a traditional state of society in the following section. The hyotheses which I present to explain the change from this state to one of continuing technological progress may be relevant also to the analysis of other types of social change.

The theory does not suggest some one key factor as causing social change independently of other forces. Rather, it presents a general model of society, and deals with interrelationships among elements of the physical environment, social structure, personality, and culture. This does not imply a thesis that almost anything may cause something, so that one must remain eclectic and confused. Rather, certain factors seem of especial importance in initiating change, but their influence can be understood only by tracing interrelationships through the society. It is implied that general system analysis is a fruitful path to advance in societal theory. Since presented in brief compass, the model is necessarily presented rather starkly here.[1]

The purely economic theories of barriers which explain the absence of

From Everett E. Hagen, "How Economic Growth Begins: A Theory of Social Change," *Journal of Social Issues,* 19:1:20–34 (January 1963). Reprinted by permission of The Society for the Psychological Study of Social Issues, Ann Arbor, Mich.

[1] The model is present at greater length in E. E. Hagen, *On The Theory of Social Change* (Homewood, Illinois: Dorsey Press, 1962). This paper is in essence an abstract of various chapters of that book.

growth seem inadequate. The assumption that the income of entire populations is too low to make saving easy; that markets in low-income countries are too small to induce investment; that costly lumps of expenditure for transport facilities, power plants, etc., which low-income countries cannot provide, are a requisite to growth—these and related theories are internally consistent but seem without great relevance to reality. Empirical study of low-income societies demonstrates that the supposed conditions and requirements do not in fact exist or are not of great importance.

Neither are the differences among nations with respect to growth explained by differences in the degree of contact with the West. Contact with the technical knowledge of the West is a requisite for growth, but forces quite independent of the degree of contact determine whether a nation uses that knowledge. The most spectacular example of this fact is that among the four great Asian nations, Indonesia and India had the most contact with the West during the period 1600–1900, China had an intermediate amount, and Japan the least. Moreover, Indonesia and India experienced the most Western investment, China an intermediate amount, and Japan none whatever until her economic growth was already well under way. Yet among the four countries Japan began to develop first, and has developed rapidly; Indonesia is the laggard; and if China solves her agricultural problem her growth will probably be faster than that of India.

These facts suggest some hypotheses which a theory of growth should not emphasize. Certain other facts give more positive indications of the elements with which a plausible theory must deal.

Economic growth has everywhere occurred interwoven with political and social change. Lipset and Coleman have demonstrated the correlation between economic change and the transition from authoritarian to "competitive" politics in Asia, Africa, and Latin America, and the same relationship is found in every country elsewhere that has entered upon economic growth.[2] The timing is such that it is clear that the economic growth does not occur first and cause the political-social change. Rather, the two are mutually dependent. Whatever the forces for change may be, they impinge on every aspect of human behavior. A theory of the transition to economic growth which does not simultaneously explain political change, or explains it merely as a consequence of the economic change, is thus suspect.

One last consideration will serve to lead up to the exposition of the model. It is this: the concept is rather widely held in the West that the present low-income societies can advance technically simply by imitating the technical

[2] S. Lipset, "Some Social Requisites of Democracy: Economic Development and Political Legitimacy," *American Political Science Review*, Vol. 53 (March 1959); G. A. Almond, J. S. Coleman *et al.*, *The Politics of the Developing Areas* (Princeton: University Press, 1960). Adapting their method slightly, I used it in "A Framework for Analyzing Economic and Political Change," in R. Asher and others, *Development of the Emerging Countries: An Agenda for Research* (Washington, D.C.: Brookings Institution, 1962).

methods already developed in the West. That concept is ethnocentric and incorrect. Mere imitation is impossible. A productive enterprise or process in the West depends for its efficiency on its position in a technical complex of facilities for supplies, services, transportation, and communication, and on a complex of economic, legal, and other social institutions. The management methods which work well within the plant and in its relationships to other units, depend on a complex of attitudes toward interpersonal relationships which are not closely paralleled by attitudes elsewhere. When the process is lifted out of its complex, to adapt it so that it will function in an underdeveloped economy requires technical and especially social and cultural creativity of a high order.

Requirements for the transition to economic growth, then, are (a) fairly widespread creativity—problem-solving ability, and a tendency to use it—and (b) attitudes toward manual-technical labor and the physical world such that the creative energies are channeled into innovation in the technology of production rather than in the technology of art, war, philosophy, politics, or other fields. I believe that exploration of these facets of the process of economic growth is a useful approach to a theory of social change.

What is in point is not widespread genius but a high degree of creativity in a few individuals and a moderately high level in a larger number. I shall suggest reasons to believe that the traditional state of a society is associated with a rather low level of creativity among the members of the society. Further, the persons in traditional society who are in position to innovate are the elite—perhaps the lower elite, but certainly not the peasants and urban menials. It is well known that being concerned with tools, machinery, and in general physical processes seems demeaning to the elite and is repugnant to them. It seems to me that a theory of economic growth must give considerable attention to the forces which change those two aspects of personality.

I. THE STABILITY OF TRADITIONAL SOCIETY

When I refer to a traditional society I have in mind a traditional agricultural society, for while there have also been traditional hunting and fishing societies and traditional pastoral societies,[3] they can hardly accumulate many artifacts and hence continuing technical progress is hardly possible in them. A traditional agricultural society is of course one in which things are done in traditional ways, but two other characteristics which have been typical of the world's traditional societies and turn out to be essential qualities of the type are also worthy of note here.

First, the social structure is hierarchical and authoritarian in all of its aspects—economic, political, religious. The existence of an authoritarian hierarchy does not refer merely to a large mass who were submissive and to

[3] Industrial societies will probably also become traditional in time, which is to say that technical progress will come to an end, at least for a time.

a small class who rule. Rather, every individual in a traditional hierarchy except perhaps for one or a few at the very apex is submissive to authoritarian decisions above him, and in turn exercises authority on persons below him. And this is true even of the lowliest peasant, who as he grows older and becomes a husband, a father, and an elder in his village, becomes increasingly an authority in some aspects of his social relations.

Secondly, one's status in the society is, with little qualification, inherited. One does not earn it; one is born to it. The families of the politically dominating groups, who usually also are economically powerful landed groups, provide the officers of the armed forces and the professional classes as well as the political leaders. Lesser elites also perpetuate their status, though with somewhat greater mobility.

These characteristics of the society as well as its technique of production are traditional and change very slowly. While the model of a completely unchanging traditional society is a construct, an ideal type, it is sufficiently relevant to reality to be useful. From the beginning of agriculture in the world until say 1600 the traditional state of society persisted everywhere except that occasionally, here and there, there was a bursting out of the traditional mode for a few hundred years, then a lapse back into it, sometimes at the original technical level, sometimes at a higher one. The present-day transition to economic growth is such a bursting out. We must ask, Why has the traditional state of society been so persistent? and then, Why have the bursts of change occurred? Or at least, Why have the modern bursts of change occurred?

One condition sometimes suggested as an answer to the first question is that the instruments of power were in the hands of the elite. The traditional authoritarian hierarchical state persisted, it is suggested, because the elite kept the simple folk in subjection by force. This explanation seems inadequate. It is possible for a small group to keep an unwilling ninety-seven percent of a society in subjection by force for a decade or two, or perhaps for a generation or two, though if the subjection persists even this long one must ask whether it really was entirely unpleasing. But that the masses were kept in subjection primarily by force for many centuries seems improbable. The authoritarian hierarchical traditional social structure must have persisted because submitting to authority above one, as well as exercising authority, was satisfying, and secondly because the conditions of life re-created personalities, generation after generation, in which it continued to be so.

Creative and Uncreative Personality

To suggest probable reasons why authoritarian social structure was satisfying, let me digress to discuss certain aspects of personality.

Many elite individuals in traditional societies are prevented from using their energies effectively in economic development by their repugnance to being concerned with the grubby material aspects of life. The repugnance includes being concerned with the details of running a business effectively, as well as performing manual-technical labor—"getting their hands dirty." Often the repugnance is largely unconscious; the individuals concerned often deny it, because it does not occur to them that any middle- or upper-class person anywhere would have any more favorable attitude toward engaging in such activity than they have. Why does this attitude exist?

It is deep-rooted. I would explain it as follows. Every person in any society who holds or gains privileged position in life must justify it to himself, in order to be comfortable. If he has gained it by his abilities, justification is easy. The person who gains it by the accident of birth is forced to feel that it is due him because he is essentially superior to the simple folk. Typically, the elite individual in traditional societies feels that his innate superiority consists in being more refined than the simple folk. One evidence of his greater refinement is that he does not like the grubby attention to the material details of life which is one of their distinguishing characteristics. However this attitude may have developed historically, once it exists ·the elite child acquires it from infancy on by perceiving the words, the attitudes, the tone of voice of his elders. By the time he is six or eight years old, it is deeply bred into his personality.

This attitude alone would not contribute to the lack of innovation in social and political fields. Presence of a low level of creativity, however, would help to explain absence of innovation in these fields as well as in techniques of production.

The explanation of a low level of creativity and justification for the assertion that it exists are more complex.

One component of creativity is intelligence, and intelligence is in part due to biological characteristics. However, although individuals differ greatly in inherited intellectual capacity, the best evidence suggests no reason to assume any appreciable average difference in this respect between the individuals of traditional societies and those of other societies. There are varying degrees of innate intelligence in both. Persons in traditional societies are not less creative because they are less intelligent.

A more relevant component is certain attitudes. In formal psychological terms, I would suggest as characteristics central to creativity high need (for) achievement, high need autonomy, high need order (though this needs further definition), and a sense of the phenomena about one as forming a system which is conceptually comprehensible, rather than merely being arbitrary external bundles.

A person who has high need achievement feels a sense of increased pleasure (or quite possibly a lessening of chronic anxiety, which is the same thing) when he faces a problem or notes a new and irregular phenomenon in a field of interest to him; by the pleasure he anticipates in using his capacities he is drawn to use his energies to understand and master the situation. A person with high need autonomy takes for granted that when he has explored a situation in an area of interest to him, his evaluation of it is satisfactory. He does not think he "knows it all"; he seeks ideas; but when he has thus gained a perspective he assumes that his discriminations and evaluations are good; he feels no anxiety about whether the judgments of other persons differ from his. He does not rebel against the conventional view for the sake of rebelling, but neither does he accept it because it is generally accepted. In Rogers' phrase, the "locus of evaluative judgment is within him."[4]

A person with high need autonomy and also high need order, in the sense in whch I use that phrase here, tolerates disorder without discomfort, because sensing that the world is an orderly place, he knows that within the disorder there is complex and satisfying order, and he is willing to tolerate the disorder, and in fact even enjoys it somewhat, until the greater order shall suggest itself to him. Such a person is alert to phenomena which contradict his previous assumptions about the scheme of things, for he assumes that he will be able to perceive the order implicit in them and thus gain an enlarged understanding of the world. In Poincaré's terms, he has a "capacity to be surprised"; in Rogers', "openness to experience."[5]

These characteristics are not fully independent of each other. In technical jargon, they may not be orthogonal. This categorization of personality therefore does not quite go to the roots of things. But it will do for my present purpose.

This personality complex may be contrasted with one which for the moment I shall term merely uncreative. It includes low need achievement and need autonomy, high need dependence, high need submission-dominance, and a sense of the world as consisting of arbitrary forces.

If an individual does not trust his own capacity to analyze problems, then when he faces a problem, anxiety rises in him. He anticipates failure, and avoids problems. He will find comfort in the consensus of a group (not on a majority decision opposed by a minority, for this involves a clash of judgment and the necessity of choosing between the two judgments). He will find it comfortable to rely on authority for guidance—the authority of older men or of the appropriate person in the hierarchy of authority and status which is always found in a traditional society. He will enjoy having a position of authority himself; one reason for this is that if he must make a decision, he can give it the sanction of his authority; persons below him, if they in turn find it comfortable to rely on authority, will not question his decision, and

---

[4] H. H. Anderson, ed., *Creativity and Its Cultivation* (New York: Harper & Bros., 1959), p. 76.
[5] Poincaré's phrase is quoted by Erich Fromm in H. H. Anderson, *op. cit.*, p. 48; Rogers' is at *ibid.*, p. 75.

he does not need to feel anxiety lest analysis of it would prove it to have been wrong. It is right because a person with the proper authority made it.

A person with such needs will avoid noting phenomena that do not meet his preconceptions, for their existence presents a problem. In any event, since he senses the world as consisting mainly of arbitrary forces, an unexpected phenomenon provides no clue to him. It is simply a possible source of failure or danger.

I shall suggest below that the experiences in infancy and childhood which give a person this perception of the world inculcate rage and need aggression in him, but also fear of his own need aggression, and therefore anxiety in any situation within his group in which power relationships are not clearly defined and conflict leading to aggressiveness might occur. Hence he likes a clearly defined structure of hierarchical authority, in which it is obviously proper for him to submit to someone above him or give orders to persons below him, without clash of judgment. In addition, his need aggression also causes him to feel pleasure in dominating those below him—his children, his juniors, his social inferiors.

Thus there are dual reasons why the authoritarian hierarchy is satisfying. It is appropriate to give this personality type not merely the negative label "uncreative" but also the positive one "authoritarian."[6]

While it is evident that these two personality types exist, to this point it is purely an assumption that authoritarian personality is typical in traditional societies. One reason for thinking that this is true is that this hypothesis explains many things about traditional societies which otherwise are puzzling. It explains, for example, why many persons in traditional societies not only follow traditional methods, but seem to cling almost compulsively to them, even though to an outsider trial of a new method seems so clearly to their advantage. It explains why the method of decision of local problems in so many traditional societies is by consensus of the village elders, through a long process of finding a least-common-denominator solution on which all can agree, rather than by majority vote. It explains, too, why authoritarian social and political systems have persisted in such societies for such long periods.

That a hypothesis explains a number of phenomena which are otherwise puzzling is strong reason for accepting it. However, there is also more direct reason for believing that authoritarian personality is unusually prevalent in traditional societies. This reason lies in the existence of some evidence that childhood environment and childhood training in traditional societies are of the kind which tend to produce such personality.

Perhaps the factor which is most important in determining whether childhood environment will be such as to cause the formation of creative personality or such as to cause the formation of authoritarian personality is the opinions of the parents concerning the nature of infants and children.

[6] It is not congruent in all respects with the one portrayed by Adorno and associates in *The Authoritarian Personality.*

Suppose that the parents take for granted that infants are organisms which, while delicate and in need of protection for a time, have great potentials; organisms which as they unfold will develop capacity for understanding and managing life. A mother who regards this as an axiomatic fact of life will if she is sensible take precautions to keep her child's explorations of the world around him from causing harm or alarm to him, but she will let him explore his world and will watch with interest and pleasure as his muscular capacities develop, his range of activity expands, and he accomplishes in endless succession the hundreds of new achievements which occur during infancy and childhood.

His repeated use of his new physiological capacities, as they unfold, is from his viewpoint problem solving—intensely interesting problem solving. Assume that it is successful because his mother has taken safeguards so that he will not fall out of his crib, cut himself, break the glassware, fall down stairs, etc., and because his mother offers advice and restraint when necessary. Assume, however, that his venturings do not meet repeated restraint, because his mother trusts his developing capacities and does not check his every step. Then he will repeatedly feel joy at his own successful problem solving and pleasure in his mother's pleasure. There will be deeply built into him the pattern that initiative is rewarded, that his judgment is adequate, that solving problems is fun.

If his mother wants him to be self-reliant, presses him to do things as soon as his capacities have developed, usually refuses to let him lapse into babyhood after he has gained capacities, and shows displeasure when he does not do things for himself, then the stimulus of her displeasure when he does not show initiative will be combined with that of her pleasure when he does so. I have mentioned only his mother. During the first year or more of his life, her attitude is the most important one in his life; after that the attitude of his father (and also that of his siblings) toward his behavior will also be important.

Suppose, alternatively, that the child's parents have as a part of their personalities the judgment that children are fragile organisms without much innate potential capacity to understand or manage the world. Then during the first two years or so of life the mother is apt to treat the child oversolicitously, and to shield him somewhat anxiously from harm. In doing so, unintentionally she also keeps the child from using his unfolding initiative. The use of initiative comes to alarm him, because it alarms her. Then, after these first few years of life, when the parents think the child is old enough to be trained, parents with the view that children are without much potential inner capacity train the child by a continual stream of commands and instructions concerning what is good to do and not good to do, the proper relationships to them and to others, and in general how he should live. Exercise of initiative on his part frequently brings alarm and displeasure and hence causes him anxiety. He can avoid anxiety only by passively obeying the instructions of these powerful persons so important in his life. The instructions will often seem arbitrary to him, and the repeated frustration of his initiative will create anger in him. He will repress it, but this does not mean that it disappears.

The practices and attitudes of older siblings and playmates who have been brought up under the same influences will provide models which in various ways will reinforce the same lesson.

The impact of these parental attitudes on the child may be reinforced by certain related attitudes of the parents. The existence of any child restricts the freedom of his parents, and interferes with their relations to each other. Moreover, the child exerts a will independent of theirs, and they are not always sure that they can control him. If the parents, especially the mother, are relaxed confident people, they will not be disturbed by these problems. Suppose, however, that they are somewhat anxious persons who feel that they themselves do not understand the world (as they are apt to feel if their own childhood was like that which I have just described). Then their child may repeatedly make them anxious, and unconsciously they may hate him for causing them anxiety and also interfering with their freedom. The child is sure to sense their hostility; it will both make him more afraid to venture and increase his pleasure in venting his frustration by controlling someone below him later in life.

Exposure to the one or the other of these parental attitudes will have an impact on the child through infancy and childhood, but for brevity I shall mention specifically only the most conspicuous manifestation, that during the "period of infantile genitality," which usually occupies about the fourth and fifth years of life. At this age a boy knows that he is a male, like his father, and that he will become big, like his father, and he begins to wonder whether he can successfully rival his father. Specifically, he becomes a rival of his father for his mother's attentions. If his father and mother are perceptive and understanding persons, they will accept him into their fellowship and let him gain an adequate degree of the feminine attention he needs. However, without anxiety or arbitrariness, they will teach him that he can postpone his demands when the circumstances require it, and need not feel anxiety at the postponement. He will learn, as before, that one's initiative must be judicious, and he will also reinforce powerfully the earlier lesson that the exercise of his initiative is safe and brings pleasure.

If the father is weak and the mother is not arbitrary and somewhat rejecting, the son may gain his mother's attention not because his parents understand his needs and meet them but because his father gives up at the boy's aggressive persistence. In this case too the son will learn that initiative is successful, though he will learn it with overtones of anxiety.

Suppose, however, that the parents doubt their own ability to manage problems, and, having no faith in the capacities of children, regard the boy's initiative as a danger rather than a valuable attribute. Then they will be disturbed by the boy's emerging rivalry with his father during the period of infantile sexuality, will resent the boy's encroachment, and will "put the boy in his place." The experience will reinforce the anxiety and alarm that the boy felt earlier at the exercise of initiative. It will also reinforce the anger that the boy felt earlier at his parents' arbitrary restrictions, and since he cannot vent his anger at his parents, there is apt to build up in him an un-formed desire to exercise arbitrary authority himself, and lord it over someone under him, later in life—just as the college freshman humiliated by hazing at the hands of sophomores often waits his turn to vent his humiliation on the new freshmen the next year.

The impact of the one or other type of parental personality on girls during this period is not quite parallel to that on boys, because of the different sexual role which girls have already learned. The differences will not be discussed here.

In these ways, creative or authoritarian personality is formed. There are many other aspects to the process, and many other aspects of authoritarian and creative personalities, which cannot be discussed here.[7] This brief discussion will, I hope, give the general flavor of both the personality types and the process which forms them.

I think that the reader may already have realized that the parental attitudes which tend to create authoritarian personality in the children are themselves components of authoritarian personality in the parents. That is, persons in whom authoritarian personality was created by the circumstances of their childhoods are apt to have such a view of life that they will in turn create an environment which will cause authoritarian personalities to appear in their children. The type, like most other personality types, tends to be self-perpetuating.

It is of great importance, then, that the scattered evidence which is available suggests that precisely the sort of childhood environment and training sketched above as conducive to the emergence of authoritarian personality is the sort prevalent in traditional societies. Fairly intensive sketches of childhood environment in Burma by Hazel Hitson[8] and in Java by Hildred Geertz,[9] and more fragmentary sketches relating to many Latin societies, indicate

---

[7] For example, models are important in personality formation, and it is of interest to ask where the son of a weak father obtains models of successful behavior. There are several possibilities. This and other complexities must be passed over here.

[8] "Family Patterns and Paranoidal Personality Structure in Boston and Burma" (Ph.D. dissertion, Radcliffe College, April 1959).

[9] *The Javanese Family* (New York: Free Press of Glencoe, Inc., 1955) and "The Vocabulary of Emotion: A Study of Javanese Socialization Processes," *Psychiatry*, Vol. XXII (August 1959), pp. 225–37.

that in all of these cases childhood environment is precisely of this type. These sketches refer primarily to the simple folk, but there is some empirical evidence to suggest that they are true of personality and childhood environment among the elite as well.

And there is even more convincing evidence that various of the conspicuous characteristics of authoritarian personality are present in many traditional societies in Latin America and Asia. Though our knowledge concerning African countries is more limited, they are probably present in those countries as well. Hence it seems likely that a low level of creativity is also characteristic of such societies.

Presumably this personality type developed initially because the every day phenomena of the physical world were bewildering to unscientific man. Convinced of his inability to fathom the world, man began to protect his children jealously when they were infants and then train them minutely in the way in which they should behave to be safe. And so authoritarian personality appeared and perpetuated itself. Repugnance to concerning oneself with the humble material matters of life and with manual-technical labor also appeared among the elite, in the way sketched earlier in this essay, and tended to perpetuate itself.

II. SOCIAL CHANGE

How, then, did social change ever occur? and technological progress and economic development ever begin?

Study of a number of countries in which there has occurred a transition from a traditional state to continuing economic development suggests that an important factor initiating change was some historical shift which caused some group or groups of the lesser elite, who previously had had a respected and valued place in the social hierarchy, to feel that they no longer were respected and valued. This derogation in some societies consisted of explicit indication of contempt for the functions or position of the lesser elite, in others of behavior by a new higher elite which seemed immoral, unmanly, or irreligious to the groups below them, and thus indicated contempt for the moral standards of the lesser elite.

I shall omit the example of England, which is complex and difficult to mention briefly, and shall refer briefly to highlights of three other examples. In the 1650's the Tsar of Russia and Patriarch of Moscow, to attain diplomatic ends by adopting Greek practices, ordered certain changes in the ritual of the Orthodox church which the faithful felt to be heretical and to endanger their souls. There followed conflict and persecution, in waves of varying severity, even down to 1900. The Old Believers, who were the victims of this withdrawal of respect for their status in the society, were prominent in economic development in Russia in the nineteenth century. Concerning the twentieth I have no information.

In Japan the feudal group known as the Tokugawa, who gained national power in 1600, imposed a peace which deprived the samurai of their traditional function; imposed rigid distinctions among social classes which had the effect of relegating the so-called "wealthy peasants," descendants of the lesser elite, to the rank of peasant; and to some extent demeaned other feudal groups, the so-called outer clans. It was the lesser samurai and wealthy peasants, apparently especially of the outer clans, who were the innovators in Japan's industrial revolution.

In Colombia, in the 1530's the Spanish settled on a high plateau around Bogotá and in the valleys around Cali and Medellín. Through historical developments I shall not sketch, during the next two centuries the settlers of the other two areas came to look down on those in Antioquia, the valley around Medellín. The social friction continues to the present; and the Antioqueños have been the leaders in economic innovation out of all proportion to their numbers in the population.

I shall call such events "withdrawal of status respect" from the group no longer accorded its old place. It is important to note that the situation is one in which a group of the elite once had full status respect and later lost it. What are the results? Let me speculate concerning them.

I suggest that among the adults of the first generation so affected, the reaction is anger and anxiety. Their children, however, seeing that their parents' role in life causes anxiety, do not find it a fully satisfying model. Alternative roles are in general not open to them, and so they respond by repressing somewhat within themselves their parents' values—by ceasing to have *any* role values with the same clarity and intensity their parents did. The process, I suggest, is cumulative in successive generations, and in the second or third or fourth generation there appears pronounced "normlessness," shiftlessness, anomie, or, in Merton's term, retreatism. It can be observed, for example, in Negroes of the southern United States, American Indians on any reservation, first and second generation immigrants, and colonial subjects.[10] Historical records suggest that it also characterized the Antioqueños, the samurai, and the Old Believers.

There is reason to suspect that retreatism affects men more than women because of the differences between the normal social roles of the sexes. After several generations, then, there will appear men who are retreatists and weak, but women who are less so. The women will probably feel some pity for their children's lot in life, and will cherish them tenderly. But, reacting to the ineffectiveness of their husbands, the women will have an intense desire

---

[10] In groups who are not of the lower elite, but instead are of the "simple folk," the later reaction may be not creative innovation but violent social revolt. For lack of space, that branch of the theory cannot be expounded here.

that their sons shall be more effective, and will respond with delight to each achievement in infancy and boyhood. During the period of infantile sexuality, the boy will win in the rivalry with his father, both because his initiative pleases his mother and because his father is weak.

Obviously not all home environments in some generation of a group of the lesser elite from whom status respect has been withdrawn will be like this, but it is plausible to believe that some such environment will appear occasionally, or even fairly often. Some combinations and intensities of such maternal attitudes, combined with weakness in the father, provide an almost ideal environment for the formation of an anxious driving type of creativity.

Where a considerable degree of creativity is inculcated, but the anxiety is great, a variant type of individual may appear, one who gives himself security by being traditional and authoritarian in most aspects of his behavior, and then dares to be bold and creative in some other aspect. Henry Ford was such a person, as was J. Pierpont Morgan. And this type has been important in economic development in Japan, the Soviet Union, and Germany.

Thus, I suggest, there gradually emerges a group of individuals, creative, alienated from traditional values, driven by a gnawing burning drive to prove themselves (to themselves, as well as to their fellows), seeking for an area in which to do so, preferably an area in which they can gain power, and preferably also one in which in some symbolic way they can vent their rage at the elites who have caused their troubles. Moreover, their (perhaps unconscious) rage at the group disparaging them will cause them to turn against some of the values of the group disparaging them. The fact that the disparaging group, in the cases cited above, was traditional, is one of the reasons why the disparaged group rejected traditional values and turned to innovation.

What they turn to will be determined in part by the models they find during their childhood somewhere in their history or their folklore or the tales their elders tell them of the life around them, and in part by the objective opportunities of the world around them. In the modern world, to few socially rebellious groups of traditional societies will any other road to power, recognition, and proof to oneself of one's ability seem as inviting as economic prowess, and creative individuals in most such groups will become economic innovators. In the cases of England, Japan, and Colombia, which I have examined in some detail, such groups have provided a disproportionate share of the leaders in the transition to economic growth.

A word is in point concerning the complexity of the situation in colonial societies. Here there has been rather harsh withdrawal of status respect, but by invading groups from the West who became colonial conquerors. These groups have not traditional but "modern" values toward manual-technical work. The tendency of disparaged groups to reject the values of the disparaging group may cause them to reject engaging their energies in the occupations of the conquerors. Thus even though they desire to gain symbols of economic power, an additional emotional block is put in the way of the indigenous elite becoming effective industrialists. This fact may explain some of the ambivalence and erratic behavior sometimes manifested.

The theory some of whose central points have been sketched so briefly above proceeds in broad sweeps, and of course is subject to a corresponding margin of error. It seems plausible to me because it is internally consistent and because it explains many aspects of social, political, and economic behavior in low-income countries for which no other very logical explanation seems available.

If it is correct it does not follow that economic growth will succeed only where certain rather special historical conditions have existed. For the forces of modern history have caused social tensions among the social classes of low-income societies themselves, by virtue of which some degree of withdrawal of status respect has existed among the indigenous social classes of almost all of them, and what values various groups are alienated from or drawn to is confused and uncertain. However, innovational personality is clearly appearing, in varying degree. The drive for security, self-reassurance, and power will surely lead many innovational individuals to technological innovation, though frequently within social forms differing from those of the West.

THE ACHIEVEMENT MOTIVE
IN ECONOMIC GROWTH[1]

David C. McClelland

From the beginning of recorded history, men have been fascinated by the fact that civilizations rise and fall. Culture growth, as Kroeber has demonstrated, is episodic, and sometimes occurs in quite different fields.[2] For example, the people living in the Italian peninsula at the time of ancient Rome produced a great civilization of law, politics, and military conquest; and at another time, during the Renaissance, the inhabitants of Italy produced a great civilization of art, music, letters, and science. What can account for such cultural flowerings? In our time we have theorists like Huntington, who stresses the importance of climate, or Toynbee, who also feels the right amount of challenge from the environment is crucial though he conceives of the environment as including its psychic effects. Others, like Kroeber, have difficulty imagining any general explanation; they perforce must accept the notion that a particular culture happens to hit on a particularly happy mode of self-expression, which it then pursues until it becomes overspecialized and sterile.

My concern is not with all culture growth, but with economic growth. Some wealth or leisure may be essential to development in other fields—the

From David C. McClelland, "The Achievement Motive in Economic Growth," *Industrialization and Society*, pp. 74–96 (The Hague: UNESCO & Mouton, 1963). Reprinted by permission of UNESCO & Mouton.

[1] This paper is a summary of the author's book, *The Achieving Society*, published by Van Nostrand Co. in Princeton, N.J., in the fall of 1961.

[2] A. L. Kroeber, *Configurations of Culture Growth* (Berkeley, California, 1944).

arts, politics, science, or war—but we need not insist on it. However, the question of why some countries develop rapidly in the economic sphere at certain times and not at others is in itself of great interest, whatever its relation to other types of culture growth. Usually, rapid economic growth has been explained in terms of "external" factors—favorable opportunities for trade, unusual natural resources, or conquests that have opened up new markets or produced internal political stability. But I am interested in the *internal* factors—in the values and motives men have that lead them to exploit opportunities, to take advantage of favorable trade conditions; in short, to shape their own destiny.

This interest is not surprising; I am a psychologist—and, furthermore, a psychologist whose primary research interest is in human motivation, in the *reasons* that people behave as they do. Of course, all people have always, to a certain extent, been interested in human motivation. The difference between their interest and the twentieth-century psychologist's interest is that the latter tries to define his subject matter very precisely and, like all scientists, to measure it. How can human motives be identified, or even measured? Psychologists' favorite techniques for conducting research in this area have always been the interview and the questionnaire. If you want to know what a man's motives are, ask him. Of course, you need not ask him directly; but perhaps, if you talk to him long enough in an interview, or ask him enough in a questionnaire, you can infer what his motives are—more or less the same way that, from a number of clues, a detective would infer who had committed a crime.

Whatever else one thinks of Freud and the other psychoanalysts, they performed one extremely important service for psychology: once and for all, they persuaded us, rightly or wrongly, that what people said about their motives was not a reliable basis for determining what those motives really were. In his analyses of the psychopathology of everyday life and of dreams and neurotic symptoms, Freud demonstrated repeatedly that the "obvious" motives—the motives that the people themselves thought they had or that a reasonable observer would attribute to them—were not, in fact, the real motives for their often strange behavior. By the same token, Freud also showed the way to a better method of learning what people's motives were. He analyzed dreams and free associations: in short, fantasy or imaginative behavior. Stripped of its air of mystery and the occult, psychoanalysis has taught us that one can learn a great deal about people's motives through observing the things about which they are spontaneously concerned in their dreams and waking fantasies. About ten or twelve years ago, the research group in America with which I was connected decided to take this insight quite seriously and to see what we could learn about human motivation by coding objectively what people spontaneously thought about in their waking fantasies.[3] Our method was to collect such free fantasy, in the form of brief stories written about pictures, and to count the frequency with which certain themes appeared—rather as a medical technician counts the frequency with which red or white corpuscles appear in a blood sample. We were able to demonstrate that the frequency with which certain "inner concerns" appeared in these fantasies varied systematically as a function of specific experimental conditions by which we aroused or induced motivational states in the subjects. Eventually, we were able to isolate several of these inner concerns, or motives, which, if present in great frequency in the fantasies of a particular person, enabled us to know something about how he would behave in many other areas of life.

Chief among these motives was what we termed "the need for Achievement" (*n* Achievement)—a desire to do well, not so much for the sake of social recognition or prestige, but to attain an inner feeling of personal accomplishment. This motive is my particular concern in this paper. Our early laboratory studies showed that people "high" in *n* Achievement tend to work harder at certain tasks; to learn faster; to do their best work when it counts for the record, and not when special incentives, like money prizes, are introduced; to choose experts over friends as working partners; etc. Obviously, we cannot here review the many, many studies in this area. About five years ago, we became especially interested in the problem of what would happen in a society if a large number of people with a high need for achievement should happen to be present in it at a particular time. In others words, we became interested in a social-psychological question: What effect would a concentration of people with high *n* Achievement have on a society?

It might be relevant to describe how we began wondering about this. I had always been greatly impressed by the very perceptive analysis of the connection between Protestantism and the spirit of capitalism made by the great German sociologist, Max Weber.[4] He argues that the distinguishing characteristic of Protestant business entrepreneurs and of workers, particularly from the pietistic sects, was not that they had in any sense invented the institutions of capitalism or good craftmanship, but that they went about their jobs with a new perfectionist spirit. The Calvinistic doctrine of predestination had forced them to rationalize every aspect of their lives and to strive hard for perfection in the positions in this world to which they had been assigned by God. As I read Weber's description of the behavior of these people, I concluded that they must certainly have had a high level of *n* Achievement. Perhaps the new spirit of capitalism Weber describes was none

[3] J. W. Atkinson (Ed.), *Motives in Fantasy, Action, and Society* (Princeton, N.J., 1958).

[4] Max Weber, *The Protestant Ethic and the Spirit of Capitalism,* trans. Talcott Parsons (New York, 1930).

other than a high need for achievement—if so, then n Achievement has been responsible, in part, for the extraordinary economic development of the West. Another factor served to confirm this hypothesis. A careful study by Winterbottom had shown that boys with high n Achievement usually came from families in which the mothers stressed early self-reliance and mastery.[5] The boys whose mothers did *not* encourage their early self-reliance, or did not set such high standards of excellence, tended to develop lower need for achievement. Obviously, one of the key characteristics of the Protestant Reformation was its emphasis on self-reliance. Luther stressed the "priesthood of all believers" and translated the Bible so that every man could have direct access to God and religious thought. Calvin accentuated a rationalized perfection in this life for everyone. Certainly, the character of the Reformation seems to have set the stage, historically, for parents to encourage their children to attain earlier self-reliance and achievement. If the parents did in fact do so, they very possibly unintentionally produced the higher level of n Achievement in their children that was, in turn, responsible for the new spirit of capitalism.

This was the hypothesis that initiated our research. It was, of course, only a promising idea; much work was necessary to determine its validity. Very early in our studies, we decided that the events Weber discusses were probably only a special case of a much more general phenomenon—that it was n Achievement as such that was connected with economic development, and that the Protestant Reformation was connected only indirectly in the extent to which it had influenced the average n Achievement level of its adherents. If this assumption is correct, then a high average level of n Achievement should be equally associated with economic development in ancient Greece, in modern Japan, or in a preliterate tribe being studied by anthropologists in the South Pacific. In other words, in its most general form, the hypothesis attempts to isolate one of the key factors in the economic development, at least, of all civilizations. What evidence do we have that this extremely broad generalization will obtain? By now, a great deal has been collected—far more than I can summarize here; but I shall try to give a few key examples of the different types of evidence.

First, we have made historical studies. To do so, we had to find a way to obtain a measure of n Achievement level during time periods other than our own, whose individuals can no longer be tested. We have done this—instead of coding the brief stories written by an individual for a test, we code imaginative literary documents: poetry, drama, funeral orations, letters written by sea captains, epics, etc. Ancient Greece, which we studied first, supplies a good illustration. We are able to find literary documents written during three different historical periods and dealing with similar themes:

[5] M. R. Winterbottom, "The Relation of Need for Achievement to Learning and Experiences in Independence and Mastery," in Atkinson, *op. cit.*, pp. 453–478.

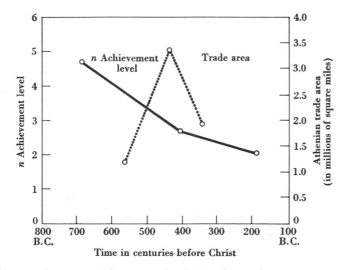

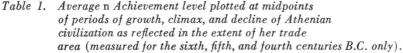

Table 1. *Average* n *Achievement level plotted at midpoints*
of periods of growth, climax, and decline of Athenian
civilization as reflected in the extent of her trade
area (measured for the sixth, fifth, and fourth centuries B.C. only).

the period of economic growth, 900 B.C.–475 B.C. (largely Homer and Hesiod); the period of climax, 475 B.C.–362 B.C.; and the period of decline, 362 B.C.–100 B.C. Thus, Hesiod wrote on farm and estate management in the early period; Xenophon, in the middle period; and Aristotle, in the late period. We have defined the period of "climax" in economic, rather than in cultural, terms, because it would be presumptuous to claim, for example, that Aristotle in any sense represented a "decline" from Plato or Thales. The measure of economic growth was computed from information supplied by Heichelheim in his *Wirtschaftsgeschichte des Altertums.*[6] Heichelheim records in detail the locations throughout Europe where the remains of Greek vases from different centuries have been found. Of course, these vases were the principal instrument of Greek foreign trade, since they were the containers for olive oil and wine, which were the most important Greek exports. Knowing where the vase fragments have been found, we could compute the trade area of Athenian Greece for different time periods. We purposely omitted any consideration of the later expansion of Hellenistic Greece, because this represents another civilization; our concern was Athenian Greece.

When all the documents had been coded, they demonstrated—as predicted—that the level of *n* Achievement was highest during the period of growth prior to the climax of economic development in Athenian Greece. (See Table 1.) In other words, the maximum *n* Achievement level preceded

[6] F. Heichelheim, *Wirtschaftsgeschichte des Altertums* (Leiden, 1938).

the maximum economic level by at least a century. Furthermore, that high level had fallen off by the time of maximum prosperity, thus foreshadowing subsequent economic decline. A similar methodology was applied, with the same results, to the economic development of Spain in the sixteenth century[7] and to two waves of economic development in the history of England (one in the late sixteenth century and the other at the beginning of the industrial revolution, around 1800).[8] The n Achievement level in English history (as determined on the basis of dramas, sea captains' letters, and street ballads) rose, between 1400–1800, *twice* a generation or two before waves of accelerated economic growth (incidentally, at times of Protestant revival). This point is significant because it shows that there is no "necessary" steady decline in a civilization's entrepreneurial energy from its earlier to its later periods. In the Spanish and English cases, as in the Greek, high levels of n Achievement preceded economic decline. Unfortunately, space limitations preclude more detailed discussion of these studies here.

We also tested the hypothesis by applying it to preliterate cultures of the sort that anthropologists investigate. At Yale University, an organized effort has been made to collect everything that is known about all the primitive tribes that have been studied and to classify the information systematically for comparative purposes. We utilized this cross-cultural file to obtain the two measures that we needed to test our general hypothesis. For over fifty of these cultures, collections of folk tales existed that Child and others had coded,[9] just as we coded literary documents and individual imaginative stories, for n Achievement and other motives. These folk tales have the character of fantasy that we believe to be so essential for getting at "inner concerns." In the meantime, we were searching for a method of classifying the economic development of these cultures, so that we could determine whether those evincing high n Achievement in their folk tales had developed further than those showing lower n Achievement. The respective modes of gaining a livelihood were naturally very different in these cultures, since they came from every continent in the world and every type of physical habitat; yet we had to find a measure for comparing them. We finally thought of trying to estimate the number of full-time "business entrepreneurs" there were among the adults in each culture. We defined "entrepreneur" as "anyone who exercises control over the means of production and produces more than he can consume in order to sell it for individual or household income." Thus an entrepreneur was anyone who derived at

---

[7] J. B. Cortés, "The Achievement Motive in the Spanish Economy between the Thirteenth and the Eighteenth Centuries," *Economic Development and Cultural Change*, IX. (1960), 144–163.

[8] N. M. Bradburn and D. E. Berlew, "Need for Achievement and English Economic Growth," *Economic Development and Cultural Change*, 1961.

[9] I. L. Child, T. Storm, and J. Veroff, "Achievement Themes in Folk Tales Related to Socialization Practices," in Atkinson, *op. cit.*, pp. 479–492.

least seventy-five per cent of his income from such exchange or market practices. The entrepreneurs were mostly traders, independent artisans, or operators of small firms like stores, inns, etc. Nineteen cultures were classified as high in n Achievement on the basis of their folk tales; seventy-four per cent of them contained some entrepreneurs. On the other hand, only thirty-five per cent of the twenty cultures that were classified as low in n Achievement contained any entrepreneurs (as we defined it) at all. The difference is highly significant statistically (Chi-square $= 5.97$, $p < .02$). Hence data about primitive tribes seem to confirm the hypothesis that high n Achievement leads to a more advanced type of economic activity.

But what about modern nations? Can we estimate their level of n Achievement and relate it to their economic development? The question is obviously one of the greatest importance, but the technical problems of getting measures of our two variables proved to be really formidable. What type of literary document could we use that would be equally representative of the motivational levels of people in India, Japan, Portugal, Germany, the United States, and Italy? We had discovered in our historical studies that certain types of literature usually contain much more achievement imagery than others. This is not too serious as long as we are dealing with time changes within a given culture; but it is very serious if we want to compare two cultures, each of which may express its achievement motivation in a different literary form. At last, we decided to use children's stories, for several reasons. They exist in standard form in every modern nation, since all modern nations are involved in teaching their children to read and use brief stories for this purpose. Furthermore, the stories are imaginative; and, if selected from those used in the earliest grades, they are not often influenced by temporary political events. (We were most impressed by this when reading the stories that every Russian child reads. In general, they cannot be distinguished, in style and content, from the stories read in all the countries of the West.)

We collected children's readers for the second, third, and fourth grades from every country where they could be found for two time periods, which were roughly centered around 1925 and around 1950. We got some thirteen hundred stories, which were all translated into English. In all, we had twenty-one stories from each of twenty-three countries about 1925, and the same number from each of thirty-nine countries about 1950. Code was used on proper names, so that our scorers would not know the national origins of the stories. The tales were then mixed together, and coded for n Achievement (and certain other motives and values that I shall mention only briefly).

The next task was to find a measure of economic development. Again, the problem was to insure comparability. Some countries have much greater natural resources; some have developed industrially sooner than others;

some concentrate in one area of production and some in another. Economists consider national income figures in per capita terms to be the best measure available; but they are difficult to obtain for all countries, and it is hard to translate them into equal purchasing power. Ultimately, we came to rely chiefly on the measure of electricity produced: the units of measurement are the same all over the world; the figures are available from the 1920's on; and electricity is the *form* of energy (regardless of how it is produced) that is essential to modern economic development. In fact, electricity produced per capita correlates with estimates of income per capita in the 1950's around .90 anyway. To equate for differences in natural resources, such as the amount of water power available, etc., we studied *gains* in kilowatt hours produced per capita between 1925 and 1950. The level of electrical production in 1925 is, as one would expect, highly correlated with the size of the gain between then and 1950. So it was necessary to resort to a regression analysis; that is, to calculate, from the average regression of gain on level for all countries, how much gain a particular country should have shown between 1925 and 1950. The actual gain could then be compared with the expected gain, and the country could be classified as gaining more or less rapidly than would have been expected on the basis of its 1925 performance. The procedure is directly comparable to what we do when we predict, on the basis of some measure of I.Q., what grades a child can be expected to get in school, and then classify him as an "under-" or "over-achiever."

The correlation between the *n* Achievement level in the children's readers in 1925 and the growth in electrical output between 1925 and 1950, as compared with expectation, is a quite substantial .53, which is highly significant statistically. It could hardly have arisen by chance. Furthermore, the correlation is also substantial with a measure of gain over the expected in per capita income, equated for purchasing power by Colin Clark. To check this result more definitively with the sample of forty countries for which we had reader estimates of *n* Achievement levels in 1950, we computed the equation for gains in electrical output in 1952–1958 as a function of level in 1952. It turned out to be remarkably linear when translated into logarithmic units, as is so often the case with simple growth functions. Table 2 presents the performance of each of the countries, as compared with predictions from initial level in 1952, in standard score units and classified by high and low *n* Achievement in 1950. Once again we found that *n* Achievement levels predicted significantly (r = .43) the countries which would perform more or less rapidly than expected in terms of the average for all countries. The finding is more striking than the earlier one, because many Communist and underdeveloped countries are included in the sample. Apparently, *n* Achievement is a precursor of economic growth—and not only in the Western style of capitalism based on the small entrepreneur, but also in economies controlled and fostered largely by the state.

Table 2. *Rate of growth in electrical output* (*1952–1958*)
and national n Achievement levels in 1950

National n Achievement levels (1950)[a]	Deviation from expected growth rates* in standard score units			
	Above expectation		Below expectation	
High n Achievement				
3.62 Turkey	+1.38			
2.71 India[b]	+1.12			
2.38 Australia	+ .42			
2.32 Israel	+1.18			
2.33 Spain	+ .01			
2.29 Pakistan[c]	+2.75			
2.29 Greece	+1.18	3.38	Argentina	− .56
2.29 Canada	+ .08	2.71	Lebanon	− .67
2.24 Bulgaria	+1.37	2.38	France	− .24
2.24 U.S.A.	+ .47	2.33	U. So. Africa	− .06
2.14 West Germany	+ .53	2.29	Ireland	− .41
2.10 U.S.S.R.	+1.61	2.14	Tunisia	−1.87
2.10 Portugal	+ .76	2.10	Syria	− .25
Low n Achievement				
1.95 Iraq	+ .29	2.05	New Zealand	− .29
1.86 Austria	+ .38	1.86	Uruguay	− .75
1.67 U.K.	+ .17	1.81	Hungary	− .62
1.57 Mexico	+1.12	1.71	Norway	− .77
.86 Poland	+1.26	1.62	Sweden	− .64
		1.52	Finland	− .08
		1.48	Netherlands	− .15
		1.33	Italy	− .57
		1.29	Japan	− .04
		1.20	Switzerland[d]	−1.92
		1.19	Chile	−1.81
Correlation of n Achievement level (1950) x deviations from expected growth rate = .43, p < .01.		1.05	Denmark	− .89
		.57	Algeria	− .83
		.43	Belgium	−1.65

* The estimates are computed from the monthly average electrical production figures, in millions of Kwh, for 1952 and 1958, from United Nations, *Monthly Bulletin of Statistics* (January, 1960), and *World Energy Supplies*, 1951–1954 and 1955–1958 (Statistical Papers, Series J).

The correlation between log level 1952 and log gain 1952–58 is .976.

The regression equation based on these thirty-nine countries, plus four others from the same climatic zone on which data are available (China-Taiwan, Czechoslovakia, Rumania, Yugoslavia), is: log gain (1952–58) = .9229 log level (1952) + .0480.

Standard scores are deviations from mean gain predicted by the regression formula (M = −.01831) divided by the standard deviation of the deviations from mean predicted gain (SD = .159).

[a] Based on twenty-one children's stories from second-, third-, and fourth-grade readers in each country. [b] Based on six Hindi, seven Telegu, and eight Tamil stories. [c] Based on twelve Urdu and eleven Bengali stories. [d] Based on twenty-one German Swiss stories, mean = .91; twenty-one French Swiss stories, mean = 1.71; over-all mean obtained by weighting German mean double to give approximately proportionate representation to the two main ethnic population groups.

For those who believe in economic determinism, it is especially interesting that n Achievement level in 1950 is *not* correlated either with *previous* economic growth between 1925 and 1950, or with the level of prosperity in 1950. This strongly suggests that n Achievement is a *causative* factor—a change in the minds of men which produces economic growth rather than being produced by it. In a century dominated by economic determinism, in both Communist and Western thought, it is startling to find concrete evidence for psychological determinism, for psychological developments as preceding and presumably causing economic changes.

The many interesting results which our study of children's stories yielded have succeeded in convincing me that we chose the right material to analyze. Apparently, adults unconsciously flavor their stories for young children with the attitudes, the aspirations, the values, and the motives that they hold to be most important.

I want to mention briefly two other findings, one concerned with economic development, the other with totalitarianism. When the more and less rapidly developing economies are compared on all the other variables for which we scored the children's stories, one fact stands out. In stories from those countries which had developed more rapidly in both the earlier and later periods, there was a discernible tendency to emphasize, in 1925 and in 1950, what David Riesman has called "other-directedness"—namely, reliance on the opinion of particular others, rather than on tradition, for guidance in social behavior.[10] *Public opinion* had, in these countries, become a major source of guidance for the individual. Those countries which had developed the mass media further and faster—the press, the radio, the public-address system—were also the ones who were developing more rapidly economically. I think that "other-directedness" helped these countries to develop more rapidly because public opinion is basically more flexible than institutionalized moral or social traditions. Authorities can utilize it to inform people widely about the need for new ways of doings things. However, traditional institutionalized values may insist that people go on behaving in ways that are no longer adaptive to a changed social and economic order.

The other finding is not directly relevant to economic development, but it perhaps involves the means of achieving it. Quite unexpectedly, we discovered that every major dictatorial regime which came to power between the 1920's and 1950's (with the possible exception of Portugal's) was foreshadowed by a particular motive pattern in its stories for children: namely, a low need for affiliation (little interest in friendly relationships with people) and a high need for power (a great concern over controlling and influencing other people).

The German readers showed this pattern before Hitler; the Japanese

[10] David Riesman, with the assistance of Nathan Glazier and Reuel Denney, *The Lonely Crowd* (New Haven, Conn., 1950).

readers, before Tojo; the Argentine readers, before Peron; the Spanish readers, before Franco; the South African readers, before the present authoritarian government in South Africa; etc. On the other hand, very few countries which did not have dictatorships manifested this particular motive combination. The difference was highly significant statistically, since there was only one exception in the first instance and very few in the second. Apparently, we stumbled on a psychological index of ruthlessness—i.e., the need to influence other people (*n* Power), unchecked by sufficient concern for their welfare (*n* Affiliation). It is interesting, and a little disturbing, to discover that the German readers of today still evince this particular combination of motives, just as they did in 1925. Let us hope that this is one case where a social science generalization will not be confirmed by the appearance of a totalitarian regime in Germany in the next ten years.

To return to our main theme—let us discuss the precise ways that higher *n* Achievement leads to more rapid economic development, and why it should lead to economic development rather than, for example, to military or artistic development. We must consider in more detail the mechanism by which the concentration of a particular type of human motive in a population leads to a complex social phenomenon like economic growth. The link between the two social phenomena is, obviously, the business entrepreneur. I am not using the term "entrepreneur" in the sense of "capitalist": in fact, I should like to divorce "entrepreneur" entirely from any connotations of ownership. An entrepreneur is someone who exercises control over production that is not just for his personal consumption. According to my definition, for example, an executive in a steel production unit in Russia is an entrepreneur.

It was Joseph Schumpeter who drew the attention of economists to the importance that the activity of these entrepreneurs had in creating industrialization in the West. Their vigorous endeavors put together firms and created productive units where there had been none before. In the beginning, at least, the entrepreneurs often collected material resources, organized a production unit to combine the resources into a new product, and sold the product. Until recently, nearly all economists—including not only Marx, but also Western classical economists—assumed that these men were moved primarily by the "profit motive." We are all familiar with the Marxian argument that they were so driven by their desire for profits that they exploited the workingman and ultimately forced him to revolt. Recently, economic historians have been studying the actual lives of such entrepreneurs and finding—certainly to the surprise of some of the investigators—that many of them seemingly were not interested in making money as such. In psychological terms, at least, Marx's picture is slightly out of focus. Had these entrepreneurs been above all interested in money, many more of them would have quit working as soon as they had made all the money that they could possibly use. They would not have continued to risk their money in further entrepreneurial ventures. Many of them, in fact, came from pietistic sects, like the Quakers in England, that prohibited the enjoyment of wealth in any of the ways cultivated so successfully by some members of the European nobility. However, the entrepreneurs often seemed consciously to be greatly concerned with expanding their businesses, with getting a greater share of the market, with "conquering brute nature," or even with altruistic schemes for bettering the lot of mankind or bringing about the kingdom of God on earth more rapidly. Such desires have frequently enough been labeled as hypocritical. However, if we assume that these men were really motivated by a desire for achievement rather than by a desire for money as such, the label no longer fits. This assumption also simplifies further matters considerably. It provides an explanation for the fact that these entrepreneurs were interested in money without wanting it for its own sake, namely, that money served as a ready quantitative index of how well they were doing—e.g., of how much they had achieved by their efforts over the past year. The need to achieve can never be satisfied by money; but estimates of profitability in money terms can supply direct knowledge of how well one is doing one's job.

The brief consideration of the lives of business entrepreneurs of the past suggested that their chief motive may well have been a high n Achievement. What evidence have we found in support of this? We made two approaches to the problem. First, we attempted to determine whether individuals with high n Achievement behave like entrepreneurs; and second, we investigated to learn whether actual entrepreneurs, particularly the more successful ones, in a number of countries, have higher n Achievement than do other people of roughly the same status. Of course, we had to establish what we meant by "behave like entrepreneurs"—what precisely distinguishes the way an entrepreneur behaves from the way other people behave?

The adequate answers to these questions would entail a long discussion of the sociology of occupations, involving the distinction originally made by Max Weber between capitalists and bureaucrats. Since this cannot be done here, a very brief report on our extensive investigations in this area will have to suffice. First, one of the defining characteristics of an entrepreneur is *taking risks* and/or innovating. A person who adds up a column of figures is not an entrepreneur—however carefully, efficiently, or correctly he adds them. He is simply following established rules. However, a man who decides to add a new line to his business *is* an entrepreneur, in that he cannot know in advance whether his decision will be correct. Nevertheless, he does not feel that he is in the position of a gambler who places some money on the turn of a card. Knowledge, judgment, and skill enter into his decision-making; and, if his choice is justified by future developments, he can certainly feel a sense of personal achievement from having made a successful move.

Therefore, if people with high *n* Achievement are to behave in an entrepreneurial way, they must seek out and perform in situations in which there is some moderate risk of failure—a risk which can, presumably, be reduced by increased effort or skill. They should not work harder than other people at routine tasks, or perform functions which they are certain to do well simply by doing what everyone accepts as the correct traditional thing to do. On the other hand, they should avoid gambling situations, because, even if they win, they can receive no sense of personal achievement, since it was not skill but luck that produced the results. (And, of course, most of the time they would lose, which would be highly unpleasant to them.) The data on this point are very clear-cut. We have repeatedly found, for example, that boys with high *n* Achievement choose to play games of skill that incorporate a moderate risk of failure. The figure below represents one study. The game was adapted from one used by the psychologist Kurt Lewin. Each child was given a rope ring and told that he could stand at any distance that he preferred from the peg, to try to throw the ring over the peg. The children with high *n* Achievement usually stood at middle distances from the peg, where the chances of success or failure were moderate. However, the children with low *n* Achievement evinced no particular preference for any position. They more frequently stood at extremes of distance—either very close to the peg, where they were sure to throw the ring over it, or very far away, where they were almost certain not to. They thus manifested behavior like that of many people in underdeveloped countries who, while they act very traditionally economically, at the same time love to indulge in lotteries—risking a little to make a great deal on a very long shot. In neither of the two last examples do the actors concentrate on the realistic *calculated* risk, as do the subjects with high *n* Achievement.

We have recently concluded a somewhat analogous study, which indicated that boys with high *n* Achievement tend to perform better and to work harder under conditions of moderate risk—boys not only in the United States, but also in Japan, Brazil, and India. In each of these countries, the boys with high *n* Achievement did not invariably perform a laboratory task better than the boys with low *n* Achievement. They did better only under conditions involving some degree of competition, some risk of doing worse than others or of not getting a sense of personal achievement. There was still another group of boys in the sample from each country. These boys were identified by their optimistic attitude toward life in general, as manifested in their answers to a questionnaire. The members of these groups always had more success than the others, no matter what the competitive or risk situation was. I like to think of these boys as the conscientious ones, who will do their work cheerfully and efficiently under any kind of incentive conditions. They may form the backbone of the civil service, because they can tolerate routine; but they

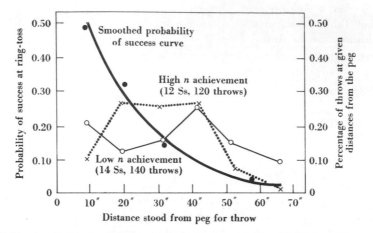

Table 3. *Percentage of throws made by 5-year-olds with high and low
"doodle" n Achievement at different distances from the peg and
smoothed curve of probability of success at those distances.
26 Ss, 10 throws each. Plotted at midpoints of intervals of 11
inches beginning with closest distance stood (4"-14", 5"-15", etc.).*

will not be the business entrepreneurs, because the latter constantly seek
situations in which they can obtain a sense of personal achievement from
having overcome risks or difficulties.

Another quality that the entrepreneur seeks in his work is that his job
be a kind that ordinarily provides him with accurate knowledge of the results of his decisions. As a rule, growth in sales, in output, or in profit
margins tells him very precisely whether he has made the correct choice
under uncertainty or not. Thus, the concern for profit enters in—profit is
a measure of success. We have repeatedly found that boys with a high *n*
Achievement work more efficiently when they know how well they are doing.
Also, they will not work harder for money rewards; but if they are asked,
they state that greater money rewards should be awarded for accomplishing
more difficult things in games of skill. In the ring-toss game, subjects were
asked how much money they thought should be awarded for successful throws
from different distances. Subjects with high *n* Achievement and those with
low *n* Achievement agreed substantially about the amounts for throws made
close to the peg. However, as the distance from the peg increased, the amounts
awarded for successful throws by the subjects with high *n* Achievement rose
more rapidly than did the rewards by those with low *n* Achievement. Here,
as elsewhere, individuals with high *n* Achievement behaved as they must if
they are to be the successful entrepreneurs in society. They believed that
greater achievement should be recognized by quantitatively larger reward.

We are now investigating to learn whether business executives do, in fact, have higher *n* Achievement. Our analysis of this question is not yet finished; but Table 4 indicates what, on the whole, we shall probably find. Four conclusions can be drawn from it. (*1*) Entrepreneurs ("junior executives") have higher *n* Achievement than do a comparable group of non-entrepreneurs ("adjusters"), whose chief job was quasi-judicial (tax claim and insurance adjusters). A very careful study in the General Electric Company has confirmed this finding: on the average, production managers have higher *n* Achievement than do staff specialists of comparable education and pay. (*2*) The more successful junior executives have higher *n* Achievement than the less successful ones. (*3*) Turkish executives have a lower *average* level of *n* Achievement than American executives. This finding supports the general impression that the "entrepreneurial spirit" is in short supply in such countries. (*4*) Nevertheless, the more successful Turkish executives have a higher level of *n* Achievement than do the less successful ones. This confirms our prediction that *n* Achievement equips people peculiarly for the business executive role—even in a country like Turkey, where business traditions are quite different from those of the West.

There are two successful, and one unsuccessful, methods by which the business community recruits people with the "entrepreneurial spirit"—with high *n* Achievement. The unsuccessful way is easiest to describe and is still characteristic of many underdeveloped countries. In a study of the occupational likes and dislikes of boys in Japan, Brazil, Germany, India, and the United States, we found that (as Atkinson had predicted on theoretical grounds) the boys with high *n* Achievement usually aspire toward the occupation of highest prestige *which they have a reasonable chance to enter and to succeed.*[11] For example, their ambitions will be centered on the professions, which are the highest prestige occupations in most countries—*if* the boys themselves are from the upper class and thus have the opportunity and backing to enter the professions. In other words, when the business leadership of a country is largely recruited from the élite (as it is in many countries, because only the élite has access to capital and to government), it will *not* tend to attract those with high *n* Achievement who are not from the upper class.

Developments in many of the Western democracies were quite different. In the most rapidly advancing countries, business leadership was drawn, at least in the early stages, largely from the middle classes. A business career was the highest prestige occupation to which a middle-class boy with high *n* Achievement could aspire—especially if he were a member of a disliked minority group, like the Protestants in France or the Jews in many countries, to whom other channels of upward mobility were closed. Thus a constant

---

[11] J. W. Atkinson, "Motivational Determinants of Risk-Taking Behavior," *Psychological Review*, LXIV (1957), 359–372.

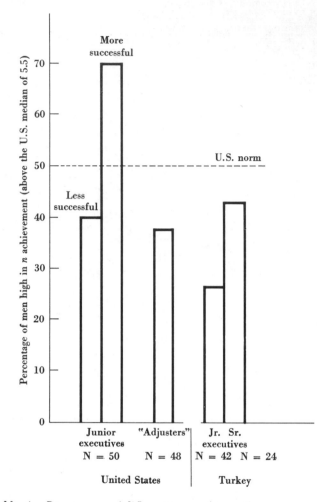

Table 4. *Percentages of different types of executives*
high in Achievement in the U.S.A. and Turkey.
(After data supplied by N. M. Bradburn).

"natural" flow of entrepreneurial talent from the middle classes provided
economic leadership of a high quality.

The other successful method of recruiting entrepreneurial talent is the
one that has been adopted, for example, in the U.S.S.R. There, the central
government took a severe, achievement-oriented, "pass-or-fail" attitude toward its plant managers, so that only the "fittest" survived. We believe that
those "fittest" were the ones with the highest *n* Achievement, although we

have no supporting evidence as yet. In the free enterprise system, the recruiting method may be compared to a garden in which all plants are allowed to grow until some crowd the others out. In the Soviet system, it is comparable to a garden in which plants that have not reached a specified height by a certain time are weeded out. In many underdeveloped countries, it is comparable to a garden where only certain plants are permitted to live in the first place, so that the gardener has to take them whatever size they attain. Of course, no country represents a pure type; but perhaps the analogy, oversimplified though it is, helps to illustrate my point.

What produces high *n* Achievement? Why do some societies produce a large number of people with this motive, while other societies produce so many fewer? We conducted long series of researches into this question. I can present only a few here.

One very important finding is essentially a negative one: *n* Achievement cannot be hereditary. Popular psychology has long maintained that some races are more energetic than others. Our data clearly contradict this in connection with *n* Achievement. The changes in *n* Achievement level within a given population are too rapid to be attributed to heredity. For example, the correlation between respective *n* Achievement levels in the 1925 and 1950 samples of readers is substantially zero. Many of the countries that were high in *n* Achievement at one or both times may be low or moderate in *n* Achievement now, and vice versa. Germany was low in 1925 and is high now; and certainly the hereditary makeup of the German nation has not changed in a generation.

However, there is substantiating evidence that *n* Achievement is a motive which a child can acquire quite early in life, say, by the age of eight or ten, as a result of the way his parents have brought him up. Winterbottom's study of the importance of early self-reliance and achievement training has been supplemented by a much more detailed inquiry by Rosen and D'Andrade.[12] They actually entered the homes of boys with high and low *n* Achievement and observed how the boys were treated by their parents while they were engaged in various kinds of work, e.g., stacking blocks blindfolded. The principal results are summarized in Table 5, which indicates the differences between the parents of the "high *n* Achievement boys" and the parents of boys with low *n* Achievement. In general, the mothers and the fathers of the first group set higher levels of aspiration in a number of tasks for their sons. They were also much warmer, showing positive emotion in reacting to their son's performances. In the area of authority or dominance, the data are quite interesting. The mothers of the "highs" were more domineering than the mothers of the "lows," but the *fathers* of the "highs" were significantly *less* domineering than the fathers of the "lows". In other words, the fathers of the "highs" set

[12] B. C. Rosen and R. G. D'Andrade, "The Psychosocial Origins of Achievement Motivation," *Sociometry*, XXII (1959), 185–218.

Parent behavior

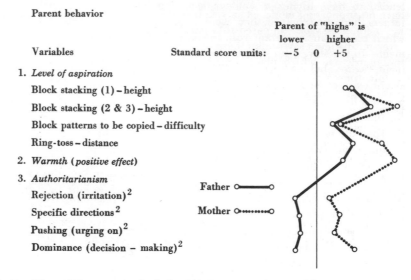

Parent of "highs" is

lower   higher

Variables   Standard score units: −5   0   +5

1. *Level of aspiration*
   Block stacking (1) – height
   Block stacking (2 & 3) – height
   Block patterns to be copied – difficulty
   Ring-toss – distance
2. *Warmth (positive effect)*
3. *Authoritarianism*
   Rejection (irritation)[2]   Father o———o
   Specific directions[2]   Mother o·······o
   Pushing (urging on)[2]
   Dominance (decision – making)[2]

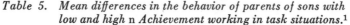

Table 5.   *Mean differences in the behavior of parents of sons with low and high* n *Achievement working in task situations.*[1]

[1] After Rosen and D'Andrade.
[2] Parents of 'highs' predicted to be lower, permitting more independence.

high standards and are warmly interested in their sons' performances, but they do not directly interfere. This gives the boys the chance to develop initiative and self-reliance.

What factors cause parents to behave in this way? Their behavior certainly is involved with their values and, possibly, ultimately with their religion or their general world view. At present, we cannot be sure that Protestant parents are more likely to behave this way than Catholic parents—there are too many subgroup variations within each religious portion of the community: the Lutheran father is probably as likely to be authoritarian as the Catholic father. However, there does seem to be one crucial variable discernible: the extent to which the religion of the family emphasizes individual, as contrasted with ritual, contact with God. The preliterate tribes that we studied in which the religion was the kind that stressed the individual contact had higher *n* Achievement; and in general, mystical sects in which this kind of religious self-reliance dominates have had higher *n* Achievement.

The extent to which the authoritarian father is away from the home while the boy is growing up may prove to be another crucial variable. If so, then one incidental consequence of prolonged wars may be an increase in *n* Achievement, because the fathers are away too much to interfere with their sons' development of it. And in Turkey, Bradburn found that those boys tended to have higher *n* Achievement who had left home early or whose fathers had died before they were eighteen.[13] Slavery was another factor which played an important role in the past. It probably lowered *n* Achievement—in the slaves, for whom obedience and responsibility, but not achievement, were obvious virtues; and in the slave-owners, because household slaves were often disposed to spoil the owner's children as a means for improving their own positions. This is both a plausible and a probable reason for the drop in *n* Achievement level in ancient Greece that occurred at about the time the middle-class entrepreneur was first able to afford, and obtain by conquest, as many as two slaves for each child. The idea also clarifies the slow economic development of the South in the United States by attributing its dilatoriness to a lack of *n* Achievement in its élite; and it also indicates why lower-class American Negroes, who are closest to the slave tradition, possess very low *n* Achievement.[14]

I have outlined our research findings. Do they indicate ways of accelerating economic development? Increasing the level of *n* Achievement in a country suggests itself as an obvious first possibility. If *n* Achievement is so important, so specifically adapted to the business role, then it certainly should be raised in level, so that more young men have an "entrepreneurial drive." The difficulty in this excellent plan is that our studies of how *n* Achievement originates indicate that the family is the key formative influence; and it is very hard to change on a really large scale. To be sure, major historical events like wars have taken authoritarian fathers out of the home; and religious reform movements have sometimes converted the parents to a new achievement-oriented ideology. However, such matters are not ordinarily within the policy-making province of the agencies charged with speeding economic development.

Such agencies can, perhaps, effect the general acceptance of an achievement-oriented ideology as an absolute *sine qua non* of economic development. Furthermore, this ideology should be diffused not only in business and governmental circles, but throughout the nation, and in ways that will influence the thinking of all parents as they bring up their children. As Rosen and D'Andrade found, parents must, above all, set high standards for their children. The campaign to spread achievement-oriented ideology, if possible, could also incorporate an attack on the extreme authoritarianism in fathers that impedes or prevents the development of self-reliance in their sons. This is, however, a more delicate point, and attacking this, in many countries, would be to threaten values at the very center of social life. I believe that a more indirect approach would be more successful. One approach would be

[13] N. M. Bradburn, "The Managerial Role in Turkey" (unpublished Ph.D. dissertation, Harvard University, 1960).

[14] B. C. Rosen, "Race, Ethnicity, and Achievement Syndrome," *American Sociological Review*, XXIV (1959), 47–60.

to take the boys out of the home and to camps. A more significant method would be to promote the rights of women, both legally and socially—one of the ways to undermine the absolute dominance of the male is to strengthen the rights of the female! Another reason for concentrating particularly on women is that they play the leading role in rearing the next generation. Yet, while men in underdeveloped countries come in contact with new achievement-oriented values and standards through their work, women may be left almost untouched by such influences. But if the sons are to have high n Achievement, the mothers must first be reached.

It may seem strange that a paper on economic development should discuss the importance of feminism and the way children are reared; but this is precisely where a psychological analysis leads. If the motives of men are the agents that influence the speed with which the economic machine operates, then the speed can be increased only through affecting the factors that create the motives. Furthermore—to state this point less theoretically—I cannot think of evinced substantial, rapid long-term economic development where women have not been somewhat freed from their traditional setting of "Kinder, Küche and Kirche" and allowed to play a more powerful role in society, specifically as part of the working force. This generalization applies not only to the Western democracies like the United States, Sweden, or England, but also to the U.S.S.R., Japan, and now China.

In the present state of our knowledge, we can conceive of trying to raise n Achievement levels only in the next generation—although new research findings may soon indicate n Achievement in adults can be increased. Most economic planners, while accepting the long-range desirability of raising n Achievement in future generations, want to know what can be done during the next five or ten years. This immediacy inevitably focuses attention on the process or processes by which executives or entrepreneurs are selected. Foreigners with proved entrepreneurial drive can be hired, but at best this is a temporary and unsatisfactory solution. In most underdeveloped countries where government is playing a leading role in promoting economic development, it is clearly necessary for the government to adopt rigid achievement-oriented standards of performance like those in the U.S.S.R.[15] A government manager or, for that matter, a private entrepreneur, should have to produce "or else." Production targets must be set, as they are in most economic plans; and individuals must be held responsible for achieving them, even at the plant level. The philosophy should be one of "no excuses accepted." It is common for government officials or economic theorists in underdeveloped countries to be weighed down by all the difficulties which face the economy and render its rapid development difficult or impossible. They note that there is too rapid population growth, too little capital, too few technically com-

[15] David Granick, *The Red Executive* (New York, 1960).

petent people, etc. Such obstacles to growth are prevalent, and in many cases they are immensely hard to overcome; but talking about them can provide merely a comfortable rationalization for mediocre performance. It is difficult to fire an administrator, no matter how poor his performance, if so many objective reasons exist for his doing badly. Even worse, such rationalization permits, in the private sector, the continued employment of incompetent family members as executives. If these private firms were afraid of being penalized for poor performance, they might be impelled to find more able professional managers a little more quickly. I am not an expert in this field, and the mechanisms I am suggesting may be far from appropriate. Still, they may serve to illustrate my main point: if a country short in entrepreneurial talent wants to advance rapidly, it must find ways and means of insuring that only the most competent retain positions of responsibility. One of the obvious methods of doing so is to judge people in terms of their *performance*—and not according to their family or political connections, their skill in explaining why their unit failed to produce as expected, or their conscientiousness in following the rules. I would suggest the use of psychological tests as a means of selecting people with high n Achievement; but, to be perfectly frank, I think this approach is at present somewhat impractical on a large enough scale in most underdeveloped countries.

Finally, there is another approach which I think is promising for recruiting and developing more competent business leadership. It is the one called, in some circles, the "professionalization of management." Harbison and Myers have recently completed a world-wide survey of the efforts made to develop professional schools of high-level management. They have concluded that, in most countries, progress in this direction is slow.[16] Professional management is important for three reasons. (1) It may endow a business career with higher prestige (as a kind of profession), so that business will attract more of the young men with high n Achievement from the élite groups in backward countries. (2) It stresses *performance* criteria of excellence in the management area—i.e., what a man can do and not what he is. (3) Advanced management schools can themselves be so achievement-oriented in their instruction that they are able to raise the n Achievement of those who attend them.

Applied toward explaining historical events, the results of our researches clearly shift attention away from external factors and to man—in particular, to his motives and values. That about which he thinks and dreams determines what will happen. The emphasis is quite different from the Darwinian or Marxist view of man as a creature who *adapts* to his environment. It is even different from the Freudian view of civilization as the sublimation of man's primitive urges. Civilization, at least in its economic aspects, is neither adapta-

[16] Frederick Harbison and Charles A. Meyers, *Management in the Industrial World* (New York, 1959).

tion nor sublimation; it is a positive creation by a people made dynamic by a high level of *n* Achievement. Nor can we agree with Toynbee, who recognizes the importance of psychological factors as "the very forces which actually decide the issue when an encounter takes place," when he states that these factors "inherently are impossible to weigh and measure, and therefore to estimate scientifically in advance."[17] It is a measure of the pace at which the behavioral sciences are developing that even within Toynbee's lifetime we can demonstrate that he was mistaken. The psychological factor responsible for a civilization's rising to a challenge is so far from being "inherently impossible to weigh and measure" that it has been weighed and measured and scientifically estimated in advance; and, so far as we can now tell, this factor is the achievement motive.

---

[17] Arnold J. Toynbee, *A Study of History* (abridgment by D. C. Somervell; Vol. I; New York, 1947).

REFLECTIONS
ON THE PROTESTANT
ETHIC ANALOGY
IN ASIA

Robert N. Bellah

The work of Max Weber, especially the so-called "Protestant Ethic hypothesis", continues to exercise an impressive influence on current research in the social sciences, as a glance at recent journals and monographs will quickly show.[1] The great bulk of this research is concerned with refining the Weberian thesis about the differential effects of Protestant compared with Catholic religious orientations in the sphere of economic activity. In recent years, however, there have been increasing though still scattered attempts to apply Weber's argument to material drawn from various parts of Asia. The present paper will not undertake to review these attempts with any completeness. Rather it will be devoted to a selective consideration of several different approaches to the problem with a view to determining some of their possibilities and limitations.

Perhaps the commonest approach has been to interpret the Weber hy-

From Robert N. Bellah, "Reflections on the Protestant Ethic Analogy in Asia," *Journal of Social Issues*, 19:1:52–60 (January 1963). Reprinted by permission of The Society for the Psychological Study of Social Issues, Ann Arbor, Mich.

[1] For example the current (April 1962) issue of the *American Sociological Review* contains two articles explicitly claiming to shed light on "the Weberian hypothesis." Among last year's more important books in which the Influence of Weber's work is very evident are Gerhard Lenski's *The Religious Factor*, New York: Doubleday and David C. McClelland's *The Achieving Society*, Princeton, New Jersey: van Nostrand. One might also mention Kurt Samuelson's scurrilous attack *Religion and Economic Action*, New York: Basic Books. That Weber can at this date generate such irrational hostility is in itself a kind of indication of his importance.

pothesis in terms of the economists' emphasis on the importance of entrepreneurship in the process of economic development. Weber's "Protestant
Ethic" is seen as an ideological orientation tending to lead those who hold it
into an entrepreneurial role where they then contribute to economic growth.
We will consider shortly how serious this oversimplification of Weber's view
distorts his intention. At any rate those who have taken this interpretation
have proceeded to analyze various Asian religious groups to see whether
examples of this-wordly asceticism, the religious significance of work in a
calling and so forth have been associated with successful economic activity.
Cases in which the association has been claimed include in Japan Jōdo and
Zen Buddhists, the Hōtoku and Shingaku movements; in Java the Santri
Muslims; in India the Jains, Parsis and various business or merchant castes
and so forth.[2] David C. McClelland has recently subsumed a number of such
examples under the general rubric of "Positive Mysticism" within which he
finds Weber's Protestant example to be merely a special case.[3]

Whether or not the claim to have discovered a religious ethic analogous
to Weber's type case can be substantiated in all of these Asian examples, this
general approach has much to recommend it. For one thing it calls attention

[2] The influence of Jōdo Buddhism and the Hōtoku and Shingaku movements in
Japan was discussed by Robert N. Bellah in *Tokugawa Religion*, Glencoe, Ill.: Free
Press, 1957, Chapter 5. The Zen case in Japan was discussed by David C. McClelland,
op. cit., pp. 369–370 under the mistaken impression that the samurai in the Meiji Period
were devotees of Zen Buddhism. The Santri Muslims of Java were treated by Clifford
Geertz in *The Religion of Java*, Glencoe, Ill.: Free Press, 1960 and more especially in
terms of the present context in "Religious Belief and Economic Behavior in a Central
Javanese Town: Some Preliminary Considerations," *Economic Development and Cultural
Change*, Volume IV, Number 2, 1956. McClelland has discussed the Jains and the Parsis
in *op. cit.*, pp. 368–369 and Milton Singer has discussed several Indian examples in
"Cultural Values in India's Economic Development," *The Annals*, Volume 305, May, 1956,
pp. 81–91. The latter article received further comment from John Goheen, M. N. Srinivas,
D. G. Karve and Mr. Singer in "India's Cultural Values and Economic Development: A
Discussion," *Economic Development and Cultural Change*, Volume VII, Number 1, 1958,
pp. 1-12. Nakamura Hajime in a brief article entitled "The Vitality of Religion in Asia"
which appeared in *Cultural Freedom in Asia*, Herbert Passin, Ed., Rutland, Vt.: Tuttle,
1956, pp. 53–66 argued for the positive influence of a number of Asian religious currents
on economic development. In his more comprehensive *The Ways of Thinking of Eastern
Peoples*, Tokyo: UNESCO, 1959 (An inadequate and partial translation of *Tōyōjin no
Shii Hoho*, Tokyo: Misuzu Shobo, 1949, 2 vols.) Nakamura takes a position very close to
that of Weber. The types of argument put forward in the above very partial rating of
work on this problem are quite various. In particular Clifford Geertz was careful to point
out that the Santri religious ethic seemed suited to a specifically pre-capitalist small
trader mentality which Weber argued was very different from the spirit of capitalism.
This distinction could perhaps be usefully applied to many of the above cases of traditional merchant groups which seem to have some special religious orientation supporting
their occupational motivations.

[3] *Op. cit.*, pp. 367–373, 391.

to the motivational factor which historians, economists and sociologists have often overlooked. For another it calls attention to subtle and non-obvious connections between cultural and religious beliefs and behavioral outcomes. This latter point is one which some readers of Weber have consistently failed to understand, Kurt Samuelson being merely one of the more recent examples. The latter claims in refutation of Weber that since the puritan fathers did not espouse a materialistic dog-eat-dog capitalism their theology could not possibly have led to its development.[4] Milton Singer on the other hand proves himself a more discerning pupil of Weber when he argues that economic development is not supported merely by "materialistic" values but may be advanced by an "ethic of austerity" based perhaps in the case of India on the tradition of religious asceticism.[5]

But the application of the "entrepreneurship model" or motivational approach to Weber's thesis has, I believe, certain grave limitations. Some of the difficulty lies in the original essay itself when it is not grasped in its proper relation to the whole of Weber's work. One of the most serious of these limitations is emphasis on the importance of the motivational factor at the expense of the historical and institutional setting.

However important motivational factors may be they have proven time and again to be highly sensitive to shifts in institutional arrangements. The consequences for economic development depend as much on the institutional channeling of motivation as on the presence or absence of certain kinds of motivation. For example the entrepreneurial potential of the Japanese samurai, who from at least the 16th century comprised what most observers would agree was the most achievement oriented group in Japan, could not be realized until the Meiji period when legal restraints on their entering trade were abolished and their political responsibilities eliminated. Chinese merchants who made an indifferent showing within the institutional limitations of imperial China turned into a vigorous capitalist class under more favorable conditions in Southeast Asia. Clifford Geertz has shown how the Muslim Santri group in Java, characterized by a long merchant tradition and a favorable religious ethic, began to burgeon into entrepreneurship under favorable economic conditions early in this century only to wither on the vine when economic conditions worsened markedly during the great depression.[6] Gustav Papanek in a recent paper has indicated how several relatively small "communities" (quasi-castes) of traditional traders were able to spearhead Pakistan's remarkable industrial growth in recent years by taking

[4] *Op. cit.*, pp. 27–48.

[5] "India's Cultural Values and Economic Development: A Discussion," *Economic Development and Cultural Change*, Volume VII, No. 1 (1958), p. 12.

[6] "The Social Context of Economic Change: An Indonesian Case Study," Center for International Studies (MIT, 1956) (mimeo), pp. 94–119.

advantage of highly favorable economic conditions which had not previously existed.[7] On the basis of such examples one might argue that there exists in most Asian countries a small but significant minority which has the motivation necessary for entrepreneurial activity. If this is the case, then, it would be advisable to consider motivation in close connection with institutional structure and its historical development.

In *The Protestant Ethic and the Spirit of Capitalism,* Weber himself seems to lean rather heavily on the motivational variable and this may be what has led some of his readers astray. In the later comparative studies in the sociology of religion, however, we get a much more balanced view and an implicit correction of emphasis in the earlier work. Following Weber's comparative studies a number of students have undertaken what might be called an "institutional approach", attempting to discern institutional factors favorable or unfavorable to economic development. Examples of this kind of study are Albert Feuerwerker's monograph *China's Early Industrialization,*[8] my *Tokugawa Religion,* about the inadequacies of which I will speak in a moment, Joseph Elder's dissertation on India,[9] and perhaps the most comprehensive in scope and historical coverage, Clifford Geertz's work on Java contained in a number of published and unpublished writings.[10] In all of these studies Weber's emphasis on the religious ethic continues to receive a central focus. It is seen, however, not simply in relation to personal motivation but also as embodied in or related to a wide range of institutional structures. Feuerwerker writes, ". . . one institutional breakthrough is worth a dozen textile mills or shipping companies established within the framework of the traditional society and its system of values."[11] And Geertz says in a similar vein:

> The extent and excellence of a nation's resources, the size and skill of its labor force, the scope and complexity of its productive "plant," and the distribution and value of entrepreneurial abilities among its population are only one element in the assessment of its capacity for economic growth; the institutional arrangements by means of which these various factors can be brought to bear on any particular economic goal is another . . . It is for this reason that economic development in "underdeveloped" areas implies much more than capital transfers, technical aid, and ideological exhortation: it demands a deep going transformation of the basic structure of society and,

[7] "The Development of Entrepreneurship," *The American Economic Review,* Vol. LII, No. 2 (May 1962).

[8] Albert Feuerwerker, *China's Early Industrialization* (Cambridge, Mass.: Harvard University Press, 1958).

[9] Ph.D. Dissertation, Department of Social Relations, Harvard University, Joseph Elder, *Industrialism in Hindu Society: A Case Study in Social Change* (June 1959).

[10] In addition to writings already cited see especially "The Development of the Javanese Economy: A Socio-Cultural Approach," Center for International Studies (MIT, 1956) (mimeo).

[11] *Op. cit.,* p. 242.

beyond that, perhaps even in the underlying value-system in terms of which that structure operates.[12]

My study of Tokugawa Japan taking a somewhat more optimistic approach to traditional society, stressed the extent to which traditional Japanese institutions were or could under certain circumstances be made to be favorable to economic development. In so doing I drew a number of parallels between certain aspects of "rationalization" in Japan and the rationalization Weber was talking about in the West. It was precisely on this point that Maruyama Masao's review on the April 1958 issue of *Kokka Gakkai Zasshi* was sharply critical.[13] Without denying that a number of the mechanisms I discussed, for example the concentration of loyalty in the emperor, may have been effective in bringing about certain social changes contributing to economic growth, he points out that they were far from rational in Weber's sense and indeed had profoundly irrational consequences in subsequent Japanese development, not the least of which were important economic inefficiencies.

With Maruyama's strictures in mind one is perhaps better able to deal with some remarks of Milton Singer near the end of his sensitive and illuminating review article on Weber's *Religion of India:*

> To evaluate Weber's conclusions is not easy. In view of the complexity of Hinduism, and of Asian religions generally, any characterization of them or any comparison of them with Western religion is going to involve large simplifications. Certainly Weber has brilliantly constructed a characterization based on an impressive knowledge of both textual and contextual studies. But one may wonder whether the construction does justice to elements of Asian religions. Some of these are: a strand of this-worldly asceticism; the economic rationality of merchants, craftsmen, and peasants; the logically-consistent system of impersonal determinism in Vedānta and Buddhism, with direct consequences for a secular ethic; the development of "rational empirical" science; religious individualism; and personal monotheism. Weber is certainly aware of all these elements and discusses them in his study. . . . But in the construction of the "Spirit" he does not give very much weight to these elements. With the evidence today before us of politically independent Asian states actively planning their social, economic, and scientific and technical development, we would attach a good deal more importance to these elements and see less conflict between them and the religious "spirit."[14]

For Maruyama the mere *presence* of rational elements for which I argued in the Japanese case along lines quite parallel to those of Singer is simply not enough if they exist passively side by side with irrational elements (as they

---

[12] "The Developments of the Javanese Economy . . . ," pp. 105–106.

[13] *Kokka Gakki Zasshi* (The Journal of the Association of Political and Social Sciences), Vol. LXXII, No. 4 (April 1958), Tokyo.

[14] *American Anthropologist*, Volume 63, No. 1 (1961), p. 150.

do in both Japanese and Indian cases) and are not pushed through "methodically and systematically" to their conclusion as they were in Weber's paradigmatic case of Protestantism. If Maruyama is right, and I am coming increasingly to believe that he is, then it becomes necessary to press beyond both the motivational and the institutional approaches and to view matters in an even broader perspective as the above quote from Geertz already hinted.

Concretely, this means that we are forced to take seriously Weber's argument for the special significance of Protestantism. The search through Asia for religious movements which here and there have motivational or institutional components analogous to the Protestant Ethic ultimately proves inadequate. The Protestant Reformation is not after all some mere special case of a more general category. It stands in Weber's whole work, not in the *Protestant Ethic* essay alone, as the symbolic representation of a fundamental change in social and cultural structure with the most radical and far-reaching consequences. The proper analogy in Asia then turns out to be, not this or that motivational or institutional component, but reformation itself. What we need to discern is the "transformation of the basic structure of society" and its "underlying value-system," to use Geertz's language. Before trying to discover some examples of this structural approach to the Protestant Ethic analogy in Asia it is necessary to note briefly that we see here an example of what must occur in any really serious confrontation with Asian examples: we are forced back to a reconsideration of the European case which provides us so many of the conscious and unconscious categories of our investigation.

The first consideration is that the development in Europe is neither even nor uniform. Developments in different countries and at different times have very different significance. As Reinhard Bendix has so clearly indicated it was Weber's growing discernment of the failure of structural transformation in important sectors of German society which led him to the Protestant Ethic problem.[15] As every reader of the famous essay knows the material is derived from England primarily, and not from Germany where the Reformation remained abortive in important respects and its structural consequences stunted. This is indeed the background for Weber's profound cultural pessimism. Interestingly enough one of the first Japanese to penetrate deeply into the structure of Western culture, Uchimura Kanzō, made a similar diagnosis. Writing in 1898 he said:

> One of the many foolish and deplorable mistakes which the Satsuma-Chōshū Government have committed is their having selected Germany as the example to be followed in their administrative policy. Because its military organization is well-nigh perfect, and its imperialism a gift of its army, therefore they thought that it ought to be taken as the pattern of our own Empire. . . .
> Germany certainly is a great nation, but it is not the greatest, neither is

15 *Max Weber: An Intellectual Portrait* (New York: Doubleday, 1960), Chapter II.

it the most advanced. It is often said that Art, Science, and Philosophy have their homes in Germany, that Thought has its primal spring there. But it is not in Germany that Thought is realized to the fullest extent. Thought may originate in Germany, but it is actualized somewhere else. The Lutheran Reformation bore its best fruit in England and America.[16]

These suggestions about European developments, which must in the present brief paper remain without adequate elaboration, have a further important implication. Germany is certainly one of the most economically developed nations in the world, yet it lagged, according to Weber, in some of the structural transformations which he discovered to be crucial in the development of modern society. Once the crucial breakthroughs have been accomplished it becomes possible for other nations to take some of them over piecemeal without the total structure being transformed. Possible, but at great cost, as the German case indicates.

These considerations bring us back to Maruyama's criticism of my work and the criticism of a number of Japanese intellectuals of American analyses of Japan in general.[17] Japan too, comparatively speaking, is one of the world's most economically advanced nations. Looking at economic growth as our sole criterion, we are inclined to consider Japan as a rather unambiguous success story. But to Japanese intellectuals who feel as acutely as Weber did the failure of modern Japan to carry through certain critical structural transformations which are associated with modern society, the evaluation of Japan's modern history is much more problematic. It would be convenient for social scientists and policy makers if economic growth were an automatic index to successful structural transformation. This does not, however, seem to be the case. Indeed where economic growth is rapid and structural change is blocked, or as in the Communist cases distorted, social instabilities result which under present world conditions are serious enough to have potentially fatal consequences for us all. A broader perspective than has often been taken would seem then to be in order.

As examples of the structural approach, which I believe to be the most adequate application of the Weberian problem to Asia, I may cite again the work of Clifford Geertz on Indonesia and especially a very suggestive recent article on Bali,[18] together with a highly interesting study of recent religious and social developments in Ceylon by Michael Ames.[19] In the Balinese case only the beginnings of the questioning of traditional assumptions are evident and the degree to which rationalization at the value level will have social consequence is not yet clear. In Ceylon Ames documents the existence of

[16] *Uchimura Kanzō Zenshū* (Tokyo: Iwanami Shoten, 1933), Vol. 16, p. 361–362.

[17] Some illuminating remarks on this topic are to be found in John Whitney Hall's "Japan and the Concept of Modernization: Hakone and Aftermath" (Mimeo, 1962).

[18] "Internal Conversion in Contemporary Bali," Mimeo (1961).

[19] "An Outline of Recent Social and Religious Changes in Ceylon," *Human Organization*, forthcoming.

movements of religious reform which have gone far in changing some of the most fundamental assumptions of traditional Buddhism and replacing them with orientations supporting social reform. The degree to which the structural reform itself has gotten under way is not as yet clear. In Japan a century of ideologcal ferment has given rise to a number of tendencies and potentialities which need much more clarification, a problem on which the writer is currently working.[20]

There are indications from a number of Asian countries that traditional elements are being reformulated as part of new nationalist ideologies. Joseph Elder has presented some evidence that the Indian caste ethic is being transformed into a universalistic ethic of occupational responsibility detached from its earlier anchorage in the hereditary caste structure.[21] Such examples would seem to support Singer's argument as quoted above, as indeed in a sense they do. But it should not be forgotten that these reformulations have occurred under Western impact (not infrequently under Protestant Christian impact as Ames shows in Ceylon) and involve fundamental alterations in pattern even when based on traditional material, making them often formally similar to Western paradigms. This is not to imply that Asian cultures are inherently imitative but rather that modern Western societies are not fortuitous cultural sports. Since they represent the earliest versions of a specific structural type of society it is inevitable that Asian societies should in some patterned way come to resemble them as they shift toward that type. Another set of problems arising from the structural approach have to do with the extent to which nationalism or communism can supply the ideological underpinning, the cultural Reformation if you like, for the necessary structural transformations. It is not possible to review here all the work done on these topics, some of which is certainly relevant to the present problem concern.

In conclusion let me say that the whole range of problems having to do with social change in Asia would be greatly illuminated if we had a comprehensive social taxonomy based on evolutionary principles of the sort that Durkheim called for in 1895.[22] Among recent sociologists I can think only of S. N. Eisenstadt as having made significant contributions to this end.[23] With such a taxonomy in hand we would be in a much stronger position to interpret the meaning of the results obtained by those currently concentrating on motivational and institutional research. We might also be in a better position to clear up profound problems both of science and policy which hover around the definition of the concept of modernization.

[20] "Ienaga Saburo and the Search for Meaning in Modern Japan," Mimeo (1962), is the first study concerned with this problem which the writer has completed.

[21] *Op. cit.*

[22] *The Rules of Sociological Method* (Glencoe, Ill.: Free Press, 1950), Chapter 4.

[23] See his *From Generation to Generation* (Glencoe, Ill.: Free Press, 1958), and especially *The Political Systems of Empires*, Free Press, 1963.

THE TAKE-OFF
INTO SELF-SUSTAINED
GROWTH[1]

W. W. Rostow

I

The purpose of this article is to explore the following hypothesis: that the process of economic growth can usefully be regarded as centering on a relatively brief time interval of two or three decades when the economy and the society of which it is a part transform themselves in such ways that economic growth is, subsequently, more or less automatic. This decisive transformation is here called the take-off.[2]

The take-off is defined as the interval during which the rate of investment increases in such a way that real output *per capita* rises and this initial increase carries with it radical changes in production techniques and the disposition of income flows which perpetuate the new scale of investment and perpetuate thereby the rising trend in *per capita* output. Initial changes in

From W. W. Rostow, "The Take-Off into Self-Sustained Growth," *The Economic Journal*, 66:261:33–48 (March 1956). Reprinted by permission of the Royal Economic Society, Cambridge, England.

[1] I wish to acknowledge with thanks the helpful criticisms of an earlier draft by G. Baldwin, F. Bator, K. Berrill, A. Enthoven, E. E. Hagen, C. P. Kindleberger, L. Lefeber, W. Malenbaum, E. S. Mason and M. F. Millikan.

[2] This argument is a development from the line of thought presented in *The Process of Economic Growth* (New York, 1952), Chapter 4, especially pp. 102–5. The concept of three stages in the growth process centering on the take-off is defined and used for prescriptive purposes in *An American Policy in Asia* (New York, 1955), Chapter 7.

method require that some group in the society have the will and the authority to install and diffuse new production techniques;[3] and a perpetuation of the growth process requires that such a leading group expand in authority and that the society as a whole respond to the impulses set up by the initial changes, including the potentialities for external economies. Initial changes in the scale and direction of finance flows are likely to imply a command over income flows by new groups or institutions; and a perpetuation of growth requires that a high proportion of the increment to real income during the take-off period be returned to productive investment. The take-off requires, therefore, a society prepared to respond actively to new possibilities for productive enterprise; and it is likely to require political, social and institutional changes which will both perpetuate an initial increase in the scale of investment and result in the regular acceptance and absorption of innovations.

In short, this article is an effort to clarify the economics of industrial revolution when an industrial revolution is conceived of narrowly with respect to time and broadly with respect to changes in production functions.

1. *A* Prima Facie *Case*

If we take the aggregate marginal capital–output ratio for an economy in its early stage of economic development at 3.5–1 and if we assume, as is not abnormal, a population rise of 1–1.5% per annum it is clear that something between 3.5 and 5.25% of NNP must be regularly invested if NNP *per capita* is to be sustained. An increase of 2% per annum in NNP *per capita* requires, under these assumptions, that something between 10.5 and 12.5% of NNP be regularly invested. By definition and assumption, then, a transition from relatively stagnant to substantial, regular rise in NNP *per capita*, under typical population conditions, requires that the proportion of national product productively invested move from somewhere in the vicinity of 5% to something in the vicinity of 10%.

[3] We shall set aside in this article the question of how new production techniques are generated from pure science and invention, a procedure which is legitimate, since we are examining the growth process in national (or regional) economies over relatively short periods. We shall largely set aside also the question of population pressure and the size and quality of the working force, again because of the short period under examination; although, evidently, even over short periods, the rate of population increase will help determine the level of investment required to yield rising output *per capita*. . . . By and large, this article is concerned with capital formation at a particular stage of economic growth; and of the array of propensities defined in *The Process of Economic Growth* it deals only with the propensity to accept innovations and the propensity to seek material advance, the latter in relation to the supply of finance only.

2. *The Swedish Case*

In the appendix to his paper on international differences in capital formation, Kuznets gives gross and net capital formation figures in relation to gross and net national product for a substantial group of countries where reasonably good statistical data exist. Excepting Sweden, these data do not go back clearly to pretake-off stages.[4] The Swedish data begin in the decade 1861–70; and the Swedish take-off is to be dated from the latter years of the decade.

Kuznets' table of calculations for Sweden follows:

Decade	Domestic GCF GNP (%)	Domestic NCF NNP (%)	Depreciation to DGCF (%)
1. 1861–70	5.8	3.5—	(42)
2. 1871–80	8.8	5.3	(42)
3. 1881–90	10.8	6.6	(42)
4. 1891–1900	13.7	8.1	43.9
5. 1901–10	18.0	11.6	40.0
6. 1911–20	20.2	13.5	38.3
7. 1921–30	19.0	11.4	45.2

Note (Kuznets): Based on estimates in Eric Lindahl, Einar Dahlgren and Karin Kock, *National Income of Sweden, 1861–1930* (London: P. J. Kingston, 1937), Parts One and Two, particularly the details in Part Two.

These underlying totals of capital formation exclude changes in inventories.

While gross totals are directly from the volumes referred to above, depreciation for the first three decades was not given. We assumed that it formed 42% of gross domestic capital formation.

[4] The Danish data are on the margin. They begin with the decade 1870–79, probably the first decade of take-off itself. They show net and gross domestic capital formation rates well over 10%. In view of the sketch of the Danish economy presented in Kjeld Bjerke's "Preliminary Estimates of the Danish National Product from 1870–1950" (Preliminary paper mimeographed for 1953 Conference of the International Association for Research on Income and Wealth), pp. 32–4, it seems likely that further research would identify the years 1830–70 as a period when the preconditions were actively established, 1870–1900 as a period of take-off. This view is supported by scattered and highly approximate estimates of Danish National Wealth which exhibit a remarkable surge in capital formation between 1864 and 1884.

Estimates of National Wealth in Denmark

	1,000 millions of kroner.	Source.
1864	3.5	Falbe-Hansen, *Danmarks statistik*, 1885.
1884	6.5	Falbe-Hansen, *Danmarks statistik*, 1885.
1899	7.2	Tax-commission of 1903.
1909	10.0	Jens Warming, *Danmarks statistik*, 1913.
1927	24.0	Jens Warming, *Danmarks erhvervs- or samfundsliv*, 1930.

3. *The Canadian Case*

The data developed by O. J. Firestone[5] for Canada indicate a similar transition for net capital formation in its take-off (say, 1896–1914); but the gross investment proportion in the period from Confederation to the mid-nineties was higher than appears to have marked other periods when the preconditions were established, possibly due to investment in the railway net, abnormally large for a nation of Canada's population, and to relatively heavy foreign investment, even before the great capital import boom of the pre-1914 decade:

Canada: Gross and Net Investment in Durable Physical Assets as Percentage of Gross and Net National Expenditure (for Selected Years).

	GCF GNP	NCF NNP	Capital consumption as percentage of gross investment.
1870	15.0	7.1	56.2
1900	13.1	4.0	72.5
1920	16.6	10.6	41.3
1929	23.0	12.1	53.3
1952	16.8	9.3	49.7

4. *The Pattern of Contemporary Evidence in General*[6]

In the years after 1945 the number of countries for which reasonably respectable national income (or product) data exist has

| 1939 | 28.8 | Economic expert committee of 1943 *Økonomiske efterkrigsproblemer*, 1945. |
| 1950 | 54.5 | N. Banke, N. P. Jacobsen og Vedel-Petersen, *Danske erhvervsliv*, 1951. |

(Furnished in correspondence by Einar Cohn and Kjeld Bjerke.) It should again be emphasised, however, that we are dealing with a hypothesis whose empirical foundations are still fragmentary.

[5] O. J. Firestone, *Canada's Economic Development, 1867–1952, with Special Reference to Changes in the Country's National Product and National Wealth*, paper prepared for the International Association for Research in Income and Wealth, 1953, to which Mr. Firestone has kindly furnished me certain revisions, shortly to be published. By 1900 Canada already had about 18,000 miles of railway line; but the territory served had been developed to a limited degree only. By 1900 Canada already had a net balance of foreign indebtedness over $1 billion. Although this figure was almost quadrupled in the next two decades, capital imports represented an important increment to domestic capital sources from the period of Confederation down to the pre-1914 Canadian boom, which begins in the mid-1890s.

[6] I am indebted to Mr. Everett Hagen for mobilising the statistical data in this section, except where otherwise indicated.

grown; and with such data there have developed some tolerable savings and investment estimates for countries at different stages of the growth process. Within the category of nations usually grouped as "underdeveloped" one can distinguish four types.[7]

(*a*) *Pretake-off economies*, where the apparent savings and investment rates, including limited net capital imports, probably come to under 5% of net national product. In general, data for such countries are not satisfactory, and one's judgment that capital formation is low must rest on fragmentary data and partially subjective judgment. Examples are Ethiopia, Kenya, Thailand, Cambodia, Afghanistan and perhaps Indonesia.[8]

(*b*) *Economies attempting take-off*, where the apparent savings and investment rates, including limited net capital imports, have risen over 5% of net national product.[9] For example, Mexico (1950) NCF/NDP 7.2%; Chile (1950) NCF/NDP 9.5%; Panama (1950) NCF/NDP 7.5%; Philippines (1952) NCF/NDP 6.4%; Puerto Rico (1952) NCF (Private)/NDP 7.6%; India (1953) NCF/NDP, perhaps about 7%. Whether the take-off period will, in fact, be successful remains in most of these cases still to be seen.

(*c*) *Growing economies*, where the apparent savings and investment rates, including limited net capital imports, have reached 10% or over; for example, Colombia (1950) NCF/NDP, 16.3%.

[7] The percentages given are of net capital formation to net domestic product. The latter is the produce net of depreciation of the geographic area. It includes the value of output produced in the area, regardless of whether the income flows abroad. Since indirect business taxes are not deducted, it tends to be larger than national income; hence the percentages are lower than if national income was used as the denominator in computing them.

[8] The Office of Intelligence Research of the Department of State, Washington, D.C., gives the following estimated ratios of investment (presumably gross) to GNP in its Report No. 6672 of August 25, 1954, p. 3, based on latest data available to that point, for countries which would probably fall in the pretake-off category:

	%		%
Afghanistan	5	Pakistan	6
Ceylon	5	Indonesia	5

[9] The Department of State estimates (*ibid.*) for economies which are either attempting takeoff or which have, perhaps, passed into a stage of regular growth include:

	%		%
The Argentine	13	Colombia	14
Brazil	14	Philippines	8
Chile	11	Venezuela	23

Venezuela has been for some time an "enclave economy," with a high investment rate concentrated in a modern export sector whose growth did not generate general economic momentum in the Venezuelan economy; but in the past few years Venezuela may have moved over into the category of economies experiencing an authentic take-off.

(*d*) *Enclave economies* (1) cases where the apparent savings and investment rates, including substantial net capital imports, have reached 10% or over, but the domestic preconditions for sustained growth have not been achieved. These economies, associated with major export industries, lack the third condition for take-off suggested above. . . . They include the Belgian Congo (1951) NCF/NDP 21.7%; Southern Rhodesia (1950) GCF/GDP 45.5%, (1952) GCF/GDP 45.4%. (2) Cases where net capital exports are large. For example, Burma (1938) NCF/NDP, 7.1%; net capital exports/NDP, 11.5%; Nigeria (1950–51) NCF/NDP 5.1%; net capital exports/NDP, 5.6%.

5. *The Cases of India and Communist China*

The two outstanding contemporary cases of economies attempting purposefully to take-off are India and Communist China, both operating under national plans. The Indian First Five Year Plan projects the growth process envisaged under assumptions similar to those in paragraph 1, p. 34, above. The Indian Planning Commission estimated investment as 5% of NNP in the initial year of the plan, 1950–51.[10] Using a 3/1 marginal capital–output ratio, they envisaged a marginal savings rate of 20% for the First Five Year Plan, a 50% rate thereafter, down to 1968–69, when the average proportion of income invested would level off at 20% of NNP. As one would expect, the sectoral composition of this process is not fully worked out in the initial plan; but the Indian effort may well be remembered in economic history as the first take-off defined *ex ante* in national product terms.

We know less of the Chinese Communist First Five Year Plan than we do of the concurrent Indian effort, despite the recent publication of production goals for some of the major sectors of the Chinese economy.[11] Roundly, it would appear that, from a (probably) negative investment rate in 1949, the Chinese Communist regime had succeeded by 1952 in achieving a gross rate of about 12%; a net rate of about 7%.

On arbitrary assumptions, which have a distinct upward bias, these figures can be projected forward for a decade yielding rates of about 20% gross, 17% net by 1962.

So far as the aggregates are concerned, what we can say is that the Indian planned figures fall well within the range of *prima facie* hypothesis and historical experience, if India in fact fulfils the full requirements for take-off, notably the achievement of industrial momentum. The Chinese Communist

[10] Government of India, Planning Commission, *The First Five Year Plan* (1952), Vol. I, Chapter 1.
[11] These comments are based on the work of Alexander Eckstein and the author in *The Prospects for Communist China* (New York and London, 1954), Part 5, pp. 222 ff. The statistical calculations are the work of Mr. Eckstein.

figures reflect accurately an attempt to force the pace of history, evident throughout Peking's domestic policy, whose viability is still to be demonstrated. In particular, Peking's agricultural policy may fail to produce the minimum structural balance required for a successful take-off, requiring radical revision of investment allocations and policy objectives at a later stage.

We have, evidently, much still to learn about the quantitative aspects of this problem; and, especially, much further quantitative research and imaginative manipulation of historical evidence will be required before the hypothesis tentatively advanced here can be regarded as proved or disproved. What we can say is that *prima facie* thought and a scattering of historical and contemporary evidence suggests that it is not unreasonable to consider the take-off as including as a necessary but not sufficient condition a quantitative transition in the proportion of income productively invested of the kind indicated here.

II. THE INNER STRUCTURE OF THE TAKE-OFF

Whatever the importance and virtue of viewing the take-off in aggregative terms—embracing national output, the proportion of output invested, and an aggregate marginal capital–output ratio—that approach tells us relatively little of what actually happens and of the causal processes at work in a take-off; nor is the investment-rate criterion conclusive.

Following the definition of take-off . . . we must consider not merely how a rise in the investment rate is brought about, from both supply and demand perspectives, but how rapidly growing manufacturing sectors emerged and imparted their primary and secondary growth impulses to the economy.

Perhaps the most important thing to be said about the behavior of these variables in historical cases of take-off is that they have assumed many different forms. There is no single pattern. The rate and productivity of investment can rise, and the consequences of this rise can be diffused into a self-reinforcing general growth process by many different technical and economic routes, under the ægis of many different political, social and cultural settings, driven along by a wide variety of human motivations.

The purpose of the following paragraphs is to suggest briefly, and by way of illustration only, certain elements of both uniformity and variety in the variables whose movement has determined the inner structure of the take-off.

1. *The Supply of Loanable Funds*

By and large, the loanable funds required to finance the take-off have come from two types of sources: from shifts in the control over income flows, including income-distribution changes and capital imports;[12] and from the plough-back of profits in rapidly expanding particular sectors.

The notion of economic development occurring as the result of income shifts from those who will spend (hoard[13] or lend) less productively to those who will spend (or lend) more productively is one of the oldest and most fundamental notions in economics. It is basic to the *Wealth of Nations*,[14] and it is applied by W. Arthur Lewis in his recent elaboration of the classical model.[15] Lewis builds his model in part on an expansion of the capitalist sector, with the bulk of additional savings arising from an enlarging pool of capitalist profits.

Historically, income shifts conducive to economic development have assumed many forms. In Meiji Japan and also in Czarist Russia the substitution of government bonds for the great landholders' claim on the flow of rent payments lead to a highly Smithian redistribution of income into the hands of those with higher propensities to seek material advance and to accept innovations. In both cases the real value of the government bonds exchanged for land depreciated; and, in general, the feudal landlords emerged with a less attractive arrangement than had first appeared to be offered. Aside from the confiscation effect, two positive impulses arose from land reform: the state itself used the flow of payments from peasants, now diverted from landlords' hands, for activity which encouraged economic development; and a certain number of the more enterprising former landlords directly invested in commerce and industry. In contemporary India and China we can observe quite different degrees of income transfer by this route. India is relying to only a very limited extent on the elimination of large incomes unproductively spent by large landlords; although this element figures in a small way in its program. Communist China has systematically transferred all non-governmental pools of capital into the hands of the State, in a series of undisguised or barely disguised capital levies; and it is drawing heavily for capital resources on the mass of middle and poor peasants who remain.[16]

In addition to confiscatory and taxation devices, which can operate

12 Mr. Everett Hagen has pointed out that the increase in savings may well arise from a shift in the propensity to save, as new and exciting horizons open up, rather than merely from a shift of income to groups with a higher (but static) propensity to save. He may well be right. This is, evidently, a matter for further investigation.

13 Hoarding can, of course, be helpful to the growth process by depressing consumption and freeing resources for investment if, in fact, non-hoarding persons or institutions acquire the resources and possess the will to expand productive investment. A direct transfer of income is, evidently, not required.

14 See, especially, Smith's observations on the "perversion" of wealth by "prodigality" —that is, unproductive consumption expenditures—and on the virtues of "parsimony" which transfers income to those who will increase "the fund which is destined for the maintenance of productive hands." (Routledge edition, London, 1890), pp. 259–60.

15 *Op. cit.*, especially pp. 156–9.

16 *Prospects for Communist China*, Part 4.

effectively when the State is spending more productively than the taxed individuals, inflation has been important to several take-offs. In Britain of the late 1790s, the United States of the 1850s, Japan of the 1870s there is no doubt that capital formation was aided by price inflation, which shifted resources away from consumption to profits.

The shift of income flows into more productive hands has, of course, been aided historically not only by government fiscal measures but also by banks and capital markets. Virtually without exception, the take-off periods have been marked by the extension of banking institutions which expanded the supply of loanable funds, may be the decisive element in the take-off, as op- range of long-range financing done by a central, formally organised, capital market.

Although these familiar capital-supply functions of the State and private institutions have been important to the take-off, it is likely to prove the case, on close examination, that a necessary condition for take-off was the exist- ence of one or more rapidly growing sectors whose entrepreneurs (private or public) ploughed back into new capacity a very high proportion of profits. Put another way, the demand side of the investment process, rather than the supply of loanable funds, may be the decisive element in the take-off, as op- posed to the period of creating the preconditions, or of sustaining growth once it is under way. The distinction is, historically, sometimes difficult to make, notably when the State simultaneously acts both to mobilise supplies of finance and to undertake major entrepreneurial acts. There are, nevertheless, periods in economic history when quite substantial improvements in the machinery of capital supply do not, in themselves, initiate a take-off, but fall within the period when the preconditions are created: *e.g.*, British banking developments in the century before 1783; Russian banking developments before 1890, etc.

One extremely important version of the plough-back process has taken place through foreign trade. Developing economies have created from their natural resources major export industries; and the rapid expansion in ex- ports has been used to finance the import of capital equipment and to service the foreign debt during the take-off. United States, Russian and Canadian grain fulfilled this function, Swedish timber and pulp, Japanese silk, etc. Currently Chinese exports to the Communist Bloc, wrung at great adminis- trative and human cost from the agricultural sector, play this decisive role. It should be noted that the development of such export sectors has not in itself guaranteed accelerated capital formation. Enlarged foreign-exchange proceeds have been used in many familiar cases to finance hoards (as in the famous case of Indian bullion imports) or unproductive consumption outlays.

It should be noted that one possible mechanism for inducing a high rate of plough-back into productive investment is a rapid expansion in the effec- tive demand for domestically manufactured consumers' goods, which would direct into the hands of vigorous entrepreneurs an increasing proportion of income flows under circumstances which would lead them to expand their own capacity and to increase their requirements for industrial raw materials, semi-manufactured products and manufactured components.

A final element in the supply of loanable funds is, of course, capital imports. Foreign capital has played a major role in the take-off stage of many economies: e.g., the United States, Russia, Sweden, Canada. The cases of Britain and Japan indicate, however, that it cannot be regarded as an essential condition. Foreign capital was notably useful when the construction of railways or other large overhead capital items with a long period of gestation, played an important role in the take-off. After all, whatever its strategic role, the proportion of investment required for growth which goes into industry is relatively small compared to that required for utilities, transport and the housing of enlarged urban populations. And foreign capital can be mightily useful in helping carry the burden of these overhead items either directly or indirectly.

What can we say, in general, then, about the supply of finance during the take-off period? First, as a precondition, it appears necessary that the community's surplus above the mass-consumption level does not flow into the hands of those who will sterilise it by hoarding, luxury consumption or low-productivity investment outlays. Second, as a precondition, it appears necessary that institutions be developed which provide cheap and adequate working capital. Third, as a necessary condition, it appears that one or more sectors of the economy must grow rapidly, inducing a more general industrialisation process; and that the entrepreneurs in such sectors plough back a substantial proportion of their profits in further productive investment, one possible and recurrent version of the plough-back process being the investment of proceeds from a rapidly growing export sector.

The devices, confiscatory and fiscal, for ensuring the first and second preconditions have been historically various. And, as indicated below, the types of leading manufacturing sectors which have served to initiate the take-off have varied greatly. Finally, foreign capital flows have, in significant cases, proved extremely important to the take-off, notably when lumpy overhead capital construction of long gestation period was required; but take-offs have also occurred based almost wholly on domestic sources of finance.

2. The Sources of Entrepreneurship

It is evident that the take-off requires the existence and the successful activity of some group in the society which accepts borrowers' risk, when such risk is so defined as to include the propensity to accept innovations. As noted above, the problem of entrepreneurship in the take-off has not been profound in a limited group of wealthy agricultural nations whose populations derived by emigration mainly from north-western Europe. There the problem of take-off was primarily economic; and when economic incentives for industrialisation emerged commercial and banking groups moved over easily into industrial entrepreneurship. In many other countries, however, the development of adequate entrepreneurship was a more searching social process.

Under some human motivation or other, a group must come to perceive it to be both possible and good to undertake acts of capital investment; and, for their efforts to be tolerably successful, they must act with approximate rationality in selecting the directions toward which their enterprise is directed. They must not only produce growth but tolerably balanced growth. We cannot quite say that it is necessary for them to act as if they were trying to maximise profit; for the criteria for private profit maximisation do not necessarily converge with the criteria for an optimum rate and pattern of growth in various sectors.[17] But in a growing economy, over periods longer than the business cycle, economic history is reasonably tolerant of deviations from rationality, in the sense that excess capacity is finally put to productive use. Leaving aside the question of ultimate human motivation, and assuming that the major overhead items are generated, if necessary, by some form of state initiative (including subsidy), we can say as a first approximation that some group must sucessfully emerge which behaves as if it were moved by the profit motive, in a dynamic economy with changing production functions; although risk being the slippery variable, it is under such assumptions Keynes' dictum should be borne in mind: "If human nature felt not temptation to take a chance, no satisfaction (profit apart) in constructing a factory, a railway, a mine or a farm, there might not be much investment merely as a result of cold calculation."[18]

In this connection it is increasingly conventional for economists to pay their respects to the Protestant ethic.[19] The historian should not be ungrateful for this light on the grey horizon of formal growth models. But the known cases of economic growth which theory must seek to explain take us beyond the orbit of Protestantism. In a world where Samurai, Parsees, Jews, North Italians, Turkish, Russian, and Chinese Civil Servants (as well as Huguenots, Scotsmen and British North-countrymen) have played the role of a leading *élite* in economic growth John Calvin should not be made

[17] For a brief discussion of this point see the author's "Trends in the Allocation of Resources in Secular Growth," Chapter 15, *Economic Progress*, ed. Leon H. Dupriez, with the assistance of Douglas C. Hague (Louvain, 1955), pp. 378–9. For a more complete discussion see W. Fellner, "Individual Investment Projects in Growing Economies" (mimeographed), paper presented to the Center for International Studies Social Science Research Council Conference on Economic Growth (October 1954), Cambridge, Massachusetts.

[18] *General Theory*, p. 150.

[19] See, for example, N. Kaldor, "Economic Growth and Cyclical Fluctuations," *Economic Journal* (March 1954), p. 67.

to bear quite this weight. More fundamentally, allusion to a positive scale of religious or other values conducive to profit-maximising activities is an insufficient sociological basis for this important phenomenon. What appears to be required for the emergence of such *élites* is not merely an appropriate value system but two further conditions: first, the new *élite* must feel itself denied the conventional routes to prestige and power by the traditional less acquisitive society of which it is a part; second, the traditional society must be sufficiently flexible (or weak) to permit its members to seek material advance (or political power) as a route upwards alternative to conformity.

Although an *élite* entrepreneurial class appears to be required for take-off, with significant power over aggregate income flows and industrial investment decisions, most take-offs have been preceded or accompanied by radical change in agricultural techniques and market organisation. By and large the agricultural entrepreneur has been the individual land-owning farmer. A requirement for take-off is, therefore, a class of farmers willing and able to respond to the possibilities opened up for them by new techniques, land-holding arrangements, transport facilities, and forms of market and credit organisation. A small purposeful *élite* can go a long way in initiating economic growth; but, especially in agriculture (and to some extent in the industrial working force), a wider-based revolution in outlook must come about.[20]

Whatever further empirical research may reveal about the motives which have led men to undertake the constructive entrepreneurial acts of the take-off period, this much appears sure: these motives have varied greatly, from one society to another; and they have rarely, if ever, been motives of an unmixed material character.

3. *Leading Sectors in the Take-off*

The author has presented elsewhere the notion that the overall rate of growth of an economy must be regarded in the first instance as the consequence of differing growth rates in

[20] Like the population question, agriculture is mainly excluded from this analysis, which considers the take-off rather than the whole development process. Nevertheless, it should be noted that, as a matter of history, agricultural revolutions have generally preceded or accompanied the take-off. In theory we can envisage a take-off which did not require a radical improvement in agricultural productivity: if, for example, the growth and productivity of the industrial sector permitted a withering away of traditional agriculture and a substitution for it of imports. In fact, agricultural revolutions have been required to permit rapidly growing (and urbanizing) populations to be fed without exhausting foreign exchange resources in food imports or creating excessive hunger in the rural sector; and as noted at several points in this argument, agricultural revolutions have in fact played an essential and positive role, not merely by both releasing workers to the cities, and feeding them, but also by earning foreign exchange for general capital-formation purposes.

particular sectors of the economy, such sectoral growth rates being in part derived from certain overall demand parameters (*e.g.*, population, consumers' income, tastes, etc.), in part from the primary and secondary effects of changing supply factors, when these are effectively exploited.[21]

On this view the sectors of an economy may be grouped in three categories:

(*a*) *Primary growth sectors,* where possibilities for innovation or for the exploitation of newly profitable or hitherto unexplored resources yield a high growth rate and set in motion expansionary forces elsewhere in the economy.

(*b*) *Supplementary growth sectors,* where rapid advance occurs in direct response to—or as a requirement of—advance in the primary growth sectors; *e.g.*, coal, iron and engineering in relation to railroads. These sectors may have to be tracked many stages back into the economy, as the Leontief input–output models would suggest.

(*c*) *Derived growth sectors,* where advance occurs in some fairly steady relation to the growth of total real income, population, industrial production or some other overall, modestly increasing parameter. Food output in relation to population, housing in relation to family formation are classic derived relations of this order.

Very roughly speaking, primary and supplementary growth sectors derive their high momentum essentially from the introduction and diffusion of changes in the cost–supply environment (in turn, of course, partially influenced by demand changes); while the derived-growth sectors are linked essentially to changes in demand (while subject also to continuing changes in production functions of a less dramatic character).

At any period of time it appears to be true even in a mature and growing economy that forward momentum is maintained as the result of rapid expansion in a limited number of primary sectors, whose expansion has significant external economy and other secondary effects. From this perspective the behaviour of sectors during the take-off is merely a special version of the growth process in general; or, put another way, growth proceeds by repeating endlessly, in different patterns, with different leadings sectors, the experience of the take-off. Like the take-off, long-term growth requires that the society not only generate vast quantities of capital for depreciation and maintenance, for housing and for a balanced complement of utilities and other overheads, but also a sequence of highly productive primary sectors, growing rapidly, based on new production functions. Only thus has the aggregate marginal capital–output ratio been kept low.

---

[21] *Process of Economic Growth,* Chapter 4, especially pp. 97–102; and, in greater detail, "Trends in the Allocation of Resources in Secular Growth," see above, p. 41, n. 1.

Once again history is full of variety: a considerable array of sectors appears to have played this key role in the take-off process.

The development of a cotton-textile industry sufficient to meet domestic requirements has not generally imparted a sufficient impulse in itself to launch a self-sustaining growth process. The development of modern cotton-textile industries in substitution for imports has, more typically, marked the pretake-off period, as for example in India, China and Mexico.

There is, however, the famous exception of Britain's industrial revolution. Baines' table on raw-cotton imports and his comment on it are worth quoting, covering as they do the original leading sector in the first take-off:[22]

Rate of Increase in the Import of Cotton-wool, in Periods of Ten Years from 1741–1831

	%		%
1741–1751	81	1791–1801	67½
1751–1761	21½	1801–1811	39½
1761–1771	25½	1811–1821	93
1771–1781	75¾	1821–1831	85
1781–1791	319½		

From 1697 to 1741, the increase was trifling; between 1741 and 1751 the manufacture, though still insignificant in extent, made a considerable spring; during the next twenty years, the increase was moderate; from 1771 to 1781, owing to the invention of the jenny and the water-frame, a rapid increase took place; in the ten years from 1781 to 1791, being those which immediately followed the invention of the mule and the expiration of Arkwright's patent, the rate of advancement was prodigiously accelerated, being nearly 320%; and from that time to the present, and especially since the close of the war, the increase, though considerably moderated, has been rapid and steady far beyond all precedent in any other manufacture.

Why did the development of a modern factory system in cotton textiles lead on in Britain to a self-sustaining growth process, whereas it failed to do so in other cases? Part of the answer lies in the fact that, by the late eighteenth century, the preconditions for take-off in Britain were very fully developed. Progress in textiles, coal, iron and even steam power had been considerable through the eighteenth century; and the social and institutional environment was propitious. But two further technical elements helped determine the upshot. First, the British cotton-textile industry was large in relation to the total size of the economy. From its modern beginnings, but notably from the 1780s forward, a very high proportion of total cotton-textile output was directed abroad, reaching 60% by the 1820s.[23] The evolution of this

[22] E. Baines, *History of the Cotton Manufacture* (London, 1835), p. 348.

[23] The volume (official value) of British cotton goods exports rose from £355,060 in 1780 to £7,624,505 in 1802 (Baines, *op. cit.*, p. 350). See also the calculation of R. C. O. Matthews, *A Study in Trade Cycle History* (Cambridge, 1954), pp. 127–9.

industry was a more massive fact, with wider secondary repercussions, than if it were simply supplying the domestic market. Industrial enterprise on this scale had secondary reactions on the development of urban areas, the demand for coal, iron and machinery, the demand for working capital and ultimately the demand for cheap transport, which powerfully stimulated industrial development in other directions.[24]

Second, a source of effective demand for rapid expansion in British cotton textiles was supplied, in the first instance, by the sharp reduction in real costs and prices which accompanied the technological developments in manufacture and the cheapening real cost of raw cotton induced by the cotton gin. In this Britain had an advantage not enjoyed by those who came later; for they merely substituted domestic for foreign-manufactured cotton textiles. The substitution undoubtedly had important secondary effects by introducing a modern industrial sector and releasing in net a pool of foreign exchange for other purposes; but there was no sharp fall in the real cost of acquiring cotton textiles and no equivalent lift in real income.

The introduction of the railroad has been historically the most powerful single initiator of take-offs.[25] It was decisive in the United States, Germany and Russia; it has played an extremely important part in the Swedish, Japanese and other cases. The railroad has had three major kinds of impact on economic growth during the take-off period. First, it has lowered internal transport costs, brought new areas and products into commercial markets and, in general, performed the Smithian function of widening the market. Second, it has been a prerequisite in many cases to the development of a major new and rapidly enlarging export sector which, in turn, has served to generate capital for internal development; as, for example, the American railroads of the 1850s, the Russian and Canadian railways before 1914. Third, and perhaps most important for the take-off itself, the development of railways has led on to the development of modern coal, iron and engineering industries. In many countries the growth of modern basic industrial sectors can be traced in the most direct way to the requirements for building and, especially, for maintaining substantial railway systems. When a society has developed deeper institutional, social and political prerequisites for take-off, the rapid growth of a railway system with these powerful triple effects has often served to lift it into self-sustaining growth. Where the prerequisites have not existed, however, very substantial railway building has failed to

[24] If we are prepared to treat New England of the first half of the nineteenth century as a separable economy, its take-off into sustained growth can be allocated to the period, roughly, 1820–50 and, again, a disproportionately large cotton-textile industry based substantially on exports (that is, from New England to the rest of the United States) is the regional foundation for sustained growth.

[25] For a detailed analysis of the routes of impact of the railroad on economic development see Paul H. Cootner, *Transport Innovation and Economic Development: The Case of the U.S. Steam Railroads* (1953), unpublished doctoral thesis, M.I.T.

initiate a take-off, as, for example, in India, China, pre-1895 Canada, pre-1914 Argentine, etc.

It is clear that an enlargement and modernisation of Armed Forces could play the role of a leading sector in take-off. It was a factor in the Russian, Japanese and German take-offs; and it figures heavily in current Chinese Communist plans. But historically the role of modern armaments has been ancillary rather than central to the take-off.

Quite aside from their role in supplying foreign exchange for general capital-formation purposes, raw materials and foodstuffs can play the role of leading sectors in the take-off if they involve the application of modern processing techniques. The timber industry, built on the steam saw, fulfilled this function in the first phase of Sweden's take-off, to be followed shortly by the pulp industry. Similarly, the shift of Denmark to meat and dairy products, after 1873, appears to have reinforced the development of a manufacturing sector in the economy, as well as providing a major source of foreign exchange. And as Lockwood notes, even the export of Japanese silk thread had important secondary effects which developed modern production techniques.[26]

> To satisfy the demands of American weaving and hosiery mills for uniform, high-grade yarn, however, it was necessary to improve the quality of the product, from the silkworm egg on through to the bale of silk. In sericulture this meant the introduction of scientific methods of breeding and disease control; in reeling it stimulated the shift to large filatures equipped with machinery; in marketing it led to large-scale organization in the collection and sale of cocoons and raw silk . . . it exerted steady pressure in favor of the application of science, machinery, and modern business enterprise.

The role of leading sector has been assumed, finally, by the accelerated development of domestic manufacture of consumption goods over a wide range in substitution for imports, as, for example, in Australia, the Argentine and perhaps in contemporary Turkey.

What can we say, then, in general about these leading sectors? Historically, they have ranged from cotton textiles, through heavy-industry complexes based on railroads and military end products, to timber, pulp, dairy products and finally a wide variety of consumers' goods. There is, clearly, no one sectoral sequence for take-off, no single sector which constitutes the magic key. There is no need for a growing society to recapitulate the structural sequence and pattern of Britain, the United States or Russia. Four basic factors must be present:

1. There must be enlarged effective demand for the product or products of sectors which yield a foundation for a rapid rate of growth in output. Historically this has been brought about initially by the transfer of income from

[26] W. W. Lockwood, *The Economic Development of Japan* (Princeton, 1954), pp. 338–9.

consumption or hoarding to productive investment; by capital imports; by a sharp increase in the productivity of current investment inputs, yielding an increase in consumers' real income expended on domestic manufactures; or by a combination of these routes.

2. There must be an introduction into these sectors of new production functions as well as an expansion of capacity.

3. The society must be capable of generating capital initially required to detonate the take-off in these key sectors; and especially, there must be a high rate of plough-back by the (private or state) entrepreneurs controlling capacity and technique in these sectors and in the supplementary growth sectors they stimulated to expand.

4. Finally, the leading sector or sectors must be such that their expansion and technical transformation induce a chain of Leontief input–output requirements for increased capacity and the potentiality for new production functions in other sectors, to which the society, in fact, progressively responds.

III. CONCLUSION

This hypothesis is, then, a return to a rather old-fashioned way of looking at economic development. The take-off is defined as an industrial revolution, tied directly to radical changes in methods of production, having their decisive consequence over a relatively short period of time.

This view would not deny the role of longer, slower changes in the whole process of economic growth. On the contrary, take-off requires a massive set of preconditions going to the heart of a society's economic organisation and its effective scale of values. Moreover, for the take-off to be successful, it must lead on progressively to sustained growth; and this implies further deep and often slow-moving changes in the economy and the society as a whole.

What this argument does assert is that the rapid growth of one or more new manufacturing sectors is a powerful and essential engine of economic transformation. Its power derives from the multiplicity of its forms of impact, when a society is prepared to respond positively to this impact. Growth in such sectors, with new production functions of high productivity, in itself tends to raise output per head; it places incomes in the hands of men who will not merely save a high proportion of an expanding income but who will plough into highly productive investment; it sets up a chain of effective demand for other manufactured products; it sets up a requirement for enlarged urban areas, whose capital costs may be high, but whose population and market organisation help to make industrialisation an on-going process; and, finally, it opens up a range of external economy effects which, in the end, help to produce new leading sectors when the initial impulse of the take-off's leading sectors begins to wane.

We can observe in history and in the contemporary world important changes in production functions in non-manufacturing sectors which have powerful effects on whole societies. If natural resources are rich enough or the new agricultural tricks are productive enough such changes can even outstrip population growth and yield a rise in real output per head. Moreover, they may be a necessary prior condition for take-off or a necessary concomitant for take-off. Nothing in this analysis should be read as deprecating the importance of productivity changes in agriculture to the whole process of economic growth. But in the end take-off requires that a society find a way to apply effectively to its own peculiar resources what D. H. Robertson once called the tricks of manufacture; and continued growth requires that it so organise itself as to continue to apply them in an unending flow, of changing composition. Only thus, as we have all been correctly taught, can that old demon, diminishing returns, be held at bay.

ON THE POLITICAL
ECONOMY
OF BACKWARDNESS

Paul A. Baran

The capitalist mode of production and the social and political order concomitant with it provided, during the latter part of the eighteenth century, and still more during the entire nineteenth century, a framework for a continuous and, in spite of cyclical disturbances and setbacks, momentous expansion of productivity and material welfare. The relevant facts are well known and call for no elaboration. Yet this material (and cultural) progress was not only spotty in time but most unevenly distributed in space. It was confined to the Western world; and did not affect even all of this territorially and demographically relatively small sector of the inhabited globe. Germany and Austria, Britain and France, some smaller countries in Western Europe, and the United States and Canada occupied places in the neighbourhood of the sun. The vast expanses and the multitude of inhabitants of Eastern Europe, Spain and Portugal, Italy and the Balkans, Latin America and Asia, not to speak of Africa, remained in the deep shadow of backwardness and squalor, of stagnation and misery.

Tardy and skimpy as the benefits of capitalism may have been with respect to the lower classes even in most of the leading industrial countries,

From Paul Baran, "On the Political Economy of Backwardness," *The Manchester School of Economics and Social Studies,* 20:66–84 (January 1952). Reprinted by permission of the University of Manchester.

they were all but negligible in the less privileged parts of the world. There productivity remained low, and rapid increases in population pushed living standards from bad to worse. The dreams of the prophets of capitalist harmony remained on paper. Capital either did not move from countries where its marginal productivity was low to countries where it could be expected to be high, or if it did, it moved there mainly in order to extract profits from backward countries that frequently accounted for a lion's share of the increments in total output caused by the original investments. Where an increase in the aggregate national product of an underdeveloped country took place, the existing distribution of income prevented this increment from raising the living standards of the broad masses of the population. Like all general statements, this one is obviously open to criticism based on particular cases. There were, no doubt, colonies and dependencies where the populations profited from inflow of foreign capital. These benefits, however, were few and far between, while exploitation and stagnation were the prevailing rule.

But if Western capitalism failed to improve materially the lot of the peoples inhabiting most backward areas, it accomplished something that profoundly affected the social and political conditions in underdeveloped countries. It introduced there, with amazing rapidity, all the economic and social tensions inherent in the capitalist order. It effectively disrupted whatever was left of the "feudal" coherence of the backward societies. It substituted market contracts for such paternalistic relationships as still survived from century to century. It reoriented the partly or wholly self-sufficient economies of agricultural countries toward the production of marketable commodities. It linked their economic fate with the vagaries of the world market and connected it with the fever curve of international price movements.

A *complete* substitution of capitalist market rationality for the rigidities of feudal or semi-feudal servitude would have represented, in spite of all the pains of transition, an important step in the direction of progress. Yet all that happened was that the age-old exploitation of the population of underdeveloped countries by their domestic overlords, was freed of the mitigating constraints inherited from the feudal tradition. This superimposition of business *mores* over ancient oppression by landed gentries resulted in compounded exploitation, more outrageous corruption, and more glaring injustice.

Nor is this by any means the end of the story. Such export of capital and capitalism as has taken place had not only far-reaching implications of a social nature. It was accompanied by important physical and technical processes. Modern machines and products of advanced industries reached the poverty stricken backyards of the world. To be sure most, if not all, of these machines worked for their foreign owners—or at least were believed by the population to be working for no one else—and the new refined appurtenances of the good life belonged to foreign businessmen and their domestic counterparts. The bonaza that was capitalism, the fullness of things that was modern industrial civilization, were crowding the display windows—they were protected by barbed wire from the anxious grip of the starving and desperate man in the street.

But they have drastically changed his outlook. Broadening and deepening his economic horizon, they aroused aspirations, envies, and hopes. Young intellectuals filled with zeal and patriotic devotion travelled from the underdeveloped lands to Berlin and London, to Paris and New York, and returned home with the "message of the possible."

Fascinated by the advances and accomplishments observed in the centers of modern industry, they developed, and propagandized the image of what could be attained in their home countries under a more rational economic and social order. The dissatisfaction with the stagnation (or at best, barely perceptible growth) that ripened gradually under the still-calm political and social surface was given an articulate expression. This dissatisfaction was not nurtured by a comparison of reality with a vision of a socialist society. It found sufficient fuel in the confrontation of what was actually happening with what could be accomplished under capitalist institutions of the Western type.

II

The establishment of such institutions was, however, beyond the reach of the tiny middle-classes of most backward areas. The inherited backwardness and poverty of their countries never gave them an opportunity to gather the economic strength, the insight, and the self-confidence needed for the assumption of a leading role in society. For centuries under feudal rule they themselves assimilated the political, moral, and cultural values of the dominating class.

While in advanced countries, such as France or Great Britain, the economically ascending middle-classes developed at an early stage a new rational world outlook, which they proudly opposed to the medieval obscurantism of the feudal age, the poor, fledgling bourgeoisie of the underdeveloped countries sought nothing but accommodation to the prevailing order. Living in societies based on privilege, they strove for a share in the existing sinecures. They made political and economic deals with their domestic feudal overlords or with powerful foreign investors, and what industry and commerce developed in backward areas in the course of the last hundred years was rapidly moulded in the straitjacket of monopoly—the plutocratic partner of the aristocratic rulers. What resulted was an economic and political amalgam combining the worst features of both worlds—feudalism and capitalism—and blocking effectively all possibilities of economic growth.

It is quite conceivable that a "conservative" exit from this impasse might have been found in the course of time. A younger generation of enterprising and enlightened businessmen and intellectuals allied with moderate leaders of workers and peasants—a "Young Turk" movement of some sort—might have succeeded in breaking the deadlock, in loosening the hide-bound social and political structure of their countries and in creating the institutional arrangements indispensable for a measure of social and economic progress.

Yet in our rapid age history accorded no time for such a gradual transition. Popular pressures for an amelioration of economic and social conditions, or at least for some perceptible movement in that direction, steadily gained in intensity. To be sure, the growing restiveness of the underprivileged was not directed against the ephemeral principles of a hardly yet existing capitalist order. Its objects were parasitic feudal overlords appropriating large slices of the national product and wasting them on extravagant living; a government machinery protecting and abetting the dominant interests; wealthy businessmen reaping immense profits and not utilizing them for productive purposes; last but not least, foreign colonizers extracting or believed to be extracting vast gains from their "developmental" operations.

This popular movement had thus essentially bourgeois, democratic, anti-feudal, anti-imperialist tenets. It found outlets in agrarian egalitarianism; it incorporated "muckraker" elements denouncing monopoly; it strove for national independence and freedom from foreign exploitation.

For the native capitalist middle-classes to assume the leadership of these popular forces and to direct them into the channels of bourgeois democracy—as had happened in Western Europe—they had to identify themselves with the common man. They had to break away from the political, economic, and ideological leadership of the feudal crust and the monopolists allied with it; and they had to demonstrate to the nation as a whole that they had the knowledge, the courage, and the determination to undertake and to carry to victorious conclusion the struggle for economic and social improvement.

In hardly any underdeveloped country were the middle-classes capable of living up to this historical challenge. Some of the reasons for this portentous failure, reasons connected with the internal make-up of the business class itself, were briefly mentioned above. Of equal importance was, however, an "outside" factor. It was the spectacular growth of the international labor movement in Europe that offered the popular forces in backward areas ideological and political leadership that was denied to them by the native bourgeoisie. It pushed the goals and targets of the popular movements far beyond their original limited objectives.

This liaison of labor radicalism and populist revolt painted on the wall the imminent danger of a social revolution. Whether this danger was real or imaginary matters very little. What was essential is that the awareness of this threat effectively determined political and social action. It destroyed whatever chances there were of the capitalist classes joining and leading the popular anti-feudal, anti-monopolist movement. By instilling a mortal fear of expropriation and extinction in the minds of *all* property-owning groups the rise of socialist radicalism, and in particular the Bolshevik Revolution in Russia, tended to drive all more or less-privileged, more or less well-to-do elements in the society into one "counterrevolutionary" coalition. Whatever differences and antagonisms existed between large and small landowners, between monopolistic and competitive business, between liberal bourgeois and reactionary feudal overlords, between domestic and foreign interests, were largely submerged on all important occasions by the over-riding *common* interest in staving off socialism.

The possibility of solving the economic and political deadlock prevailing in the underdeveloped countries on lines of a progressive capitalism all but disappeared. Entering the alliance with all other segments of the ruling class, the capitalist middle-classes yielded one strategic position after another. Afraid that a quarrel with the landed gentry might be exploited by the radical populist movement, the middle-classes abandoned all progressive attitudes in agrarian matters. Afraid that a conflict with the church and the military might weaken the political authority of the government, the middle-classes moved away from all liberal and pacifist currents. Afraid that hostility toward foreign interests might deprive them of foreign support in a case of a revolutionary emergency, the native capitalists deserted their previous anti-imperialist, nationalist platforms.

The peculiar mechanisms of political interaction characteristic of all underdeveloped (and perhaps not only underdeveloped) countries thus operated at full speed. The aboriginal failure of the middle-classes to provide inspiration and leadership to the popular masses pushed those masses into the camp of socialist radicalism. The growth of radicalism pushed the middle-classes into an alliance with the aristocratic and monopolistic reaction. This alliance, cemented by common interest and common fear, pushed the populist forces still further along the road of radicalism and revolt. The outcome was a polarization of society with very little left between the poles. By permitting this polarization to develop, by abandoning the common man and resigning the task of reorganizing society on new, progressive lines, the capitalist middle-classes threw away their historical chance of assuming effective control over the destinies of their nations, and of directing the gathering popular storm against the fortresses of feudalism and reaction. Its blazing fire turned thus against the entirety of existing economic and social institutions.

III

The economic and political order maintained by the ruling coalition of owning classes finds itself invariably at odds with all the urgent needs of the underdeveloped countries. Neither the social fabric that it embodies nor the institutions that rest upon it are conducive to progressive economic development. The only way to provide for economic growth and to prevent a continuous deterioration of living standards (apart from mass emigration unacceptable to other countries) is to assure a steady increase of total output—at least large enough to offset the rapid growth of population.

An obvious source of such an increase is the utilization of available unutilized or underutilized resources. A large part of this reservoir of dormant productive potentialities is the vast multitude of entirely unemployed or ineffectively employed manpower. There is no way of employing it usefully in agriculture, where the marginal productivity of labor tends to zero. They could be provided with opportunities for productive work only by transfer to industrial pursuits. For this to be feasible large investments in industrial plant and facilities have to be undertaken. Under prevailing conditions such investments are not forthcoming for a number of important and interrelated reasons.

With a very uneven distribution of a very small aggregate income (and wealth), large individual incomes exceeding what could be regarded as "reasonable" requirements for current consumption accrue as a rule to a relatively small group of high-income receivers. Many of them are large landowners maintaining a feudal style of life with large outlays on housing, servants, travel, and other luxuries. Their "requirements for consumption" are so high that there is only little room for savings. Only relatively insignificant amounts are left to be spent on improvements of agricultural estates.

Other members of the "upper crust" receiving incomes markedly surpassing "reasonable" levels of consumption are wealthy businessmen. For social reasons briefly mentioned above, their consumption too is very much larger than it would have been were they brought up in the puritan tradition of a bourgeois civilization. Their drive to accumulate and to expand their enterprises is continuously counteracted by the urgent desire to imitate in their living habits the socially dominant "old families," to prove by their conspicuous outlays on the amenities of rich life that they are socially (and therefore also politically) not inferior to their aristocratic partners in the ruling coalition.

But if this tendency curtails the volume of savings that could have been amassed by the urban high-income receivers, their will to re-invest their funds in productive enterprises is effectively curbed by a strong reluctance to damage their carefully erected monopolistic market positions through creation of additional productive capacity, and by absence of suitable investment opportunities—paradoxical as this may sound with reference to underdeveloped countries.

The deficiency of investment opportunities stems to a large extent from the structure and the limitations of the existing effective demand. With very low living standards the bulk of the aggregate money income of the population is spent on food and relatively primitive items of clothing and household necessities. These are available at low prices, and investment of large funds in plant and facilities that could produce this type of commodities more cheaply rarely promises attractive returns. Nor does it appear profitable to develop major enterprises the output of which would cater to the requirements of the rich. Large as their individual purchases of various luxuries may be, their aggregate spending on each of them is not sufficient to support the development of an elaborate luxury industry—in particular since the "snob" character of prevailing tastes renders only imported luxury articles true marks of social distinction.

Finally, the limited demand for investment goods precludes the building up of a machinery or equipment industry. Such mass consumption goods as are lacking, and such quantities of luxury goods as are purchased by the well-to-do, as well as the comparatively small quantities of investment goods needed by industry, are thus imported from abroad in exchange for domestic agricultural products and raw materials.

This leaves the expansion of exportable raw materials output as a major outlet for investment activities. There the possibilities are greatly influenced, however, by the technology of the production of most raw materials as well as by the nature of the markets to be served. Many raw materials, in particular oil, metals, certain industrial crops, have to be produced on a large scale if costs are to be kept low and satisfactory returns assured. Large-scale production, however, calls for large investments, so large indeed as to exceed the potentialities of the native capitalists in backward countries. Production of raw materials for a distant market entails, moreover, much larger risks than those encountered in domestic business. The difficulty of foreseeing accurately such things as receptiveness of the world markets, prices obtainable in competition with other countries, volume of output in other parts of the world, etc., sharply reduces the interest of native capitalists in these lines of business. They become to a predominant extent the domain of foreigners who, financially stronger, have at the same time much closer contacts with foreign outlets of their products.

The shortage of investable funds and the lack of investment opportunities represent two aspects of the same problem. A great number of investment projects, unprofitable under prevailing conditions, could be most promising in a general environment of economic expansion.

In backward areas a new industrial venture must frequently, if not always, break virgin ground. It has no functioning economic system to draw upon. It has to organize with its own efforts not only the productive process *within* its own confines, it must provide in addition for all the necessary *outside* arrangements essential to its operations. It does not enjoy the benefits of "external economies."

There can be no doubt that the absence of external economies, the inadequacy of the economic milieu in underdeveloped countries, constituted everywhere an important deterrent to investment in industrial projects. There is no way of rapidly bridging the gap. Large-scale investment is predicated upon large-scale investment. Roads, electric power stations, railroads, and houses have to be built *before* businessmen find it profitable to erect factories, to invest their funds in new industrial enterprises.

Yet investing in road building, financing construction of canals and power stations, organizing large housing projects, etc., transcend by far the financial and mental horizon of capitalists in underdeveloped countries. Not only are their financial resources too small for such ambitious projects, but their background and habits militate against entering commitments of this type. Brought up in the tradition of merchandizing and manufacturing consumers' goods—as is characteristic of an early phase of capitalist development—businessmen in underdeveloped countries are accustomed to rapid turnover, large but short-term risks, and correspondingly high rates of profit. Sinking funds in enterprises where profitability could manifest itself only in the course of many years is a largely unknown and unattractive departure.

The difference between social and private rationality that exists in any market and profit-determined economy is thus particularly striking in underdeveloped countries. While building of roads, harnessing of water power, or organization of housing developments may facilitate industrial growth and thus contribute to increased productivity on a national scale, the individual firms engaged in such activities may suffer losses and be unable to recover their investments. The nature of the problem involved can be easily exemplified: starting a new industrial enterprise is predicated among other things upon the availability of appropriately skilled manpower. Engaging men and training them on the job is time-consuming and expensive. They are liable to be unproductive, wasteful, and careless in the treatment of valuable tools and equipment. Accepting the losses involved may be justifiable from the standpoint of the individual firm if such a firm can count with reasonable certainty on retaining the services of those men *after* they go through training and acquire the requisite skills. However, should they leave the firm that provided the training and proceed to work for another enterprise, that new employer would reap the fruits of the first firm's outlays. In a developed industrial society this consideration is relatively unimportant. Losses and gains of individual firms generated by labor turnover may cancel out. In an underdeveloped country the chances of such cancellation are very small, if not nil. Although society as a whole would clearly benefit by the increase of skills of at least some of its members, individual businessmen cannot afford to provide the training that such an increase demands.

But could not the required increase in total output be attained by better utilization of land—another unutilized or inadequately utilized productive factor?

There is usually no land that is both fit for agricultural purposes and at the same time readily accessible. Such terrain as could be cultivated but is actually not being tilled would usually require considerable investment before becoming suitable for settlement. In underdeveloped countries such outlays for agricultural purposes are just as unattractive to private interests as they are for industrial purposes.

On the other hand, more adequate employment of land that is already used in agriculture runs into considerable difficulties. Very few improvements that would be necessary in order to increase productivity can be carried out within the narrow confines of small-peasant holdings. Not only are the peasants in underdeveloped countries utterly unable to pay for such innovations, but the size of their lots offers no justification for their introduction.

Owners of large estates are in a sense in no better position. With limited savings at their disposal they do not have the funds to finance expensive improvements in their enterprises, nor do such projects appear profitable in view of the high prices of imported equipment in relation to prices of agricultural produce and wages of agricultural labor.

Approached thus *via* agriculture, an expansion of total output would also seem to be attainable only through the development of industry. Only through increase of industrial productivity could agricultural machinery, fertilizers, electric power, etc., be brought within the reach of the agricultural producer. Only through an increased demand for labor could agricultural wages be raised and a stimulus provided for a modernization of the agricultural economy. Only through the growth of industrial production could agricultural labor displaced by the machine be absorbed in productive employment.

Monopolistic market structures, shortage of savings, lack of external economies, the divergence of social and private rationalities do not exhaust, however, the list of obstacles blocking the way of privately organized industrial expansion in underdeveloped countries. Those obstacles have to be considered against the background of the general feeling of uncertainty prevailing in all backward areas. The coalition of the owning classes formed under pressure of fear, and held together by the real or imagined danger of social upheavals, provokes continuously more or less threatening rumblings under the outwardly calm political surface. The social and political tensions to which that coalition is a political response are not liquidated by the prevailing system; they are only repressed. Normal and quiet as the daily routine frequently appears, the more enlightened and understanding members of the ruling groups in underdeveloped countries sense the inherent instability of the political and social order. Occasional outbursts of popular dissatisfaction assuming the form of peasant uprisings, violent strikes or local guerrilla warfare, serve from time to time as grim reminders of the latent crisis.

In such a climate there is no will to invest on the part of monied people; in such a climate there is no enthusiasm for long-term projects; in such a climate the motto of all participants in the privileges offered by society is *carpe diem*.

IV

Could not, however, an appropriate policy on the part of the governments involved change the political climate and facilitate economic growth? In our time, when faith in the manipulative omnipotence of the State has all but displaced analysis of its social structure and understanding of its political and economic functions, the tendency is obviously to answer these questions in the affirmative.

Looking at the matter purely mechanically, it would appear indeed that much could be done, by a well-advised regime in an underdeveloped country, to provide for a relatively rapid increase of total output, accompanied by an improvement of the living standards of the population. There is a number of measures that the government could take in an effort to overcome backwardness. A fiscal policy could be adopted that by means of capital levies, and a highly progressive tax system would syphon off all surplus purchasing power, and in this way eliminate non-essential consumption. The savings thus enforced could be channelled by the government into productive investment. Power stations, railroads, highways, irrigation systems, and soil improvements could be organized by the State with a view to creating an economic environment conducive to the growth of productivity. Technical schools on various levels could be set up by the public authority to furnish industrial training to young people as well as to adult workers and the unemployed. A system of scholarships could be introduced rendering acquisition of skills accessible to low-income strata.

Wherever private capital refrains from undertaking certain industrial projects, or wherever monopolistic controls block the necessary expansion of plant and facilities in particular industries, the government could step in and make the requisite investments. Where developmental possibilities that are rewarding in the long-run appear unprofitable during the initial period of gestation and learning, and are therefore beyond the horizon of private businessmen, the government could undertake to shoulder the short-run losses.

In addition an entire arsenal of "preventive" devices is at the disposal of the authorities. Inflationary pressures resulting from developmental activities (private and public) could be reduced or even eliminated, if outlays on investment projects could be offset by a corresponding and simultaneous contraction of spending elsewhere in the economic system. What this would call for is a taxation policy that would effectively remove from the income stream amounts sufficient to neutralize the investment-caused expansion of aggregate money income.

In the interim, and as a supplement, speculation in scarce goods and excessive profiteering in essential commodities could be suppressed by rigorous price controls. An equitable distribution of mass consumption goods in short supply could be assured by rationing. Diversion of resources in high demand to luxury purposes could be prevented by allocation and priority schemes. Strict supervision of transactions involving foreign exchanges could render capital flight, expenditure of limited foreign funds on luxury imports, pleasure trips abroad, and the like, impossible.

What the combination of these measures would accomplish is a radical change in the structure of effective demand in the underdeveloped country, and a reallocation of productive resources to satisfy society's need for economic development. By curtailing consumption of the higher-income groups, the amounts of savings available for investment purposes could be markedly increased. The squandering of limited supplies of foreign exchange on capital flight, or on importation of redundant foreign goods and services, could be prevented, and the foreign funds thus saved could be used for the acquisition of foreign-made machinery needed for economic development. The reluctance of private interests to engage in enterprises that are socially necessary, but may not promise rich returns in the short-run, would be prevented from determining the economic life of the backward country.

The mere listing of the steps that would have to be undertaken, in order to assure an expansion of output and income in an underdeveloped country, reveals the utter implausibility of the view that they could be carried out by the governments existing in most underdeveloped countries. The reason for this inability is only to a negligible extent the nonexistence of the competent and honest civil service needed for the administration of the program. A symptom itself of the political and social marasmus prevailing in underdeveloped countries, this lack cannot be remedied without attacking the underlying causes. Nor does it touch anything near the roots of the matter to lament the lack of satisfactory tax policies in backward countries, or to deplore the absence of tax "morale" and "discipline" among the civic virtues of their populations.

The crucial fact rendering the realization of a developmental program illusory is the political and social structure of the governments in power. The alliance of property-owning classes controlling the destinies of most underdeveloped countries, cannot be expected to design and to execute a set of measures running counter to each and all of their immediate vested interests. If to appease the restive public, blueprints of progressive measures such as agrarian reform, equitable tax legislation, etc., are officially announced, their enforcement is wilfully sabotaged. The government, representing a political compromise between landed and business interests cannot suppress the wasteful management of landed estates and the conspicuous consumption on the part of the aristocracy; cannot suppress monopolistic abuses, profiteering, capital flights, and extravagant living on the part of businessmen. It cannot curtail or abandon its lavish appropriations for a military and police establishment, providing attractive careers to the scions of wealthy families and a profitable outlet for armaments produced by their parents—quite apart from the fact that this establishment serves as the main protection against possible popular revolt. Set up to guard and to abet the existing property rights and privileges, it cannot become the architect of a policy calculated to destroy the privileges standing in the way of economic progress and to place the property and the incomes derived from it at the service of society as a whole.

Nor is there much to be said for the "intermediate" position which, granting the essential incompatibility of a well-conceived and vigorously executed developmental program with the political and social institutions prevailing in most underdeveloped countries, insists that at least *some* of the requisite measures could be carried out by the existing political authorities. This school of thought overlooks entirely the weakness, if not the complete absence, of social and political forces that could induce the necessary concessions on the part of the ruling coalition. By background and political upbringing, too myopic and self-interested to permit the slightest encroachments upon their inherited positions and cherished privileges, the upper-classes in underdeveloped countries resist doggedly all pressures in that direction. Every time such pressures grow in strength they succeed in cementing anew the alliance of all conservative elements, by decrying all attempts at reform as assaults on the very foundations of society.

Even if measures like progressive taxation, capital levies, and foreign exchange controls could be enforced by the corrupt officials operating in the demoralized business communities of underdeveloped countries, such enforcement would to a large extent defeat its original purpose. Where businessmen do not invest, unless in expectation of lavish profits, a taxation system succeeding in confiscating large parts of these profits is bound to kill private investment. Where doing business or operating landed estates are attractive mainly because they permit luxurious living, foreign exchange controls preventing the importation of luxury goods are bound to blight enterprise. Where the only stimulus to hard work on the part of intellectuals, technicians, and civil servants is the chance of partaking in the privileges of the ruling class, a policy aiming at the reduction of inequality of social status and income is bound to smother effort.

The injection of planning into a society living in the twilight between feudalism and capitalism cannot but result in additional corruption, larger and more artful evasions of the law, and more brazen abuses of authority.

V

There would seem to be no exit from the impasse. The ruling coalition of interests does not abdicate of its own volition, nor does it change its character in response to incantation. Although its individual members occasionally leave the sinking ship physically or financially (or in both ways), the property-owning classes as a whole are as a rule grimly determined to hold fast to their political and economic entrenchments.

If the threat of social upheaval assumes dangerous proportions, they tighten their grip on political life and move rapidly in the direction of unbridled reaction and military dictatorship. Making use of favourable international opportunities, and of ideological and social affinities to ruling groups in other countries, they solicit foreign economic and sometimes military aid, in their efforts to stave off the impending disaster.

Such aid is likely to be given to them by foreign governments regarding them as an evil less to be feared than the social revolution that would sweep them out of power. This attitude of their friends and protectors abroad is no less shortsighted than their own.

The adjustment of the social and political conditions in underdeveloped countries to the urgent needs of economic development can be postponed; it cannot be indefinitely avoided. In the past, it could have been delayed by decades or even centuries. In our age it is a matter of years. Bolstering the political system of power existing in backward countries by providing it with military support may temporarily block the eruption of the volcano; it cannot stop the subterranean gathering of explosive forces.

Economic help in the form of loans and grants given to the governments of backward countries, to enable them to promote a measure of economic progress, is no substitute for the domestic changes that are mandatory if economic development is to be attained.

Such help, in fact, may actually do more harm than good. Possibly permitting the importation of some foreign-made machinery and equipment for government or business-sponsored investment projects, but not accompanied by any of the steps that are needed to assure healthy economic growth, foreign assistance thus supplied may set off an inflationary spiral increasing and aggravating the existing social and economic tensions in underdeveloped countries.

If, as is frequently the case, these loans or grants from abroad are tied to the fulfilment of certain conditions on the part of the receiving country regarding their use, the resulting investment may be directed in such channels as to conform more to the interests of the lending than to those of the borrowing country. Where economic advice as a form of "technical assistance" is supplied to the underdeveloped country, and its acceptance is made a prerequisite to eligibility for financial aid, this advice often pushes the governments of underdeveloped countries toward policies, ideologically or otherwise attractive to the foreign experts dispensing economic counsel, but not necessarily conducive to economic development of the "benefitted" countries. Nationalism and xenophobia are thus strengthened in backward areas—additional fuel for political restiveness.

For backward countries to enter the road of economic growth and social progress, the political framework of their existence has to be drastically revamped. The alliance between feudal landlords, industrial royalists, and the capitalist middle-classes has to be broken. The keepers of the past cannot be the builders of the future. Such progressive and enterprising elements as exist in backward societies have to obtain the possibility of leading their countries in the direction of economic and social growth.

What France, Britain, and America have accomplished through their own revolutions has to be attained in backward countries by a combined effort of popular forces, enlightened government, and unselfish foreign help. This combined effort must sweep away the holdover institutions of a defunct age, must change the political and social climate in the underdeveloped countries, and must imbue their nations with a new spirit of enterprise and freedom.

Should it prove too late in the historical process for the bourgeoisie to rise to its responsibilities in backward areas, should the long experience of servitude and accommodation to the feudal past have reduced the forces of progressive capitalism to impotence, the backward countries of the world will inevitably turn to economic planning and social collectivism. If the capitalist world outlook of economic and social progress, propelled by enlightened self-interest, should prove unable to triumph over the conservatism of inherited positions and traditional privileges, if the capitalist promise of advance and reward to the efficient, the industrious, the able, should not displace the feudal assurance of security and power to the well-bred, the well-connected and the conformist—a new social ethos will become the spirit and guide of a new age. It will be the ethos of the collective effort, the creed of the predominance of the interests of society over the interests of selected few.

The transition may be abrupt and painful. The land not given to the peasants legally may be taken by them forcibly. High incomes not confiscated through taxation may be eliminated by outright expropriation. Corrupt officials not retired in orderly fashion may be removed by violent action.

Which way the historical wheel will turn and in which way the crisis in the backward countries will find its final solution will depend in the main on whether the capitalist middle-classes in the backward areas, and the rulers of the advanced industrial nations of the world, overcome their fear and myopia. Or are they too spell-bound by their narrowly conceived selfish interests, too blinded by their hatred of progress, grown so senile in these latter days of the capitalist age, as to commit suicide out of fear of death?

Section 3
POPULATION
GROWTH
AND ECONOMIC
DEVELOPMENT

Introduction: *The Demographic Transition: West and East*

The movement from high birth and death rates to low birth and death rates is known as the *demographic transition*. Death rates fall first while birth rates remain high. Later, birth rates fall to a position close to the death rates. The intervening period thus experiences relatively rapid population growth, giving us the well-known "S"-shaped curve of population growth. In Figures 1 and 1a the two-century record of England and Wales is used to illustrate the transition.

The remarkable thing about this transition is that it has been experienced by almost every society that has achieved sustained increases in output per capita.[1] Neither the massive emigration from Europe, the massive immigration into the Americas and Oceania, nor the "oriental culture" of Japan has appreciably altered this pattern. *Modern* economic development implies both a significant and sustained increase in output per capita *and* a significant increase in population. It is this dual aspect of growth that leads Simon Kuznets to mark off the present period (already about two centuries old) as a distinct epoch.[2]

---

[1] The case of the Soviet Union is less clear, partly because of the fantastic loss of life caused by World War I, the revolution and civil war, the great purge, and finally by World War II. It may also be, however, that the Socialist revolution has in other respects altered the more common pattern of the demographic transition.

[2] Simon Kuznets, *Modern Economic Growth* (New Haven, 1966), pp. 1–8.

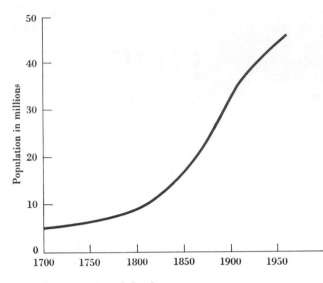

Figure 1. Crude birth and death rates
for England and Wales 1700–1960.

Like economic development itself, the demographic transition reflects a major change in social organization. The change is also essentially that from traditional to modern, from the old to the new, from the small-scale rural, agrarian, subsistence societies to the large-scale, urban, industrial, market societies. Further, what is known as demo-

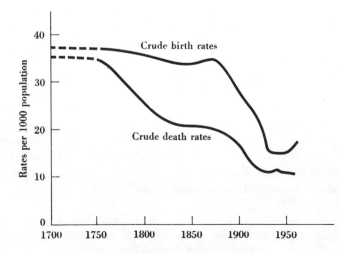

Figure 1a. Population growth in England
and Wales 1700–1960.

graphic transition theory provides a general explanation for the differential fall in death and birth rates, which produces the period of
rapid population growth.

The human species is relatively precarious. Its long gestation period,
the normal production of only one offspring at a time, and especially the
long period of infancy place the species in considerable jeopardy.[3] Given
these conditions it is only those societies that produce powerful institutional supports for sustaining life and reproduction that manage to
survive at all. These institutional supports include a negative value
placed upon death, a high value placed upon reproduction, and a set of
organizational constraints that get women into the reproductive business
relatively early and keep them there through most of the reproductive
period, and provides additional support in the form of a sexual division
of labor that protects both mother and infant. With such institutional
supports for species reproduction it is understandable that death rates
can be lowered without immediately affecting birth rates. Only after
considerable experience with low mortality will pressures emerge to
change reproductive behavior. When these pressures build up, the
change in fertility can come rather rapidly.

We have already suggested, from the cross-sectional data in Section
1, that the pattern experienced by the currently developed economies
may not be exactly reproduced in the currently developing economies.
In our English and Welsh example the death rates fell rather gradually,
taking almost two centuries, from the latter part of the 18th century to
the mid-twentieth century. Birth rates, on the other hand, fell rather
rapidly, taking less than a century, from the late 19th to the middle of
the 20th century. The decline of mortality was brought about by a series
of changes that gradually increased the standard of living. New crops
from the New World, a revolution in agriculture, and the replacement
of gin by tea and coffee as standard items of liquid consumption all
raised the general level of nutrition. The production of cheap cotton
cloth that could be easily washed and more frequently changed raised
the general level of personal hygiene. Also, the gradual control of water
supplies and sewage increased the level of public health. All of these
changes came gradually and required a general increase in the level of
wealth. The more rapid changes in a readily transplantable medical
technology came later. For the currently developed economies, then, the
decline in mortality was rather closely associated with an increase in
output per capita.

It appears that the currently developing economies will not have to
pass through this same lengthy transition. We have already witnessed a

---

[3] It is also these conditions that give the human organism such tremendous adaptive
and survival capacity.

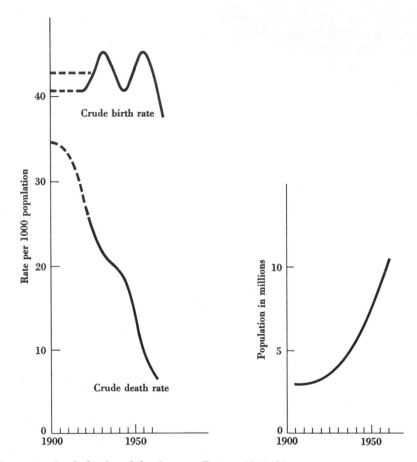

Figure 2. Crude birth and death rates: Taiwan 1920–64.
Figure 2a. Population growth in Taiwan 1905–60.

much more rapid decline in mortality in much of the rest of the world. The decline in mortality that required from one to two centuries in the West is currently being experienced by a number of countries in less than half a century. Figures 2 and 2a use the experience of Taiwan to illustrate this process.

It is this current pattern of the uncompleted demographic transition that is reflected in the lower correlation between death rates and Gross National Product per capita found in cross-sectional analysis.

This rapid decline in mortality has come about largely through the development and importation into poorer economies of an advanced medical and public health technology produced in the wealthier economies. The mid-twentieth century has experienced a very rapid development of antibiotic drugs, vaccines, and pesticides to control disease-bearing insects. This technology can be imported quite easily into poorer economies, partly because the technological development came after a period in which relatively effective administrative structures were built under the colonial impetus in a large number of poor economies. In addition, there has been a rapid increase of international administrative structures capable of diffusing the new technology throughout a greater part of the world.

Figure 2 shows an uncompleted demographic transition, a condition that obtains for a large portion of the world's population. Since fertility has not yet declined, we are in the period of rapid population increase. And since both birth and death rates in these populations appear to have been higher at the early stages of the transition than was the case for the currently developed economies, the rates of population growth that now occur in the poor countries are considerably higher than they were for the currently developed economies at an earlier stage in their histories. The rapid rates of population growth that the developed economies experienced through much of the 19th century were between 1 percent and 2 percent. It is not unusual today to find rates of population growth in excess of 3 percent in the poor economies.

This is, of course, the core of the current population explosion. For our analysis of social and economic change this raises two fundamental issues. How does this rapid rate of population growth affect economic development? And, under what conditions can we expect the rapid decline in fertility that will complete the demographic transition in the underdeveloped countries?

In regard to the impact of population growth on economic development, we must first be aware of the limitations of a simple accounting definition of the problem. Since we measure economic development by output per capita, any increase in population will, *ceteris paribus*, reduce the rate of economic development. If we find that total output has increased by 5 percent per year over a decade, and population has increased by 3 percent per year, we are left with approximately a 2 percent per year growth in output per capita. If over the same period population had increased by only 2 percent, and total output had grown by the same 5 percent per year, we would have had an increase in output per capita by approximately 3 percent per year. At 2 percent per year, increase per capita output will double in approximately 35 years, at 3 percent, it will require only about 27 years. Hence, *other things being equal* (especially rates of increase in output) it is clearly advantageous to have lower rates of population growth.

In these terms, population growth is an obstacle to economic development *by definition.* While this is, to be sure, no real solution to the problem, and certainly avoids the main issue, it is characteristic of an important element of current thinking on population growth and development. As such this general orientation has had a marked impact on public policy formation in the area of population growth, an issue to which we shall return shortly.

The more fundamental issue, however, is that of the organic (as opposed to the arithmetic) relation between population growth and economic development. We open this set of readings with a selection by J. J. Spengler, which draws attention to the complexity of the relationship. Population growth is at once a cause, an effect, and an indicator of economic growth. This is at least in part because population growth has implications for the individual family, for the collection of firms that make up the market (whether private or public makes little difference), and for the total economy. Further the implications are not always the same for all levels. Nonetheless, the overall argument presented by Spengler is rather clearly on the side of population growth as an obstacle to development. That is, the costs appear more important than the benefits.

Nathan Keyfitz gives greater detail to the cost argument in his focus on the age structure. This clearly an area in which population growth appears to constitute a brake on the development process. Rapid population growth that is brought about by a decline in mortality (rather than by migration) produces an almost immediate lowering of the average age of the population, or in increase in the proportions of infants and young people. We can assume that the normal life cycle of an individual begins with almost pure consumption through a rather long period of infancy. Only gradually does the productive capacity of the individual increase, with adulthood marked in some sense by a predominance of productive capacity over consumption. This is then followed in old age by a decline in productive capacity and an increase in consumption. In this general sense a younger population experiences greater pressures on consumption and less productive capacity than an older population. It is also possible to identify in greater detail the specific pressures on consumption, in the demands for infant care, followed by the demands currently widespread for schools and public education, all of which come before the individuals are ready to begin a productive life in society.

In the age distribution, then, we have an area in which the rapid population growth accompanying the demographic transition clearly appears to obstruct economic development.

In what has become one of the most frequently cited arguments, Albert Hirschman suggests that population growth can also be a stimulant to economic development. He points out that people at all levels normally resist a lowering in their standards of living. This takes us back to Spengler's family level for the analysis of the relation between population growth and economic development. For the family, more children clearly constitute an increased pressure for consumption. Rather than meeting these pressures by spreading more thinly the limited resources available, Hirschman argues there is a clear tendency to produce or earn more. People are producers as well as consumers and have a tendency to relate their performance as producers to their needs as consumers. But apparently the discovery that more can be produced can have a stimulating effect on output beyond the immediate needs of consumption to care for more people. That is, the pressures to provide more for the increased number of family consumers spills over into a more generalized increase in output. In this sense population growth can act as a stimulant to economic growth.[4]

Although the actual process of this spill-over effect is not clear, it is obvious that many populations have experienced both an increase of output at the same time that they have experienced an increase of population. Thus population growth is not always a decisive brake upon economic development, however much we may be able to identify specific costs at one point in time. Probably the only resolution possible at this time is the indeterminate one of noting that under some conditions population growth may constitute a greater cost than benefit, and at other times it may constitute a greater benefit than cost. It is also clear, however, that such things as population density, and the political processes of mobilization for development stimulation are significant variables that stand between population growth and economic development.

Irma Adelman provides a slightly different approach to the problem in her "Economic Analysis of Population Growth." Using regression analysis of cross-sectional data, Adelman draws out some of the variables significantly associated with age specific birth and death rates. As might be expected from other studies, this shows that fertility is lower where the population is more educated and where it is engaged in nonagricultural industries. Mortality is lower in the more wealthy, rapidly growing, nonagricultural economies, which also have higher general levels of health.

A somewhat unusual finding is that higher levels of per capita real income are associated with higher fertility, especially at ages 15–19 and

[4] Esther Boserup has presented a similar argument, though for populations with very low levels of agricultural technology. She also suggests that population density is a critical determinant of the specific impact of population growth on agricultural growth. See her *Conditions of Agricultural Growth* (Chicago, 1966).

above 35. It is difficult to relate this finding to the aggregate analysis that shows higher levels of fertility in countries with lower levels of per capita income, because the age structure is an important variable in the aggregate analysis. This does suggest, however, that increases in output per capita might produce general rises in overall fertility especially at the early stages of the demographic transition, where levels of income are lower and where the younger reproductive age groups (15–19) increase more rapidly than the subsequent age groups.

Another finding in this regression analysis is also quite suggestive. The only two variables consistently and negatively associated with age-specific birth rates are education and *population density*. The former is not a unique finding and agrees with most of what we know about the process of fertility decline. The latter suggests that population growth itself may bring pressures for reduced fertility. This is in accord with demographic transition theory, but it still leaves unanswered a number of questions on how the decline in fertility at the close of the demographic transition comes about.

Ronald Freedman takes up the issue of fertility decline in the next article in this section. He makes rather sweeping prognoses about the prospects of widespread fertility decline in the underdeveloped economies over the next generation, and draws attention to the opportunities and promise this offers for students of social change. Freedman offers six conditions of fertility decline, the conceptualization of which provides an excellent summary of current thinking on the process of social and demographic change.

The first and fourth of these conditions argue that a certain level of social development must be achieved before fertility decline will be widespread. Social development can perhaps best be measured by the use of the variety of communication variables, including education and literacy, that we discussed earlier. The second and third conditions reflect population pressures: low mortality and a growing desire for smaller families and fewer births.

It is also suggested that these conditions constitute a threshold for fertility change. Until a certain level of social development and population pressure is reached, the net balance of a wide range of forces will be to sustain high fertility. Once this threshold is reached, we can expect rather rapid fertility decline. The idea of a threshold is clearly supported by past patterns of fertility decline in the countries that have passed through the demographic transition. In these cases once fertility began to decline, it came down rather rapidly, and was clearly associated with population pressure and social and economic development.

The last two of Freedman's conditions relate to the technology of fertility decline and offer the real possibility of large-scale direct social and political intervention in the process of fertility decline. In the past generation we have witnessed a technological breakthrough in the development of techniques of contraception. The interuterine device and the oral contraceptive are currently the most dramatic manifestations of this breakthrough. When such new and individually highly effective techniques are made available to a population through large scale effective programs for family planning, we can expect rather rapid declines in fertility. As Freedman points out this process is already underway in such rapidly growing populations as Taiwan, Korea and Singapore. And with the rapid increase in the commitment to fertility limitation programs throughout the world, it is highly likely that the next generation will see a closing of the demographic transition probably more rapid than that experienced in the currently developed economies.

The recent interest in and commitment to widespread fertility decline ranks along with the interest in and commitment to economic development as among the most significant and pervasive social goals of the mid-twentieth century. Prior to 1950 there was scarcely a nation in the world with a serious commitment to a program of induced fertility decline. In less than two decades family planning programs have become common features of development plans in most underdeveloped economies. From the limited efforts of private voluntary organizations with minute budgets, family planning has advanced to large-scale public efforts with budgets increasing at virtually astronomical rates. Some of the dimensions of the emergence of this new social goal are dealt with in the selection by Dudley Kirk and Dorothy Norton.

The final article in this section raises some critical questions on the efficacy of the programs evolved under this new social goal. Kingsley Davis argues that family planning programs have not yet been very successful and do not in their present form offer significant hope for bringing about widespread and rapid fertility decline. Davis argues that even the most successful current programs have only succeeded in bringing the average family size of contraceptive users down to the level of about four children. While this may be a significant reduction from an average family size of six or more children, it is not sufficient to bring about the extent of fertility decline that Davis and many others believe the world needs. That is, many social observers currently consider that a zero level of population growth must be achieved by the world rather shortly if mankind is to avoid disastrous ecological pressures. And to achieve this level of population growth average family size must be brought considerably below the level of four children.

Davis' arguments on this issue are essentially static and are countered by a dynamic argument by the proponents of modern family planning programs. They point out that reducing the average family size to a level of four children is only the first step in a process of social change that will almost inevitably be followed by further fertility reductions. The character of the social changes required to bring about the subsequent fertility decline is, however, suggested by Kingsley Davis and raises what is perhaps one of the most profound issues of modern social and demographic change.

Most studies of the conditions of fertility decline indicate that the emancipation of women is closely associated with reductions in fertility. In micro studies we find that female education and literacy, and female readership of newspapers and other literature, or husband-wife discussions of fertility are strongly and negatively related to fertility. On the macro level, Islam, the world religion with the most marked subordinate position of women, is consistently related with high fertility. Davis suggests that the complete reduction of fertility that the world now needs will only be brought about by a more complete emancipation of women. This will include the virtual elimination of current patterns of sexual division of labor, with equal pay for female work, and widespread opportunities for women to engage in careers other than child raising.

It is possible to conceive of the demographic transition as we know it in the history of the developed economies as a significant but incomplete model of the demographic changes that will eventually come with widespread economic development. The model is significant because it portrays a common change from small, agrarian societies with poor economies to large-scale industrial societies with highly productive economies. It also indicates some of the patterns of change that are quite likely to occur in other economies that achieve sustained increases in human productivity. The model is incomplete in that it only suggests but does not fully indicate the depth of the changes in human institutions that will eventually come with economic development. And it seems likely that some of the most profound changes will come with those institutions, those value-ladened patterned relationships that are broadly associated with human reproduction.

POPULATION CHANGE:
CAUSE, EFFECT, INDICATOR

Joseph J. Spengler

It is possible to study a given problem, in some
degree of approximation, without first taking into account
the infinity of factors that are needed for a perfectly
precise prediction of any given result.

David Bohm, in *Causality and Chance
in Modern Physics*, p. 14.[1]

Population movements are of significance to the student of economic growth
because population change and economic change interact. Population change
may function as cause, as effect, and as equilibrating agent when economic
growth is under way. It may serve also as an indicator of the behavior of
phenomena connected with economic growth, provided that adequate allow-

From Joseph J. Spengler, "Population Change: Cause, Effect, Indicator," *Economic
Development and Cultural Change*, 9:3:249–266 (April 1961). Reprinted by permission of
The University of Chicago Press.

[1] London, 1953.

Bibliographical Note:
I have made very great use of J. R. Russell, "Late Ancient and Medieval Population,"
Transactions of the American Philosophical Society, n.s., XLVIII, Part 2 (June, 1958);
idem, British Medieval Population (Albuquerque, 1948); Roger Mols, S.J., *Introduction*

ance is made for the great changes that have taken place since (say) 1700 in demographic and output-producing processes and in the variables connecting or conditioning them.

I. TYPES OF POPULATION CHANGE

Population movements assume three main forms.

Form (i), change in an area's population, results because births (deaths) exceed deaths (births), and this excess is not offset by net migration.

Form (ii), redistribution of population in space, results when persons immigrating into (emigrating from) an area exceed in number those emigrating from (immigrating into) it, and their arrival (departure) does not generate offsetting changes in fertility.

Form (iii), change in the proportions in which a population is distributed among social or demographic categories, may be affected or even dominated by migratory or reproductive selection. Disbalance in sex composition, generally under the empire of sexually selective migration, in the past

---

à la démographie historique des villes d'Europe du XIVe au XVIIIe siècle, 3 vols. (Louvain, 1953–1956).

I have also made considerable use of the following works:

W. Abel, Die Wüstungen des ausgehenden Mittelalters (Jena, 1943), and "Bevölkerungsgang und Landwirtschaft im ausgehenden Mittelalter im Lichte der Preis- und Lohnbewegung," Schmollers Jahrbuch, LVIII, 1 (1934), 33–62.

E. H. Phelps Brown and Sheila V. Hopkins, "Wage-rates and Prices: Evidence for Population Pressure in the Sixteenth Century," Economica, XXIV, No. 96 (1957), 289–306, and "Builders' Wage-rates, Prices and Population: Some Further Evidence," ibid., XXVI, No. 101 (1959), 18–38.

Cambridge Economic History of Europe, I–II (Cambridge, 1941, 1952); F. de Dainville, "Grandeur et population des villes au XVIIIe siècle," Population, XIII, 3 (1958), 459–480.

L. I. Dublin et al., Length of Life, rev. ed. (New York, 1949); J. D. Durand, "The Population Statistics of China A.D. 2–1953," Population Studies, XIII, 3 (1960), 209–256.

P. M. Hauser and O. D. Duncan, eds., The Study of Population (Chicago, 1959); J. T. Krause, "Changes in English Fertility and Mortality," Economic History Review, XI, 1 (1958), 52–70.

Simon Kuznets, "Quantitative Aspects of the Economic Growth of Nations," Economic Development and Cultural Change, V, 1 (1956); Friedrich Lütge, "Das 14./15. Jahrhundert in der Sozial- und Wirtschaftsgeschichte," Jahrbücher für Nationalökonomie und Statistik, CLXII, Heft 3 (1950), 161–213; Richard Nelson, "Growth Models and the Escape from the Low-Level Equilibrium Trap: The Case of Japan," Economic Development and Cultural Change, VIII, 4 (1960), 378–388.

Ping-ti Ho, Studies in the Population of China 1368–1953 (Cambridge, 1959); J. J. Spengler and O. D. Duncan, eds., Demographic Analysis (Glencoe, 1956); Brinley Thomas, ed., The Economics of International Migration (London, 1958); United Nations, Demographic Yearbook.

was occasioned much more than now by sexual selection in survivorship. Change in genetical structure (i.e., changes in gene or genotypic frequencies) is dominated by reproduction selection, since a given genetically distinguishable fraction of a population (say, a cohort) may give rise to a disproportionate fraction of its successor population. The composition of a population's values and aspirations may be affected similarly, though never so completely. Changes in racial structure may result from both migratory and reproductive selection.

The change in composition of most concern in this essay, that in age structure, results in the long run from changes in mortality and/or fertility, though it can be produced in the short run by migratory selection. Change in age composition exemplifies, as probably does change in genetic structure, a type of demographic change that has become significant only in modern times. Before 1800 changes in fertility and mortality seldom were sufficiently marked and persistent to modify age composition greatly, though they might augment natural increase. Gross reproduction rates usually fell within the range 2.5–3. Life was typically short; "death was at the center of life, as the cemetery was at the center of the village." "Average durations of life in excess of 30–35 years were exceptional, and life expectancies of 20–30 years were the norm."[2] Not until the 1700s, if then, did this norm begin to be exceeded significantly. The ratio of persons aged 15–59 to all persons in a stable population would increase only about 5–6 percent in consequence of a decline in gross reproduction from 3 to 2.5; it would decline only about 5 percent as the result of an increase in life expectancy at birth from 20–25 years to 30–35 years.[3]

II. POPULATION CHANGE AS CAUSE

The role of population change as a causal agency in economic growth may be dealt with in stimulus-response terms. The responding is done by three sets of decision-makers (households, firms, and agencies of the state) whose relevant responding behavior is dealt with in Sub-section II. B. The stimuli to which these decision-makers respond are changes in the macro-economic environment in which they carry on economic activity. The stimuli or changes of concern in Sub-section II. A (which follows) are those produced in this macro-economic environment by population movements. The significance attached by decision-makers to these

[2] The quotations are from J. Fourastié, "De la vie traditionelle à la vie tertiaire," *Population*, XIV, 3 (1959), 418, and from A. J. Coale, "Increases in Expectation of Life and Population Growth," in Union internationale pour l'etude scientifique de la population, *International Population Conference* (Vienna, 1959), p. 36. See also J. D. Durand, "Mortality Estimates from Roman Tombstone Inscriptions," *American Journal of Sociology*, LXV, 4 (1960), 365–373; works of Mols and Russell.

[3] United Nations, *The Aging of Populations and Its Economic and Social Implications* (Population Studies, No. 26) (New York, 1956), pp. 26–27.

changes, together with their responses thereto, is conditioned by variables or constraints which lie outside the stimulus-response circuit propèr and which may be treated as exogenous elements. These intermediate variables tend to change in character and importance over time even as do components of the macro-economic environment and capacities of decision-makers.

A. *Macro-Economic Environment*

One may distinguish at least ten dimensions of a modern macro-economic environment which are sensitive to population change, and to modifications in which modern economic decision-makers are likely to be sensitive. Because population growth has been the rule in modern times, attention will be focused upon the effects of population increase instead of upon the effects of population decrease, even though the latter may differ from the former in more than mere change of sign.

Empirical treatment of interaction between changes in population and changes in various dimensions of a population's macro-economic environment is handicapped in two ways. First, the quantitative data available seldom fit nicely into the analytical categories or boxes employed by economists. Second, relations and findings are often space-bound or time-bound. Economies have changed greatly in organization, structure, technology, and resource base, and decision-makers have experienced great increases in the range of choice open to them. As a result the comparative importance of the ten dimensions discussed below has changed markedly over time. Only dimension 3 was more important formerly than now; dimensions 4, 9, and 10 were less significant formerly; dimensions 1–2, 5–8 were probably of little significance until modern times.

1. *Producer-population ratio.* The ratio of persons of productive age in a population to the whole of that population depends (*ceteris paribus*) solely upon its age composition. This ratio, representable (say) by the fraction of a population in the age group 15–59, is not often greatly affected by migration even in the short run, though it was so affected in nineteenth century America and other newly settled lands. It declines as mortality falls; e.g., about 6–7 percent when life expectancy at birth rises in a stable population from 35 to 60 years. In increases as fertility falls; e.g., about 10–12 percent when the gross reproduction rate declines from 2.5 to 1.5. It varies little from one stable population to another, the fraction aged 15–60 always approximating six-tenths.[4]

[4] *Ibid.*, pp. 26–27; see also Conseil National de Statistique du Brésil, "Sur la durée moyenne de la vie économiquement active," in United Nations, *Proceedings of the World Population Conference, 1954*, III (New York, 1955), 370–381.

During the past 160 years increase in the average duration of life has largely counterbalanced such improvement in age composition as is attributable to decline in fertility. For example, given a gross reproduction rate of 2.5 and a life expectancy of 30 years as of 1800, and corresponding values of 1.25 and 70 as of 1960, the ratio would have increased only a percent or so. Had gross reproduction not declined as postulated, the relative number of persons aged 15–59 would have been about 11 percent lower. Should life-expectancy be extended appreciably beyond 70, with gross reproduction given, the relative number of persons aged 15–59, would decline accordingly. Average income would be adversely affected since, as Johansen found, the upper limit of productive ages needs to rise in order that increase in average lifetime may appreciably elevate average income.[5]

The economic significance of the ratio of persons aged 15–59 to the total population is affected by the correlation obtaining between age and labor-force participation and by that found between age and productivity among persons participating in the labor force. While these correlations depend largely upon a country's technology, educational composition, industrial structure, degree of urbanization, income levels, and social-security conventions, they are affected also by factors responsible for increase in life expectancy. These factors make for decline in morbidity, for increase in a population's general health, and, hence, for increase in its capacity to work hard and regularly. Increase in life expectancy, unlike increase in fertility, is thus accompanied, within limits, by a compensatory change in the working capacity of labor-force participants.

2. *Dependency ratio.* The ratio of persons of unproductive age to those of productive age (say, of persons aged under 15 and over 65 to those between 15–64) fell in most developed countries between 1800 and 1950 when it approximated 0.54. It was only about two-thirds as high as that found in the underdeveloped world (around 0.81 in 1950).[6] Eventually, of course, declining mortality counterbalances improvement occasioned by declining fertility; e.g., in a stable population with a gross reproduction rate of 1.5 and a life expectancy of 70.2, the ratio differs little from that found in a stable population with corresponding values of 2.5 and 30.

Difficulties attendant upon the supply of education in high-fertility countries may be represented by the ratio of persons aged 15–64 to those under 15. This ratio, in the neighborhood of 1.3 in such countries, is about

[5] Coale, *op. cit.*, pp. 38–41; Leif Johansen, "Death Rates, Age Distribution, and Average Income," *Population Studies*, XI, 1 (1957), 77; Spengler and Duncan, *op. cit.*, pp. 497–517.

[6] United Nations, *The Aging of Populations*, pp. 8–9, 15; also V. G. Valaoras, "A Reconstruction of the Demographic History of Modern Greece," *Milbank Memorial Fund Quarterly*, XXXVIII, 2 (1960), 128.

half that found in low-fertility countries. It thus takes about twice as large a fraction of the labor force in a high-fertility as in a low-fertility country to supply comparable education (e.g., 4 percent of the labor force as compared with 2 percent, given a pupil-teacher ratio of 20 to 1). The advantage low-fertility countries enjoy in respect of teacher-supply is partly offset by the greater cost of supporting their aged; it could be wholly offset, given sufficiently high life expectancy.

3. *Man-land ratio.* Because population growth, together with net immigration, increases the ratio of population to land and to other raw-material sources, it may depress output per variable input in affected industries. Inasmuch as outlay upon raw materials other than products of land, though of increasing importance since the mid-nineteenth century, still remains small in relation to gross national product, the impact of population growth upon the availability of raw materials may be treated in terms of the man-land ratio, and agricultural land may be assigned the role played by limitational factors in demographic models.

Population growth elevates the demand curve for output into whose production the services of agricultural land enter. Accordingly, if unexploited sources of these services (similar to sources already in use) are not easily accessible, population growth tends to be followed by increase in the intensity with which land is utilized. In consequence variable inputs per unit of output increase at the margin and (*ceteris paribus*) output per worker in the economy as a whole falls; or, if technical progress is being realized, variable inputs per unit of output do not decline as much as they might otherwise have done.

This statement was applicable in Malthus' day and long before.[7] It remains applicable in various densely populated countries in which agricultural land has not diminished in importance and the agricultural labor force has not yet begun to decline appreciably.[8] It has proven of use in the analysis of income determination in agriculture (though at times movement of capital into low-wage areas can be more important than movement of labor out of these areas),[9] and it helps to explain migration from land-short to land-long regions and countries. It is pertinent to the utilization of non-agricultural land, though difficult to employ empirically because of imperfections in the urban property market, and because in many countries the land absorbed by

[7] See Colin Clark, *Conditions of Economic Progress,* 2nd ed. (London, 1951), pp. 225–226; W. R. Robinson, "Money, Population and Economic Change in Late Medieval Europe," and M. M. Poston's reply, *Economic History Review,* XII, 1 (1959), 63–82.

[8] See B. F. Hoselitz, "Population Pressure, Industrialization and Social Mobility," *Population Studies,* XI, 1 (1957), 124–127.

[9] Frank T. Bachmura, "Man-Land Equalization through Migration," *American Economic Review,* XLIX, 5 (1959), 1004–1017; G. H. Borts, "Returns Equalization and Regional Growth," *ibid.,* L, 2 (1960), 319–347.

urbanization, recreation, and transportation still forms only a small fraction (about 5 percent in the U.S.A.) of that used in the supply of forest and farm products. Comparison over time of the role played by urbanization in making for economy in the use of non-agricultural land is complicated by the fact that change in urban transport has greatly modified the urban population-land ratio (which is usually lower today than it was in ancient and medieval times, or in the eighteenth century when it often rose above earlier levels).

4. *Structure of demand.* The composition of demand reflects the incidence of many forces, among them rate of population growth and age composition of population. Under *ceteris paribus* conditions an increase in the requirement of some products (e.g., food) is associated with increase in population, and of others, (e.g., dwelling units, furnishings) with increase in number of households. Population growth particularly stimulates the consumption of products, the elasticity of household demand for which is below unity, and the absorption of the services of lumpy products, the elasticity of whose supply is likely to be low periodically in a slowly expanding economy. Population growth may shape demand indirectly in so far as demand is a function of population concentration and such concentration is a function of size of population. Changes in age composition affect the structure of demand in two ways: by their impact upon man's age-connected needs, and by modifying the ratio of households to population. The incidence of population movements, both upon investment in population-sensitive capital and upon the structure of demand in general, tends to be reflected, albeit imperfectly, in the composition of gross national product so long as consumer sovereignty and freedom of choice prevail (as is unlikely in state-dominated economies).[10]

Here structure of demand is described as mirroring the impact of population change. This structure also mirrors the impact of technological, income, and related changes. These in turn may modify the response of population movements to changes in per capita income.

5. *Time horizon of decision-makers.* When a population is growing, the time horizons of decision-makers tend to be longer than when it is not growing. This is true of entrepreneurial and governmental decision-makers and it may be true of household decision-makers. For a prospectively positive rate of population growth projects the impact of currently utilized resources farther into the future than does a prospectively zero rate of population growth. On balance, the prospect of population growth probably diminishes the development-retarding influence of uncertainty respecting the future, since

[10] Simon Kuznets, "Long Swings in the Growth of Population and Related Economic Variables," *Proceedings of the American Philosophical Society*, CII, 1 (1958), 33–35, 49; Clark, *Conditions*, p. 410.

it tends to swell entrepreneurial estimates of future demand more than entrepreneurial estimates of future supply.

6. *Ratio of ex-ante investment to ex-ante saving.* Population growth
tends to increase this ratio. Equipping increments to a population with industrial, consumers', and public capital requires investment; a 1 percent rate
of population growth will absorb savings supplied by a 3–5 percent rate of
saving. At the same time the addition of children to a household, income
being given, tends to reduce its capacity to save and its actual rate of saving.

7. *Labor-supply-demand relations.* When a population is growing appreciably (instead of remaining approximately stationary), its dependency
ratio is comparatively high and its relative number of persons of productive
age is comparatively low. On the assumption that the size of a country's labor
force corresponds closely to the size of its population, one would therefore
expect the ratio of a country's labor force to its population to be inversely
associated with its rate of natural increase. Labor-force participation, together with the supply of labor, is not entirely under the governance of age
composition, however, although in a number of advanced countries the ratio
of the labor force to the population of working age seems not to vary
greatly.[11] Labor force data reveal much international disparity in the labor-
force-population ratio which cannot be attributed to disparity in age composition; but these data, together with the economies to which they relate,
are too heterogeneous to permit precise isolation of the demographic and
economic influences at work.

An increase in the dependency ratio may give rise to a certain amount
of compensatory change and it tends to do so. In most countries employed
workers can easily supply additional man-hours, since they work far fewer
hours than they are capable of working (e.g., in 1950 the work-week averaged 40 and 48 hours, respectively, in the U.S.A. and Europe; in 1850–90,
62–70 and 69–84 hours); much larger numbers of women can participate in
the labor force than do; and entry into the labor force can be accelerated and
withdrawal delayed. There is, in short, a reserve of labor power that may be
tapped.

A rise in the dependency ratio may be interpreted as a rightward shift
in the potential demand curve for labor that will not be met by the existing
labor force should its demand for income in terms of effort not be such as to
generate a fairly elastic supply of man-hours. Then additional man-hours
must be sought elsewhere, either through the employment of additional
women, or, as happens in underdeveloped agricultural countries, by deferring

---

[11] C. D. Long, *The Labor Force Under Changing Income and Employment* (Princeton, 1958), Chs. 1, 5–7, 12–13.

retirement and reducing the age of entry into the labor force.[12] Undoubtedly, if increase in the number of dependents per household reduces per capita income therein, or greatly slows down its advance, many households will be disposed to supply more man-hours even at current wage-rates, by working longer hours or by setting more of their members to work. This disposition operates to slow down the tendency of the average number of man-hours worked per adult to fall, and it could even increase it.

The increasing entry of women into the labor force appears to be dominated by forces other than changes in age-composition and in number of dependents per family. It has accompanied decline in the participation of males in the labor force as well as decline in both fertility and the length of the standard work-week. It has been governed, above all, by the spread of industrialization, modernization, and urbanization.[13]

8. *Flexibility.* Population growth makes for greater flexibility in an economy so long as overall population density remains below levels at which constraints on freedom of choice are deemed increasingly necessary, given prevailing technology. Underlying this greater flexibility is the fact that, when population is growing, additions to demand and supply are more important, in comparison with replacements (of products no longer considered serviceable), than when a population is stationary. For then gross national product, capital and wealth, and the labor force are growing faster, with the result that adjustments to technical progress, style and fashion change, purposeful obsolescence, etc., are easier to accomplish. Moreover, since entrepreneurs seemingly assume population growth to augment demand more than supply, they are more inclined to make adjustments, to undertake new and relatively untried ventures, and to count on population growth to correct overestimates of future demand.

(i) Suppose that the average life of gross national product is 5 years and that per capita income is increasing 2 percent per year. Then, if population is stationary, the ratio of additions (i.e., increment in total realized demand or output) to replacements will approximate 10 percent. This ratio becomes 15 percent if population and the labor force are growing 1 percent per year. Now suppose a two-percent-per-year decline in the per capita demand for a given product, or for the labor incorporated into it. The 1 percent increase in population will offset half this decline and thus make the required adjustment to the decline slower and, hence, somewhat easier.

12 *Ibid.*, pp. 72–82; J. D. Durand, "Population Structure as a Factor in Manpower and Dependency Problems of Under-developed Countries," *Population Bulletin of the United Nations*, No. 3 (1953), pp. 1–16, esp. 6–8, 13.

13 United Nations, *The Determinants and Consequences of Population Trends* (Population Studies, No. 17) (New York, 1953), pp. 200–203; Long, *op. cit.*, Ch. 1; C. E. V. Leser, "Trends in Woman's Work Participation," *Population Studies*, XII, 2 (1958), 100–110.

(ii) Suppose a stationary male population with a life expectancy of 70. Each year approximately 2 percent of the labor force withdraw from it for reasons of death, retirement, and disability, and their places are taken by an equal number of males newly entering the labor force. Accordingly, in the absence of recruits, the set of individuals attached to a given employment would diminish 2 percent in the first year and at progressively higher rates in subsequent years. The males newly entering the labor force (but not shrinking employments) constitute a mobile reserve whose members enter expanding employments and enable these to grow even though the aggregate male labor force remains unchanged. This reserve would be appreciably larger, however, if the labor force were growing 1 percent per year, and it would accordingly be somewhat easier to keep workers distributed optimally among employments. How important this advantage is turns on the extent to which the younger members of the labor force are interoccupationally mobile when its total membership remains constant.

(iii) When a population is growing, its aggregate stock of capital and durable wealth grows faster than when its numbers are stationary, though probably not enough faster to make capital and wealth per head grow faster. This tendency is associated with the fact that income growth is positively correlated with population growth, and that capital needs to be provided for increments in the population as well as for improvement of the capital-population ratio; and it is somewhat reenforced by the fact that the ratio of capital-replacement to depreciation varies inversely with the rate of growth of gross national product.[14] The average age of equipment in use will be somewhat lower, therefore, and a larger fraction of the stock of equipment will incorporate recent "know-how," given that the economy is technically progressive. Moreover, since a larger fraction of the stock of capital equipment will have been installed recently, its composition will be better adapted to current demands. In consequence of the seemingly greater opportunity to install new equipment, the rate of innovation may be somewhat higher, and, as a result, the rate of invention would tend to be higher.

An economy tends (ceteris paribus) to be technologically more progressive if its population is growing instead of non-growing. The pattern of invention will not be quite the same, however, since invention is more likely to be capital-saving when the rate of population growth is relatively high than when it is relatively low. Furthermore, in so far as economic fluctuation is associated with fluctuation in the output of durable assets, increase of the latter in relative importance could intensify economic fluctuation.

9. *Size of population versus size of country.* It is essential to distinguish between size of population and size of country. Within limits increase in size of a country's population permits release of economies associated with increase in scale, division of labor, and so on. Moreover, it is accompanied

[14] E. D. Domar, *Essays in the Theory of Economic Growth* (New York, 1957), Ch. 7.

by increase in the ratio of the size of relevant regional or national markets to the capacity of firms of optimum size in various industries. In consequence, elasticity of demand and (probably) industrial elasticity of supply increase, with the result that the economy becomes more competitive and inputs are utilized under more nearly optimal conditions. Population growth tends to accentuate this tendency.

In contrast, with overall population density given, increase in size of a country is accompanied, within limits, by increase in the size and diversity of its economy. It is accompanied by increase in the size of the stream of inputs that may be made subject to a single and essentially sovereign set of market and political mechanisms which, acting in combination, are capable of optimally transforming these inputs into output. For, as a rule, under otherwise similar conditions, mobility of factors is greater within than between countries; moreover, competition is more intense, and entrepreneurial estimates of profit-prospects tend to be more favorable in larger than in smaller economies. Presumably a point might be reached when further increase in the size of a country and its economy would no longer be a source of economic advantage, though it might not yet be a source of disadvantage.[15]

10. *Population concentration.* The forces which make for population growth also make for population concentration and, hence, for such economic changes as are associated therewith. Two processes are involved. (i) Expansion of the agricultural sector is limited (in the absence of exportation) by the inelasticity of domestic demand for agricultural produce. Accordingly, the (surplus) agricultural population beyond what is required (given current technology) to supply a community's demand for produce must seek employment outside agriculture. Much of this surplus, which functions as an industrial reserve army, tends to emigrate to the economy's nonrural communities, or abroad where it may increase demand for the output of these communities. So long as the rural population is much larger than the nonrural and rural natural increase is relatively high, the rural industrial reserve army declines very slowly and the flow of rural migrants into the nonrural sector serves to hold down nonrural wages and to augment nonrural profits; this circumstance has been largely responsible for the slowness with which wages have risen in the early stages of industrialization. This flow may also intensify and protract urban boom conditions, thereby making for greater contraction and, hence, for greater amplitude of fluctuation.[16]

---

[15] Austin Robinson, ed., *The Consequences of the Size of Nations* (London, 1960).

[16] Dorothy S. Thomas, *Social and Economic Aspects of Swedish Population Movements* (New York, 1941), Chs. 8–9, 12; D. Mazumdar, "Under-employment in Agriculture and the Industrial Wage Rate," *Economica*, XXVI, 4 (1959), 328–340; N. Georgescu-Roegen, "Economic Theory and Agrarian Economics," *Oxford Economic Papers*, XII, 1 (1960), 11–29; Nicholas Kaldor, *Essays on Economic Stability and Growth* (London, 1960), pp. 288–297.

(ii) The migrating surplus, together with such population growth as it subsequently generates, tends to become concentrated in relatively large urban centers, though not in a regular enough way to permit simple formulation of the association between the size of population and summary indices of the concentration of nonrural population.[17]

B. Micro-Economic Response

We now inquire into the probable responses of strategically situated decision-makers to the dimensional changes, or stimuli, just described. These decision-makers are of three sorts: (1) family households; (2) business firms whose primary concern is the profitable transformation of inputs into output; and (3) governmental agencies empowered to determine how certain inputs are used. We are here concerned only with responses affecting the supply and/or the use of inputs over which the decision-makers exercise control in the shorter run.

1. *Household.* Changes in a population's rate of growth and age composition affect the disposition of households to supply labor-service in two ways. (i) An increase in the number of children, or dependent members, of a household, tends to increase its aggregate outlay upon consumption, to diminish its current rate of saving, and to affect the uses to which its savings are put.[18] Such increase is roughly equivalent, in analytical terms, to a decrease in family income. It often animates a household's nondependent members (other than mother) to supply more labor-service at given prices than they would otherwise have been ready to supply. It may even affect the labor-service supply curve of the mother similarly, though in lesser measure and usually after the children have advanced in age sufficiently to diminish the mother's double burden of caring for them and working outside the household. Unfortunately, empirical data bearing upon the shifts of household labor-service supply curves are not abundant, particularly those relating to women. For researchers have been largely concerned with the correlation between membership of wives in the labor force and their relative infertility, and with that between number of children and freedom of wives to participate in the labor force.[19]

[17] Otis Dudley Duncan et al., *Metropolis and Region* (Baltimore, 1960).

[18] E.g., see R. W. Goldsmith, Dorothy S. Brady, and Horst Mendershausen, *A Study of Saving in the United States*, III (Princeton, 1956), 202–223; A. M. Henderson, "The Cost of a Family," *Review of Economic Studies*, XVII, 2 (1949–50), 127–148; *idem* (with J. Hajnal), "The Economic Position of the Family," in Royal Commission on Population, *Papers*, V (London, 1950), 9–19; Janet A. Fisher, "Postwar Changes in Income and Savings among Consumers in Different Age Groups," *Econometrica*, XX, 1 (1952), 47–50.

[19] E.g., see Jeanne Ridley, "Number of Children Expected in Relation to Non-Familial Activities of the Wife," *Milbank Memorial Fund Quarterly*, XXXVII, 3 (1959),

(ii) Change in the dependency ratio tends to affect fullness of employment under *ceteris paribus* conditions. Thus, a rise in this ratio tends to accompany an increase in the rate of natural increase and to be accompanied by an upswing in the potential demand for labor-service. This upswing tends to offset the upswing in supply discussed under (i), particularly since the latter has been partly counter-balanced already by the tendency of motherhood to remove women temporarily from the labor force. The negative income effect of the increase in dependents reduces the chance that the labor supply curve will be backward bending in the relevant range.

2. *Business-firm.* Whether the effects described eventuate in greater employment depends upon the response business firms make to increases in potential demand for labor-service associated with increases in the dependency ratio and in the need for additional durable assets. For the business firm will be responding to all the changes in the economy's macro-economic dimensions described under (A), together with its estimate of the probable response of competing and complementary business firms to these same changes. In the absence of a temporary downswing in overall economic activity, movement to a higher level of fertility is more likely than movement to a lower level of fertility to actualize potential demand for labor, at least in developed countries. After population growth has become stable and an economy has become adjusted thereto, however, the significance of the rate of population growth diminishes, though not enough to offset entirely (under *ceteris paribus* conditions) the tendency of a higher rate of growth to be more favorable than a lower rate to full employment (given sufficiency of capital).

3. *State-agencies.* The responses described under (1) and (2) are conditioned by the responses made by agencies of the state, which in the aggregate enjoy considerable autonomy. Let C, G, and I represent, in aggregate terms, private demand for consumer goods and services, governmental absorption of goods and services, and private investment (or offsets to "savings"); and let these aggregates be expressed in terms of average hours of labor-service, of which L would normally be forthcoming under conditions of full employment. Accordingly, if L should exceed $C + G + I$, it would be necessary only to manipulate the magnitude and the content of G to eliminate the disparity. Of course, the impact of such manipulation upon the capacity of the economy to produce in the future would depend largely, as would its

277–296; R. K. Kelsall and Sheila Mitchell, "Married Women and Employment in England and Wales," *Population Studies*, XIII, 1 (1959), 23, 30–31; Alain Girard, "Le budget-temps de la femme mariée dans les agglomerations urbaines," *Population*, XIII, 4 (1958), 590–618; Durand, "Population Structure as a Factor . . . ," *loc. cit.*, p. 7; Long, *op. cit.*, pp. 114–116, 123–133.

impact upon population growth, upon the content of the change made in the magnitude of G. Similarly, the capacity of the state to manipulate G would depend *ceteris paribus* upon the nature of the state's institutional and agency structure. A state's agencies thus may constitute an effective lever wherewith to supplement or counterbalance the response-mechanisms discussed under (1) and (2). Our discussion has run in terms of sustaining full employment. It could also run in terms of preventing inflation, since population growth might generate increases in I in excess of the amount of savings the economy stood ready to supply; in this event C or G might be reduced, or L could be augmented.

III. POPULATION CHANGE AS EFFECT

Migration, mortality, and fertility are sensitive to economic change. Regarding migration it need only be said, that in the absence of restraints, a person will move from his current situation in space to some other if he expects his economic welfare to be increased thereby in sufficient measure more than to offset the costs of movement and the uncertainties involved. Before 1800, legal and other restraints, costs of movement, and uncertainties respecting what a migrant might achieve probably operated, together with the fact that income disparity was much smaller than in modern times, to limit individual and very small-scale migration. As these conditions changed, largely because of changes in the macro-economic environment, the disposition to migrate was affected accordingly.

The relationship between economic conditions and mortality is not a simple one. First, this relationship may change as a result of changes in the socio-economic composition of a population, since mortality usually is higher among the relatively less well rewarded or housed elements of the population. Second, mortality may eventually prove sensitive to a cumulation of minor economic changes, though not to any one such change. Third, mortality may be sensitive to a major economic change (e.g., famine), but not to minor changes; this sort of relationship is likely when economic conditions are hard and mortality already is very high (e.g., life expectancy in the low 20s). Fourth, mortality may no longer be very sensitive to minor economic changes if economic conditions are very good (as in some modern societies), or if highly effective methods of death control have been introduced (e.g., in post-1930 Ceylon). Finally, a great deal of mortality has been attributable to catastrophes (war, famine, pestilence, etc.) which, while they produced adverse economic effects, were only partly if at all of economic origin. Most important of these catastrophes was epidemic pestilence and the pronounced upsurges in abnormal mortality which accompanied it. Such mortality greatly reduced Europe's population several times (e.g., A.D. 200–600, and again in the fourteenth century) ; in fact, Europe's population did not begin to grow at a sustained and accelerated rate until in the eighteenth century when pestilential mortality greatly declined. Such mortality continued, however, to interrupt growth in large non-European countries (e.g., India, China).[20]

Even though the relationship between economic conditions and mortality is not a simple or linear one, a portion of mortality has been quite sensitive to economic change. So long as population remained largely at the mercy of the elements, as was true even in eighteenth century Europe, a turn for the worse in weather and other economically-oriented conditions would be accompanied by marked upturns in mortality. In the course of this century, however, at least in England, mortality began to fall significantly as a result of improvement in economic conditions, and this double improvement continued, though not without interruption, throughout the nineteenth century.[21]

Gross reproduction has always been somewhat subject to social control, but, prior to the contraceptive revolution of the nineteenth century, it could not be modified greatly or rapidly. The maximum gross reproduction rate may be put at 4; this implies crude birth rates of roughly 60–64 and 56–57, respectively, in stable populations with life expectancies of 20–30 and 40–50 years.[22] Given a gross reproduction rate of 4 and an average effective reproductive life of 22–23 years, a representative woman completing this period would average a birth every 2.8–2.9 years. Even though a married woman survived to complete her reproductive period, however, she might have produced less than 8 births. For her period of exposure to reproduction commonly was reduced by deferment of her initial marriage, or by its premature termination (e.g., because of death of spouse, etc.), together with her failure to remarry promptly. How much her production of children would be reduced thereby would depend upon whether or not reduction of exposure at earlier ages diminished fertility more than did reduction at higher ages and on whether this reduction came early (e.g., because of deferment of marriage)

[20] Karl F. Helleiner, "The Vital Revolution Reconsidered," *Canadian Journal of Economics and Political Science*, XXIII, 1 (1957), 1–9; *idem*, "Population Movements and Agrarian Depression in the Later Middle Ages," *ibid.*, XVII, 4, 368–377; *idem*, *Readings in Economic History* (Toronto, 1946), Introduction; G. Utterström, "Some Population Problems in Pre-Industrial Sweden," *Scandinavian Historical Review*, II, 2 (1954), 103–165; works of Mols and Russell.

[21] E.g., see Helleiner, "The Vital Revolution Reconsidered," *loc. cit.*, pp. 1–2; M. M. Poston and J. Titow, "Heriots and Prices on Winchester Manors," *Economic History Review*, XI, 3 (1959), 399–410; J. Titow, "Evidence of Weather in the Account Rolls of the Bishopric of Winchester, 1209–1350," *ibid.*, XII, 3, 362–365.

[22] Joseph W. Eaton and Albert J. Mayer, *Man's Capacity to Reproduce* (Glencoe, 1954), pp. 38–42; George Sabagh, "The Fertility of the French-Canadian Women During the Seventeenth Century," *American Journal of Sociology*, XLVII, 2 (1942), 683–687; F. Lorimer, *Culture and Human Fertility*, Unesco (Paris, 1954), Ch. 1.

or later in her reproductive period (e.g., because of the death of her spouse).[23]

Because of these and other restraints, gross reproduction rates have seldom approximated 4. Prior to the 1800s (when new methods of fertility control became available in medically advanced parts of the world) these rates usually remained within the range 2.5–3.0, yielding birth rates in the 40s. Even so, a rate of population growth of 0.5 to 1.0 percent per year could easily be attained, at least for a short time; a birth rate in the 40s would suffice, given a death rate in the middle or high 30s. Russell's observation that medieval society could produce "more than enough children to maintain its numbers except under the most severe circumstances" seems applicable to the Roman and to many oriental societies.[24]

Of the eleven intermediate variables which, according to Davis and Blake, govern fertility by conditioning exposure to intercourse and conception, together with gestation and successful parturition, only some are both significantly sensitive to economic changes and quantitatively important.[25] Involuntary abstinence, voluntary control over fecundity (e.g., by castration), involuntary sterility (apparently somewhat sensitive to economic conditions), coital frequency, and voluntary abstinence within unions (which is greater in preindustrial than in industrial societies) are not of this sort. The adverse effect of unfavorable economic conditions upon foetal viability is partly offset by the resulting reduction in interval between pregnancies. Voluntary control over foetal mortality through recourse to abortion, while sensitive to economic change (among other factors), was prohibited, though not with complete success, in the Christian world as was its functional equivalent, infanticide (a form of mortality). The amount of time spent outside a sexual union by a member of a terminated union depends upon mortality, upon the frequency of separation and divorce, and upon the opportunity of victims of broken unions to remarry; of these factors the first and the last are somewhat sensitive to economic change.

Three variables, each sensitive to economic affairs and aspirations, have been primarily responsible, along with abortion, for the fact that gross reproduction has usually fallen short of its theoretical maximum. They are contraceptive practice, age of entry into marriage, or other sexual unions,

[23] W. Brass, "The Distribution of Births in Human Populations," *Population Studies*, XII, 1 (1958), 56–58, 61–63, 67–68; Chi-Hsien Tuan, "Reproductive Histories of Chinese Women in Rural Taiwan," *ibid.*, pp. 40–50; H. Hyrenius, "Fertility and Reproduction in a Swedish Population Group without Family Limitation," *ibid.*, XII, 2, 121–130; Louis Henry, *Fécondité des mariages* (Paris, 1953), Chs. 7–8; Christopher Tietze, "Reproductive Span and Rate of Reproduction among Hutterite Women," *Fertility and Sterility*, VIII, 1 (1957), pp. 89–97.

[24] *Late Ancient and Medieval Population*, p. 22.

[25] See Kingsley Davis and Judith Blake, "Social Structure and Fertility: An Analytic Framework," *Economic Development and Cultural Change*, IV, 3 (1956), 211–235.

and permanent celibacy. The first of these, while it played a role of some importance before the nineteenth century when folk methods predominated, became quite important only in the later 1800s.[26] Until then deferment of marriage and (in lesser measure) non-marriage constituted the main curbs on fertility. In a society little subject to contraception, postponement of a woman's marriage until in the middle or late 20s might reduce by 1.5–2 or more the number of children she would bear. This curb was primarily operative in those parts of the world (especially Europe) in which the nuclear family predominated and young people could not, as a rule, marry until the prospective spouse had access to support for a family in the form of cultivable land or employment; it sometimes was found, however, even in familistic societies (e.g., Japan). Deferment of marriage was much less common, as was non-marriage, in areas (e.g., much of Asia and Africa) in which the joint family system prevailed and acquisition of economic independence was not a precondition to marriage.[27] In these parts, therefore, fertility usually was higher than in Western Europe, as apparently was mortality.

The fertility-affecting variables which serve, together with mortality, to condition a household's size and composition are interrelated, constituting an equilibrium system that is subject to exogenous constraints and influences. Within a household, therefore, a change in any one of these variables may substitute for a change in another. Similarly, within the world at large one sort of change sometimes offsets another, as when the sometimes greater ease of marriage in cities was offset by the fact that urban mortality commonly exceeded urban natality. In general, the disposition of a household to modify any one fertility- or mortality-affecting variable has been affected by what has taken place in the external economic world, as well as by changes in other variables internal to the household viewed as a system.

Changes in a household's aspirations may greatly modify its disposition to control fertility. Such change is much more characteristic, however, of modern than of traditional or other pre-1800 societies in which very few people were optimistic respecting their futures. Before the late eighteenth century the dynamic components of most societies were comparatively small. It was not anticipated that the real income of more than a small fraction of the population would improve appreciably. Not many individuals were likely to be animated by high and rising aspirations, in the light of which their

---

[26] *Ibid.*, pp. 223–225; works of Russell; United Nations, *The Determinants and Consequences*, pp. 75–77; A. Sauvy, "La prévention des naissances dans la famille," *Population*, XV, 1 (1960), 115–120; Irene B. Taeuber, *The Population of Japan* (Princeton, 1958), pp. 29–31.

[27] K. Davis, *The Population of India and Pakistan* (Princeton, 1951), p. 108; Taeuber, *op. cit.*, pp. 30–31, 169; Davis and Blake, *op. cit.*, pp. 214–223; T. H. Hollingsworth, "A Demographic Study of the British Ducal Families," *Population Studies*, XI, 1 (1957), 13–14, 25–26; works of Mols and Russell.

reproductive conduct ought to be determined. Moreover, the likelihood that high aspirations might give rise to "fertility planning" was much reduced by the high mortality prevailing and the consequential inference that mere replacement of a household would probably prove difficult.

Inasmuch as some of the determinants of mortality and the main determinants of fertility are sensitive to changes in economic and related conditions, natural increase will be sensitive thereto. Prior to the nineteenth century, however, mortality was both more volatile than natality and more immediately sensitive to changes in economic conditions. Some mortality (other than infanticide) responded almost tropismatically to economic change, whereas fertility usually responded only in so far as individuals of reproductive age were disposed to modify it through variation in age at marriage or recourse to abortion or contraception. Natural increase, of course, fluctuated more than either fertility or mortality which tended to move in opposite directions as economic conditions changed.

If, for expository convenience, we use the concept population elasticity e (where $e = dP \cdot Y/dY \cdot P$, P denotes aggregate population, and Y denotes some index of aggregate economic conditions such as total output or income), it may be said that prior to the nineteenth century e was positive and probably close to unity except when the movement of population was dominated by abnormal mortality. In the course of this century, however, the value of e fell. For the forces making for increase in Y also made for change in the socio-economic composition of populations, for increasing knowledge of contraception, and for supersession of traditional modes of life by a highly rational one. Within some components of the population, furthermore, materially-oriented aspirations rose faster than income and intensified the pressure households already were under (e.g., because of diminution in infant and child mortality, increase in the number of dependents per household, child labor and related legislation, etc.) to regulate family size.

Decline in e signifies that a population may be escaping from a Malthusian trap in which high fertility keeps household incomes depressed. Escape entails three steps. (i) Income must be made to increase faster than population, by increasing the work-week, by making fuller and more efficient use of available agents of production, and by augmenting savings and importing capital. (ii) This upward movement of income must be sustained by increasing the rate of innovation, the marginal propensity to save, and the capital-labor ratio. (iii) In time fertility must be reduced, since otherwise limitational factors may slow down the increase of income and permit e to rise. Step (iii) may prove easier to realize today than formerly because methods of fertility control are much more effective now than formerly, and men are as indisposed as ever to relinquish a scale of living once attained, or even one intensely desired.

Steps (i) and (ii) may prove more difficult to take, however. Today the populations of underdeveloped countries may be increasing 2–3 percent per year, whereas 175 years ago they were increasing 1 percent or less.[28] Today, therefore, increasing per capita income 1 percent per year may call for savings of 9–16 percent of income, whereas before 1800 the bulk of savings (perhaps 3–5 percent) often could be used to increase per capita income. The presence of limitational factors may even operate, especially in densely populated lands, as they often did in less densely peopled pre-1800 economies, to make realization of the required annual increase in output (at least 3–4 percent) difficult. Escape may prove possible, however, through the introduction of tested innovations, through orienting investment to the supply of producer goods, and through the avoidance of unproductive use of those inputs which are not required to satisfy current minimal needs. Even then income may not rise rapidly enough to transform a society's social structure and aspirations and thereby set in motion a pronounced and rapid decline in gross reproduction. Yet it is upon such decline as well as upon initially successful efforts to increase per capita income that escape from a Malthusian trap ultimately depends.

IV. POPULATION MOVEMENTS AS INDICATORS

Because before 1800 population growth implied income growth and income growth usually signified population growth, certain inferences may be drawn from pre-1800 population movements.

1. Continuing "pull" migration (i.e., movement *toward* centers of attraction) signified rising aggregate and per capita real income, since "free" migrants usually seek higher income and since urban expansion improves the demand for rural produce.

2. Persisting rural population growth in a traditional society (in contradistinction to one capitalistically and rationally organized) has been compatible with overall economic retardation when this growth absorbed the surplus produce that would otherwise have been available to a more dynamic non-rural population.[29]

3. Long-run swings in population have signified swings in the affected economy, though these usually have been partly of demographic origin.

4. In the past when the rate of innovation was much lower than today, population growth, together with its spread, was the main absorber of newly formed capital; it thus tended to stiffen both profits and real interest rates (though the movement of monetary rates was sometimes cushioned by the associated tendency of money prices to fall, as noted in [10] below).

5. A continuing and fairly stable increase in population signified con-

[28] Colin Clark, "World Population," *Nature*, CLXXXI (May, 1958), pp. 1235–1236.
[29] N. Keyfitz, "Développement économique et accroissement de population: un exemple actuel en Indonesie," *Population*, XIII, 3 (1958), 407–433.

tinuing increase in total output and at least the maintenance of per capita income.

6. The gradual slowing down of population growth (e.g., in the late 1200s and early 1300s) signified the increasing operation of formerly quite powerful limitational factors (e.g., diminishing returns in agriculture, deceleration in growth of strategic markets) and approach to a population ceiling fixed largely by the prevailing technology, mode of agricultural organization, and socio-economic structure of society.

7. Inasmuch as the "normal" tendency, in the absence of catastrophe or of economic collapse, was for numbers to grow until the ceiling noted in (6) had been reached, a sharp but non-persisting decline in population, though associated with economic contraction, merely signified the incidence of catastrophes, whereas an initially marked and subsequently persisting decline signified collapse of the existing politico-economic organization.

8. Prior to the nineteenth century persistently falling real wages must usually have signified a rising man-land ratio in agriculture and a turning of the terms of trade against the non-agricultural sector. Of course, as implied in (6), growth of population might long persist before limitational factors became effective and began to depress the marginal productivity of labor and (eventually) real wages.

9. Persisting population growth, particularly when not associated with extension of settlement, signified increase in the real agricultural rental share.

10. Since the movement of aggregate output almost always was positively associated with population growth, such growth tended to make for falling money prices in the absence of sufficient accessions to the stock of hard money. For while increase in the exchange value of the monetary unit usually makes for increasing economy in its use, the resulting increase in velocity could have offset only partially the increasing pressure of the volume of activity upon that of available hard money.

Decline in population and total output produced opposite effects. Rising (falling) prices did not necessarily reflect population growth (decline) since the supply of hard money of standard quality sometimes changed markedly for reasons not closely associated with population movement.[30]

11. While the economic implications of pre-1800 population growth seem clear, interpretation of the impact of population decline is not always easy, since the conditions responsible for this decline may also affect directly the economic variables responding to population decline (e.g., business confidence, money supply, gross interest rates, economic organization).

Even given that these inferences are generally tenable and that demographic indicators may be employed to help determine the current state of

[30] For an excellent account of price movements see E. J. Hamilton, "The History of Prices before 1750," *XIᵉ Congress Internationale des Sciences Historiques* (Stockholm, 1960), pp. 144–164.

economic development of backward economies,[31] it does not follow that inferences may be similarly drawn today, or that quite rigid growth models incorporating population movements are nearly so applicable in today's advanced economies as in yesterday's relatively primitive and static societies. Today the range of choice open to men is much wider than it was before 1800, and the functional connections between population and economic movements are much more variable. Thus, since population growth is now dominated by fertility which is both volatile and relatively unpredictable, the response of population growth to output growth is susceptible of wide variation. Moreover, because technological change plays so large and increasing though somewhat variable a role in the formation of output, and because both the volume and the composition of capital formation may vary greatly, the response of output to population growth is also susceptible of wide variation.

[31] P. M. Hauser, "Demographic Indicators of Economic Development," *Economic Development and Cultural Change*, VII, 2 (1959), 98–116; E. G. Stockwell, "The Measurements of Economic Development," *ibid.*, VIII, 4 (1960), 419–432.

AGE DISTRIBUTION
AS A CHALLENGE
TO DEVELOPMENT

Nathan Keyfitz

ABSTRACT

The 1961 census of Indonesia suggests that the number of entrants into the labor force will double during the next five years and that their literacy rate will be 75 per cent. Literate citizens with high expectations will be impatient with the minute division of labor and product in village agriculture; even those willing to work along traditional lines will find no land remaining. A large movement to the cities can be anticipated, but it will encounter the difficulty that the generation of potential managers is relatively small, for demographic and other reasons. These facts can be expected to modify Indonesian life sharply, the direction of modification depending on whether or not the crisis is interpreted as an issue of production in relation to population.

Much attention is being given in the new countries to the creation of new men; the most malleable material out of which to make national citizens is the young adult population. The demographic fact of a relative surplus of young adults combines with the molding of them by national civilian and military agencies and the educational system to create directions of economic and social pressure whose effects are becoming visible in certain countries. In this paper the age distribution of Indonesia will be presented in some detail; comparison will be made with other countries of Asia; finally some

From Nathan Keyfitz, "Age Distribution as a Challenge to Development," *American Journal of Sociology,* 70:6:659–668 (May 1965). Reprinted by permission of The University of Chicago Press.

of the economic and social consequences of the changing distribution will be traced out.

1961 AGE DISTRIBUTION OF INDONESIA

The Indonesian census of 1961 has now been tabulated on a 1 per cent sample, of which the classification by age and sex is reproduced below as Table 1. Following down the column for both sexes together we note the drop from over 15 million in each of the first two age groups to about 8 million subsequently, and the fact that the age distribution is very nearly flat from ten to thirty-five. (Ages from twenty-five onward must be divided by two because they are in ten-year age groups.) The flatness or emptiness of these ages has been cited as a disadvantage under which Indonesia suffered in the 1950's;[1] the percentage of the population in the labor force was smaller than it would be with a more normal distribution.

Table 1. Population of Stated Age by Sex, Indonesia, 1961

Age	Male	Female	Total
0– 4	8,462,000	8,580,000	17,042,000
5– 9	7,684,000	7,639,000	15,323,000
10–14	4,318,000	3,861,000	8,179,000
15–19	3,834,000	3,874,000	7,708,000
20–24	3,452,000	4,339,000	7,791,000
25–34	7,334,000	8,542,000	15,876,000
35–44	5,720,000	5,363,000	11,083,000
45–54	3,559,000	3,483,000	7,042,000
55–64	1,898,000	1,850,000	3,748,000
65–74	796,000	829,000	1,625,000
75+	377,000	407,000	784,000
Total	47,434,000	48,767,000	96,201,000

Source: Central Statistical Office, *1961 Census, 1% Sample* (Djakarta, 1964).

The empty ages, as well as the over-full ages below ten in 1961, fit with well-known historical facts. The decade of the 1950's was relatively healthy and prosperous. Malaria had been in considerable part eliminated; food was far more available than in the 1940's, according to the recollections of those who passed through these periods (unfortunately, one of the evils of war and revolution, although by no means the greatest, was the fact that no one had the time to collect statistics). One can surmise that births as well as deaths differed between the 1940's and the 1950's; certainly during the

[1] K. Horstmann, *Ekonomi dan Keuangan Indonesia* (1959).

occupation and the revolution marriages were delayed, and this, as well as separation of married couples, would have brought the birth rate down.

ACCURACY OF THE DATA

Could there be some error in the enumeration of the census sufficiently gross to account for the notch at age ten? Fortunately some evidence on the accuracy of the census is at hand, covering this particular point on which the entire succeeding argument will be based. We have a separate and independent labor force survey, taken in 1958, whose results for the crucial ages are shown in Table 2. We also have

Table 2. Population of Rural Java and Madura at Three Dates

Age	Labor force survey, 1958	Census, 1961	Demographic survey, 1962
0– 4	7,901,000	9,332,000	9,068,000
5– 9	6,919,000	8,492,000	8,518,000
10–14	3,958,000	4,229,000	4,828,000
15–19	3,914,000	3,868,000	3,714,000
Total, all ages	48,339,000	53,186,000	54,782,000
0–9 as percentage of total	30.7	33.5	32.1
5–9 as multiple of 10–14	1.75	2.01	1.76
0–10 as multiple of 10–19	1.88	2.20	2.06

a demographic survey of December, 1962; although this survey was not entirely independent of the census, the figures are worth examining. The three sets of data are available most conveniently for rural Java and Madura, and it is to this important part of Indonesia that Table 2 is confined. Since the main phenomenon we are concerned with is common to both rural and urban parts, according to the census, we will be satisfied if the census is confirmed for rural Java and Madura.

In its main lines it is indeed amply confirmed. We see that the numbers in the first two age groups are in all cases much larger than the numbers in the next two. Moreover, the ratio of the 5–9 to the 10–14 age group is higher for the census date, 1961, than for either of the other two dates. This is what one would expect if the break between the reproduction of the war and revolution on one side and of the peaceful period of the republic occurred exactly in the period 1950–51. For this would make the 5–9 age group in 1958 somewhat short because it contains about two years of the low 1940's; it would make the 10–14 age group of 1962 somewhat high because it contains one or two years of the high 1950's. The 0–4 of the labor force survey is not quite as high as the census would have us think;

the discrepancy is of the order of 10 per cent. But the study of the three sets of data both confirms the census and permits us to locate the moment of change as centered on the year 1950.

It is of interest to see whether another country with a similar history of difficulties in the 1940's and relative security in the 1950's shows a similar age distribution. Pakistan meets the requirement of approximate similarity of conditions, and Table 3 shows for the first twenty years of age somewhat the same profile as does Indonesia. However, it appears that the Pakistani enumerator was required to fill an extra labor force form for those over ten, and this could have resulted in some distortion. I have no evidence on which to judge this point.

Table 3. *Population Aged 0–19 Pakistan, 1961*

0– 4	15,722,021
5– 9	16,001,151
10–14	8,455,346
15–19	7,438,928

The censuses are certainly not exact; in fact those who have been closest to the operations speak with the greatest modesty about the accuracy they have succeeded in attaining. Further work on the tabulations and perhaps further surveys or even the next census will have to be awaited before the last word can be said. But one does not need this last word to be certain that a considerable difference exists between the number of persons under ten and those aged 10–19. Even if the figures have departed from the reality by being 10 per cent in excess for the younger group and 10 per cent short for the older, the statements concerning the pending increase would still be more than two-thirds true, and this would suffice for the present discussion.

THE IMPENDING EXPANSION

We can probably do better than this on estimating the moment of change from the regime of low increase to that of high increase. For we also have at our disposal the census figures by single years of age; these are given in Table 4. The original census figures do not move smoothly from age to age; the strongest champion of the census must admit the possibility, for example, that many children of age eleven were given as age twelve. In order to get around this, one can perform a graduation with the use of Sprague multipliers[2] and obtain the results shown in the third column of Table 4. The reader who prefers some

2 See U.S. Bureau of the Census, *Handbook of Statistical Methods for Demographers* (Washington, D.C.: Government Printing Office, 1951), pp. 95, 96.

other graduation, who perhaps wishes to do his own by graphical means, is advised to do so; he can hardly reach conclusions very different from those that follow.

Table 4. Population Aged 0–14 as Reported in Census and as Smoothed by Sprague Multipliers,* Indonesia, 1961

Age in 1961	Census	Smoothed	Year in which attain age 17
− 1	3,171,000		1978
1	3,009,000		1977
2	3,516,000		1976
3	3,769,000		1975
4	3,578,000		1974
5	3,296,000		1973
6	3,073,000	3,360,000	1972
7	3,327,000	3,108,000	1971
8	2,884,000	2,812,000	1970
9	2,743,000	2,492,000	1969
10	2,381,000	2,139,000	1968
11	1,341,000	1,742,000	1967
12	1,912,000	1,466,000	1966
13	1,344,000	1,389,000	1965
14	1,200,000	1,444,000	1964

* See text, n. 2.
Source: *1961 Census, 1% Sample.*

The striking feature of the table is the drop from over 3 million at age seven to under 1½ million by age twelve or thirteen. But to call this a drop is correct only when the table is read from top to bottom. In the book of real history this table is read from the bottom upwards. The successive ages are successive classes or cohorts, and they file past the grandstand from the bottom of our list to the top. Those who were age fourteen in 1961 are nineteen in 1966 and twenty-four in 1971. It is convenient to take one single age as the point at which to stand in reviewing the march-past of the cohorts, and we chose age seventeen. This is not the earliest that Indonesians start to work, especially in the villages, but one can say that by that age the large majority have left school and are in the labor market. The table shows that at the present time, as Table 1 shows for the past, the number that reach seventeen year by year is less than 1½ million; in 1966 it is still less than 1½ million. But then it takes a sudden jump—on the graduated figures it goes to 1,742,000 in 1967. By 1968 it has passed the 2 million mark; in 1969 it is close to 2½ million; in 1970 it is approaching 3 million, and in 1971 it has passed that figure. The witness of this march-past of the generations may well watch with breathless suspense. Is the increase going to continue? We cannot be sure, but it will probably not surpass 3½ million for a considerable period, perhaps not until the 1990's. Some uncertainty on this score arises as the result of the smaller numbers below two years of age; whether these reflect a real drop in births, the omission of infants in the census, or the overstatement of their ages is not possible at the moment to say.

Table 5. *Index of Demographic Change Between Cohorts Following 1950 and Those Preceding 1950, Derived from Censuses About 1960*

	Population 0–9 ÷ Total population (per cent)	Population 0–9 ÷ Population 10–19 (ratio)
Cambodia, 1959	33.0	1.54
Indonesia, 1961	33.6	2.04
Rural Java and Madura, 1961	33.5	2.20
Malaya, 1957	33.0	1.60
Pakistan, 1961	35.1	2.00
Philippines, 1960	33.0	1.43
Singapore, 1957	33.4	1.78
United States, 1960	21.8	1.30

A NUMERICAL MEASURE OF SUDDENNESS OF CHANGE

The phenomenon of sudden increase in the number of young adults noted for Indonesia and Paskistan ought to be measurable in terms of some single index. In casting about for such an index one thinks first of the percentage of the population under age ten. But this does not measure what we have in mind, for we are thinking of a phenomenon of transition from high to low death rates rather than of any possible stable condition, and it is easy to find instances of stable populations with as high a percentage under ten years of age (33–35 per cent) as is shown in Indonesia and Pakistan. If it is the rapidity of change between the 0–9 and the 10–19 age groups which is the essence of the situation in these two countries, then we ought to consider the ratio of the second of these to the first. Both of these measures are given in Table 5 for a number of the countries of South Asia and for the United States.

The Asian countries shown are uniform in their percentage under ten years of age, and all are half as high again as the United States figure of

21.8 per cent. But the countries of Asia differ considerably from one another in the steepness of declines of numbers as one proceeds up the pyramid of ages. Indonesia and Pakistan are uniquely steep; they show twice as many individuals under ten years of age as between ten and nineteen. Here again we must be aware of possible enumeration error.

EDUCATION

The entrants into the labor force in all new countries from now on will have more formal education than the entrants of the past. There is abundant evidence of this fact as far as Indonesia is concerned in the 1961 census; some figures of simple literacy are reproduced in Table 6. The ability to read (in Roman,

Table 6.   Literacy by Age, Indonesia, 1961 (per cent)

| | Males | | Females | | |
Age	Urban	Rural	Urban	Rural	Total
10–14	89.8	73.5	84.7	64.0	72.1
15–19	92.3	72.9	79.9	54.3	67.7
20–24	89.0	70.2	64.4	40.1	57.5
25–34	79.2	58.5	47.8	26.9	44.6
35–44	74.3	49.4	37.1	18.2	37.4
45–54	65.1	38.2	24.2	9.4	26.6
55–64	57.7	29.0	17.5	6.1	19.9
65–74	50.6	20.6	12.2	5.0	14.9
75+	40.7	21.3	9.5	6.0	14.7

Source: *1961 Census, 1% Sample.*

Arabic, or other characters) is sharply differentiated by age, sex, and rural-urban residence; but the differential that seems to stand out most is that by age. The enormous success of the educational process in reaching the young appears especially in the fact that 70 per cent of rural males under twenty-five are literate, as against only 20 per cent of those over sixty-five. The investment in human capital, especially for the cohorts born in 1930 and onward, is impressive by any standards. Considerable effort is now being made to expand the educational system in accord with the increase in numbers of children, but little statistical evidence is available on its exact extent. Aside from the self-judged literacy declared to the census taker of Table 6, nothing is in print regarding the effect of the educational system on productive competence. But there can be no question regarding its effectiveness in inculcating a national outlook and attitude.

ENTRY INTO THE LABOR FORCE

The number of persons entering the age groups at which the labor force is recruited, now about 1½ million annually, will rise to over 3 million per year very early in the 1970's. The evidence for this is essentially what we saw in Table 1 for ages 0–14, where some 8 million in 1961 are replaced by 15 million in 1966. We are here using census figures for the ages 5–14 in 1961 without deducting deaths; the justification for this is that deaths at these ages are low everywhere, and they seem to be particularly low with the level of health that has been attained in Indonesia.

What ordinarily happens is that an age cohort moves up through the labor force each year; people are promoted, retire, or die, and their places are taken by the young entrants who come in at the bottom of the hierarchy. This is how most of the 1½ million have been absorbed in Indonesia year by year up to now and will continue to be absorbed up to 1966. But by the beginning of the new decade the annual number of potential entrants will be double the number to which the country is now accustomed. Each entrant will literally bring his brother along, and the brother will want a job as well. What sort of jobs will they want?

For the countryside the answer depends on the degree to which such youth, with training often including middle school, will be willing to share in the minute division of labor and of the crop which characterizes village life in Central and East Java, for instance, and whether there will be places for them. This question applies even today to the smaller numbers who are finishing their schooling and going back to the village. They are having trouble locating themselves in the economic circuit. The census throws light on this problem: Table 7 shows unemployment data for rural areas. We see

Table 7. *Male Labor Force Unemployed in Rural Areas, by Age, 1961 (per cent)*

Age	Indonesia	Java and Madura
10–14	22.4	24.3
15–19	15.6	18.4
20–24	7.5	8.9
25–34	1.9	2.0
35–44	0.8	0.7
45–54	0.8	0.6
55–64	1.0	0.8
65–74	1.9	1.6
75+	2.6	2.7

Source: *1961 Census, 1% Sample.*

that unemployment is predominantly a problem of those under twenty-five; the men beyond that age are evidently located on the land in one way or another. For better or worse, their place in society is determined; even though in a bad season they may face starvation, they do not describe themselves as unemployed to the census enumerator. The census figures indicate that, on the other hand, either there is no work for one-fifth of the young, or else they are not willing to undertake the tasks that sufficed for their parents. This superfluity or dissatisfaction of the young appeared even in 1961, when they constituted an "empty" age group, abnormally depleted by the war and revolution.

MIGRATION

What about the enlarged age groups that are expected from 1967 onward? They will clearly be tempted to migrate, and to this subject we now turn our attention. The census shows how much net migration there has been, particularly in the rural-urban direction, during the past thirty years. Its figures will suggest the movement likely to occur during the late 1960's and 1970's.

Growth of cities has been rapid during the thirty-one years preceding the census. Djakarta Raya increased from 533,000 residents in 1930 to 2,973,000 in 1961, a growth of five and a half times. Bandung increased at an even higher rate, coming close to the million mark. Surabaya multiplied by three to exceed one million. These figures are impressive, especially when one bears in mind that the ages at which migration takes place, say fifteen to twenty-five, were underrepresented in the Indonesian pyramid during the period in question.

The doubling that is in prospect at these ages therefore permits the safe prediction that cityward migration will shortly be intensified. The youth who are being turned out by the rural and small-town schools, educated and upwardly mobile, will move where opportunity seems to beckon. The idea that there is opportunity in the cities is inevitably given by the construction which has taken place during the past few years. New boulevards, stadiums, hotels, government buildings, especially in Djakarta, all suggest to the young man of the *desa* that the city is the place to come for the opportunity to introduce oneself into the economic circuit of production and consumption.

COMPLEMENTARITY OF AGES IN PRODUCTION

Clearly the doubling of the youthful cohorts within the five-year period 1966–71 represents an enormous opportunity for development. The major question will be the availability of organizing skill and capital to put it to work productively. One cannot expect that people of seventeen years of age will provide their own opportunities. A kind of complementarity of ages operates in production, which requires certain proportions of skilled and experienced people along with the young. This applies whether enterprise is private or governmental; the organizing of production is never an easy matter. Indonesia is handicapped at this stage of its development by the fact that the older generation continues to be relatively small in numbers, as has been stressed above; its proportion literate is relatively small and its proportion with higher education, especially higher technical education, is smaller yet. The smaller old generation will have to guide the productive effort of the large new generation. Needless to say, if a spirit of enterprise proves to be sufficient, the great increase of youth, its education and determination to make something of life whether in agriculture or the city are nothing but advantages for the country.

THE ELITE AND ITS OBJECTIVES

An elite that has come into existence through political struggle is likely to see its continuing success in terms of the qualities and actions that brought it to the forefront to begin with. The giving of authority to owners and managers on the basis of skill in production would constitute a major change. An elite may develop an ideology which is especially adverse to industry in proportion as its career has consisted in argument or warfare with foreigners whose claim to domination was their superiority in managing production. Such a history may bring about an incapacity to perceive the role of management or the fact of talent for productive organization. We are all partially blind, and people choose what they will and will not perceive in accord with social need. It requires especially strong pressures and very patent needs for a class or nation to perceive the role of management in production.

It is frequently assumed that the most urgent social need facing a governing elite in a poor country is to alleviate the poverty and suffering of its people, especially of its peasants. But this assumption underestimates the capacity of rulers everywhere to tolerate misery in their subjects, a capacity which the whole course of history demonstrates. Sensitivity in rulers may lead to expressions of sympathy for the poor, and to symbolic acts of charity, but hardly to the neglect of all other values in the interest of development. We must reflect that the measures necessary for development attack poverty only indirectly and show results not immediately but after a period of years. Mere sympathy with the poor is more likely to show itself in the distribution of alms, either in old-fashioned style or as social security measures and other such immediate alleviation of misery, which is often quite the opposite of a long-term policy that will lead to development—as seen in nineteenth-century

England, where people were urged not to give alms so that able-bodied beggars would be forced to seek factory work.

Thus while poverty is always in some sense a challenge to government, it is not one to which a positive response at the level of effective action is inevitable. That poverty which arises from the high density and rapid growth of population would seem to be as tolerable as any other. What sort of challenge can find a response in development? Presumably one that somehow enmeshes the self-interest of powerful groups or individuals. Thus a military threat from the outside world was accepted as a challenge to Japan's existence by samurai bureaucrats after the Meiji restoration.

If poor, aging peasants can be left to misery or even starvation without serious political consequences, the case is different with the young generation whose numerical importance in the coming years is revealed by the census figures. The literacy, mobility, and incipient organization of these young people make them politically important, capable of exercising a pressure for goods which government will find it hard to deny.

POPULATION AS AN OBSTACLE AND A CHALLENGE

The relation of population growth to economic development has been studied extensively and deeply. Coale and Hoover, in what is the classic work on the subject,[3] show the very different consequences for Indian development of different rates of population growth, these rates operating through their effect on the process of capital accumulation and in other ways. Any increase in income which a country struggles to attain must be rapid so that population growth may be outdistanced and reversion to stability avoided, as Leibenstein has shown.[4] But the somewhat opposite possibility that population growth might provide a healthy challenge, or otherwise awaken people to reality, is not entirely absent from the literature. Hirschman develops this point, citing a series of suggestions from Malthus (the incentive effect of having to provide for one's wife and children), from Schumpeter (that population may have an energizing effect), and from other writers. He suggests that "the possibility of a strong reaction is greater if the population increase comes as a sudden shock."[5] The present writer is less optimistic about the chances that population pressure in general will arouse the necessary action toward development, largely because it can only lower per capita incomes at the rate of 3 percent or so per year in the country as a

---

[3] A. J. Coale and E. M. Hoover, *Population Growth and Economic Development in Low-Income Countries* (Princeton, N.J.: Princeton University Press, 1955).

[4] Harvey Leibenstein, *Economic Backwardness and Economic Growth* (New York: John Wiley & Sons, 1957).

[5] A. O. Hirschman, *The Strategy of Economic Development* (New Haven, Conn.: Yale University Press, 1956), pp. 176–83.

whole. This is too gradual for people to have a point at which to take a stand. If there are any circumstances in which population can offer a shock treatment, they should be in the situation where a critical age group—that of the entrants into the labor force—doubles in numbers within a five-year period.

YOUTH AND NATION-BUILDING

The significance of the advent of a host of young people in Indonesia arises not only from their numbers but from the circumstances of political, economic, and social life. First among these is the nation-building effort of the authorities. Nations are very different social groups from those governed by tradition. To establish a nation is not merely to legitimate the indigenous culture as against that imposed by a now-rejected colonial power. In many of its aspects, indeed, the underdeveloped nation stands in even sharper opposition to the precolonial culture and society than it does to the colonial.

Nation-building is a frequent theme of Indonesian public speeches.[6] The set of ideas unfolded under this theme includes the importance of getting away from the variegated indigenous culture (except on such points as Islam, which can help unify a modern Republic) ; Indonesian nation-building is seen to depend on the Javanese ceasing to be Javanese, the Minangkebau ceasing to be Minangkebau. Even intermarriage among the several *suku-bangsa* or cultures of which Indonesia is made up is counseled. All formal political discourse is in the neutral Indonesian language which is the new national speach, created out of antecedents in a trader's *lingua franca* throughout the archipelago and as far away as Madagascar. This language has the advantage for a modern state of dispensing with the inflections for indicating respect that are integral features of the more deeply rooted local languages; it is thus suited to be a means of communication among nominally equal citizens recently liberated from their ancient fixed societies. It is spreading with the very rapid spread of education at the primary level and upward, for school education stresses the national language at the expense of the local languages. This education includes a much larger measure than is usual in older countries of what we would call "civics," an inculcation of the themes which make up the official national belief system—invariably referred to as the Indonesian Revolution. Aside from the social homogenization which is represented by the playing-down of regional cultures and their social hierarchies, there is also a more visible homogenization in the military-style training which hundreds of thousands, perhaps millions, of volunteers

[6] For example, that given by General Nasution at the University of Indonesia in May, 1964.

for the enterprise of crushing Malaysia are now undergoing. Leaders are much in favor of physical fitness, of citizens taking daily exercise individually and in groups.

It is hardly necessary to stress how alien to the adult peasant are all these elements. The peasant can no more appreciate the importance of training in civics than he can that of doing physical jerks. Only his children of an age to have attended school after the mid-1940's can even understand the national language. He has no national preoccupations; in the expression commonly used in Indonesia today, he is wholly "feudal." To make him a national product is the aim of much intense effort, but one that can hardly succeed in any considerable measure for individuals already at middle age or beyond.

It is largely the young who are susceptible of being formed in the national mold through the educational and political system. It is the young who have the ambition to rise within the new social systems being formed of political parties, trade unions, army groups, in which the pressure of upward mobility is so strong. The old, at least those in the countryside, are mentally located within a hierarchical system, and materially they have some greater or lesser claim to the land. The claim may be only the privilege of sowing and weeding an area of half a hectare, for which they obtain one-quarter of the crop; but this is enough in general to keep them alive, and they are not easily alerted to the possibility of improving their position by leaving their claim and going elsewhere.

RURAL YOUTH AND PRESSURE ON THE LAND

If we remember that Java is about three-quarters rural; that the number of rural young people reaching age seventeen every year will rise from about 800,000 to about 1,600,000 during the next six years; that the attitudes of the young, determined by their education, must include impatience with the fragmentation of labor and of the crop which is the best that the Javanese village can offer them; and that even this kind of entrance into economic life will not be available to most of them since the land is already wholly taken up in most places, then it seems safe to predict that there will be movement to the cities. We reflect that the cities have been growing by over 200,000 persons per year during the period in which those reaching the age of entrance into economic life in rural Java numbered only 800,000 annually and the villages were less crowded than they have now come to be. It becomes plain that the cities will grow very fast indeed with the doubling of the numbers coming to labor-force-entry age, which is everywhere the age of greatest propensity to migrate.

A SYSTEM WHOSE OUTPUT IS SPIRITUAL RATHER THAN MATERIAL

What will the city offer the new immigrants? Is the activity of training for the invasion of west Irian of three years ago and for guerilla action in north Borneo today the ideal occupation? From some points of view it is; it puts the youth into green uniforms which well represent the cultural homogeneity so much desired by the authorities of the Republic; they learn the civic virtues now being inculcated as constituting the permanent Indonesian Revolution; they maintain a high degree of physical fitness. For Marx, men are made what they are by the relations of production into which they enter; for guided democracy they are shaped by military-style exercises, by mass rallies, by mass organizations, by the school system.

There is of course one difficulty with these last-named means: although they may be analogous to a productive system in making new men, as well as in the various kinds of input they use, they differ in having no material output. The spiritual output or satisfaction is not to be disregarded, but it is a complement to, rather than a substitute for, material goods. However much individuals may think when they are gathered on the drill ground that the satisfactions of the activity itself suffice for them, there will certainly be moments when they will individually observe the shortage of food, clothing, and other necessities.

A CHALLENGE BECOMES SUCH ONLY WHEN SUITABLY INTERPRETED

Whether this essentially unemployed younger generation is a difficulty or an opportunity for the republic will depend on how the increase in numbers is interpreted. For the first time since 1950 Indonesia will face a genuine problem—the demands of a new and self-conscious group, insistent in a way that an excess population consisting of illiterate peasants could never be. Attempts will certainly be made to interpret the problem as one of division of the product rather than of its insufficiency in total. On the other hand the pressure may be so great as to bring a moment of truth: that the republic's troubles are not to be solved by the rectification of unequal or unjust division of the national product, but by increasing it. Some few Indonesians have pointed this out, circumspectly and under the banner of guided democracy and its need to crush Malaysia, but the attention of the public and the authorities is not yet effectively focused on it. A widespread recognition of the solution through production, both agricultural and industrial, would force recognition of the need for management and organization. It would lead to a selection of talent among the young away from political and toward economic organization. It could accentuate and unconditionally support the many constructive activities now going on throughout the country. But any historical prediction based on pressure and a challenge must face the fact that in human society a challenge becomes such only when appropriately interpreted. Whether the educated youth descending on the cities will impose a production-mindedness—not hitherto called for—depends on the interpretations and ideologies with which that youth is received. A first sign that the population crisis has forced the country into constructive action will be the initiation of energetic measures to bring down the birth rate.

POPULATION PRESSURES

A. O. Hirschman

Few topics in the theory of economic development have evoked such unanimity as population growth. With increases in per capita income widely accepted as the objective of development or as the best available approximation to it, population is firmly relegated to the denominator of the expression which we want to maximize and any increase in numbers can only be considered a set back on the road to development. Such expressions as the population growth that "swallows up" increases in output in whole or in part, such images as walking up a downward moving escalator,[1] and the virtually obligatory quotation from Lewis Carroll: "Here it takes all the running you can do, to keep in the same place,"—all testify to the universal assumption that the exclusive effect of population growth is to frustrate economic development. Some writers are of course aware of the fact that demographic stagnation or declining population growth were high on the list among the explanations for the falling behind of France as a major political and economic power, and were one of the three pillars of the stagnation thesis in the United States. But any disturbing ideas on that account could be quickly discarded by the reassuring, if somewhat shapeless, thought that the problems of developed and underdeveloped countries are entirely distinct.

---

[1] Singer, "Economic Progress in Underdeveloped Countries," p. 7.

In the face of such unanimity, we shall present with considerable reluctance some reasons which make us think that population pressures are to be considered forces that may stimulate development. We are fully aware that this is a dangerous thought—dangerous not so much for the world at large as for the reputation of the author; and in order not to expose ourselves too long to the heavy fire which will certainly be opened on us, we shall dispose of what we have to say with the utmost brevity.

Let us start out by again invoking Duesenberry's "fundamental psychological postulate," which says that people will resist a lowering in their standard of living. If they do this as a result of a cyclical depression why should they not also react in some way against their incomes being squeezed by an increase in population? Our first proposition is therefore that *population pressure on living standards will lead to counterpressure, i.e., to activity designed to maintain or restore the traditional standard of living of the community.* Leaving the validity of this proposition for later consideration, we shall assume for the moment that this counterpressure is partially or wholly successful in restoring per capita incomes. Thus far, then, the psychological postulate yields at best a mechanism of equilibrium, i.e., of stagnation rather than development.

But the situation is not really the same after this process, for in its course the community has *learned,* through wrestling successfully with new tasks. Our second proposition is therefore that *the activity undertaken by the community in resisting a decline in its standard of living causes an increase in its ability to control its environment and to organize itself for development.* As a result, the community will now be able to exploit the opportunities for economic growth that existed previously but were left unutilized.

In short, the learning a community does when it reacts to population pressures increases the total stock of its resources much as investment adds to total productive capacity. To revert to the images mentioned earlier: walking up downward escalators or running in the same place is excellent exercise and practice for people who need to improve their walking or running performance. Anyone who has watched attempts by public and private bodies to cope with the traffic, water supply, electric power, housing, school, and crime problems of a growing city can have little doubt that the qualities of imagination and organization developed in these tasks of *maintaining* standards of living in the face of population pressures are very similar to those that are needed to *increase* per capita incomes. The basic determinant of development which we have called the "ability to invest" is decisively enhanced in the course of the struggle to accommodate more people.

Returning to our first proposition, we cannot claim that it is more than a variant of an old idea. Many writers, Malthus among them, have remarked on the incentive effects of the need to provide for one's wife and children. Others have examined the stimulating effect of population increases, not on the individual's "natural indolence," but on society's. In this respect, much that is incisive has been said, in particular by the Belgian sociologist and philosopher Dupréel who has traced the many ways in which an increasing population leads to improved performance of the administrative, political, and cultural processes.[2] But while these direct positive influences and actions of population growth on individual motivations and economic and political developments are of interest, we think it more useful to stress the *reaction* mechanism that is set up when population growth depresses, or is about to depress, living standards, for the recognition of this reaction mechanism permits us to go beyond the following, somewhat unsatisfactory summary of the problem by Schumpeter: "Sometimes an increase in population actually has no other effects than that predicted by classical theory—a fall in per capita real income; but at other times it may have an energizing effect that induces new developments with the result that per capita income rises."[3] By viewing the "energizing" effect as potentially induced by the "classical" effect, we can at least attempt to reduce the complete indeterminateness of this statement.

Our affirmation that a society will attempt to react to the "dilution" of total income that comes with larger numbers is of interest only if the reaction can be successful, i.e., if there is some "slack" in the economy that can be taken up. This assumption is of course contrary to the basic hypothesis of the neo-Malthusian models, *viz.* "all productive forces are fully utilized, i.e., there are no unemployed resources—the supply of land and capital is fixed."[4] This formulation is not even sufficiently strong if we wish to stipulate that it is impossible to squeeze more output from the available resources without a prior increase in per capita incomes out of which new savings can be extracted. We must then also suppose that production is *optimally* organized, that all existing technological and organizational knowledge that does not require capital outlays is fully applied. Obviously, even in densely populated underdeveloped areas, such a situation will be exceedingly rare.[5]

[2] E. Dupréel, "Population et progrès" in *Deux essais sur le progrès* (Brussels, 1928).

[3] J. Schumpeter, "The Creative Response in Economic History," *Journal of Economic History*, 7 (Nov. 1947), 149.

[4] Alan T. Peacock, "Theory of Population and Modern Economic Analysis," *Population Studies*, 6 (1952–53), 115.

[5] Malthus can be quoted in support of this view: "There are few large countries, however advanced in improvement, the population of which might not have been doubled or tripled, and there are many which might be ten or even a hundred times as populous, and yet all the inhabitants be as well provided for as they are now, if the institutions of society and the moral habits of the people, had been for some hundred years the most favourable to the increase of capital, and the demand for produce and labour." *A Summary View of the Principle of Population*, reprinted in *Introduction to Malthus*, ed. D. V. Glass (London, Watts, 1953), pp. 151–2.

The panorama changes abruptly if it is granted that a margin of possible improvements exists, and if, more generally, we revert to our diagnosis of underdevelopment as a state where labor, capital, entrepreneurship, etc. are potentially available and can be combined, provided a sufficiently strong "binding agent" is encountered. Then an increase in incomes is by no means the only way of starting the economy on an upward course. Nevertheless, there is some question whether population pressure can be considered an "inducement mechanism" in the sense in which we have used this term. How will it cause the possible improvements to be made? How will it call forth the latent resources of the economy?

Among the inducement mechanisms we have studied, from the various complementarity effects on down, population pressure must rank as the least attractive one. In the first place, it works through an initial decline in per capita income rather than through, e.g., an uneven expansion in output. Secondly, it is less reliable than the other mechanisms we have considered. In our previous, vaguely similar mechanism, i.e., losses in foreign exchange income leading to industrialization, we could point to several solid links in the reaction chain: specific, now unsatisfied, needs; "forced savings" of a kind; the interest of the heretofore importers or foreign suppliers, etc.[6]

In the case of population pressures, on the other hand, we are provided only with an aspiration to return to the status quo ante, but generally not with specific means or intermediate reaction links for doing so. Nevertheless, in some of the following situations, the passage from aspiration to reality becomes plausible or is more readily visualized than in others.

1. The probability of a strong reaction is greater if the population increase comes as a sudden shock. A community may not feel impelled to "make a stand" when population increases and declines in living standards are slow, just as workers will sometimes experience greater difficulty in maintaining their real wages in the face of creeping inflation than when prices rise a good 20% a year. For this reason, the dramatic decline in mortality rates and the consequent massive increase in numbers that is taking place today in underdeveloped areas holds greater promise of a vigorous reaction than the far slower increases of previous epochs.

2. A population increase is likely to be more action-stimulating if it is combined with increased urbanization and therefore leads to obvious needs and pressures for more overhead facilities, such as housing, schools, and public utilities.

3. Again, the reaction may be facilitated if population growth takes place in underdeveloped countries which as a result of the increase in num-

[6] Note that this mechanism is in turn less reliable than the one utilized in Duesenberry's construction. In the case of a sudden absence of a desired good because of balance-of-payments difficulties, consumers cannot protect their previous standard of living just by saving less as Duesenberry's consumers are wont to do in a depression.

bers pass minimum production thresholds in a number of important industries, as compared to more populous countries where these thresholds have
long been passed or to much smaller countries where they remain far away.

4. The reaction may be easier to accomplish if the increase affects primarily the upper classes of society, or at least the upper classes along with
the lower classes, for the need to provide for one's children is in this case
more likely to take the form of increased entrepreneurial activity.

5. Finally, the closer a country actually is to the rigid assumptions of
the neo-Malthusian models which we mentioned above, i.e., the more fully
and perfectly its resources are already utilized, the less room there is for
any reactions outside of the most direct ones—namely, birth control and
postponement of marriage. Precisely because of the assumption of fixed resources, this reaction to population pressures has virtually monopolized the
attention of demographers. From our point of view, the "preventive checks"
are only one of the many forms which the reaction mechanism can take.
Under present conditions, in fact, it is in many countries more difficult to
visualize population pressures resulting in effective birth control measures
than in improvements of agricultural techniques and in stepped-up capital
formation in industry and public utilities. In any event, our second proposition applies here also, even though perhaps somewhat indirectly: for a people that is induced to exercise foresight to the point of adopting effective
birth control techniques is again learning that one's environment can be
controlled and changed and will therefore be better equipped for coping
with the tasks of development.

All in all, population pressure still qualifies as an inducement mechanism
in the sense that it presents the developmental forces within a society with
an opportunity to assert themselves. It supplies "the motive and the cue for
passion" (though admittedly it fails to provide many cues for action). Thus
it seems wrong to say that population pressures act as an obstacle to development. There are circumstances under which these pressures are unsuccessful in performing their stimulating role just as relative price increases
are at times ineffective in calling forth increases in the supply of the "sig-
naled" commodities.

The view that has been presented is consistent with the fact that population pressures have demonstrably been an integral part of the development
process in all countries that are economically advanced today. It would
surely be most unrealistic to look at the population increases in Europe in
the nineteenth century and at those in, say, Brazil and Mexico today as a
depressing influence on economic development. But if this is granted, then
we must ask the partisans of the classical view to explain why population
growth, like some of the lesser Homeric gods who throw their support to
the winning side at the height of battle, suddenly becomes a stimulant to
economic development after having long played the role of obstacle. In our

view, no such switch ever occurs; rather we are able to account by a single hypothesis for a stream of events within which we might distinguish three periods: during the first, per capita incomes do not increase, but countries, in reacting to population pressures, acquire the abilities to launch undertakings that will lead to genuine economic growth; during a second period, per capita incomes begin to rise, with economic growth continuing to draw strength from population growth; and only at a later stage does economic growth wean itself from population growth and becomes self-sustained.[7]

What conclusion can be drawn from the preceding remarks for population policy in underdeveloped countries? Certainly not that they should institute a system of generous family allowances. In the first place, we have already stated our view that population pressures are a clumsy and cruel stimulant to development. Actually, underdeveloped countries are today abundantly supplied with this stimulant, whether they want it or not, as a result of the universal and rapid decline in mortality rates. Secondly, we consider the spread of birth control as one important form which the reaction to population pressure can take, and one that, if it occurs, brings with it basic attitude changes that are favorable to development.

Our policy conclusions, then, are somewhat anticlimactic. Any practical usefulness of our reasoning lies in the fact that it leads to a less alarmist attitude toward the population problems than is displayed by the current literature with its "traps" and the need for a huge jump to break out of them. This kind of reasoning derives of course from the comparisons of population growth with output growth rates. A highly sophisticated version of this approach is given by Leibenstein; he demonstrates that if a country has a population growth rate of, say, one per cent per year, it is not sufficient for it to achieve an output growth rate in excess of one per cent; for when output and therefore income rise, population may rise even more; so that to overtake population growth for good, the country may have to achieve a rate of output growth that is a multiple of the initial rate of population growth; and it must achieve this rate not gradually but in one jump, for at any intermediate point the country's rate of income growth will be dragged down again to its low-level starting point.[8]

Our approach leads us to take a far calmer view of the situation. We have shown that if a country is at all able to offset, be it even partially at first, the effect of the population increase, then we may have confidence that, through the learning acquired in this process, it will be able to do progressively better in marshaling its productive forces for development so that eventually output growth will overtake population growth. If a com-

---

[7] With population still growing in all economically progressive countries, we actually have no conclusive empirical evidence about the existence of this stage.

[8] Leibenstein, *Economic Backwardness and Economic Growth*, pp. 170–2. See also Ch. 2, n. 16.

munity makes a genuine effort to defend its standard of living in the face of population pressures, it need not be afraid of imaginary traps, for cumulative growth is then already in the making: just as income can rise in advance of consumption, so can economic progress get under way before being registered in per capita income increases.

AN ECONOMETRIC ANALYSIS
OF POPULATION GROWTH

Irma Adelman

There has been remarkably little theoretical or empirical analysis of the effects of economic development upon population change.[1] While the existence of an interaction between the economic and the demographic evolution of a society has long been acknowledged by authorities in both fields, only the impact of population growth on economic development has received any significant amount of attention in the economic literature.

The present paper attempts to illuminate the other side of the coin. Specifically, this manuscript constitutes an economic analysis of fertility and mortality patterns as they are affected by economic and social forces. First, age specific birth and death rates in various countries are correlated with several economic and sociocultural indicators. As a partial test of the validity of this approach, the derived relations are then used to estimate crude birth and death rates in 1953 in the various continents. Finally, a quantitative feeling for the relative impact of changes in economic and social variables upon the demographic features of a society is obtained by calculating the changes in the equilibrium age distribution and in the

---

From Irma Adelman, "An Econometric Analysis of Population Growth," *American Economic Review* (June 1963), pp. 314–339. Reprinted by permission of The American Economic Association.

[1] Some notable exceptions to this statement are to be found in the work of G. S. Becker [24, pp. 209–31], R. A. Easterlin [4], E. E. Hagen [6], H. Leibenstein [9], B. Okun [12], and G. H. Orcutt, M. Greenberger, J. Korbel, and A. M. Rivlin [13].

equilibrium rate of population growth which would result (*ceteris paribus*) from a permanent change in each of the socioeconomic variables.

I. THE STATISTICAL APPROACH

In principle, long-run relationships between demographic and socioeconomic factors can be investigated statistically from either of two points of view [4, pp. 629–630]. One possibility is to study one or more geographical units over time and determine the variations in fertility and mortality which are, on the average, associated with changes in the per capita income, degree of industrialization, education, and other relevant characteristics of each unit. For conclusions of general validity to be drawn from this approach, a similar analysis must be repeated for several countries over long periods of time.

Alternatively, a number of geographical units can be investigated at the same point in time. The influence of income, industrial development, and other socioeconomic indicators upon fertility and mortality can then be established quantitatively, in some average sense. One advantage of this approach is that the greater range of variation in characteristics among countries and the lesser degree of interaction among the explanatory variables permit a much more accurate determination of regression coefficients than does time-series analysis. However, there is a fundamental difficulty inherent in this cross-section technique: in order to draw any conclusions from the data it must be assumed that, regardless of any differences in environmental and historical conditions, each human population, from a demographic point of view, responds to a small number of more or less quantifiable socioeconomic variables as if it were drawn from a homogeneous environment. In view of the tremendous variations in values, outlook, and other sociocultural imponderables throughout the world, this condition is a very severe one; fortunately, it is open to empirical test. For, whenever specific cultural factors lead to systematic deviations in demographic behavior in different countries, low correlation coefficients, large standard errors, and significant differences in regression coefficients among individual subsamples will be observed.

In choosing between the techniques it must also be recognized that variations in the over-all (or crude) birth and death rates reflect not only changes in fertility and mortality conditions, but also differences in the age and sex distribution of the populations. In order to isolate the impact of socioeconomic forces upon fertility and mortality patterns, therefore, one must eliminate those variations in general birth and death rates which occur for purely demographic reasons; for it is the response of *age specific* birth and death rates to changes in economic and social factors that constitutes the focus of our study.

Since extended time series for age specific birth and death rates are unavailable even for the United States [4, p. 876], the time-series approach cannot effectively be used. The present study must therefore rely upon cross-country analysis to establish long-term effects of economic and sociocultural factors on age specific birth and death rates.

II. INPUT DATA

The data upon which this study is based are primarily the result of a concerted effort by the United Nations to maximize the number of countries for which good demographic and other statistical information would exist. All countries for which roughly comparable demographic and economic data were available at some date in the period from 1947–57 were included in the study.

For each country in our sample the most recent year for which age specific demographic statistics could be found was determined, and the values of the independent (economic and sociocultural) variables were centered on or around that date. The sample used for the fertility study consists of 37 countries, whose annual per capita incomes range from $125 (Morocco) to $1900 (United States), with about half the incomes below $350. The geographic distribution of the observations is also wide, even though Africa and Asia are relatively underrepresented. The mortality study was performed on a similar sample of 34 nations. The list of countries included in the fertility and mortality samples, the data used for each study, and the sources and methods of computation are given in detail in tables available upon request from the author.

III. FERTILITY ANALYSIS

A. *Determinants of Fertility*

Effects of economic conditions upon birth rates, at least in the short run, have often been observed by demographers. For example, Yule [15] found a weak-lagged positive correlation between the course of the business cycle in Great Britain during the latter half of the 19th century and the deviation of birth rates from their secular trend. Similar results were obtained by Ogburn and Thomas [11] for the United States for 1870–1920. From the years 1920–41, Kirk and Nortman [8], working with percentage deviations from the trend, found a correlation coefficient of +.77 between birth per thousand women of child-bearing age and real per capita income. Their results were confirmed by Galbraith and Thomas [5], and, more recently, by Becker [24, pp. 209–231]. The long-run relationship between fertility and economic conditions is less clearly established. On the one hand, the normal pattern of fertility differentials among social and economic classes is that of negative association between socioeconomic status and fertility [20, pp. 86–88] [24, p. 5]. Moreover, casual empiricism suggests that, at least up to World War II, differences in fertility among countries were negatively correlated with their levels of economic development. On the other hand, the postwar baby boom experienced by the high-income Anglo-Saxon countries in sparsely populated areas argues in the opposite direction. In addition, Easterlin [4] has adduced strong evidence for the existence of a positive long-run relationship between births and economic conditions in the United States from 1890 to the present. Since the direction and extent of long-run association between childbearing and living standards is unclear, it would appear that one of the socioeconomic variables whose long-run effects upon fertility ought to be analyzed in this study is the level of real per capita national income (or some similar indicator).

A second set of factors commonly credited with responsibility for the continued decline in fertility which occurred prior to 1930 in northwestern Europe is the social and economic transformation brought about by the Industrial Revolution [17, pp. 76–80]. The resulting urbanization and industrialization process appears to have led to persistent changes in fundamental attitudes towards family limitation. Indeed, in all countries, the historical decline in fertility has been preceded by or accompanied by a great shift of the population from country to city. And both the urban-rural differential in fertility and the agricultural-industrial differential have persisted through time [24, pp. 77–87].

A logical indicator of urbanization is, of course, the percentage of the total population living in cities. Similarly, it is reasonable to choose as an indicator of industrialization the percentage of nonagricultural employment of the labor force. From preliminary tests on our sample data, however, it became apparent that there is a very high degree of correlation between these two indicators. Since, in addition, data on urban and rural populations are not internationally comparable because of national differences in the definitions of "urban" residents [23, pp. 1–2], it was decided to use the nonagricultural employment figures alone to represent the variety of socioeconomic forces related to the urbanization-industrialization complex.

Another major influence upon childbearing behavior is the mother's level of education [17, p. 89]. While the net direction of the effect of education upon fertility for college graduates is somewhat uncertain, at lower education levels a clear inverse correlation between the number of years of schooling of the wife and family size is well established from cross-sectional studies [24, pp. 155–70]. Unfortunately, there exist no international data on education for the female population alone; instead, an educational index for the over-all population is included in our regression analysis. This index was constructed by computing the unweighted arithmetic average of the literacy index and an index of newspaper circulation (tons per year) per capita, each based on U.S. = 100. These particular indicators of the educational level of a population were chosen primarily because of their ready availability. The averaging procedure was adopted in order to gain some discrimination among high-income countries, since the literacy index reported for most developed nations is 100.

A measure of population density is also included in the analysis. This was done because, ever since the days of Malthus, the concept of a stable optimum population size which maximizes the per capita income of a nation for a given set of techniques, resources, tastes, and institutions has played a central role in demographic theories.[2] For smaller than optimal populations the extent of the market is too limited to permit full benefits to be derived from division of labor and economies of scale. With too large a population diminishing returns set in, since fewer cooperating resources are available per worker. There exists, therefore, an intermediate population density which optimizes the average real income per capita.

Obviously, these more or less static considerations are not completely appropriate in a dynamic setting. However, in many underdeveloped regions, actual population numbers are so far out of balance with existing arable land resources, given their almost static techniques and their essentially fixed endowments of other cooperating factors, that the population-resource ratio may actually exert some practical influence upon reproductive behavior. Admittedly, population density is only a very crude index of the extent of population pressure upon available resources. In and of itself, a high (or low) ratio of people to land is not synonymous with over- (or under-) population. For it fails to take account of nonland resources and makes no allowance for differences in natural soil fertility, climate, crops and techniques, and the related institutional arrangements. A more refined measure of the population-land ratio, such as the number of people per square mile of cultivable or of arable land, would still be very far from the mark. Nonetheless, some indication of the influence of the population-resource ratio upon fertility may be obtained by including the average population density in the regression equations.

The decline in mortality among infants and young children has sometimes been advanced as another factor responsible for the decrease in fertility [17, pp. 81]. To the extent that families strive towards some optimal size, a greater rate of survival among the young may cause couples to limit the number of children born. In addition, the level of infant mortality may also serve as an index of the general social situation, insofar as the latter bears upon attitudes and practices related to childbearing. For these reasons infant

---

[2] For a more detailed discussion of this point, see [9, pp. 171–91].

mortality was incorporated into our preliminary regression analysis. Moreover, since infant mortality is highly correlated with per capita income, the partial regression coefficient of age specific birth rates upon infant mortality was not statistically significant and fluctuated in direction. This variable was therefore eliminated from the ultimate set of equations.

The final factor whose influence upon fertility was tested in our investigation is the percentage rate of growth of real per capita income. Leibenstein [9, pp. 173–75] argues that this variable has a direct effect upon the rate of population growth since, at a given level of per capita income, a higher rate of growth implies a higher percentage of investment goods and a lower percentage of consumer products. According to his theory, this shift in the composition of output leads to higher mortality and (perhaps) lower birth rates than would otherwise prevail. This variable, however, was ultimately dropped from the fertility study, as some of the earlier calculations indicated that it would not be statistically significant in the form of the regression equations chosen for our analysis.[3]

B. *The Regression Model*

From preliminary least-squares regression calculations using the indicators suggested by the discussion of the last section, it was found that the highest coefficients of determination and most consistent regression coefficients were obtained by using regression equations of the form:

$$(1) \quad \log_e b_i = a_{oi} + a_{1i} \log_e Y + a_{2i} \log_e I + a_{3i} \log_e E + a_{4i} \log_e P + u_i.$$

In these equations, b represents the number of live births per 1000 females in the ith age group, Y stands for the level of real national income per capita in 1953 U.S. dollars, I indicates the per cent of the labor force employed outside of agriculture, E is the index of education, P is the number of inhabitants per square mile, and u_i is a random disturbance term. Since, in (1), all the socioeconomic variables are expressed in logarithmic terms, the regression coefficients a_{ji} ($j = 1, 2, 3, 4$) measure the elasticities of the birth rate in the ith age group with respect to the jth variable.

In the computation of the regression coefficients from the cross-section data, it was recognized that there are significant differences in the statistical accuracy of the information available from each country. For this reason the data from each country were weighted; the weights were computed from information published in the 1956 *Demographic Yearbook* [19, pp. 9–23, 26–28]. Each weight is the product of three quantities:

1. The reciprocals of the Whipple Index. This index represents a measure of the inaccuracy of the age statistics [19, pp. 26–28].

---

[3] The percentage rate of growth of real per capita income was sometimes statistically significant in some of the nonlogarithmic forms of the regression equations.

2. A measure of the birth registration procedure. This factor is 100 if births and deaths are recorded as they occur (continuous register) and 70 otherwise.

3. A measure of the completeness of the data. This factor is 100 if the data are based on a census covering more than 90 per cent of the population and is taken as 80 otherwise.

The resulting weights (available upon request from the author) vary from 28 for El Salvador and the Dominican Republic to 100 for Morocco, Algeria, and most of the European countries.

It was assumed in the calculations that the u_i, corrected by weighting for intercountry differentials in the quality of the statistics, are normally distributed around the regression surface defined by equation (1) with zero mean and constant variance. Therefore a_{ji} are unbiased estimates of the regression coefficients.

The validity of the cross-country approach was tested by computing separate regression equations—one for the developed lands and one for the undeveloped ones. No statistically significant differences in regression coefficients emerged, a result which indicates that the basic postulate of the cross-section technique—homogeneity of population response—is satisfied.

C. The Regression Results

The regression results derived with the aid of the statistical model described in the previous section are summarized in Table 1. The upper entry in the ith row and the jth column of this table is an unbiased estimate of the regression coefficient a_{ji}. The standard error of this estimate is listed in parentheses below the corresponding coefficient.

It is apparent from the last two columns of this table that our regression model accounts for roughly 50 to 70 per cent of the total variance in age specific birth rates among countries. The values of R^2 are all statistically significant, and the standard errors of estimate (column 6) are satisfactorily small. In addition, the signs of the individual regression coefficients are all internally consistent and in accord with a priori expectations.

A closer look at the table reveals that our results support the hypothesis that, *ceteris paribus*, age specific birth rates tend to vary directly with per capita income in the long run. Since the sign of the partial regression coefficient of births upon income is consistently positive, this conclusion appears to be valid even though the income coefficient is significantly different from zero for only the first two age groups. The dependence of births upon income, however, is not very strong even in the two lowest age groups; in fact, the calculated income elasticity never exceeds .55.

These results of our regression analysis are consistent with the findings of Easterlin [4] for the United States from 1870 to 1960. Easterlin observed

Table 1. *Age Specific Birth Rate Regressions*

Age of Mother	ln Y	ln I	ln E	ln P	Constant	S	R^2	$\bar{R}^2$
15–19	.553 (.207)	−.209* (.366)	−1.229 (.315)	−.180 (.057)	6.896	.094	.497	.434
20–24	.202 (.086)	−.086* (.152)	−.533 (.125)	−.079 (.024)	6.782	.040	.527	.468
25–29	.075* (.065)	−.110* (.116)	−.332 (.100)	−.044 (.018)	6.765	.030	.480	.415
30–34	.061* (.074)	−.150* (.130)	−.380 (.112)	−.045 (.020)	6.892	.034	.513	.452
35–39	.089* (.092)	−.284 (.163)	−.490 (.141)	−.047 (.025)	7.213	.042	.530	.472
40–44	.084* (.130)	−.559 (.230)	−.540 (.198)	−.070 (.036)	7.622	.060	.507	.445
45–49	.268* (.197)	−1.182 (.350)	−1.472 (.301)	−.057 (.054)	10.816	.091	.700	.663

* Not significant at the 5 per cent level.
Symbols:
   Y = per capita income, converted into U.S. dollars at purchasing parity exchange rate.
   I = per cent of labor force employed outside of agriculture
   E = an index of education
   P = population density
   Dependent variable is the natural log of the number of live births per 1000 females in
      age group specified.

a positive correlation between long swings in white urban births and Kuznetz cycles in nonagricultural economic activity. He also found that the amplitude of the long waves in birth rates is much smaller than that of the corresponding long cycles in economic indicators.

Our findings are also consistent with the short-run results of Becker, whose estimates of average income elasticities for the short business cycles for first- and second-order births were .56 and .42, respectively [24, pp. 224–25].

There appears to be a systematic variation in income effects with age. The impact of income upon births, which tends to be strongest for women between 15 and 19, declines with age for a while and then rises again from age 35. This pattern of variation suggests the hypothesis that both desired family size and the timing of childbearing tend to react to economic factors. At the early ages, there is a strong tendency to adjust the family size to short-run variations in family income by temporarily postponing or accelerating childbearing in response to changes in economic conditions. As would-be mothers age, however, the strength of the timing effect diminishes, leading to a declining income elasticity to about age 34. The rising income elasticity at higher ages, on the other hand, represents primarily the increasing influence of the "permanent" effect of changes in per capita income.

As expected, the socioeconomic phenomena associated with the urbanization process tend to reduce birth rates in the long run. It is apparent from column 2 of Table 1 that the age specific elasticity of birth rates with respect to nonagricultural employment is negative throughout. It is not statistically significant up to age 35. The calculated values, however, decline to age 25 and then begin to rise; the elasticity is greater than unity for the 45–49 age group. The progressively stronger impact of industrialization upon age specific birth rates is thus quite marked. A reasonable interpretation of this pattern is that the reduction in crude birth rates which has historically accompanied the process of urbanization has been achieved, in part, by a shortening of that portion of the life span devoted to childbearing activities by an average woman. Further, the strongest effect appears among the older women.

The well-known negative correlation of birth rates with the level of education is also apparent in our results. The regression coefficient of birth rates with respect to the educational index is always negative and statistically significant. Furthermore, as indicated by the analogous age specific pattern of variation of the relevant elasticities, the impact of the level of education upon fertility is qualitatively similar to that of the degree of industrialization. Quantitatively, among all the variables, a 1 per cent change in the index of education appears to exert the largest absolute influence upon age specific birth rates.

In view of the rough degree of approximation to which the population density figure represents the theoretical concept of the population-resource ratio, the unequivocal significance of P in the regression analysis is somewhat surprising. To a certain extent, as indicated by the negative sign of the regression coefficient in column 4, overpopulation tends to generate its own antidote. However, the over-all elasticity of birth rates with respect to population density is rather small.

The regression equations for age specific birth rates for the subsample of developed countries taken by themselves are reproduced in Table 2 for comparison purposes. Since for this subsample the correlation coefficient between the logarithms of per capita income and of the degree of industrialization was quite high ($r = .81$), the latter variable had to be omitted from the regression equations. As stated above, the results of the regression for the developed subsample are consistent with those for the combined group of countries. Indeed, in no case is the difference in regression coefficients significant at the 5 per cent level. In developed countries, the influence of income levels upon births seems to decline more rapidly with age, and becomes negative from the age of 30 onward. The educational level exercises its pri-

Table 2. *Age Specific Birth Rate Regressions*
Developed Countries

Age of mother	ln Y	ln E	ln P	Constant	S	R^2
15–19	.703	−.965	−.127*	3.502	.099	.617
	(.224)	(.523)	(.077)			
20–24	.179*	−.227*	−.809	5.179	.050	.519
	(.112)	(.262)	(.038)			
25–29	.175	−.121*	−.050*	4.678	.040	.216
	(.090)	(.210)	(.030)			
30–34	−.0051*	−.282*	−.045*	6.519	.042	.206
	(.094)	(.219)	(.032)			
35–39	−.0015*	−.519	−.042*	6.651	.046	.284
	(.104)	(.243)	(.136)			
40–44	−.0392*	−.735	−.060*	6.799	.065	.286
	(.148)	(.345)	(.051)			
45–49	−.0923*	−1.212	−.081*	6.897	.095	.327
	(.214)	(.501)	(.074)			

* Not significant at the 5 per cent level.
Symbols:
  Y = per capita income, converted into U.S. dollars at purchasing parity exchange rates
  E = an index of education
  P = population density
  Dependent variable is the natural log of the number of live births per 1000 females in
    age group specified.

mary impact at early ages and from 30 onwards, as before. And the impact of population density is statistically less significant for the developed sub-group than for all countries combined. In addition, R^2 declines more rapidly with age in the developed subsample than for the entire group of countries.

IV. THE ANALYSIS OF MORTALITY

A. *Determinants of Mortality*

There is general agreement among demographers that the determinants of changes in mortality in both developed and underdeveloped areas are of two kinds: (1) those related to the standard of living of the population, and (2) those associated with public health programs for the control of epidemic and endemic diseases. The relative importance of these two classes of factors in both the short and the long run, however, and the extent to which they are interdependent are still unclear.

For example, in discussing recent trends and determinants of mortality in developed countries Stolnitz argues that, "To a significant degree, the great mortality movements of the West appear to have been initiated by medical advances, particularly as applied to governments. Improving economic conditions were important, but much more as permissive elements than as precipitating factors" [16, p. 34]. Similarly, with respect to underdeveloped areas, Bourgeois-Pichat and Chia-Liu Pau point out that, "In the short run the steep mortality decline during the postwar period in, for example, Ceylon, Formosa and Japan stressed that the drop was attributable more to the development of public health programs with a wide use of new drugs than to any possible rising level of living of the people" [16, p. 25].

Clearly, the immediate impact upon death rates in underdeveloped countries of such public health measures as the control and purification of the water supply, the disposal of sewage, the use of new drugs, large-scale innoculations against communicable diseases, and progress in environmental sanitation is bound to be dramatic. On the other hand, once the major benefits from these improvements have been reaped, it may well be that economic conditions play the primary role in determining the subsequent rate of progress in mortality. For it stands to reason that such factors as better nutrition, improved housing, healthier and more humane working conditions, and a somewhat more secure and less careworn mode of life, all of which accompany economic growth, must contribute to improvements in life expectancy. In addition, as pointed out by Spiegelman, "Fundamentally, health progress depends upon economic progress. By the rapid advance in their economies in the postwar period, the highly developed countries have produced wealth for the development of health programs. Also, more efficient technologies in industry are releasing the manpower needed for an extension of medical care and public health services. The intangible contribution of economic progress to lower mortality is derived from the advantage of a high standard of living —more abundant, better and more varied food—a more healthful work and home environment—and more time for healthful recreation" [16, p. 59].

In our study of mortality, the indicator of public health conditions used was the number of physicians per thousand inhabitants. It might be argued that the sum of real per capita expenditures on public health and social security would have been a preferable criterion. However, as pointed out by the United Nations [18, p. 489], the significance of this item in the total health picture varies from country to country depending upon the type of state organization and the scope of the government's share in economic activity. In socialist economies and in centralized states, for example, the national government is almost completely responsible for the health of the public. In private enterprise economies, on the other hand, the degree of public responsibility for health assumed by the government varies significantly from country to country and, in some, constitutes only a minor share of the total. The number of physicians per capita was therefore considered to be a more satisfactory indicator.

As before, economic conditions were represented in our mortality analysis by the level of real per capita income. The percentage of nonagricultural employment of the labor force was used as a measure of the degree of industrialization and urbanization. And the percentage rate of growth of real per capita income was introduced in order to investigate the empirical relevance of one of Leibenstein's population theories [9, pp. 173–75].

The same considerations which suggested the incorporation of population density into the birth rate analysis also led us to test the effects of this variable upon mortality. To our surprise, however, the partial regression coefficient of age specific death rates upon population density was never statistically significant in either the logarithmic or the nonlogarithmic forms of the equations calculated. This variable was therefore dropped.

The influence of the degree of education upon mortality patterns was also investigated by means of an index of education analogous to that used in the fertility study. This factor might be expected to affect especially postneonatal mortality for infants and of young children because survival probabilities at early ages are largely affected by the socially and educationally conditioned techniques which mothers employ in the feeding and care of babies. Indeed, our regression results indicate that, in the logarithmic form of the equations, the partial regression coefficient of death rates with respect to the educational index E was statistically significant up to the age of 25. Moreover, in accord with expectations, the effect of educational forces upon mortality after the first five years was found to diminish steadily with age. It was observed in the preliminary calculations that E and the health indicator H were never both statistically significant for the same regression surface, except in the case of infant mortality. Since H is the better indicator for most of the age groups, and since it was felt desirable to have a uniform set of explanatory variables for mortality at all ages, the number of physicians per capita (H) was used instead of the educational index (E) throughout the entire mortality calculation.

B. *The Regression Model*

The regression equations fitted by least squares to the data were of the form:

$$(2) \quad \log_e m_i = c_{0i} + c_{1i} \log_e Y + c_{2i} \frac{\Delta Y}{Y} + c_{3i} \log_e I + c_{4i} \log_e H + \delta_i.$$

In (2) m_i represents the number of deaths per 1000 people in the ith age group; Y and I have the same meanings as in the birth rate questions; $\Delta Y/Y$ is the percentage rate of growth of per capita real income; H is our health indicator—the number of physicians per 10,000 inhabitants; and δ_i is a random error term. The variable $\Delta Y/Y$ was not represented in logarithmic form since, for some countries, it takes on zero or negative values.

As before, in order to achieve a homoscedastic distribution of the δ_i, the least-square fits were computed with country weights derived in the same manner as in the birth rate analysis.

Nonlogarithmic forms of the regression equations with nonlinear terms in income were also fitted to the data. The nonlogarithmic alternatives re sulted in slightly poorer fits than (2) up to the age of 40 and somewhat better fits afterwards. The decision to adopt the logarithmic version was made primarily for consistency with the birth rate study.

Disaggregation of the sample into developed and underdeveloped sub-groups led to no significant differences in regression coefficients. This time, however, the values of R^2 for the underdeveloped countries were significantly higher than for the developed ones. This observation tends to bear out the contention of Ansley Coale that, "The course of mortality in *industrialized* areas can safely be discussed without reference to prospective variation in strictly economic forces" [24, p. 9].

C. *The Regression Results*

Table 3 presents a summary of the regression results derived with the statistical model just described. As before, the upper entry in the *i*th row and the *j*th column of this table is an estimate of the regression coefficient a_{ji}. The standard error of this estimate is listed in parentheses below the corresponding coefficient.

It is evident from the last 2 columns of the table that, up to the age of 50, medical and socioeconomic forces account for something like 50 to 85 per cent of the total variance among countries in age specific death rates. Up to the age of 70, the values of R^2 are all statistically significant. In addition, the signs of the individual regression coefficients are all internally consistent.

One interesting feature of our calculations is the steadily diminishing importance of economic, social, and medical factors in explaining inter-country death rate differentials at higher ages. (From the age of 35 onwards, the values of R^2 decrease continuously.) Similar results were obtained by Moriyama and Guralnick [16, pp. 61–73] in a cross-sectional study of differences in mortality between occupational and social strata in the United States; they found that the gap in mortality rates between socioeconomic classes narrows with age, especially after 55. This observation may be related to some suggestions from recent medical research that the physiological quality of human organisms is largely determined at a very early stage in life. Economic and social conditions during early childhood, therefore, may well play a more significant role in determining differences in mortality rates after age 55 than do current variations in socioeconomic and medical factors.

A more detailed examination of our regression results leads to the following generalizations:

1. *Ceteris paribus*, there exists a negative long-run association between death rates and economic conditions. Column 1 of Table 3 indicates that the

Table 3. Age Specific Death Rate Regressions

Age group	ln Y	ΔY/Y	ln I	ln H	Constant	S	R²	R̄²
0–1	−.275 (.116)	+.025* (.030)	−.664 (.255)	−.149* (.129)	8.417	.0571	.686	.643
1–4	−.583 (.034)	−.035 (.008)	1.284 (.074)	−.311 (.037)	10.681	.0166	.857	.838
5–9	−.420 (.138)	−.033* (.035)	−.610 (.303)	−.336 (.153)	5.776	.0679	.721	.683
10–14	−.304 (.089)	−.065 (.023)	−.713 (.196)	−.157* (.099)	4.916	.0437	.771	.740
15–19	−.433 (.092)	−.093 (.024)	−.476 (.203)	+.044* (.103)	5.014	.0455	.653	.606
20–24	−.372 (.105)	−.043 (.026)	−.362* (.231)	−.203 (.117)	4.808	.0519	.702	.661
25–29	−.341 (.103)	−.045 (.026)	−.637 (.225)	−.135* (.114)	5.738	.0504	.717	.678
30–34	−.274 (.100)	−.045 (.026)	−.615 (.220)	−.178* (.111)	5.470	.0493	.699	.658
35–39	−.240 (.098)	−.050 (.025)	−.514 (.214)	−.198 (.108)	5.175	.0481	.670	.625
40–44	−.137 (.098)	−.047 (.025)	−.528 (.214)	−.175* (.109)	4.878	.0484	.562	.502
45–49	−.207 (.097)	−.038* (.025)	−.185* (.211)	−.185 (.106)	4.252	.0472	.478	.372
50–54	−.065* (.090)	−.031* (.023)	−0.220* (.198)	−.198 (.100)	3.976	.0448	.444	.368
55–59	−.017* (.080)	−.016* (.020)	−.144* (.175)	−.194 (.088)	3.717	.0393	.358	.270
60–64	−.031* (.066)	−.015* (.016)	−.114* (.146)	−.170 (.072)	4.074	.0324	.410	.329
65–69	−.0008* (.085)	−.004* (.022)	−.060* (.187)	−.170 (.095)	4.082	.0422	.255	.153
70–74	−.048* (.066)	−.002* (.016)	+.008* (.146)	−.098 (.072)	4.409	.0323	.199	.089*

* Not significant at 5 per cent level.
Symbols:

Y = per capita income, converted into U.S. 1953 dollars at purchasing parity exchange rates

ΔY/Y = the percentage rate of growth of per capita real income

I = the percentage of the labor force employed outside agriculture

H = health indicator, the number of physicians per 10,000 inhabitants

Dependent variable is the number of deaths per 1000 people in the appropriate age group.

regression coefficient of deaths upon income is negative throughout and statistically significant up to the age of 50. The elasticity of death rates with respect to income is considerably below unity, however. These results are in accord with the conclusions of Moriyama and Guralnick in the study previously cited.

2. Urbanization and industrialization seem to play a significant direct role in the reduction of mortality (col. 3). Much of the apparent effect of urbanization may be due to differences between city and country in environmental sanitation (water supply, sewage, etc.), type of housing, and availability of professional (as opposed to traditional) medical care and the willingness of the population to utilize it. In addition, differences in occupational structure and in per capita income between urban and rural communities may also contribute to the negative correlation between mortality rates and the percentage of nonagricultural employment.

3. As expected, mortality is negatively associated with differentials in medical care (col. 4). Indeed, from the age of 50 onwards, variations in mortality are largely accounted for by differences in medical services. None of the other socioeconomic factors is statistically significant after that age.

4. Finally, our results also indicate the existence of a negative partial correlation between the rate of growth of real per capita income and death rates (col. 2). This finding is in direct conflict with that theory of Leibenstein which suggests that, *ceteris paribus*, a more rapid rate of economic growth will, on the average, be correlated with an *increase* in mortality [9, pp. 173–75].

The explanation of the latter phenomenon may be much more classical in nature than Leibenstein's argument would indicate. As pointed out by Adam Smith, "It is not the actual greatness of national wealth, but its continual increase, which occasions a rise in the wages of labour. It is not, accordingly, in the richest countries, but in the most thriving or in those which are growing rich the fastest that the wages of labour are highest" [14, p. 69]. Now, at a given level of income and within a given sociocultural context, the over-all death rate of the population might be expected to vary with the distribution of income between classes. Even when the over-all average standard of living is low, the per capita income of profit receivers is so high that mortality rates within the entrepreneurial classes are not particularly sensitive to changes in income. In contrast, at low levels of income, a higher wage rate reduces mortality among the laboring population through the better nutritional, health, and sanitation standards that accompany improved wages. As a result, an increase in the rate of growth of income, which augments the relative share of wages in the total product by increasing demand for labor, diminishes death rates. By the same token, by increasing the share of profit receivers, a decline in the rate of economic expansion leads to an increase in mortality.[4]

The flaw in Leibenstein's contention would appear to be that, even

[4] A similar argument is made in I. Adelman [1, pp. 110–11].

though a higher rate of growth of per capita income is associated with a decrease in over-all consumption, it is also associated with an increase in the amount of consumer products accruing to the lower income groups. This decreases mortality among the laboring classes without a corresponding increase in the mortality rate of upper income groups. The result is, of course, a net reduction in mortality for the community as a whole.

V. ESTIMATES FOR 1953

To obtain a partial indication of the usefulness of the above regression approach to natality and mortality phenomena, the regression coefficients of Tables 1 and 3 were used to estimate the crude birth and death rates in 1953 in the six inhabited continents. The year 1953 was used as a bench-mark date because good estimates of per capita income were available for that year and because empirical demographic data for 1950–55 have been published by the United Nations. In addition, for this period, the socioeconomic regression estimates can also be compared with estimates of crude birth and death rates computed by the United Nations Population Division on the basis of purely demographic phenomenological models of population growth [20] [21] [22].

Before our regression analysis can be used for this purpose, however, the values of the independent variables in our equations have to be estimated. For North America, Oceania, and Europe, our estimates are the arithmetic averages of the single country data for 1953, weighted by population; but for Latin America, Asia, and Africa, statistics are notoriously scanty. Our estimates for these regions were therefore necessarily based upon fragmentary data, and are consequently much less reliable. Also, in the absence of better information, a uniform figure of 2 per cent was chosen for the rate of growth of real per capita income in order to avoid a suggestion of spurious accuracy. The values of the independent variables assumed for the 1953 estimates are given in Table 4.

The resulting age specific birth and death rates are indicated in Tables 5 and 6 respectively. Since, from the age of 70 onwards, our death regressions were not statistically significant, the United Nations model mortality tables were used to estimate death rates for the uppermost age groups [22, pp. 72–73]. The pattern of birth and death rates estimated is consistent with later empirical data and a priori expectations. In our estimates, birth rates are lowest in Europe, higher and fairly similar in North America and Oceania, and higher still in Asia, Latin America, and Africa. Death rates in North America and in Oceania are somewhat lower than those in Europe. They are high in both Africa and Asia, and intermediate in Latin America. In accord with observation, Europe, in our estimates, appears to be in a low-birth-and-low-death-rate demographic state; North America and Oceania are of a

Table 4. *Values of Independent Variables Assumed for 1953 Estimates*

Region	Popula-tion density P[a]	Per capita income Y	% rate of growth of per-cap. income ΔY[c]$/Y$	Physicians per 10,000 population H	Educa-tional index E	% of labor force out-side agriculture I
North America	7.8	1800[c]	2.0	12.5[c]	94[c]	87[c]
Latin America	8.1	265[d]	2.0	2.0[f]	30[f]	40[f]
Asia	51[b]	75[d]	2.0	1.0[f]	20[f]	30[f]
Europe	59	770[c]	2.0	11.0[c]	95[c]	78[c]
Oceania	1.3	1120[c]	2.0	12.7[c]	100[c]	84[c]
Africa	6.5	105[d]	2.0	0.5[e]	20[f]	35[f]

Sources: [a] *Demographic Yearbook* 1956, p. 151. Population per km[2] in 1950.

  [b] Corrected in the light of later estimates, back to 1950.

  [c] Averages, weighted by population, of data for 1953 for countries in the region.

  [d] Estimates taken from T. Kristensen and Associates, *The World Economic Balance* (North Holland, 1960), p. 250.

  [e] Hypothetical figure.

  [f] Estimate based on fragmentary data.

Table 5. *Age Specific Birth Rates Estimated for 1953*

Age of mother	Asia	Africa	Latin America	North America	Oceania	Europe
15–19	66	111	106	64	63	28
20–24	234	291	274	206	209	149
25–29	256	283	259	188	193	163
30–34	206	226	199	129	133	113
35–39	145	158	134	73	74	63
40–44	66	72	57	23	25	20
45–49	28	28	17	2	2	2

low-death-rate and intermediate-birth-rate type; and Latin America is in a transition phase, with both mortality and natality intermediate between those of the Asian and African continents and the much lower birth and death rates of the more developed continents. In addition, the age specific pattern of variation of both birth and death rates in each continent is consistent with that found in the real world.

Our estimates of the crude birth and death rates for each continent in 1953 are summarized in Table 7. These estimates are based upon population age distributions derived by interpolation from the actual data for age groups 0–14, 15–64, 65 and over listed in the 1956 *Demographic Yearbook*. The ratio of females to total population used for these estimates was calculated

Table 6. Estimated Age Specific Death Rates (1953)

Age groups	North America	Africa	Latin America	Asia	Europe	Oceania
0–1	21.4	138	120.0[a]	152	29.6	24.9
1–4	.76	34.8	11.1	41.5	1.49	1.04
5–9	.36	6.17	2.42	6.19	.58	.45
10–14	.34	2.57	1.42	2.85	.49	.40
15–19	.65	2.98	1.99	3.82	.98	.81
20–24	.82	6.32	3.22	6.58	1.20	.99
25–29	.91	6.62	3.68	7.45	1.33	1.09
30–34	1.14	7.69	4.30	8.20	1.57	1.32
34–39	1.62	9.65	5.49	9.88	2.15	1.84
40–44	2.59	10.90	7.03	11.0	3.16	2.82
45–49	3.78	14.60	9.12	14.2	4.71	4.19
50–54	6.98	19.40	13.50	17.9	7.76	7.24
55–59	11.30	25.20	18.60	22.8	11.90	11.40
60–64	17.70	37.10	28.00	33.9	18.88	18.0
65–69	27.2	49.75	39.00	44.6	30.00	27.2
70–74	46.10	72.10	65.00	68.4	48.6	47.0
75–79[a]	74	118	99	108	77	75
80–84[a]	118	176	152	163	122	118
85[a]	232	277	255	265	234	232

[a] Estimated on the basis of U.N. model mortality tables, Methods for Population Projection by Sex and Age, Manual III, U.N. 1956, pp. 72–73.

Table 7. Comparison of Birth and Death Rate Estimates 1950–55

Continent	Crude birth rate			Crude death rate			Natural increase		
	Actual*	Our estimate	U.N.** estimate	Actual*	Our estimate	U.N.** estimate	Actual*	Our estimate	U.N.** estimate
	1951–55	1953	1950	1951–55	1953	1950	1951–55	1953	1950
Africa	45	43	47	25	20	33	20	23	14
North America	25	23	22	9	9	0	16[a]	14	13
Latin America	42	41	40	18	13	19	24[a]	28	21
Asia	39	39	46	22	19	33	17	20	13
Europe[b]	20	21	20	11	9	9	9[a]	12	11
Oceania	25	23	26	8	9	12	17	14	14

* Source: Demographic Yearbook 1956, Table A, p. 2.
** Source: The Future Growth of World Population, U.N. 1958, Table 11, p. 32.
Rates are estimated on annual averages for 1951–55.
[a] This rate excludes the effect of migration.
[b] Excluding USSR.

from individual country data on sex distribution by age given in the 1957 *Demographic Yearbook*. From Table 7 one can see that our birth rate estimates are close to the actual figures and compare very favorably with those of the United Nations. Our death rate estimates are less satisfactory. They are still considerably better than the U.N. estimates, but they tend to be low. Since crude death rates are quite sensitive to the details of the age distribution of the population, especially at ages above 45, a large part of the discrepancy between our calculations and empirical observations can be ascribed to inaccuracies and approximations in our assumed age structure. This hypothesis is supported by the fact that life expectancy at birth (see Table 8), which is independent of age structure, is consistent with observation.

One would expect, of course, that even better agreement with real world birth and death rates could be achieved if crude vital statistics were estimated from the regression equations country by country and averaged (using relative populations as weights) for each continent. Unfortunately, however, the scarcity of data, especially in the underdeveloped regions, precluded this approach.

Table 8. Comparisons of Life Expectancy and Reproduction Rate Estimates, U.N. and Ours

Continent	Life expectancy at birth			Gross reproduction rate			NRR
	U.N. estimate 1950	Our estimate 1953[i]	Actual[g]	U.N. estimate 1950	Our estimate 1953[i]	Actual[g]	Our estimate[1]
Africa	31.5[a]	46.5	49	3.0[a]	2.89	h	2.33
North America	68.2[b]	71.9	71	1.5[b]	1.70	1.74	1.66
Latin America	46.8[c]	56.7	50	2.75[c]	2.59	3.08	2.31
Asia	32.2[d]	45.2	h	2.92[d]	2.47	h	1.95
Europe	68.2[e]	69.9	66	1.29[e]	1.33	1.22	1.29
Oceania	68.2[f]	71.2	69	1.5[f]	1.73	1.59	1.69

[a] Source: *The Future Growth of World Population* (p. 12), Model AB for Middle Africa and Models CG and DH for Northern and Southern Africa.

[b] *Loc. cit.*, Model LMS.

[c] *Loc. cit.*, Model DH for Central, Tropical and Southern America and Model LMS for Temperate America.

[d] *Loc. cit.*, Model CG for Asia excluding Japan and Model LRVW for Japan.

[e] *Loc. cit.*, Model QRS for Northern and Central Europe and average QRS and LRS Models for Southern Europe.

[f] *Loc. cit.*, Model LMN.

[g] Estimated from available country data on or about 1953 in *Demographic Yearbook*. Averages weighted by population. Figures are rounded to nearest year.

[h] Sample available too unrepresentative to use.

[i] For this computation the regression death rates were converted into life table mortality rates with the aid of the Reed & Merrell Tables reproduced in [7, pp. 19–26].

[1] In this computation it is assumed that .495 of all births are females.

VI. EQUILIBRIUM DISTRIBUTIONS AND DEMOGRAPHIC MULTIPLIERS

A. *Some General Considerations*

One important problem which our regression analysis enables us to attack is: how sensitive is the rate of population growth to changes in each of the socioeconomic variables? In attempting to answer this question, one cannot simply compare elasticities. For a given percentage change in one of the independent variables does not, in general, have the same a priori probability as the same percentage change in another independent variable. One must instead compute the effect on population growth of each of a set of equiprobable percentage changes in the independent variables in order to achieve a more or less objective inter-variable comparison.

A more basic difficulty arises when one tries to determine the relevant whole-population elasticities (elasticities averaged over all age groups), as the averaging process depends of necessity on the age distribution assumed for the population. One can bypass this problem by rephrasing the question in a manner similar to that used in comparative statics analysis. Thus we shall not ask: what changes in the *actual* demographic features of a community will be brought about by a given percentage variation in a particular socioeconomic quantity? Instead, we shall compare the *equilibrium* configurations which correspond to the age specific birth and death rates of the society before and after the change.

This alternative approach leads us to the calculation of demographic multipliers, conceptually analogous to the more familiar multipliers of modern economics. These demographic multipliers indicate the differences in the equilibrium demographic features of a society before and after a change in the value of some particular social or economic variable. A demographic multiplier is derived by (1) calculating the equilibrium age distribution corresponding to a certain set of initial values of those socioeconomic variables which determine the age specific birth and death rates; (2) changing one of our independent variables, such as per capita income, by a certain percentage; (3) calculating the new age specific birth and death rates; (4) calculating the new equilibrium age distribution; and (5) comparing the demographic characteristics of the two equilibria.

Before these demographic multipliers can be calculated, therefore, we must derive the equilibrium configuration implied by a given pattern of age specific birth and death rates. The equilibrium age distribution of a society is that age distribution which would ultimately tend to establish itself under unchanging birth and death conditions [3, pp. 236–51].[5] It can be shown that, if the fertility of women at each age were to remain constant for a sufficient length of time, the age structure of the population would assume a definite pattern which is independent of the initial age distribution of the population. In addition, it can also be proved that, given a set of fertility and mortality rates, the equilibrium configuration is stable with respect to large displacements as well as to small. The nature of the implied equilibrium age distribution is therefore of demographic interest both intrinsically and as a means of obtaining a better representation of the inherent power for growth of a population. From an economic point of view, the equilibrium age distribution is also of interest, as such important features of an economy as its consumption pattern, the savings tendencies of the community, the attitudes of the society towards risk, the labor-force participation rate, and the average productivity of the employed are all age-dependent phenomena [24, pp. 287–522].

B. *Equilibrium Distributions and Multipliers*

Some of the significant demographic features of the calculated equilibrium distributions are given in Table 9 for the six continents. For each continent the predicted age configuration in equilibrium consists of a larger proportion of younger people than was observed in 1953, and, except possibly for Europe, it implies a reversal of the current tendencies towards an older population. Since the decrease in the aged is more than counterbalanced by the increase in the proportion of children, the economic burden upon the working population rises in equilibrium. In Table 9 this effect is measured by the dependency ratio, an indicator which is obtained by dividing the proportion of the population under 15 and over 59 by the working age population. These projected changes are obviously related to the dramatic difference in death rates between the actual and the predicted populations.

The demographic multiplier calculations summarized in Tables 10 and 11 were carried out for four continents, chosen to represent four different demographic situations. North America is an example of a high-birth-rate and low-death-rate society. Asia represents a community with both birth and death rates high. Europe is more or less typical of a low-death-rate and low-birth-rate region; and Latin America has an intermediate death rate and a high birth rate. The changes for which the multiplier calculations were carried out were of a magnitude which might be expected to result

[5] This equilibrium age distribution is identical with the "stable age distribution" first introduced by Lotka in 1911 [10]. The approximation technique suggested [3, pp. 240–42] was used for its calculation.

Table 9.   Equilibrium Demographic Features by Continent

Continent	Conditions	Age distribution %			Depend-ency	Crude birth rate	Crude death rate[c]	Natural in-creased[d]
		0–14	15–60	>60				
Africa	Actual '53[a]	42	52	6	.92	45	25	20
	Equilibrium	46	50	4	1.00	42	11	30
	Regression Est. 1953	—	—	—	—	43	20	23
Asia	Actual '53[a]	38	56	6	.78	39	22	17
	Equilibrium	41	53	5	.86	36	13	23
	Regression Est. 1953	—	—	—	—	39	19	20
Latin America	Actual '53[a]	40	55	5	.82	42	18	24
	Equilibrium	44	51	5	.94	38	8	30
	Regression Est. 1953	—	—	—	—	41	13	28
North America	Actual '53[a]	27	61	12	.64	25	9	16
	Equilibrium	33	57	10	.75	25	7	19
	Regression Est. 1953	—	—	—	—	22	9	14
Oceania	Actual '53[a]	30	59	11	.69	25	8	17
	Equilibrium	34	56	10	.78	26	7	19
	Regression Est. 1953	—	—	—	—	23	9	14
Europe[b]	Actual '53[a]	25	62	13	.61	20	11	9
	Equilibrium	27	59	15	.70	19	10	9
	Regression Est. 1953	—	—	—	—	21	9	12

[a] Source: *Demographic Yearbook* 1956, p. 8, Table B.
[b] Excluding USSR.
[c] Calculated by the method given in [25, p. 32].
[d] Excluding the effect of migration.

from a reasonably successful 5-year development program. Inasmuch as neither the literacy index nor the degree of nonagricultural employment in Europe and North America is likely to change very much, no educational or industrialization multipliers were calculated for these continents. In addition, it was not obvious what assumption could reasonably be made about changes in the number of physicians per capita and changes in population density. Therefore, no multipliers were calculated for these variables.

From Tables 10 and 11 it would appear that the demographic characteristics of a society are most sensitive to changes in the educational level of the population. Some of the demographic indicators, such as the rate of natural increase, also respond noticeably to changes in per capita income.

Table 10. Demographic Multipliers by Continent

Continent	Demographic quantity	Equilibrium value based on 1953 data	Effect of 25% increase in			Effect of change in $\Delta Y/Y$ from 2% to 4%
			Y	I	E	
North America	Birth rate (%)	2.55	+.12	*	*	0
	Death rate (%)	.69	−.04	*	*	0
	Rate of natural increase (%)	1.86	+.16	*	*	0
	Doubling period (years)	37.61	−2.95	*	*	0
	Life expectancy (years)	71.88	+.34	*	*	+.31
Europe	Birth rate (%)	1.92	+.08	*	*	0
	Death rate (%)	1.03	−.05	*	*	−.01
	Rate of natural increase (%)	.89	+.14	*	*	+.01
	Doubling period (years)	78.23	−10.59	*	*	−.87
	Life expectancy (years)	69.94	+.43	*	*	+.35
Latin America	Birth rate (%)	3.82	+.15	−.14	−.47	0
	Death rate (%)	.78	−.05	−.05	+.09	−.02
	Rate of natural increase (%)	+3.03	+.21	−.08	−.55	+.02
	Doubling period (years)	23.22	−1.48	+.62	+5.07	+.15
	Life expectancy (years)	56.72	+1.08	+2.45	*	+.47
Asia	Birth rate (%)	3.60	+.12	−.14	−.41	0
	Death rate (%)	1.27	−.09	−.12	+.20	−.05
	Rate of natural increase (%)	+2.33	+.22	−.02	−.20	+.05
	Doubling period (years)	30.09	−2.56	+.26	+8.13	−.62
	Life expectancy (years)	45.17	+1.83	+4.04	*	+.97

* Not calculated.

The net effect of changes in industrialization per se or in the rate of increase of per capita income is, in general, quite small. On the other hand, the degree of industrialization has a significant influence upon life expectancy. Perhaps the major surprise in the results is the apparently paradoxical observation that the crude death rate increases as the educational level of the society is raised. The explanation of this effect is that, in the long run, the decreased

Table 11. Equilibrium Age Structure and Dependency Ratios by Continent[a]

Continent	Age group	Equilibrium value	Effect of 25% increase in Y	I	E	Effect of change in $\Delta Y/Y$ from 2% to 4%
North America	0–14 (%)	33.14	+1.12	*	*	−.06
	15–35 (%)	31.65	+.19	*	*	−.04
	35–60 (%)	24.92	−.69	*	*	+.02
	>60 (%)	10.29	−.63	*	*	+.09
	Dependency ratio	.75	+.04	*	*	0
Europe	0–14 (%)	26.70	+.85	*	*	−.08
	15–35 (%)	29.96	+.29	*	*	−.06
	35–60 (%)	28.84	−.49	*	*	+.02
	>60 (%)	14.50	−.65	*	*	+.11
	Dependency ratio	.70	+.01	*	*	0
Latin America	0–14 (%)	43.79	+1.24	−.94	−3.86	−.08
	15–35 (%)	32.94	−.10	+.01	+.08	−.05
	35–60 (%)	18.51	−.73	+.63	+2.42	+.09
	>60 (%)	4.76	−.41	+.30	+1.36	+.04
	Dependency ratio	.94	+.03	−.02	−.09	0
Asia	0–14 (%)	41.33	+1.12	−.79	−3.46	−.05
	15–36 (%)	33.29	−.02	−.02	−.07	−.03
	35–60 (%)	19.99	−.68	+.55	+2.20	+.03
	>60 (%)	5.39	−.42	+.25	+1.32	+.05
	Dependency ratio	.86	+.04	−.003	−.06	0

[a] Percentages may not add up to 100 due to rounding.

birth rate accompanying an improvement in education leads to an older population, with its associated higher mortality rates.

VII. CONCLUSIONS

The results of this study suggest that there is a systematic dependence of age specific birth and death rates upon some of the important socioeconomic variables. This relationship can be utilized to estimate the potential demographic changes which may be induced by national development programs. The demographic effects of changes in per capita income and in its rate of growth, however, do not appear to be very dramatic.

For economic development, the implications of this study are therefore rather encouraging. They indicate, for example, that the increase induced in the ratio of population growth by a 25 per cent improvement in per capita income would not raise the population by more than 1 per cent over a 5-year period. Furthermore, if the development program were accompanied by an effective educational effort, the rate of population expansion might actually decline.

All in all, it would seem that the influence of socioeconomic variables upon the demographic features of a society is very much smaller than the effect of population growth upon economic development.

REFERENCES

[1] I. ADELMAN, *Theories of Economic Growth and Development.* Stanford 1961.

[2] H. B. CHENERY, "Patterns of Industrial Growth," *Amer. Econ. Rev.*, Sept. 1960, *50*, 624–54.

[3] L. I. DUBLIN, A. J. LOTKA, AND M. SPIEGELMAN, *Length of Life.* New York 1949.

[4] R. A. EASTERLIN, "The Baby Boom in Perspective," *Amer. Econ. Rev.*, Dec. 1961, *51*, 869–911.

[5] V. L. GALBRAITH AND D. S. THOMAS, "Birth Rates and the Interwar Business Cycles," *Jour. Amer. Stat. Assoc.*, Dec. 1941, *36*, 465.

[6] E. E. HAGEN, "Population and Economic Growth," *Am. Econ. Rev.*, June 1959, *49*, 310–27.

[7] A. J. JAFFE, *Handbook of Statistical Methods for Demographers.* U.S. Department of Commerce, Washington 1951.

[8] D. KIRK AND D. L. NORTMAN, "Business and Babies: The Influence of the Business Cycle on Birth Rates," *Proc. Am. Stat. Assoc.*, Soc. Stat. Sec., 1958, pp. 151–60.

[9] H. LEIBENSTEIN, *Economic Backwardness and Economic Growth.* New York 1957.

[10] A. J. LOTKA, *Analyse demographique avec application particulère à l'espèce humaine.* Paris 1939.

[11] W. F. OGBURN AND D. S. THOMAS, "The Influence of the Business Cycle on Certain Social Conditions," *Jour. Amer. Stat. Assoc.*, 1922, *18*, 324–40.

[12] B. OKUN, *Trends in Birth Rates in the United States Since 1870.* Baltimore 1958.

[13] G. H. ORCUTT, M. GREENBERGER, J. KORBEL AND A. M. RIVLIN, *Microanalysis of Socio-Economic Systems: A Simulation Study.* New York 1961.

[14] ADAM SMITH, *The Wealth of Nations.* New York 1937.

[15] G. U. YULE, "On the Changes in the Marriage and Birth Rates in England and Wales during the Past Half Century with an Inquiry as to Their Probable Causes," *Jour. Roy. Stat. Soc.*, 1906, *69*, 88–132.

[16] MILLBANK MEMORIAL FUND *Trends and Differentials in Mortality.* New York 1956.

[17] UNITED NATIONS, Department of Social Affairs, *The Determinants and Consequences of Population Trends*, Population Studies 17. New York 1953.

[18] ——, Department of Economic and Social Affairs, *Statistical Yearbook.* New York 1959.

[19] ———, Department of Economic and Social Affairs, *Demographic Yearbook*. New York, various years.

[20] ———, Department of Social Affairs, *Age and Sex Patterns of Mortality Model Life Tables for Underdeveloped Countries*, Population Studies 22. New York 1955.

[21] ———, Department of Economic and Social Affairs, *The Future Growth of World Population*, Population Studies 28. New York 1958.

[22] ———, Department of Economic and Social Affairs, *Methods for Population Projections by Sex and Age*, Manual III, Population Studies 25. New York 1956.

[23] ———, Department of Social Affairs. *Data on Urban and Rural Population in Recent Censuses*. New York 1950.

[24] *Universities-National Bureau*, Committee for Economic Research, *Demographic and Economic Change in Developed Countries*, Spec. Conf. 11. Princeton 1960.

THE TRANSITION FROM HIGH TO LOW FERTILITY: CHALLENGE TO DEMOGRAPHERS

Ronald Freedman

Demographers have a great opportunity to study the demographic transition now beginning in some high fertility countries. In the next five to fifteen years fertility is likely to decline sharply in many more countries, where the process of change can be studied and even accelerated under planned experimental conditions. The more quickly demographers gain new knowledge about the whole process of change, the greater the probability that they can make practical contributions to social and economic development. The opportunity is unique. None of the previous major fertility declines in the West or in Japan was studied in detail as it occurred, and much of their demographic and social history is forever lost.[1] Moreover, previously there was not the opportunity to observe the effects of large-scale planned pro-

From Ronald Freedman, "The Transition from High to Low Fertility: Challenge to Demographers," *Population Index*, 31:4:417–430. Reprinted by permission of Princeton University.

[1] Of course, a great deal of important work has been done on Japanese demography. These include the work on family planning by Dr. Y. Koya, many important publications of the Institute of Population Problems of the Ministry of Health and Welfare in Japan, the public opinion surveys of the Mainichi Press, and Irene Taeuber's monumental *The Population of Japan*. However, we do not have detailed studies on many aspects of the Japanese fertility decline. For example, we do not know for either the past or present the proportion of the child-bearing population who have had abortions in different social strata, at what stage of married life, and with what specific effects.

grams to bring family planning to masses of the population and, thus, to accelerate the decline of the birth rate.

The evidence that fertility is declining in at least some high fertility countries now is varied and partial, but convincing. I believe the present declines in a few countries are precursors of things to come in other high fertility areas, as favorable conditions develop. The decline is probably best documented for Taiwan where birth rates have fallen 17 per cent from 42 in 1958 to 35 in 1964.[2] In Hong Kong, birth rates fell below 30 for the first time in 1964 from 32 in 1963 and 37 in 1958.

We cannot document a fertility decline in Korea directly from the vital statistics, which are sadly deficient. Nevertheless, on the basis of evidence about family limitation practices, it is highly probable that the birth rate has begun to decline there. In Seoul, which has about ten per cent of South Korea's population, it is likely that more than 30 per cent of all pregnancies were intentionally aborted in 1963, an increase from perhaps 16 per cent 10 years earlier.[3] Among women aged 35–39 the induced abortion rate was probably 58 per 100 pregnancies in 1959–64, as compared with 14 in the preceding five-year period. While induced abortion rates probably are not so high in other parts of Korea, rates in two rural districts indicate that about 20 per cent of all pregnancies were ended by induced abortion in the period 1962–64 as compared with about 5 per cent in 1960–61.[4] In South Korea as a whole the proportion who have begun recently to limit family size by contraception, sterilization, and abortion is, probably, enough to have started a fertility decline, although the size of the decline is still unknown.[5] In Singapore birth rates have fallen from 44 in 1956 to 32 in 1964. A recorded decline in Puerto Rican birth rates from 41 in 1945–49 to 30 in 1964 is difficult to interpret because of the effects of migration, but it is likely that a genuine fertility decline has occurred there, too.

For several of the areas in which the fertility decline has begun already I venture to predict acceleration of the decline within the next five years to levels of 20–25 births per thousand.

[2] Data on vital rates for Taiwan are from the Taiwan Provincial Department of Civil Affairs. All other vital data cited are from the United Nations Demographic Yearbooks or official publications of the countries concerned.

[3] The data on abortion in Seoul are from an unpublished study by Dr. Sung-Bong Hong of Sudo University, sponsored by the Population Council. They are from one district of Seoul, but it is unlikely to differ greatly from Seoul as a whole.

[4] Data from the Koyang study being conducted by Dr. Jae Mo Yang and Dr. Sook Bang of Yonsei University with support from the Population Council. The rates for the earlier period may represent more retrospective "forgetting," but there is little reason to doubt a major increase.

[5] See T. I. Kim, F. H. Choe, K. S. Lee, D. R. Koh, *The Early Stage of Family Planning in Korea*, Seoul (1964).

THE CONDITIONS FOR FERTILITY DECLINE

Before discussing the specific basis for these audacious predictions, I want to review the broad assumptions on which they are based, not so much because I am certain of their truth, as because testing the assumptions themselves is an important part of the needed research agenda.

Let me say in summary that I expect fertility to decline first and most rapidly under the following conditions:[6] (1) where significant social development has already occurred; (2) where mortality has been relatively low for some time; (3) where there is evidence that many people, wanting moderate-sized families, are beginning to try to limit family size; (4) where there are effective social networks transcending local communities through which family-planning ideas and services and other modernizing influences can be disseminated; (5) where there are large-scale, effective *organized* efforts to disseminate family-planning ideas and information; (6) where such new contraceptives as the intrauterine devices or contraceptive pills are effectively available.

I do not assert that all of these are necesary preconditions for *any* fertility decline. I do not know what the necessary mix is for the beginning or for accelerations of fertility decline. That is precisely one of the important general questions on which we need research. Obviously, the first four conditions are relevant both to the past and to current situations. The last two conditions, organized programs and the new contraceptives, introduce new elements for which history provides no specific guide-lines. I want to comment briefly on each of these six conditions that I assume are favorable for fertility decline.

First, fertility is likely to decline most rapidly where there has been a significant beginning of the kind of social development that decreases dependence on local kinship and community ties. As long as getting the things worth having in a society depends mainly on local kinship-based institutions, rapid fertility decline is unlikely. More generally, declining fertility has been associated in the past with various types of modernization or development. The important questions are: why should these changes affect fertility? how much change in which development variables is necessary for one or another rate of fertility decline?

The United Nations has recently completed an impressive comparative review[7] of how current fertility rates are related to various development

---

[6] Some of the ideas presented briefly in this address are developed more fully in "The Sociology of Human Fertility," *Current Sociology* 10/11(2):35–38 (1961–62); and in "Norms for Family Size in Underdeveloped Areas." *Proceedings of the Royal Society, B,* 159(974):220–245 (March 17, 1964).

[7] *Population Bulletin of the United Nations, No. 7—1963* (St/SOA/Series N/7). Sales No: 64. XIII. 2.

measures. The report indicates that almost all countries with adequate data have either high to very high fertility or quite low fertility. There are essentially no cases in the middle. The U.N. report also finds that a variety of measures of development sharply distinguish the high from the low fertility countries, but that there is practically no correlation between these development measures and fertility *within* each of these two groups of countries. The United Nations publication offers the interpretation that, under historically observed conditions, a combination of development measures must pass a minimum threshold to make low fertility possible. I find this plausible and would expect the threshold to be that combination of development changes that will produce both low mortality and a sufficient erosion of the primacy of kinship to make important aspirations attainable in ways for which high fertility is irrelevant or burdensome. The need for research to replace this speculation with data is obvious.

My second assumption specifies that mortality decline may be an important precondition for fertility decline. Since in all societies some minimum number of children is regarded as essential for married couples, it is unlikely that fertility will fall much until parents are reasonably confident that this minimum number will survive and that excess children are unnecessary. The survival of almost all children imposes increasing pressure on traditional housing, familial, and other arrangements developed over a long time-period as adaptions to high child mortality.

Clearly, I disagree with the final conclusions of those who lament that if mortality and fertility declines do not occur simultaneously there is a serious population problem. Of course, there is. This is precisely one of the "population problems" which induces, and is solved by, the fertility decline. Probably, it is desirable from a policy point of view to begin family-planning programs early in the development process. Nevertheless, while I think the lag between mortality and fertility decline can be reduced substantially by appropriate action, I doubt that such programs will become effective until married couples feel reasonably certain that the number of living children they want will survive, if born, and until the parents observe about them and experience, themselves, the problems of excess fertility, when mortality is low. Certainly I may be wrong in this view, and the stakes are high.[8] Why not run experimental tests trying to use the best family-planning programs

---

[8] After this address was delivered Ansley Coale reminded me that fertility apparently began to decline in a number of European countries prior to or simultaneously with the mortality decline. It is probably unnecessary for a mortality decline to precede a fertility decline if some of the other necessary conditions change; e.g. changes in the economic situation or social organization may reduce the value of marriage or of a certain number of children, without any change in mortality. Then, the desired number of children might be attained with lower fertility and without a reduction in mortality.

in field organizations under varying mortality conditions that exist now? This will serve both science and social policy.

The third condition I specify as a sign of incipient fertility decline is that married couples should want only a moderate number of children and that an increasing minority of them should have made some efforts to limit family size, if only crudely and ineffectively. In sample surveys in many high fertility countries women have stated preferences for only moderate numbers of children.[9] Such statements of fertility desires are at best approximate, and may or may not discount the effects of child mortality. We know that in many places where such statements are made the opportunity to obtain contraceptives does not evoke any significant response. However, if the populations making such verbal responses also have begun to make more use of abortion, contraception, or other means to limit family size, we may take this as an indication of the existence of a family-size problem great enough to move some groups of people to seek a solution. Such groups should be especially relevant for family-planning programs.

The fourth assumption I make is that the idea and the means of family planning will spread most rapidly in a society in which there are effective social networks transcending the local community for interaction and communication. Such networks were crucial in the decline of fertility in the West and in Japan, even without organized family-planning programs. It is likely that information and social validation for family-limitation practices developed over time through interactions in informal networks of friends, relatives, and neighbors, linked in turn to sources of information and supplies by the mass media and commercial networks, and rather later by the private health network.

This again is, at best, a plausible speculation. We need research now in the developing societies on just how information, social support, and validation for new family-limitation ideas and practices are disseminated and how they affect particular components of fertility.

My fifth assumption is that when the other conditions are favorable, a well organized program to bring family planning to a population will accelerate fertility decline by speeding up the diffusion of family-planning practices. Such programs do appear to be accelerating this process, at least in Taiwan, Hong Kong, and Korea.[10] I believe that they do so by providing

---

[9] For a review of some of these findings see Parker Mauldin, "Application of Survey Techniques to Fertility Studies" to be published in a forthcoming volume of the papers presented at a symposium on Research Issues on Public Health and Population Change, University of Pittsburgh, June, 1964.

[10] For a summary view of the programs in Taiwan and Korea, see S. M. Kleenex, "Korea and Taiwan: Two National Programs." *Studies in Family Planning*, No. 6 (March 1965), pp. 1–6.

better information to circulate in the widening social networks, by rationalizing service and supplies, and by providing important social legitimation for the new ideas.

There is a vast area for important research on whether and how various kinds of family-planning programs affect family-limitation norms and practices and, through them, fertility. Time permits only one example. In the fertility declines of the West and Japan the most modernized strata of the population adopted family limitation practices first, thus producing the well known differential fertility patterns. But what will happen if there is a well organized large-scale family-planning program, absent in these earlier situations? In Taiwan, and probably in Korea, for example, the situation before any organized program was like that of the West earlier.[11] Fertility had begun to decline; it was lowest and family-planning practices were most common in the modernized sectors of the population. With large-scale programs, however, a surprising number of those in the less modernized strata have adopted family planning—such groups as illiterates, farmers, members of joint families, etc.

My interpretation of this situation is that during the early stages of the transition the problem which family planning solves is rather widespread in all parts of the population, but it is those in the modern advanced strata who are able to define their problem in relation to available solutions, to seek out the solution, and to use it with minimal assistance or support. Those in the less modern strata need a large-scale, well organized program to accelerate their adoption of the solution, because they need help in defining their problem, in knowing that a solution is available, and in receiving social reassurance that this new activity is safe and socially acceptable. This is, of course, interpretative speculation. Comparative research is needed on whether the facts observed in Taiwan and Korea are general and what they mean.

My final assumption is that the availability of such modern contraceptives as the intrauterine devices or the contraceptive pills will accelerate the adoption of family planning and the fertility decline. Until recently I was among those who believed that improvement of contraceptive technology is irrelevant for fertility decline, since the major declines in countries like England and France occurred mainly through the use of coitus interruptus. It now seems to me that when minimal favorable conditions exist, fertility decline will be accelerated, if there are available contraceptives which are inexpensive, effective, not connected with the sexual act, trouble-free, and requiring little forethought or care, once use is initiated. At any given

[11] For Korea, see Kim et. al. *op. cit.* For Taiwan see R. Freedman, J. Takeshita, and T. H. Sun. "Fertility and Family Planning in Taiwan: A Case Study of the Demographic Transition." *American Journal of Sociology* 70(1):16–27 (July 1964); and B. Berelson and R. Freedman. "A Study in Fertility Control." *Scientific American* 210(5):29–37 (May 1964).

level of motivation such contraceptives should increase the probability that those under cross-pressures between old and new values will adopt the new values and persist in them. I still believe, however, that type of method is largely irrelevant until there have been certain minimal changes in mortality and social organization, but that view, too, needs testing.

Observations in at least three countries make it appear that the introduction of the intrauterine devices in large scale programs does accelerate acceptance greatly. Information about these new methods appears to be particularly suitable for diffusion by word of mouth or mass media in informal networks.[12] Yet, I must admit that we don't know whether under the same social conditions the same large-scale effort could be effective with traditional contraceptive methods. Probably, there will be opportunities for experimental tests.

PROSPECTS FOR FERTILITY DECLINES

I return now to my predictions of large fertility declines soon, at least in Taiwan, Hong Kong, and Korea. I base my predictions on the fact that in these places the six favorable conditions I have specified are present in reasonable measure.

In Taiwan, which I know best, there is low mortality and considerable social development of the type relevant to fertility decline. While fertility decline is general throughout the island, it is significant that fertility does vary systematically in relation to social and economic development and inversely to mortality in the 362 local areas of the island.[13] The majority of the married couples want three or four children, and most have that number by the time the wife is 30. Given rising aspirations for self and children, the result is increasing action to limit family size after age 30. At ages 35–39 fertility declined by 30 per cent between 1958 and 1963. This fertility decline occurred before the beginning of large-scale organized programs, now underway. It resulted from the efforts of individual couples to do something in various ways about family size after having the desired number of children. People learned about what to do from friends, neighbors, and relatives, from the drug stores and private doctors, and to some extent from the mass media. Significant minorities used induced abortion or sterilization.

All of these conditions would have led me to expect a significant decline of fertility in Taiwan even without an organized program, but a decline

---

[12] In experiments in both Korea and Taiwan a majority of women coming to clinics for intrauterine devices have heard about them through mass media or through informal communications, although in each country there were substantial programs for direct communication by health workers.

[13] From an unpublished M. A. paper in economics at the University of Michigan by Paul K. Liu.

likely to be rather slow. My prediction of a rapid decline is based on the expectation that the organized program recently begun will greatly accelerate the decline already underway. We know that a major experimental effort in one city, Taichung, in 1963 was followed in 1964 by a 6 per cent decline in its birth rate as compared with an average decline of less than 3 per cent in the four other large cities.[14] In 1964 the large-scale organized program was extended to many other parts of the island. In that year 50,000 intra-uterine devices were inserted as part of this planned effort, although the program was not yet fully staffed, was unable to use the mass media, and did not yet operate in some of the major population centers. The program goals for 1965 are for 100,000 IUD insertions and the five-year goal is for 600,000 insertions, estimated to reduce the birth rate to about 24 by 1970. On the basis of the favorable conditions and the success to date, I have little doubt that the 1965 goals will be met. The five-year goal of 600,000 insertions may be high, but its attainment is not out of the question. A report for March 1965 indicates that more than 10,000 IUD insertions were made, although the average monthly goal is only about 8,500.

In South Korea although some aspects of the situation are not so favor-able, there is high literacy and use of the mass media, a market orientation, and mobility. Here, too, there is considerable evidence that desired family size is moderate and that recent individual efforts to achieve this goal have been considerable. The organized effort here, more recent than in Taiwan, is strongly supported by the government and is systematically utilizing the national mas media in a substantial way for the first time in the history of any country.[15]

The opening months of the large scale program last year were very successful. More than 100,000 intrauterine devices were inserted under the official program, almost entirely in the last six months of 1964. An experi-mental program in one part of Seoul is demonstrating that more intensive efforts can be even more successful, especially with the use of the mass media.[16]

While the specific conditions in Hong Kong are somewhat different, especially in the fact that the organized program is under a voluntary agency, the basic conditions making for fertility decline are similar to those pre-viously cited, in my judgment.

[14] These data and plans are from unpublished reports of the Taiwan Population Studies Center of the Provincial Health Department of Taiwan and the University of Michigan Population Studies Center.

[15] The data and plans for Korea are from unpblished reports by the Health Ministry of Korea, and from conversations with responsible Korean officials.

[16] From unpublished reports of the Sun Dong Gu Action Research Project of the school of Public Health of Seoul National University, directed by Dr. E. Hyock Kwon.

In at least these three places, Hong Kong, South Korea, and Taiwan, a demographic event of great importance is occurring now—a fertility decline of major proportions in a short time, accelerated by organized social effort. The great challenge to demographers is to study the conditions and processes of the decline with all the tools of modern social science.

So far, I have purposely used as examples a few small countries in which the conditions are especially favorable for fertility decline. What about the rest of the high fertility areas where most of the world's population lives? Here, the relevant conditions are much less favorable. Nevertheless, I venture to predict that a majority of the world's population will be living in countries with declining fertility within the next five to ten years. I do not mean to say that the declines will occur without organized and vigorous efforts, and I do not predict that the "population problem" will be solved, but I am predicting that the fundamental social conditions will bring forth the necessary effort to initiate and accelerate fertility declines. Where the declines will occur, and how rapidly, will depend on many factors, only some of which we can specify now. One of our urgent research tasks is to undertake to keep track of the relevant social, economic, and demographic variables in as many countries as possible, so as to make possible both regularly revised predictions and sound *ex-post-facto* studies. With a humble acknowledgment of inadequacy for the task, I want now to canvass the other major-high fertility areas in a quick, presumptuous, global survey.

In Africa as a whole the prospects for fertility decline seem small. Apart from the theoretical availability of modern contraceptives, none of the favorable conditions I have specified seems present for any substantial parts of the indigenous populations.

In Latin America the conditions do seem favorable for major fertility declines in some places, so that we may expect at least moderate declines for the area as a whole. Significant parts of the Latin American population have relatively low mortality and considerable social and economic development. Recent surveys indicate strong preferences for small families in parts of the population.[17] Evidence of high illegal induced abortion rates in some places[18] indicates that many couples are looking for solutions to pressing family problems. In many areas the necessary health and other social networks exist. It seems likely that access to these networks by organized programs and a more permissive attitude may be developing with the deepening reinter-

[17] For examples, see Carmen Miró and Ferdinand Rath. "Preliminary Findings of Comparative Fertility Surveys in Three Latin American Countries." Paper No. 2 of the 1965 Milbank Memorial Fund Conference. To be published.

[18] For example, see Rolando Armijo and Tegualda Monreal. "The Problem of Induced Abortion in Chile." Paper No. 11 of the 1965 Milbank Memorial Fund Conference.

pretation of the Catholic position now underway. After all, even without such a reinterpretation low birth rates were achieved in such Catholic countries as Argentina and Italy.

In Asia, where most of the world's population lives, the situation is complex. Japan has already gone through the fertility decline, and it is underway at least in Hong Kong, Korea, Taiwan, and Singapore. Even my audacity this evening does not extend to systematic, country-by-country predictions for Asia. Almost the whole range of possibilities can be found in Asia, because the necessary conditions are so variable between and within countries. However, I do believe that in three of the major populations—India, Pakistan, and mainland China—conditions are sufficiently favorable to make fertility decline likely in the next ten years, probably not as quickly or as uniformly as in Taiwan or South Korea, but of vast significance nevertheless.

In India and Pakistan significant mortality declines already underway are likely to continue. In parts of these populations and in particular places there has been significant social and economic development and a vast expansion of the mass media influence and of links to the wider world. The desire for families of moderate size appears in both urban and rural sample surveys.[19] However, evidence that people are doing something to limit family size is found mainly in urban areas. The necessary social networks to transcend local and familial dependence exist in many places, but many other places remain isolated. In both countries official action recently has made intrauterine devices available for use on a mass scale. In short, my hurried estimate is that there are significant parts of the Indian and Pakistani populations in which the pertinent conditions are favorable but others in which they are not. Therefore, I expect fairly rapid fertility decline in some parts of these populations, which on balance will produce only moderate declines in the national rates in the near future.

If I were asked for advice about the Indian family-planning program I would recomemnd concentrating first the limited personnel resources available on those tens of millions of couples who are in the areas and strata with the favorable conditions. However, at the same time, I would select for the most careful immediate study a number of less promising areas varying in respect to the conditions I have specified. In these areas I would utilize the best workers and services possible to try to discover the threshold levels at which unfavorable conditions can be overcome by efficient organization, services, and supplies. Many will disagree with my diagnosis of this particular situation. Some feel that such populations always have been ready for family planning, so that it is only necessary to bring them information and supplies

19 For examples, see Mauldin, *op. cit.*, and S. N. Agarwala. "A Family Planning Survey in Four Delhi Villages." *Population Studies* 15(2):110–120 (Nov. 1961).

in effective ways. Others agree that at least minimal changes in basic conditions are necessary, but argue that these have already taken place all over countries like India and Pakistan.[20]

Both for science and social policy, these positions should be tested by experimental studies now. We need to know particularly whether changes in how people perceive themselves and their world are a sufficient basis for fertility decline prior to substantial changes in their objective social and economic situation. For example, suppose the members of a peasant population are linked to the wider world through the mass media or education. Suppose that they begin to identify with institutions and ideas and social roles outside of the local, the familial, and traditional. Is this a basis for fertility decline before the institutions in which they actually live are changed? I don't think so, but this certainly needs study. We need to know, too, whether such changes in self-perception and identification do in fact precede other objective changes for any substantial number.

Speculation about mainland China is perilous, foolhardy, and necessary. After all we are talking about twenty to twenty-five per cent of the world's population. It would be foolish to allow disagreements with communist ideology and political practice to prevent us from making the best assessment possible of the demographic trends and possibilities. Admittedly, even the China experts must speculate about important trends, and I am not even that kind of expert on China. Nevertheless, I think we can say something meaningful about the prospects for fertility decline. First of all, there is evidence that the communists have created a considerable medical and public-health network which probably has reduced mortality to levels as low as those of India and Pakistan, and perhaps lower.[21] This health network, while staffed with many people with insufficient training by best Western standards, is, probably, adequate as a potential means for bringing family planning to the masses. How much economic and social development of various kinds has taken place is very debatable. However, there seems to be little doubt that literacy has been increased considerably and that there is a considerable capability for reaching masses of people with communications. There have been many changes which probably are eroding further the strength of the extended family, whose earlier universality is in serious question anyway. Recently, we have had some evidence that there is not only considerable government interest in family limitation but that there is already significant provision for contraception and induced abortion, at least in the

[20] For example, see Donald Bogue's 1964 Presidential Address to the Population Association of America, "The Demographic Breakthrough: From Projection to Control." *Population Index* 30(4):449–453 (Oct. 1964).

[21] E.g., Lee Robert Worth. "Health Trends in China Since the Great Leap Forward." *American Journal of Hygiene* 78(3):349–357 (Nov. 1963).

cities.[22] While there is no evidence that such newer contraceptives as the intrauterine devices are being used extensively, such devices are easily copied, and the Chinese certainly can make them in quantity and distribute them to millions if they wish to do so. I expect that they will and that fertility will decline.

I want to emphasize that I am *not* predicting that *major* fertility declines are inevitable in the large populations of Latin America and Asia. I have been predicting only moderate declines in the next 10–15 years for these populations as a result of large declines in some parts of them balanced by much more modest declines in the larger rural populations. How large the declines will be and when they will occur will depend to a considerable extent on the size and effectiveness of the organized effort to bring family planning to the masses and to legitimate it in the society as a whole. But, I doubt that any organized effort concentrating on fertility alone can produce *large* fertility declines where the other necessary conditions are missing.[23]

THE TASKS FOR DEMOGRAPHERS

One of the perils and glories of demographic work is that our projections can be checked against the facts. I'm not sure that the quick surveys I have made should be dignified by the terms "prediction" or "projection." I certainly expect that I will be proved wrong in many particulars. This would be true of even the most careful and painstaking projections at present. Nevertheless I issue a call for making such projections much more carefully, so that we can learn from careful diagnosis of both errors and successes about the basic forces at work.

Whether I am right or wrong about particular places, it seems safe to

[22] See "Family Planning in China." *Japan Economy News* (*Nippon Kerzai Shinbun*) (20 Jan. 1965). Also for a report of the observations of a Japanese medical team on their observations of family-planning clinics, abortions, etc., in mainland China see Dr. Kan Majima. "Chugoke de no sanji seigen ronso [Discussions on Birth Control in China]." *Bungei Shunjei* 42(2):144–148 (Feb. 1965). Edgar Snow reports the following comment by Chou En Lai, "We are encouraging family planning, especially in schools, factories, and government offices, we have had pretty good results. Young people at these places know the advantages of late marriage and after marriage they have the desire to plan their families. Thus, family planning can be spread, if we try, but since it does require proper propaganda and education, it will take time. I feel that we should be satisfied with China's rate of population growth can be brought down to below 1 per cent within this century." P. 16 in "She On-lai shusho kaikeni [An interview with Premier Chou En Lai]." *Asahi Jyanaru*, Vol. 7, No. 10 (March 1965).

[23] This paragraph was added after the address was delivered, because so many newspapers and even some scholars interpreted the address as a flat prediction of major fertility declines all over the world in the near future. Apparently the eagerness for such a decline and its potential news value makes it necessary to emphasize again what I thought was clear in the address itself.

say that fertility changes will be occurring at various rates and under varying conditions in different countries in the next five to twenty-five years. Probably, we can learn most about the social and demographic processes in fertility change if we observe them under such varying conditions, before, during, and after the major changes.

The tools of modern science and demography and the computer make it possible for us to study the coming fertility declines in ways that were never possible before. Despite ingenious and energetic efforts by those working with historical data we know very little about the fertility decline of the West and Japan. What we know does not permit us to link together directly the major variables at work. For example, in his brilliant address two years ago, Kingsley Davis discussed the importance of abortion in the fertility declines of the West and Japan.[24] Unfortunately, he had to rely on fragmentary evidence about the incidence of abortion. He could not link precisely even the evidence available to specific social strata and to specific effects on fertility. We can collect such detailed and systematic data today.

Demographers generally believe that the fertility declines in England and France resulted from the adoption of contraceptive practices. But what is the evidence? For England, we have a sample survey based on a rather unsatisfactory hospital sample of women reporting retrospectively for periods as long as 50 years.[25] Our French colleagues have ingeniously used diaries, letters, and other historical documents to buttress the plausible argument that the fertility decline began early in France and resulted mainly from the use of coitus interruptus.[26] For neither England or France is the prevalence and effectiveness of the practices well documented nor are there data on the links to the rest of the social-demographic structure. Even for the most recent dramatic fertility decline in Japan we do not have much detailed knowledge of the change process.

What I am suggesting is that we plan boldly to study the whole array of pertinent social and demographic variables so that we can study their variations over time and link them into chains of influence for individuals, groups, regions, and countries. The programs of research which I am suggesting must be viewed in their broadest context. As I see it, we need comparative research on a time-series basis on four broad groups of variables.

1. As our end point we need data on fertility itself to include, as far as

---

[24] "The Theory of Change and Response in Modern Demographic History." *Population Index* 29(4) :345–366 (Oct. 1963).

[25] Lewis-Faning, E. *Report on an Enquiry into Family Limitation and Its Influence on Human Fertility During the Past Fifty Years.* Papers of the Royal Commission on Population, Vol. I (London, H. M. Stationary Office, 1949).

[26] Bergues, H., et al. *La prévention des naissances dans la famille.* Institut National d'Etudes Démographiques, Cahiers de Travaux et Documents, 35 (Paris: Presses Universitaires de France, 1959).

possible, both period and cohort measures of the number and timing of births in major population strata.

2. We need measures of what Kingsley and Judith Davis[27] call the "intermediate variables"—those through which any social variables must work to affect fertility—for example, age at marriage or first sexual union, periods of separation, contraception, fecundity, voluntary or involuntary fetal deaths, etc. We need to have measures of these for significant strata of the population and to know how each affects the number and spacing of children.

3. We need to know what the social norms are about these intermediate variables as well as about family size and child spacing. We also need to know how these norms about what ought to be done influence the intermediate variables and through them fertility itself.

4. Finally, we need to know which elements of social and economic organization affect these norms, these intermediate variables, and finally fertility itself. A new crucial element in the set of causal *social* variables is the operation of the new programs designed specifically to modify family size.

Presumably, lines of causation run from the social and economic organization to the intermediate variables either directly or through the social norms and then from the intermediate variables to the fertility variables themselves. Of course, biological variability in fecundity also enters into the final result.

This total system of variables is complex. No single investigator or institution can study the whole. Even collectively we may not fill in the outline of the whole structure in our life time. Others may conceptualize the basic framework in radically different ways. But, I hope that many of us, individually or in working groups, will try to do our research in such a way as to gather cumulative and comparative data on whole clusters of these variables in relation to *some* view of the whole process. It is a large task, but not impossible, if we think and work boldly and if we can bring in a larger number of young first-rate workers who see the task as an exciting scientific challenge.

Fortunately, the task is made simpler by the opportunity for large-scale experimental studies in connection with family-planning programs. Such experimentation is both feasible and ethical in a situation in which the mass of the population wants help in limiting family size and the indigenous leadership sees this as a desirable goal. The possibilities of disentangling cause and effect relationships in experiments conducted under almost classical condi-

[27] Kingsley Davis and Judith Blake. "Social Structure and Fertility: An Analytic Framework." *Economic Development and Cultural Change* 4(3):211–235 (April 1956).

tions is a great opportunity for imaginative researchers. Unfortunately, many of the action programs underway do not take advantage of these unique opportunities.

Social demographers who are willing to assist in the practical evaluation of these family-planning action programs have a unique opportunity to collect simultaneously demographic and social data in detail for the periods preceding, during, and following the action programs. The demographer who helps to establish ways of measuring vital rates where registration is imperfect, helps to evaluate an existing program, while developing the data needed for basic demographic analysis.

Sometimes, demographers look at those working on the action side of family-planning programs as far away from basic demographic concerns, more emotional than scientific, more concerned with operational details than general knowledge. On the other side, the family-planning activists sometimes see the demographers as unable to contribute to the solution of immediate problems, diverting energy and resources from these problems. On balance, both views are incorrect, in my opinion. The demographer must recognize that the family-planning action programs on the scale now under way are going to be a significant element in the set of social forces determining fertility and other demographic trends. They are one of the facts of life today. They are properly a subject of research and provide unique opportunities for basic demographic studies. On the other hand, the family-planning "activists" will be short-sighted if they do not encourage basic demographic research as part of the evaluation of specific programs. The demographers who can be attracted to this work are uniquely equipped to assist in the evaluation studies. Figures of distribution of supplies or intrauterine device insertions are important, but they are, after all, only measures of some intervening variables. What is wanted ultimately is data on how these affect birth rates and family-building patterns. Then, too, what we learn today in basic research activities may be useful in guiding programs later in Latin America or in Africa.

There is also a responsibility to the scientific community and to posterity to learn everything we can about the important demographic changes now underway. We cannot always precisely specify how what we learn can be applied now, but the growth of the central body of scientific knowledge is of value for its own sake, and its useful applications are difficult to foresee in advance.

Finally, none of us should be under the illusion that if all countries achieve low fertility, practical "population problems" will be solved forever and there will be no scientific problems about human fertility. The problems will be rather different, to be sure, but I cannot imagine a society in which the relations of man to man and to his environment do not have demographic aspects involving the patterns of reproduction. After all, not too long ago both demographers and activists were concerned with the problems of declining and aging populations. What we learn in this generation about the transition from high to low fertility will help the next generation to work on the new demographic problems—whatever those may be.

POPULATION POLICIES
IN DEVELOPING COUNTRIES

Dudley Kirk and Dorothy Nortman

Population policy is rapidly becoming an accepted part of development programs. This is very recent, and its origin can readily be traced to the thwarting of development plans by high rates of population growth. Those of us who have followed this subject closely over the last decade are not surprised at this interest among economic planners, but like the rest of the world, we are astounded at the rapidity with which the climate of world opinion has changed on the subject of population control. Indeed, it may be that the people have been ahead of their leaders, and that the change in attitude toward limiting family size is more apparent than real. At any rate, a decade ago, only one country—India—had a "population policy," in the sense of promoting family planning. Today the roster of nations with such programs is rapidly growing. If we include Mainland China, some five-eighths of the 2.3 billion people in the developing regions live in countries that now have policies favoring population control or, more specifically, the adoption of family planning.

This outburst of interest and action in the field of population is related to growing recognition of: (1) the fact that rates of population growth in the developing countries are generally high, generally rising, and generally higher than those experienced by the industrial countries at a comparable

From Dudley Kirk and Dorothy Nortman, "Population Policies in Developing Nations," *Economic Development and Cultural Change*, 15:2:1:129–142 (January 1967). Reprinted by permission of the University of Chicago Press.

stage of economic development; (2) the extent to which high birth rates and rapid population growth are handicaps to social and economic development; and (3) the legitimacy of government action in this field—that governments both can and should do something about family planning. This paper will assume the first proposition, summarize the arguments relating to the second, and give principal attention to the third.

The whole problem of population is increasingly being viewed as a question of dynamic relationships between population growth and economic development, rather than in terms of static man-land ratios. The impact of rapid population growth is most obvious in densely populated agricultural countries such as India, but even where potential resources seem plentiful in relation to population, as in Latin America and Africa, we are coming to see that high rates of population growth impede the accumulation of sufficient capital for the exploitation of those resources.

At the most elementary level, it is of course necessary that socio-economic progress at least keep up with population growth; i.e., if population is growing at 2.5 per cent per year (the present average in the developing countries), the economy must grow by at least this pace just to stand still insofar as per capita income is concerned. Or viewed the other way, population growth is a major drag on raising per capita income. Equally important, rapid population growth forces a hard choice in the allocation of resources. Planners are pulled between meeting the immediate consumption needs of the growing population and the demands for investment to raise the economic potential and future productive capacity of the country.

For the developing countries, this question of priorities is at the heart of their problems in mapping plans. Affluent nations living well beyond the subsistence level have relatively wide latitude in allocating their resources. In the countries of Asia, Africa, and Latin America, where 80 percent of family income goes for food alone—and at that the people are undernourished—to divert even 10 percent of the national income from consumption to investment involves mass suffering.

Yet investment is imperative, if these nations are to modernize. Even assuming that the capital/output ratio, i.e., the number of investment units needed to produce an additional income unit, is as low as three in agrarian economies undergoing development,[1] it would still take an investment of 9 percent of the national income to add 3 percent to aggregate income. In the absence of population growth, an annual investment of 9 percent of the national income would represent a considerable achievement, for it would result in doubling per capita income in 23 years. If, however, population is growing at 3 percent per year, a figure already surpassed in several developing coun-

[1] This ratio is the subject of great speculation among economists. See, for example, Simon Kuznets, "Toward a Theory of Economic Growth," in *Economic Growth and Structure* (New York: W. W. Norton, 1965), p. 33.

tries and rapidly being approached in others, an annual investment of 9 percent represents no per capita gain whatsoever.

In their comprehensive analysis of the relationship between population growth and economic development in low income countries, Coale and Hoover arrived at the startling conclusion that in India *"total* output would grow faster with reduced fertility than with continued high fertility."[2] In other words, a slower rate of population growth would produce a greater total product. The explanation for this seeming anomaly is that a decline in the birth rate does not immediately affect the size of the labor force, but it does immediately reduce the number of dependents to be provided for. With fewer dependents, there is less pressure to consume; therefore more funds are immediately available for investment purposes, and a greater output results.[3] Here, then, is the dilemma. If developing countries could modernize, birth rates would presumably fall; but if birth rates would fall, developing countries could more readily modernize.

Confronted with high rates of population growth that are thus a major drag on economic development, the governments of developing countries are now endorsing population control policies at a rate and in a climate of world approval unimaginable even a few years ago. As evidenced at international conferences, it is not a case of the West pushing the rest of the world toward population control. Rather, the situation is one in which the developing countries are turning for knowledge and means to the nations with long experience in the control of family size.[4]

[2] Ansley J. Coale and Edgar M. Hoover, *Population Growth and Economic Development in Low-Income Countries* (Princeton University Press, 1958), p. 285.

[3] It is true, as pointed out by Kuznets, *op. cit.*, p. 124, that "the empirical evidence, at least in its present state, is insufficient for a detailed analysis of the impact of population growth on the growth of aggregate output." The above argument relating to *total* output is of course more controversial than the proposition that a lower rate of growth would contribute to higher *per capita* income.

[4] The subject of population control first reached the floor of the United Nations General Assembly in December 1962. In debating Resolution 1838 (XVII), it was clear that, with the exception of some Latin American countries, developing nations strongly supported the clause that the UN "give technical assistance, as requested by Governments, for national projects and programmes dealing with the problems of population." UN General Assembly 7–17 December 1962. *Provisional Summary Record.*

At the UN Asian Population Conference, to which the participating countries sent official representatives, the delegates approved the recommendation that "the U.N. and its specialized agencies should expand the scope of the technical assistance which they are prepared to give at the request of governments in the development of statistics, research, experimentation and action programmes relating to population problems." ECAFE, *The Asian Population Conference 1963* (New York, 1964), p. 50.

At the UN World Population Conference in Belgrade in September 1965, although there was neither vote nor resolution on any issue, the general conviction was that rapid population growth is now a major impediment to fulfillment of the economic goals of the UN Development Decade. A growing roster of developed countries supported this view,

Developed nations can offer technical experts, supplies and equipment, and financial assistance, but their own experience in reducing rates of population growth presents no historical precedent upon which to draw. This is so because fertility decline in the West resulted from the individual decisions of married couples to limit the size of their families, which they did by resorting to abortion and to folk methods of contraception that had been known for centuries. Organized society frowned on these practices and often strongly denounced birth control movements and jailed their leaders.[5] Nevertheless, as economies industrialized, as people moved from village to town to city, and as the traditionally subordinate status of women was modified, the small family became the norm in spite of public exhortations and laws against the sale and distribution of contraceptive information and supplies.[6] Even Japan is no model for direct emulation, for despite the fact that she is an Asian country with one of the lowest birth rates in the world, in terms of industrialization, urbanization, literacy, and the like, Japan is more at an occidental than oriental level. Moreover, Japanese advocates of family planning prefer contraception to abortion, which still plays a prominent role in Japan's control of births. Clearly, each developing country must cope with its high rate of population growth in its own way, consistent with its own particular values and circumstances.

Although countries are now proceeding by declarations of policy at high governmental levels, formal policy statements are neither necessary nor sufficient to achieve a reduction in birth rates. Contraceptive practices are widespread in countries without policies, notably in the Western world. In some rapidly developing areas of Asia, such as Singapore, Hong Kong, and Taiwan, widespread practice pre-dates policy. The adoption of a formal policy does

---

which was voiced strongly by the demographic, economic, and other experts from most of the developing nations.

Finally, it may be noted that in response to its "Inquiry among Governments on Problems Resulting from the Interaction of Economic Development and Population Changes," the UN Secretary-General reports that "Many of the responses received from Governments of developing countries manifest more or less serious concern with the high rate at which the population of their countries is increasing, considering this as an important handicap to economic and social development." UNESCO, E/3895/Rev. 1 (24 November 1964), p. 19.

[5] For a recent concise discussion of birth control movements in the West, see D. V. Glass, "Fertility and Birth Control in Developed Societies, and Some Questions of Policy for Less Developed Societies" in *Proceedings of the Seventh Conference of the International Planned Parenthood Federation*, Singapore, 1963, Excerpta Medical Foundation, International Congress Series No. 72, pp. 38–46.

[6] In the U.S., for example, it was only in May 1966 that the Massachusetts Legislature repealed its 1847 law according to which the sale, distribution, and advertising of contraceptives were criminal offenses. The new law legalizes birth control information and supplies for married, but not unmarried, persons.

not insure a reduction of the birth rate. Even success in specific programs thus far has made little impact on the national birth rate. Examples of this can be found among some of the largest countries in the world, notably India and Pakistan and possibly Mainland China.

By contrast there are countries which have no official family planning policies, but whose governments provide or support birth control services in the interests of health and welfare. Many nations will find this the easiest route to take, whether they are developing countries concerned with high rates of population growth or advanced nations concerned with high fertility among low income groups. In some emerging nations without formal policies, family planning services are becoming available in the proliferation of experimental and pilot family planning programs which have tended to be forerunners of larger national programs and formal policies.

Among the countries that have officially decided to foster family planning, besides India, Pakistan, and Mainland China, are South Korea, Ceylon, Singapore, Hong Kong, Malaysia, Turkey, Egypt, Tunisia, Morocco, and Honduras. Taiwan has no formal policy, but the government has given full cooperation to an island-wide program that has already reached a substantial part of the population. In many other countries, at least the beginning of governmental interest is visible—The Philippines, Thailand, Nepal, Afghanistan, Iran, Kenya, Mauritius, Chile, Colombia, Peru, and Venezuela.[7]

How does a country implement a population control policy? With the desensitization of the subject, a growing group of institutions stands ready to help. The major bottlenecks, however, are less a matter of finances and supplies than of internal organization and administration. A review of some specific programs and developments is instructive, not only as a narrative of their achievements to date, but also for an understanding of their difficulties. We begin with Asia, partly because in numerical terms this is the chief home of mankind, and partly because this is the region where the new national population policies first appeared.

ASIAN COUNTRIES

India, the second largest country in the world next to Mainland China, was the first to declare a national program to control population growth. A modest allocation of funds for family planning was included in the First Five Year Plan (1951–56), but the program was not implemented on a large scale before the Second Plan (1956–61). The increase in tempo of activity is suggested by the following information on expenditures:

[7] See Population Council, *Studies in Family Planning*, No. 16 (December 1966), for formal governmental policy statements.

Five-year plan	Rupees (millions)
First (1951–56)	1.5
Second (1956–61)	21.6
Third (1961–66)	261.0
Fourth (1966–71)	950.0 (tentative allocation)

Note: In June 1966, the rupee was devaluated from $.21 to $.1335.

A memorandum[8] dated 21 May 1966 from Secretary S. R. Sen of the Government of India Planning Commission (Health Division), to the Planning Secretaries of all state governments, advises that states will be reimbursed with 90 percent instead of the previous 75 percent of their expenditures. The memorandum states further: "In view of the national importance of the family planning programme, the State Governments, it is hoped, will make every effort to utilize fully the funds allocated for Family Planning and ensure that there is no diversion of these funds to any other programmes."

Thus far, the establishment of family planning clinics has been the main channel for providing contraceptive supplies and services to the people. This has been supplemented by sterilization "camps," in which this simple but definitive method of family planning was offered to men who desired it. The voluntary response has been surprisingly large; since 1963, over 100,000 men and women have sought sterilization each year, and the total is approaching one million. Some contraceptive supplies are now manufactured in India, and distribution is through private as well as public channels.

Despite difficulties the program is gaining momentum, and a great increase of activity is planned for the Fourth Five Year Plan (1966–71). The first year's goal is to insert one million of the new intra-uterine devices (IUD's), with 20 million planned for the five-year period. The "camp" technique which proved successful for sterilization procedures is contemplated for IUD service and training. The plan also anticipates five million vasectomies and ten million effective users of traditional contraceptives. If these goals are attained, the yearly number of births prevented is expected to be nine million by 1975. The emphasis on newer methods of contraception may well accelerate the progress of the program.

While provision of services and supplies is the heart of the family planning program, effective education, publicity, record-keeping, research, and evaluation are integral aspects. Training in demography, biomedical research, and communications is given in Indian medial schools and the universities and in five Demographic Training and Research Centers. The need to improve the collection of vital statistics and to develop more sensitive indicators of fertility trends is urgent. Finally, the Indian program hopes to get down to the local level, to use village doctors and midwives, as well as more specialized personnel, to advocate and provide family planning services. It is also

[8] No. HLH 4 (14)/65.

expected that other social changes such as marrying at a later age will be encouraged to help establish a norm of small families.[9]

The objective of the program is to achieve as rapidly as possible a decline in the annual birth rate from 42 per thousand population, as currently estimated from national sample surveys, to 25 per thousand.[10] While the achievements of India's family planning program have been important, they have probably not yet had an appreciable effect on the national birth rate, although the means of measuring changes in the birth rate are too defective to detect year-to-year trends.

The urgency of the population problem in India is suggested by the current crisis in food. In January 1966, the Indian government reported it will need ten to fourteen million tons of imported food grains to meet the famine caused by the worse drought of the century. Because of the severe drought, India's crop is expected to be 80 million tons this past year, compared with 88 million the year before.[11] The famine is a catastrophe, but the food crisis is chronic. For several years now the U.S. has been sending 20 percent of its total wheat crop to India, providing 7 percent of that nation's food grain consumption.

Pakistan's efforts to implement a national family planning program have encountered many of the problems noted in India. Expenditures on family planning (chiefly for the establishment of clinical service) have averaged only about one cent per person each year. But as in India, the problems have centered on organization and administration, rather than on lack of funds.

As of July 1, 1965, Pakistan adopted a plan for upgrading and reorganizing the Family Planning Directorate with a five-year budget of 300 million rupees. The new plan as implemented would raise annual per capita expenses on family planning to twelve cents.

A major innovation is to be the insertion of intra-uterine devices by midwives under general medical supervision.[12] The local midwives will receive incentive payments for referrals and insertions, presumably to compensate them for loss of income in the prevention of births.[13] No less than 50,000 village midwives are to be recruited and given a five-week training course by 1970.[14]

The target is to make family planning available to everyone. In drawing up the present plan, weaknesses revealed in the program under the Second Five Year Plan (1960–65) were carefully studied. That plan reached 100 percent of its target in the establishment of clinics, but only 31 percent in

[9] Government of India, *Third Five Year Plan*, p. 678, paragraph 68.

[10] Col. B. L. Raina, Past Director of Family Planning, *Annual Report, 1962–1963*.

[11] *The New York Times*, December 10, 1965.

[12] *Family Planning Scheme for Pakistan during the Third Five Year Plan Period 1965–1970*, p. 3, paragraph 8.

[13] *Ibid.*, p. 10, paragraph 12.

[14] *Ibid.*, p. 3, paragraph 8.

patients attending clinics and 42 percent in personnel projected for training. Failure to reach goals was attributed, among other reasons, to the clinic orientation of the program, emphasis on the urban population (who constitute only 13 percent of the total), and the addition of family planning to existing health and medical services already concerned with other responsibilities.

Korea is seeking to reduce the annual growth rate from a current estimate of about 2.9 percent to 1.82 percent by 1971.[15] The Economic Planning Board estimates that by 1980, implementation of its population policy will result in a growth rate of 1.16 percent per annum, compared with 3.15 percent under a *laissez-faire* situation, and will produce a per capita income 36 percent above the level that would otherwise prevail.

The 1966 level of expenditures on family planning in Korea, at 6.8 cents per capita in the last budget, is at this time the highest in the world. Some 2,200 full-time field workers have been trained and equipped, or an average of one for each 2,500 women in the childbearing ages. The new plastic intrauterine devices figure largely in the Korean program, and the annual rate of insertions is reaching something on the order of 15 percent of the "target" women, i.e., those exposed to risk of unwanted pregnancy. Because of poor vital statistics, the effects of the program on the birth rate cannot be determined at the present time with any high degree of certainty, but the impact of the program is surely being felt.

In Taiwan, an island-wide network of family planning services has been established through the Provincial Health Ministry. The cost of educating the children and providing other services if there were no family planning in part motivated the Economic Planning Board to authorize funds for a ten-year omnibus health program, including family planning services.[16]

The feasibility of a national program was demonstrated by a mass action research project in family planning in the city of Taichung, which has become rather a classic study.[17] The principal feature of the program in Taiwan is to insert 600,000 IUD's within five years, with the object of reducing the birth rate to 19.7 by 1968. This would mean a loop for about one-third of the married women of childbearing age, including those who would marry in the period. Insertions for 1965 fell just short of the initial target of 100,000.[18]

An outstanding feature of the Taiwan program is the excellent statistical evaluation. Performance against targets can be compared at the level of the individual worker, and there is detailed evaluation of the program in relation

[15] *Korea, Summary of First Five-Year Economic Plan 1962–1966*, p. 30.

[16] Taiwan, *Ten Year Health Plan 1966–1975*, p. 15.

[17] It is described by Bernard Berelson and Ronald Freedman in "A Study in Fertility Control," *Scientific American*, CCX, No. 5 (May 1964), pp. 3–11.

[18] The total of monthly insertions for the twelve months of 1965 came to 99,253. There is now developing a considerable body of empirical data on retention, explosion, removal, and pregnancy rates.

to different areas, the acceptability of different contraceptive methods, the age and other characteristics of women accepting the IUD, etc.

Compared with India and Pakistan, Korea and Taiwan are small countries. In addition, they are relatively advanced, particularly Taiwan, when measured by such indices as literacy and education. Nevertheless, the rapid development of family planning in these countries from pilot projects into national action programs is of great importance. In neither country has the program been in effect on a sufficient scale long enough to say *how* successful it has been, but each effort is clearly moving forward rapidly.

Elsewhere in Asia, there are formal programs in Ceylon, Singapore, Hong Kong, and Malaysia. In Singapore, which has one of the most successful private family planning associations in the world, "An Act [No. 32 of 1965] to create a statutory authority to be the sole agency for promoting and disseminating information pertaining to family planning" was signed by President Yusof Bin Ishak in January 1966. The widespread services provided by the hitherto private association in Singapore may well have been a factor in the rapid fall of the crude birth rate from 45.4 per thousand in 1952 to 29.9 per thousand in 1965.[19] The birth rate in Hong Kong, 26.9 per thousand in 1965, is also relatively low for Asia, but this is in major part attributable to distortion of the age structure of the population associated with the influx of refugees from Mainland China.

In Malaysia also, the birth rate is falling, especially among people of Chinese background. According to the First Malaysia Plan 1966–1970 (adopted in 1965), "The main objectives . . . are to lay the groundwork for less rapid population growth by instituting an effective programme of family planning . . ." Ceylon has received technical assistance from the Swedish government in pilot projects implementing family planning in several communities. The program is now to be extended to the country as a whole by stages over a period of years.[20] The results, limited to project locations thus far, have been encouraging. In Thailand, a major action experiment has been conducted under the sponsorship of the National Research Council, and others are under consideration. The first, in the rural district Pho-tharam, has been in operation little more than a year, but the results already suggest a wide acceptance in Thailand of contraceptive services if they are made readily available by the government.[21]

In Mainland China, family planning information and materials are sup-

[19] UN Statistical Office, *Population and Vital Statistics Report*, Series A, XVIII, No. 2 (1 April 1966).

[20] Ceylon, *Provisional Scheme for a Nationwide Family Planning Programme in Ceylon, 1966–1976*.

[21] Amos H. Hawley and Visid Prachuabmoh, "Family Growth and Family Planning in a Rural District of Thailand," in *Family Planning and Population Programs: A Review of World Developments*, Proceedings of the International Conference on Family Planning Programs, Geneva, 1965 (Chicago: University of Chicago Press, 1966), pp. 523–44.

plied as a part of the public health services. Directives have been issued for instruction in birth control to many of the 17 million Communist Party members and 25 million Young Communists, and they in turn are expected to become models and teachers. One son and one daughter are now considered ideal.[22]

As early as 1956 and 1957, Premier Chou En-lai and President Mao Tze-tung were quoted as making statements favorable to the adoption of family planning, and subsequently it was reported that a birth control campaign was initiated and services provided in government health centers. In 1958, however, political winds shifted, and the birth control campaign was brought to a halt, although contraceptives continued to be available. In 1962, there was a resumption of the birth control campaign, and in January of that year the state council revised import duties to permit contraceptive supplies to enter China duty-free. At the same time, the government began to advocate later age at marriage. Japanese doctors who visited China in March and April 1964 and in July 1965 reported that family planning was promoted as part of the maternal and child health program, and that all methods of contraception, including sterilization and induced abortion, were available. Oral contraceptives were used, as well as various forms of the intra-uterine device, which had become quite a popular method.

The official attitude was presumably stated by Premier Chou En-lai during his African tour in 1964. In Conakry, Guinea, where he was interviewed by Edgar Snow, he was quoted as follows:

> . . . Our present target is to reduce population growth to below 2 percent; for the future we aim at an even lower rate. . . . However, I do not believe it will be possible to equal the Japanese rate [of about one percent] as early as 1970. . . . For example, with improved living conditions over the past two years, our rate of increase again rose to 2.5 per cent. . . . We do believe in planned parenthood, but it is not easy to introduce all at once in China. . . . The first thing is to encourage late marriages. . . .[23]

An annual rate of increase at 2.5 percent would mean some 17 million additional population each year. Birth control practice is now common in the cities and in the last three years has gradually moved into the countryside. As Director Madame Huang Ching-wan of the Health Ministry said to Edgar Snow, "We plan production of material things and we must plan to avoid chaos in human reproduction."[24] This may be a revision of traditional Marxist doctrine, but it is compatible with the concept of central planning.

[22] *The Sunday Times* (London), January 23, 1966.
[23] *The New York Times,* February 3, 1964.
[24] *The Sunday Times* (London), January 23, 1966.

THE MIDDLE EAST AND NORTH AFRICA

Four governments of this region have initiated mass action programs to implement their national policies, and more seem likely to do so in the near future.

In Turkey, a new law providing the legal framework for financing and implementing a nation-wide family planning program was signed by the president in April 1965. The goal is a 10 percent decline in fertility in each five-year period during the next 15 years. Operationally the program will utilize the existing facilities of the Health Ministry, but full-time family planning personnel will be added, including mobile family planning teams to take the program to the people. Supplies will be offered free or at cost. Although supplies are now imported, local manufacture is contemplated. An interesting feature of the Turkish program is an education campaign among the armed forces, not merely for their personal edification, but for the "ripple" effect among the population at large, as the conscripted men return to civilian life.

Turkey has several advantages. It is homogeneous in nationality and language, which suggests a rapid cultural diffusion once family planning practice begins to take hold. In a national survey conducted in 1964, women were found to support the idea of family planning 3 to 1. Moreover, 70 percent of the men and 79 percent of the women answered affirmatively the question, "Should the government have a program to give information to those people who want to keep from having too many children?" The Turkish program thus will have the support of the people.[25]

In Tunisia, an experimental program designed to develop a practical family planning service was initiated in 1964. Clinical trials with the IUD were established in the city of Tunis in three maternal and child health centers. The success of this program has led to the formulation of a national campaign with a goal of 120,000 women using the IUD within a two-year period. A unique feature of the Tunisian program is the use of workers in the major political party as a major source of information and publicity.

In the United Arab Republic, the government's interest in family planning goes back at least a decade, to the time when the National Population Commission, formed in 1953, opened four planned parenthood clinics. Policy, however, dates from the May 1962 draft of the National Charter, in which President Nasser declared: "Population increase constitutes the most dangerous obstacle that faces the Egyptian people in their drive towards raising the standard of production. . . . Attempts at family planning deserve the most sincere efforts supported by modern scientific methods."[26]

[25] "Turkey: National Survey on Population" in *Studies in Family Planning*, No. 5 (Population Council, December 1964).

[26] United Arab Republic Information Department, *The Charter*, draft presented by President Gamal Abdel Nasser on 21st May 1962, p. 53.

Until now there has not been a substantial governmental program, but on February 1, 1966, a widespread campaign utilizing the oral contraceptives was launched. The government has also requested foreign assistance in obtaining 50,000 IUD's and the molds for their manufacture. There is a resurgence of interest in governmental and private circles, and it is believed that these new contraceptives may make a full-scale government program more feasible and acceptable.

At the opening of the Seminar on Family Planning in Rabat, Morocco, on October 11, 1966, the Minister of Development and Planning declared, "We must settle down to this problem of birth control all the more because, according to the economists and statisticians, we have to fear a serious reduction of our per capita material investments."

Other countries in the region have been following these programs and developments with interest. Iran, for example, is considering expanding the family planning services in its maternity and child health centers into a national program. The Middle East area is of particular interest because of all cultural and religious groups Moslems characteristically have the highest fertility.

AFRICA SOUTH OF THE SAHARA

No formal population policies or national family planning programs yet exist in Africa below the Sahara, but there is considerably greater official readiness for such programs than had been suspected. Kenya requested an advisory mission from the Population Council which prepared a report to the government in 1965. Its 1966–1970 Development Plan includes "measures to promote family planning education," such as the establishment of a Family Planning Council, and to provide services in family planning clinics in government hospitals and health centers.[27] In Mauritius, at the opening of the Legislative Assembly on 15 March 1966, the governor called attention to the problems of unemployment and the high rate of population growth and asked the Legislature to vote funds in the capital budget for a sustained campaign for education in family planning. According to Premier Ramgoolam, programs are now under way "with the assistance of Government and the International Planned Parenthood Federation . . . both in the urban and rural areas."[28] Additional assistance is expected from the Swedish Government.

African countries firmly believe in economic and health planning by government. It is quite possible that they entertain fewer doubts about government guidance in development than do the new nations of any other continent.

[27] Kenya, *1966–1970 Development Plan*, p. 324.

[28] Sir Seewoosagur Ramgoolam, "Mauritius and Its Problems," *Commonwealth Journal*, IX, No. 4 (August 1966), p. 144.

With the growing awareness that the reduction of infant and other deaths produces rapid population growth, there is increasing appreciation of the key importance of population growth, as opposed to population density, as a factor affecting the dynamics of economic development. Considerable interest in population problems and policies was expressed at the First African Population Conference, held at the University of Ibadan, Nigeria, in January 1966.

LATIN AMERICA

This region has the most rapid rate of population growth of any major part of the world. Until quite recently this has not been a cause of much public concern, partly because of the predominancy of Catholicism, and partly because these countries have a traditional image of themselves as underpopulated, with a large area capable of new settlement.

Two developments seem to be bringing an important change in the attitudes of governments in the region. The first of these is a realization that in Latin America, as in many other parts of the world, population growth is eating up a large share, in some cases all, of the economic growth being achieved. A second factor is the growing consciousness of the problem of abortion. The reaction of the medical profession has been an important stimulus toward more liberal attitudes on contraception. Comparable fertility surveys, conducted in eight Latin American capitals and coordinated by the UN Latin American Demographic Centre in Santiago, Chile, have revealed favorable attitudes toward family planning in a large segment of the population concerned.

Until recently it was thought unlikely that governments of the region would adopt national population policies because of the opposition of the Church. However, it now seems that a number of countries will institute family planning as a regular public health service. This has already occurred in Chile, is to be instituted in Jamaica and Honduras, and is under serious consideration in Colombia. The Jamaica Five-Year Independence Plan 1962–68 calls attention to both the rapid population growth and population pressure in the island and the effects of excessive childbearing on the lives and prospects of individuals. Most recently, Haiti has also expressed interest in population control. In Peru a recent presidential statement decreed that population development "should be systematically studied in order to formulate programs of action with which to face the problems of population and socio-economic development."[29]

[29] December 5, 1964, No. 244/64–DSG.

INTERNATIONAL ACTION AND REACTION

These policies and programs designed to reduce rates of population growth are novel, not only for the recency of their origin, but because they seem to fly in the face of historical experience. In the presently developed nations, economic growth was accompanied in almost all cases by a sustained and substantial increase in population. To meet the challenge of development under today's circumstances of rapidly declining death rates, the official world has therefore had to reverse its historic attitude toward population growth.

If one considers the newness of the problem, reversal in attitude is occurring swiftly; but because of their multi-national character, the international agencies have moved less rapidly than many of the developing nations in taking action. Up to now, private agencies—foundations and the International Planned Parenthood Federation—have provided most of the foreign aid and technical assistance in population programs. But with the rapidly growing awareness that the dimensions of the problem are beyond the capacity of private groups, official agencies are showing increasing willingness to meet the need for technical assistance.

THE UN AND ITS AFFILIATES

The UN has long had a program to stimulate demographic research and training and to improve the registration, collection, and analysis of vital data. With its recent mission to India (1965),[30] sent in response to that government's request to advise on steps to accelerate the impact of the national program on the country's birth rate, the UN moved from an investigatory phase to readiness to give technical assistance in the matter of population control. The stage for this development was set in July 1965 when the Economic and Social Council endorsed the recommendations of the Population Commission to increase "the amount of technical assistance in population fields available to Governments of developing countries upon their request." The Council also called to the attention of the General Assembly "the need to provide the necessary resources . . . to carry out the intensified and expanded programme of activities in the field of population . . ."

Perhaps the UN position is best exemplified by the statement of Philippe de Seynes, the Undersecretary for Economic and Social Affairs, to the 1965 Belgrade World Population Conference, that the UN is ready "to respond to all requests for assistance from any country" interested in a birth control

---

[30] See UN Department of Economic and Social Affairs, *Report on the Family Planning Programme in India,* TAO/IND/48 (20 February 1966).

policy, although it would maintain its traditionally neutral attitude in deference to "respect for all beliefs."

Other notable events by UN-related agencies include the World Health Organization's resolution approved unanimously last year (1965) on the occasion of its 18th annual assembly empowering the organization to give assistance to its members on birth control programs, short of actually engaging in "operational activities." A recent request by the UNICEF governing council to its director to prepare a statement on possible UNICEF activities in the area of population control also indicates the direction in which international agencies are now moving.

The impetus to move is stimulated to no small extent by the recent finding of the UN Food and Agriculture Organization that "In the six years since [1958/59] production [of food] has barely kept up with population growth . . ."[31] In his address to the 1965 World Population Conference, FAO Director-General B. R. Sen stated "if . . . large-scale breakdowns are to be brought within a measure of control, then, side by side with a concerted effort to increase productivity of agriculture in the developing countries, population stabilization must be undertaken simultaneously as a social policy of urgent priority without further delay."

THE U.S. AND OTHER DEVELOPED COUNTRIES

The timidity and caution of the international agencies in this field was until very recently paralleled in the bilateral programs of most countries giving foreign aid. But that too is changing rapidly. In the United States the official attitude has within the past year or so turned from non-involvement in family planning programs to one of approbation and assistance. The administration is now contemplating an increase in outlay for technical assistance to foreign countries for population matters from about $2 million expended in the fiscal year ending June 1965 to $5.5 million in the fiscal year 1966, and up to $20 million in the next few years.

Funds expended thus far have been used mainly for maternal and child health programs, demographic research and surveys, and improvement of census procedures and analyses. Now, however, the Agency for International Development has advised its missions that, in line with President Johnson's decision[32] "to seek new ways to use our knowledge to help deal with the explosion of world population and the growing scarcity of world resources . . . we are ready to entertain requests for technical assistance."[33] The memorandum states that "A.I.D. does not advocate any particular method of

---

[31] FAO, *The State of Food and Agriculture 1965*, p. 7.

[32] Stated in his January 1965 State of the Union Message.

[33] U.S. Department of State Circular 280, subject "Population Programs," 2/25/65, signed by Secretary of State Rusk.

family regulation." Korea and Taiwan are already drawing on counterpart funds to support health and family planning clinics. Turkey, Honduras, Pakistan, and Tunisia are reported to be seeking direct aid for population control programs. Assistance may take any form short of providing contraceptives or the equipment for their manufacture.

On the domestic scene, the Supreme Court's ruling on June 7, 1965, that Connecticut's anti-birth-control law was unconstitutional, on the ground that it denied the right to privacy, has been followed by widespread action to make birth control services available through tax-supported as well as private channels. Other notable recent developments affecting both the national and international scene include: (1) reversal by the American Medical Association of its former policy with a new declaration, the first since 1938, that "child-spacing measures should be made available to all patients who require them . . . whether they obtain their medical care through private physicians or tax or community supported health services"; (2) reinforcement by the National Academy of Sciences and the American Public Health Association of their earlier proposals that governmental and private organizations take effective measures to make the benefits of family planning available to all; (3) inclusion of birth control services in the U.S. anti-poverty program; and (4) recommendation by the Committee on Population of the White House Conference on International Cooperation Year in November (1965) that the U.S. government give greater support to other governments requesting help in family planning programs.

The U.S. is, of course, the chief source of foreign aid funds, but other countries have also announced interest in assisting population programs. The Ministry of Overseas Development, Great Britain's counterpart of the U.S.'s AID, is ready to participate in such programs and has offered Mauritius, for example, "financial assistance . . . on a substantial scale."[34] The Swedish International Development Authority has long been active, notably in Ceylon and Pakistan.

THE CHURCH

While the deliberations of the Roman Catholic Church have captured much of the attention of the world on religious attitude toward contraception, it should be noted that among the more than two billion people in the underdeveloped areas, the Buddhist, Hindu, and Moslem religions predominate. In these religions, interpretations are conveyed to the people by numerous priests and scholars, the force of the ruling depending upon the personal following

[34] Speech by His Excellency the Governor at the opening session of the First Legislative Assembly of Mauritius on the 15th of March 1966.

of its conveyor. Attitudes toward family planning derive from custom and tradition, rather than from formal religious doctrine. Among Buddhists, Hindus, and Moslems, there appears to be no doctrinal prohibition against the use of mechanical or chemical methods to limit births.

The Roman Catholic Church, subject to growing pressure to reverse its traditional ban on the use of methods other than periodic or total abstinence, has been re-examining its position. This fact alone has been interpreted by some as a weakening of its traditional proscription of modern methods. A special commission of experts appointed by the Pope during the Ecumenical Council Vatican II failed to make a specific recommendation, and the Council ended with this question still unsettled. Final authority on this matter rests with the Pope, who can be expected to come to some decision after reviewing the report recently submitted by the papal commission reorganized in March 1966.

CONCLUSIONS

It must be evident from the foregoing discussion that with developments so rapid, any review of population policies will be out of date almost by the time it is written. It is also clear that measurable progress so far relates more to attitude and policy than to action and achievement. But in most cases, government-sponsored family planning programs are so new that it would be unreasonable to expect them to have yet had a major and measurable impact on birth rates, and hence on rates of population growth. Except in Korea and in Taiwan, the programs have not yet taken hold in the rural areas, where most of the people in the developing countries live. Not unnaturally, the first successes in such programs are most likely in the more advanced of the developing countries (e.g., Taiwan and Korea) and among urban and better educated groups. Nevertheless, new reasons give important grounds for optimism.

(1) *Improvement in contraceptive technology.* The discovery and rapidly expanding use of oral contraceptives (the "pill") and of the new plastic intra-uterine devices (IUD's) have revolutionized the practice of birth control. Both have the great advantage of being dissociated from the sex act, and the latter has the additional advantage of often requiring only sufficient motivation to obtain the initial insertion. These make family planning much more practicable for the populations of the developing countries. Ongoing research promises to improve these methods (e.g., in reducing the cost and side effects of the oral contraceptives; in reducing expulsions and increasing the efficiency of IUD's). It is also likely that even better methods will be developed in the next few years. Private foundations (e.g., the Ford Founda-

tion and the Population Council), drug companies, and now the U.S. government are investing large sums in these endeavors.

(2) *Evidence of widespread interest and willingness to practice family planning.* Field surveys on knowledge of, attitudes towards, and practices of family planning in general populations have now been conducted in nine Asian countries, three African countries, and nine Latin American countries. The "KAP Studies," as they have come to be called, all reveal a substantial proportion of couples who would like to limit the size of their families and who are prepared to practice contraception, but who do not do so now because of ignorance and unavailability of methods suitable for their way of life. These studies show that governments have usually been more conservative on this subject than the people. The proportion of potential users of contraception of course varies from country to country, and one must recognize the gap between an expression of attitude and a willingness to take action. Nevertheless, the studies reveal a tremendous potential "market" for birth control, if suitable methods and services can be provided.[35]

(3) *Growing success of pilot projects and experiments in providing family planning services.* Historically these have met with varying success in developing countries, the results being closely related to the socio-economic level of the population concerned. With the new contraceptives, several such projects have shown striking success in obtaining acceptance among populations not previously practicing contraception.[36]

It would be quixotic to expect population policies to eliminate population growth quickly, and indeed this is not usually the objective. National targets are much more likely to be set at reducing population growth to an annual rate of, say, one percent fifteen years hence. The objective is to check runaway growth and at a minimum to induce declines in the birth rate comparable to those occurring in the death rate. The effectiveness of population policies to achieve even these more limited objectives is still to be tested. But they are swimming with the tide of socio-economic progress and awareness on many fronts.

Until the present, the monetary investments in family planning programs have been small, and this may in part be responsible for their modest effects. Even with gathering momentum, the costs of such programs will be a minor part of development budgets. We do not yet know the minimal mix of social and economic ingredients for a take-off in reductions of the birth rate, but thus far problems of organization and administration have proved as difficult as the question of finance. It is most unlikely that the needs of family planning programs will seriously compete with other forms of socio-

[35] A review of these studies is given by W. Parker Mauldin, "Fertility Studies: Knowledge, Attitude and Practice," in *Studies in Family Planning*, No. 7 (June 1963).

[36] The results of such projects are reviewed in various issues of *Studies in Family Planning*, Nos. 1–10 (July 1963–February 1966).

economic investment. By the same token, it is probable that modest investments in such programs will bring future returns disproportionately large in relation to the size of the investment.

With two-thirds of the world's people living in underdeveloped economies, the problem engendered by their high birth rates is a global one. Birth control, hitherto a topic not fit for public discussion, let alone as a proper function of government, is now increasingly an aspect of anti-poverty programs everywhere in the world. Birth rates can no longer be regarded as a "given" factor not subject to change. It is apparent that the great majority of the world's families would like to control their size, given the proper information, the services, and methods appropriate to their ways and conditions of life. There is increasing evidence that the "population dilemma" of the modern world is at least partly amenable to solution by government action in providing voluntary family planning services and in otherwise facilitating the adoption of family planning.

POPULATION POLICY: WILL PRESENT PROGRAMS SUCCEED?

Kingsley Davis

Throughout history the growth of population has been identified with prosperity and strength. If today an increasing number of nations are seeking to curb rapid population growth by reducing their birth rates, they must be driven to do so by an urgent crisis. My purpose here is not to discuss the crisis itself but rather to assess the present and prospective measures used to meet it. Most observers are surprised by the swiftness with which concern over the population problem has turned from intellectual analysis and debate to policy and action. Such action is a welcome relief from the long opposition, or timidity, which seemed to block forever any governmental attempt to restrain population growth, but relief that "at last something is being done" is no guarantee that what is being done is adequate. On the face of it, one could hardly expect such a fundamental reorientation to be quickly and successfully implemented. I therefore propose to review the nature and (as I see them) limitations of the present policies and to suggest lines of possible improvement.

THE NATURE OF CURRENT POLICIES

With more than 30 nations now trying or planning to reduce population growth and with numerous private and inter-

From Kingsley Davis, "Population Policy: Will Present Programs Succeed," *Science*, 158:3802:730–739 (November 1967). Copyright 1967 by the American Association for the Advancement of Science. Reprinted by permission of the author.

national organizations helping, the degree of unanimity as to the kind of measures needed is impressive. The consensus can be summed up in the phrase "family planning." President Johnson declared in 1965 that the United States will "assist family planning programs in nations which request such help." The Prime Minister of India said a year later, "We must press forward with family planning. This is a programme of the highest importance." The Republic of Singapore created in 1966 the Singapore Family Planning and Population Board "to initiate and undertake population control programmes".[1]

As is well known, "family planning" is a euphemism for contraception. The family-planning approach to population limitation, therefore, concentrates on providing new and efficient contraceptives on a national basis through mass programs under public health auspices. The nature of these programs is shown by the following enthusiastic report from the Population Council:[2]

> No single year has seen so many forward steps in population control as 1965. Effective national programs have at last emerged, international organizations have decided to become engaged, a new contraceptive has proved its value in mass application, . . . and surveys have confirmed a popular desire for family limitation. . . .
>
> An accounting of notable events must begin with Korea and Taiwan . . . Taiwan's program is not yet two years old, and already it has inserted one IUD [intrauterine device] for every 4–6 target women (those who are not pregnant, lactating, already sterile, already using contraceptives effectively, or desirous of more children). Korea has done almost as well . . . has put 2,200 full-time workers into the field, . . . has reached operational levels for a network of IUD quotas, supply lines, local manufacture of contraceptives, training of hundreds of M.D.'s and nurses, and mass propaganda. . . .

Here one can see the implication that "population control" is being achieved through the dissemination of new contraceptives, and the fact that the "target women" exclude those who want more children. One can also note the technological emphasis and the medical orientation.

What is wrong with such programs? The answer is, "Nothing at all, if they work." Whether or not they work depends on what they are expected to do as well as on how they try to do it. Let us discuss the goal first, then the means.

GOALS

Curiously, it is hard to find in the population-policy movement any explicit discussion of long-range goals. By implication the policies seem to

[1] *Studies in Family Planning, No. 16* (1967).
[2] *Ibid., No. 9* (1966), p. 1.

promise a great deal. This is shown by the use of expressions like *population control* and *population planning* (as in the passages quoted above). It is also shown by the characteristic style of reasoning. Expositions of current policy usually start off by lamenting the speed and the consequences of runaway population growth. This growth, it is then stated, must be curbed—by pursuing a vigorous family-planning program. That family planning can solve the problem of population growth seems to be taken as self-evident.

For instance, the much-heralded statement by 12 heads of state, issued by Secretary-General U Thant on 10 December 1966 (a statement initiated by John D. Rockefeller III, Chairman of the Board of the Population Council), devotes half its space to discussing the harmfulness of population growth and the other half to recommending family planning.[3] A more succinct example of the typical reasoning is given in the Provisional Scheme for a Nationwide Family Planning Programme in Ceylon:[4]

> · The population of Ceylon is fast increasing. . . . [The] figures reveal that a serious situation will be created within a few years. In order to cope with it a Family Planning programme on a nationwide scale should be launched by the Government.

The promised goal—to limit population growth so as to solve population problems—is a large order. One would expect it to be carefully analyzed, but it is left inmprecise and taken for granted, as is the way in which family planning will achieve it.

When the terms *population control* and *population planning* are used, as they frequently are, as synonyms for current family-planning programs, they are misleading. Technically, they would mean deliberate influence over all attributes of a population, including its age-sex structure, geographical distribution, racial composition, genetic quality, and total size. No government attempts such full control. By tacit understanding, current population policies are concerned with only the *growth* and *size* of populations. These attributes, however, result from the death rate and migration as well as from the birth rate; their control would require deliberate influence over the factors giving rise to all three determinants. Actually, current policies labeled population control do not deal with mortality and migration, but deal only with the birth input. This is why another term, *fertility control*, is frequently used to describe current policies. But, as I show below, family planning (and hence current policy) does not undertake to influence most of the determinants of human reproduction. Thus the programs should not be referred to as population control or planning, because they do not attempt to influence the factors responsible for the attributes of human populations, taken generally;

[3] The statement is given in *Studies in Family Planning* (*1*, p. 1), and in *Population Bull. 23*, 6 (1967).

[4] The statement is quoted in *Studies in Family Planning* (*1*, p. 2).

nor should they be called fertility control, because they do not try to affect most of the determinants of reproductive performance.

The ambiguity does not stop here, however. When one speaks of controlling population size, any inquiring person naturally asks, What is "control"? Who is to control whom? Precisely what population size, or what rate of population growth, is to be achieved? Do the policies aim to produce a growth rate that is nil, one that is very slight, or one that is like that of the industrial nations? Unless such questions are dealt with and clarified, it is impossible to evaluate current population policies.

The actual programs seem to be aiming simply to achieve a reduction in the birth rate. Success is therefore interpreted as the accomplishment of such a reduction, on the assumption that the reduction will lessen population growth. In those rare cases where a specific demographic aim is stated, the goal is said to be a short-run decline within a given period. The Pakistan plan adopted in 1966[5] aims to reduce the birth rate from 50 to 40 per thousand by 1970; the Indian plan[6] aims to reduce the rate from 40 to 25 "as soon as possible"; and the Korean aim[7] is to cut population growth from 2.9 to 1.2 percent by 1980. A significant feature of such stated aims is the rapid population growth they would permit. Under conditions of modern mortality, a crude birth rate of 25 to 30 per thousand will represent such a multiplication of people as to make use of the term *population control* ironic. A rate of increase of 1.2 percent per year would allow South Korea's already dense population to double in less than 60 years.

One can of course defend the programs by saying that the present goals and measures are merely interim ones. A start must be made somewhere. But we do not find this answer in the population-policy literature. Such a defense, if convincing, would require a presentation of the *next* steps, and these are not considered. One suspects that the entire question of goals is instinctively left vague because thorough limitation of population growth would run counter to national and group aspirations. A consideration of hypothetical goals throws further light on the matter.

Industrialized Nations as the Model

Since current policies are confined to family planning, their maximum demographic effect would be to give the underdeveloped countries the same level of reproductive performance that

---

[5] *Hearings on S. 1676, U.S. Senate, Subcommittee on Foreign Aid Expenditures, 89th Congress, Second Session, April 7, 8, 11* (1966), pt. 4.

[6] B. L. Raina, in *Family Planning and Population Programs*, B. Berelson, R. K. Anderson, O. Harkavy, G. Maier, W. P. Mauldin, S. G. Segal, Eds. (Univ. of Chicago Press, Chicago, 1966).

[7] D. Kirk, *Ann. Amer. Acad. Polit. Soc. Sci.* 369, 53 (1967).

the industrial nations now have. The latter, long oriented toward family planning, provide a good yardstick for determining what the availability of contraceptives can do to population growth. Indeed, they provide more than a yardstick; they are actually the model which inspired the present population policies.

What does this goal mean in practice? Among the advanced nations there is considerable diversity in the level of fertility.[8] At one extreme are countries such as New Zealand, with an average gross reproduction rate (GRR) of 1.91 during the period 1960–64; at the other extreme are countries such as Hungary, with a rate of 0.91 during the same period. To a considerable extent, however, such divergencies are matters of timing. The birth rates of most industrial nations have shown, since about 1940, a wavelike movement, with no secular trend. The average level of reproduction during this long period has been high enough to give these countries, with their low mortality, an extremely rapid population growth. If this level is maintained, their population will double in just over 50 years—a rate higher than that of world population growth at any time prior to 1950, at which time the growth in numbers of human beings was already considered fantastic. The advanced nations are suffering acutely from the effects of rapid population growth in combination with the production of ever more goods per person.[9] A rising share of their supposedly high per capita income, which itself draws increasingly upon the resources of the underdeveloped countries (who fall farther behind in relative economic position), is spent simply to meet the costs, and alleviate the nuisances, of the unrelenting production of more and more goods by more people. Such facts indicate that the industrial nations provide neither a suitable demographic model for the nonindustrial peoples to follow nor the leadership to plan and organize effective population-control policies for them.

Zero Population Growth as a Goal

Most discussions of the population crisis lead logically to zero population growth as the ultimate goal, because *any* growth rate, if continued, will eventually use up the earth. Yet hardly ever do arguments for population policy consider such a goal, and current policies do not dream of it. Why not? The answer is evidently that zero population growth is unacceptable to most nations and to most religious and

[8] As used by English-speaking demographers, the word *fertility* designates actual reproductive performance, not a theoretical capacity.

[9] K. Davis, *Rotarian 94*, 10 (1959); *Health Educ. Monographs 9*, 2 (1960); L. Day and A. Day, *Too Many Americans* (Houghton Mifflin, Boston, 1964); R. A. Piddington, *Limits of Mankind* (Wright, Bristol, England, 1956).

ethnic communities. To argue for this goal would be to alienate possible support for action programs.

Goal Peculiarities Inherent in Family Planning

Turning to the actual measures taken, we see that the very use of family planning as the means for implementing population policy poses serious but unacknowledged limits on the intended reduction in fertility. The family-planning movement, clearly devoted to the improvement and dissemination of contraceptive devices, states again and again that its purpose is that of enabling couples to have the number of children they want. "The opportunity to decide the number and spacing of children is a basic human right," say the 12 heads of state in the United Nations declaration. The 1965 Turkish Law Concerning Population Planning declares:[10]

> *Article 1.* Population Planning means that individuals can have as many children as they wish, whenever they want to. This can be ensured through preventive measures taken against pregnancy. . . .

Logically, it does not make sense to use *family* planning to provide *national* population control or planning. The "planning" in family planning is that of each separate couple. The only control they exercise is control over the size of *their* family. Obviously, couples do not plan the size of the nation's population, any more than they plan the growth of the national income or the form of the highway network. There is no reason to expect that the millions of decisions about family size made by couples in their own interest will automatically control population for the benefit of society. On the contrary, there are good reasons to think they will not do so. At most, family planning can reduce reproduction to the extent that unwanted births exceed wanted births. In industrial countries the balance is often negative—that is, people have fewer children as a rule than they would like to have. In underdeveloped countries the reverse is normally true, but the elimination of unwanted births would still leave an extremely high rate of multiplication.

Actually, the family-planning movement does not pursue even the limited goals it professes. It does not fully empower couples to have only the number of offspring they want because it either condemns or disregards certain tabooed but nevertheless effective means to this goal. One of its tenets is that "there shall be freedom of choice of method so that individuals can choose in accordance with the dictates of their consciences,"[11] but in practice this amounts to limiting the individual's choice, because the "conscience" dictating the method is usually not his but that of religious and governmental officials. Moreover, not every individual may choose: even the so-called

10 *Official Gazette* (15 Apr. 1965); quoted in *Studies in Family Planning* (*1*, p. 7).
11 J. W. Gardner, Secretary of Health, Education, and Welfare, "Memorandum to Heads of Operating Agencies" (Jan. 1966), reproduced in *Hearings on S. 1676* (*5*), p. 783.

recommended methods are ordinarily not offered to single women, or not all offered to women professing a given religious faith.

Thus, despite its emphasis on technology, current policy does not utilize all available means of contraception, much less all birth-control measures. The Indian government wasted valuable years in the early stages of its population-control program by experimenting exclusively with the "rhythm" method, long after this technique had been demonstrated to be one of the least effective. A greater limitation on means is the exclusive emphasis on contraception itself. Induced abortion, for example, is one of the surest means of controlling reproduction, and one that has been proved capable of reducing birth rates rapidly. It seems peculiarly suited to the threshold stage of a population-control program—the stage when new conditions of life first make large families disadvantageous. It was the principal factor in the halving of the Japanese birth rate, a major factor in the declines in birth rate of East-European satellite countries after legalization of abortions in the early 1950's, and an important factor in the reduction of fertility in industrializing nations from 1870 to the 1930's.[12] Today, according to *Studies in Family Planning*,[13] "abortion is probably the foremost method of birth control throughout Latin America." Yet this method is rejected in nearly all national and international population-control programs. American foreign aid is used to help *stop* abortion.[14] The United Nations excludes abortion from family planning, and in fact justifies the latter by presenting it as a means of combating abortion.[15] Studies of abortion are being made in Latin America under the presumed auspices of population-control groups, not with the intention of legalizing it and thus making it safe, cheap, available, and hence more effective for population control, but with the avowed purpose of reducing it.[16]

Although few would prefer abortion to efficient contraception (other things being equal), the fact is that both permit a woman to control the size of her family. The main drawbacks to abortion arise from its illegality. When performed, as a legal procedure, by a skilled physician, it is safer than childbirth. It does not compete with contraception but serves as a backstop

[12] C. Tietze, *Demography 1*, 119 (1964); *J. Chronic Diseases 18*, 1161 (1964); M. Muramatsu, *Milbank Mem. Fund Quart. 38*, 153 (1960); K. Davis, *Population Index 29*, 345 (1963); R. Armijo and T. Monreal, *J. Sex Res. 1964*, 143 (1964); Proceedings World Population Conference, Belgrade, 1965; Proceedings International Planned Parenthood Federation.

[13] *Studies in Family Planning, No. 4* (1964), p. 3.

[14] D. Bell (then administrator for Agency for International Development), in *Hearings on S. 1676 (5)*, p. 862.

[15] *Asian Population Conference* (United Nations, New York, 1964), p. 30.

[16] R. Armijo and T. Monreal, in *Components of Population Change in Latin America* (Milbank Fund, New York, 1965), p. 272; E. Rice-Wray, *Amer. J. Public Health 54*, 313 (1964).

when the later fails or when contraceptive devices or information are not available. As contraception becomes customary, the incidence of abortion recedes even without its being banned. If, therefore, abortions enable women to have only the number of children they want, and if family planners do not advocate—in fact decry—legalization of abortion, they are to that extent denying the central tenet of their own movement. The irony of anti-abortion-ism in family-planning circles is seen particularly in hair-splitting arguments over whether or not some contraceptive agent (for example, the IUD) is in reality an abortifacient. A Mexican leader in family planning writes:[17]

> One of the chief objectives of our program in Mexico is to prevent abortions. If we could be sure that the mode of action [of the IUD] was not interference with nidation, we could easily use the method in Mexico.

The questions of sterilization and unnatural forms of sexual intercourse usually meet with similar silent treatment or disapproval, although nobody doubts the effectiveness of these measures in avoiding conception. Steriliza-tion has proved popular in Puerto Rico and has had some vogue in India (where the new health minister hopes to make it compulsory for those with a certain number of children), but in both these areas it has been for the most part ignored or condemned by the family-planning movement.

On the side of goals, then, we see that a family-planning orientation limits the aims of current population policy. Despite reference to "population control" and "fertility control," which presumably mean determination of demographic results by and for the nation as a whole, the movement gives control only to couples, and does this only if they use "respectable" con-traceptives.

THE NEGLECT OF MOTIVATION

By sanctifying the doctrine that each woman should have the number of children she wants, and by assuming that if she has only that number this will automatically curb population growth to the necessary degree, the leaders of current policies escape the necessity of asking why women desire so many children and how this desire can be in-fluenced.[18, 19] Instead, they claim that satisfactory motivation is shown by the popular desire (shown by opinion surveys in all countries) to have the means of family limitation, and that therefore the problem is one of invent-ing and distributing the best possible contraceptive devices. Overlooked is the

---

[17] E. Rice-Wray, in "Intra-Uterine Contraceptive Devices," *Excerpta Med. Intern. Congr. Ser. No. 54* (1962), p. 135.

[18] J. Blake, in *Public Health and Population Change*, M. C. Sheps and J. C. Ridley, Eds. (Univ. of Pittsburgh Press, Pittsburgh, 1965).

[19] J. Blake and K. Davis, *Amer. Behavioral Scientist*, 5, 24 (1963).

fact that a desire for availability of contraceptives is compatible with *high* fertility.

Given the best of means, there remain the questions of how many children couples want and of whether this is the requisite number from the standpoint of population size. That it is not is indicated by continued rapid population growth in industrial countries, and by the very surveys showing that people want contraception—for these show, too, that people also want numerous children.

The family planners do not ignore motivation. They are forever talking about "attitudes" and "needs." But they pose the issue in terms of the "acceptance" of birth control devices. At the most naive level, they assume that lack of acceptance is a function of the contraceptive device itself. This reduces the motive problem to a technological question. The task of population control then becomes simply the invention of a device that *will* be acceptable.[20] The plastic IUD is acclaimed because, once in place, it does not depend on repeated *acceptance* by the woman, and thus it "solves" the problem of motivation.[21]

But suppose a woman does not want to use *any* contraceptive until after she has had four children. This is the type of question that is seldom raised in the family-planning literature. In that literature, wanting a specific number of children is taken as complete motivation, for it implies a wish to control the size of one's family. The problem woman, from the standpoint of family planners, is the one who wants "as many as come," or "as many as God sends." Her attitude is construed as due to ignorance and "cultural values," and the policy deemed necessary to change it is "education." No compulsion can be used, because the movement is committed to free choice, but movie strips, posters, comic books, public lectures, interviews, and discussions are in order. These supply information and supposedly change values by discounting superstitions and showing that unrestrained procreation is harmful to both mother and children. The effort is considered successful when the woman decides she wants only a certain number of children and uses an effective contraceptive.

In viewing negative attitudes toward birth control as due to ignorance, apathy, and outworn tradition, and "mass-communication" as the solution to the motivation problem,[22] family planners tend to ignore the power and com-

---

[20] See "Panel discussion on comparative acceptability of different methods of contraception," in *Research in Family Planning*, C. V. Kiser, Ed. (Princeton Univ. Press, Princeton, 1962), pp. 373–86.

[21] "From the point of view of the woman concerned, the whole problem of continuing motivation disappears, . . ." [D. Kirk, in *Population Dynamics*, M. Muramatsu and P. A. Harper, Eds. (Johns Hopkins Press, Baltimore, 1965)].

[22] "For influencing family size norms, certainly the examples and statements of public figures are of great significance . . . also . . . use of mass-communication methods which help to legitimize the small-family style, to provoke conversation, and to establish

plexity of social life. If it were admitted that the creation and care of new human beings is socially motivated, like other forms of behavior, by being a part of the system of rewards and punishments that is built into human relationships, and thus is bound up with the individual's economic and personal interests, it would be apparent that the social structure and economy must be changed before a deliberate reduction in the birth rate can be achieved. As it is, reliance on family planning allows people to feel that "something is being done about the population problem" without the need for painful social changes.

Designation of population control as a medical or public health task leads to a similar evasion. This categorization assures popular support because it puts population policy in the hands of respected medical personnel, but, by the same token, it gives responsibility for leadership to people who think in terms of clinics and patients, of pills and IUD's, and who bring to the handling of economic and social phenomena a self-confident naiveté. The study of social organization is a technical field; an action program based on intuition is no more apt to succeed in the control of human beings than it is in the area of bacterial or viral control. Moreover, to alter a social system, by deliberate policy, so as to regulate births in accord with the demands of the collective welfare would require political power, and this is not likely to inhere in public health officials, nurses, midwives, and social workers. To entrust population policy to them is "to take action," but not dangerous "effective action."

Similarly, the Janus-faced position on birth-control technology represents an escape from the necessity, and onus, of grappling with the social and economic determinants of reproductive behavior. On the one side, the rejection or avoidance of religiously tabooed but otherwise effective means of birth prevention enables the family-planning movement to avoid official condemnation. On the other side, an intense preoccupation with contraceptive technology (apart from the tabooed means) also helps the family planners to avoid censure. By implying that the only need is the invention and distribution of effective contraceptive devices, they allay fears, on the part of religious and governmental officials, that fundamental changes in social organization are contemplated. Changes basic enough to affect motivation for having children would be changes in the structure of the family, in the position of women, and in the sexual mores. Far from proposing such radicalism, spokesmen for family planning frequently state their purpose as "protection" of the family—that is, closer observance of family norms. In addition, by concentrating on *new* and *scientific* contraceptives, the movement escapes taboos attached to old ones (the Pope will hardly authorize the condom, but

a vocabulary for discussion of family planning." [M. W. Freymann, in *Population Dynamics*, M. Muramatsu and P. A. Harper, Eds. (Johns Hopkins Press, Baltimore, 1965)].

may sanction the pill) and allows family planning to be regarded as a branch of medicine: overpopulation becomes a disease, to be treated by a pill or a coil.

We thus see that the inadequacy of current population policies with respect to motivation is inherent in their overwhelmingly family-planning character. Since family planning is by definition private planning, it eschews any societal control over motivation. It merely furnishes the means, and, among possible means, only the most respectable. Its leaders, in avoiding social complexities and seeking official favor, are obviously activated not solely by expediency but also by their own sentiments as members of society and by their background as persons attracted to the family-planning movement. Unacquainted for the most part with technical economics, sociology, and demography, they tend honestly and instinctively to believe that something they vaguely call population control can be achieved by making better contraceptives available.

THE EVIDENCE OF INEFFECTIVENESS

If this characterization is accurate, we can conclude that current programs will not enable a government to control population size. In countries where couples have numerous offspring that they do not want, such programs may possibly accelerate a birth-rate decline that would occur anyway, but the conditions that cause births to be wanted or unwanted are beyond the control of family planning, hence beyond the control of any nation which relies on family planning alone as its population policy.

This conclusion is confirmed by demographic facts. As I have noted above, the widespread use of family planning in industrial countries has not given their governments control over the birth rate. In backward countries today, taken as a whole, birth rates are rising, not falling; in those with population policies, there is no indication that the government is controlling the rate of reproduction. The main "successes" cited in the well-publicized policy literature are cases where a large number of contraceptives have been distributed or where the program has been accompanied by some decline in the birth rate. Popular enthusiasm for family planning is found mainly in the cities, or in advanced countries such as Japan and Taiwan, where the people would adopt contraception in any case, program or no program. It is difficult to prove that present population policies have even speeded up a lowering of the birth rate (the least that could have been expected), much less that they have provided national "fertility control."

Let us next briefly review the facts concerning the level and trend of population in underdeveloped nations generally, in order to understand the magnitude of the task of genuine control.

RISING BIRTH RATES IN UNDERDEVELOPED COUNTRIES

In ten Latin-American countries, between 1940 and 1959,[23] the average birth rates (age-standardized), as estimated by our research office at the University of California, rose as follows: 1940–44, 43.4 annual births per 1000 population; 1945–49, 44.6; 1950–54, 46.4; 1955–59, 47.7.

In another study made in our office, in which estimating methods derived from the theory of quasi-stable populations were used, the recent trend was found to be upward in 27 underdeveloped countries, downward in six, and unchanged in one.[24] Some of the rises have been substantial, and most have occurred where the birth rate was already extremely high. For instance, the gross reproduction rate rose in Jamaica from 1.8 per thousand in 1947 to 2.7 in 1960; among the natives of Fiji, from 2.0 in 1951 to 2.4 in 1964; and in Albania, from 3.0 in the period 1950–54 to 3.4 in 1960.

The general rise in fertility in backward regions is evidently not due to failure of population-control efforts, because most of the countries either have no such effort or have programs too new to show much effect. Instead, the rise is due, ironically, to the very circumstance that brought on the population crisis in the first place—to improved health and lowered mortality. Better health increases the probability that a woman will conceive and retain the fetus to term; lowered mortality raises the proportion of babies who survive to the age of reproduction and reduces the probability of widowhood during that age.[25] The significance of the general rise in fertility, in the context of this discussion, is that it is giving would-be population planners a harder task than many of them realize. Some of the upward pressure on birth rates is independent of what couples do about family planning, for it arises from the fact that, with lowered mortality, there are simply more couples.

UNDERDEVELOPED COUNTRIES WITH POPULATION POLICIES

In discussions of population policy there is often confusion as to which cases are relevant. Japan, for instance, has been widely praised for the effectiveness of its measures, but it is a very advanced industrial nation and, besides, its government policy had little or nothing to do with the decline in the birth rate, except unintentionally. It therefore offers no test of population policy under peasant-agrarian conditions. Another case of questionable relevance is that of Taiwan, because Taiwan is sufficiently developed to be placed

[23] O. A. Collver, *Birth Rates in Latin America* (International Population and Urban Research, Berkeley, Calif., 1965), pp. 27–28; the ten countries were Colombia, Costa Rica, El Salvador, Ecuador, Guatemala, Honduras, Mexico, Panama, Peru, and Venezuela.

[24] J. R. Rele, *Fertility Analysis through Extension of Stable Population Concepts.* (International Population and Urban Research, Berkeley, Calif., 1967).

[25] J. C. Ridley, M. C. Sheps, J. W. Lingner, J. A. Menken, *Milbank Mem. Fund Quart. 45*, 77 (1967) ; E. Arriaga, unpublished paper.

Table 1. Decline in Taiwan's Fertility Rate, 1951 through 1966

Year	Registered births per 1000 women aged 15–49	Change in rate (percent) *
1951	211	
1952	198	−5.6
1953	194	−2.2
1954	193	−0.5
1955	197	+2.1
1956	196	−0.4
1957	182	−7.1
1958	185	+1.3
1959	184	−0.1
1960	180	−2.5
1961	177	−1.5
1962	174	−1.5
1963	170	−2.6
1964	162	−4.9
1965	152	−6.0
1966	149	−2.1

* The percentages were calculated on unrounded figures. Source of data through 1965, *Taiwan* Demographic Fact Book (1964, 1965) ; for 1966, *Monthly Bulletin of Population Registration Statistics of Taiwan* (1966, 1967).

in the urban-industrial class of nations. However, since Taiwan is offered as the main showpiece by the sponsors of current policies in underdeveloped areas, and since the data are excellent, it merits examination.

Taiwan is acclaimed as a showpiece because it has responded favorably to a highly organized program for distributing up-to-date contraceptives and has also had a rapidly dropping birth rate. Some observers have carelessly attributed the decline in the birth rate—from 50.0 in 1951 to 32.7 in 1965—to the family-planning campaign,[26] but the campaign began only in 1963 and could have affected only the end of the trend. Rather, the decline represents a response to modernization similar to that made by all countries that have become industrialized.[27] By 1950 over half of Taiwan's population was urban, and by 1964 nearly two-thirds were urban, with 29 percent of the population living in cities of 100,000 or more. The pace of economic development has been extremely rapid. Between 1951 and 1963, per capita income increased by 4.05 percent per year. Yet the island is closely packed, having

[26] "South Korea and Taiwan appear successfully to have checked population growth by the use of intrauterine contraceptive devices" [U. Borell, *Hearings on S. 1676 (5)*, p. 556].

[27] K. Davis, *Population Index 29*, 345 (1963).

870 persons per square mile (a population density higher than that of Belgium). The combination of fast economic growth and rapid population increase in limited space has put parents of large families at a relative disadvantage and has created a brisk demand for abortions and contraceptives. Thus the favorable response to the current campaign to encourage use of the IUD is not a good example of what birth-control technology can do for a genuinely backward country. In fact, when the program was started, one reason for expecting receptivity was that the island was already on its way to modernization and family planning.[28]

At most, the recent family-planning campaign—which reached significant proportions only in 1964, when some 46,000 IUD's were inserted (in 1965 the number was 99,253, and in 1966, 111,242)[29, 30]—could have caused the increase observable after 1963 in the rate of decline. Between 1951 and 1963 the average drop in the birth rate per 1000 women (see Table 1) was 1.73 percent per year; in the period 1964–66 it was 4.35 percent. But one hesitates to assign all of the acceleration in decline since 1963 to the family-planning campaign. The rapid economic development has been precisely of a type likely to accelerate a drop in reproduction. The rise in manufacturing has been much greater than the rise in either agriculture or construction. The agricultural labor force has thus been squeezed, and migration to the cities has skyrocketed.[31] Since housing has not kept pace, urban families have had to restrict reproduction in order to take advantage of career opportunities and avoid domestic inconvenience. Such conditions have historically tended to accelerate a decline in birth rate. The most rapid decline came late in the United States (1921–33) and in Japan (1947–55). A plot of the Japanese and Taiwanese birth rates (Fig. 1) shows marked similarity of the two curves, despite a difference in level. All told, one should not attribute all of the post-1963 acceleration in the decline of Taiwan's birth rate to the family-planning campaign.

The main evidence that *some* of this acceleration is due to the campaign comes from the fact that Taichung, the city in which the family-planning effort was first concentrated, showed subsequently a much faster drop in

[28] R. Freedman, *ibid. 31*, 421 (1965).

[29] Before 1964 the Family Planning Association had given advice to fewer than 60,000 wives in 10 years and a Pre-Pregnancy Health Program had reached some 10,000, and, in the current campaign, 3650 IUD's were inserted in 1965, in a total population of 2½ million women of reproductive age. See *Studies in Family Planning, No. 19* (1967), p. 4, and R. Freedman *et al., Population Studies 16*, 231 (1963).

[30] R. W. Gillespie, *Family Planning on Taiwan* (Population Council, Taichung, 1965).

[31] During the period 1950–60 the ratio of growth of the city to growth of the non-city population was 5:3; during the period 1960–64 the ratio was 5:2; these ratios are based on data of Shaohsing Chen, *J. Social. Taiwan 1*, 74 (1963) and data in the United Nations *Demographic Yearbooks*.

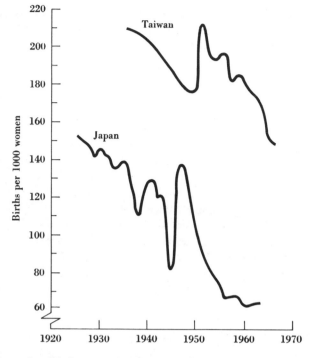

*Figure 1.   Births per 1000 women aged 15
through 49 in Japan and Taiwan.*

fertility than other cities.[30, 32] But the campaign has not reached throughout
the island. By the end of 1966, only 260,745 women had been fitted with an
IUD under auspices of the campaign, whereas the women of reproductive
age on the island numbered 2.86 million. Most of the reduction in fertility
has therefore been a matter of individual initiative. To some extent the campaign may be simply substituting sponsored (and cheaper) services for
those that would otherwise come through private and commercial channels.
An island-wide survey in 1964 showed that over 150,000 women were already using the traditional Ota ring (a metallic intrauterine device popular
in Japan); almost as many had been sterilized; about 40,000 were using
foam tablets; some 50,000 admitted to having had at least one abortion; and
many were using other methods of birth control.[30]

The important question, however, is not whether the present campaign
is somewhat hastening the downward trend in the birth rate but whether,

---

[32] R. Freedman, *Population Index 31,* 434 (1965). Taichung's rate of decline in
1963–64 was roughly double the average in four other cities, whereas just prior to the
campaign its rate of decline had been much less than theirs.

even if it is, it will provide population control for the nation. Actually, the campaign is not designed to provide such control and shows no sign of doing so. It takes for granted existing reproductive goals. Its aim is "to integrate, through education and information, the idea of family limitation *within the existing attitudes, values, and goals* of the people"[30] (italics mine). Its target is *married* women who do not want any more children; it ignores girls not yet married, and women married and wanting more children.

With such an approach, what is the maximum impact possible? It is the difference between the number of children women have been having and the number they want to have. A study in 1957 found a median figure of 3.75 for the number of children wanted by women aged 15 to 29 in Taipei, Taiwan's largest city; the corresponding figure for women from a satellite town was 3.93; for women from a fishing village, 4.90; and for women from a farming village, 5.03. Over 60 percent of the women in Taipei and over 90 percent of those in the farming village wanted 4 or more children.[33] In a sample of wives aged 25 to 29 in Taichung, a city of over 300,000, Freedman and his co-workers found the average number of children wanted was 4; only 9 percent wanted less than 3, 20 percent wanted 5 or more.[34] If, therefore, Taiwanese women used contraceptives that were 100-percent effective and had the number of children they desire, they would have about 4.5 each. The goal of the family-planning effort would be achieved. In the past the Taiwanese woman who married and lived through the reproductive period had, on the average, approximately 6.5 children; thus a figure of 4.5 would represent a substantial decline in fertility. Since mortality would continue to decline, the population growth rate would decline somewhat less than individual reproduction would. With 4.5 births per woman and a life expectancy of 70 years, the rate of natural increase would be close to 3 percent per year.[35]

In the future, Taiwanese views concerning reproduction will doubtless change, in response to social change and economic modernization. But how far will they change? A good indication is the number of children desired by couples in an already modernized country long oriented toward family planning. In the United States in 1966, an average of 3.4 children was considered ideal by white women aged 21 or over.[36] This average number of births would give Taiwan, with only a slight decrease in mortality, a long-run rate of natural increase of 1.7 percent per year and a doubling of population in 41 years.

Detailed data confirm the interpretation that Taiwanese women are in

[33] S. H. Chen, *J. Soc. Sci. Taipei 13*, 72 (1963).

[34] R. Freedman *et al.*, *Population Studies 16*, 227 (1963); *ibid.*, p. 232.

[35] In 1964 the life expectancy at birth was already 66 years in Taiwan, as compared to 70 for the United States.

[36] J. Blake, *Eugenics Quart. 14*, 68 (1967).

the process of shifting from a "peasant-agrarian" to an "industrial" level of reproduction. They are, in typical fashion, cutting off higher-order births at age 30 and beyond.[37] Among young wives, fertility has risen, not fallen. In sum, the widely acclaimed family-planning program in Taiwan may, at most, have somewhat speeded the later phase of fertility decline which would have occurred anyway because of modernization.

Moving down the scale of modernization, to countries most in need of population control, one finds the family-planning approach even more inadequate. In South Korea, second only to Taiwan in the frequency with which it is cited as a model of current policy, a recent birth-rate decline of unknown extent is assumed by leaders to be due overwhelmingly to the government's family-planning program. However, it is just as plausible to say that the net effect of government involvement in population control has been, so far, to delay rather than hasten a decline in reproduction made inevitable by social and economic changes. Although the government is advocating vasectomies and providing IUD's and pills, it refuses to legalize abortions, despite the rapid rise in the rate of illegal abortions and despite the fact that, in a recent survey, 72 percent of the people who stated an opinion favored legalization. Also, the program is presented in the context of maternal and child health; it thus emphasizes motherhood and the family rather than alternative roles for women. Much is made of the fact that opinion surveys show an overwhelming majority of Koreans (89 percent in 1965) favoring contraception,[38] but this means only that Koreans are like other people in wishing to have the means to get what they want. Unfortunately, they want sizable families: "The records indicate that the program appeals mainly to women in the 30–39 year age bracket who have four or more children, including at least two sons. . . ."[38]

In areas less developed than Korea the degree of acceptance of contraception tends to be disappointing, especially among the rural majority. Faced with this discouragement, the leaders of current policy, instead of reexamining their assumptions, tend to redouble their effort to find a contraceptive that will appeal to the most illiterate peasant, forgetting that he wants a good-sized family. In the rural Punjab, for example, "a disturbing feature . . . is that the females start to seek advice and adopt family planning techniques at the fag end of their reproductive period".[39] Among 5196 women coming to rural Punjabi family-planning centers, 38 percent were over 35 years old, 67 percent over 30. These women had married early, nearly a third of them

[37] Women accepting IUD's in the family-planning program are typically 30 to 34 years old and have already had four children. [*Studies in Family Planning No. 19* (1967), p. 5].

[38] Y. K. Cha, in *Family Planning and Population Programs*, B. Berelson *et al.*, Eds. (Univ. of Chicago Press, Chicago, 1966).

[39] H. S. Ayalvi and S. S. Johl, *J. Family Welfare 12*, 60 (1965).

before the age of 15;[40] some 14 percent had eight or more *living* children when they reached the clinic, 51 percent six or more.

A survey in Tunisia showed that 68 percent of the married couples were willing to use birth-control measures, but the average number of children they considered ideal was 4.3.[41] The corresponding averages for a village in eastern Java, a village near New Delhi, and a village in Mysore were 4.3, 4.0, and 4.2, respectively.[42, 43] In the cities of these regions women are more ready to accept birth control and they want fewer children than village women do, but the number they consider desirable is still wholly unsatisfactory from the standpoint of population control. In an urban family-planning center in Tunisia, more than 600 of 900 women accepting contraceptives had four living children already.[44] In Bangalore, a city of nearly a million at the time (1952), the number of offspring desired by married women was 3.7 on the average; by married men, 4.1.[43] In the metropolitan area of San Salvador (350,000 inhabitants) a 1964 survey[45] showed the number desired by women of reproductive age to be 3.9, and in seven other capital cities of Latin America the number ranged from 2.7 to 4.2. If women in the cities of underdeveloped countries used birth-control measures with 100-percent efficiency, they still would have enough babies to expand city populations senselessly, quite apart from the added contribution of rural-urban migration. In many of the cities the difference between actual and ideal number of children is not great; for instance, in the seven Latin-American capitals mentioned above, the ideal was 3.4 whereas the actual births per woman in the age range 35 to 39 was 3.7.[46] Bombay City has had birth-control clinics for many years, yet its birth rate (standardized for age, sex, and marital distribution) is still 34 per 1000 inhabitants and is tending to rise rather than fall. Although this rate is about 13 percent lower than that for India generally, it has been about that much lower since at least 1951.[47]

[40] Sixty percent of the women had borne their first child before age 19. Early marriage is strongly supported by public opinion. Of couples polled in the Punjab, 48 percent said that girls *should* marry before age 16, and 94 percent said they should marry before age 20 (H. S. Ayalvi and S. S. Johl, *ibid.*, p. 57). A study of 2380 couples in 60 villages of Uttar Pradesh found that the women had consummated their marriage at an average age of 14.6 years [J. R. Rele, *Population Studies 15*, 268 (1962)].

[41] J. Morsa, in *Family Planning and Population Programs*, B. Berelson *et al.*, Eds. (Univ. of Chicago Press, Chicago, 1966).

[42] H. Gille and R. J. Pardoko, *ibid.*, p. 515; S. N. Agarwala, *Med. Dig. Bombay 4*, 653 (1961).

[43] *Mysore Population Study* (United Nations, New York, 1961), p. 140.

[44] A. Daly, in *Family Planning and Population Programs*, B. Berelson *et al.*, Eds. (Univ. of Chicago Press, Chicago, 1966).

[45] C. J. Goméz, paper presented at the World Population Conference, Belgrade, 1965.

[46] C. Miro, in *Family Planning and Population Programs*, B. Berelson *et al.*, Eds. (Univ. of Chicago Press, Chicago, 1966).

[47] *Demographic Training and Research Centre (India) Newsletter 20*, 4 (Aug. 1966).

IS FAMILY PLANNING THE "FIRST STEP"
IN POPULATION CONTROL?

To acknowledge that family planning does not achieve population control is not to impugn its value for other purposes. Freeing women from the need to have more children than they want is of great benefit to them and their children and to society at large. My argument is therefore directed not against family-planning programs as such but against the assumption that they are an effective means of controlling population growth.

But what difference does it make? Why not go along for awhile with family planning as an initial approach to the problem of population control? The answer is that any policy on which millions of dollars are being spent should be designed to achieve the goal it purports to achieve. If it is only a first step, it should be so labeled, and its connection with the next step (and the nature of that next step) should be carefully examined. In the present case, since no "next step" seems ever to be mentioned, the question arises, Is reliance on family planning in fact a basis for dangerous postponement of effective steps? To continue to offer a remedy as a cure long after it has been shown merely to ameliorate the disease is either quackery or wishful thinking, and it thrives most where the need is greatest. Today the desire to solve the population problem is so intense that we are all ready to embrace any "action program" that promises relief. But postponement of effective measures allows the situation to worsen.

Unfortunately, the issue is confused by a matter of semantics. "Family *planning*" and "fertility *control*" suggest that reproduction is being regulated according to some rational plan. And so it is, but only from the standpoint of the individual couple, not from that of the community. What is rational in the light of a couple's situation may be totally irrational from the standpoint of society's welfare.

The need for societal regulation of individual behavior is readily recognized in other spheres—those of explosives, dangerous drugs, public property, natural resources. But in the sphere of reproduction, complete individual initiative is generally favored even by those liberal intellectuals who, in other spheres, most favor economic and social planning. Social reformers who would not hesitate to force all owners of rental property to rent to anyone who can pay, or to force all workers in an industry to join a union, balk at any suggestion that couples be permitted to have only a certain number of offspring. Invariably they interpret societal control of reproduction as meaning direct police supervision of individual behavior. Put the word *compulsory* in front of any term describing a means of limiting births—*compulsory sterilization, compulsory abortion, compulsory contraception*—and you guarantee violent opposition. Fortunately, such direct controls need not be invoked, but conservatives and radicals alike overlook this in their blind opposition to the idea of collective determination of a society's birth rate.

That the exclusive emphasis on family planning in current population policies is not a "first step" but an escape from the real issues is suggested by two facts. (i) No country has taken the "next step." The industrialized countries have had family planning for half a century without acquiring control over either the birth rate or population increase. (ii) Support and encouragement of research on population policy other than family planning is negligible. It is precisely this blocking of alternative thinking and experimentation that makes the emphasis on family planning a major obstacle to population control. The need is not to abandon family-planning programs but to put equal or greater resources into other approaches.

NEW DIRECTIONS IN POPULATION POLICY

In thinking about other approaches, one can start with known facts. In the past, all surviving societies had institutional incentives for marriage, procreation, and child care which were powerful enough to keep the birth rate equal to or in excess of a high death rate. Despite the drop in death rates during the last century and a half, the incentives tended to remain intact because the social structure (especially in regard to the family) changed little. At most, particularly in industrial societies, children became less productive and more expensive.[48] In present-day agrarian societies, where the drop in death rate has been more recent, precipitate, and independent of social change,[49] motivation for having children has changed little. Here, even more than in industrialized nations, the family has kept on producing abundant offspring, even though only a fraction of these children are now needed.

If excessive population growth is to be prevented, the obvious requirement is somehow to impose restraints on the family. However, because family roles are reinforced by society's system of rewards, punishments, sentiments, and norms, any proposal to demote the family is viewed as a threat by conservatives and liberals alike, and certainly by people with enough social responsibility to work for population control. One is charged with trying to "abolish" the family, but what is required is selective restructuring of the family in relation to the rest of society.

The lines of such restructuring are suggested by two existing limitations on fertility. (i) Nearly all societies succeed in drastically discouraging re-

---

[48] K. Davis, *Population Index 29*, 345 (1963). For economic and sociological theory of motivation for having children, see J. Blake [Univ. of California (Berkeley)], in preparation.

[49] K. Davis, *Amer. Economic Rev. 46*, 305 (1956); *Sci. Amer. 209*, 68 (1963).

production among unmarried women. (ii) Advanced societies unintentionally reduce reproduction among married women when conditions worsen in such a way as to penalize childbearing more severely than it was penalized before. In both cases the causes are motivational and economic rather than techno-logical.

It follows that population-control policy can de-emphasize the family in two ways: (i) by keeping present controls over illegitimate childbirth yet making the most of factors that lead people to postpone or avoid marriage, and (ii) by instituting conditions that motivate those who do marry to keep their families small.

POSTPONEMENT OF MARRIAGE

Since the female reproductive span is short and generally more fecund in its first than in its second half, postpone-ment of marriage to ages beyond 20 tends biologically to reduce births. Sociologically, it gives women time to get a better education, acquire interests unrelated to the family, and develop a cautious attitude toward pregnancy.[50] Individuals who have not married by the time they are in their late twenties often do not marry at all. For these reasons, for the world as a whole, the average age at marriage for women is negatively associated with the birth rate: a rising age at marriage is a frequent cause of declining fertility during the middle phase of the demographic transition; and, in the late phase, the "baby boom" is usually associated with a return to younger marriages.

Any suggestion that age at marriage be raised as a part of population policy is usually met with the argument that "even if a law were passed, it would not be obeyed." Interestingly, this objection implies that the only way to control the age at marriage is by direct legislation, but other factors gov-ern the actual age. Roman Catholic countries generally follow canon law in stipulating 12 years as the minimum *legal* age at which girls may marry, but the actual average age at marriage in these countries (at least in Europe) is characteristically more like 25 to 28 years. The actual age is determined, not by law, but by social and economic conditions. In agrarian societies, postponement of marriage (when postponement occurs) is apparently caused by difficulties in meeting the economic prerequisites for matrimony, as stipu-lated by custom and opinion. In industrial societies it is caused by housing shortages, unemployment, the requirement for overseas military service, high costs of education, and inadequacy of consumer services. Since almost no research has been devoted to the subject, it is difficult to assess the relative weight of the factors that govern the age at marriage.

[50] J. Blake, *World Population Conference* [*Belgrade, 1965*] (United Nations, New York, 1967), vol. 2, pp. 132–36.

ENCOURAGING LIMITATION OF BIRTHS WITHIN MARRIAGE

As a means of encouraging the limitation of reproduction within marriage, as well as postponement of marriage, a greater rewarding of non-familial than of familial roles would probably help. A simple way of accomplishing this would be to allow economic advantages to accrue to the single as opposed to the married individual, and to the small as opposed to the large family. For instance, the government could pay people to permit themselves to be sterilized;[51] all costs of abortion could be paid by the government; a substantial fee could be charged for a marriage license; a "child-tax"[52] could be levied; and there could be a requirement that illegitimate pregnancies be aborted. Less sensationally, governments could simply reverse some existing policies that encourage childbearing. They could, for example, cease taxing single persons more than married ones; stop giving parents special tax exemptions; abandon income-tax policy that discriminates against couples when the wife works; reduce paid maternity leaves; reduce family allowances;[53] stop awarding public housing on the basis of family size; stop granting fellowships and other educational aids (including special allowances for wives and children) to married students; cease outlawing abortions and sterilizations; and relax rules that allow use of harmless contraceptives only with medical permission. Some of these policy reversals would be beneficial in other than demographic respects and some would be harmful unless special precautions were taken. The aim would be to reduce the number, not the quality, of the next generation.

A closely related method of de-emphasizing the family would be modification of the complementarity of the roles of men and women. Men are now able to participate in the wider world yet enjoy the satisfaction of having several children because the housework and childcare fall mainly on their wives. Women are impelled to seek this role by their idealized view of marriage and motherhood and by either the scarcity of alternative roles or the difficulty of combining them with family roles. To change this situation women could be required to work outside the home, or compelled by circumstances to do so. If, at the same time, women were paid as well as men and given equal educational and occupational opportunities, and if social life were organized around the place of work rather than around the home or neighborhood, many women would develop interests that would compete

---

[51] S. Enke, *Rev. Economic Statistics 42*, 175 (1960) ; ——, *Econ. Develop. Cult. Change 8*, 339 (1960) ; ——, *ibid. 10*, 427 (1962) ; A. O. Krueger and L. A. Sjaastad, *ibid.*, p. 423.

[52] T. J. Samuel, *J. Family Welfare India 13*, 12 (1966).

[53] Sixty-two countries, including 27 in Europe, give cash payments to people for having children [U.S. Social Security Administration, *Social Security Programs Throughout the World, 1967* (Government Printing Office, Washington, D.C., 1967), pp. xxvii–xxviii].

with family interests. Approximately this policy is now followed in several Communist countries, and even the less developed of these currently have extremely low birth rates.[54]

That inclusion of women in the labor force has a negative effect on reproduction is indicated by regional comparisons.[18, 55] But in most countries the wife's employment is subordinate, economically and emotionally, to her family role, and is readily sacrificed for the latter. No society has restructured both the occupational system and the domestic establishment to the point of permanently modifying the old division of labor by sex.

In any deliberate effort to control the birth rate along these lines, a government has two powerful instruments—its command over economic planning and its authority (real or potential) over education. The first determines (as far as policy can) the economic conditions and circumstances affecting the lives of all citizens; the second provides the knowledge and attitudes necessary to implement the plans. The economic system largely determines who shall work, what can be bought, what rearing children will cost, how much individuals can spend. The schools define family roles and develop vocational and recreational interests; they could, if it were desired, redefine the sex roles, develop interests that transcend the home, and transmit realistic (as opposed to moralistic) knowledge concerning marriage, sexual behavior, and population problems. When the problem is viewed in this light, it is clear that the ministries of economics and education, not the ministry of health, should be the source of population policy.

THE DILEMMA OF POPULATION POLICY

It should now be apparent why, despite strong anxiety over runaway population growth, the actual programs purporting to control it are limited to family planning and are therefore ineffective. (i) The goal of zero, or even slight, population growth is one that nations and groups find difficult to accept. (ii) The measures that would be required to implement such a goal, though not so revolutionary as a Brave New World or a Communist Utopia, nevertheless tend to offend most people reared in existing societies. As a consequence, the goal of so-called population control is implicit and vague; the method is only family planning. This method, far from de-emphasizing the family, is familistic. One of its stated goals is that of helping sterile couples to *have* children. It stresses parental aspirations and responsibilities. It goes along with most aspects of conventional morality, such as condemnation of abortion, disapproval of premarital intercourse,

[54] Average gross reproduction rates in the early 1960's were as follows: Hungary, 0.91; Bulgaria, 1:09; Romania, 1:15; Yugoslavia, 1:32.

[55] O. A. Collver and E. Langlois, *Econ. Develop. Cult. Change 10*, 367 (1962); J. Weeks, [Univ. of California (Berkeley)], unpublished paper.

respect for religious teachings and cultural taboos, and obeisance to medical and clerical authority. It deflects hostility by refusing to recommend any change other than the one it stands for: availability of contraceptives.

The things that make family planning acceptable are the very things that make it ineffective for population control. By stressing the right of parents to have the number of children they want, it evades the basic question of population policy, which is how to give societies the number of children they need. By offering only the means for *couples* to control fertility, it neglects the means for societies to do so.

Because of the predominantly pro-family character of existing societies, individual interest ordinarily leads to the production of enough offspring to constitute rapid population growth under conditions of low mortality. Childless or single-child homes are considered indicative of personal failure, whereas having three to five living children gives a family a sense of continuity and substantially.[56]

Given the existing desire to have moderate-sized rather than small families, the only countries in which fertility has been reduced to match reduction in mortality are advanced ones temporarily experiencing worsened economic conditions. In Sweden, for instance, the net reproduction rate (NRR)has been below replacement for 34 years (1930–63), if the period is taken as a whole, but this is because of the economic depression. The average replacement rate was below unity (NRR = 0.81) for the period 1930–42, but from 1942 through 1963 it was above unity (NRR = 1.08). Hardships that seem particularly conducive to deliberate lowering of the birth rate are (in managed economies) scarcity of housing and other consumer goods despite full employment, and required high participtation of women in the labor force, or (in freer economies) a great deal of unemployment and economic insecurity. When conditions are good, any nation tends to have a growing population.

It follows that, in countries where contraception is used, a realistic proposal for a government policy of lowering the birth rate reads like a catalogue of horrors: squeeze consumers through taxation and inflation; make housing very scarce by limiting construction; force wives and mothers to work outside the home to offset the inadequacy of male wages, yet provide few child-care facilities; encourage migration to the city by paying low wages in the country and providing few rural jobs; increase congestion in cities by starving the transit system; increase personal insecurity by encouraging conditions that produce unemployment and by haphazard political arrests. No government will institute such hardships simply for the purpose of controlling population growth. Clearly, therefore, the task of contemporary population policy is to develop attractive substitutes for family interests, so

[56] Roman Catholic textbooks condemn the "small" family (one with fewer than four children) as being abnormal [J. Blake, *Population Studies 20*, 27 (1966)].

as to avoid having to turn to hardship as a corrective. The specific measures required for developing such substitutes are not easy to determine in the absence of research on the question.

In short, the world's population problem cannot be solved by pretense and wishful thinking. The unthinking identification of family planning with population control is an ostrich-like approach in that it permits people to hide from themselves the enormity and unconventionality of the task. There is no reason to abandon family-planning programs; contraception is a valuable technological instrument. But such programs must be supplemented with equal or greater investments in research and experimentation to determine the required socioeconomic measures.

Part II
ECONOMIC DEVELOPMENT IN THE MID-TWENTIETH CENTURY: DEVELOPMENT IN BACKWARD ECONOMIES

Introduction

One of the most central issues currently faced in the sociology of economic development is that of economic development in the backward economies. Since World War II the attention of scholars and statesmen has turned to the dramatic demand and hope for achieving long-term sustained increases in human productivity in the poorer nations of the world. Men have been concerned with the question of why these economies have remained backward, and with the question of how they can be transformed into advanced economies. In the course of this new social awareness and of the myriad action programs designed to induce social change, the student has an excellent opportunity to increase his understanding of the sociological aspects of economic development.

We should emphasize once again the implication of the use of the term *backward economies*. It has become much more common to use a wide array of euphemisms: less developed, developing, emerging, or the more advanced Orwellian attempt to sterilize the language, LDC's (for Less Developed Countries). It has often been pointed out that ours is an age accustomed to calling a spade an agricultural implement. Our argument is that in the economy, we do have the opportunity to use an underlying quantitative and more or less unidimensional measure for change. Thus we can usefully speak of progressive change, development, and advanced and backward stages or conditions. This is an advantage we should use, not one from which we should flee in embarrassment.

We have opened this part with an essay that attempts to set the current issue of economic development in the backward economies in its larger historical context. It is this context that has shaped and continues to exercise considerable influence over the process of economic development today. This essay also points to what we consider the central determinants of economic development in the backward economies today. For want of better terms, we call these *political* and *bureaucratic* forces in economic development. The remaining two sections are designed to deal with what we consider to be central issues in the political and bureaucratic determinants of modern economic development.

COLONIALISM, NATIONALISM AND ECONOMIC DEVELOPMENT

Gayl D. Ness

The expansion of the West from the sixteenth through the nineteenth centuries, which brought the West to a position of dominant influence in the world,[1] can be viewed in two major phases. In the first three centuries the rise of the European nation-state and the revolutions in transportation produced a great physical expansion of Western Europe into the Americas, Asia, and Africa. The more accessible and empty lands of the Americas received a massive European outmigration and became real colonies of Europe. In this way the Americas were drawn integrally into the boundaries of the Western world itself. In Asia and Africa, on the other hand, the Western penetration came by means of trade. The major mechanisms of this penetration were private capitalist merchant companies, best exemplified in the great British East India Company and the Dutch East India Company, both established at the beginning of the seventeenth century. The points of contact and penetration into the non-Western world were ports and trading stations, with little direct involvement in the control of land and populations until the second phase.

The second phase began when the dramatic economic development of the Western world in the nineteenth century, fostered by industrialization, brought two significant changes. One was an increase of trade and more or less peaceful interaction among the industrializing countries of the West. The other was an increasing political penetration into the lands of Asia and

[1] See William J. McNeill, *The Rise of the West* (Chicago, 1962), especially Part III, for the detailed historical argument on which this statement is based.

Africa. The growing industrial organization of the West developed an apparently insatiable, if not always stable, appetite for raw materials and food products.[2] The demand for such goods grew to such proportions that it could no longer be satisfied by the crude and sporadic gathering capacities of the small-scale social organization that had proved sufficient for providing Europe with spices and other exotic products. The demand could be satisfied, however, by another social invention of the European world, the rationally organized bureaucratic structure. Chinese overseas clan capitalism, working under unstable relations with unstable Malay sultans, had been sufficient to produce the small amounts of tin consumed up to the mid-nineteenth century. For the massive demands of the late nineteenth and twentieth centuries larger scale organizational capacities were required. Similarly, Western adventurers using brute force over native Brazilian slaves had been sufficient to produce the relatively small amounts of natural rubber that were needed for such novelties as rubber balls and footwear through the end of the nineteenth century. But for the massive demands of a motorized age the infinitely greater capacity of a rationally organized plantation agriculture was needed.

The great advantages of large-scale rational calculation in the bureaucratic organization require a specific social and political setting. The modern bureaucratic structure requires a legal rational organization of public authority, a system that itself admits of long-term rational calculation. This was the organizational imperative by which the Western industrialization that produced an insatiable demand for raw materials brought about a transformation in the character of Western penetration into Asia and Africa. In the nineteenth century the industrializing Western nations increasingly moved to assume direct control over the lands and peoples of Asia, producing what we can call modern *colonial systems*. This direct control would produce the social and political setting that permitted the new Western organizations to be used to their fullest advantage.

In some areas, such as India and Indonesia (then the Dutch East Indies) the earlier private capitalist companies had already assumed considerable control over land and peoples. In these cases the companies were dissolved and transformed into explicit state instruments. The Dutch East India Company was dissolved in 1800. The British East India Company was not dissolved until after the Indian Sepoy Mutiny of 1857 dramatized the inadequacy of the private company for dealing with the responsibilities

---

[2] While I do not wish to discount the search for markets as an imperialist motive, I consider this far less important in the creation of the colonial systems described here than was the demand for raw materials. It is often overlooked that the merchant groups in the pre-colonial port cities often provided a major impetus for the assumption of land control in the hinterlands. These groups were largely motivated by the promise of high profits to be gained from the new mining and agricultural enterprises that could produce the raw materials for which demand increased rapidly in the nineteenth century.

of public authority that had grown along with the more intensive penetration brought by nineteenth century industrialization.

In most of Asia and Africa, however, Western commercial penetration had not brought direct control over lands and peoples. In these areas the late nineteenth century saw something approaching a land rush as Western powers moved to assume direct control over peoples heretofore touched only by the penetration of markets.

The rapidity with which this happened is quite remarkable. The last quarter of the nineteenth century was a brief and highly concentrated period of imperialist expansion. By the end of the century the process was largely complete, with Germany and the United States arriving somewhat late on a scene dominated by the British, Dutch, and French. In the process, the trader or merchant gave way to the district officer as the key functionary, and the Western bureaucratic form of organization extended control over most areas of Southeast and South Asia and Africa.

The colonial systems established by the West can be described in terms common to the analysis of social systems.[3] In the first place they had *dependent polities.* That is, the major decisions on the articulation of interests, the mobilization and allocation of collective resources, the definition and control of boundaries and the maintenance of internal order were made by outsiders in centers outside of the territory being governed. The distinction between the rulers and the ruled became highly crystallized along lines of territorial origin and location, race, language, culture, and economic interests.

The arrangement was not without considerable benefit to indigenous populations as well as to the metropolitan powers. Many areas into which the Western powers moved had been marked by small-scale chronic warfare and a generally low level of peace and order. This was in fact often one of the more compelling reasons for moving into direct control over the land. Western merchant interests in the trading posts urged metropolitan intervention in the hinterland because the indigenous lack of order was an obstacle to trade and to the exploitation of the natural resources that existed in the hinterlands.

In some cases the Western intervention was direct, with Westerners forcibly or otherwise deposing local rulers and assuming for themselves the power to rule. In other cases the intervention was indirect. Treaties could be made with local chiefs, kings or sultans that kept many of the indigenous forms and functionaries of rule, though the predominant interest of govern-

---

[3] It should be emphasized that I am using only the terminology here. The concept of social system assumes self-sufficiency of a collectivity. The systems that I am describing here were hardly self-sufficient. On the contrary their distinctive feature was that they were dependent outposts of the metropolitan systems. The terminology is useful, however, even without the equilibrium assumptions, because it provides some systematic and comprehensive coverage of critical social characteristics.

ment would henceforth always be that of the foreign or metropolitan power. In the larger sense the difference between direct and indirect rule was not significant in that it did not affect the real exercise of power. It did, however, make some difference in the pattern of articulation between the social structure and the new colonial bureaucracy that was developed, but that is an issue that must be neglected for the moment.

In all cases the development of a dependent polity was accomplished by the gradual construction of bureaucratic instruments of rule. The histories of administration in the colonial systems show a clear trend toward a progressive differentiation and specialization of government functions. The earliest residents, advisers, and district officers performed a vast array of tasks, including codifying native law and adjusting the imposed metropolitan legal code to the local situation, collecting revenues, providing order, building roads and other items of public infrastructure, and promoting agricultural development and public health. Gradually as the colonial experience proved economically successful, as it usually did, these functions began to be differentiated. A central secretariat emerged with a set of specialized agencies for agriculture, public works, police and legal functions, commerce, education, public health, and social welfare. Such administrative systems normally developed on models taken from the metropolitan power itself. The dependent polity became the setting for the emergence of a highy developed government bureaucracy.

Foreign rule brought both the internal stability and the financial incentives that permitted the Western economic agencies to work at a high level of effectiveness. The result was a period of economic development whose rapidity is unlikely to be matched in the modern period. Literally millions of acres of unused land were brought under cultivation to provide such goods as tea, rice, sugar, cocoa, bananas, cotton, sisal, hemp, coconuts, and rubber to the rest of the world. Untapped sources of minerals were opened to provide the world with oil, tin, bauxite, and a host of other minerals in smaller but no less critical quantities. All of this happened in a period of less than half a century.

The products of the dependent polities were not destined for indigenous consumers. They were export products, destined primarily for the peoples of the more advanced economies. Nor were the returns or the profits of these export economies destined or even significantly shared with the native populations of the colonial territories. The agency houses, plantations, and mines of the colonial territories provided rich returns to the investors and the managers from the metropolitan countries, and often to the metropolitan governments themselves. Ownership in the hands of foreigners and goods destined largely for foreign markets mark the significant characteristics of the *colonial export economies*.[4] The territories of much of Asia and Africa

---

[4] See Jonathan Levin's *The Export Economies* (Cambridge, Mass., 1960), for a fuller exposition of this model, illustrated by a comparative analysis of Peru and Burma.

were drawn into the modern world in politically and economically subordinate positions.

The rapid pace of development in the export colonial economies was
associated, and perhaps necessarily, with a highly unbalanced pattern of development. An export sector emerged, integrally related to the metropolitan
power and the world market. This was the sector of the towns, mines and
plantations producing for the world market. It evolved an allied social infrastructure that included commercial and financial houses, the center of the
government bureaucracy, and the schools, churches, and clubs by which the
metropolitan society controlled its own functionaries in the outpost and
brought some few indigenous peoples into its own cultural orbit. Alongside
of this export sector remained a traditional peasant sector, not by any means
untouched by the export sector, but less touched by it. This was the world
of the village, of an organization of production that bore powerful resem-
blances to what it had been for centuries in the past. It was a world where
the indigenous language was used and indigenous gods were worshipped.
The extent to which this traditional peasant sector had been changed by and
integrated into the export sector varied considerably. In some cases the
peasant sector was actually created by the emergence of the export sector
as the growth of the latter brought an increased demand for the foodstuffs
that could be produced cheaply and easily with traditional means of production. In virtually all cases, however, the two sectors could be distinctly
identified. The term dual economy, which has been so common in the
literature, was in fact a product of the colonial export economy.[5]

The process of colonial economic development placed powerful strains
upon population and labor supply in the colonial territories. For the most
part the territories were underpopulated by modern standards and the indigenous peoples lived in a rather effective adjustment with their environments, given their levels of technology and organization. The shortage of
labor was in fact often a critical obstacle to the process of development in
colonial territories. In some cases it was necessary to institute a head tax to
force native people into a position where they needed money and would thus
present themselves on the commercial labor market created by the emerging
export economy.[6]

More often, however, the supply of labor was provided by immigration.
The densely populated areas of Southern Asia and Southeast China provided
millions of migrants to the less densely settled and rapidly growing areas of
East Africa and Southeast Asia.

[5] The term was first used by Dr. J. H. Boeke, a Dutch economist and colonial officer.
See *Indonesian Economics, Selected Studies by Dutch Scholars*, Vol. 6 (The Hague,
1961), for a selection of arguments aroused by the term and its conceptual implications.

[6] See Wilbur Moore, *Industrialization and Labor* (Ithaca, 1951), for an early attempt
to provide a conceptual framework for a large selection of studies on the labor market in
nonindustrial societies.

Although the metropolitan powers permitted and even fostered this migration into their colonial territories, they also made a distinction between the migrants and the natives, who were in some sense to be protected from the ravages of the migrants. The migrants were on the whole viewed as itinerants in a great migrant labor camp. Colonial policy often attempted to keep migrants from owning land and gaining a legitimate place in the territory.

The migrants seldom were assimilated into the indigenous populations. They kept their religions and languages, their foods and dress, and a wide range of cultural characteristics. They often lived in different places from the native populations, either as isolated residents on plantations, estates and mines, or in the urban centers that grew up with the development of the export economies. In addition, they engaged in occupations that were in the larger pattern different from those of the indigenous populations. Thus, the Indians in East Africa and in Southeast Asia, and the Chinese in Southeast Asia were more concentrated in urban commercial and financial pursuits, while the indigenous populations were more concentrated in traditional peasant or nomadic activities. A whole series of socially integrative patterns, activities, and identities were thus crystallized along ethnic lines. In this way the dependent polity and the colonial export economy brought with their development *ethnic plural societies*. Like the term *dual economy,* the term *plural society* is a product of the colonial system.[7]

The unity of the colonial system was essentially provided by force; it was a *coercive unity*. The military superiority of the Western powers, which had both technological and organizational aspects, provided for the rapid assumption of control over land and peoples that marked the emergence of the colonial systems. Subsequently, the military and police capacities of the metropolitan powers provided a firm foundation for the operation of the colonial systems throughout their lives.

The amount of coercion required to establish and to maintain colonial rule varied considerably. The British annexations of Burmese territory in the wars of 1852 and 1885–86 were bloody affairs, the latter at one time requiring as many as 32,000 troops, with the formal ending of the wars followed by years of guerrilla resistance. In Malaya, on the other hand, a small punitive expedition up-river was all that was necessary to demonstrate to native chiefs the advisability of accepting their Sultan's treaty with the British, which brought Western control into the peninsula.

It is a long-standing sociological observation that no system of authority rests on force of arms alone; all systems seek to legitimize themselves in some manner. And so it was with the basically coercive authority of the colonial systems. For the metropolitan populations the "white man's burden,"

---

[7] See J. S. Furnivall, *Colonial Policy and Practice* (New York, 1956), for an excellent account of the impact of the colonial system on the plural society of Burma.

derived from a social interpretation of Charles Darwin's evolutionary theory, provided a sense of legitimacy for the coercive extension of rule over colonial lands and peoples.

In the colonies another type of legitimacy emerged from the success of the coercive rule itself. The extension of Western bureaucratic structures brought an appreciation of their inherent capacities and an indigenous belief in their rightness of rule. In addition, the penetration of Western culture brought an acceptance of Western political philosophies that was supportive of the colonial systems in the short run, but proved ultimately subversive to those systems. Indigenous peoples came gradually into the institutional extensions of the Western world. Through the schools, the government bureaucracies, and the communications networks that developed with colonial rule, indigenous peoples came to accept both the rightness of Western administrative and political forms, and a belief in the ultimate moral as well as physical superiority of colonial rule. This belief was gradually undermined by an acceptance of Western political philosophies, which based legitimacy on the consent of the governed, and provided an ideological base for the growing nationalist movements. Until World War II, however, the nationalist forces and ideologies were essentially outweighed by the belief, shared by Western rulers and many indigenous peoples, in the legitimacy of the existing system.

The basic characteristics of the colonial systems—the dependent polity, the colonial export economy, the ethnic plural society, and the coercive unity—were largely mutually supportive and held the colonial systems more or less in equilibrium. The dependent polity brought the setting required for the successful emergence of an export economy, which in turn made the maintenance of that polity highly profitable for the metropolitan political leadership. The polity and the economy produced the ethnic plural society, which in turn provided a sufficient and docile labor force for the economy and precluded the emergence of cohesive mass pressure against the external rule. All three characteristics provided the organization, the financial resources, and the group structure that made coercion both necessary and effective in maintaining sufficient cohesion to allow the system to continue.

This is not to argue that the equilibrium of the colonial systems was absolute. There were, to be sure, forces generated within these systems that were essentially subversive. The education that was designed to produce clerks for the colonial bureaucracy brought along with it the political philosophies of the West on which the subsequent successful independence movements were based. And the very creation of an effective instrument of rule brought a visible target for the focus of indigenous independence movements. Colonial governments became not something to be destroyed to allow the return of older systems of power, but places that could be physically occupied by indigenous people desirous of self-rule. Still, the forces of equilibrium were in balance overpowering. Independence movements were defined essentially as illegitimate and were put down, often with considerable brutality. Even where the legitimacy of colonial rule was beginning to crack, as it was in India, for example, the perceived coming of independence was "not in my lifetime and not in yours."

Despite the balance of the colonial systems, they did come to an end and, often, rather abruptly. Consistent with the view of equilibrium, however, is the view that the colonial systems were destroyed by external forces rather than by internal forces. These forces were brought to the surface of world history in World War II, which marks the end of the era of colonial dominance just as World War I marked the end of the old regimes in Europe.[8]

If the unity of the colonial systems was based on military force and a belief in their legitimacy, the forces that destroyed those systems necessarily acted on both military and ideological levels. The Japanese defeat of the Western powers in Southeast Asia brought to an abrupt end the superiority of the Western powers in that region, with implications that reached far beyond. The defeat came as a great shock to indigenous peoples and Westerners alike. As might be expected, the racial and national implications of the defeat were at least as important as the military implications. The military bases could be rebuilt; and during the post-1945 reoccupation, there were often more Western troops on the scene than were ever seen during the great imperialist drive for land control in the nineteenth century. None of this, however, could erase the image of small brown men from Asia overwhelming, destroying, and humiliating the white giants from the West, whose technical, organizational, and military superiority had almost come to be viewed, by native and Westerner alike, as innate. By a military victory over the West, the Japanese struck a blow at both the military and the ideological underpinnings of the colonial systems.

The war in Europe played its part as well, though primarily on the ideological level. One of the most relevant aspects of that war for the colonial systems was the struggle between competing political ideologies. In a real sense the symbol of democracy was at stake. The German National Socialists openly denigrated the idea of democracy, equating it with the decadence of the Allied powers. The Nazis proposed an autocratic elitist pattern of rule, with legitimacy resting on genetic grounds. Against this the Allies represented an ideology in which the consent of the governed, manifest through empirical electoral mechanisms, provided the ultimate legitimacy of rule. The Allies won, and with that victory the ideological grounds of the colonial systems were fatally undermined. The military victory over the Axis powers brought an ideological victory for the symbol of democracy,

---

[8] See especially Rupert Emerson, *From Empire to Nation* (Boston, 1960).

which made the metropolitan rulers of the colonial systems highly vulnerable to the demands of the nationalists in the colonies for self-rule, for rule based upon the consent of the governed.

Of these two attacks on colonial rule, the military and the ideological, the latter was ultimately more significant. The Japanese destruction of the Western military power in the Southeast Asian colonies was, of course, only short-lived. The ideological victory of the democratic symbol was more permanent. The Western powers returned victorious to the colonies with a far superior military power, but they found in all cases more energetic nationalist movements against whose demands for self-rule the Western powers themselves were rendered vulnerable by their own victories. This determined to a large extent how and where the struggle for independence would be carried out, with powerful implications for the course of modern economic development in the colonies.

The demands for self-rule in the colonial systems were based on the Western political ideology, which gave legitimacy to rule based on the consent of the governed. This meant that indigenous political elites had to demonstrate a popular following in order to claim legitimacy. The nationalist movements mobilized mass followings with openly chauvinistic and ethnic symbols, but also with material promises. Independence would bring the better life that the colonial masters had demonstrated was within human reach. Thus independence came to be associated with economic progress, and political elites committed the emerging independent systems to collective goals of economic development.

Another set of post-independence forces reinforced the political commitment to economic development. These lay primarily in the disequilibrium introduced into the colonial territories by independence. If the characteristics of the colonial systems had been mutually supportive, the change from dependent to independent polities brought widespread strains into the territories containing the local residues of those systems. A colonial export type of economy might support a dependent polity, but it was intolerable in an independent polity based on democratic patterns. Where the citizens were also producers and consumers the political pressures would work in the direction of a change in the character of the economy. Similarly, if an ethnic plural society usefully precluded pressures for representation in the dependent polity, it was intolerable in a dependent polity, which required that the state be a major object of identification and loyalty of the citizens. Thus the basic characteristic of the new states of Asia and Africa—the recent independence gained from democratic metropolitan powers—brings powerful political forces to the center of the arena of modern social and economic change.

Another aspect of the new states also gives their modern economic development a distinctive character. Under the colonial systems they all experienced considerable development of bureaucratic instruments of rule.

These provided the visible organizations by which changes in the economic and social structure could be induced. Further, the imbalanced nature of the colonial system meant that the agencies of government were overwhelming in their dominance of the organizational environment. Government agencies not only created the physical infrastructure and the order of the colonial systems, they also created and quite thoroughly dominated the entire educational, welfare, and communications institutions, and were closely articulated with the foreign commercial organizations that so thoroughly dominated the economy. Thus when indigenous leaders took over the establishment of public authority, they gained control of an organizational network that was predominant in every aspect of the society. No large leap of the imagination was required to suggest that the changes implicit in the new goals established in the polity should be fostered and directed by the specific organizations of the polity. The government bureaucracy became quite naturally the mechanism by which the new collective goals would be realized.

This raises, then, a new and somewhat distinctive set of issues for the analysis of modern economic development in the new states that encompass so much of the backward economies of the world today. The issues are those of the character of the polity and the bureaucracy. For the new states in the mid-twentieth century the degree of political commitment to economic development, and the specific models of development to which the commitment is made, will exercise a powerful influence over the speed and direction of economic development. In addition the character and capacity of the administrative instruments used to translate public commitment into action will exercise a powerful influence on the course of development. It is to these issues that we turn our attention in the following sections.

Section 1
THE POLITICS
OF ECONOMIC
DEVELOPMENT

Introduction: *Conflicting Demands of Flexibility and Discipline*

The most fundamental question in the politics of economic development is the *extent* to which specialized political institutions will be directly involved in making specific decisions about the production and distribution of goods and services. In the advanced economies, this is commonly defined as the issue of *command* versus *demand* in economic systems.[1]

Classical economics made the distinct theoretical break from the rationale of mercantilism with the argument for a separation of political and economic institutional spheres. The argument held a powerful position until a series of political and conceptual changes in the early twentieth century, most noticeably the Russian Revolution and Socialist theory, proposed a reintegration of political and economic institutional spheres.[2] Against the demand economies of classical theory, command economies have reemerged as viable theoretical and organizational alternatives.

It is now quite common to speak of the great difference between centrally planned economies with a wide range of production and

---

[1] See a collection of readings edited by Shanti Tangri, *Command vs. Demand* (Boston, 1967).

[2] See Neil J. Smelser, *Economy and Society* (Englewood Cliffs, New Jersey, 1963), for a brief but penetrating analysis of these theoretical changes.

distribution decisions made by commands from a planning body, and economies in which those decisions are made by discrete individuals, using market prices as indicators of demand. The analysis of these types of systems has produced considerable agreement on some of their relative capacities. It has almost become a commonplace that the Soviet (command) economy can put men on the moon but cannot put men into adequate housing on earth, while the American (demand) economy can put a television set in the room of every child, but cannot put children into adequate school rooms.[3] The command economies have proved quite successful at forced capital mobilization and at inducing the type of social discipline that is necessary to meet many public wants or to work for the achievement of some collective goal. Demand economies, on the other hand, have proved quite successful in drawing out individual initiative and action. This essentially provides a high degree of flexibility in economic and social organizations that is necessary if individual and private demands are to be met.

To this literature on comparative performance, there has been added another on *convergence*. It is often argued that the imperatives of large-scale industrial organization push demand economies toward a greater exercise of central control to achieve a necessary level of co-ordination; and push command economies toward greater utilization of (decentralizing) market mechanisms to achieve a higher level of efficiency. The American economy shows an increase in the proportion of gross national product that flows through the government sector, and an increase in public mechanisms, such as taxation, welfare, and other public distribution schemes, to influence both the production and distribution of goods and services. On the other hand, the Soviet economy moves more to the use of price incentives and the price market to influence the production and distribution of goods and services. In both cases these central figures have not converged as much as some of their smaller allied systems. Central planning is certainly more advanced in most of western Europe than in the United States, and parts of eastern Europe, especially Yugoslavia, have moved more rapidly to decentralized market mechanisms than has the Soviet Union.

Some of the analysis of economic development in backward economies has taken over this concern with *command* and *demand* systems. In the period following World War II, the Soviet model of economic development was very much in vogue, with its emphasis on social mobilization for heavy industrialization, to be paid for by holding back on consumption, and especially on consumer-oriented industries. Further, the capitalist or market systems were discredited through their association with colonialism in a period when colonialism was being deliber-

---

[3] The specific analogies are from John K. Galbraith, *The Affluent Society* (Boston, 1961).

ately and pervasively dismantled. For many indigenous elites in the new states, the old equation: colonialism equals capitalism equals economic backwardness, exploitation, and poverty, was replaced with the new equation: independence equals socialism equals economic development, equality, and affluence. State-owned steel mills became the heroes of economic development; the private enterprise became the villain.

As is often the case, the simple transfer of a set of concepts from one setting to another obscured as much as it clarified, and perhaps more. To a large extent, the issue of command versus demand systems assumes a large-scale complex organizational setting for production, which does not exist in most of the backward economies. Without such a broadly supportive environment, the political decision to create a state-owned steel industry may constitute (and often has) a fantastic waste of public resources. Further, as many political elites in the new states have discovered, the actual ownership of the means of production may be less important than the mechanisms of control and the orientations of the enterprise. The simple fact of public ownership does not insure that resources will be used for the public good. On the other hand, though the agency houses of the colonial systems were privately owned, this did not prevent them from gaining political support for policies and profit levels that the market conditions alone would not justify.

In both cases another set of issues lies behind the issue of ownership. An article by Hla Myint opens this section with a statement of the fundamental issue of *discipline* and *flexibility*, a conflicting set of demands in the current condition of most backward economies. Using Rostow's stage terminology, Myint argues that the stage of social organization of the new states implies a conflicting set of demands for the achievement of economic development. He avoids the issue of nationalization versus private ownership, and heavy versus light industry. He observes that some social discipline is required to provide the mobilization of effort needed to increase productive capacity, but some flexibility is also needed to provide adaptable skills for a social and economic organization whose form and specific needs are not yet known. Further, by focusing on the issue of conceptualization, Myint provides a formulation that is generally applicable. At certain stages in an economy's development political forces may be necessary to provide the setting that allows market forces to work for the broader public good. Although this is generally overlooked, the same argument was made by the imperial powers in the last century. Military and political forces had to be used to provide by force the kind of setting in which rational market calculations could be made, which would in the long run provide higher productivity and increased public welfare.

Alexander Eckstein reinforces Myint's analysis on the side of flexibility. Shanti Tangri focuses on the issue of efficiency in economic organization. Morris Watnik reinforces it on the side of discipline. And Bert Hoselitz joins the two together again with a slightly different formulation. Nationalism, he points out, has both positive, inclusive aspects and negative, exclusive aspects. A dilemma is reached when we observe that in the backward economies, nationalism often produces a powerful ideology for development and for greater equality, while the great social cleavages between masses and a small elite produce tendencies toward autocratic rule for greater social discipline.

Finally, Bruce Glassburner and Hans Schmidt illustrate an important aspect of the problem with two slightly different analyses in the specific case of Indonesia. In that case a series of highly complicating and conflicting issues was raised: between foreign and indigenous private ownership and activity in the economy, between interests of consumption and of economically rational investment, and between specific groups—indigenous bureaucrats, agriculturalists, foreign owners, and indigenous private business interests. Ultimately, the failure to resolve the conflicts was a political one. The political system failed to provide mobilization and long-term support for any program or any positive policy. Cabinets moved into and out of power so rapidly that economic policy never had the opportunity to move beyond short-range fiscal policy. This produced a series of failures and crises that led to a complete expulsion of the Dutch foreign interests. In the long run this may have been necessary for the development of the Indonesian economy, but in the short run it produced widespread economic failure. One of the results of this failure, which goes beyond the period of the Glassburner–Schmidt analyses, was the breakdown of order and the widespread violence that attended the fall of President Sukarno in late 1965 and early 1966.

The analysis of Indonesia provides an illustration of a useful classification of the new states. Some, as Indonesia, obtained independence in a period of outright struggle and violence. Their subsequent policies have emphasized the break with the metropolitan power and the social and economic organization that it produced. In these cases the dominant goals of the polity have been goals of change. The public rhetoric and much of the specific policy has emphasized the necessity of destroying the evils of the old system and of producing a new type of system.

Other new states, such as Malaysia and the Philippines and to a lesser extent India, have experienced a more peaceful transition to independence. Consequently, the political emphasis has been on development, on working to increase the productive and distributive capacity of the existing economic system, with the long-run aim of changing the distribution of wealth between foreign and indigenous elements.

Whatever the long run may show, the short run displays a moving irony. The emphasis on change seems normally to have produced only a destruction of the economy, with changes primarily in a negative direction. Thus, Schmidt asks whether there may not be a necessary association between the observed historical association between the expulsion of Dutch economic interests and the stagnation of the economy in Indonesia. States that have been more concerned with development than with change, on the other hand, may well have laid the foundation for a more profound long-term change based on the powerful forces of economic development as well as producing higher levels of welfare in the short run.

Whatever the final outcome, it is clear that political forces now play a dominant role in determining the rate and direction of economic development.

SOCIAL FLEXIBILITY,
SOCIAL DISCIPLINE
AND ECONOMIC GROWTH

Hla Myint

There are wide variations in the general level of social and economic development, not only between different underdeveloped countries but also within each underdeveloped country. The anthropologists have concentrated on one end of the scale and have mainly concerned themselves with the countries at the earlier stages of development or with the economically backward sectors within these countries. The economists, on the other hand, tend to concentrate on the opposite end of the scale and have mainly concerned themselves with underdeveloped countries at the later stages of development or with the more advanced sectors within these countries. Unfortunately, some of the more important and interesting problems of development arise within the wide no-man's-land of the intermediate stages of development, those which have passed beyond the purview of the anthropologists but have not come squarely into the purview of the economists.

The economist's view of the no-man's-land can be best illustrated in terms of Professor Rostow's theory of the 'take-off' into self-sustained economic growth. Most underdeveloped countries aspire to 'take off' in the manner described by Professor Rostow, but only a few are ready for the

From Hla Myint, "Social Flexibility, Social Discipline and Economic Growth," *International Social Science Journal*, 16:2:252–260 (1964). Reprinted by permission of UNESCO, Paris.

process in the sense that they are anywhere near fulfilling all three of the related conditions he has laid down for a successful take-off. These are: '(a) a rise in the rate of productive investment from (say) 5 per cent or less to over 10 per cent of national income (or net national product); (b) the development of one or more substantial manufacturing sectors, with a high rate of growth; (c) the existence or quick emergence of a political, social and institutional framework which exploits the impulses to expansion in the modern sector and the potential external economy effects of the take-off and gives to growth an ongoing character.'[1]

The underdeveloped countries trying to accelerate their economic growth generally turn their attention to Professor Rostow's conditions (a) and (b). They tend to ignore the elusive condition (c) which turns out to be the most important of the three in the sense that unless it is fulfilled to some degree it is not possible to keep the two other conditions fulfilled for long. Thus, according to the historical instances given by Professor Rostow of the countries which have successfully taken off in the past, condition (a) means not merely raising the rate of capital formation above 10 per cent of the national income as a once-for-all effort, but keeping the economy at this high level of capital formation for at least two or three decades before it can hope to attain a self-sustaining momentum of growth. This requires a capacity not only to mobilize savings but also to 'absorb' capital and invest it productively to yield a high enough rate of return to sustain the continuous process of a high rate of reinvestment, which is beyond the present capabilities of the institutional and organizational framework of many underdeveloped countries. Similarly, condition (b) does not merely mean setting up a few factories which are indifferently run and managed and have to be maintained by heavy subsidy or protection from the government. It requires the development of the 'primary growth sectors', based on innovations, new methods of production, discoveries of new resources and new ways of exploiting existing resources which will serve as the 'leading sectors' to the rest of the economy. Here again the important role of the institutional framework both in stimulating these vital points of growth and in transmitting their effects to the rest of the economy is fairly obvious.

The truth of the matter is that although economic writings on the underdeveloped countries are full of proposals to launch them into self-sustained growth, only a few of these countries are ready for it. Many of them are handicapped by the lack of an effective institutional framework required for the process. To expand Professor Rostow's metaphor: a few of the underdeveloped countries, ready for the take-off, are already taxiing along the runway. For them the final spurt of speed in investment and general economic activity, if properly carried out and sustained, might conceivably enable them

[1] W. W. Rostow, *The Stages of Economic Growth* (Cambridge, The University Press, 1960), p. 39.

to become airborne. But many other underdeveloped countries have not yet got to this stage; they are still in the process of building their runways. Now, whether we are talking about aeroplanes or developing economies, we should expect the problems of getting airborne to be very different from the problems of building the runway. But unfortunately Professor Rostow does not give us very much help about the second type of problem. He has merely stated that before the underdeveloped countries are ready for the final take-off they have to pass through a long 'pre-take-off' period, which in the case of the Western countries, for instance, took about a century or more. Beyond this, we are left to our own devices to try to identify the various sub-stages of the pre-take-off period at which many of the underdeveloped countries seem to be situated at the present moment, and to try to assess how far economic policies designed to assist the take-off at a later stage of development are relevant for the problems of building the runway at the earlier stages of development.

This tendency to neglect the earlier pre-take-off stages of the underdeveloped countries is of course not peculiar to Professor Rostow but is fairly widespread among economists. We have chosen his theory as our example because it is well known and also because it is explicitly stated in terms of stages of development, thus clearly revealing the gap in our knowledge about the earlier stages of economic development represented by the no-man's-land between anthropology and economics.

From the economist's side of the border, however, two distinct lines of approach have been made to explore the no-man's-land. The first consists in the various studies of the process of the spread of the money economy in the markets for commodities and for factors of production, notably labour, breaking down the self-sufficiency of the subsistence economies of the traditional societies. In this approach, the problem of stimulating economic development is looked upon mainly in terms of the growth of free market institutions and the growth of competitive economic individualism, breaking down the traditional communalism of the village, the tribe or the extended family. The general direction of development is conceived in terms of greater flexibility and adaptability of the social and economic framework, stimulating and responding to further changes. The second line of approach consists in extending the ideas of investment and capital formation originally used in relation to material capital, to 'social and human capital'. In this approach, the problem of economic growth is looked upon mainly in terms of increasing the rate of investment, not only in improving the physical infrastructure such as transport and communications and public utilities, but also in improving what may be called the 'social infrastructure', notably in the level of education, research, technical skills and health. In order to increase the rate of investment, an increasing amount of resources has to be mobilized, and in order effectively to carry out this programme of investment both in material and human capital, the social and institutional framework must be capable of enforcing some degree of consistency and coherence both in the mobilization and in the allocation of resources. Thus the general direction of development is conceived in terms of a greater degree of social discipline and authority to push through the desired pattern of economic planning. We are faced then with the conflicting requirements of social flexibility and social discipline, a conflict which seems particularly sharp at the earlier, pre-take-off stages of development.

II

Since the broad patterns of the growth of the money economy in the underdeveloped countries are familiar, we shall concentrate on the second line of approach based on investment in social and human capital. This idea has proved attractive to many people, both economists and non-economists, and there have been attempts to consider how to strike a correct balance between investment in material capital and investment in human capital, between economic development and social development. Unfortunately, however, as currently stated this idea remains rather vague, based upon an analogy which has not been systematically drawn. Thus, as a possible subject for discussion among social scientists of different disciplines, we may begin by drawing attention to some of the conceptual problems as they appear to an economist.

To begin with, even with respect to material capital, there is no simple mechanical relationship between the amount of resources invested and the *value* of the capital formation which results from it. Although national income statistics automatically equate the two, it can readily be seen that, say, an amount of one million pounds of savings invested may result in capital goods which may be worth many times more or many times less than one million pounds, depending on how and where it is invested and how far the resultant capital goods serve the future productive requirements of the country, and how far people value the products which these capital goods can help to produce. In the extreme case, it has not been unknown that large sums of money have been so wrongly invested as to serve no useful purpose so that the value of capital formation resulting from them is zero. The problems of trying to establish a causal quantitative relation between the expenditure on resources invested and the value of capital formation which results from it are multiplied many times when we move from material capital to human capital. To start with the most general difficulty: in dealing with material capital the economists have a reasonably clear idea of what they mean by the productive structure and how an additional piece of material capital may contribute to it, either by changing and improving its efficiency or by fitting into an identifiable gap. But no such established conceptual framework exists when we move to human capital. By analogy, we must suppose that the value of a given investment in human capital will depend on its contribution to the 'social infrastructure', either by improving and changing this infrastructure or by fitting into a gap in it. But what is this 'social infrastructure' and in what direction do we wish to change and improve it?

At this point the economist will look askance at the social scientists from other disciplines, many of whom have been using the fashionable concept of 'social and human capital' as much as some of the economists. If hard pressed to define the 'social infrastructure' further, the economist can only carry the analogy one or two stages further. He would suppose that in the same way as there is an intimate connexion between the material production structure of a country and its natural resources, there would be a similar connexion between the social infrastructure and the social conditions and characteristics of a country. Material production structure represents the adaptation and improvement of natural resources through investment in material capital. Some investment would exploit the special advantages of these natural resources and other investment would make up for the deficiencies in these natural resources. He would then have to ask the other social scientists whether this analogy is meaningful when extended to cover the relationship between the social infrastructure and the social conditions of a country.

Carrying the analogy a stage further, the economist would point out that the consequences of a wrong choice of investment project may be very different between material capital and human capital. Frequently, a wrong investment in material capital and attempts to salvage it have a distorting effect on the whole production structure. For instance, a wrongly sited railway system or a factory which is a 'show piece' but uneconomic may be maintained by government subsidy, grants of exclusive monopolistic privileges or protection against foreign competitors. But as a last resort a wrong investment in material capital can be scrapped when it proves too expensive to salvage. Wrong choice of investment in human capital will presumably have similar distorting effects on the social infrastructure, but wrong pieces of human capital cannot be scrapped; they tend to be self-perpetuating and have the habit not merely of distorting but actually of disrupting the social infrastructure. For instance, the growing problem of graduate unemployment in Asian countries, owing to the production of too much of the wrong type of 'human capital' is a very clear illustration of this danger.[2]

In this connexion, it may be noted that for the economist the material production structure of a country is a different thing from the economic institutions which mobilize resources and feed them into the production

[2] H. Myint, 'The Universities of South-East Asia and Economic Development', *Pacific Affairs* (Summer 1962).

structure. But when we come to the concept of social infrastructure, the distinction between these two different functions is blurred. As currently used, the idea of social infrastructure seems both to serve as the social equivalent of the production structure which absorbs resources and also to have the more active function of the social and institutional framework which mobilizes and allocates resources. This makes assessment of the productivity of investment in human capital doubly difficult. For instance, increased educational opportunities, say through films, radio and other mass media, may widen the horizons of the people and stimulate the growth of new wants (through demonstration effects) and new ideas. This may possibly increase the long-run productivity of the people and thus may be regarded as an improvement in the social infrastructure in the first sense. But on the other hand, the effect of these new educational opportunities may also weaken and disrupt the ability of existing social values and social hierarchies to mobilize resources and thus undermine the social infrastructure in the second sense.

III

We started by saying that the conflicting requirements of social flexibility and social discipline in promoting economic development at the earlier, pre-take-off stages of development can be illustrated by two approaches: the first in terms of the growth of the money economy, and the second in terms of increasing investment in social and human capital. It now appears that this conflict is latent even if we concentrate on the second approach only, although to some extent it is hidden by the vagueness in the concept of the 'social infrastructure'. Certain changes which might widen the educational horizon of a people, and thus increase their longer-run productivity, might at the same time undermine the capacity of the social and institutional framework to mobilize resources for the increase of capital formation, both human and material.

This conflict may be further illustrated by human investment in higher education for economic development where the greatest long-run increases in productivity have been frequently claimed. When people make this claim, they have two distinct ideas at the back of their minds. First, they are thinking of the dynamic effects of higher education in stimulating new discoveries and innovations and in adopting new methods of production. This implies a sort of intellectual yeast which will ferment and change the whole of the production structure and presumably the social infrastructure with it. Here the productivity of investment in human capital is conceived in terms of greater flexibility and adaptability of the social and institutional framework, which will create favourable conditions both in stimulating changes and for receptiveness and adaptability to these changes. Secondly, they are also thinking of shortages of skilled people of particular types who are needed as 'missing components' to be fitted into a desired pattern of economic development. Of course, some flexibility has to be allowed even in the most rigid and comprehensive type of planning. But it is fair to say that the *basic* reasons for c'aiming high productivity as a result of investment in education are different in these two types of argument. In popular terms, the first type of argument is thinking in terms of creating square pegs to fit into round holes with the hope that the pattern of holes will be stretched and changed into more productive directions. The second type of argument is thinking in terms of trying to create round pegs to fit into round holes, as though fitting the missing pieces into a jigsaw puzzle within the framework of a given and fixed pattern of production and planning requirements.

These conflicting considerations become bewildering when we look closely at the skilled manpower problems of any newly independent countries. First, there is an obvious need to fill up the gaps left in the civil service, and those left in all sectors of the economy by departing foreign personnel. The missing components have to be produced to maintain the old economic and administrative structure. But at the same time there is a great desire to change very quickly 'the old colonial structure', not only politically but also economically and socially. Logically, one might perhaps expect a great upsurge of a liberal educational policy encouraging individualism, enterprise and innovations to break down the rigidities both of the traditional and of the colonial systems. But given the prevailing intellectual view that such quick change can be forced through only by economic planning, the prevailing bias is against both economic liberalism and 'liberal education' in favour of detailed skilled manpower planning integrated with programmes of technical education which ideally should specify the exact type of training and the exact number of trainees. Thus we get back to the problem of manufacturing the 'missing components' for the jigsaw puzzle, the only trouble being that the old puzzle has been torn down and the new puzzle has not been constructed.

If the newly independent countries are vague and ambivalent about the general direction in which they wish to change their 'social infrastructure', the social forces and the social and institutional framework which they can use to carry out these changes are weak and diffused and in varying stages of disintegration. On the economic side, it is well known that the growth of the money economy, while imparting flexibility, has undermined the coherence of the traditional societies. On the political side, even indirect rule through indigenous authorities has frequently had the same effect. With the new countries which have gone through an intense phase of nationalistic revolt against colonialism, this process itself has further undermined the framework of social authority and discipline. Thus the difficulties which new countries have in trying to implement their plans is not only due to the lack of technical skills and know-how, but also to a disintegration, if not a complete breakdown, of cohesive social values which contribute to social discipline.

The value of a cohesive force of social discipline in promoting economic development is now becoming increasingly recognized. The classical illustration of this is perhaps the role of the Japanese 'feudal discipline' which enabled Japan's ruling classes to carry out a fairly ruthless but effective process of economic development behind a protective shell against disruptive outside influences. It would be an interesting task to find out how far the surviving traditional social institutions in a continent like Africa are capable of serving this role in promoting economic development both at the local or tribal level, such as in co-operative societies and community development schemes, and for larger units which can take advantage of the economies of scale and complementary projects. One obvious difficulty about using the traditional social forces such as 'feudalism' or the caste system is the prevailing political idea of equality which raises the well known conflict between economic equality and economic growth, not only with respect to income distribution but also with respect to the distribution of economic activities and economic and social roles. To illustrate from our example of investment in education: many people, even when they stress the importance of investment in human capital, look upon the resources to be invested mainly as sums of money or material resources, such as college buildings, laboratories, libraries, hospitals, etc. But as every university teacher knows, the really scarce resource is the 'human input': teachers of suitable ability and qualifications, the supply of whom cannot be expanded quickly in the short run, perhaps not dramatically even in the longer run. On the other hand, the production of further such high-quality human capital requires some restriction of entry to universities and training colleges so that those who are admitted get proper intensive training. But this conflicts with the prevailing ideals of new countries to provide university education for almost everyone, and few of the countries have been able to exercise the necessary social and political discipline to restrict numbers in this really vital process of supplying further human capital goods of suitable quality. That is to say, although most people talk about increasing 'investment in education', few of them are prepared to 'tighten their belts' to save the scarce teaching capacity for the training of further human capital to the minimum degree of 'capital intensity' necessary to make this process a success.[3]

IV

Our analysis in this paper is admittedly brief and impressionistic, but it is hoped that it has been sufficient for the purpose of establishing two propositions.

[3] H. Myint, *op. cit.*

The first and narrower proposition is that there are a number of conceptual problems in speaking about investment in 'social and human capital' which those who use this fashionable approach have not adequately explored. It would be nice if we could say that in a given situation the rate of return on investment, say in technical education, is 20 per cent and that since it is higher than the rate of return on investment in transport and communications, say 15 per cent, a larger proportion of investible funds should be transferred to the former from the latter to obtain a more correct balance between social and economic development. But we are nowhere near this blissful state of quantification. In fact in our present imperfect stage of knowledge, to try to make premature and somewhat pseudo-quantitative statements may distract attention from the important and complex qualitative problems about the relationship between economic growth and the social and economic framework in the countries at the earlier pre-take-off stages of general social and economic development. We have suggested that one convenient way of sorting out these qualitative problems is the conflicting requirements of social flexibility and social discipline which seem to have relevance for a large number of social situations at different stages of economic development.

The second and broader proposition is the existence of the wide no-man's-land of intermediate stages of social and economic development, of societies in transition, which seem to have passed the purview of conventionally-minded anthropologists and have not come within the purview of conventionally-minded economists even when they are concerned with the underdeveloped countries. We have suggested that some of the interesting and important problems of promoting economic development at this pre-take-off period, notably the problems of building the runway as distinct from the problems of the take-off, fall within this no-man's-land which needs to be jointly explored by economists and other social scientists. No doubt there are laggards on both sides of the borderland. Some economists still think in terms of bulldozing away the traditional social institutions of the underdeveloped countries as so many outmoded obstacles to development, and of substituting in their place their own special brand of mechanistic Utopia either in terms of atomistic perfect competition or completely integrated economic planning. Some anthropologists still think in terms of retreating further and further away from the borders of social and economic change so that they may study the dwindling areas of unspoilt primitive cultures intact. But the social reality facing the majority of the underdeveloped countries in a state of transition, with all its complex and conflicting drives, is somewhat more challenging and interesting than is suggested by the stereotype models of the economists and the anthropologists.

INDIVIDUALISM
AND THE ROLE OF THE STATE
IN ECONOMIC GROWTH

Alexander Eckstein

I

Economic growth can be viewed as a broadening of the range of alternatives open to society. Clearly, technological and resource constraints are likely to be so compelling and overriding in primitive or underdeveloped economies as to leave comparatively little scope for the exercise of choice—either individual or social. On the other hand, the situation is quite different—at least in degree—at more advanced stages of economic development. At these stages, one of the principal manifestations of this broadening in the range of alternatives is precisely the greater opportunity to exercise choice over the form in which choices in the economy become institutionalized. This, in turn, requires a delineation of the spheres of public vs. private choice and a determination of the relative weight of each sphere.

One of the aspects of individualism, and possibly the one most relevant for our purposes, is the scope for individual choice and decentralized decision-making in the economic sphere. In a preponderantly free enterprise market economy the institutionalization of these ingredients of individualism is more or less automatically assured. This does not, however, mean that this system necessarily assures equal scope for the exercise of choice on the

From Alexander Eckstein, "Individualism and the Role of the State in Economic Growth," *Economic Development and Cultural Change*, 6:2:81–87 (January 1958). Reprinted by permission of The University of Chicago Press.

part of all individuals in the economic system, or that it provides a greater scope for individual choice than an alternative system might. In contrast to preponderantly free enterprise market systems, in economies in which the public sector looms quite large, the scope for individual choice and decision making may be more a function of the political rather than the economic system. Thus the mechanism through which economic policy is formulated and the role of the ballot box in economic policy formulation become major conditioning factors.

In essence, what this suggests is that there is a potentially positive correlation between individualism and economic development. The extent to which this potential is translated into reality will depend upon the role played by individual choice and initiative in resource allocation, regardless of whether the choices and decisions are in fact arrived at primarily within the confines of the economic or political process. With this context in mind, let us attempt to spell out some of the factors and variables that are likely to condition the role the state may be expected or forced to play in the process of economic growth and its impact upon the position of the individual.

II

In analyzing the role of the state in the process of economic growth, the following elements may be considered as essential:

1. *The hierarchy of objectives, goals, and ends of economic development.* This necessarily involves an examination of both the qualitative and quantitative aspects, that is, the character, range, and variety of the ends sought as well as the level to be attained. The interplay of these dimensions of content, range, and level will be one of the principal factors defining the ambitiousness of the particular economic development program. In respect to content, several broad categories of objectives or motivations may be cited, for instance, those revolving around nationalism and those related to a striving for rising standards of living. In a sense, these might be considered as ultimate ends which need to be, and are in fact, broken down into a series of derived and possibly more concrete goals. Thus, at the stage when these objectives are disaggregated and sorted out as to the ranges and levels involved, they inevitably tend to become competitive rather than complementary entities in the sense that under *ceteris paribus* assumptions, the wider the range, the lower will have to be the level, and *vice versa*.

2. *The time horizon in economic development.* This entails a definition of the rate at which the goals are to be attained. In a sense, it is but

another aspect of the hierarchy of objectives, since rapid or leisurely growth may be an explicitly stated end in and of itself.

3. *The means available for attaining—at the desired rate—the content, range, and level of ends explicitly or implicitly formulated.* Here one would have to consider such variables as resource and factor endowments and the state of the arts prevailing in the particular economy.

4. *The structure and character of institutions: social, economic, and political.* This is possibly the most complex of all the categories listed here. The considerations most relevant for our purposes revolve around the rigidity of the institutional framework, its capacity to generate, absorb, and adapt itself to economic change and to the disruptive forces of industrialization. This would mean investigating factors such as the prevailing value system, class structure, social mobility, contractual and legal arrangements, degree and character of urbanization, land tenure system, degree of commercialization and monetization, character and structure of state organization, structure of political power, etc. However, analysis of these variables is greatly complicated by virtue of the fact that some of them are rather intangible, while their particular chemical mix—that is, the nature of combinations and interaction between the different institutional factors—and the reaction produced may be quite unpredictable. In effect, it is much easier to provide *ex post facto* rationalizations or explanations as to why and in what ways certain types of institutional structure were more conducive to industrialization than others, than to assess *ex ante* the height and the tensile strength of institutional barriers and their resistance to economic development.

5. *The relative backwardness of the economy.* From an economic point of view, relative backwardness—and the emphasis should be on relative—involves certain advantages and disadvantages. The disadvantages lie principally in the field of foreign trade, while the so called "advantages of backwardness" may be found in the realm of technology. Thus industrially advanced countries enjoy certain competitive advantages in world markets, and particularly in the markets of the underdeveloped areas themselves. This in and of itself can under certain conditions become a major handicap in the industrialization of backward countries. On the other hand, as Professor Gerschenkron has pointed out, one of the essential ingredients of relative backwardness is a gap in the levels of technology used and applied. Therefore the backward country can reap large potential gains by importing advanced technology from abroad and thus, in effect, make a technological leap from comparatively primitive to highly advanced levels.

At this point another aspect of relative backwardness may be usefully introduced, namely the gap in material welfare or standards of living, and the gap in national power produced by differences in levels of industrialization. All three of these gaps—in consumption, technology, and power—could be viewed as different aspects of a "demonstration effect" through which the gulf between a potential and actual state is forcefully brought home. Characteristically, it is in this shape that the pressure for industrialization of backward countries is manifested. Once the disequilibrating and innovating forces of modernization, industrialization, and urbanization have been introduced on an appreciable scale,[1] one could say that, *ceteris paribus*, the greater the relative backwardness, the more acute will tend to be the "tension" arising from this chasm between the potential and the actual, and thus the greater will be the pressure for industrialization.

Given the five categories of elements and variables considered above, we are now in a position to state our hypothesis concerning the conditions under which the state will tend to play a greater or lesser role in the process of economic growth. On this basis then one could say that:

a. The greater the range of ends and the higher the level of attainment sought;

b. the shorter the time horizon within which the ends are to be attained, that is, the more rapid the rate of economic growth desired;

c. the more unfavorable the factor and resource endowments;

d. the greater the institutional barriers to economic change and industrialization; and

e. the more backward the economy in relative terms

the greater will tend to be the urge, push, and pressure for massive state intervention and initiative in the process of industrialization, and at the same time, the greater will be the need for such intervention if a breakthrough, rather than a breakdown, is to be attained.

III

Assuming that the state is compelled to make a major commitment on behalf of industrialization, what types of measures may the state be expected to adopt and what effect may these have upon the position of the individual, or more specifically, upon the individual choice and decentralized decision-making in the economic sphere? From this point of view, a sharp distinction needs to be made between the elements and the degree of state power applied in the process of economic growth.

In analyzing the qualitative aspects of state intervention affecting the

[1] This scale effect is, of course, both crucial and indeterminate, in the sense that what will be the operationally significant range will inevitably vary from country to country, depending upon size, institutional framework, etc.

economic sphere, one could perhaps distinguish between five categories of action: provision of social overhead, provision of economic overhead, application of direct and indirect levers and controls, government operation of enterprises extending beyond the overhead sectors, and central planning.

Provision of social overhead might entail maintenance of law and order in the society, provision and enforcement of legal and contractual obligations, supply of educational, health, and social welfare facilities, assumption of military and defense functions, etc. In effect, these are categories of action which to the extent that they are provided at all, are usually furnished by public rather than private agencies.

Provision of economic overhead may involve the institution of central banking and of monetary and fiscal facilities, the development of a highway and railroad network and of other public utilities.

Application of direct or indirect levers and controls may be based on a wide variety of measures, such as introduction of tariffs, railroad rate discrimination, tax privileges and other types of subsidies, rationing of goods and of credit, price controls, etc.

Government operation of enterprises extending beyond the overhead sectors may range from management of some industries, or a few firms in different industries, to public ownership of all means of production.

Central planning may involve more or less total concentration of economic decision-making in the hands of a national planning board.

Admittedly, this fivefold classification is arbitrary, and the line of demarcation between the different categories is quite blurred. Yet, in terms of their effect upon the exercise of individual choice and initiative, they present qualitatively rather significant differences. Thus, most of the items in the first two categories belong to what, in industrializing societies at least, are usually considered as the minimal and essential functions of a state. In contrast, centralized and comprehensive planning combined with total government operation of the economy may be regarded as maximum functions. One of the key questions that needs to be posed in this context is which one, or which combination, of categories will the state use to promote economic development? Whichever means it uses, how massively, to what degree, and with what intensity will it apply its power to the provision of these different categories? Moreover, how will particular kinds and degrees of state intervention affect factor supply, particularly the supply of capital and entrepreneurship?

It may turn out that the more massively and rapidly the state provides what can be considered its minimum functions, the less may be the pressure or the need for it to provide the maximum functions. Therefore, the reliance upon maxima may in effect be a function of past and current failure to provide the minima. In these terms, then, one could say that a necessary precondition for the broadening of opportunities for the exercise of individual choice, individual initiative, and the growth of individual values in underdeveloped countries, launched on a development program, is a high degree and rapid application of state power for the supply of social and economic overhead, combined with partial controls and planning as circumstances may demand them.

Theoretically one could, of course, visualize a system in which amidst public ownership of the means of production, national planning, and resource allocation was—within wide limits—based upon the operation of free consumer choice and consumer autonomy. Realistically, however, it would be extremely difficult to build sufficient checks and balances into such a Lange-like model to prevent it from slipping into a totalitarian mold. On the other hand, this is much less true in the case of partial planning and partial government operation of enterprises, which in many situations is needed to reinforce the provision of social and economic overheads, if comprehensive government planning and management is to be avoided.

The failure of the state in the minimum fields tends to be more or less directly reflected in capital formation and the growth of entrepreneurship. Thus, in many traditional societies, accumulations of merchant and other forms of capital tend to be dissipated because of: (a) the absence of adequate and contractual arrangements to protect these holdings from the more or less arbitrary ravages of officialdom, and (b) the failure of the state to institute a social security system, so that old age assistance, poor relief, and similar functions must be privately assumed through the family and kinship system. At the same time, condition (a) tends to reinforce the economic risks of various types of business and industrial investments. Moreover, the same condition further encourages the flow of capital into land investment, which in an environment of acute population pressure and agrarian value orientation, represents one of the safest and most profitable forms of holding. However, from the standpoint of the economy, this is merely a transfer payment, ultimately representing a leakage of investment into consumption. In effect, then, this is a milieu in which the state—through sins of commission and omission—tends to undercut actual and potential sources of capital accumulation, while at the same time making its contribution to the narrowing of business opoprtunities. Under these conditions the scarcities of entrepreneurial and technical talent tend to be further intensified through the neglect of education facilities. Morover, to the extent that some education is provided, its orientation is frequently inhospitable to the growth of scientific and technical knowledge.

Viewed in these terms, perhaps one of the most important contributions the pre-industrial European city made to the industrialization of the continent was that it provided a legally and more or less militarily protected haven for the accumulation and conservation of capital, and for its investment in fields that were eminently productive from a point of view of economic development.

Amidst such circumstances, the formidable barriers to modernization and industrialization are likely to be perpetuated, while economic, social, and political tensions mount under the impact of innovating influences ushered in—as a rule—through foreign contact. Unless some means are found for alleviating these tensions through a process of change and adaptation, the potentially explosive forces in society may be expected to burst forth, sweeping away the old order, capturing the state, and using it as a total and far-reaching instrument for mounting an industrial revolution.

On this basis, one could argue that if India, for instance, wishes to avoid a totalitarian path to industrialization, her current plans and efforts do not provide for enough, rather than for too much, state intervention. Thus the large gap in the financial resources available for the implementation of the Second Five Year Plan may be a symptom of the inability and the reluctance of the Indian state to mobilize the means adequate for the implementation of the ends sought. But, even more fundamentally, perhaps, the inadequacy of the government efforts to spread adult education—both basic and technical education—rapidly, may be an important factor in inhibiting the attainment of certain economic objectives, while at the same time it serves to reinforce the great gulf between the small elite and the rural masses—a factor representing marked potential dangers in the political realm.

To sum up this phase of my argument, it may perhaps be useful to attempt to work with the concept of an "optimum level and pattern of state intervention" parallelling other optima—e.g., the optimum propensity to consume—incorporated in different types of economic and social science models. For our present purposes, this optimum would have to be defined in relation to two broad sets of objectives, i.e., striving for rising standards of living combined with an increase and/or preservation of the scope for the exercise of individual choice and initiative. The definition would also have to take account of the specific circumstances in each case, particularly in relation to the qualitative and quantitative aspects of state intervention, and to the variables listed in Section II above.

IV

We have discussed thus far the role the state may need to play in the process of economic growth without any reference to the character of the state and its capacity to perform the tasks required of it. Historically, however, particularly in the underdeveloped countries, the state—and the social structure on which it was based—was one of the very agencies hampering economic development. The same conditions that create the need for massive state intervention, in one form or another, also tend to breed a type of state which is singularly unequipped to intervene effectively on behalf of economic development. That is, economic backwardness is usually associated with political and other forms of backwardness.

Thus in China, for instance, the state has played a passive to actively negative role *vis à vis* the economy. The very concept of economic change and economic dynamism was alien to such a society with the nexus between economic growth and national power and/or welfare only very dimly understood, if perceived at all. The function of the economy was a largely static one, being charged with the primary task of supporting the ruling elite. Therefore, the state assumed very few responsibilities in the economy, beyond assuring that it would provide a stable, continuing, and adequate source of revenue for the imperial household and the gentry-bureaucracy.

The continuing failure of the traditional Chinese state to respond to the challenge of modernization, the institutional rigidities permeating the traditional social structure, the incapacity and unwillingness of the ruling classes to come to terms with change, their inability to understand the character of the innovating influences and to follow a policy of enlightened self-interest, have all served to retard the process of industrialization for so long that cumulative tensions of such explosive proportions were generated that they could no longer be contained, while at the same time perhaps nothing short of such an explosive force could have broken the shackles of the old order and swept away the barriers to economic growth. The violent eruption of the Chinese economy into what seems to bear the earmarks of an industrial revolution under totalitarian control can thus be viewed as an illustration of a resort to maximum solutions in the face of repeated and continued failure of the old state to perform and furnish the minimal functions referred to in the preceding section.

This course of development contrasts sharply with that experienced in Japan, where the breakdown of the old order accelerated by innovating influences produced a realignment of elites. The new elite, which bore some continuity with the old, then set out very deliberately to use the state as an instrument for modernization and industrialization. In doing this, the state from the outset paid major attention to developing rapidly the social and economic overhead sectors and to provide a general framework within which all types of enterprises, private and public, large and small, would grow. The state in effect conceived its role as initiator and promoter of the development process, leaving much of the execution to private enterprise.

While this is not intended to suggest that the Japanese experience can necessarily be duplicated in other countries, and in different circumstances, it is worthwhile to note that the state was able to perform this kind of a role amidst conditions which *ex ante* would have seemed exceptionally unfavorable. Not only were factor and resource endowments poor—in many respects poorer, perhaps not only absolutely but relatively, than those of some major underdeveloped areas today—but institutional barriers were formidable too.

However, an analysis of the conditions under which the state would or would not be *capable* of performing the functions required of it would be beyond the scope of this paper. Rather, I have tried to confine myself more specifically to a spelling out of the conditions under which and the ways in which the state may be *required* to assume a large role in initiating and promoting economic development without jeopardizing the growth of opportunities for the exercise of individual choice and initiative in the economic sphere.

ECONOMIC SYSTEMS
AND ECONOMIC EFFICIENCY

Shanti S. Tangri

All economic systems share some ends and some means for attaining those ends though the emphasis placed on the attainment of different ends and the use of different means varies in different systems and indeed in different economies within each system. If systems had nothing in common, it would be meaningless to compare them.[1]

Efficiency means the achievement of given ends (output) with minimum means (input) or getting maximum output with a given input. This general definition, however, needs to be adapted according to the nature of both means and ends. Thus, economic efficiency for a household usually implies its maximization of income with the services and resources it wants to sell and the maximization of its satisfaction from its expenditure and saving decisions. For a firm, similarly, economic efficiency means the maximization of profits—the difference between the value of its output and the cost of inputs. The profit to be maximized, however, may be for the current period, or for a finite time span, or may represent the discounted present value of all future profits.

Maximization of current net income by firms or of utility by households is the most commonly used meaning of economic efficiency and may be called

From Shanti S. Tangri, "Economic Systems and Economic Efficiency," *Asian Economic Review*, 10:1:18–29 (November 1967). Reprinted by permission of The Indian Institute of Economics.
[1] See Carl Landauer, *Contemporary Economic Systems* (Lippincott, Philadelphia, New York 1964), pp. 6–11, 17–23.

micro-static efficiency. Under certain conditions, such maximization in each period is necessary for maximization over time. Under other conditions short-run or microstatic efficiency conflicts with long-run or microdynamic efficiency.[2] The same argument applies to the efficiency of an economy as a whole. Macrostatic and macrodynamic efficiency may or may not be consistent.

Stability, full employment, social security, education, rising standards of living and health, economic growth, and decreased income inequalities have become some of the common goals of contemporary economic systems. The achievement of these goals provides criteria for measuring the economic efficiency of systems. It appears that most systems are also increasingly accepting the notion that widening opportunities for individuals in the development of their latent aptitudes and in the choice of their vocation, place of work and residence and in the disposition of their incomes is an important goal of social and economic development.

Yet another meaning of efficiency at the micro or the macro level may be borrowed from cybernetics. A system or sub-system which needs minimal control and supervision, once it is in operation, is more efficient than one which needs continuous and intensive manipulation to keep it on course. It was, perhaps, this that Lange had in mind when he remarked that the extensive and crude physical controls which are necessary in centrally planned economies in their earlier stages of development become barriers to efficiency once these economies have been launched successfully on the course of sustained growth.[3] In this sense command economies are inefficient. As these economies grow and become more complex, the persistence of older ways of centralized physical planning and controls become increasingly anachronistic resulting in what might be called "system inefficiency" or perhaps "servo-mechanistic inefficiency".

Demand economies, until the second world war, had a poor record of stability, whereas, command economies performed rather efficiently in this sense. Since the war, however, demand economies have produced a remarkable record of stability. Governments have been building more and more automatic fiscal and monetary stabilizers into their economies. The public

[2] John Kenneth Galbraith thus argues that the microstatic inefficiencies implicit in monopolistic market structures in the U.S. are more than offset by the dynamic efficiency of monopolies, while highly competitive industries such as textiles and agriculture which allocate resources very efficiently at any given point of time are dynamically inefficient; see, *American Capitalism: The Concept of Countervailing Power* (Houghton Mifflin, Boston, 1956), rev. ed. Earlier, Joseph A. Schumpeter, in several of his writings had defended the role of patent rights and other transitory monopolistic practices as necessary for innovation and growth. See e.g., *Capitalism, Socialism in a Democracy* (1942) (Harper, 1950), 3rd. ed., pp. 87–106.

[3] Oskar Lange, "The Role of Planning in Socialist Economy," in Oskar Lange (ed.), *Problems of Political Economy of Socialism* (People's Publishing House, New Delhi, 1962), pp. 16–30.

and politicians are increasingly committed to the belief that the promotion of full employment, stability and growth are legitimate and essential functions of government. Economists and econometricians are increasingly refining their policy instruments.

The continuing improvement in the system efficiency of the demand economies is reflected in two decades of high rates of growth. Economic fluctuations of the fifties, mild as they were compared to those of the pre-war period, have become even more damped in the sixties. There are good reasons to believe that this upward trend in systems-efficiency will continue in demand economies.

Even in an underdeveloped economy like India's, in which automatic stabilizers and fiscal monetary instruments are far less developed, there has been a much better record of stability than in Communist China. Thus, India's economic growth over the past fifteen years has been rather steady, whereas, the Communist Chinese economy has displayed considerable instability. In the thirteen years from 1952 to 1965 per capita output in both economies seems to have risen by about 25 per cent. In the first seven years, Chinese growth was about twice as fast as India's; in the next two years, per capita output declined to levels below that of 1952; by 1965, per capita output had recovered to the 1957 level.[4]

Totalitarian societies, with their passion for total commitment to causes, and their penchant for doing things in a big way, seem to register colossal achievements and gigantic failures. A Great Leap Forward gone wrong becomes a Great Leap Backward. Indeed, instability seems to have been more a characteristic of command economies than of demand economies in the post second world war era.

One of the common and most important goals of all contemporary economic systems is economic growth, which enables many of their other goals to be achieved over time, even though in the short run these goals may be competitive rather than complementary. In the rest of this paper I will be concerned with the relative efficiency of economic systems in achieving this goal.

The nature and pace of economic growth, to a large measure, is dependent on how a society answers the questions that face all societies: what to produce? how much? for whom? and how? The questions can be answered in three ways:[5]

(1) by following the dictates of a single individual such as a king, a general, a patriarch, or a priest, or the dictates of a small group of people

---

[4] For tables and sources see, Clair Wilcox, Willis D. Weatherford, Holland Hunter, and Morton S. Baratz, *Economies of the World Today* (Harcourt, Brace and World, Inc., New York) (2nd ed.), p. 123.

[5] Gregory Grossman, "Notes for a Theory of the Command Economy," *Soviet Studies*, Vol. XV; No. 2 (Oct. 1963), pp. 101–123 and Robert L. Heilbroner, *The Making of Economic Society* (Prentice-Hall, Englewood Cliffs, N.J., 1962), pp. 9–17.

such as a military junta, a party committee, an oligarchy of wealth or of old families;

(2) by following the dictates of all the individuals and groups in or outside the geographical or political boundaries of the community who enter the market as buyers and suppliers of goods and services; and

(3) by following the dictates of tradition and custom handed down from generation to generation.

While all systems use elements of all three mechanisms, systems can be classified according to the mechanism they are most: command, demand, or tradition.

The traditional system is not well suited to the tasks of economic change. If "what was good enough for Jonah is good enough for me" is a basic tenet of belief in a society it is unlikely by its own efforts to achieve a standard of living much above that of Jonah.

Communist nations rely largely on command mechanisms. Demand plays a role in these economies but at the behest of the power elite who stand ready to restore the hegemony of command mechanisms. If they permit market forces to operate in vast areas of the economy for a generation or more it might, indeed, not be easy to restore command mechanisms. But there is a conjecture about the future. Meanwhile, even significant decentralization, as in Yugoslavia since 1957 or in Czechoslovakia since 1962, does not amount to autonomy of consumers and producers. It constitutes delegation of powers which can be withdrawn.

Influenced by the writings of classical economists and Utilitarian Radicals of the 18th and 19th century such as Adam Smith and John Stuart Mill, economists (and large numbers of laymen in the west) had come to believe that individual liberty is a necessary and often a sufficient condition for economic growth and conversely slavery in any form is an inefficient economic institution.

Much of the discussion about the comparative economic merits of alternative systems has suffered from the fact that many writers have assumed, often implicitly, that the only valid meaning of economic efficiency is the efficiency of individual production and consumption units. In a pure exchange economy without production and uncertainty, and with the usual and rigorous assumptions made in models of perfect competition, at any given point of time if all units are behaving efficiently, indeed the system as a whole would also be efficient and *vice-versa*. Micro-static efficiency in other words, then, also implies macro-static efficiency. One could argue that this holds for a primitive or traditional static economy based largely on barter. This conclusion, however, becomes debatable once production, investment, uncertainty, change, structural and institutional rigidities, imperfect knowledge and imperfect foresight are introduced into the picture.

In such a world of reality, all producers and consumers may be efficient in the micro-static sense yet the system as a whole may be operating with significant levels of unemployment of land, labour, capital and other resources. The system, in other words, may be inefficient macro-statically. Again the system may be efficient in both the micro and the macro sense but only statically. Individuals and communities could be very efficient in the production and consumption of current incomes. They could, however, consume all the current income and even their accumulated capital and in doing so, destroy their own or their children's future. Destruction of natural resources, inadequate conservation, and insufficient saving and capital formation in many economies are examples of this macro-dynamic inefficiency.

One could similarly speak of micro-dynamic efficiency, whereby, individual economic units, as producers and consumers, allocate their resources efficiently over time, and not simply at a point of time. Command economies severely limit the autonomy of individual economic units in making such decisions. Until the perfect computer with perfect information and with perfect controls over the population arrives on the scene to make and enforce all such decisions for individual economic units, command economies are unlikely to achieve such micro-dynamic efficiency.

Some economists, such as Von Mises, argued in the 1930's that a command economy in which individuals and private groups could not own property and buy and sell their material and non-material resources (land, labour, and capital) would have no genuine economic markets.[6] Consequently, they reasoned, production units would have no idea of the real (opportunity) costs of inputs or values of outputs, or, as Hayek argued, it would be extremely difficult to find these costs and values in practice even if these could be computed in theory.[7] Hence, efficient rational resources allocation (micro-static efficiency) would be impossible in such economies. This in turn meant, many believed, little or no growth in the economy (macro-dynamic inefficiency). Such neo-classical thought ignored or was unaware of the gains a command system could obtain from full, or fuller, employment of its resources (macro-static efficiency).[8]

The early dislocation of the Soviet economy under War Communism and its consequent recovery under a partial return to capitalistic markets

[6] Ludwig Von Mises, "Economic Calculation in the Socialist Commonwealth," in F. A. Hayek (ed.), *Collectivist Economic Planning* (Routledge, London, 1935), pp. 87–130.

[7] F. A. Hayek, "The Present State of the Debate," in Hayek, *op. cit.*

[8] John Maynard Keynes writings, such as *The General Theory of Employment, Interest and Money* (Harcourt, Brace, New York, 1936), shifted the attention of economists from problems of resource allocation to the macro problems of resource utilization (full employment) and were only peripherally concerned with problems of growth. Schumpeter deviated from classical and neo-classical thought in recognizing that capitalism may operate with less than full employment for long periods of time; but considered this a virtue. "A system—any system, economic or other—that at *every* point of time fully utilizes its possibilities to the best advantage may yet in the long run be inferior to a system that does so at *no* given point of time, because the latter's failure to do so may be a condition for the level or speed of long-run performance," *op. cit.*, p. 83.

under the New Economic Policy in the 1920's lent support to such views. However, the rapid growth of the Soviet economy, under planning since 1928, has belied these expectations. Most economists now believe that a command economy can force the pace of development by full mobilisation of its resources and by producing very high rates of investment (financed by forced savings) which could more than offset any decreases in output resulting from misallocation of resources over space and time, organizational inefficiency, and lack of adequate incentives for the mass of people. Soviet planning, it may be said, is inefficient micro-statically and micro-dynamically, but efficient macro-statically and macro-dynamically.

If the earlier view that a command system could not be efficient has been disproved by events and ideas it would be a mistake to go to the other extreme and assume that any command system, at any stage of development, is more efficient than a demand system. Many of the feudal and military command systems of the Middle East and Latin America have been and are being used effectively to sustain traditional ways of life inimical to change and growth. Command produces what the commander desires—change or stagnation. Communists inevitably, and military dictators occasionally, such as Kamal Ataturk in Turkey or Ayub Khan in Pakistan, desire change and economic growth intensely. Where a command system sustains, and is sustained by a "universalistic" ideology and a monolithic party structure and organized cadres as under Communism or Nazism, it is more likely to achieve its goals than a command system based only on military power, "particularistic" value systems and narrow interests of some families or clans.

If the system is totalitarian, i.e., it controls the social life in its totality, it is able to concentrate resources on a few chosen goals such as defense, space exploration, or heavy industry. Successes in a few selected areas overshadow the sluggishness or failures in sectors which tend to be neglected. The politically distrusted and powerless peasantry is usually the segment of population which suffers the most in such systems and the agricultural sector performs poorly.

Authoritarian systems, as under some Latin military dictatorships do not, by definition, have control over the totality of social life of the community. Their capacity to marshall resources for achieving ends is more limited than that of totalitarian systems. However, this weakness may be more than offset by gains of productivity resulting from the relative freedom and initiative of the peasantry and other productive groups if the ruling elite are interested in economic growth. The authoritarian governments of Japan were more successful in generating agricultural progress by teaching the peasant how to produce better while Stalin's totalitarian techniques yielded poor agricultural results.[9]

[9] W. Arthur Lewis, *The Theory of Economic Growth* (Irwin, Homewood, Ill., 1955), pp. 136, 188–189, 244, 279, 388, 407.

It is debatable whether the command systems of the Russian and other Communist economies are logical derivations of the Marxist-Leninist ideology or are the children of historical circumstances including chance.

A command system may be quite efficient, as Arthur Lewis has pointed out, when the economy is simple, its goals are few (as during a war), the mass of people are ignorant and the chief knows better. The same command system however may become very inefficient when the economy, as a result of growth, becomes complex and people more informed and the chief then cannot know better than millions of reasonably informed consumers and producers.[10] Patterns of paternal care which make for healthy homes and growing children if maintained beyond childhood, may produce rebellious adolescents or apathetic adults.

This indeed may be the lesson that the Russians are learning as their economy moves into a complex industrial society manned by skilled, urbanized, and educated workers and professions. Also, when there is sufficiency of quantity in goods, quality comes to the fore. Output is output only if the buyer wants it, otherwise it represents wasted resources. The buyers become increasingly more selective with economic growth. With rising levels of income, therefore, the efficient allocation of resources for the production of goods in demand (micro-static efficiency) may indeed again become a crucial condition for the continuation of rapid growth (macro-dynamic efficiency).

Historically, capitalist economies have solved their economic problems largely as dictated by the changing patterns and volumes of market demand for various goods and services. While there has been a tendency to equate market demand with private demand (of consumers and producers), this is neither technically necessary nor historically correct. Governments in all capitalist systems have affected, and affect, the volume and composition of demand significantly. Traditionally government demand has been largely in the areas of defense, internal security, justice and a few other essential services which the community could not be supplied with adequately through the workings of the market mechanism. Japan represents perhaps the best example of activist governments which have used the market mechanism for transforming a feudal economy into a modern industrial economy. She has produced perhaps the most rapid rates of growth for almost a century. Most capitalist governments are increasingly expanding their role in controlling, regulating and sustaining market forces.

Individuals and groups whose poverty prevents their needs from being translated into demand in the economic markets have come to make their demands felt in the political markets, especially where free voting and po-

[10] *Ibid.*, pp. 80–84; also see Wilfred Malenbaum and Wolfgang Stolper, "Political Ideology and Economic Progress; The Basic Question," World Politics, XII, 3 (April 1960), pp. 413–421.

litical competition have become well established. Fiscal and monetary policies for full employment, social security, health insurance, unemployment insurance, subsidized farming, education, and health care are some of the measures adopted to satisfy the demands articulated in political markets.

Even nationalization reflects aspects of a demand system in a democratic community. Thus, the voters whose demand led to the nationalization of steel in post-war Britain, were able, when their demand changed, to bring about denationalization of the industry.

Economic and political markets complement and correct each other. The egalitarian political market (one man, one vote) tends to temper the harsh results of the weighted voting of the economic markets (more money, more influence), just as the economic markets are needed to set standards of costs, returns, and therefore, of efficiency which act as norms restraining bureaucracies from becoming economically irresponsible and wasteful.

But even if one kept to the conventional meaning of demand, nationalization of industry need not mean suppression of the market. As Lange, Taylor, Lerner[11] and others have argued, this may be a pattern for socialist economies in which consumers retain their sovereignty while a planning board sets prices (and only prices) to clear the markets. Yugoslavia was the first Communist country to introduce strong features of such a model of market Socialism. Czechoslovakia has plunged headlong into a variant of this system recently.[12] Other Eastern European economies are debating the issues and are experimenting piecemeal with market demand and decentralization. The success of Yugoslavia, which a decade ago could certainly have been classified as underdeveloped, suggests that centralized planning of the Russian variety need not be the best system even for a poor country,[13] and that simple economies in which the chief knows best may be rarer than we think.

Just as the centrally planned economies are learning the value of market forces for improving their micro-static and micro-dynamic efficiency, the capitalist economies have been learning the value of aggregative planning for improving their macro-static and macro-dynamic efficiency. Capitalism in Post-War Europe and Post-Eisenhower America has experienced accelerated rates of economic growth just at the time when the command systems are experiencing deceleration of their growth rates. Whether these new trends

[11] Oskar Lange and Fred M. Taylor, *On the Economic Theory of Socialism*, ed. and with an introduction by Benjamin E. Lippincott (University of Minnesota Press, Minneapolis, 1938), (McGraw Hill, New York, 1961), paperback edition, Abba P. Lerner, *Economics of Control* (Macmillan, New York, 1944).

[12] See Harry G. Shaffer, "Out of Stalinism: Czechoslovakia's New Economic Model," *Problems of Communism* (Sept.–Oct., 1965), pp. 31–40.

[13] See, especially, the discussion of the Yugoslavian economy in Rudolph Bicanic "Economic Growth Under Centralized and Decentralized Planning—A Case Study," *Economic Development and Cultural Change* (October, 1957).

will continue in the future and the narrowing gap between the growth rates of command and demand systems will disappear or even reverse itself is a matter for speculation.

The increasing use of national planning policies in demand systems and of markets and market criteria in command systems could lead to convergence of the two systems in a purely technical sense. Whether that will diminish or intensify the competition between the two economic and political systems is a matter of debate.

That culture and folklore can be independent factors affecting economic growth of systems is reflected in the slowness with which Americans have experimented with the budget as a stabilizing and expansionary tool and the Communists have approached the use of market prices and profits as instruments of economic policy.

It would be hazardous to make guesses about the future. At the moment, it appears both systems are learning how to rectify their internal deficiencies; which system will learn faster is hard to say. Both systems are in flux and systems like men usually learn from experience and change their goals with age and maturation. But not all social changes, Marx and Marxist notwithstanding, are predictable.

Purists often insist that all planning is coercive and inconsistent with a demand system[14] (or conversely that profit and interest are capitalistic evils which have no place in a socialist planned economy).[15] But planning and markets are consistent both with systems of demand and of command. If the people through their demand can introduce, modify and then eliminate planning, the system should be considered a demand system. It is centralized physical or quantitative planning which has shown itself to be inconsistent with a demand system. After all, some form of planning is necessary for any organized society. In any demand system, individual firms and local State and Central Governments need short or long run plans. Even a *laissez-faire* government, as Robbins has pointed out, needs to plan the legal and judicial framework of the economy very carefully.[16]

---

[14] The most forceful attack on planning is by F. A. von Hayek, *The Road to Serfdom* (University of Chicago Press, Chicago, 1944). A variation on the theme is Milton Friedman, *Capitalism & Freedom* (University of Chicago Press, Chicago, 1962).

[15] Most Marxists and many anti-Marxists have often confused the nature of interest, rents and profits as prices for the proper allocation and use of scarce resources—capital, land and entrepreneurial talent with the economic desirability of paying out interest, rents and profits to individuals and groups. The moral justification of these payments is yet another question which has only added to the voluminous and confusing literature. Recently Soviet economists have shown increasing awareness of these distinct issues. Polish economists have long treated these problems with theoretical astuteness and sophistication.

[16] Lionel Robbins, *Economic Planning & International Order* (MacMillan, London, 1937), especially pp. 221–229, 259–268.

THE APPEAL
OF COMMUNISM
TO THE UNDERDEVELOPED
PEOPLES

Morris Watnick

If time is a power dimension in any political strategy, the odds facing the West in the underdeveloped areas of the world today are heavily weighted against it. The effort to capture the imagination and loyalties of the populations of these areas did not begin with the West in President Truman's plea for a "bold new program" of technical aid to backward areas. It began more than a generation earlier when the Communist International at its second world congress in 1920 flung out the challenge of revolution to the peoples of colonial and dependent countries and proceeded to chart a course of action calculated to hasten the end of Western overlordship. We thus start with an initial time handicap, and it is a moot question whether we can overcome the disadvantage by acquiring the radically new appreciation of the human stakes involved necessary to meet the challenge of the Communist appeal to the peoples of these areas.

Fortunately, there is no need to trace out the tortuous course of the careers of the various Communist parties in the backward areas of the world in order to gain some appreciation of the extent and intensity of their indigenous appeal. For purposes of this discussion we can confine ourselves to China, India, and the area of Southeast Asia, where they have had their greatest successes to date. Despite the blunders and ineptitudes which marked

From Morris Watnick, "The Appeal of Communism to Underdeveloped Peoples," B. F. Hoselitz (ed.), *The Progress of Underdeveloped Areas* (Chicago, 1952), pp. 152–172. Reprinted by permission of The University of Chicago Press.

their initial grand play in China in 1924–27, ending in almost complete disaster for their most promising single party organization in these areas, they have emerged today as a political magnitude of the first order, boasting a seasoned leadership, a core of trained cadres, and a mass following recruited mainly from the peasant masses of the region. It is the purpose of the remarks which follow to indicate the nature of the Communist appeal to the peoples of these areas and to suggest some of the sociological factors which have made that appeal so effective.

It was once the wont of certain Continental writers, preoccupied with the problem of imperialism, to refer to the peoples who form the subject of our deliberations as the "history-less" peoples. Better than the Europacentric term, "underdeveloped peoples," it delineates in bold relief all the distinctive features which went to make up the scheme of their social existence: their parochial isolation, the fixity of their social structure, their tradition-bound resistance to change, their static subsistence economies, and the essential repetitiveness and uneventfulness of their self-contained cycle of collective activities. With a prescience which has not always received its due, these theorists of imperialism also called the right tune in predicting that the isolated careers of these archaic societies would rapidly draw to a close under the impact of economic and social forces set in motion by industrial capitalism and that these history-less peoples would before long be thrust onto the arena of world politics, impelled by a nascent nationalism born of contact with the West and nurtured by a swelling resentment against the exaction of its imperialism.[1]

The final result of this process is unfolding today with a disconcerting force and speed in almost all the backward regions of the world. We can see its culmination most clearly among the classic exemplaries of history-less peoples in China, India, and the regions of Southeast Asia where the political and economic predominance of western Europe is being successfully challenged by forces unmistakably traceable to the forced absorption of these societies into the stream of world history. Their internal cohesiveness, largely centered on self-sufficient village economies, has been disrupted by enforced contact with the West, giving way to a network of commercialized money transactions in which the strategic incidence of economic activity has shifted from subsistence agriculture to plantation production of raw materials and foodstuffs for the world market. Their economies thus took on a distorted character which rendered the material well-being of the native populations peculiarly subject to the cyclical fluctuations of the world market. All this, coupled with rapid population increases which the existing state of primitive technique, available area of cultivation, and customary allocation of soil

[1] For typical discussions see Otto Bauer, *Die Nationalitätenfrage und die Social-demokratie* (Vienna, 1907), pp. 494–97 *et passim;* Rudolf Hilferding, *Das Finanzkapital* (Vienna, 1910; Berlin, 1947), p. 441.

could not adjust to the requirements of maximum output, has conspired to create widespread rural indebtedness, abuses of plantation and tenant labor, and other excrescences traditionally associated with the prevalence of a raw commercial and financial capitalism superimposed on a predominantly agricultural economy.[2]

Given the fact that the new economic dispensation in these regions was fashioned under the aegis if not active encouragement of the Western imperialisms, it should occasion no surprise that these regions, particularly Southeast Asia, have seen the efflorescence of a distinctive type of nationalism, especially after the debacle of Western rule during the second World War, differing in many crucial respects from the historical evolution of nationalism as experienced by western Europe. Indeed, the employment of a term like "nationalism" with all its peculiarly Western connotations to describe what is going on in Southeast Asia today is in a sense deceptive precisely because it diverts our attention from some of the distinctive attributes of native sentiment which set it apart from the nineteenth-century manifestations of nationalism in Europe. It is, moreover, a particularly inappropriate characterization because it inhibits a full appreciation of the potency of the Communist appeal among the populations of these regions. Historically, nationalism in western Europe has flourished with the burgeoning of an industrial technology, the urbanization of the population, the growth of a self-conscious middle class and an industrial proletariat, the spread of literacy, and the multiplication of media of mass communication. Now it is one of the distinctive features of the movements of revolt in Southeast Asia today that they lack any of these marks of Western nationalism. The indigenous "nationalism" of Southeast Asia today, lacking any of these props, nevertheless derives its peculiar potency from a universal reaction of personalized resentment against the economic exploitation of foreign powers. Whether all the economic and social dislocations of this region are directly attributable in refined analytic terms to Western rule is quite beside the point. The simple and crucial datum which we must take as the point of orientation in all our thinking is that to the mind of the masses of indigenous peoples they do stem from this common source. The Indo-Chinese peasant victimized by usurers, the plantation worker in Malaya periodically deprived of his income by a drop in world price of rubber, the Indonesian intellectual debarred from a higher post in the government service, the Burmese stevedore underpaid by the *maistry* system of contract labor—all tend to attribute the source of their grievances to the systems of government and economy imposed on them from without. The distinctive and novel aspect of the native movements of Southeast Asia, then, is that they represent a mass collective gesture of rejec-

---

[2] For an excellent analysis of the economic impact of the West on the rural economies of Southeast Asia, where the results are most clearly apparent today, see Erich Jacoby, *Agrarian Unrest in Southeast Asia* (New York, 1949).

tion of a system of imposed economic and social controls which is compelled by historic circumstances to take the form of a nationalist movement of liberation from foreign rule.[3]

It is this distinctive coalescence of two sources of resentment which offers the Communist parties the opportunities they lack elsewhere to any comparable degree. The two-dimensional direction of native resentment lends itself ideally to Communist appeal and manipulation for the simple reason that Communists can successfully portray Soviet Russia both as a symbol of resistance to political imperialism imposed from without as well as a model of self-directed and rapid industrialization undertaken from within.[4] This twin appeal gains added strength from the multinational composition of the U.S.S.R., which enables indigenous Communists of Southeast Asia to confront their audience with the glaring disparity between the possibilities of ethnic equality and the actualities of Western arrogance and discrimination. Communist propaganda has accordingly exploited this theme in almost all important policy pronouncements directed to the people of Asia.[5]

With the victory of the Chinese Communists, the incidence of these appeals has perceptibly shifted the symbolism of successful resistance and internal reconstruction from Russia to China, which is now being held up as a model for emulation by the other areas of Southeast Asia.[6] The shift is not without its tactical and propaganda value, since the adjacent region of Southeast Asia is now regarded as the "main battle-front of the world democratic camp against the forces of reaction and imperialism."[7] Success in this case carries its own rewards beyond the frontiers of China itself, for it is altogether probable that Mao Tse-tung will take his place alongside Lenin and Stalin as

[3] Bauer (op. cit., pp. 262–63) has given the classic formulation of this relationship in his analysis of the problem of national conflicts in the old Austro-Hungarian Empire which showed some formal resemblance to the situation in the backward regions today. The resemblance was superficial, however, since the lines of conflict were far less clearly drawn in Austria-Hungary, especially as regards professional and intellectual groups.

[4] It is noteworthy that variations of both types of Communist propaganda have also been attempted in western Europe in the last three years. The Marshall Plan, for example, has been presented to Europeans as an attempt on the part of the United States to impose its political rule over the Continent and to throttle its industries, without, however, carrying the conviction it enjoys in Asia.

[5] See the report of L. Soloviev at the Congress of Asian and Australasian Trade Unions at Peking, November 19, 1949, in World Trade Union Movement (organ of the WFTU), No. 8 (December, 1949), pp. 25–27. Also cf. "Manifesto to All Working People of Asia and Australasia," ibid., pp. 43–46.

[6] "Mighty Advance of National Liberation Movements in Colonial and Dependent Countries," For a Lasting Peace, for a People's Democracy! (organ of the Cominform) (January 27, 1950); cf. speech by Liu Shao-chi at the Trade Union Conference of Asian and Australasian countries, Peking, 1949, World Trade Union Movement, No. 8 (December, 1949), pp. 12–15.

[7] R. Palme Dutt, "Right Wing Social Democrats in the Service of Imperialism," For a Lasting Peace, for a People's Democracy! (November 1, 1948), p. 6.

a font of revolutionary sagacity for these movements in India and Southeast Asia.[8]

Unfortunately, recent discussions of the Communist movement in Asia have done more to obscure than to clarify the nature and direction of its appeal to the indigenous populations. All too frequently, the tendency has been to fall back on the blanket formula that Communists have sought to identify themselves with local nationalism and demands for agrarian reform. We have already seen that their identification with nascent nationalism, if such it must be called, derives its peculiar strength from certain of its unique qualities. It is no less important to an appreciation of the problem to recognize that the Communist appeal does not by mere virtue of this process of identification acquire the same uniform access to all sectors of the population. Indeed, the most striking and disconcerting feature of much of the propaganda appeal emanating both from Moscow, Peking, and other centers is that it is not, and in the nature of the case cannot be, designed for peasant or worker consumption. The appeal of communism as such in these areas is first and foremost an appeal which finds lodgment with indigenous professional and intellectual groups. Its identification with native nationalism and demands for land reform turns out to be, when carefully scrutinized, not so much a direct appeal to specific peasant grievances, powerful though its actual results may be, as it is an identification with the more generalized, highly conscious, and sharply oriented outlook of the native intelligentsia.[9]

Given the entire range of sociological and economic forces at work in these areas, the very logic and terms of the Communist appeal must of necessity filter through to the peasant masses by first becoming the stock in trade of the intellectual and professional groups. To revert to the terminology suggested at the outset of this paper, we may say that, by and large, it is the old history-less style of social existence which still claims the loyalty and

[8] See statement of Ho Chi Minh's newly constituted Laodong party, which "pledges itself to follow the heroic example of the Communist party of China, to learn the Mao Tse-tung concept which has been leading the peoples of China and Asia on the road to independence and democracy" (Viet-Nam News Agency, English Morse to Southeast Asia, March 21, 1951). Likewise, the ruling body of the Indian Communist party fell into line with the general trend by declaring its adherence to Mao's strategy (*Crossroads* [Bombay], March 10, 1950).

[9] Failure to appreciate the true direction of the Communist appeal in these areas frequently causes some observers to commit the mistake of minimizing its effectiveness. Thus, Mr. Richard Deverall, the AF of L representative in these areas and an otherwise very perceptive student of the subject, ventures the opinion that Communist propaganda in these areas is mere "rubbish" because it is for the most part couched in terms which hold no interest for the masses, having meaning only for intellectuals (see his "Helping Asia's Workers," *American Federationist* [September, 1951], p. 16). Mr. Deverall's account of the nature of Communist propaganda is quite accurate, but, if the thesis presented above is a valid estimate of the current situation in Asia, he has not drawn the conclusion which follows from the evidence.

outlook of the bulk of the indigenous populations. It is still the old village community which serves as the center of peasant and worker aspirations, and, if they have taken to arms, it is because European rule has destroyed the old securities and values without replacing them by new ones.[10] Without leadership and organization, their unrest would be without direction and certainly without much chance for success, quickly dissipating itself in spontaneous outbursts against individual landowners and achieving no lasting goals. Whatever else it may be that we are facing in Southeast Asia today, it certainly does not resemble the classic uprisings of peasant *Jacquerie* but a highly organized and well-integrated movement, with a leadership that has transcended the immediate urgencies of its mass following and can plan ahead in terms of long-range perspectives.

That leadership is supplied by the new indigenous intelligentsia. It is from this group that native Communist and non-Communist movements alike recruit their top leadership as well as the intermediate layers of cadres, for, of all the groups which make up the populations of these areas, it is the intelligentsia alone (taking the term in its broadest sense) that boasts an ideological horizon which transcends the history-less values of the bulk of the population and makes it the logical recruiting ground for the leadership of political movements. For this, it can thank the formal schooling and intellectual stimulus provided by the West, which not only brought such a group into existence but also—and this is crucial—condemned large sections of that intelligentsia to a form of *déclassé* existence from the very beginnings of its career. The new intelligentsia was in large measure consigned by the imperial system to hover uneasily between a native social base which could not find accommodation for its skills and ambitions and the superimposed imperial structure which reserved the best places for aliens. There were, of course, considerable variations and differences in the various areas of Southeast Asia—India, for example, did succeed in absorbing a good many of its professionally trained native sons—but, by and large, the picture is one of a rootless intellectual proletariat possessing no real economic base in an independent native middle class. The tendency in all these areas, moreover, has been to train technicians, lawyers, and other groups of professional workers

---

[10] In most backward areas the tie to the countryside is still apparent in the tendency of laborers engaged in industry and mining periodically to drift back to the village (W. E. Moore, "Primitives and Peasants in Industry," *Social Research*, XV, No. 1 [March, 1948], 49–63). See also the observations of Soetan Sjahrir in his *Out of Exile*, trans. C. Wolf (New York, 1949), pp. 74–75, concerning the mental outlook of the masses in these regions. This fact was not lost on the leaders of the Communist movement. In the 1928 resolution on colonial strategy the Sixth Comintern Congress noted that the proletariat "still have one foot in the village," a fact which it recognized as a barrier to the development of proletarian class consciousness (see *International Press Correspondence* [Vienna], VIII, No. 88 [December 12, 1928], 1670).

in numbers far out of proportion to the absorptive capacity of the social structures of the home areas, even if more of the higher posts in industry and administration were thrown open to native talent. In any case, those who did find such employment were frozen in minor posts, the most coveted positions going to Europeans.[11]

But if these groups could not be integrated into the social structure of these dependent areas, the same does not hold true of their acclimatization to the cross-currents of political doctrine. Western education exposed many of them to the various schools of social thought contending for influence in Europe, and from these they distilled the lessons which seemed to offer the best hope for their native communities. Western capitalism was necessarily excluded from their range of choices if for no other reason than that its linkage with imperialist rule over their own societies debarred it from their hierarchy of values. The anticapitalist animus is common to the intellectual spokesmen of these areas, whatever their specific political allegiance or orientation may be.[12] Nor does it appear that any populist variety of Gandhiism, with its strong attachment to the values of a static subsistence economy, has won any considerable following among these intellectual groups. Soetan Sjahrir voiced a common sentiment when he wrote:

> We intellectuals here are much closer to Europe or America than we are to the Boroboedoer or Mahabrata or to the primitive Islamic culture of Java or Sumatra. . . . For me, the West signifies forceful, dynamic and active life. I admire, and am convinced that only by a utilization of this dynamism of the West can the East be released from its slavery and subjugation.[13]

The sole possibility, then, which appeared acceptable to them was one or another of the forms of state-sponsored reconstruction and industrialization, for which liberation from the rule of European states was naturally considered to be a prerequisite. Liberation and internal reconstruction thus came to be

[11] Some interesting data on this score for Indonesia are offered by J. M. van der Kroef's "Economic Origins of Indonesian Nationalism," in *South Asia in the World Today,* ed. Phillips Talbot (Chicago, 1950), pp. 188–93, and his "Social Conflicts and Minority Aspirations in Indonesia," *American Journal of Sociology* (March, 1950), 453–56. Cf. L. Mills (ed.), *New World of Southeast Asia* (Minneapolis, 1949), pp. 293–95.

[12] For a typical rejection of the capitalist solution coming from anti-Communist sources see D. R. Gadgil, "Economic Prospect for India," *Pacific Affairs,* XXII (June, 1949), 115–29; Sjahrir, *op. cit.,* pp. 161–62; and the remarks of H. Shastri, of the Indian Trade Union Congress at the Asian Regional Conference of the International Labor Office, Ceylon, January 16–27, 1950, *Record of Proceedings* (Geneva, 1951), p. 112. Cf. van der Kroef's article, "Social Conflicts and Minority Aspirations in Indonesia," *op. cit.,* pp. 455–56, and J. F. Normano, *Asia Between Two World Wars* (New York, 1944), pp. 83–87.

[13] Sjahrir, *op. cit.,* pp. 67 and 144.

two inseparable operations, intimately tied together as they seldom have been before.

We can now appreciate the enormous initial advantage which was thus offered the Communist movements in these backward areas. The Russian Revolution of 1917 and the subsequent course of planned industrialization could not but fail to impress native intellectuals as offering a model pattern of action by which they could retrieve their communities from precapitalist isolation and backwardness without paying the price of continued foreign exploitation. There is doubtless a large measure of self-revelation in Mao's reaction to the Russian experience in his statement:

> There is much in common or similar between the situation in China and prerevolutionary Russia. Feudal oppression was the same. Economic and cultural backwardness was common to both countries. Both were backward. China more so than Russia. The progressives waged a bitter struggle in search of revolutionary truth so as to attain national rehabilitation; this was common to both countries. . . . The October Revolution helped the progressive elements of the world, and of China as well, to apply the proletarian world outlook in determining the fate of the country. . . . The conclusion was reached that we must advance along the path taken by the Russians.[14]

It should also be noted, in passing, that the Comintern lost no time in launching a large number of international front organizations such as the Red International of Trade Unions, International League against Imperialism, International of Seamen and Dockers, International Red Aid, etc.—all of which furnished the necessary organizational scaffolding and support for facilitating the dissemination of propaganda. Finally, as will be noted presently, the Comintern provided a rallying point for their aspirations by outlining a program of revolutionary action in the colonies and dependent areas which was ideally calculated to provide them with a mass peasant following.

The result, though viewed with some misgivings by the leadership of the Comintern, was merely what might have been expected under the circumstances. The Communist parties of these underdeveloped areas of Asia were from their very beginnings initiated, led by, and predominantly recruited from (prior to their conversion into mass organizations as has been the case in China after 1949) native intellectual groups. Though this vital sociological clue to the nature of the Communist appeal in the colonial areas has not received the recognition it deserves, amid the general preoccupation with the theme of Communist appeals to the peasantry, its implication was perfectly plain to the leaders of the Comintern. One of the most revealing (and

---

[14] Mao Tse-tung, *On People's Democratic Rule* (New York: New Century Publishers, 1950), pp. 2–4. For the same reaction of M. N. Roy, one of the earlier leaders of the Indian Communists who later broke with the Comintern, see his *Revolution and Counter-revolution in China* (Calcutta, 1946), p. 522.

to date largely unnoticed) admissions on this score is contained in the Sixth Comintern Congress in 1928 in its resolution on strategic policy in the colonies and semicolonies in which the point is very clearly made that

> experience has shown that, in the majority of colonial and semi-colonial countries, an important if not a predominant part of the Party ranks in the first stage of the movement is recruited from the petty bourgeoisie, and in particular, from the revolutionary inclined intelligentsia, very frequently students. It not uncommonly happens that these elements enter the Party because they see in it the most decisive enemy of imperialism, at the same time not sufficiently understanding that the Communist Party is not only the Party of struggle against imperialist exploitation . . . but struggle against all kinds of exploitation and expropriation. Many of these adherents of the Party, in the course of the revolutionary struggle will reach a proletarian class point of view; another part will find it more difficult to free themselves to the end, from the moods, waverings and half-hearted ideology of the petty bourgeoisie.[15]

The fact that this did not accord with the *idée fixe* of this and all other Comintern pronouncements that leadership of colonial revolutionary movements is properly a function of the industrial urban workers should in no way blind us to the fact which Comintern leadership was realistic enough to acknowledge, namely, that membership of these Communist parties is heavily weighted in favor of the intelligentsia. One may, in fact, go one step further and say that, in accepting the predominance of the "colonial" intelligentsia, the Comintern was closer to the genus of Leninist doctrine than were any of its indorsements of the leadership role of the urban proletariat. No other group in these areas but the intelligentsia could be expected to undertake the transformation of the social structure under forced draft and in a predetermined direction and thus fulfil the main self-assigned historical mission of Leninism.[16]

If we bear this key factor in mind, it throws a new light on the nature of the grip which Communists exercise on the political movements of these areas. The usual formulation of the character of these movements is that they stem from mass discontent with the prevailing system of land distribution, with the labor practices in force, with the overt or indirect political control of these areas by foreign governments, etc. These are perfectly valid empiri-

---

[15] "The Revolutionary Movement in the Colonies and Semi-colonies; Resolution of the Sixth World Congress of the Communist International" (adopted September 1, 1928), *International Press Correspondence*, VIII, No. 88 (December 12, 1928), 1670.

[16] Though cognizant of the role of the intellectuals in the Chinese part, Benjamin Schwartz's illuminating study, *Chinese Communism and the Rise of Mao* (Cambridge, 1951), falls short of an appreciation of its significance by focusing attention on a purely strategic problem—Mao's peasant-oriented movement—and concluding from this that Mao's ideology represents a radical break with classical Leninism.

cal descriptions of the necessary conditions for the rise of liberation movements in these areas. But they obviously fail to take notice of the specific
social groups that give these movements their *élan,* direction, and whatever
measure of success they have had thus far. As matters stand today, the intellectuals are the sole group in these areas which can infuse these raw social
materials of agrarian discontent, etc., with the organization and leadership
necessary for their success. And it is largely this group which has acted as
the marriage broker between the international Communist movement and
the manifestations of indigenous revolt.

Enough empirical material exists to warrant the conclusion that the
"colonial" Communist parties of Asia today, as in the 1920's, are the handi-
work of native intellectuals. Since 1940, they have, of course, greatly expanded their mass following and membership, but their leadership is still
drawn overwhelmingly from the intelligentsia. As regards China, this elite
character of Communist party leadership was expressly recognized by Mao
Tse-tung in 1939,[17] and the entire history of the party from its founding by
Li Ta-chao and Ch'en Tu-hsu to Mao Tse-tung and Liu Shao-chi is virtually
an unbroken record of a party controlled by intellectuals.[18] India illustrates
the same trend. Its earliest Communist leadership is exemplified in M. N. Roy
(who later broke with the movement), a high-caste Brahmin of considerable
intellectual attainments. Also indicative of the predominance of intellectuals
in the leadership of the Indian Communist party is the fact that, at its first
All-Indian Congress in 1943, 86 of a total attendance of 139 delegates were
members of professional and intellectual groups.[19] And in the postwar period
the leading position of this social group in the affairs of the Indian Communist party finds expression in men like Joshi, Ranadive, and Dange.[20] The
same pattern also holds good for the Communist parties of Indochina, Thailand, Burma, Malaya, and Indonesia, all of which show a heavy preponderance of journalists, lawyers, and teachers among the top leadership.[21] The
Burmese Communists afford an especially pointed illustration in this respect,
since the parent-organization, the Thakens, originated in the early 1930's
among university students who today comprise the leadership of both rival

[17] Mao Tse-tung, *The Chinese Revolution and the Communist Party of China* (New
York: Committee for a Democratic Far Eastern Policy, n.d.), pp. 13–14.

[18] Mao Tse-tung's excursion into an instrumentalist approach to Marxian philosophy is one manifestation (see his "On Practice," *Political Affairs* [organ of the United
States Communist Party] (April, 1951), pp. 28–42.

[19] *People's War* (organ of the CPI) (Bombay) (June 13, 1943).

[20] See a review of Dange's *India, from Primitive Communism to Slavery* (Bombay,
1949), in *The Communist* (organ of the CPI) (Bombay), III, No. 4 (October–November,
1950), 78–91. Cf. M. R. Masani, "The Communist Party in India," *Pacific Affairs*
(March, 1951), 31–33.

[21] See, e.g., biographic data in V. Thompson and R. Adloff, *The Left Wing in South
East Asia* (New York, 1950), pp. 231–86.

Communist factions.[22] If any doubt exists as to the extent to which the leadership of these movements is dominated by intellectual groups, it is quickly dispelled by an examination of the top echelons of trade-unions, as instanced, for example, by the names of those attending the WFTU-sponsored Congress of Asian and Australasian Unions in Peking in 1949. Here, at least, we can appreciate the full impact of the trend by noting that, while European trade-union leadership (in contrast to the leadership of parties) has been largely recruited from within membership ranks, the reverse is true in Southeast Asia. The trade-union movement in that region is largely a newborn post-war phenomenon, and the various bodies (whether Communist-dominated or controlled by other political groups) have been fashioned and directed by professionals with no direct experience in the occupations concerned.[23]

This, in its larger perspectives, is the structure of leadership for both the Communist and the non-Communist groups in the entire region. More detailed research might serve to throw some light on the sociological factors which determine the distribution of these professional groups among Communist and anti-Communist movements. But, even if a completely detailed analysis is still lacking, enough is already known of the larger trends to indicate that these sections of the native populations constitute the key operational factor in the Communist appeal. It is they who spearhead the propaganda drive, organize the unions, youth groups, and other organizations, plan the tactics of their parties, etc.

As matters stand, then, the organization and leadership of Communist parties in colonial areas do not accord with their accepted doctrinal precepts. For over a generation now it has been a standard item of doctrine, reiterated again and again, that the leadership of these parties must rest with the industrial working class.[24] The realities of the situation in these areas have not been very obliging to this formula, though it still occupies its customary niche in all their pronouncements. From the standpoint of their own strategic imperatives and long-term objective, however, the Communist parties of these areas have not hesitated to draw the necessary practical conclusions. They have acquiesced in the primacy of the intellectuals in the movement because the acceptance of any alternative leadership coming from the ranks of the peasantry or the industrial workers (assuming the possibility of such

[22] *Ibid.*, pp. 80–82.

[23] *New York Times*, May 21, 1950; see also Institute of Pacific Relations, *Problems of Labor and Social Welfare in South and Southeast Asia* ("Secretariat Paper No. 1 Prepared by Members of the ILO" [New York, 1950]), p. 20. Cf. statements of delegates from India and Ceylon to Asian Regional Conference of the ILO, Ceylon, January 16–27, 1950, *Record of Proceedings*, pp. 98, 113.

[24] See, e.g., "The Revolutionary Movement in Colonies and Semi-colonies; Resolution of the Sixth Congress of the Communist International" (adopted September 1, 1928), *International Press Correspondence*, VIII (1928), 1670–72 *et passim*; and Mao's pamphlet, *The Chinese Revolution and the Communist Party of China*, pp. 15–16.

leadership) would entail the sacrifice of the prime objectives of the party— viz., the seizure of power and the launching of a long-range plan for internal planning and reconstruction. Gradual and piecemeal reforms and certainly basic reforms designed to bring immediate economic relief to the masses (for instance, in the credit structure of an area) undertaken by non-Communist regimes would be welcomed by the mass of the peasantry because they are in accord with their immediate and most pressing interests.[25] A program of seizing political power followed by prolonged industrialization, economic planning, recasting of the social structure, realignment of a country's international position in favor of the U.S.S.R.—these are considerations of the type which can attract intellectuals only.[26]

Accordingly, if the main appeal of communism per se, in underdeveloped areas, has been to the native intelligentsia, a transgression has apparently been committed against an expendable item of party dogma, but the fundamental spirit of the Leninist position with regard to the relation between leadership and the masses has actually been preserved in its pristine form. There is no need to labor this point, since there is enough evidence to indicate that the leadership of Communist parties in underdeveloped areas is acutely aware of the conflict between its own long-range objectives and the "interests" of its mass following, as well as of the conclusions to be drawn for the practical guidance of their parties' activities. Thus a recent party document issued by the Malaya Communist party to cope with internal criticism of its leadership and policies contains this cogent passage:

> Regarding these masses, our responsibility is not to lower the Party's policy and to accede to the selfish demands of small sections of the backward elements, but to bring out a proper plan to unite and direct them courageously to carry out the various forms of struggle against the British. If this course is not followed we will retard the progress of the national revolutionary war, and will lose the support of the masses. The proper masses route is not only to mix up with them [mingle with them(?)—M.W.] but to resolutely and systematically lead them to march forward to execute the Party's policy and programme. By overlooking the latter point, we will not be able to discharge the historical duty of a revolutionary Party.[27]

[25] This is all the more true of large sections of Southeast Asia, where the land problem is not identical with the structure of ownership distribution and where no direct correlation prevails between tenancy and poverty. In large sections of this region the problem arises largely from the primitive credit and marketing facilities rather than from concentration of land titles.

[26] Communist leaders are not loath to recognize that this cleavage exists between the immediate interests of the masses and the party's long range perspectives (see Liu Shao-chi, "On the Party," *Political Affairs* [October, 1950], 88).

[27] The document from which this passage is taken is contained in a Malaya Communist party publication titled *How To Look After the Interests of the Masses* ("Emancipation Series," No. 5), published secretly by the Freedom Press in Malaya, December

If we discern the central driving force of communism in the under-developed areas to be its appeal to a considerable number of the indigenous intelligentsia, we are also in a position to reassess the meaning and changes of its mass appeal, most notably its program of land redistribution. To no inconsiderable extent, much of the confusion which attends thinking and discourse on the subject in this country can be traced to a widespread impression still current that the Communist movement in underdeveloped areas owes its success to the fact that it is finely attuned to the most urgent and insistent "land hunger" of millions of the poorest peasants living on a submarginal level of existence. There is just enough historical truth in this impression to make it a plausible explanation of Communist strength. It is unquestionably true that the mass base of the Communist parties in Southeast Asia can be accounted for by the almost universal prevalence of local agrarian unrest which thus constitutes the necessary precondition for the activities of the Communists. But if—as is not infrequently done—this is offered as the crucially strategic element in the complex of circumstances which have served the cause of the Communist parties, we are once again confronted with the old confusion of necessary with sufficient causes.[28] For there is no intrinsic reason which compels the ground swell of agrarian discontent to favor the fortunes of the Communist parties—unless that discontent can be channeled and directed in predetermined fashion by the intervention of a native social group capable of giving organized shape to its various amorphous and diffused manifestations. If the foregoing analysis has any merit, the balance of the sociological picture in these areas will have to be redressed in our thinking to give greater weight to the Communist-oriented intelligentsia and to its role as the prime mover of the native Communist movements.

A more balanced picture of the sociological roots of the Communist movement in the underdeveloped areas would also serve to throw some light on the shift which has recently taken place in their agrarian reform program and therefore, too, in the direction of their appeal.

In its original form the agrarian program of the Comintern was an outright bid for the support of the poorest and therefore the numerically preponderant sections of the peasantry. At the Second Congress of the Comintern in 1920, Lenin placed the question of agrarian reform at the very center of

---

15, 1949, and made public after its seizure by the local authorities. Another document titled "Resolution To Strengthen Party Character" reaffirms the doctrine of democratic centralism against the more "extremist democratic" demands of some of the members. For an expression of the same standpoint regarding the relation between the party and the masses from a Chinese source see Liu Shao-chi, "On the Party," *op. cit.*, p. 78.

[28] An otherwise excellent discussion by Miss Barbara Ward verges on this error, especially in its opening remarks. See her article in the *New York Times Magazine*, March 25, 1951.

the Communist appeal and dismissed as utopian any notion that a Communist movement in these areas was even conceivable without an appeal to the masses of peasantry.[29] The resolution adopted by that congress repudiated any attempt to solve the agrarian problem along Communist lines and instead accepted the inevitable fact that, in its initial stages, the agrarian revolution in these areas would have to be achieved by a "petty bourgeois" program of land distribution, directed "against the landlords, against large landowner-ship, against all survivals of feudalism."[30] Eight years later the Sixth Con-gress of the Comintern was more specific. Its resolution on the strategy of the Communist movement in colonial areas called attention to the presence of a "hierarchy of many stages, consisting of landlords and sublandlords, parasitic intermediate links between the laboring cultivator and the big land-owner or the state" who were destroying the basis of the peasant's livelihood. More particularly, "the peasantry . . . no longer represents a homogeneous mass. In the villages of China and India . . . it is already possible to find exploiting elements derived from the peasantry who exploit the peasants and village laborers through usury, trade, employment of hired labor, the sale or letting out of land." While the Comintern was willing to collaborate with the entire peasantry during the first period of the liberation movement, the upper strata of the peasantry was expected to turn counterrevolutionary as the movement gained momentum. When the chips were down, therefore, the program would have to shift to "a revolutionary settlement of the agrarian question."[31]

The "revolutionary settlement of the agrarian question" was never ac-complished, save in the case of Korea. Wherever the Communists have achieved power in these areas, the program of agrarian revolution, stipulated in the resolution of the Sixth Comintern Congress, soon became a dead letter.[32] Except for North Korea, where its application was dictated by the previous expropriation of native lands in favor of the Japanese, its place was taken by a series of moderate reforms designed to mollify the poorer sections of the peasantry without alienating the "parasitic intermediate links" or impairing the productive capacity of agriculture. During the period when the Chinese Communists held sway in the border regions, for example, steps were

[29] For the text of Lenin's remarks see *Selected Works*, X, 239–40.

[30] "Theses on National and Colonial Questions," *ibid.*, pp. 231–38. See also the speech of Zinoviev at the Congress of Eastern Peoples held in Baku, 1920 (*I. S'zed Narodov Vostoka September 1–8, 1920, Baku Stenograficheskii Otchety* [Petrograd, 1920]).

[31] "The Revolutionary Movement in the Colonies and Semi-colonies; Resolution of the Sixth Congress of the Communist International" (adopted September 1, 1928), *International Press Correspondence*, VIII (1928), 1663–67.

[32] Except in Kiangsi and Fukien in the late 1920's and later discontinued. Simi-larly, the radical confiscatory program of 1946–49 was abandoned with the Communist's final accession to power.

taken to alleviate the lot of the poorer peasantry in such matters as rentals and interest rates; but wholesale confiscation and redistribution were not attempted to any great extent. Similarly, under the present regime in China, the revolutionary formula has been virtually dismissed as a propaganda appeal, once useful for enlisting the support of the poorer peasantry in the period before the Communist accession to power, but having no relevance to the problems of agriculture today. In fact, the propaganda appeal is now designed to reconcile the middle and wealthier sections of the Chinese peasantry to the new regime in political terms and to promote increased output and land improvements as prerequisites to a program of industrialization.[33] Without the active intervention of a Communist-oriented intelligentsia, a large-scale peasant movement in China as well as in the region of Southeast Asia, if successful, would not go beyond agrarian reform pure and simple. The end goal would be Sun Yat-sen's and Stambulisky's rather than Lenin's, given the essentially static and conservative temper of the bulk of the peasant populations. As matters stand now, however, the schedule of agrarian reform under Communist sponsorship has definitely been subordinated to the long-range perspectives of industrialization with a program of collectivization in store for the future when conditions are more favorable to its success.[34] Accordingly, the imperatives of the "New Democracy" require a shift in the main incidence of Communist appeal to secure for the regime a base of support more in accord with its long-range plans.

The shift is equally apparent in the industrial field, where attempts are being made to enlist the support of the "national burgeoisie" during an indefinite transition period pending the introduction of "genuine" socialism. The present program envisions a form of limited state-sponsored and state-regulated capitalist enterprise to promote the process of industrializations,[35] and the attractions now being employed to enlist entrepreneurial co-operation are strangely reminiscent of the "infant-industry" argument so familiar in "imperialist" countries.[36]

[33] Liu Shao-chi, "On Agrarian Reform in China," *For a Lasting Peace, for a People's Democracy!* (July 21, 1950), pp. 3–4; see also Teh Kao, "Peasants in the New China," *For a Lasting Peace, for a People's Democracy!* (October 13, 1950), p. 2. For a summary of the history of the Communist agrarian program see F. C. Lee, "Land Redistribution in Communist China," *Pacific Affairs* (March, 1948), 20–32.

[34] Mao Tse-tung, *On the Present Situation and Our Tasks* (East China Liberation Publishers, 1946); see also remarks of Liu Shao-chi in *People's China* (July 16, 1950).

[35] See, e.g., Mao Tse-tung, *On People's Democratic Rule*, p. 12, and the text of the "Common Program of the People's Political Consultative Conference of 1949" included as an appendix to Mao's speech, esp. p. 19.

[36] Wu Min, "Industry of People's China Grows," *For a Lasting Peace, for a People's Democracy!* (November 17, 1950), p. 4. This outright nationalistic appeal to the interests of domestic business groups is also plainly apparent in the latest draft program of the Indian Communist party (see *For a Lasting Peace, for a People's Democracy!* [May 11, 1951], p. 3).

An identical transposition of appeal may also be detected in the program of Ho Chi-minh's newly organized Laodong (Worker's) party in Viet-Nam.[37] Its program proclaims it the leader of a national united front comprising *all* classes, parties, and races, and its leading motif is the need to oust the French oppressors who are charged not only with exploiting Viet-Namese workers but also native landlords and capitalists who must pay a tribute to the French in the form of high prices for imports and the sale of their own products at depressed prices.[38] The socialist regime is indefinitely postponed until such time as the country is ready for it, and in the meantime

> the national bourgeoisie must be encouraged, assisted and guided in their undertakings, so as to contribute to the development of the national economy. The right of the patriotic landlords to collect rent in accordance with the law must be guaranteed.
>
> Our agrarian policy mainly aims at present in carrying out the reduction of land rent and interest . . . regulation of the leasehold system, provisional allocation of land formerly owned by imperialists to poorer peasants, redistribution of communal lands, rational use of land belonging to absentee landlords.[39]

To say, then, that the Communist program in the underdeveloped areas of Asia is designed purely and simply as an appeal to the poorest and landless sections of the peasant population is to indulge in an oversimplification of the facts. The Communist appeal is rather a complicated function of the total interplay of political forces in these areas and has therefore tended to shift both in direction and in content with the degree of influence and political power exercised by the Communist parties. The only constant element among all these changes has been the abiding appeal of the Communist system to certain sections of the intelligentsia. Whether the new dispensation of the appeal can be expected to evoke the same degree of sympathetic response from the "national bourgeoisie" and the more prosperous peasantry as the discarded slogan of outright land confiscation had for the impoverished peasants is open to considerable doubt. The avowed transitional character of the program of the "People's Democracy" is alone sufficient to rob these appeals of any sustained response. It does not require any high degree of political sophistication on the part of the "national bourgeoisie," for example, to realize that a full measure of co-operation with a Communist-controlled regime would only serve to hasten its own extinction. How seriously such a withdrawal of support would affect the fortunes of a Communist regime would depend to a crucial extent on the speed with which it could find a sub-

---

[37] Actually a revival of the Communist party dissolved in 1945.

[38] Viet-Nam News Agency in English Morse to Southeast Asia, April 12, 1951.

[39] Viet-Nam News Agency in English Morse to Southeast Asia, March 18 and April 10, 1951.

stitute support in newly evolved social groups with a vested stake in its continued existence. Some indication of how the problem is visualized by the leaders of the Communist regime in China may be gleaned from the following remarks made by Liu Shao-chi in a speech to Chinese businessmen last year:

> As Communists we consider that you are exploiting your workers; but we realize that, at the present stage of China's economic development, such exploitation is unavoidable and even socially useful. What we want is for you to go ahead and develop production as fast as possible and we will do what we can to help you. You may be afraid of what will happen to you and your families when we develop from New Democracy to Socialism. But you need not really be afraid. If you do a really good job in developing your business, and train your children to be first-class technical experts, you will be the obvious people to put in charge of the nationalized enterprise and you may find that you earn more as managers of a socialized enterprise than as owners.[40]

For the time being the challenge which confronts the West in its efforts to deny the underdeveloped areas of Southeast Asia to the Communist appeal is therefore compounded of two distinct elements. The more obvious of these is, of course, the problem of depriving the Communists of their actual and potential "mass base" by an adequate program of technical aid and economic reform designed to remove the blight of poverty and exploitation from the scheme of things heretofore in force in these areas. The other and more imponderable aspect of this twofold challenge requires the development of an ethos and system of values which can compete successfully with the attraction exercised by communism for those sections of the native intelligentsia which have been the source and mainstay of its leadership. To date, there is little evidence that the West is prepared to meet either of these challenges on terms commensurate with their gravity.

[40] Quoted by M. Lindsay in *New China*, ed. O. van der Sprenkel (London, 1950), p. 139.

NATIONALISM, ECONOMIC DEVELOPMENT AND DEMOCRACY

Bert F. Hoselitz

An often observed characteristic of the newly emerging societies in Asia, Africa, and other parts of the economically less advanced portions of the world is the sharp and undisguised nationalism prevailing in these countries. Sentiments of nationalism are loudly proclaimed in countries which have recently gained independence as well as in those which are still under some form of foreign colonial domination. They are present also in countries which have gained independence some time ago, such as the republics of Latin America, and in those in which foreign domination has never succeeded in establishing itself. Even the form of government of a country, its membership in the Communist bloc or among the free nations of the world, does not seem to make any difference: Chinese nationalism is as strong and as dynamic in its aspirations as Indian or Indonesian nationalism.

To be sure, the actual forms which nationalist movements take are dependent upon the narrower political conditions under which these movements exist. In some countries the attainment of independence is the immediate goal; in others it is the full integration and consolidation of a country's territory; in still others, an expansionist, aggressive type of nationalism is discernible; and in some countries national sentiment is directed primarily towards cultural integration rather than political ends.

From Bert F. Hoselitz, "Nationalism, Economic Development, and Democracy," *The Annals*, 305:1–11 (May 1956). Reprinted by permission of The American Academy of Political and Social Science and the author.

Since apart from political or cultural objectives all these countries also have the economic objective of increasing the level of living of the members of the society, the question may be asked what relationships exist between the processes leading to higher welfare aspirations on the part of the people and the nationalist sentiment prevailing among them. Moreover, both the implementation of a planned program of economic advancement and the spreading of an ideology of nationalism require agencies which often overlap and supplement one another. The men and agencies that advocate most vociferously the need for economic advancement also stress the common national objectives of their societies; indeed the ideology of nationalism seems to be one of the requirements for the achievement of devlopmental goals in societies on a relatively low level of economic advancement.

LIVING STANDARDS AND NATIONALISM

This paper is devoted to an examination of the relationships between aspirations for higher levels of welfare and nationalist movements and trends. First, I shall describe the negative and the positive aspects of nationalism in underdeveloped countries. The former defines the separateness and exclusiveness of a group; it often stresses its antagonism to others, especially those who are, or are felt to be, opponents of indigenous national aspirations. The second attempts to give meaning to the communality of interests of a given group and to define the rights of membership in the group of all those who are said to belong to it. It tends to break down loyalties to particularistic sub-groups, such as clans, tribes, or specific ethnic or linguistic groups in a country, and to replace them by loyalty to the nation as a whole. Next, I shall attempt to relate the positive aspects of indigenous nationalism to forms of economic development and trace the interrelations between them. Finally, I shall try to relate the social processes involved in economic development and the growth of a common national consciousness in an underdeveloped country to its sociopolitical structure. In this way I hope to clarify the interaction between exigencies of maintaining social privileges arising out of a stratified society and democratic implications associated with the improvement of mass living standards supported by a common nationalist ideology. If the problem is posed in this fashion it may be possible to discover what are the chances of democratic developments in these countries, as against the likelihood of some form of authoritarian government.

COMMON CHARACTERISTICS

A nationalist ideology and a welfare-oriented program of economic development have as common characteristics, on the one hand, the aim of affecting the life of all members of a given society and, on the other, stress on the interrelation between the welfare and security of each member of the society and the welfare and security of the society as a whole. Let us analyze these two features somewhat more in detail.

Programs of economic development may have various more or less immediate objectives, but one common goal of most of them is a general rise in mass levels of living. In some countries this objective is stressed much more strongly than any other, but even in those countries in which more emphasis is placed upon the building up of capital equipment or a military machine, some stress is laid on the ultimate benefits which economic development programs will have on the general level of economic welfare of the masses. Economic development is thus commonly declared to be an essentially democratic process. Its benefits are expected to accrue to all members of the society, and even where collective aims are given preference, the impact upon the private personal welfare of the members of society is stressed as a concomitant development.

Just as programs of economic development are represented to be matters of concern for all members of a society, so the equal partnership of all members of that society is "legitimized" by increased emphasis on their common nationality. A nationalist ideology normally presents a Janus-faced appearance. On the one hand it delineates a series of features which are common to all members of a given nationality, which tie them together, and which establish a special kind of solidarity between them. On the other hand it lists a series of factors which divide this nationality from others, which indicate its separateness, its exclusiveness, and often its alleged superiority over others.

NEGATIVE ASPECTS OF NATIONALISM

In countries which still lack independence the foreigner is easily discerned. The dominant metropolitan power is the representative of all that is foreign to the subject nation; the common positive tie is the struggle to emancipate all members of the indigenous population from the foreign yoke. Once independence has been achieved, the image of the foreign dominating power disappears from the immediate scene, and with it a convenient scapegoat on whom could be placed all the ills from which the indigenous society suffered.

But the image of the domineering foreigner is too good a symbol in nationalist propaganda to be let go altogether. Thus we observe a not infrequent technique employed by Communist parties, especially in former colonial countries, of discovering at various times the workings of alleged oppressors in their midst. The fact that even today in Russia and China the actual presence of "imperialist warmongers and their native stool pigeons" is every now and then discovered is eloquent testimony to the powerful role which the foreign dominating power plays in the process of building a nationalist ideology in these countries. Similarly, though admittedly in less crude fashion, the sins of imperialism are still today appealed to in many countries of Asia and even Latin America, even though the former imperialists have lost control and, in many cases, have completely withdrawn from these countries.

The loss of significance of these negative aspects of nationalism and the dilemma created for native leaders by the weakening and gradual withdrawal of the dominant foreign power can be well seen in West Africa. Technically the British territories of that part of the world are still in a colonial status. But in Nigeria and, above all, the Gold Coast, a rather high degree of self-government has been attained. The purely political nationalist objectives have been won to a large extent, and although these countries have not yet attained *de jure* independence, many powers, especially in the economic field, are exercised now by natives rather than Europeans. This has weakened the negative appeal of nationalism and has introduced a number of difficulties for the more doctrinaire and above all the irresponsibly inclined nationalists. Just as in the fully independent countries it is becoming more difficult to place economic failures at the doorstep of the former dominant power, so in these semi-independent countries nationalist leaders have been forced more and more to stress the positive aspects of nationalism rather than its defensive features, its opposition against the foreign oppressor.

POSITIVE ELEMENTS

Through the attainment of full independence or a larger or smaller measure of local autonomy, the main aspects of nationalist ideology shifted. Its features as a movement of opposition and defiance were weakened, and its positive elements became more and more important. The main positive element of nationalism is the proposition that all members of a given country belong to one and the same in-group, which is distinct from the various out-groups surrounding it. This aspect of nationalism is of considerable importance also as a factor of economic development. Since among the goals of economic development programs the attainment of higher levels of mass welfare is stressed, membership in a national group assures participation in this improvement of private economic conditions. Moreover, it also enhances the second aspect of nationalist ideology in stressing the interdependence of the economic and political goals of all members of the in-group and in supporting the proposition that what benefits the community also benefits each individual member of it.

This positive aspect of nationalism in many underdeveloped countries seems to be an indispensable aspect of the actual achievement of higher levels of living. It must not be forgotten that many of these countries exhibited until recently a high degree of heterogeneity in social structure and institutions. Some writers in discussing the social arrangements of these countries have spoken of dual or of plural societies. But even if we disregard these abstractions as too general, when we look at underdeveloped countries more closely we find that almost all of them comprise several ethnic or linguistic communities and that, apart from such divisive elements as castes and deep class lines, there are sharp differences between city and country, between occupational groups, and between persons belonging to certain clans, fraternities, or other groups and those outside such groups.

DIVISIVE FORCES IN NATIONALISM

In fact, the rise of nationalist sentiment in underdeveloped countries has strengthened some of these divisive tendencies. In India, for example, the attempt to make Hindi the common national language has met with increased opposition from other language groups and, in fact, the language question has brought to the fore a kind of local "nationalism" which seeks to go beyond the dispute over a national language and to establish additional political goals, notably a higher degree of local autonomy. In other words, the linguistic controversy, which could be regarded as a symptom of cultural nationalism, becomes tinged with political aims that tend to strengthen the divisive internal forces. A similar development is discernible in Nigeria, where the political leaders of the three major ethnic groups, the Ibo, the Yoruba, and the Hausa, waver between supporting an all-Nigerian nationalism and a tribal nationalism.

EFFECT ON ECONOMIC DEVELOPMENT

Such divisive forces in nationalist movements have unfavorable consequences for economic development. In Nigeria the primary problem before the native leaders is the issue of full independence. Though Nigeria is, in a sense, an artificial state, with boundaries which do not correspond to any ethnic or natural lines of division, the most successful policy in attaining the goal of independence is the fostering of a common Nigerian nationalist ideology rather than an ethnically divided one. Yet the existence of separatist nationalist movements shows that common Nigerian national sentiment is relatively weak, and there is a definite likelihood that the three peoples may form separate states once the goal of indpendence is reached. Separation was also one of the results of the attainmnt of political independence of British India, although the divisive force there was religion rather than linguistic or ethnic differences. In Burma division has only been avoided after a long and destructive civil war, which delayed economic development greatly, and the granting of far-reaching powers of local autonomy to some ethnic groups within the Union of Burma. This process of "balkanization," even where it does not lead to internal struggles, has doubt-less an unfavorable impact upon economic development. Not only does it impede the optimum harnessing of all human and nonhuman resources of a given region, and thus interfere with their optimum allocation, but also it tends to maintain particularistic relations in many fields of social action and slows up in this manner the development of fully rational, efficient forms of political and economic administration.

TRANSFER OF LOYALTY TO THE LARGER GROUP

Thus the penetration of attachments and loyalties to par-ticularistic entities and their replacement by loyalty to the whole nation is the most important positive effect of nationalist ideologies in underdeveloped countries. If we consider that in most of these countries the great majority of the people are still engaged in subsistence agriculture and therefore living in villages to a large degree economically self-contained, the paucity of in-teraction between them becomes plain. Their limited economic horizon affects their world view and their political awareness. Anthropological studies in many parts of the world have shown that the common understanding of the villagers of their place in the world usually does not reach far beyond the limits of their village. They maintain relations with persons living in the surrounding region and occasionally may go to a nearby town, but their loyalty is to their own home community, and people in other parts of their country are regarded by them as strangers. The function of nationalism in such a society is the transference of loyalty from the narrow village or kinship group to the larger national group.

To be sure, in many underdeveloped countries a number of factors which facilitate this process have been operating, some for a long time and others more recently. The establishment of Western enterprises in parts of under-developed countries has tended to break down the isolation of the villages. They have attracted workers from the villages and have brought them in contact with persons from other villages, towns, and often also other parts of the country. The growth of urban centers has had a similar effect. Villagers have migrated to the cities and settled there, permanently or temporarily. There they have been thrown with persons from other parts of the country, have worked and often lived with them, and have attained membership in clubs, trade unions, or other voluntary organizations composed of many people with whom they had no previous tie, kinship or regional. A similar melting-pot effect was exercised by service in the army or sometimes in work gangs, and the effects of warfare which forced many people to flee their homes and settle among strangers also brought about the establishment of new contacts and the general enlargement of the horizon of simple people, whose previous world was confined to the boundaries of their village or district.

All these processes which tended to make people more mobile geo-graphically and to enhance the number and frequency of contacts between them led to an increased awareness that beyond those persons with whom one customarily maintained face-to-face relations were others who had some things in common with the members of the in-group, and yet were strangers. It was this faintly felt tie that received its most powerful support from nationalist ideology. Nationalist symbols provided a meaning and an interpretation for the very imprecise and blurred sentiments of community of interest and destiny which people in many underdeveloped countries began to experience. They drew a firmer boundary around the new in-group and defined in more expressive forms the differences between that in-group and the various out-groups. And they showed how the activities of each member of the in-group interrelate with, and are dependent upon, what others of the same in-group are doing, even though the various actors may not know each other personally. In the course of this process the main goal of nationalism tended to be achieved, namely, the gradual transference of primary loyalties from the village or kinship group to the larger society.

Difference from Earlier Large States

In this, the modern sentiment of nationalism differs from analogous ideologies held in the earlier large societies in underdeveloped countries. The establishment of large states in the territories of many underdeveloped countries is nothing new. The Mogul Empire in India, the empire of Majapahit in Java, even the kingdom of Dahomey in West Africa, were large states covering the major part of present nations or peoples aspiring to independent nationhood. Like the monarchies of early mediaeval Europe, however, they were not built upon nationality as a common bond but rather upon submission to a common ruler and assignment of places in a sociopolitical hierarchy with this ruler at the apex. In this sense the upsurge of a nationalist ideology in Asia and Africa is an outgrowth of the contact of these peoples with Europe and the West. Nationalism provides a means by which strong common ties can be established without hierarchical subordination and with maintenance of the principle of equality as a significant political value. This is the reason why programs of improvement of mass welfare, buttressed by a nationalist ideology, have, in principle, an egalitarian, democratic hue, and this is the chief feature by which modern nation-states in underdeveloped countries are distinguished from their monarchical predecessors.

LEADERSHIP

But although this phase of nationalism combined with aspirations to higher levels of welfare on a mass basis appears to offer a fertile soil for democratic political

institutions, the very need for the institutionalization of these processes requires strong centralized leadership, which in turn makes possible the development of autocratic and, in extreme cases, even totalitarian government.

Requirements of National Propaganda

Although nationalism attains and pre-
serves a momentum of its own in the societies of the West, the very newness
of nationalist ideology in many underdeveloped countries requires that it be
attended to and supported constantly. In spite of the persistence of processes
of social and economic change which tend to break down the isolation of the
villages, and in spite of the buttressing of these processes by an officially
promulgated nationalist ideology, the attachments of the kinship group or the
local community in many underdeveloped countries are strong enough to
make necessary the constant maintenance of nationalist propaganda and
agitation. This requires a staff of skilled and devoted persons who become
the chief manipulators of nationalist symbols and the elite personnel in the
promulgation and diffusion of these symbols.

The logical group to undertake this task in an underdeveloped country
is the leadership of political parties both in and out of government office. In
fact, the manipulation of nationalist symbols might be regarded as one of
the two or three most significant and appropriate functions of political party
leadership in underdeveloped countries. This statement applies to all parties
which wish to maintain and enlarge their influence and extends from the
parties on the radical right to those on the radical left, that is, the Communists. The association in underdeveloped countries between nationalism
and Communist ideology has often been observed, in spite of the pretensions
of Communists to an ideology of internationalism. Resentment against those
alleged to have kept large colonial populations in a state of poverty and hence
to have "exploited" them and resentment against the foreign powers which
until recently have supplied the political machinery maintaining this condition of exploitation have combined to offer these Communist parties a fruitful soil for action and propaganda. It should be noted that the Communist
appeal depends upon this two-pronged resentment: on the one hand against
the "exploiters" and on the other against the foreigners who are either
identified with the exploiters or presented as supporting them.

But the Communist leaders are not the only ones who use nationalism
as a plank in their party propaganda. In fact, the ability of a party to
manipulate the nationalist symbols and appear in the eyes of the masses as
the true representative of nationalist aspirations seems to be an important
factor of its success. For example, the relatively poor showing of the Socialists in the Indonesian elections of 1955 must be attributed in large part to
inability to make optimum use of nationalist propaganda.

If the proposition is granted that nationalist propaganda requires ceaseless activity because of the still somewhat ambivalent loyalties of many simple people in underdeveloped countries, and if it is granted that the persons in positions of political leadership in the government and political parties are the primary carriers of this nationalist propaganda, the ultimate political effect of nationalist trends and their association with economic development programs will depend upon the aims and objectives of the leaders. For this reason it is important to ask not only what these aims are but also what the social composition of the new political leadership in underdeveloped countries is and what the relation of the leaders to the mass of peoples over whom they exercise power.

Gap Between the Elite and the Masses

One of the outstanding characteristics of the political elite in underdeveloped countries is the wide cultural and educational distance which separates them from the masses of the people. The exigencies of government, administration of economic and political bureaucracies, and control of media of mass communication require a degree of technical and organizational skill which could only be acquired in the West or in Western dominated institutions. Thus in those countries in which independence has been attained the political elite are to a considerable degree Western educated and have adopted not only Western forms of behavior but in many instances also Western values. Even in countries which are still lacking full independence, as, for example, Nigeria and the Gold Coast, many members of the native political elite conform to this pattern. The social distance between these persons and the mass of their followers is often greater than that between them and the Western foreigners designated by nationalist propagandists as the main representatives of the inimical out-groups.

The result of this situation is, first, a sharp class division between the common people on the one hand and members of the government and leading political figures on the other. Another result of the conflicting cultural orientations of the elite and the masses is the monopolization of many functions of leadership by the members of the elite. Modern administration, in the political as well as the economic field, requires rationalized, impersonal bureaucracies. Their optimum performance depends upon the assignment of roles on a universalistic, achievement-oriented basis. But in view of the fact that traditionalist, often strongly particularistic, norms are widely observed among the popular masses, the political and to some minor extent the economic elite occupy a favored position with respect to leadership. Although widespread extension of education would gradualy make it possible for increasing numbers to compete for leadership roles, most underdeveloped countries lack the necessary educational facilities and hence are deficient in suitably trained technical personnel with qualifications necessary for the fulfillment of administrative tasks on the higher or even medium levels.

The social characteristics of the political leadership group therefore tend to place it in a position somewhat apart from and on top of the mass of the people, and the often observed absence of a middle class in underdeveloped countries is perhaps not so much a true description of actual facts as a reflection of the social distance between those who are leaders in some political or economic area and those who are not. Since it takes a long time to develop adequate educational institutions, the members of the present elite are able to maintain the social differentiation which endows them with positions of leadership. Correspondingly, we can understand why in most underdeveloped countries education is so highly prized. It is perhaps the most important, though not the only, means of social advancement.

Aids to Social Advances

Besides education, there exist several other avenues of social ascent. One of them, as in Western countries, is the acquisition of wealth, and another the attainment of positions in the bureaucracies of religious and voluntary organizations. The former usually requires educational attainments of a high order. The latter, among which positions in trade unions and some semipolitical bureaucracies are the most important, has on the whole greater significance in underdeveloped countries than in the West, since there the ties between trade unbalance and political partisanship are stronger and more obvious.

An aid to rising in the social scale is the fact that the economic expansion of the countries, even if gradual and halting, and the increase in political and administrative tasks require the gradual enlargement of the social elite. In countries where pressures to move upwards are strong, because there is a relatively greater abundance of trained personnel or because economic development is slow and stagnant, the supply of "intellectuals," especially intellectuals of certain kinds—for example, lawyers—may exceed the demand for them and force them into accepting leadership in political counterelites, such as radical political parties or popular movements with real or alleged charismatic objectives. This development has, for example, occurred in India and is one of the reasons for the violent political radicalism of many Indian intellectuals.

ECONOMIC DEVELOPMENT AND SOCIAL STRUCTURE

The general picture presented by the social structure in underdeveloped countries thus is one in which there exists a wide gap between the upper and the lower classes. The upper classes have adopted many Western values and forms of behavior; they are familiar with the operations of a money economy; and many things bought from the West become status symbols. The lower classes frequently follow traditional indigenous values, often have little skill in monetary transactions, and live to a considerable extent still in an economy in which the village or a more or less clearly defined local region is largely self-sufficient. As a consequence of this dichotomy in values and behavioral norms, the upper classes enjoy an almost exclusive monopoly of access to those "goods" in society which are most highly prized: political power, education, and wealth.

Centralized Planning

The power of this group is enhanced by the fact that economic development in almost all underdeveloped countries is fostered to a large extent by the central government. This is not the place to discuss whether centralization of developmental planning is a matter of choice or necessity for these countries. In view of the fact that they still lack most of the capital equipment which is usually referred to as "social overhead"—transport and communications networks, power stations, educational and health facilities, and the like—and in view of 'the further fact that these installations are of primary importance for economic development, a high degree of centralized developmental planning may be unavoidable. At any rate the prevailing inclination of governments to undertake the function of programming economic development can easily be understood. But the result of this centralization of developmental planning is the enhancement of the power of the socio-political elite and the increased dependence of the large mass of the people upon decisions made by this relatively small section of the population.

Conflicting Forces

The main dilemma of political, and with it economic, development in underdeveloped countries results from this divergence between, on the one hand, the actual structure of social relations, which is rigorously hierarchical and associated with deep social cleavages, and, on the other, the collectivity-oriented values expressed by nationalism in its positive aspects and the ideology of elevation of mass living standards. The pressure of these ideologies tends to push in the direction of greater democracy and mass participation in political and economic processes. The interests inculcated in the members of the political elite and buttressed by the inequalities in the social structure tend to push in the direction of authoritarianism and a high degree of centralization of governmental powers.

It is difficult to predict the outcome of these conflicting forces. In different countries different results may ensue. For example, some observers who have noted the pressures discussed in this essay in the emerging societies of Africa have expressed the fear that the attainment of independence may there be associated with the coming to power of a highly authoritarian black elite rather than with a democratization of political and social relations. Such an outcome seems not improbable since, as may be seen in Central and Eastern Europe, a nationalist ideology can be diverted to the support of totalitarian or quasi-totalitarian governments as well as democratic ones.

As against this alternative must be held the potentialities for greater equality and freedom which stem from the struggle for political independence. Although the internal class relations in the societies of underdeveloped countries provide a fruitful soil for authoritarian political developments, the forces unleashed by the struggle for independence may lead in the opposite direction. The actual course of political developments in these countries appears to me to depend upon two factors, which are operative with varying force in different underdeveloped countries. One is the rapidity of economic development, and the other is the success of transforming the many particularistic hierarchical relations now existing on the social and political levels into a system in which the different interest groups become co-ordinated, with power distributed among them, rather than subordinated within one hierarchy.

Rapidity of Economic Development

The impact of rapid economic development upon the potentialities of democratic political institutions is not very difficult to see. If the economy, especially in its consumption goods sector, grows rapidly, the goal of improved mass living standards can be implemented more fully. Although economic growth, and especially industrialization and urbanization, remain associated with recurring episodes of social disorganization, the visible increase in consumption standards compensates for this to some extent, and the implementation of developmental programs can count upon a greater degree of consensus. The government needs to use fewer constraints, and there tends to develop less conflict between the leaders and the mass. Moreover, a rapidly growing economy has a greater and more insistent demand for skilled personnel, and the rising members of the lower social strata are less frequently frustrated in their desire for social and economic advancement.

Remolding the Social Structure

But economic development alone, even if it stresses and actually succeeds in bringing about an elevation of consumption standards, does not guarantee the evolution of democratic political forms unless the sociopolitical structure is remolded at the same time. It has been argued that a nationalist ideology tends to break down particularistic loyalties and interests. But if its over-all effect is to bring the various groups, once they are robbed of their traditionalist values, into a rigorous hierarchy with a small group of nationalistic, sometimes charismatic, leaders at the top, democratic political forms will have a negligible chance of evolving. The main problem before these societies is not merely the abolition of particularist elements in their sociopolitical structure, but the replacement of these elements by groupings which, though universalistically oriented in their over-all values, nevertheless maintain independence of action and the power to represent the interests of functionally diverse social elements on an approximately equal level.

Two Possibilities

In more concrete terms, this can be expressed by saying that there are two possible ways of eliminating the existing particularistic structures in underdeveloped countries.

1. They may become rigorously subordinated to a central hierarchy. The leaders of the various village and regional communities, even of ethnic and linguistic groups, are assigned positions on various lower levels of this hierarchy and exercise their power roles through it. The society returns to the type prevailing in earlier monarchical periods, only with the difference that modern methods of communication and the addition of a nationalist ideology provide this structure with increased strength and resilience as compared with its monarchical forebears. The similarities to these earlier structures are even enhanced if, and to the extent to which, the leadership in the new hierarchy is endowed with charismatic qualities.

2. Democratic development, on the contrary, is aided if the dissolution of particularistic groups leads to their replacement by functionally specialized groupings among which power is distributed in a more or less co-ordinate fashion. Or, more concretely: if the present petty elite in the village, the region, the ethnic or linguistic group, are robbed of their positions of leadership in these particularist groupings and new groups are formed along political party lines, occupational interests, or social class lines, leadership in these new groups depends not upon undifferentiated localized control and power but upon adequate representation of the interests of the members of the new group.

It does not matter greatly whether the leaders in these new groups are identical with those in the old ones or not. In general, the universalistic values which are forced, as it were, upon the leaders of the new interest groups, will tend to bring about a gradual replacement of the old elite by new leaders, and thus will tend to encourage a circulation of the elite. New leaders will attain positions in the functionally differentiated groups not because of the position of their family or the accidents surrounding their birth (in other words, not because of genealogical or magical qualities), but rather because of achievement in representing the group interest. This, in turn, will contribute to the greater degree of circulation of the elite and also to the distribution of power among the various interest groups, since each of them, provided it maintains its independence of action, will find a place in the total social structure in accordance with the success with which it can uphold the special interests of its members as against the claims of other competing interest groups.

Given an essentially universalist orientation of the members of these groups, the competition for influence and power need not lead to a rupture of society but will rather eventuate in an over-all rough balance of the power positions of these groups. In the most common-sense terms, one might say that if and to the extent to which tribal chiefs and village heads can be transformed into or replaced by secretaries of competing political parties or trade unions, officers of independent chambers of agriculture, industry, or labor, or chairmen of regional welfare or health committees, the over-all chances of democratic development in underdeveloped countries will be much enhanced. It goes without saying that this development will take place only if this change is one in substance rather than one in name.

THE DEMOCRATIC ALTERNATIVE

In general, economic development sets a framework in which these sociopolitical changes may take place. It affords opportunities for the evolution of less tradition-oriented and more rationalized social and economic action. But whether these opportunities will be grasped and implemented so as to lead to democratic political institutions will also depend upon whether the nationalist symbols are used to enthrone a centralized bureaucratic authoritarian leadership or to provide new avenues for political expression of diverse functionally oriented interest groups in a sociopolitical framework in which power is not centralized but widely distributed.

ECONOMIC POLICY-MAKING IN INDONESIA, 1950-1957

Bruce Glassburner

The period beginning with the transfer of Dutch sovereignty over the East Indian Islands to the government of the United States of Indonesia in December 1949, and ending with the so-called "take-over" of Dutch-owned business property in December 1957, seems clearly destined to become one of those times of struggle and crisis which historians of the nation will analyze and re-analyze over the generations, interpreting and re-interpreting the known facts as the perspective of time changes. We are, of course, still much too close to that period to be able to understand its historical significance at all well. It is nevertheless of great importance to make an effort to understand the recent past in a highly dynamic situation such as that which now exists in this new nation.

It is the intent of this article to analyze the period in terms of just one aspect—namely, the making and implementation of economic policy—not only because the author is an economist rather than a historian or political scientist, but also because the disappointing record of economic policy during that period clearly reflects the underlying political conflict which eventually resulted in the drastic action of December 1957. This record, therefore, makes the dramatic attempt at re-ordering which is now in progress in the nation somewhat more easy to understand than is possible if it is viewed only as a series of current events.

From Bruce Glassburner, "Economic Policy-Making in Indonesia, 1950–1957," *Economic Development and Cultural Change*, 10:2:1:113–133 (January 1963). Reprinted by permission of The University of Chicago Press.

I would like to begin this analysis of the period by asserting that, from the point of view of economic policy, the years 1950–57 in Indonesia are best understood as years of a hopeless losing battle on the part of a very small group of pragmatically conservative political leaders against an increasingly powerful political opposition of generally radical orientation.

This statement, while it is my own way of putting the point, is by no means entirely original. The same general idea has been more or less clearly stated by six other writers. In order to give proper credit where due, and to indicate clearly the eclectic nature of this analysis, it will be useful to look at the statements of this general hypothesis which have been made in several analyses of the Indonesian economic and political scene which have appeared in the last few years.

Dr. John Sutter, in his extensive descriptive study of Indonesian economic policy,[1] sees the period as being divided into two parts, which are, roughly, the times of political ascendancy of two major factions in the struggle. The period of the first four cabinets, from December 1949, when Dr. Mohammed Hatta took office as prime minister, until June 1953, when the cabinet of Mr. Wilopo[2] fell, is referred to by Sutter as "the *Masjumi* period." He regards it as such in spite of the fact that Dr. Hatta and Mr. Wilopo were not members of the *Masjumi* political party, because, in his view, during this period the dominating outlook among members of the cabinet was the "Sjafruddin-*Masjumi*" outlook. (Mr. Sjafruddin Prawiranegara was first minister of finance, and later the governor of the Bank of Indonesia. He was also quite consistently the *Masjumi* party's outstanding spokesman on matters of economic policy.)

The period following the fall of the Wilopo cabinet is referred to by Sutter as "the PNI period"[3] and as having been dominated in outlook by "the less tolerant ultra-nationalist and socialist politicians."[4]

Although Dr. Sutter uses these labels as major time categories, he does not dwell on their significance at length, nor does he explicitly make use, except very occasionally,[5] of the idea of the conflict implied in the distinction as a means of analyzing the economic policies of the post-revolutionary pe-

---

[1] John O. Sutter, *Indonesianisasi, Politics in a Changing Economy, 1940–55*, Data Paper No. 36–1, Southeast Asia Program (Ithaca: Cornell University, Department of Far Eastern Studies, 1959).

[2] The designation "Mr." (for *Meester in Rechten,* or Master of Laws) is a Dutch title, still widely used in Indonesia.

[3] PNI being the initials of the *Partai Nasional Indonesia* (Indonesian Nationalist Party).

[4] Sutter, *op. cit.,* p. 1190.

[5] He does speak at one point of a tendency for the two sides to cancel each other out, "and [leave the] Government on a dead center of inactivity or . . . [following] the moderate rationalist-socialist middle course of which Djuanda and Sumitro were exponents." *Ibid.*

riod. Aside from the fact that he gives brief and casual treatment to this basic idea, it seems to me that he overemphasizes the importance of the *Masjumi* and the quite highly conservative (by Indonesian standards) Mr. Sjafruddin. The emphasis on Sjafruddin indicates a tendency on Dr. Sutter's part to regard the leadership of the earlier period as being more conservative in outlook than it really was, an emphasis which is necessary if his two periods are to be clearly distinct. This tendency to overemphasize the differences in the ideological orientation of the leadership of the two periods is also reflected in his reference to the leadership of the "PNI period" as being in the hands of "socialist politicians," when in fact, socialism is basic to the political ideology of virtually all shades of the Indonesian political spectrum. It might be added that the use of the party labels is unfortunate, in view of the fact that by no means all members of the *Masjumi* party think along the lines of Mr. Sjafruddin—Dr. Sukiman, who was prime minister from March 1951 to March 1952, appears to be one major exception. Similarly, the PNI has its "economics-minded" intellectuals, who fail to fit the description of "ultra-nationalist"—Mr. Wilopo and Mr. Sumanang (Wilopo's minister of economic affairs) being important examples.

Benjamin Higgins has suggested terminology which describes the basic antagonism somewhat better than that of Dr. Sutter. Higgins suggests that "economics-minded" or "development-minded" persons provided leadership on the one hand, and "history-minded" persons on the other.[6] The former turn out to be essentially Western-oriented, and the latter to be "a mixture of Communists and of a larger number who are nationalist, conservative (in Western terms), and isolationist."[7] The orientation of the latter group Higgins sees as being more militantly anti-foreign and more concerned with the retention of Indonesia's traditional linguistic, cultural, and religious institutions. The main advantage of this terminology over Sutter's is that the awkward connection of such attitudes to party labels is avoided. The disadvantage is that the terminology is unfair to the radicals of the left who opposed the leadership and policies of the first four cabinets.

The same criticism can be made of the terminology used by John Meek, who feels that the split occurs between those emphasizing "Indonesianization" of the economy and those who emphasized economic development.[8] Meek makes the difference in orientation between the two groups the center of his analysis of economic policy from 1950 to 1954, concluding, incidentally, that those interested in "Indonesianization first" achieved considerably more success than the other group, in spite of the fact that four of the five cabinets

[6] Benjamin Higgins, *Indonesia's Economic Stabilization and Development* (New York: Institute of Pacific Relations, 1957), p. 103.

[7] *Idem.*

[8] John Paul Meek, *The Government and Economic Development in Indonesia, 1950–54*, Ph.D. thesis (University of Virginia, 1956), microfilm, p. 185.

in the time period which he analyzed were led by the group that have been referred to here as pragmatic conservatives. The main point implicit, in all of the writers thus far discussed, is that the group in opposition from 1950 to 1957 refused to accept the basic premise of the cabinet leadership, i.e., that the main outlines of the structure of the economy, both in terms of ownership and function, had to be lived with for a relatively long period of time, and that policy had to be designed to improve its functioning. This much can be accepted as correct, but it does not follow from this that demands for "completion of the revolution" in the economy and insistence on Indonesian control over economic institutions are to be regarded as backward-looking (as they are by both Meek and Higgins).

The most ambitious attempt to deal with the relationship of this conflict to economic policy is that of Hans Schmitt.[9] Schmitt sees the basic cause of economic and political strife in Indonesia as stemming from the economic interests of the "bureaucratic elite" of the Indonesian community, who were faced with a frustrating obstacle in the form of continued domination of the industrialized-commercialized sector of the economy by foreign interests—primarily Dutch. Schmitt bases his analysis on a drastic premise:

> It seems . . . plausible to argue that extensions in the capital stock enhance the power of those who control it. This is a consideration which leads to a contemporaneous conflict between interests of power and of consumption. Maximum consumption (and leisure) is apt to be in the immediate interests of people not in control of accumulated capital, and maximum investment of those that are. The rate of economic development would then reflect the balance of power between them. The rate is maximized, *ceteris paribus*, when one group is firmly in control and in fact sees its power enhanced by further accumulation. Unfortunately, neither has been the case in Indonesia, and this is reflected in the course of Indonesian monetary policy.
>
> The capital stock in Indonesia has been predominantly in the hands of foreigners, reflecting pre-war colonial conditions.[10]

The bureaucratic elite is not well identified by Schmitt, but from context it would appear to mean the broad mass of employees of government and the government-created group of *nasional* (i.e., indigenous) entrepreneurs—the bulk of whom were importers. These people had considerable political power and little control over economic activity, and were because of this both desirous and able to raise their own standards of "consumptions and leisure" by becoming economic parasites. Thus their interests were in direct conflict with "rational" economic goals, and they formed an intransigent opposition to cabinet-led attempts at fiscal retrenchment. Domestic inflation was

[9] Hans O. Schmitt, *Monetary Policy and Social Conflict in Indonesia* (Djakarta, 1958), multilithed. A later version of this paper was submitted as a Ph.D. thesis to the University of California (Berkeley, in 1959).

[10] Schmitt, *op. cit*, p. 1–14.

in the interest of the importer group, for one thing, and, since government expenditure on a high level meant high government employment and also opportunities to favor interests in close relation to this elite, streamlining of government finance aroused ready opposition.

The Schmitt version of the conflict raises several difficult questions. First, one is inclined to ask why the early cabinets made any attempt at all to devise policies that would bring fiscal stability and economic growth. In connection with the Wilopo cabinet's retrenchment program, Dr. Schmitt is bothered by this question himself:

> Since these interests [i.e., those challenged by the retrenchment policy] were those of the elite taken as a unit, . . . it is curious to find any political orientation developing at all that would be prepared to challenge them.[11]

The answer which Dr. Schmitt found was that (a) the *Masjumi* party anticipated very wide popular support in the general elections, and could therefore ignore the interests of the elite, and (b) failing the materialization of popular support, "the support which . . . [retrenchment's] proponents could muster in the army."

But this reply does not really answer the question. Why, even with popular and/or military support, should the *Masjumi* leadership wish to foster the interests of entrenched Dutch capital and ignore the interests of its countrymen? *Masjumi* party members in large numbers were to be found among the *nasional* importers, if not so strongly among the civil servants— all this aside from the fact that the cabinet in question was under the leadership of the "liberal" wing of the Nationalist Party, not the *Masjumi*. Finally, what would motivate the army leadership to support fiscal retrenchment? Surely its leadership was no less nationalistic than that of the bureaucracy.

A second difficult question raised by this formulation is that of the identification of the interests of the elite. As George Kahin has said:

> The Indonesian bureaucracy was not a harmonious and unified group . . . although the bureaucracy can be regarded as a force of some consequence in the Indonesian political scene, its impact has not been as great as might be expected on the basis of the high proportion of the Western-educated Indonesian elite it has incorporated. Where the influence of its members has been felt, it has frequently been in terms of party advantage rather than calculated to promote views or interests of the bureaucracy as a whole.[12]

Thus, it appears plain that any attempt to explain the pattern of politics and economic policy in terms of a simple theory of economic interest runs afoul of the complexities of multiple economic interests, and the quite ap-

[11] *Ibid.,* p. 3–18.
[12] George McT. Kahin, "Indonesia," in Kahin, ed., *Major Governments of Asia* (Ithaca: Cornell University Press, 1958), p. 521.

parent presence in the community of elite group members who were interested enough in economic stabilization and development to make modest efforts at appropriate policy proposals, and even to fight for them politically to some extent.

But Dr. Schmitt's analysis contains a basically correct insight—namely, that the economic elements in the basis of power of the opposition to these cabinets, and their policies, lay in the fact of the continued existence of an entrenched Dutch economic interest and in the economic impotency of the Indonesian elite in general.

J. A. C. Mackie, in a recent article,[13] deals with the same issue in still different terms, though basically it is the same as the Schmitt analysis. Mackie says that the government in this period (1950–57) did not represent "productive interests," but "consumers" instead. Hence, policy was not "productive." In the absence of a strong government, the "conditions appropriate to a free-enterprise development policy" could not be expected. This formulation, too, would seem to put the matter rather too firmly in terms of economic interest to avoid the problems of the Procrustean bed.

Last in this gallery of analysts of the schism of Indonesian leadership is Herbert Feith, who, in a remarkably fine M.A. thesis, has examined the problem entirely from the point of view of the political scientist. Feith, like Sutter, sees the period as being divided by the fall of the Wilopo cabinet. Until that event took place (June 1953), "the political elite was substantially united on fundamentals."[14] But by that time, according to Mr. Feith, a serious political polarization had taken place, and the failure of that cabinet swung control decisively to the other pole—i.e., to the "mass leaders." Before the pendulum swing, he argues, policy was largely in the hands of the "intellectuals" of the *Masjumi,* PNI, and Indonesian Socialist Party (PSI).[15] The position of strength which this group held in 1950 was eroded by a continued discrepancy between expectations and performances, a discrepancy which was, in large measure, the result of the efforts of the so-called mass leaders themselves, who were able to make ready use of the anti-Dutch, anti-liberal sentiments that were deeply rooted in the community. While Feith's analysis of the schism is far more complete than that of any of the others, it is primarily an analysis of political events and thus, properly enough, tends to place its relationship to economic policy in a position of secondary interest. Secondly, his emphasis on the intellectual leadership of the one pole and the mass

[13] "The Political Economy of Guided Democracy," *Australian Outlook* (December 1959), esp. pp. 287–88.

[14] Herbert Feith, *The Wilopo Cabinet, 1952–53: Turning Point in Post-Revolutionary Indonesia* (Ithaca: Cornell University Southeast Asia Program Monograph Series, 1958), pp. 210–11.

[15] In Feith's terminology, "intellectuals" are persons "of Western university or senior secondary education" (p. 19), and "mass leaders" are those whose positions of power rest on "narrowly political skills," rather than on any claim to administrative expertise or knowledge of government.

orientation of the other tends to prejudice the case against the latter.

The radical left and right do not entirely lack rationale for their positions, however alien their premises may be to Western observers. The Marxian point of view, for example, rests on the argument that the state is inevitably controlled by those who control the economy; and that private capital is inherently exploitative. Refusal to cooperate with governments which made even tentative gestures toward rehabilitation of the colonial economy was consistent with this argument—which, incidentally, originates with Western academics.

The radically conservative point of view is that Indonesian culture has been badly diluted by more than three centuries of Western overlordship, and that the only hope of salvaging Indonesian institutions is to prevent their further dilution. The continued presence of Dutch business and government personnel meant to many Indonesians the continued existence of the colonial social structure, in which the Dutchman sat atop a pyramid whose base was "native." They hope to see free Indonesia develop her own institutions, "consistent with the Indonesian spirit." Pragmatically, the fact that the "mass leaders" were able to enlist mass support would seem to suggest that their political premises, if not their economic logic, might be more nearly correct for the longer view than those on which the leaders of the opposite pole felt compelled to operate.

In support of my restatement of the idea that runs through all of these analyses in terms which seem to fit my problem best, it is necessary to start with the Round Table Conference held at The Hague in the autumn months of 1949. At that conference, Holland agreed to grant Indonesia her sovereignty, politically, but at the same time established conditions in the agreement which were designed to preserve her economic interests in the archipelago. The following are the relevant passages:

SECTION A

Article 1

1. In respect of the recognition and restoration of the rights, concessions, and licenses properly granted under the law of the Netherlands East Indies (Indonesia) and still valid on the date of transfer of sovereignty, the Republic of the United States of Indonesia will adhere to the basic principle of recognizing such rights, concessions, and licenses. The Republic of the United States of Indonesia also recognizes, insofar as this has not been done, that the rightful claimants be restored to the actual exercise of their rights under the proviso referred to in the following paragraphs of this article. . . .[16]

---

[16] Article 1, paragraph 3, specifically qualified this paragraph to take account of the problem of squatters on estate lands, noting that removal of population from the lands might cause "too much unrest," and that each case must be judged on its individual merits in this regard.

Article 2

The rights, concessions, and licenses referred to in Article 1, paragraph 1, may be infringed only in the public interest, including the welfare of the people, and through amicable settlement with the rightful claimants, and if the latter cannot be achieved, by expropriation for the public benefit, such in accordance with the provisions of Article 3.

Article 3

Expropriation, nationalization, liquidation, compulsory cession, or transfer of properties or rights, shall take place exclusively for the public benefit, in accordance with the procedure prescribed by law and, in the absence of an agreement between the parties, against previously enjoyed or guaranteed indemnity to be fixed by judicial decision at the real value of the object involved, such in accordance with provisions to be prescribed by law.[17]

These provisions in the agreement were the basis of perpetuation of an economic system which even the most tolerant of Indonesian patriots must have found difficult to accept agreeably, for the degree of foreign domination of the economy (aside from peasant agriculture) was extreme. Nan Amstutz cites a prewar estimate that only 19 percent of the privately owned non-agricultural capital was in the hands of indigenous Indonesians, while 52% was held by Dutch owners.[18] In 1952 it was estimated that 50% of all consumer imports were still being handled by four Dutch firms, and 60% of exports by eight firms.[19] The bank of issue was a largely Dutch-owned corporation, controlled by Dutch officers. Private banking was largely in the hands of seven foreign banks, three of which were Dutch. Under such circumstances it is little wonder that even the moderate leaders felt that the Indonesian revolution had not yet entered its economic phase.[20]

Thus, the situation which confronted the economic leaders of the new national community was one which they inevitably had strong inclinations to change. It can be taken for granted that any successful Indonesian politician is, first of all, a nationalist, and secondly, a socialist;[21] while the task which

[17] Round Table Conference results as accepted in the second plenary meeting held on 2 November 1949 in the "Ridderzaal" at The Hague, published by the Secretariat-General of the Round Table Conference (no date), pp. 23–24.

[18] Nan G. Amstutz, *Development of Indigenous Importers in Indonesia, 1950–55,* Ph.D. thesis, Fletcher School of Law and Diplomacy, 1958, unpublished, p. 8.

[19] Meek, *op. cit.,* p. 168n.

[20] Higgins, *op. cit.,* p. 102, quotes Hadji Agus Salim to this effect.

[21] The question often arises in discussions of Indonesian politics as to whether the nation's Communist Party leadership is not perhaps Communist first and Nationalist second—and if then only as a matter of political convenience. Confronted by this question in personal conversation, a close associate of D. N. Aidit, Secretary General of the Indonesian Communist Party, emphatically stated that Aidit has always said that he is a Communist because he is Indonesian. It is fair to say, furthermore, that the Party in Indonesia has taken a consistently nationalist position for many years—and particularly so since President Sukarno has assumed the position of prime minister.

the government faced in 1950 was to stabilize and expand an economy that was (a) foreign-dominated and (b) privately owned. They were expected to devise policy which, if successful, would benefit the interests of their ideological enemies at least as much as their allies, and, anticipating the general elections, to attempt to gain the support of the politically sensitive part of the electorate—a group more radically inclined than they. Examined in retrospect, it is not surprising that they made so little progress in formulating successful economic policy. As Feith aptly puts it, "the fiery idealism of Jogjakarta and the days of guerilla fighting had to be accommodated in the Dutch-established structure of Djakarta."[22]

In terms of accomplishing that accommodation, it was fortunate that, in 1950, a virtual monopoly of economic expertise was held by sober-minded, Dutch-trained pragmatic socialists. In the first four cabinets, only Dr. Hatta and Dr. Sumitro Djojohadikusumo were trained economists, but the general direction of their economic ideology was followed by several others whose experience and inclinations perhaps qualified them as economic experts, namely, Sjafruddin Prawiranegara, Djuanda Kartawidjaja, Jusuf Wibisono, and perhaps others. Of this group, Sjafruddin was the one most clearly inclined to accept the circumstances and to be willing to make the necessary accommodation, and Sumitro was undoubtedly the least inclined in that direction. Sjafruddin's cautious variety of socialism was clearly stated by him in 1948 in the following words:

> The ideology which is suitable to our society is Religious Socialism, an ideology which is in harmony with the Constitution. Religious Socialism does not abolish individualism, individual initiative, and individual responsibility . . . Competition arising out of private initiative as such is not bad, but the contrary, because competition increases production and improves the quality of goods . . . Only at a certain stage does this liberal economy not increase production and is there a tendency to limit production. At that stage the government must intervene by nationalizing certain private enterprises or establishing enterprises itself.[23]

This was, indeed, the voice of conservatism. But the more dynamic, and, I think it is safe to say, more effective, Dr. Sumitro took a position farther left, and more clearly nationalistic:

> In general in the states of Asia, in my view, the effort to surmount stagnation and retrogression, and later to encourage increasingly fast development, must be planned and consciously arranged. Here comes to the forefront the state which takes the role of the pioneer in the process of development. It is a fact

[22] *Op. cit.,* p. 3.
[23] Quoted from Kahin, *Nationalism and Revolution in Indonesia* (Ithaca: Cornell University Press, 1952), p. 310. The original is Sjafruddin's pamphlet, *Politik dan Revolusi Kita* (Jogjakarta, 1948).

that, in the states of Asia, there are not yet, or not yet sufficient, groups of creative entrepreneurs from within the society itself . . . The state must play an important role, particularly in the beginning stage . . . unless development is to be left absolutely to the foreign entrepreneurs which are [now] in our countries . . . In my opinion, this last road is not the intention and goal of development which is desired in the states of Asia. Both for the creation of autonomous investment and of skills, the state must and can play an important role by means of direct or indirect policy.[24]

Sumitro expressed his leftward nationalistic bent more directly in policy six months after joining the Natsir cabinet by directing the development of the Economic Urgency Program of 1951, a plan for quite extensive economic intervention in an attempt to establish indigenous industries.[25] And later, as minister of finance in two cabinets, Sumitro took drastic action to weaken the position of foreign enterprise. Sumitro, I think, represented more nearly the attitude of the leadership group of the time than did Sjafruddin (Sutter's nominee for the guiding spirit), for even Sjafruddin's own *Masjumi* party proposed a comprehensive, if cautious, program of nationalization of vital enterprises in 1950, and was directly responsible for the nationalization of the Java Bank under the Sukiman cabinet, with Mr. Sjafruddin rather reluctantly replacing the Dutch president, A. Houwink. But whether the consensus among the leaders was nearer the views of Sjafruddin or of Sumitro is really of little moment, for the range was not wide in view of the circumstances. The orientation of both of these men was at least nominally socialist and essentially pragmatic—toward making the system work. No cabinet undertook a major program of economic re-ordering. And it was Sumitro, whose inclinations were radical, who turned out to be the most ingenious at "tinkering around the edges" of the economic system.[26]

As for the persons charged with economic responsibility after the fall of the Wilopo cabinet, the possibility of their designing and implementing economic policy that was "rational" in terms of the existing economic system was almost non-existent. There was no longer even a vague positively-oriented consensus, since they, in opposition, had repudiated the very steps that such rationality would call for. Ultimately, then, the only way out was the radical way—namely, nationalization of the Dutch enterprises.

[24] Sumitro Djojohadikusumo, *Ekonomi Pembangunan* (Pembangunan, Djakarta, 1957), pp. 128–29, my translation.

[25] Sumitro Djojohadikusumo, ed., "The Government's Program on Industries," *Ekonomi dan Keuangan Indonesia* (November 1954). While the plan was strongly interventionist, its impact on the structure of the economy was slight, since (as Sumitro's article shows) implementation of the program was never carried far.

[26] Sumitro and Sjafruddin debated their differences freely in newspaper articles, in books, and in Indonesia's economic journals. E.g., Sjafruddin's careful, considered annual reports as governor of the Bank of Indonesia (1951–56), and Dr. Sumitro's collection of articles, *Persoalan Ekonomi*.

With this orientation to the situation, let us now turn to the pattern of economic policy. The appended table and the following discussion give a summary of that pattern.

THE HATTA CABINET[27]

The cabinet led by Dr. Mohammed Hatta has been the only one in Indonesia's political history to be led by a professional economist. Unfortunately, however, its focus was narrow and its view restricted very much to the short run. The primary concern of this brief cabinet was with political unification. At the time of the transfer of sovereignty (December 1949), the new nation was known as the Republic of the United States of Indonesia, a federation of sixteen states, of which the Republic of Indonesia was one. Over the following nine months these states merged with the Republic of Indonesia to become a "unitary state."

Despite this atmosphere of political defiance of Dutch advice and influence, the cabinet gave its attention to many matters of economic policy. The most important measure undertaken was an attempt at monetary reform through simultaneous currency devaluation and the literal cutting of the money supply, in March 1950. The "money cut" involved the actual cutting in half of all Java Bank notes in denominations larger than 2.50 Indonesian guilders,[28] and the reduction of all bank deposits larger than 400 guilders by half. Compensation for losses incurred in this purge were made in long-term government bonds.

The results of this reform were disappointing. President Houwink of the Java Bank claimed that the purge had reduced the money supply by 1.6 billion guilders—41 percent of the money supply! But, amazingly, the monthly data on money in circulation published by the Java Bank show a reduction from March to April of only 170 million guilders, and prices of food and textiles actually rose over the period.[29]

Aside from these quite. drastic efforts at monetary and fiscal control,

[27] The following sections, summarizing the performances of the various cabinets, are largely the result of many hours of newspaper scanning undertaken by Wagiono, Ho Ing Thong, and Kenneth D. Thomas.

[28] The Indonesian currency was known as the guilder until the nationalization of the Java Bank on May 22, 1951, at which time the bank of issue became the Bank of Indonesia, and the currency became the rupiah.

[29] *Report of the Java Bank, 1950–51*, p. 29. Schmitt argues (op. cit., p. 2–43) that the differential exchange rate system, which was introduced with the devaluation as a means of correcting the deficit in the balance of payments, counteracted both the money-reducing and the deflationary impact of the purge. While this system would indeed have this effect in a small way, no conceivable change in the trade balance could account for the huge discrepancy between the president's stated estimate of the reduction in money in circulation and the modest (4 percent) change shown in the monthly statistics. For this writer the discrepancy remains unexplained.

little else was undertaken during this cabinet's short tenure. Foreign assistance received during 1950 was larger than at any time from 1949 to 1954, reflecting, perhaps, Dr. Hatta's firm belief that the main sources of development capital must be foreign. Also, by the end of 1950, the bulk of Java's railway network had been placed under the operation of the Indonesian government, replacing the Dutch private owners.

THE NATSIR CABINET

The first cabinet of the unitary Republic of Indonesia was led by Mohammed Natsir of the *Masjumi* party. This cabinet was probably the most distinctly dedicated toward action in economic affairs of any in Indonesian republican history. Dr. Sumitro was named minister of trade and industry, and Mr. Sjafruddin, minister of finance.

This cabinet was fortunate in taking over in the period of the full development of the Korean boom. It was thus blessed with very strong export demand, which provided at once a solution to the problem of the balance of payments, as well as a rising source of government revenue. The cabinet reacted to this situation by liberalizing imports as a means of keeping domestic prices down, raising standards of consumption, and encouraging the development of indigenous enterprise.

Credit was tight for the foreign-owned firms that dominated the economy, though easy for the burgeoning *nasional* firms. In an attempt to broaden the fiscal system, a 2.5% turnover tax was imposed. A combination of fiscal prudence and high revenues produced a sizeable budget surplus in 1951.

This cabinet also designed, but did not have time to initiate, an Economic Urgency Program. This was a highly nationalistic attempt to diminish the nation's dependence on foreign economic interests in several ways: by developing small, *nasional* (i.e., indigenous) industry to produce import substitutes in the hope of reducing dependence on foreign trade; by means of capital assistance to indigenous enterprise; and by restricting certain markets to indigenous sellers. The latter aspect of the program is often referred to as the *"benteng* program."[30] The Urgency Program was opposed from within the cabinet because of its highly nationalistic aspect—by Mr. Sjafruddin.[31]

The "historical rights" to shares of the foreign exchange allocation which had been used by the Dutch government to re-establish the prewar pattern of trade were abandoned by the Natsir cabinet, since it was their avowed intention to change that pattern in such a way as to diminish the degree of foreign domination.

As a means of supporting the economic program, the government reorganized the *Bank Rakjat* (People's Bank) and directed its activities toward

[30] *Benteng* is the Indonesian word for protected or fortified.
[31] Java Bank, *Report for the Year 1951–52*, pp. 39–42.

support of small business. At the same time the *Bank Industri Negara* (State Industrial Bank) was established to provide credit for reconstruction and development projects. The *Bank Negara Indonesia* was also greatly expanded and given the direct responsibility for providing capital for the *benteng* importers. Both the *Bank Rakjat's* reorganization and the establishment of the *Bank Industri Negara* actually took place in April 1951, just after the fall of the cabinet on an issue of regional autonomy.[32] This was, clearly, a very active cabinet, but with only six months of life, it could make little genuine progress. It was followed by a cabinet divided in control between the *Masjumi* and the *Nationalist* parties, though still led by the *Masjumi*.

THE SUKIMAN CABINET

The Sukiman cabinet served for ten months, from April 1951 to February 1952—a period of several significant landmarks in the economy's history. The finance minister was Jusuf Wibisono, and Mr. Wilopo was minister of economic affairs during most of this period. The most significant developments were the nationalization of the Java Bank and the collapse of the fiscal situation. The peak of the Korean boom was passed by mid-1951, and Indonesia's exports began to decline. The 1952 budget deficit was nearly three billion rupiahs, as compared with a surplus of 1.7 billion rupiahs for the preceding year. The deficit would have been larger still, had not a substantial revision of fiscal policy followed in the Wilopo cabinet later in the year.

The multiple exchange rate system which had been part of the fiscal trappings of the economic system since the reforms of 1950 were abandoned on the advice of Hjalmar Schacht, who had been invited to Indonesia by Dr. Sumitro as financial adviser. The "Sumitro plan" for small industries was partially implemented during the same year. The *benteng* program was continued, but, as a result of less careful screening of applicants for import licenses, the proportion of legitimate importing businesses initiated declined, and the disastrous fate of the program was thereby foreshadowed.

The Sukiman cabinet fell in February 1952, over the issue of the signing of the Mutual Security Agreement with the United States.

THE WILOPO CABINET

After some political difficulty, the Wilopo cabinet was formed in early April 1952, with retrenchment as its initial economic theme. Dr. Sumitro returned to the cabinet, as finance

---

[32] Although implemented late, the policy is properly called the Natsir cabinet's. Lags in implementation, e.g., in the case of the foreign investment law, often make responsibility for a particular policy difficult to assign. But in this case the responsibility belongs plainly to Natsir's cabinet.

minister, and Mr. Sumanang became minister of economic affairs. Despite heavy expenditure commitments which carried over from the Sukiman cabinet, the estimated 1952 deficit as of June 1952 of Rp. 4 billion was pared down to a realized deficit at the year's end of slightly less than Rp. 3 billion. This was accomplished mainly by ingenious gadgeteering, mainly with the taxes and exchange regulations in the foreign trade sector, although some effort at austerity in government expenditure was made as well.

The most spectacular effort at economy was made in connection with rationalization of the army. Conservative factions within the army combined with conservative political elements to oppose attempted renovation, resulting in the abortive effort on the part of the rationalization's supporters to force the issue by use of arms, in October 1952. The attempt failed, and the results were disastrous for the proponents of the rationalization, and a blow to the cabinet leadership and their supporters as well. This fiasco, incidentally, is often pointed to by persons familiar with the Indonesian political scene as the actual turning point, rather than the fall of the cabinet, which came several months later.

Less spectacularly, but more significantly, the ministry of finance sought a budget for 1953 that would call for an aggregate reduction in government expenditures of more than Rp. 4 billion—more than 25% of total expenditures in 1952. Implementation would have resulted in the dismissal of at least 150,000 persons on the government payroll, according to an estimate by the ministry of finance.[33] In point of fact, expenditures were not greatly reduced, but the Wilopo cabinet actually succeeded in maintaining a deficit less than that which they had projected until June 1953, when the cabinet fell on the issue of use of force to remove squatters from Sumatran estate lands.

THE FIRST ALI SASTROAMIDJOJO CABINET

The fiscal stringency of the Wilopo cabinet was promptly abandoned with the accession of the first cabinet in free Indonesia's history that did not have *Masjumi* representation. This was the longest-lived cabinet of any which preceded Ir. Djuanda's[34] *Karja* cabinet of 1957–59. From a fiscal point of view, this cabinet's first nine months were catastrophic. The government's debt was trebled and foreign exchange reserve was eliminated altogether.[35]

This unfortunate performance in the financial field was complemented by the open perversion of the *benteng* policy. Under the minister of economic affairs, Mr. Iskaq Tjokrohadisurjo, the issuing of licenses became primarily

[33] Cited by Higgins, *op. cit.*, p. 10n.

[34] The title "Ir." (*Ingenieur*) is commonly used in Indonesia to designate persons holding degrees in engineering.

[35] Schmitt, *op. cit.*, p. 3–48, Table III:6.

a means of financial support for the Nationalist Party. The government was bitterly criticized for its fiscal failures on the one hand and its perversion of the *benteng* policy on the other, and in November 1954, several major cabinet changes were made, including the replacement of Mr. Iskaq with Ir. Rooseno Surjohadikusumo. Reforms were immediately undertaken in the importers' screening process by Ir. Rooseno, but the reputation of the *nasional* importer group had been irreparably damaged. Thereafter little faith was placed in this means of displacing foreign enterprise.

The main efforts at restabilization following the November 1954 cabinet shake-up were directed toward import restrictions. These efforts met with considerable success. Efforts to curb the rise in the money supply, however, were less successful.

Although under the first Ali cabinet a draft bill on foreign investment regulations was brought forth, the general atmosphere and attitude of the government at the time was anything but congenial toward foreign enterprise. In particular, the abrogation of the trade policy section of the Round Table Agreement could be, and was, rather generally regarded as a negative gesture in this respect. Thus, the Ali government presented a confusing and disturbing face toward the supporters of private foreign enterprise in Indonesia.

But despite these policy failures, the cabinet successfully maneuvered its parliamentary strength until July 24, 1955, when the political repercussions of difficulties in the appointment of a new army chief of staff brought the government down.

THE HARAHAP CABINET

Following a cabinet crisis of less than three weeks, Dr. Hatta, as acting president, brought the *Masjumi* Party back to government leadership by inducing Mr. Burhanuddin Harahap, the *Masjumi* parliamentary leader, to accept the position of prime minister. Dr. Sumitro Djojohadikusumo returned to the post of minister of finance.

This cabinet was generally recognized as an interim cabinet, in office to maintain government until the general elections, which were scheduled for the month of September 1955, and until a new parliament could be installed. In spite of this situation, or perhaps because of it, this cabinet was one of the most active and most successful in the field of economic policy. The confusing import certificate system was swept away, along with all special import taxes, and a relatively simple system of tax categories took their place, graduated according to the nation's need for the imported commodity to be taxed. The licensing system was depersonalized to eliminate corruption, and a new Foreign Exchange Board (BDP) was created to displace the old KPUI. Screening of *nasional* importers was improved, and an attempt was made to give the same privileges to all businessmen who were citizens of Indonesia, regardless of ethnic origin. This latter move was morally and economically laudable, but politically very dangerous, in view of the common fear of the traders of Chinese descent.

At the same time, importers were required to advance the full value of the goods they intended to purchase abroad at the time application was made for an import license. Importer's prepayments of this sort had been used by previous governments, but never so severely. The results of this rapid action were quickly in evidence. By November the money supply had been reduced by nearly Rp. 600 million (almost 5%),[36] and prices of imported goods, which had risen nearly 13% in the first six months of 1955, fell almost 15% in the second half. The gold value of the rupiah rose by nearly 8% between April and September.[37] Food prices, however, continued to rise with increasing rapidity—largely due to a very bad crop year.

Aside from this vigorous resumption of *ad hoc* fiscal discipline, the only major accomplishment of the Harahap cabinet was the decision to abrogate the Round Table Agreement unilaterally. This took place only a month before the cabinet returned its mandate, in March 1956.

THE SECOND ALI CABINET

Ali Sastroamidjojo returned to cabinet leadership in late March 1956, and it shortly became evident that his second term was to be little better than the first from the point of view of economic policy, even though the *Masjumi* was this time to be represented.[38] Jusuf Wibisono, who had presided over the inflationary policies of the Sukiman cabinet as minister of finance, resumed the post.

The results were a prompt resumption of a large current budget deficit and an almost immediate crisis in foreign exchange. The shortage of foreign exchange, it should be noted, would have been much less a problem for Mr. Wibisono if it had not been for the eagerness with which Dr. Sumitro and his associates had increased imports in their enthusiasm for price reduction. However, the response of the government was feeble, and the crisis steadily deepened. A loan of $55 million from the International Monetary Fund was negotiated in August 1956, as a means of partial rescue.

Several important economic matters which had been long pending came to a head under this cabinet. One was the foreign investment bill, which was finally submitted formally to parliament. This was a limited accomplishment, however, since the bill was not actually passed until three years later.[39] The

---

[36] Schmitt, *op. cit.*, pp. 4–7.

[37] Bank Indonesia, *Report for the Year 1955–56.*

[38] Indicating, as the Sukiman cabinet's record had, that *Masjumi* participation was no guarantee of performance.

[39] With minor alterations.

second was the abrogation of the debt to Holland, signifying the end of all semblance of the economic agreement on which the transfer of sovereignty had been based.

The record of the second Ali cabinet, like the first, was a mixed one as far as its attitude toward foreign capital was concerned. The new export inducement certificates (*Bukti Pendorong Expor*) were issued to foreign as well as to Indonesian exporters, whereas in former versions of this scheme, the foreigners were excluded. Also, anti-strike and anti-squatter legislation was proposed by the government as measures to protect the estates, which were largely foreign-owned and operated.

Finally, the long-awaited five year plan appeared in May 1956 and was approved by the cabinet in September. This plan, however, was the product of effort expended over four years and at least five cabinets. Little credit is due to the Ali cabinet for the timing of its appearance.

In February 1957, President Sukarno announced his famed "Conception" of "Guided Democracy" in an atmosphere of virtual revolt. Incidents multiplied in the various provinces thereafter, and in March the second Ali cabinet fell. Djuanda Kartawidjaja, the minister of planning in the second Ali cabinet, accepted the leadership of a non-party "business cabinet" (or *Karja* cabinet, as it is often referred to in Indonesia).

THE DJUANDA CABINET

The Djuanda cabinet had little opportunity to formulate new economic measures before the West Irian action of December 1957 ended the period which is under discussion here. It was mainly concerned with the rapidly deteriorating political situation which threatened to develop into civil war.[40] This challenge, however, was economic as well as political and military.

The most significant economic response on the part of the cabinet leadership was a new version of the exchange certificate system, known simply as the *Bukti Expor* or "BE" system. The essence of the system was that exporters were issued par value in certificates rather than currency in return for their foreign exchange earnings. At the outset of the program, these certificates were saleable for whatever the market would bring minus a twenty percent tax. Importers were required to present sufficient certificates of par value to cover any foreign exchange request. The effect of this measure was, of course, a *de facto* devaluation. The market value of the certificates had reached 332 percent of par value by April 1958, far in excess of the anticipated ceiling, when their price was pegged. This attempt to placate the exporting outer islands did not succeed as a political move, nor was it notably successful as an

[40] In fact, a "State of War and Siege" was declared just prior to the formation of the cabinet.

economic measure. However, the BE certificates were required for import as late as August 1959, when the system was abolished as part of a new monetary reform.[41]

The Djuanda cabinet also fought a hard but losing battle with government finance under the minister of finance, Sutikno Slamet. A halt was ordered in further hiring of government personnel, and an attempt was made at increasing general taxation. The result for the year, however, was a deficit of Rp. 5.5 billion, or nearly 22% of total government expenditures.[42]

A three-day national conference, or *Musjawarah Nasional* (Munas), was held in mid-September 1957. This conference was primarily political, being largely concerned with the attempt to re-establish the dual leadership of Dr. Hatta and President Sukarno as a means of reuniting the nation. However, there also emerged a suggestion of a program for regional autonomy in development of the economy and decentralization of foreign exchange control. A follow-up National Planning Conference (Munap), held in November 1957, set out this program more fully. Subsequent political events—the West Irian action and the open rebellion in Sumatra and Sulawesi—all but erased the memory of these proposals for the remainder of the Djuanda term of office.

On November 29, 1957, Indonesia's resolution in the United Nations General Assembly calling for cession of West Irian (West New Guinea) to the Indonesian Republic was defeated. In early December there began a series of demonstration strikes against Dutch firms. One of these, at the Dutch inter-island shipping company, KPM, turned into a worker *coup* of management prerogatives. Other worker groups followed suit in short order. During the next two weeks, under military supervision, the movement became a *de facto* expulsion of all Dutch management. The Djuanda cabinet neither sponsored nor resisted the "take-over" movement. There was little public criticism of the action of the army and the worker groups.

The Djuanda cabinet remained in office until the political reorganization of June 1959, at which time President Sukarno himself became prime minister, returning to the 1945 Constitution of the revolutionary Republic as his legal basis.[43] Thus was the stage set for the development of "Socialism a la Indonesia."

What general characteristics emerge from the pattern? First of all, it is

[41] Of course, the basic, "liberal," aspect of the BE system had been abandoned in April 1958, when the upward spiral of the price of the certificates had been blocked by pegging. Between that date and August 1959, Indonesia was in fact operating with a multiple exchange rate system, with the BE certificates as so much excess baggage. This was apparently not clearly understood in Djakarta prior to the 1959 money purge, judging from the heated attacks on the BE system on the part of businessmen, economists, and members of parliament.

[42] Source: Central Statistical Bureau, Djakarta.

[43] Ir. Djuanda is still often referred to, erroneously, as prime minister. He is now, in fact, the "first minister."

very evident that, outside the financial fields, there wasn't much activity. There is a marked absence of policies that would have led to major changes in the economy. A glance down the left-hand column of the appendix table at the dates of the various cabinets gives one very quickly a good answer for that. There was not sufficient time to get very far with formulation of big plans.

More explicitly, there is no clear-cut, consistent march toward elimination of the Dutch economic interests. There are several moves in this direction: the *benteng* program, the Sumitro Plan for indigenous industries, and the abrogation of the Round Table Agreement. None of these made major inroads.

Also, there is no striding forward into socialism. Aside from the socialization of the Bank of Indonesia, there was only the taking-over of the railway companies, the utilities companies, and the establishment of a variety of government enterprises under the *Bank Industri Negara*—and perhaps a few others.

Aside from the Sumitro Plan, the five year plan, and the suggestions for regional development that came out of the National Conference in 1957, named here in order of decreasing degree of implementation, there has been no program for economic development.

Apart from three separate intervals of successful control of the budget and the balance of payments, fiscal irresponsibility is general. And these intervals provide the relief in the general picture, because otherwise, there is a marked sameness in the economic policy activities of cabinet after cabinet. These three cabinets, in which financial policy was quite successful, are the three out of the eight that are usually regarded by Western observers as the good ones. The main thing that all three had in common was the active participation of Dr. Sumitro. Two of them were *Masjumi*-led, one PNI-led. The outstanding failure in this respect, on the other hand, was the one PNI cabinet in which the *Masjumi* did not participate. At the same time, other cabinets, which did include *Masjumi* people (one, the Sukiman, was led by *Masjumi*), did not perform notably better.

Why, aside from the three almost quixotic attempts to deal with financial crises, did all cabinets do so little in any direction? If they were all nationalists, why did they not vigorously attack the vested Dutch interests? Since they all called themselves socialists, why was there no vigorous program of building of state enterprise? Why, when the more pragmatic intellectual clique was defeated, was there no clear repudiation of their policies and marked swing to reflect the polar political swing which Herbert Feith finds?

The answer, I think, is simply that little else *could* be done so long as the economy retained its colonial pattern of ownership. The Indonesian leaders felt that they could not eliminate the Dutch owners and their administrative staffs because they had little or nothing to put in their place. There were no funds with which to compensate the nationalized owners; and there were no Indonesian experts to operate the firms. Practical policy thus called for attempting to build an Indonesian commercial and industrial economy alongside the foreign one. This huge task was attempted in only a small way, via the unfortunate *benteng* program, and through in-service training in the larger Dutch firms.

The same general problem arose in connection with building new state enterprise. The new capital was not available, nor was the expertise. In short, the legacy of colonialism paralyzed them.

The general fiscal irresponsibility stemmed from a variety of causes. Schmitt believes that they lived with deficits because deficits were in the interest of the bureaucratic elite. Indeed, government employees could not accept retrenchment policies that would endanger or eliminate their jobs. However, it is dubious that inflation was in the interest of the dominant political group in general. More likely explanations are to be found in the archaic tax system, the inadequate civil service, the expensive defense establishment, and the anti-colonial abandonment of taxation of landed interests. Sumitro's fiscal success was the result of ingenious financial *"ad-hocery,"* to use Higgins' term. Most of his devices were once-over palliatives. Fiscal reform never came.

Also, there was always the threat of the general elections, the effect of which was to stifle inclinations toward action. Since no one really knew what the Indonesian electorate would respond to, the sensible tactic for any cabinet was to play it safe.[44] It has been suggested that the Harahap cabinet was an exception to this, having, apparently, staked a great deal on making the *Masjumi* appear to be the honest, expert party, cleaning up in the wake of the disastrous PNI cabinet of Ali Sastroamidjojo.[45]

Finally, there was the recognized fact that financial stability would serve the interest of the Dutch businessmen and bankers; that rehabilitation of the estates would serve the purposes of the Dutch plantation owners; that a larger amount of produce had to flow through Dutch distribution channels and float in Dutch boats and ships. Or, if these improvements did not serve the Dutch, then they would serve the Chinese—if they did not serve both. The argument that they would also serve Indonesians was justifiably called *Kolonial denken,*

[44] Regarding the elections from hindsight, apparently the electorate need not have been feared by national policy makers. Local issues seem to have determined non-urban voting patterns. But even if this had been understood beforehand by the leadership of the pragmatic conservatives, their actions would have been little, if any, less hampered, for the power of their opposition in parliament, the civil service, and the active political public was such that any major effort toward improving economic performance within the established structure could be defeated.

[45] The Harahap cabinet had only a few weeks in which to project this image prior to the elections, and most of the program necessarily was undertaken after it could conceivably have had any effect on their outcome.

a version of what Americans call the "percolator" or "trickle-down" theory.

Summarizing, I find several differences with other analyses of this period and these problems. First, viewing the situation in Indonesia historically, it is debatable whether the "pragmatic conservatives" can be regarded as correct in their attempt to live with the established economic structure. Secondly, these leaders, when in power, succeeded in making no great attempt at this accommodation because (a) their political opposition was too effective to permit it, and (b) their own ideological orientation, being nationalist and socialist, made them hesitant to move vigorously in that direction. Thirdly, Western observers generally have tended to regard the political opposition to this group from a jaundiced point of view. Both strong nationalism and rapid socialization have their intelligent, intellectual proponents in Indonesia, as elsewhere. From the short-term point of view, their opposition had demonstrably unfortunate economic effects and, if they had had the patience of Dr. Hatta, they could have perhaps seen their ends achieved by evolutionary means with much less political and economic disruption. But who is to say that Dr. Hatta's gradual way would involve less social cost, even if *all* costs were to be fully considered? And it is to be expected that Indonesians would count that part of the cost which the Dutchmen had to pay at a sharp discount.

Thus it appears to this writer that Dr. Schmitt was basically right in asserting, in effect, that there was a one-way road to expulsion of the Dutch interests. Having accomplished that, however, Indonesia has by no means solved her economic problems. Indeed, she has created many in the process. Also, the divisive forces which emerged during the last ten years have raised such problems of security and political stability that it may be many years before an atmosphere can be established in which it will be possible to consider development of economic policy on anything but the crisis level. The most that can be said is that a major block was removed from the path of the policy maker with the crushing of Dutch economic interests in the West Irian action of 1957.

Table 1. *The Pattern of Economic Policy, 1950–57*

Cabinet	Commercial, monetary, and fiscal policy	Nationalization	Assistance to indigenous business	Foreign investment	Other
Hatta (non-party) 12/49–9/50	1. Money cut 2. Export certificates	Railways		$100 million U.S. loan	
Natsir (*Masjumi*) 9/50–3/51 (without PNI)	1. Tight credit (foreign banks) 2. BIN, BNI, and BR banks 3. Turnover tax 4. Extended free import list, "liberal" commercial policy 5. Tight budget 6. Some success with counter-cyclical policy		1. Industries program (Urgency Plan) 2. *Benteng* 3. Abolition of "historical rights"	ECA agreement negotiated	Strike restrictions
Sukiman (*Masjumi*) 4/51–2/52 Cabinet including: 5 *Masjumi* 5 PNI	1. Abandoned differential exchange rates 2. Large deficit in budget	Bank Indonesia nationalized 5/22/51	*Benteng* loosened	MSA agreement	1. 2 year agricultural plan 2. Emergency labor law
Wilopo (PNI) 4/52–6/53 Cabinet including: 4 PNI 4 *Masjumi* 2 PSI	1. Budget balance 2. Tight import restriction 3. Import prepayments		*Benteng* tightened	Much discussion, no great success	1. Army rationalization 2. Anti-squatter action

Cabinet				

Ali I (PNI) 8/53–7/55 (without *Masjumi*)	1. Large deficits in
	  a. budget
	  b. balance of payments
	2. Trade policy section of Round Table Agreement abolished
			Draft regulations on foreign investment	

Burhanuddin Harahap (*Masjumi*-caretaker) 8/55–3/56	1. KPUI abolished; BDP established 2. Imports liberalized 3. Pre-payments raised and advanced 4. Deficit in budget virtually eliminated	1. Iskaq—very open-handed 2. Roosemo (11/1954), began careful screening	1. All Indonesian-owned businesses (*peranakan*) called *nasional* 2. General tightening of screening	1. Anti-corruption drive 2. Round Table Agreement abrogated

Ali II (PNI) 4/56–3/57	1. Large budget deficits
	2. Export certificates reintroduced
	3. Proliferation of regulations
		No major change	1. Foreign investment bill submitted to parliament
			2. $55 million IMF loan
				1. 5 year plan completed
				2. Debt to Holland abrogated
				3. Labor law
				  a. Anti-squatter
				  b. Regional mediation boards set up

Djuanda (non-party business cabinet) 3/57–8/59	1. *Bukti Expor* 2. Heavy import restriction	Dutch firms taken over, 12/57	Second Economic Congress—end of *benteng*	Munas and Munap—program for regional autonomy in economic development

FOREIGN CAPITAL AND SOCIAL CONFLICT IN INDONESIA, 1950-1958

Hans O. Schmitt

In December of 1957, after eight years of social and political turmoil following independence, Indonesia expelled Dutch economic interests from the dominant position they had retained from the colonial era. This action climaxed a trend toward economic stagnation which was in striking contrast to the hopes of rapid economic growth held by many Indonesians. The question posed in this essay is this: was there perhaps some connection between survival of foreign economic dominance on the one hand, and political turmoil and economic stagnation on the other?

THE ECONOMIC STRUCTURE

The incentives that make people save and invest for economic growth have as yet found no single and consistent explanation in economic theory. One aspect that is sometimes overlooked is that additions to the capital stock concurrently enhance the power of those who control it, and thereby induce them to forego consumption. Those who do not share in the control of capital have not the same incentive to save. They may still make provision for contingencies, such as old age and accident, but for the economy as a whole, such savings are likely to be offset

From Hans O. Schmitt, "Foreign Capital and Social Conflict in Indonesia, 1950–1958," *Economic Development and Cultural Change*, 10:3:284–293 (April 1962). Reprinted by permission of The University of Chicago Press.

by expenditures when the contingencies occur. On balance, therefore, the interests of the "propertiless" lie with maximum consumption. Aggregate savings can in consequence be maximized only to the extent that income payments to the "propertiless" are minimized.

The balance of power between those who do, and those who do not, control the capital stock may therefore be decisive in placing limits on the rate of accumulation. In Joan Robinson's terminology, it sets the "inflation barrier" beyond which further reductions in real wages are successfully resisted.[1] The rate of growth will be maximized when one group is firmly in control, and sees its power enhanced by further accumulation. Until very recently, no Indonesian group has been quite in this position. According to one estimate, before the Second World War only 19 percent of non-agricultural capital was owned by indigenous Indonesians, while 52 percent was held by Dutch interests.[2] Agriculture is the only area in which Indonesian ownership of resources has been at all substantial, and the larger part of the Indonesian population are in fact peasant small-holders. As W. A. Lewis has pointed out, however, peasant societies "may be happy and prosperous," but are not likely to show rapid accumulation of capital.[3] The reason for this, he argues, can be found in the fact that in societies where power and prestige are based on land holdings, ambition expresses itself chiefly in additions to real estate rather than to capital, with capital expansion often opposed as a threat to the vested interests of the landowners.

It is at any rate clear that in traditional Indonesian peasant society, capital accumulation has been slow and technical innovation rare, so much so that one Dutch scholar felt justified in assigning "limited needs" and an "aversion to capital" to "Oriental mentality" as inherent traits.[4] He does not seem to appreciate adequately the inhibiting effect of Dutch colonial policy, however. At its best it was designed only to preserve a "happy and prosperous" peasantry—by indirect rule through traditional chiefs and by the prohibition of sale of land to aliens—while at the same time making any escape from traditional society by Indonesians very difficult indeed. Under Dutch rule in Indonesia there existed three distinct social strata.[5] The indigenous population constituted the lowest layer; the Western managerial personnel in government, business, and the army, the highest. An intermediate

[1] Joan Robinson, *The Accumulation of Capital* (London: Macmillan, 1958), pp. 48 ff.

[2] L. A. Mills and associates, *The New World of Southeast Asia* (Minneapolis: The University of Minnesota Press, 1949), p. 352.

[3] W. A. Lewis, "Economic Development with Unlimited Supplies of Labor," *Manchester School* (May 1954), 175.

[4] J. H. Boeke, *Economics and Economic Policy of Dual Societies* (New York: Institute of Pacific Relations, 1953), pp. 40 ff.

[5] W. F. Wertheim, "Changes in Indonesia's Social Stratification," *Pacific Affairs* (March 1955), p. 41; and *Indonesian Society in Transition: A Study of Social Change* (Bandung and The Hague: W. van Hoeve, 1956), 135 ff.

position was occupied by the Chinese who largely controlled the collecting and distributing trades, acting as middlemen between the Western and the indigenous sectors of society. Social advancement from one of the three layers to another was all but impossible.

Nonetheless, not quite all Indonesians were peasants, even under Dutch rule. A small proletariat of wage laborers—about 500,000 by Communist count[6]—worked on the plantations, in the mines, in the factories, and in transport within the "Western" sector. The traditional aristocracy survived in the lower categories of the civil service which remained open to them, and a vestigial business group of pre-colonial origin was also able to maintain itself.[7] For a stagnant society to be transformed into a dynamic one, these groups would have had to acquire a vested interest in capital accumulation. It was precisely this development that foreign dominance in the non-agricultural sector effectively blocked.[8] Unfortunately, when Indonesia attained her independence in December 1949, the economic structure was not changed significantly. The non-agricultural groups, who assumed responsibility for the government, remained narrowly wedged between the traditionalist peasantry on one side, and the Western business community on the other.

The balance of power between economic sectors, however, was changed by the political revolution. Toward the peasantry, the new rulers lacked the weight of power that their colonial predecessors had enjoyed.[9] At the same time, they did not identify their interests with the growth of capital, either. It would seem that whenever indigenous capital is restricted—by market forces or by government policy—from reaching proportions competitive with foreign enterprise, opportunism if not fatalism and resignation in economic activity are the natural consequences in any society in any part of the world. The development of a "capitalist spirit" cannot reasonably be expected under such circumstances. Even "business enterprise" will be consumption-oriented, as indeed it was.[10]

The economic consequences were virtually inexorable. In 1939 the proportion of national income accounted for in the modern sector was 32 percent; by 1952 it had dropped to 24 percent, with the trend continuing in

[6] D. N. Aidit, *Indonesian Society and the Indonesian Revolution* (Djakarta: Jajasan Pembaruan, 1958), p. 61.

[7] On the pre-colonial Indonesian trading class, see J. C. van Leur, *Indonesian Trade and Society: Essays in Asian Social and Economic History* (Bandung and The Hague: W. van Hoeve, 1955), p. 191.

[8] Even Boeke writes of the Indonesian who "finds himself hindered in reaping the rewards of his labor and in developing his paltry little business by the competition of the much more powerful and efficient Western enterprise." *Op. cit.*, p. 215.

[9] "The present ruling class is hardly able to wield command over the agrarian masses." Wertheim, "Changes in Indonesia's Social Stratification," *op. cit.*, p. 52.

[10] A. H. Ballendux, *Bijdrage tot de Kennis van de Credietverlening aan de 'Indonesische Middenstand'* (The Hague: printed doctoral dissertation, 1951), pp. 79 ff.

succeeding years. One of the contributory causes was a shift in the burden of taxation between sectors, until in 1952 taxes claimed 29 percent of the income per gainfully employed in the modern sector, as compared with only 5 percent in the agrarian. The end result has been, if one can trust the figures, a level of disposable income per gainfully employed in 1952 of Rp. 3,000 in the agrarian sphere, compared with only Rp. 2,650 in the modern sector.[11] "The central fact of economic development," writes W. A. Lewis, "is that the distribution of incomes is altered in favor of the saving class."[12] The logic of Indonesia's economic structure, it appears, has moved in exactly the opposite direction. We turn now to trace the pattern of its political repercussions.

POLITICAL REPERCUSSIONS

Both the political and the economic dilemmas of the Indonesian leadership had the same root in the precarious position they occupied between the peasantry and foreign business interests. At the political apex stood a relatively small group often referred to as the intelligentsia, consisting largely of those Indonesians who had been permitted to benefit from Dutch education during the colonial period.[13] Their control over the mass of the population in the countryside was loose, as has already been pointed out. But, though the peasantry was difficult to govern, it was not sufficiently well organized for effective participation in political decision-making, either. Politics therefore reflected primarily the interests of non-agrarian population groups, more particularly of the bureaucracy, the trading interests, and the working classes. These groups can perhaps be described as occupying positions of "intermediate" leadership between the intellectual elite and the peasantry.[14] The bureaucracy was especially strong in Java, enjoying the position which a still somewhat feudal social structure accorded them. Trading groups for their part held a higher status outside Java, where a more commercial orientation had prevailed from early times.

[11] D. S. Paauw, *Financing Economic Development: The Indonesian Case* (Glencoe: The Free Press, 1960), pp. 205 ff.

[12] Lewis, *op. cit.*, p. 157.

[13] See, for example, L. H. Palmier, "Aspects of Indonesia's Social Structure," *Pacific Affairs* (June 1955); and J. H. Mysberg, "The Indonesian Elite," *Far Eastern Survey* (March 1957).

[14] The importance of "intermediate groups" between the elite and the "masses" is emphasized in G. J. Pauker, "The Role of Political Organization in Indonesia," *Far Eastern Survey* (September 1958). Though examples of intermediate organizations feature economic groupings prominently, the systematic discussion totally omits economic interest as a possible source of division. The distinction between bureaucrats, tradesmen, and labor is most sharply drawn in J. M. van der Kroef, "Economic Origins of Indonesian Nationalism," in P. Talbot, ed., *South Asia in the World Today* (Chicago: University of Chicago Press, 1950).

The labor movement, concentrated in the cities, held the balance of power between them.

Against this background, three determinants of political developments in post-independence Indonesia can be isolated: (1) the continuing dominance of foreign capital; (2) the division of indigenous society into several ethnic groups; and (3) the different social positions of economic classes within different ethnic groups. Other sources of political division—and alliance—in national politics could of course be listed, among them religious, cultural, and personality conflicts. These did not, however, affect public policy to the same extent; in fact, on balance they tended to accommodate themselves to the three factors isolated here. In combination, these factors produced a logical sequence of events that led directly to the expulsion of Dutch business interests.

Three stages of development can be identified. In the first, we find an initial clash between the Dutch business community in Indonesia and the Indonesian political leadership. The Dutch attempted to minimize the economic impact of Indonesian political independence by retaining control of the central bank and by allowing Dutch enterprises to operate in an environment of maximum *laissez faire*. The Indonesians, for their part, thought that they could acquire some share in the economic management of their country, not yet by expropriation, but by financing the entry of new Indonesian firms into markets controlled by the Dutch. A beginning was made in the import sector.[15] Control of the nation's credit system was thought essential for the success of such a program, so the central bank was nationalized.

The nationalization of the central bank aroused little controversy within the Indonesian camp. To be sure, the sort of program it was supposed to back tended to overcrowd markets and relax financial discipline—thoroughly adverse consequences from the point of view of economic development. But it had the short-run virtue of satisfying most hostile impulses toward foreign enterprise, while at the same time leaving people free to cooperate with foreign management if they wanted to. Financial policy therefore did not as yet provide an issue to divide the political elite. Political competition continued for the time being to reflect individual ambitions for position, with no consistent divisions along social or economic lines. In fact, no such lines seemed as yet to divide society at large either, at least as long as the Korean Boom sustained incomes for all.

But as soon as incomes dwindled with the end of the Korean War, the financial "offensive" against Dutch interests began to have serious domestic repercussions. These repercussions initiate the second stage of development.

---

[15] For detailed expositions of these policies, see N. G. Amstutz, *The Development of Indigenous Importers in Indonesia* (unpublished Ph.D. dissertation, Fletcher School of Law and Diplomacy, 1958); and J. O. Sutter, *Indonesianisasi: Politics in a Changing Economy, 1940–1955* (Ithaca: Cornell University Southeast Asia Program, 1959).

Without a reduction in government expenditures, dwindling receipts from foreign trade threatened to touch off severe inflation. The reaction was composed of three factors. (1) Fiscal retrenchment would have required cutbacks in the support given to young enterprises. Consequently, what first seemed to be an academic debate on the merits and demerits of fiscal orthodoxy, soon split the leadership sharply between those who preferred foreign dominance to monetary chaos and those who would jeopardize financial stability to rid the economy of Dutch control.[16]

(2) In the struggle for power between the two groups, both sides turned to the intermediate economic classes for support. This might have seemed difficult for the financial conservatives. A program of relaxing pressure against foreign interests, while imposing austerity elsewhere, could not have held much intrinsic appeal with the Indonesian public. Financial retrenchment did, however, favor at least one of the intermediate groups, the trading interests, especially those outside Java. Combined with fixed exchange rates, domestic inflation threatened the incomes of indigenous exporters in the Outer Regions, where the bulk of exports originate. Dwindling real incomes there caused increased resentment toward populous Java, where most of the nation's imports were being absorbed.

(3) The gains to Java were unevenly distributed, however. The over-valued exchange rate benefitted importers—bureaucrats who controlled exchange allocations and their friends—but did not reduce costs for trading interests outside the import sector, to whom imports were resold at high and rising prices. Price controls added further irritation. Trading groups outside Java therefore won political allies among their less powerful counterparts within Java. In combination, the trading interests provided the core of indigenous support needed to put force behind the demand for retrenchment at the top.

What backing the anti-inflationary party could muster still fell short of gaining them control of the government. Their strength merely sufficed to reduce the political base of the government parties to a precarious minimum. Progressive inflation followed, exacerbating social conflict and political instability. A showdown between exporting and importing regions was delayed as long as politicians looked to general elections for a decision in their rivalry for power. The third stage of development begins with the elections of 1955. When these elections turned out merely to reflect the pattern of conflict, without deciding its issues, the representatives of the exporting regions increasingly turned to extra-parliamentary means for defending their interests.[17]

[16] See H. Feith, *The Wilopo Cabinet, 1952–1953: A Turning Point in Post-Revolutionary Indonesia* (Ithaca: Cornell University Modern Indonesia Project, 1958), for a variant interpretation.

[17] The elections showed the Masjumi Party, which had consistently advocated financial retrenchment, strong among trading interests and dominant outside Java, and the Nationalist Party, which had been chiefly responsible for the government's inflationary

Some of them, in fact, in March of 1958, went so far as to proclaim a rival government in Sumatra, with scattered support elsewhere.

To counteract the tendency toward political disintegration, the government parties appealed more and more "recklessly" to nationalist sentiment in the pursuit of the "unfinished" revolution against imperialism. Their chief battle cry was against the continuing Dutch presence in West Irian, a fact used so effectively in inciting popular sentiment against Dutch business enterprises in Indonesia, that businessmen made representations in Holland favoring territorial concessions. However, while agitations within Indonesia intensified with the deepening of social strife, Indonesian efforts in the United Nations to force Holland to negotiate continued each year to end in failure. In reprisal, in December 1957 labor unions took the initiative in a forcible expulsion of Dutch economic interests from the capital. In a matter of a few days, the movement had spread across the whole country.

For a while it seemed the government had lost its power to direct events. The opposition thought to take advantage of this fact when it proclaimed its rival government in early 1958. The timing of the rebellion made its instigators seem more than ever to give aid to foreign interests. It was in some part for this reason that they lost much of the domestic support on which they had counted. The central government did not fall, but on the contrary launched a vigorous military campaign to restore its authority. Nonetheless, the rebels retained enough support to make active guerilla warfare seem irrepressible, for a while, especially in Sumatra and Sulawesi.

IMPLICATIONS FOR THEORY

The great deterrent to expropriation of Dutch capital had always been the disclocation it would cause—at least in the short run—in the management of the Indonesian economy. When expropriation came, the price had to be paid. In 1958 the governor of the Bank Indonesia reported that "shipping space was in short supply, marketing channels to Holland had to be shifted to other countries, and there was an exodus of Dutch technicians engaged in the production sector."[18] Foreign exchange losses were particularly severe as a recession in export markets and—perhaps most important—the Sumatra and Sulawesi rebellions coincided with the Dutch exodus. Their combined impact reduced exchange receipts of the central government by 34 percent below their 1957 levels.[19] In

policies, strong among the bureaucracy and dominant in Java. See H. Feith, *The Indonesian Elections of 1955* (Ithaca: Cornell University Modern Indonesia Project, 1957).

[18] Bank Indonesia, *Report for the Year 1957–1958* (Djakarta, July 1958), p. 128.

[19] Bank Indonesia, *Report for the Year 1958–1959* (Djakarta, July 1959), p. 145. Evidence suggests that smuggling by dissidents may have accounted for two-thirds of the drop in reported exports by volume.

response, imports were cut by 36 percent.[20] Even so, it was only the beginning of war reparations payments by Japan that prevented further declines in exchange reserves.[21]

For the maintenance of a reasonable degree of monetary stability, it was absolutely essential that the government deficit be cut to offset the drop in the flow of goods. Such a reduction in expenditures was unfortunately impossible—primarily because of the staggering cost of fighting the rebel guerillas. The government's cash deficit in 1958 increased by Rp. 5,025 million over its 1957 figure, to an all-time high of Rp. 10,858 million. The whole of the increase went to finance increases in expenditures for security —they rose by Rp. 6,064 million.[22] The money supply consequently rose by Rp. 10,453 million, or by 34 percent, in 1958.[23] Combined with import cuts, and an uncertain political future, inflation made orderly business management seem irrational. By early 1959, deterioration had gone so far that President Soekarno warned of an approaching "abyss of annihilation."[24]

It is tempting to use this result as evidence for "mismanagement" or "irresponsibility" on the part of the Indonesian government. Somewhat less sharply, perhaps, D. S. Paauw argues that the government "has placed too much emphasis upon essentially revolutionary goals—'sweeping away the vestiges of colonialism'—and too little upon national integration."[25] One can, on the other hand, detect a certain rationality in the behavior of the Indonesian leadership. The course of events looks very much like a simple cumulative process away from an unstable equilibrium. No stable equilibrium may have been possible within the economic structure. In countries where the control of the capital stock and the direction of public affairs are held by a single elite group, development is stimulated by the fact that the political elite identifies its interests with the expansion of capital. It is primarily this expansion which enhances elite power at home and abroad; politics will therefore be made to serve economic development. In countries where the expansion of capital will in the first instance benefit foreign managerial groups, the indigenous political elite—in spite of protestations to the contrary on grounds of general welfare—will on balance be opposed to it.[26]

Opposition to economic development will in all likelihood be accom-

[20] *Ibid.*, p. 151.

[21] *Ibid.*, p. 133.

[22] *Ibid.*, pp. 97 ff.

[23] *Ibid.*, p. 86.

[24] W. A. Hanna, *Bung Karno's Indonesia* (New York: American Universities Field Staff, 1960), p. 13–59–7.

[25] Paauw, *op. cit.*, p. xx.

[26] Referring to "the Government and the national leaders" in Indonesia, Soedjatmoko writes: "It is among these circles that there is a lack of desire and determination to proceed with economic development." See Soedjatmoko, *Economic Development as a Cultural Problem* (Ithaca: Cornell University Modern Indonesia Project, 1958), p. 8.

panied by a high degree of political instability. Barred from economic careers, members of the political elite find no stable channels for the consolidation and extension of such power as they may individually aspire to, but are restricted to internecine strife in their ambitions for advancement in politics alone. Such strife will tend to crystallize around personalities rather than broad social issues at first, with alignments changing kaleidoscopically and unpredictably. Insofar as consistent lines of demarcation develop among the contestants in politics, such lines will probably divide, as in Indonesia, those who are willing to live with the economic structure that obtains, from those who will insist on the need to prepare for its early destruction.[27] A showdown between the two opposing groups may be delayed. The "radicals" will have to be aware that the expulsion of foreign managerial and financial resources will cause serious economic dislocation. The "moderates," for their part, may come to realize the usefulness of political threats against established interests in winning favors and concessions from them.

The transition from stalemate to showdown may then be described as follows. As the political elite becomes increasingly divided within itself, more and more population groups will tend to lose faith in its leadership. The elite will then be faced with two alternatives: either it makes common cause with foreign interests to maintain itself against the indigenous population; or it attempts to divert the blame for economic deterioration exclusively to foreign interests, ascribing its own internal conflicts to often fictitious foreign subversion, and attempting to lead a movement of popular revolution against foreign control of the economy. The more precarious elite authority becomes, the more necessary one or the other alternative will seem, and the more irreconcilable will be the conflict between rival elite groups. The showdown will come when political strife has reached the breaking point, threatening the country with political disintegration and economic ruin.

We see, therefore, that Indonesia's present plight may not be due primarily to individual failings, but that it seems rather to have been the logical consequence of a particularly unfortunate social structure. Similar results are therefore threatened whenever an imperial power transfers political authority to a former colony without concurrently ceding economic power as well. In the process of disintegration, a new and more propitious economic order may emerge from the shambles of the old. From the point of view of economic development, a new order should unite in power those groups most dissatisfied with traditional arrangements in the agrarian sector, with those whose interests are most clearly identified with an expansion of the modern sector. In the absence of a strong indigenous managerial class, such requirements point to the industrial worker and to the "dispossessed" among the

[27] Examples of a similar rift include Egypt (Nasser versus Farouk), Iraq (Kassem versus Nuri-as-Said), Iran (Mossadegh versus the Shah), the Belgian Congo (Lumumba versus Tshombe), and Cuba (Castro versus Batista).

rural population. In conditions of social chaos, when old authorities are discredited, these new aspirants have every opportunity for success.

IMPLICATIONS FOR POLICY

For a variety of reasons, Western governments have shown themselves willing to assist in the economic development of their former colonies. Along with aid has gone advice. Much of the advice to underdeveloped countries concentrates on two points: (1) domestic savings are low; they need to be supplemented from abroad; therefore one must create conditions congenial to foreign investors. (2) Capital is scarce; its marginal product is maximized in labor-intensive industries; therefore one must apply it first of all in agriculture. The danger in such advice can now be appreciated: if followed, such counsel could easily strengthen an agrarian social structure hostile to progressive capital accumulation, and leave the development of modern industry to be the concern chiefly of foreign interests. In all likelihood, the resulting "dualistic" economy will touch off a political chain reaction that may end in economic as well as political disaster.

What then is the proper role of foreign aid in the economic development of former colonies? From an Indonesian point of view, there is a double criterion by which to measure the value of foreign capital: first, foreign contributions must of course add to productive capacity; but second, they must also assist in the development of Indonesian, not foreign, vested interests. If aid cannot meet the second criterion, any contribution under the first may well become pernicious. It can be argued, therefore, that American aid funds should first of all have been used to "buy up Stanvac, Goodyear, Proctor and Gamble, National Carbon, and any other incidental American capital interests in Indonesia, turn them over to the Indonesian government to run, retaining American technicians paid by the United States government just long enough to train Indonesian replacements."[28] Unless the plausible aspect of this proposal is first recognized, workable alternatives more palatable to Western interests are not likely to be devised.

The main objection to such a scheme might be its "negative" approach. It would be preferable, rather than merely to destroy an old order, to work out new relationships between the Western business communities and the leadership of the emerging nations. Methods can be devised whereby private capital will continue to make its contribution without threatening any reversion to "colonialism." One possibility starts with the observation that a number of foreign companies operating in Indonesia had in fact long ago amortized and repatriated their investment, showing as equity a figure close

[28] Hanna, *op. cit.*, p. 35–59–1.

to zero. One could argue that profits were being earned without the commitment of capital to justify them. Such a conviction could supply a moral justification for expropriation, but a technique is necessary to link expropriation to amortization in an orderly and institutionalized procedure to which businessmen can adapt their profit expectations and investment plans.

Suppose every firm were given the opportunity to transfer profits freely, but required each year to apply some negotiated percentage of earned profits to amortization. As soon as amortization allowances have risen to match equity, the physical plant could be considered a "natural resource" and become public domain—government property.[29] If amortization allowances are required in addition to depreciation reserves, they could perhaps take the place of the company tax. Instead of the government collecting the tax and later using it to pay compensation for expropriation, the firm would be exempt from the company tax until unpaid taxes matched the equity account.[30]

Whether such arrangements are thought feasible or not, the dilemma for which they seek a solution should not be disregarded. The scuttling of "empire" touches business empires, too. The analysis of this essay suggests that as long as Western private enterprise is unwilling to sacrifice its entrenched positions in the former colonies, it invites disaster upon itself. The task is to find a way of yielding those positions, while leaving the principle of private property intact.

[29] Compare this procedure with the arrangements used to finance the Indian railways. See D. S. Thorner, *Investment in Empire* (Philadelphia: University of Pennsylvania Press, 1950), p. 83.

[30] L. A. Doyle, "Reducing Barriers to Private Foreign Investment in Underdeveloped Countries," *California Management Review* (Fall 1958), considers accounting techniques to implement this idea.

Section 2
BUREAUCRATIC
ASPECTS
OF MODERN
ECONOMIC
DEVELOPMENT

Introduction: *The Conflicting Demands of Control and Innovation*

With the relatively highly developed systems of public administration produced by the colonial governments, it is understandable that the government bureaucracies of the new states will play a central role in their modern economic development. The question is what will that be; will it facilitate or obstruct the development process? Further, how will the bureaucratic role be articulated with political decisions for development? The bureaucracy can subvert political efforts for reform and change; it can turn political policies for development into actions that create explosive conflict on the ground; or it can be a sensitive instrument of the political center, carrying out development policies effectively and feeding back to the political center the kind of information that leads to a rational adjustment of policies to the needs of the local situation. One of the bitter lessons the indigenous leaders of the new states have learned is that planning and policy pronouncements are relatively easy to make; rational implementation is far more difficult.

Two important analytical issues are raised by the observation of this difficulty. One has to do with the goals and the organizational character of development bureaucracies. The other concerns the organizational environment of the development bureaucracy. One of the most critical dimensions of variance in organizational goals is identified by Victor Thompson in the article that opens this section. Thompson points out that much organizational analysis comes from Western countries where the emphasis has been on control; in the new states the need is for innovation. It is a common observation that the bureaucratic structures created by the colonial governments were largely concerned with maintaining order and keeping taxation low, so as to produce a favorable climate for the external investment that was required for the development of the export economies. The goal of colonial bureaucracies was largely a custodial goal.

One can see a rational process in which custodial goals emerged naturally out of the definition of the situation in colonial systems. Governments defined the territories as economically backward. The cause of the backwardness lay in the shortage of investment capital and of entrepreneurial skills. Both had to be imported from the outside. If the government could simply maintain order and keep taxes low, and thus profit incentives high, the needed capital and entrepreneurial skills would flow in from the outside and development would ensue.

Independence brought a radical change in the definition of the situation. Indigenous leaders generally agreed that their countries were economically backward, but they saw the causes in quite different directions. They argued that indigenous capital and entrepreneurial skills were existent, but latent. It required only changes in the general operation of government to draw out the local resources that were needed to stimulate indigenous development. Thus, the thrust from the newly independent governments was to change the goals of government bureaucracies from custodial to developmental or innovative goals. In the public rhetoric and in the organizational experimentation of the new leaders in most of the new states we can observe this attempt to change the orientation and character of their administrative instruments, the governing bureaucracies.

In regard to innovative organizational instruments we can identify three different types of environments. The critical dimension of variance in this classification lies in the freedom individual organizations have to formulate and to change their goals. In the first place we can observe organizations that spring in some sense *autocthonously* from the ground. These are the private agencies and organizations that emerge when entrepreneurs see some benefit to be gained by mobilizing human and material resources for a given end. Such organizations are represented by private enterprises, which have considerable autonomy in defining and changing their goals, within a rather wide and undetermined range of constraints. Second, we can isolate *countervailing* organizations, which emerge in reaction to a given parent organization. Trade unions are a good example, arising because factories or other enterprises already exist and control the allocation of rewards to the members. Countervailing organizations have less freedom to determine their goals since they must essentially demand and work for ends that can be granted by the parent organization. Still, within this narrower range of constraints, the countervailing organization is relatively free to choose and to change its goals. Finally, we can distinguish *subsidiary* organizations that are created directly by the parent to achieve some specific end. The parent defines a broader goal and creates an organization whose goals are the means by which the parent can achieve this broader end. Thus, the subsidiary organization has the least freedom to select and change its goals, since goals are essentially prescribed for it by the parent organization. Government bureaucracies are good examples of this type of organization.

This formulation identifies for us another important way in which the process of development in the new states of the mid-twentieth century differs from that of the nineteenth century. In the earlier period, the organizations that were in the vanguard of the development process were *autochthonous* private enterprise, with relative freedom to choose and change their goals within the broad constraints set by existing legal and economic conditions. In the current period the organizations in the vanguard of the development process are *subsidiary* organizations, development agencies created by the government and charged with specific tasks or goals to facilitate the process of development. This classification reinforces the argument that the articulation of political and bureaucratic operations is one of the most critical issues in modern economic development.

In addition to identifying the critical issues of order and innovative goals, Thompson goes on to suggest some of the organizational requirements for bureaucracies to play innovative roles. The article by Albert Hirschman speaks to the general issue of bureaucratic and political interplay. He observes that the complexities inherent in the development process, especially in the export economies, are such as to create almost intolerable conditions for planning. Trade cycles greatly inhibit rational planning and implementation and produce increasing frustrations among political leaders intent upon creating social and economic change. Frustrations mount to a threshold at which sweeping reforms are introduced, often at least partially irrationally, to do away with instruments designed to control the trade process for the purpose of producing innovation in the economy. Following the reforms, the complexities produce a creeping reintroduction of control procedures until the threshold is reached again. Hirschman's argument is similar to Thompson's: flexibility and a high tolerance for independence in the face of complex situations is required if bureaucratic instruments are to produce innovation in social and economic relations.

Hirschman also argues that the requirements of programming often allow the bureaucratic planners to place useful rational constraints on the demands of political leaders. This is, of course, only one form of interchange between bureaucracy and polity. Moshe Lissak uses the case of Burma to illustrate another type of interchange: the dynamics of exchange relations that in this case led to a military intervention in the political process. The political sphere provides manpower, resources, and norms to the military, in return for protection from external and internal disorder. In the specific historical process in Burma, the military developed new and larger demands along with its increasing capabilities. The political sphere on the other hand became increasingly incapable of mobilizing for the modernization it promised, failing, among other things, to meet the increasing demands of the military. The political failure was quite similar to that in Indonesia discussed by Glassburner and Schmitt in the previous section. The result was the same in both societies: a military take-over of the political process.

The final two articles by Ronald Dore and the editor deal with bureaucratic effectiveness in mobilizing masses for social and economic innovation. Dore's analysis provides for an understanding of one of the most dramatic cases of modern economic development in one of the currently industrialized economies: Japan. Japanese agriculture experienced about a half-century of rapid growth from the mid-nineteenth century to the early twentieth century. This growth was widespread, with large numbers of independent producers actively participating, and it was also of critical importance in paying for the industrialization of the nation. Dore's analysis of the role of government in the process demonstrates that the amount of government investment, which was quite low in Japan until the turn of the century, is far less critical than the quality and content of communication between the bureaucracy and the farmers.

In my analysis of a number of successful rural development programs, I have attempted to draw out some of the details of this communication in a more modern setting. This is also a setting in which the previously developed colonial bureaucracies required considerable reform or change in order to give them the capacity to play an innovative role in their environments. This analysis also demonstrates a point that Hirschman made earlier. There is much that is laudable in the rhetoric of modern leaders' attempts to stimulate economic growth and welfare advances. The critical problem for all cases of government attempts to stimulate economic development is translating the laudable rhetoric into effective action on the ground.

ECONOMIC POLICY
IN UNDERDEVELOPED
COUNTRIES

Albert O. Hirschman

Little attention appears to have been given by economists and other social scientists to any analysis, systematic or casual, of the behavior of governments of underdeveloped countries as revealed by their economic policy decisions over a period of time. Nevertheless, in view of th considerable role played today by governments in the development process, it is clear that governmental behavior should be subjected to just as close scrutiny as is being given to the motivations and conduct of entrepreneurs.

In fact, in the absence of more knowledge about probable actions and reactions of governments, our best-intentioned technical assistance efforts are liable to fail. This conclusion is inescapable to anyone who has been watching the economists and other social science "experts" who are sent on foreign assignments. At the outset of their mission, they are likely to think that the principal problem they are going to be confronted with will be that of determining what *ought* to be done, e.g., in what sector the principal investment effort should be undertaken, and what monetary, fiscal, and foreign exchange policies should be adopted. But soon they realize that they have little trouble in deciding *what* to do or rather what to advise to do, while by far the largest portion of their time is devoted to energy-consuming and often frustrating efforts to put their ideas and proposals across.

From Albert O. Hirschman, "Economic Policy in Underdeveloped Countries," *Economic Development and Cultural Change*, 5:4:1:362–370 (July 1957). Reprinted by permission of The University of Chicago Press.

Let me say that my remarks apply primarily to the important group of underdeveloped countries whose economies have already registered important advances. In such countries, a few obviously useful investment projects are always at hand; some monetary and fiscal reforms usually cry out to be taken; certain changes in the institutional and administrative structure would no doubt further stimulate development. The story of a technical assistance mission is then the story of its successes and failures in having these projects, reforms, and changes firmly adopted. The huge difficulties of this task are not always properly appreciated, partly, I suspect, because, in order to do so, one must catch the experts themselves during their unguarded moments rather than rely on their reports to headquarters; and partly, because the whole tale here is in terms of personalities and of human passions, frailties, and frustrations which the experts, once they are "back home", are liable to forget as easily and completely as physical pain. And if they reminisce, it seems to them that they were facing fortuitous circumstances which do not lend themselves to any kind of generalized analysis.

Here they could be mistaken. After all, underdeveloped countries and their governments may find themselves typically in situations which make likely the adoption of seemingly irrational economic policies. It is also conceivable that the emergence of oscillations and even of inconsistencies in such policies could be predicted with a fair degree of accuracy from a knowledge of their economic structure and problems.

An analysis that would deal with these probabilities would permit the economic adviser to gain some understanding of the economic policies—good or bad—and of the resistance that he and his proposals are likely to encounter. Not only would it thereby contribute to his mental health—by saving him from unnecessary exasperation—but it might make him into a more effective operator. Indeed, the governments may also profit from knowing more about themselves. In the following I shall attempt to give some examples of this kind of analysis from selected areas of economic policy making.

ATTITUDES TOWARD NATIONAL DEVELOPMENT PROGRAMMING

There is no field of economic policy in underdeveloped countries that stands as much in the limelight as the programming of economic development. To have a five-year plan for economic development has become a matter of prestige, second only to the importance of having a first-class international airport near the capital. In this, as in many other respects, governments are more powerfully subject to the "demonstration effect" than individuals for the simple reason that communications between governments are far more developed than between citizens of different countries.

The reasons for which the adoption of development plans has proven so attractive, are well-known: the plan or program is a concrete expression of the universal aspiration toward better living standards and the elaboration and adoption of such a program is a source of considerable popularity for any government; on various occasions, countries have found that the possession of a development program was an essential condition for being considered eligible for foreign assistance, or at least was helpful in connection with the application for such assistance; similarly, the existence of a program makes it easier for a government to secure additional *domestic* financing through taxation or other measures which by themselves would encounter considerable opposition; finally, a development program is a convenient device for the national government in dealing with the many requests for financial aid to which it is constantly subjected from its own agencies. It seems so much more convincing to tell the visiting mayor of a provincial town who comes to lobby for an aqueduct that no provision for this project is made in this year's portion of the five-year plan that simply to plead old-fashioned lack of funds, which in any event is an unsatisfactory explanation when aqueducts are being built at the same time for several other towns.

The development program is therefore a convenient restraint on the central government which permits it to push through high-priority projects without being side-tracked. This function of a development program is usually not the principal motive for adopting it in the first place, but the realization of its usefulness becomes often a major reason for continuing the experience. On the other hand, this very freedom-of-choice-limiting property of development programs can be felt as excessive and then results in the frequently observed spectacle of a government acting in contradiction to the course of action which it had laid down for itself.

Sometimes such behavior reflects nothing but the inherent impatience of most governments of underdeveloped countries with any kind of limitation of their powers, whether such limitation is inflicted from the outside or is self-imposed, and whether or not it is rational. But often the violation by the country of its own development program is due to the unreasonable and excessive character of the constraints laid down in the program. Governments of underdeveloped countries appear to have a tendency to subject themselves to overly rigid rules of conduct which, later on, they find themselves inevitably unable to follow. From this viewpoint, one may discern a genuine, though unexpected similarity between the orthodox and rigid monetary and banking legislations adopted in many Latin American countries in the twenties and the "integrated", long-term development programs of today. These programs often pretend to commit governments firmly to an all-embracing investment pattern in spite of the avowed weakness of our knowledge about appropriate investment criteria and even though the character and reality content of the estimates which make up the program differ widely from one economic sector to another.[1] If, in some sectors, the proposed spending is based only on the vaguest kind of criteria and extrapolations, then there is a good chance that the program figures should be radically revised once detailed engineering and economic studies have been undertaken. If it were made perfectly clear upon the publication and acceptance of a development program, which are the sectors where proposed spending results from careful screening of individual projects that are ready to be undertaken, and which are the ones where no such detailed planning has as yet been possible, then governments could change their minds about parts of the program without feeling that they are toppling the whole laboriously erected structure.

It should be added that provision for possible changes in the program should be made even with respect to those parts which have received careful attention and study as even here it is unlikely that all the alternatives have been fully considered. The distinction which we have made between sectors where planning has been sufficiently thorough to warrant full commitment by the government to the program, and those where the planning is of so general a nature that the government should retain considerable freedom of action to modify the tentatively-set goals as better knowledge becomes available, is clearly overdrawn. The plan will ordinarily consist of a series of sectoral programs and projects which can be ranked according to the quantity and quality of expert planning that has gone into them and which should then command corespondingly decreasing degrees of allegiance on the part of the national government.

After the many experiences with national economic planning which have not been wholly successful, it might be time to recognize that governments of underdeveloped countries exhibit side by side with a "propensity to plan", a "propensity to experiment and to improvise". If this is so, is it really wise to identify the former propensity with everything that is sensible and virtuous and the latter with all that is unreasonable and sinful? Would it not be far better to proceed in accordance with the prescriptions of any elementary textbook in psychology and provide healthy and constructive outlets for both propensities? Admittedly, there is nothing more exasperating and demoralizing than the spectacle, frequently on display in underdeveloped countries, of half-finished structures in reinforced concrete which were intended to become government buildings, hospitals, stadiums, etc. While the lack of planning and the arbitrary reversal of previously taken investment decisions that are responsible for these unsightly "modern ruins" are deplorable, improvisation and experimentation must be recognized not only as irrepressible urges of governments, but also as a force which, properly directed, can be made to play a beneficial role in the development process.

[1] On this point, see my "Economics and Investment Criteria—Reflections Based on Experience in Colombia", in Max F. Millikan, ed., *Investment Criteria and Economic Growth* (Cambridge, Mass., 1955) (planographed).

For instance, even with the best of plans, governments of underdeveloped countries certainly cannot and should not give up the permanent search for new and better ways of using the country's natural resources. If the search is successful, the investment pattern laid down in any previously adopted program *ought* to be disturbed. In our planning for certain average rates of growth, we are apt to forget that these average rates were realized in the industrial countries only because some very much higher rates were achieved in some sectors, often as a result of experimentation and improvisation. In underdeveloped countries, many dynamic growth sectors remain to be discovered; many patterns of social organization conducive to economic progress remain to be identified; and much flexibility in programming economic development must be preserved to enable governments and investors to take advantage of changing trends in world markets and of the changing whims of international development capital. Here, then, is a wide area where governments can and should make the utmost use of their urge to be imaginative, unpredictable, and uncoercible.

UNDERSTANDING RECURRING INFLATION

Let us now try to understand why inflation is still so real a problem in many underdeveloped countries. Is it not widely agreed that economic development should take place as much as possible within the framework of monetary stability? Has it not been pointed out *ad nauseam* that inflation, while typically resulting from an attempt to accelerate the development process, is actually harmful to it because of the speculative and non-productive investments in inventories, real estate, and foreign exchange boards it brings in its wake?

The fact is that when inflation proceeds at a fast and rapidly accelerating rate, its disadvantages usually become so obvious that somehow a way—and the political courage—is found to stop it. But after a short period of stability, the pressures often start to build up again and prices resume their upward course. The most obvious explanation is that in a developing economy which disposes of an elastic monetary system, the effective demand for investment funds always tends to outrun the supply of savings. While this explanation is true, I do not believe that it is particularly helpful in tracing the inflationary process and in locating the best means to curb it.

In the first place, this standard explanation implicitly tends to consider savings and consumption as more or less given and investment as the quantity which must be adjusted. Recent experience in several developing countries has shown, however, that savings are definitely "institution-elastic", i.e., that with the appropriate instruments and institutions, considerable amounts of domestic savings can be mobilized. Instead of curbing investment, it may also be possible to restrain consumption, in particular consumption of imported luxuries or their equivalent, namely foreign travel by residents.

This is really the economic rationale for the prohibition of luxury imports or the special high foreign exchange rates often applying to such imports and to foreign travel. While in advanced countries such measures may have little anti-inflationary effect as the great variety of domestic production permits considerable substitution of the prohibited imports by domestically available goods and services, the sharply limited range of quality articles produced in underdeveloped coutries makes such substitution there impractical so that import curbing measures may effectively decrease consumption.

Finally, the investments-outrun-savings analysis of inflation concentrates attention unduly not only on investment as opposed to savings and consumption, but also on public investments within the investment total. Public investments are the only ones that are reasonably well known and over which economic policy makers and advisers have some measure of direct control. Private investments are usually assumed at some given level, their composition is not known, and the way in which they can be influenced—by monetary policy—is not subject to accurate evaluation. As a result, public investments have to bear the brunt of any adjustment following the realization that there exists an excess of intended investment spending over available savings, and it is somewhat ironic to note that the modern approach to monetary stability, which relies on investment planning, is likely to result in this bias against public investments.

Let us now try to understand a little more fully why inflation is so difficult to avoid in underdeveloped countries. One reason is that the conditions for monetary equilibrium are more stringent for them than for the advanced countries. In the latter, all we need as a condition for price stability is an *overall* balance between investment and savings. In actual fact, balance has often been consciously achieved by having expected dissavings or inadequate savings by individuals and business offset by a surplus in the government accounts. In underdeveloped countries, on the other hand, it is likely that we will have to achieve monetary equilibrium by balancing separately the accounts of the government on the one hand, and of the non-government sector on the other—obviously a more difficult task. The reason is that the achievement of a budgetary surplus for any length of time is simply out of the question for the ministers of finance of a developing country.

Even in advanced countries where a considerable internal debt is outstanding and maturing every year, it is difficult to win public support for a fiscal policy aiming at a cash surplus. In underdeveloped countries, internal debts are either small or are held by the central bank, and there would be little understanding for a policy aimed at retiring this debt when so many essential projects need to be undertaken. As to the external debt, it is ordinarily rather increasing than decreasing in an active period of development. Thus, the best that can be hoped for from the public sector under these circumstances is a precarious balance which means that the private sector has to balance its accounts independently. In this respect, the business sector, beset by requests for high dividends and by strong expansion needs, can be relied upon to be a net spender. The only safety valve is represented by the traditional tendency of individuals to be net hoarders of cash. But this tendency is increasingly counteracted by the enlarged availability of mass consumption goods, by the gradual appearance of personal credit facilities, and by the conversion of cash hoards into bank deposits.

In spite of these complicating factors, monetary stability could still be achieved given a sufficiently strong will among the economic policy makers. I shall now argue that this will is none too likely to be encountered. In the first place, a shrewd finance minister of a developing economy may not be entirely unhappy to have to contend with *moderate* inflationary pressure as such pressures give him an opportunity and an excuse to reject the more extravagant among the projects that are constantly brought to him by the spending ministers, the local governments, and the autonomous development agencies. As long as monetary stability prevails, he is almost as vulnerable as though he had accumulated a large cash balance. He does not and cannot pretend to know precisely the limits of tolerance of the economy. Thus, for him to say, "This additional expenditure will start inflation again", is clearly much less convincing than, "With prices again on the rise, we cannot afford to add more fuel to the fire". Small inflation may therefore represent an effective line of defense against unplanned and unreasonable expenditures and, in fact, it may at times be needed to hold the line against big inflation.

It is not suggested that the minister of finance consciously manufactures inflation. But all he usually has to do to have some inflation is to relent just one day in his fight against it; and he may so relent because, consciously or unconsciously, he feels that he must be under some pressure to operate successfully in the particular environment of an underdeveloped, but developing economy.

A further reason for which a finance minister may not be putting up as stiff a fight as he might against some increase in the price level is that the more modern tax structure which has in recent years been introduced in many underdeveloped countries, makes their fiscal revenues less vulnerable to inflation than they used to be. Customs duties are now predominantly on an *ad valorem* basis with specific duties in a secondary or supplementary role. Lags in collection have been reduced. Most important, progressive income taxation now exists almost everywhere and this means that a rise in prices and incomes has actually the effect of continuously and irreversibly increasing the real incidence of the existing rate schedule without any need to make it steeper through legislative action.

It must be a slow rise, for if there is a galloping inflation the schedules will surely be revised; but if prices and incomes rise by say 5 to 10 per cent per year, the inflation may bring with it just about the desired degree of tax tightening. Incidentally, this effect which may be quite important over the years, ought to be taken into account when one analyzes the effect of inflation on income distribution.

CYCLES IN FOREIGN EXCHANGE AND FISCAL POLICY

Let us next consider briefly a closely allied area of economic policy, namely foreign exchange rates and controls. Here a characteristic cycle may often be observed: a country with an impossibly complex multiple rate and exchange control structure adopts one day an excellent reform which sweeps away all the complications and sets up a unitary exchange rate, possibly incorporating into revised customs duties the protection previously resulting from some features of the abolished multiple rates. As times goes on, however, differential exchange rates and controls infiltrate again here and there. This goes on for some time until the situation is once more so chaotic that the country is ripe for another thorough exchange rate reform.

A similar cycle can be observed with respect to fiscal policy. A common feature of the revenue structure of many underdeveloped countries is the excessive earmarking of taxes for specific expenditures, in other words the violation of the principle of budgetary unity. Every once in a while, the situation becomes so intricate and the general budget so anemic that a law is passed eliminating all earmarkings—but here also one may be sure that soon there will be back-sliding into the old ways.

These gyrations in economic policy are precisely what seems so discouraging to observers or advising experts who do not realize that there is some "logic in this madness", but see only the flouting of their advice and the total inability on the part of the authorities to adhere to a once elected course of action. Since the kind of policy-making we have described requires frequent disregard for principles that were just recently proclaimed as inviolate, it attracts persons who do not have any qualms about such disregard. In this way, the optical illusion is created that the frequent turn-abouts in economic policy are due to the fact that a capricious minister is in power when in actual fact the more pertinent causation may work the other way around. Unsavory jobs are usually handled by unsavory individuals. But if society wants these jobs to be done, it is surely wrong to focus on the individuals and to hold them uniquely responsible.

The tendencies that are disruptive of unitary exchange rate systems and of the unity principle in budgeting are directly related to the economic structure and problems of underdeveloped countries. For instance, special incentive export rates are bound to be tried from time to time in countries which feel that they rely too heavily on one or two commodities for their export earnings. Earlier in this paper, we have already presented one argument favoring special import prohibitions, or special exchange rates designed to deter certain imports. In case domestic inflationary pressures dictate a devaluation, it may also become necessary to grant temporary privileged status to some imports. Consider, for instance, equipment imports on the part of public utilities which are undertaking important expansion projects. Privileged exchange rate treatment for such imports may become a desirable offset to the handicap resulting for public utilities from the usual lag of their rates behind rises in the general price level.

In public finance the special earmarking of tax revenues is usually associated with the expansion of the government's activities. As a new field for governmental responsibility, say low-cost housing, is recognized, a new source of revenue must be discovered. It is only natural that at first the expenditure and the revenue which finances it, are coupled together. In this way the new fiscal device becomes far more acceptable to public opinion which always suspects "waste" in the expenditure of general treasury funds.

The conclusion I draw from this is not that to understand everything is to forgive everything. But I do think that to understand some of these real problems under which policy makers of underdeveloped countries labor will help in making our technical assistance more constructive. For instance, the preceding reasoning would seem to indicate that we should avoid those Fundamental Reforms accompanied by solemn declarations of principle and resounding commitments "never to do it again". In any reform, it would seem far wiser to circumscribe and to regulate such practices as multiple exchange rates and ear-marking of fiscal revenues than to prohibit them outright.

CYCLES IN THE ADMINISTRATION OF ECONOMIC DEVELOPMENT

Cycles in economic policy such as the ones we have just described with regard to exchange rates and fiscal policy are paralleled in the administration of economic development. They are particularly disturbing as, under the best of circumstances, public administration presents many deficiencies in underdeveloped countries. On the other hand, policy changes in this area are perhaps more easily condoned by the foreign observer, as all governments seem to experience considerable difficulties in creating a workable and durable administrative structure for the exercise of new functions in the economic field. For here lies the origin of the trouble: a government decides that it should undertake a new function or carry on an existing one much more effectively than heretofore. It finds that for this purpose administrative procedures prevailing within the government itself are too cumbersome and slow; that salaries are too low to attract the kind of talent one wants to secure; and, most important usually, that political pressure ought to be removed from the scene. As a result of all these cogent reasons, a new Institute, Corporation, Bank, or Agency, with semi-autonomous status, is created and starts on its career accompanied by many high hopes on the part of its founders and the general public.

One trouble with this solution is that the government of a developing country is liable to encounter one economic function after the other that ought to be newly undertaken or that must be carried out more efficiently. Thus the semi-autonomous Institutes soon begin to mushroom until one day a new Cabinet comes in, the economic ministers find that the existence of these Institutes—to which many important taxes are assigned—make budgetary and economic planning practically impossible, and that it sharply curtails their own power to the full exercise of which they were hopefully looking forward. The result is that a thorough reorganization is decided upon which places all the new agencies right back into the government and under the ministries.

The likelihood of such a development is enhanced by the fact that the presidents, directors, or managers of the Institutes are usually quite high-powered individuals at the start, but are soon replaced by others of lower standing, whereas no such process of progressive downgrading applies to the holders of ministerial jobs. Moreover, the autonomous Institutes do not fare so well if the governments take too seriously their autonomous status, for then they lack the political and financial support which they vitally need for their success. Finally, there exists a well-known and time-honored propensity in many underdeveloped countries to "solve" serious economic problems by means of legislation alone. This practice has often blocked real progress. Today many governments are apparently under the similar and similarly dangerous illusion that they actually solve a problem by setting up an Institute to which they delegate the task of solving the problem.

The preceding remarks are not meant to deny that the new tasks which governments need to undertake will often require institutional innovations. But they may be taken as a warning against advocating too freely the "autonomous institute free of political inferterence" as *the* solution. What is needed, besides a very few institutes of this kind, is primarily a reorganization of the economic ministries which would enable them to carry out some of the new functions efficiently through their own sub-divisions, or through institutes closely integrated with them.

CONCLUSION

We have noted here some salient examples of the apparently inherent instability of economic policy in underdeveloped countries. While the specific causes of this kind of instability are different in each case, a few general remarks may be in order by way of conclusion.

In the first place, we must understand this instability as the reflection of some very general characteristics of underdeveloped countries. After all, their political structures themselves are unstable and ill-defined, the legitimacy of their governments is often in doubt, and in general the powers of the state fail to be clearly bounded by custom or observed constitutional law.

Secondly, there is the desire to experiment and to manipulate. Anxious to use their newly won sovereignty to the full, confident that the basic potential of their economies leaves them some latitude for making mistakes, governments of underdeveloped countries are powerfully attracted by new gadgets in economic policy making. Just as they have made the transition from mule to airplane in one generation, so they pass easily from the complete absence of monetary controls to the imposition of complicated differential reserve requirements. In economic policy, however, the meaning of progress is not nearly as clear as in technology. There are many more possibilities of going too far and too fast and, unlike technical progress, policy is typically reversible. If it is reversed too often, demoralization results, not only among the foreign advisers, but—and this is far more serious—among the country's policy-makers and the general public. An impression of unpredictability and of lack of purpose is created which may even be damaging to economic progress itself. A rift develops between the business community which acquires the feeling that it is the only real creator of wealth in the country and the government with its bungling and erratic policies.

Much is therefore to be said for trying to make governmental policies more stable. Our analysis has shown that this aim cannot be achieved by once-and-for-all Reforms or Programs. Underdeveloped countries will not tolerate any straitjackets. The money doctor who prescribes a uniform financial diet or the economic advisor who lays down a rigid investment pattern may be obeyed for a while, but soon he becomes a father image that must be destroyed. Account must be taken of the propensity to change and to experiment so that, when it is indulged in, it does not come as a revolt against intolerable restraints but as an action that is foreseen as well as regulated. Economic policy in underdeveloped countries will then continue to fluctuate, but the limits of these fluctuations should gradually become narrower and the oscillation between those limits slower, as experiences with diverse policies are assimilated.

For economic policy in underdeveloped countries to become more stable, two conditions must therefore be fulfilled: first the institutional framework must be elastic and must regulate change rather than proscribe it; and second, home-grown experience must be accumulated, and made to yield a body of home-tested principles. As economists we can contribute importantly to this process: we can help underdeveloped countries to understand themselves and their experiences.

ADMINISTRATIVE
OBJECTIVES
FOR DEVELOPMENT
ADMINISTRATION

Victor A. Thompson

Today, with so many nonindustrial, low-income countries trying desperately to raise their living standards, the question of what contribution the discipline of public administration can make to economic development naturally arises. On the face of it the answer would seem to be "not very much." Economics, engineering, education, medicine, and so on, all are more important. In fact, a reader of the literature in the field of public administration might reasonably fear that public administration, as it is commonly interpreted and often practiced, would be a handicap to economic development. One shudders at the prospect of eager learners in Nairobi, Lagos, Karachi or Saïgon attempting to put into practice new learning about the proper roles of staff and line, the overriding importance of a position classification system, the need to organize by purpose or process, the importance of not overextending the span of control, the absolute centrality of clear, unambiguous lines of authority and responsibility, the indispensability of clearly defined jurisdictions and offices, the importance of a centralized planning agency, and so on.[1]

At a somewhat more sophisticated level, we are becoming conscious of the fact that administration in modern countries is permeated with behavioral

From Victor A. Thompson, "Administrative Objectives for Development Administration," *Administrative Science Quarterly*, 19:1:91–108 (June 1964). Reprinted by permission of the *Administrative Science Quarterly* and the author.

[1] As Joseph LaPalombara says, "The irony in much of this is that the principles we try to export do not even operate in the United States" (*Bureaucracy and Political Development* [Princeton, N.J., 1963], p. 20). We export our management mythology.

norms which are products of a modern culture. Such norms as rationality, the use of universalistic criteria, achievement, specificity, and impersonality are not adopted by management; they are not administrative objectives. They result from social and cultural conditions. Attempts to impose such behavioral norms upon an administrative system would only fail and would probably produce disintegrative effects upon a society. Surely it could not result in more than formalism, leaving a wide gap between administrative forms and administrative behavior. LaPalombara must be correct when he says: "Once a reasonable differentiation of administrative roles has occurred, once these roles are filled with a minimum attention to achievement criteria, once the bureaucrats themselves are persuaded to approach the tasks in hand on the basis of secular attitudes, the minimum conditions of a developmental bureaucracy are met and it can proceed with its responsibilities."[2]

Is there then no contribution at all that the discipline of public administration can make to economic development? I believe such a contribution can be made, but it most definitely will not come from the doctrines of management or administration most widely prevalent in the West. As LaPalombara says, these doctrines do not work well even here. The rituals and teachings of public administration have been fixated on *control*—almost neurotically fixated it would seem. Control is an ideal of a static world. Economic development, however, takes place within a milieu of constant change. The rituals and principles of public administration developed in a time of relative stability of environment and incorporated within themselves the ideal of perpetual stability—hence the morbid preoccupation with control.

In a situation of rapid change, control is much less relevant. The ideal must be *adaptation,* and this involves creativity and a looseness of definition and structure. Until now, a remarkably small proportion of time and effort within the administrative profession has been spent in trying to devise criteria and principles relevant to an adaptive administration as opposed to a controlled one. Consequently, a remarkably small amount either of our administrative practice or of our administrative principle is relevant to problems of development administration.

In this paper I suggest some administrative criteria which seem to have some relevance to economic development. I realize that this is the merest beginning. These criteria stem from the growing body of theory and research on organizations and human relations within the field of the behavioral sciences. In presenting them I would not be so foolish as to argue that economic development cannot take place under any other set of administrative conditions, but only that an administration which lives up to these criteria will achieve more development more quickly, with less human cost, with more imagination, with more attention to more values, and therefore with greater

[2] *Ibid.,* p. 54.

benefits. I believe this claim to be true whether the development administration is to take place in Kuala Lumpur, Ouagadougou, or upstate New York.

What are the administrative conditions necessary for the most effective development administration? To answer this question is to establish a set of purely administrative objectives for development administrators. The list of administrative objectives which I propose to discuss is undoubtedly incomplete, but it provides a beginning. It suggests the lines along which the discipline of public administration can be of some small assistance in economic development. Among the purely administrative objectives of the development administrator should be the following: an innovative atmosphere, the operationalizing and wide sharing of planning goals, the combining of planning (thinking) with action (doing), a cosmopolitan atmosphere, the diffusion of influence, the increasing of toleration of interdependence, and the avoidance of bureaupathology. These conditions are all interdependent, but it is helpful to consider them one at a time.

AN INNOVATIVE ATMOSPHERE

It seems reasonable to assume that the ability to change and create is a necessity for development administrative machinery. Innovative behavior seems to require certain prerequisite conditions, among which the following are most important: variety and richness of experience with the subject, psychological freedom, and psychological security.[3] Control-centered management, with its monocratic organization structure, denies or endangers all of these conditions. The analysis which underlies this statement will be revealed as we progress through the other administrative conditions or objectives to be discussed, and so it will not be repeated here. However, it will be worthwhile at this point to list some very likely propositions about innovativeness in organizations.

1. Innovation or "creativity" is facilitated by a group administrative effort dominated by a professional outlook.[4]

2. Innovation is facilitated by program or subject-matter uncertainty accompanied by personal security (by uncertainty without fear).[5]

3. Innovation is facilitated by a nonhierarchical climate, especially a nonhierarchical communication structure, and by "loose" organization in general.[6]

[3] Morris I. Stein and Shirley J. Heinze, *Creativity and the Individual* (Glencoe, Ill., 1960).

[4] Kurt W. Back, Decisions under Uncertainty, *The American Behavioral Scientist*, 4 (1961), 14–19.

[5] See Morris I. Stein, Creativity and Culture, *Journal of Psychology*, 36 (1953), 311–322; also Erik H. Erikson, The Problem of Ego Identity, *Journal of the American Psychoanalytic Association*, 4 (1956), 56–121.

[6] Tom Burns and G. M. Stalker, *The Management of Innovation* (London, 1961).

4. Innovative responsiveness is a function of both personality factors and cognitive or ability factors and can be influenced by appropriate training programs.[7]

OPERATIONAL AND SHARED PLANNING GOALS

Human beings need a cognitive structuring of their activities—need to know what they are doing—if regressive (childish) behaviors are to be avoided.[8] Clear goals can help to provide this cognitive structuring if they are "operational," meaning that the impact of a proposed action on the goal must be demonstrated with sufficient credulity so that a reasonable person can accept the demonstration without denying his own rational nature.

If the operational goals are also shared, planners can move toward them by using rational, analytic, decisional processes. Otherwise, bargaining, political, or power processes are necessary to resolve planning disputes.[9]

By shared and operational goals I do not mean the fixing of overall goals or the complete specification of planning goals, for this practice kills creativity, as Braybrooke and Lindblom convincingly argue.[10] I mean the kind of sharing which free communication can promote and the kind of concreteness and practicality promoted by deep knowledge of the subject. Shared, operational goals are products of a community of experts. Given certain other conditions mentioned below, shared operational planning goals, in addition to satisfying the need for a cognitive structuring of action, convert the problem of coordination into a procedural one.

COMBINATION OF PLANNING (THINKING) AND ACTION (DOING)

The separation of planning from action, of thinking from doing, is a special form of the mind-body error in earlier psychological theories. It is based on a mechanistic conception of human behavior which assumes oversimplified human motivations when it does not indeed neglect the problem of motivation entirely. Unlike machines, people do not just act when the button is pushed; they both think and act at the same time. In fact, thinking is a kind of action, and action is a kind of thinking. What people do

---

[7] Center for Programs in Government Administration of the University of Wisconsin, *Education for Innovative Behavior in Executives* (Cooperative Research Project No. 975; U.S. Office of Education).

[8] Kurt Lewin, *Resolving Social Conflicts* (New York, 1948).

[9] James G. March and Herbert A. Simon, *Organizations* (New York, 1958).

[10] David Braybrooke and Charles E. Lindblom, *A Strategy of Decision* (New York, 1963).

is a result of their own decisional, thinking processes, including their definition of the situation.

The more administrative arrangements are based upon the mechanistic dichotomy of thinking and doing—some to think, others to do—the more enforcement activities (with associated intelligence activities) must be engaged in, and the more unsolicited, unplanned,·unwanted consequences accumulate. At some point, the process is largely out of central control and the central planning becomes illusory.

It is sometimes argued that planning (thinking) must be separated from operations (doing) or planning will be pushed out by operations. However, this occasionally observed phenomenon has been misunderstood. The need for a cognitive structuring of activities leads people into those pursuits in which they can at least vaguely measure the consequences; it leads them into operational pursuits.[11] Thus, if planning goals are operationally defined, cognitive needs will not result in operations pushing out planning. In fact, other needs, such as the need for rewards or for seeing decisions eventuate as expected, can result in excited attention to planning and operations as a unity; for they are a unity: together they constitute action.

The attempt to separate thinking from doing tends to create classes: the thinkers, upper class; the doers, lower class. A gentleman does not do things: he does not dirty his hands; he tells others what to do. Within an administrative structure, self-protective reactions of the ascribed doers are likely to take the form of blocking responses to the thinker's overtures, most likely by cutting off communication with them. The thinkers are quite likely to become frustrated, ineffectual, isolates, unless they can employ unusual administrative or political power in their behalf. But even power cannot convert nonoperational thinking (planning) into effective action, and even operational planning, if organizationally segregated and hence dependent upon power, tends to become illusory, as described above.

A COSMOPOLITAN ATMOSPHERE

Development administration requires the ability to respond to feedback information in an adaptive fashion. Particularly important is the ability to perceive, understand, and respond to information about unsolicited effects of action upon a great variety of programs regardless of whether or not they are one's own. If the actions of bureau A react adversely upon the programs of bureau B, bureau A needs to be able to perceive, understand, and adapt positively to this fact. Such an ability requires a cosmopolitan point of view, and so we need to know what promotes such a point of view. A few hypotheses are suggested.

1. If the hierarchical institution is stressed, parochialism results. The

[11] March and Simon, *op. cit.*

rights of superiors include the right to control communication with the rest of the organization (going through channels) and the right to loyalty.[12] Groupings formed around authority roles result in differentiation of goals and perceptions of reality, in short, in a narrow parochialism. Conversely, free communication beyond the authority unit or grouping results in a broader sharing of goals and perceptions of reality, that is, in a more cosmopolitan outlook.

2. Professionalism tends toward the cosmopolitan viewpoint because of a professional or occupational identification rather than an authority group identification and because professional interdependence facilitates cross-channel communication.[13] Conversely, organizationally defined occupational roles—roles created out of specific program procedures—tend toward parochialism for a number of reasons: (1) occupational status or recognition is to be found only within the program unit; (2) interunit mobility and especially interorganizational mobility is low; (3) vested interests in specific procedures and programs arise; (4) program identifications restrict perceptions of, understanding of, and responsiveness to feedback information involving action effects on other programs and low evaluations of the worth of other program goals. This point will be more fully discussed below.

3. Extraorganizational associations of professionals or specialists encourage cosmopolitanism, or at least a nonprogram parochialism, and reduce the power of authority roles, further weakening the forces toward parochialism (i.e., the authoritative demand for loyalty and control of outgroup communication).[14]

THE DIFFUSION OF INFLUENCE

Development planning is a highly technical and scientific process involving a relatively large number of professionally and scientifically trained personnel. If such planning is to be undertaken seriously, such personnel must acquire positions of influence within the organization. This involves a de-emphasis on the line of command and a rather thorough rejection of a literal unity of command. Persons occupying authority roles are likely to experience a rather large gap between their expected authority and their actual authority. If primitive responsibility patterns continue to be followed under these circumstances, the performance

[12] Victor A. Thompson, *Modern Organization* (New York, 1961).

[13] Alvin W. Gouldner, Cosmopolitans and Locals, *Administrative Science Quarterly*, 2 (1957 and 1958); Harold L. Wilensky, *Intellectuals in Labor Unions* (Glencoe, Ill., 1956); Everett C. Hughes, *Men and Their Work* (Glencoe, Ill., 1958); and William J. Goode, Community Within a Community: The Professions, *American Sociological Review*, 22 (1957), 194–200.

[14] Thompson, *op. cit.*

of authority roles may become intolerable and the situation itself a source of debilitating and useless conflict.[15]

The acquisition and use of a large number of professionally, scientifically, and technically trained employees requires a rationalized reward system. The almost universal use of hierarchical authority roles as success roles forces the professionally trained out of the field of their greatest competence and into management; it also depresses the supply of these people below needs, depresses their morale within the organization, and exaggerates the friction between them and persons in authority roles as the latter lose power to the former.[16] A suggested remedy is to have two separate salary scales, related to real needs rather than the spurious need to maintain a single status hierarchy, so that specially trained persons might achieve "success" without leaving their specialty, so that more people would undertake the special training, and so that the dignity of those in authority roles would be adjusted to reality.[17]

THE TOLERATION OF INTERDEPENDENCE

Development administration is a highly interdependent activity, not only because it must use a large number of interdependent specialties, but also because it implies a concerted effort toward a national goal (or perhaps a few national goals). Interdependence creates the need for coordination which, in turn, implies cooperation—an attitude of willingness to be coordinated.[18] The administrative problem here is to ease the pains of interdependence. What are the conditions which increase the toleration of interdependence? Some answers are suggested.

1. The cohesiveness of a group increases the toleration of interdependence.[19] This proposition has much more relevance when applied to small face-to-face groups, but it does suggest that a free or permissive atmosphere with regard to communication within an organization should work in the right direction.

2. Acceptance of the reality or need for interdependence makes interdependence more tolerable. It is hypothesized that this acceptance is more likely to be forthcoming if real functions are involved rather than authori-

---

[15] *Ibid.*

[16] *Ibid.* See also Nigel Walker, *Morale in the Civil Service; a Study of the Desk Worker* (Edinburgh, Scotland, 1960).

[17] Thompson, *op. cit.*

[18] *Ibid.* See also Emile Durkheim, *The Division of Labor in Society* (Glencoe, Ill., 1933).

[19] Morton Deutsch, An Experimental Study of the Effects of Co-operation and Competition upon Group Processes, *Human Relations*, 2 (1949), 199–231, and Edwin J. Thomas, Effects of Facilitative Role Interdependence on Group Functioning, *Human Relations*, 10 (1957), 347–366.

tatively created dependencies; for example, my dependence upon a doctor as opposed to my dependence upon a control clearance point. The difference is that of dependence upon a person because of orders versus dependence upon him because of a service he can perform better than others—or dependence because of fear versus dependence because of need—or influence because of office authority versus influence because of technical skill.[20]

3. Interdependence between persons is more tolerable when communication between them is adequate. This fact helps to explain the increasing number of informal communication channels (nonhierarchical channels) to be found in modern organizations.[21] It, too, counsels an indulgent or permissive rather than a hierarchical pattern of communication within the organization.

AVOIDANCE OF BUREAUPATHOLOGY

All of the administrative conditions of development administration outlined above will be absent (or weak) in an organization dominated by personal insecurity. Personal insecurity in an authority position is likely to create personal needs of such magnitude as to dominate over organizational needs. Resulting behavior, then, will be pathological from the standpoint of the organization and so has been called "bureaupathic" (also "red tape," "bureaucratic," and so on). Bureaupathic behavior stems from needs that can be generalized as the need to control. It is manifested in such things as close supervision; failure to delegate; heavy emphasis on regulations, quantitative norms, precedents, and the accumulation of paper to prove compliance; cold aloofness; insistence on office protocol; fear of innovation; or restriction of communication.[22] It is characterized by a typical circularity in that such behavior by a superior tends to call forth responses from subordinates which seem to call for more of the same behavior. Subordinates "cannot be trusted," "will not take responsibility," "have to be told everything."[23] In an extreme bureaupathic situation, it is difficult to see how development planning can take place.

Such an atmosphere of insecurity can result from the existence of an arbitrary, nonrational, and unpredictable authority at the very top, as in the case of an authoritarian, single-party, political system;[24] or from the unfortunate impact of personality in a high authority role; or from the adoption of an official incentive system which heavily emphasizes individual competition for a few great status prizes and hence overlooks and tends to

[20] Thompson, *op. cit.*; and Peter M. Blau and W. Richard Scott, *Formal Organizations* (San Francisco, 1962).

[21] March and Simon, *op. cit.*

[22] Thompson, *op. cit.*; Burns and Stalker, *op. cit.*

[23] Alvin W. Gouldner, *Patterns of Industrial Bureaucracy* (Glencoe, Ill., 1954).

[24] Reinhard Bendix, *Work and Authority in Industry* (New York, 1956).

destroy the informal group structure with its group controls, loyalties, and rewards. It can result from impatience and inability of high authority figures to wait for rewards—to wait for results of development planning. Impatience for results on the part of political leaders in underdeveloped countries is all too humanly understandable, but it is very likely to be self-defeating.

Above I have discussed a list of purely administrative conditions as pre-requisites for an adaptive as opposed to a controlled administrative organiza-tion. As I said before, these conditions are all intimately interrelated. This interrelatedness, and the cruciality of these conditions for producing an adaptive administrative structure, can be more forcefully demonstrated by applying the foregoing analysis to a few recurrent administrative problems. I have chosen three such problems: the problem of centralization versus de-centralization; the problem of securing innovative responsiveness to feedback communication; and the problem of participation in planning.

CENTRALIZATION AND DECENTRALIZATION

The existing state of a technology decrees a techni-cal level of centralization in decision making. This is the level where the skills and equipment provided by the technology can be fully utilized—where the "market" is large enough so that the need for the highest skills can absorb the supply. However, centralization is frequently carried much further be-cause of different, nontechnical needs surrounding higher authority positions. These needs may be personal needs for power and prestige; they may arise from an unstable political situation; they may arise from the pressures of powerful organized interests. Whatever the cause, overcentralization (beyond what is technically decreed) creates poorly accepted interdependencies and hence conflict, tensions, low morale, sabotage.

Under conditions of overcentralization, the rational control of events is illusory to a greater or lesser degree. There are a number of reasons for this. In the first place, there is no necessary or even predictable relation between authority, as such, and rationality. Because persons or groups have the right or the power to make decisions does not mean that they have the ability to make rational decisions. In the second place, as was indicated above, over-centralization, based as it is on a machine model, rests on a partly false assumption about the behavior of subordinates. To be realistic, the plan or decision should be regarded as the actual behavior or action which eventuates, and there are many slips between the decision recorded on paper and the final ensuing behavior. There is nothing impelling about a plan on paper unless it represents the results of one's own analysis and decision. The paper plan is only an additional source of information about planning behavior, and not the best by any means. In the third place, communication processes do strange and often unpredictable things to plans handed down from above. Usually there is not time to read all the relevant documents and so, to that extent, the central planning might as well not have occurred. Often the documents are filed too well and are not available when needed. The only sure way of communicating planning is to incorporate it into the neural passages and memories of those to whom it must be communicated for purposes of execution. This implies participation in planning, or decentralization. Finally, motivation to act in the planned way is the absolutely crucial and controlling aspect of the whole process. Here again central offices may depend upon administrative authority and power, but, as was said before, the more that power is used, the more unsolicited response consequences accumulate until at some point the process is largely out of central planning control, which then becomes illusory. Solution of the motivation problem probably implies participation in the planning process, namely decentralization. In the final analysis, thinking cannot be separated from doing.

To apply the above analysis somewhat more concretely, compare planning by a large central planning department, divided inevitably into subject matter units, where bureaucratic patterns have been allowed to accumulate for various reasons (including frustration and isolation with resulting insecurities), with planning by divisions in several Ministries backed up by thoroughly interested and committed Ministers integrated into a politically homogeneous Cabinet under a development-conscious Chief Executive. Would not the latter arrangement make quicker and more politically viable decisions with regard to plan priorities than the former? And would not those decisions be more executable, more real, than those of the large central planning department? Here we see the very secondary nature of formal legal structure. The important considerations concern the existence or nonexistence of shared, operational, national, planning goals and an atmosphere which encourages creativity and cosmopolitanism.

The separation of thinking (planning) in a central planning department from the doing (executing) located elsewhere has a further administrative flaw which contributes to the illusory nature of this separation. This flaw involves a misconception about the role of authority in planning for others. Within the planning structure, disagreements not susceptible to rational processes for resolution are referred to administrative authority for settlement. When a group is planning for its own behavior (i.e., when thinking and doing are not separated), such authoritative decisions may aid momentarily, but they never finally settle anything, because they can always be reopened and are only settled finally by action. But when a group is planning for the behavior of others (i.e., when thinking and doing are separated), such decisions or settlements are largely meaningless. The issue still exists and will be up for resolution in the action group, under a different system of authority, and might as well be resolved this second time in the contrary way. Consequently, a central planning body will have more influence on events the more bland (issueless) its plans are. A corollary is that a bureaucratic, authoritarian, hierarchy-emphasized central planning body is administratively quixotic.

Attempts to justify overcentralization intellectually often rest on the illusion of elitism, or "managerial determinism," perhaps a psychological off-shoot of hero worship or father dependence. Involved is a confusion between right (authority) and ability. The former can be conferred; the latter is sub-ject to limitations which are amenable to human desires to only a very limited extent.

COMMUNICATION AND FEEDBACK

An administrative communications sys-tem is an attempt to assure at all relevant points in an organization the ability to detect, understand, and respond appropriately to appropriate data. Today, a new technology of decision making greatly facilitates the gathering, storage, recall, and utilization of data and the determination of what data is appro-priate. However, major communication problems are still administrative or organizational rather than technological. Put in another way, technology at the present time is far in advance of administration.

A planning activity needs original data out of which to fashion plans and needs, also, feedback data on their effects. It should be concerned both with effects regarding primary goals and also with secondary effects—the effects on other goals, both those of other governmental units and those of nongovernmental units.

Specialized detector roles are required, roles involving various special-ized and technical qualifications. If the organization is able to respond to new data, these specialized detector roles become new power roles within the organization, further exaggerating the latent conflict between the general line and the cross-line occupational specialties. Resistance to this new diminu-tion of authority, and hence to communication, will be especially pronounced in the insecure atmosphere of the bureaupathic, hierarchy-emphasized or-ganization. In that atmosphere, particularly, attempts will be made to restrict communication to channels (an exercise of the superior's right to monopolize communication), to the line of command, or to the hierarchy—a channel technically inadequate for specialized communication, increasingly over-loaded, and notoriously unreliable because of opportunities and motivations for censorship at each communication station. Development planning, on the other hand, calls for increasing specialization and hence increasing interde-pendence, the toleration of which depends in part upon the adequacy of communication. Growing pressure for new, nonhierarchical, specialized com-munication channels is likely to generate further resistance to the diminution of authority, especially in the bureaupathic or insecurity-dominated organiza-tion.

To detect and transmit data is only part of the problem. The organization must also be able to respond to it in an appropriate fashion. As was pointed out above, insecurity generates a need to control which greatly restricts innovative responses (innovation or creativity is by definition uncontrolled behavior). Thus, in a bureaupathic, hierarchy-emphasized atmosphere, one of the basic ingredients of development administration—innovative responsiveness—is either absent or very weak.

Furthermore, the authority system (the system of boss-man roles), reinforced by the practice of single subgoal assignment, stresses parochialism, a narrow loyalty to one's program unit, its boss and its personnel, and to one's own program goal to the exclusion of interest in all others. The effects of action on other goals tend to be ignored; in fact, they are usually not even perceived.

All of these phenomena are especially related to an emphasis on the hierarchical institution. They are also related, it is hypothesized, to the extent to which jobs or occupations within the organization are organizationally defined rather than socially defined, or to the extent to which they are skills in operating specific procedures of specific programs of specific organizations rather than social functions relevant to a broad range of human goals and programs. Persons whose skills are purely organizational, who were trained largely on the job, who had no relevant pre-entry training, who started as amateurs, have orientations and attitudes that differ from those of the professional, scientific and technical specialist, the person who did have relevant pre-entry training. The amateurs in organizations have been referred to conveniently as the "desk classes."[25] They have less interunit (or organization) mobility than others. They owe their function and status to the organization and thus tend to become organization men. They are perhaps more responsive to organizational authority, thereby encouraging a hierarchical emphasis. They are apt to be conservative with regard to their programs and procedures, since their personal status and function are so tied up with their programs. There may even be a tendency for them to hypostatize their programs and procedures into natural laws and to forget their purely instrumental origin. All of this adds up to a greater loyalty to program goals, units, and authority—in short, to parochialism. Parochialism can make detection of and response to second-order consequences of action, second-order feedback, much less likely to happen, thereby lessening the administrative structure's ability to carry on an integrated development planning activity over a broad spectrum of social and economic life.

Real communication is two way and is a form of mutual influence. Hence, if communication occurs, some decentralization or loss of central power occurs. These facts are equally true with regard to communication with the public, as we shall see below. The interpretation of communication

[25] Walker, *op. cit.*

with the public as restricted to "selling the plan" is based on some rather universal myths, such as "the stupidity of the masses" and "the indispensability of leadership." As would be expected, therefore, it results in considerable self-delusion in that actual public behavior is likely to deviate in unpredictable ways from planned behavior, making the planning illusory. It would seem that no political, let alone administrative, system could operate for long without some devices for articulating and aggregating public needs and interests and communicating the results to government for incorporation in the planning process.[26] If this interest articulation and aggregation is done administratively, it is almost sure to be either highly erroneous or downright spurious, a fact which stands behind the inevitable, periodic, colonial riot. Thus, central control, or the illusion of it, is going to be diluted in some way, either by real communication with the public (or any other group importantly affected by planning), or by peaceful or nonpeaceful nullification—the dilution of the desirable by the possible.

PARTICIPATION IN PLANNING

It has been stated recently that the participation hypothesis (the reduction in resistance to plans through participation in planning) should be taken as empirically established. This statement may be too strong in a strict sense, but from what has been stated thus far it would appear to be good advice for the development planner to follow.

The participation in planning by those to be importantly affected by a plan (or their representatives) has two broad general functions: providing information and moving towards consensus.[27] In both cases the participation will affect the final outcome of the plans, and hence it involves decentralization or loss of power (control) by central planning authority. The information to be secured is of two kinds: that about current conditions and practices, and that about possible future reactions to various planning devices or procedures. For the latter type of information, a representative advisory group is indicated. Both kinds of information, by influencing the plan in the direction of reality, make the final predicted behavior response come closer to the actual behavior response—the real plan, the plan in action. (The paper plan can usefully be regarded as a prediction of future behavior, and the actual resulting behavior as the test of the prediction.)

Participation, or consultation, moves toward consensus both by providing information to the planners, thereby making the plan more realistic, and by providing information to those to be affected (through their representa-

[26] Gabriel Almond and James S. Coleman, eds., *The Politics of the Developing Areas* (Princeton, N.J., 1960).

[27] Victor A. Thompson, *The Regulatory Process in OPA Rationing* (New York, 1950).

tives) about problems of the planners, thereby promoting understanding. It also involves the consultees in commitment to or identification with the results, to the extent that they actually do affect the results. For this function a representative advisory group is indicated.

It should be clear that real participation of the type described, since it involves some loss of control by the administrative authorities, is more likely to take place in a secure administrative atmosphere, one relatively free from the need to control, one in which the hierarchical institution is not unduly emphasized. This kind of participation also implies an innovative responsiveness to communication and a minimum of parochialism.

An insecure, authoritarian, planning administration is more likely to engage in ritualistic consultative processes, if any, and to try to use consultative devices to increase control rather than to share it. Appearance deviates from reality in that consultation is more form than reality. Appearance is also likely to deviate from reality in another way, however, in that the actual behavioral responses are more likely to deviate from planned behavioral responses, and the "rational central planning" to be illusory to that extent.

Above I have suggested the lines along which the discipline of public administration could make some small contribution to economic development. Theorists and practitioners interested in making such a contribution must reorient themselves to the needs of adaptive, innovative administration rather than controlled administration. Although most of the doctrines and practices in the field of management are derived from the need to control, there is a growing body of knowledge and theory which is applicable to an adaptive, innovative administration. It is precisely within the contributions of the behavioral sciences that this applicable knowledge and theory will be found. It will not be found within the fields of mathematics and decision making, which have become servants of control-oriented administration.

Control-oriented administration assumes stability—fixed conditions, goals, and resources. The administrative problem appears as the maximal allocation of these fixed resources. This model is a poor analogue for development administration. If principles or lessons are to be drawn from our administrative experiences which are applicable to development administration in underdeveloped countries, they should be drawn from crisis situations. Administration in a crisis is characterized by authority, status, and jurisdictional ambiguity; indefiniteness of assignment; uncontrolled communication; group decision; problem-orientation; and a high level of excitement and morale. In crises, good ideas are likely to be regarded as the most valuable output, regardless of source, because they are needed most. Control, or public-administration-as-usual, comes later, after the crisis has passed. Our doctrines and ideals of administration come from this later period. Development administration is in the crisis period; it desperately needs ideas. Ideas do not came from control. As John Stuart Mill said more than a hundred years ago, ideas come from freedom.

SOCIAL CHANGE, MOBILIZATION, AND EXCHANGE OF SERVICES BETWEEN THE MILITARY ESTABLISHMENT AND THE CIVIL SOCIETY: THE BURMESE CASE

Moshe Lissak

I. INTRODUCTION

Coups d'etat and military regimes are a dominant feature of the political landscape in an overwhelming number of the new nations and the developing societies. The military elites are trying directly or indirectly, with differing degrees of success, to speed the process of modernization and fulfill the commitments and pledges abrogated and nullified by politicians.

The increasing number of revolutions and coups d'etat has brought forth increasing numbers of attempts to describe the background of the revolutions, the stages of the coups d'etat, and the objective and subjective obstacles confronting the military in each case. These analyses have been, by and large, confined to chronological reports of the events and depictions of the main, though very general, breaking points of the society concerned which motivated the military elite (or a part of it) to respond to the challenge and to try to succeed where others had failed. Only a few of the works have turned the focus on the interaction between the military establishments of these countries with their peculiar features (unorthodox from the point of view of the modern military traditions of both the West and the Communist bloc)

From Moshe Lissak, "Social Change, Mobilization, and Exchange of Services Between the Military Establishment and the Civil Society: The Burmese Case," *Economic Development and Cultural Change*, 13:1:1:1–19 (October 1964). Reprinted by permission of The University of Chicago Press.

and the general and specific social changes occurring in the developing societies. Yet military revolutions, especially those entailing efforts to revolutionize the entire social system, are connected and entangled with the specific character of the military establishments which are the bearers of the revolution. We need, therefore, (1) a more systematic and embracing analysis of the military as a subsystem of the society at large (before the coup as well as in the post-revolution period); and (2) a more scholarly study of the pattern of entanglement of the subsystem with other subsystems in the society. Through these, attention can be given to difficulties and obstacles which confront the interacting subsystems in the light of the more general process of social change characterizing the country or the countries concerned.

II. THE THEORETICAL FRAMEWORK

In this paper it is intended to present some relevant data about the military establishment in Burma which might offer some light on one kind of pattern of interaction between the military and the civil society. The phenomenon primarily dealt with is the military assumption of unorthodox roles and its relation to the problem of social change and social mobilization.

Clarification about the concepts of social change and social mobilization, as far as the present issue is concerned, should be given before presenting the empirical data.

Exposure to Western or modern culture has not been equal for the various institutional spheres in underdeveloped countries, both in the colonial and post-colonial periods. Furthermore, even when, *prima facie*, it seems that the exposure has taken place on a very large scale, the predisposition to change of various social groups as represented by their elites vary considerably. Hence, adaptation of alien slogans, such as "Democracy," "Socialism," or "Economic Development," in many cases does not entail adequate and even changes in the economic structure, in the political framework, or in the stratification of the society. The emergent configurations of structural and cultural features are actually the reflection of different degrees of change in the various institutional spheres resulting primarily (but by no means only) from exposure to the alien modern regime.[1] Thus the success of transformations from a traditional society which lacks consciousness of national identity to a so-called "modern society," which usually has some verbal commitment to democratic values and patterns of policy making, will depend by and large

---

[1] We by no means are suggesting here a conception of a rigid and unchangeable relation between potential social changes in the various spheres. Nor should one take for granted any proposition about equilibrium. Our intention is only to suggest that some combinations or configurations of changes, in terms of fields and range of change, would be more favorable than others to a relatively stable development toward a modern society.

(other things being equal) on the degree of what might be called the *internal balance of change among the different institutional spheres.*[2] In a very general way, it may be said that the idea of balanced or unbalanced changes refers to the often repeated phenomenon in many countries that intensive changes in one sphere are not followed by comparable changes in other spheres, or that repercussions of the changes are undermining constructive exploitations of the successful changes in other spheres. In either case, the imbalance curtails the efforts of the political elite to mobilize and manipulate various resources for the task of building a "modern" society. The mobilization which is needed includes three main fields: (1) mobilization of material resources (such as transportation, communication, and accumulation of capital); (2) mobilization of manpower (which includes, for example, regulation of internal and external migration, the process of urbanization, and birth control); and (3) mobilization of norms and values (new symbols of identity for social classes, national and international symbols, etc.).[3]

One of the greatest obstacles, if not the greatest, standing in the way of the political elites in these countries is that they lack the frameworks for manipulation and mobilization as political parties, voluntary associations, or economic systems. Such frameworks are either absent or only beginning to emerge. In other words, they have to start almost from scratch in terms of persuading the public to identify with the new goals, building the proper instruments, and taking control of the relevant resources. Actually, in many cases the only practical framework available is the military; in some cases, a political party as well. This is obviously a great challenge for the military.

The main hypothesis in this paper is that the unbalanced changes are creating *new* patterns of *exchange of services* between the military establishment and the other sectors of society as compared with these patterns prevailing in most of the democratic or Communistic societies. It therefore seems worthwhile and interesting to study the types of military establishments emerging in various new states in terms of exchange between the military and the civil society, while taking into consideration the specific configurations of institutional changes occurring in these societies.[4] The phenomenon of exchange of services could be described also in terms of input and output of roles and functions which associate various groups in the society at large. In the case of the military, input and output refers to the need for an input of

[2] S. N. Eisenstadt, "Sociological Aspects of Political Development in Underdeveloped Countries," *Economic Development and Cultural Change*, V, No. 4 (July 1957), 290–98.

[3] See Karl W. Deutsch, "Social Mobilization and Political Development," *American Political Science Review*, LV, No. 3 (September 1961), 493–514.

[4] For a full and systematic discussion of this subject, see Edward Shils, "The Military in the Political Development of the New States," in John J. Johnson, ed., *The Role of the Military in Underdeveloped Countries* (Princeton: Princeton University Press, 1962), pp. 7–68.

manpower qualified in terms of professional qualities as well as adequate socialization and indoctrination, and also upon political support by the political elite. In return, the armed forces are expected as output, to be protectors of the country from external aggression or internal trends towards secession or other disorder. When this "classic" model of exchange is distorted for any of various reasons, other types of exchange may emerge, usually involving new definitions of roles for the military or even its assumption of new roles by force.

As it was said, the Burmese Army has been chosen as an illustration for examining the validity of some aspects of our hypothesis. Due to lack of space, the historical and cultural background of recent events will be taken for granted.[5] For the same reason, only one side of the two-directional way of exchange between the military and the society will be discussed, i.e., the services offered by the military to the Burmese society.

III. THE MILITARY ESTABLISHMENT IN BURMA

A Short History and Description

The origin of the Burmese Army is the "Burma Independence Army" (BIA) raised by General Aung San in 1941–42 for a revolt against the British.[6] Before independence there were only a few battalions composed mainly of Indians and non-Burman hill tribesmen such as the Kachins, Karens, and Chins. The nucleus of the BIA consisted of thirty men known as the "Thirty Comrades." Almost all of them were students who belonged to the famous movement founded by Aung San and U Nu which later became a part of the "Tankins," an anti-British, nationalistic, leftist political group. Under the Japanese authorities, the BIA was expanded to include between 20,000 and 30,000 men, and it participated in some of the battles launched by the Japanese Imperial Army against the

---

[5] For details of these events see, for example, Hugh Tinker, *The Union of Burma* (Oxford: Oxford University Press, 1957). Frank N. Trager, *Building a Welfare State in Burma: 1948–1956* (New York: Institute of Pacific Relations, 1956); and "The Political Split in Burma," *Far Eastern Survey*, XXVII, No. 10 (October 1958), 145–55. John H. Badgley, "Burma's Political Crises," *Pacific Affairs*, XXXI, No. 4 (December 1958), 336–52; and "Burma Military Government: A Political Analysis," *Asian Survey*, II, No. 6 (August 1962), 24–31. Richard Butwell, "The New Political Outlook in Burma," *Far Eastern Survey*, XXIX, No. 2 (February 1960), 21–27; and "Civilians and Soldiers in Burma," in Robert K. Sakai, *Studies on Asia* (Lincoln: University of Nebraska Press, 1961); and "The Four Failures of U Nu's Second Premiership," *Asian Survey*, II, No. 1 (March 1962), 3–12.

[6] See Traver N. Depuy, "Burma and Its Army: A Contrast in Motivations and Characteristics," *Antioch Review*, XX, No. 4 (Winter 1960–61), 428–40; Tinker, *op. cit.*, pp. 2–33.

British Army.[7] By 1944, the relations between the Burmese government established by the Japanese and the Japanese Army had drastically deteriorated, and the resistance movement, this time against the Japanese, was born, led again by Aung San, who was the defense minister of the Burmese government.

By the end of World War II the resistance movement of Aung San was only one of many armed groups in Burma. The Burmese forces which had returned from India with the British Army were mostly remnants of the colonial Burmese battalions. These two forces were at first united. However, since many of the British Burmese forces were drawn from minority groups, especially Karens who were opposed to Burmese nationalism, many deserted from the new army and joined their fellow tribesmen who had already rebelled against the newborn state. In addition, there were two groups of Communist rebels—the Red Flags, who were Trotskyites, and the White Flags, who were Stalinists—as well as the People's Volunteer Organization (PVO), a left-wing-oriented militia organized immediately after independence, some of whose men refused to be disarmed.[8]

In 1947 the Burmese army consisted of six regular battalions, fifteen military police battalions, and some thousands of irregulars. Today, the armed forces have 75,000 to 80,000 men; the Union Military Police, 30,000; the police force, 17,000; and the Special Police Service, 44,000.[9] This means that approximately 170,000 men are engaged in some way in military and police roles (the population of Burma is about 20,000,000). The combat experience of the army, although limited in its scope, is considerable. Some of the enlisted men, many of them officers, have had long experience in guerrilla warfare against the British and the Japanese. After independence the fighting against the insurgents was a combination of guerrilla and regular warfare. The basic combat units used to be frequently the battalion or the

---

[7] Under the Japanese it was called in a later stage (when the Independent Burmese government was established) "Burma National Army" (BNA).

[8] For further details, see Tinker, *op. cit.*, pp. 34–61.

[9] The "Union Military Police" (UMP) was recruited originally during the early stages of the insurrections by the socialists and was under the direction of the Home Minister. Technically it is a police force. It is trained, however, along military lines and is expected to give support to the army. See Josef Silverston, "Burma," in George M. Kahin, ed., *Government and Politics of South East Asia* (Ithaca: Cornell University Press, 1959), p. 98.

The Special Police Service origin is in the local defense forces (Pyusawhtis) which were created as auxiliary forces to aid the military in repelling rebel attacks. The villagers selected to serve were given a one-month course in tactics and military discipline. "In practice the pyusawhtis were difficult to control and in some districts they became unmanageable vigilante groups." In 1958 they disbanded and reformed into Special Police Reserves under the Union Military Police control. See Badgley, "Burma's Political Crises," *op. cit.*, pp. 338–39, 348–49.

company. Hence, the opportunities to develop tactical and logistic deployment of larger units were quite limited.

Recruitment and Length of Service

In the colonial period the main criteria for recruitment were ascribed status (either ethnic origins and/or family background), loyalty, and education. During the early years of independence, most of the officers came from the previous resistance movement which was closely affiliated with the political movement known later as the Anti-Fascist People's Freedom League (AFPFL). In recent years, recruitment for commissioned officers has been mainly from the ranks of college graduates, and "there is an even larger body of officers who represent professional soldiers who never were political agitators."[10] On March 3, 1959, an act called the People's Militia Act was passed, prescribing compulsory military service for periods ranging from six to 24 months for every man between the ages of 18 and 46; every woman between the ages of 18 and 36; and every doctor, engineer, or teacher between the ages of 18 and 56.[11]

The Degree of Professionalization

The degree and direction of professionalization of the Burmese army was determined by the type of the enemy, its strength and tactics, and actual combat experience. It was, of course, also dependent on the kind of manpower theoretically and actually put at the disposal of the army. Unlike many other ex-colonies, the Burmese army and the Burmese political leaders decided not to use foreign officers in command posts. The British officers were deposed immediately after independence, although a British military mission remained, and Burmese officers continued to be sent to Britain for higher training after finishing the Defense Services Academy. Disposing of the British officers opened to the Burmese non-commissioned officers and officers wonderful opportunities for promotion. However, this situation seems, to some extent, to have curbed the progress of professionalization. We know, for example, that in the first years after independence a very great shortage of officers and NCO's led the military to recruit many students who were actually politically nominated.[12] In addition, many NCO's without professional background were commissioned for having distinguished themselves in combat.[13]

[10] Butwell, "Civilians and Soldiers . . . ," *op. cit.*, p. 75.

[11] *The New York Times*, March 3, 1959. This act was never fully realized.

[12] Another reason for the shortage was the desertion of many NCO's and officers who belonged to the minorities.

[13] Tinker, *op. cit.*, p. 331.

The Burmese army is now mainly composed of infantry battalions. The other services, such as army, air force, and navy, are quite small. The technical competence of the various army units is not equal, and not all the battalions are very well equipped or trained. All these factors may explain some of the obstacles involved in the process of professionalization. However, it should be mentioned that the most educated people in the country are now in the army, and future rapid progress in the quality of the officer corps can be expected.

The Social Composition of the Military

In the prewar period, until 1937, the Burmese units were a part of the colonial Indian army and adopted its pattern of social composition; that is, the regiments and companies were organized on an ethnic religious basis. Figures from the 1931 census disclose the following picture of the ethnic composition of the "public forces."[14]

Burmese	31.3%
Other indigenous groups	15.9
Chinese	.3
Indians	46.7
European	5.8
	100.0

After the war, when Aung San asked to unite his BIA forces with the Burmese forces who fought under British command, he insisted that the army should be organized on what was called the "Class Battalion Basis;" in other words, on an ethnic principle. The aim was to establish "pure" Burmese battalions in order to counterbalance the battalions composed mainly of minorities which were considered disloyal to Burmese nationalism, and to assure the "Burmazation" of the officer corps.[15] As a matter of fact, the army was rebuilt in 1949–50. However, "although the number of regiments on racial basis have greatly increased, the long-term policy of the government, it is always emphasized, is to replace the 'class' regiments by units drawing their recruits from a medley of all the peoples of the Union."[16]

The top army leadership contrasts markedly with the bulk of the officer

[14] See Surinder K. Mehata, *The Labor Force in Urban Burma and Rangoon, 1953,* unpublished Ph.D. thesis, University of Chicago, 1959. The "public force" includes, apparently, the police. Hence, the high proportion of the Burmese which actually were represented in the army units in much smaller proportion. The Indians include Indo-Burmese and Anglo-Indians, as well.

[15] A particular minority which had very great representation in the armed forces is the Anglo-Burman. The chief of the air force and some colonels are from Anglo-Burman origins.

[16] Tinker, *op. cit.,* p. 325.

corps which has been recruited in recent years. Most of the senior officers were the cream of the resistance movement and its political counterpart before 1947. For example, 20 out of 23 colonels holding key positions in the caretaker regime in 1958–60 had been engaged in politics in the pre-independence period and were nominated by the political elite to military roles. Evidence of this is to be found in the list of defense service officers who were attached to or served on a part time basis in civil departments during the caretaker period. Unfortunately, this list gives no information on the social background of the officers but denotes only whether or not the officer received the "Star of the Revolution for Independence." This award is a token of national esteem and gratitude to all who had actively participated in the final phase of the struggle for national independence either in military service or in the political sphere.

The Order consists of three distinctive degrees, according to the period in which the recipient had served the national cause: (1) from January 6, 1942, to July 26, 1942—the BIA period; (2) from July 22, 1942, to March 26, 1945—Burma as an independent state under the Japanese; and (3) March 27, 1943, to August 15, 1945—guerrilla war against the Japanese.[17]

The most important conclusion drawn from the following table is that almost all of the top officers had taken part in political and military activities within the framework of the resistance movement led by Aung San. The colonels and lieutenant colonels who did not receive the "Star of the Revolution" belonged to the air force and the navy; they were therefore in the British Army and did not remain in Burma after the Japanese occupation. Although some of the majors and captains were honored, it seems obvious

Distribution of Recipients of the Star of the Revolution among Officers Who Were Attached to Civilian Departments during the Ne Win Government

Rank[a]	Did not receive degree	Third degree	Second degree	First degree	Total
Brigadiers	–	–	1	3	4
Colonels	3	–	6	9	18
Lt. Colonels	4	2	9	2	17
Majors	19	–	2	6	27
Captains	33	–	6	3	42
Lieutenants	35	1	–	–	36
Total	94	3	24	23	144

a These figures include equivalent ranks of the air force and navy.

17 See *Is Trust Vindicated?* (Director of Information, Government of Burma, 1960), p. 561.

that many of them entered the armed forces after 1945 and apparently even after independence. As mentioned previously, recruitment in recent years has been mainly from the ranks of college graduates. These officers received a more modern and progressive education in comparison to the civilian sector.[18]

The common background shared by the *senior* officers and the senior political leaders is also reflected in the fact that intermarriage between the two elites is a frequent phenomenon. Lucien Pye, for example, reports that one of the five most important colonels is married to a sister of one of the four top political leaders, while a sister of one of these colonels is married to another of these four politicians.[19]

The Military as a Channel for Mobility

One of the factors which contributed to the consolidation of the NCO and officer corps as a distinct status group is that the military is perhaps the most available channel of social mobility. The military has a considerable advantage in comparison to other public institutions in attracting the most qualified personnel in the country. Some of the reasons for this are listed below.

(1) The prestige of the military profession. Although there is no direct evidence on this issue, the general impression one gets is that the attitude of the Burmese people toward the military profession has changed from a negative to a much more positive one. It could be assumed that the role played by the army on the battlefield strengthened the status of the soldier in Burmese society after independence.[20]

(2) Instrumental rewards. The officers are receiving a considerable salary in comparison to other groups which are dependent upon the government and which are more or less equivalent in status. For example, note the comparisons of monthly earnings given below.[21] Furthermore, the housing provided for the NCO's and officers is the most comfortable in the country except for that of the cabinet ministers.

(3) The opportunities available to study and acquire, at the expense of the army, a profession (such as medicine, engineering, or accounting) which

[18] See Maung Maung, *Burma's Constitution* (The Hague, 1959), p. 146.

[19] Lucian W. Pye, "The Army in Burma Politics," in Johnson, *op. cit.*, p. 234. About the common background, see also Badgley, "Burma's Political Crises," *op. cit.*, pp. 344–50; Maung Maung, *op. cit.*, p. 144.

[20] It is interesting to note that the civilian government had tried all the time to fight against the flourishing of militarism and the military cult. One symbol of this attitude is that, in the Burmese army, there is no inflation of military ranks. Ne Win is only a lieutenant general; commanders of divisions are only brigadiers, etc.; whereas in Thailand there are 72 full generals. See Tinker, *op. cit.*, p. 328.

[21] *Ibid.*, pp. 154, 327. These were the rates in force in 1949. The average annual per capita income in Burma is K 250–300 ($50).

Rank	Monthly earnings
2nd lieutenant	K 395 ($80)
Assistant engineer	K 350 ($70)
Captain	K 631 to K 806 ($125 to $160)
Lt. colonel	K 1,231 to K 1,338 ($245 to $270)
Superintendent engineer	K 1,300 ($265)
Brigadier	K 1,550 ($310)
Cabinet secretary or divisional commissioner	K 1,500 to K 1,600 ($300 to $320)
Major general	K 1,975 ($395)
Chief secretary (head of civil service)	K 1,800 ($360)

is highly valued in civilian society and to which, in most cases, one can transfer. This is one of the greatest attractions of the military for young officers.

(4) Many of the economic enterprises developed and controlled by the army (to be discussed later) are apparently viewed by the military as means for securing their own futures. Retirement in the military services comes early, and "the army is the promise of a vast reservoir of future well-paid jobs for military personnel, their relatives, and their friends."[22]

(5) Political power is another attractive reward for mobility aspirants. Recent developments (the coup d'etat of March 1962) presumably will mean an extended military regime. For the senior officers, this balance of rewards means renewals of the "golden age" before and immediately after independence. Colonel Maung Maung, the number three man in Ne Win's first administration, put it in this way: "After the Second World War was over and we had obtained our independence, the cream of the resistance movement stayed with the Burma army, and most of the rest became politicians. It was irksome to find that those who could not hold their own in the army came, in time, to be our political superiors."[23]

The Military Establishment and the Civil Society: The Role Expansion of the Military

As far as many observers and obviously the military elite are concerned, the political elite didn't succeed in solving the basic problems of the Burmese society, in the economic, cultural, ideological, and political fields. Repercussions of these failures were felt in many corners of

[22] See Louis J. Walinsky, *Economic Development in Burma, 1951–60* (New York: Twentieth Century Fund, 1962), p. 261.

[23] Quoted by Butwell, "Civilians and Soldiers . . . ," *op. cit.*, p. 74.

the Burmese society, including the military. The paramount economic crisis (in 1959–60, the output per capita was 20 percent lower than that of 1939),[24] the tremendous shortage of professional manpower, the problems of national unity, the question of the basic cultural and ideological identity of the Burmese citizen (including such problems as the place of Buddhism in the Burmese society and the synthesis between Buddhism and socialism), troubled the politically conscious military elite not less than the battle against the insurgents. Moreover, a stalemate in the economic and political-ideological level prevented, in a sense, the final victory on the battlefield. It is in this context that the propensity of the officer corps to expand and enlarge the "classic roles" of the armed forces becomes a relevant issue for discussion. In other words, one may ask: has the failure of the political elite in the mobilization of its resources and "supply" of the adequate "services" to its operational organs led to the molding of a particular and unorthodox pattern of relations between the military and the civil society? This issue will be dealt with on two levels: (1) the ideological level; and (2) the application of the ideology concerned.

"The National Ideology and the Role of the Defense Services"

The above heading is taken from a section of a book issued by the *first* Ne Win government.[25] The aim of that section was to present the phases of *ideological development in the Defense Services.* It is worthwhile to consider its content in some detail. In a document issued by the Defense Services Conference at Meiktila on October 21, 1958,[26] it was stated: "Man's endeavor to build a society set free at last from anxieties over food, clothing, shelter, and able to enjoy life's spiritual satisfactions . . . must proceed from the premise of a faith only in a politico-economic system based on the eternal principles of justice, liberty, and equality. This is our belief."[27] This statement is actually the essence of the national ideology as stated in the Declaration of Independence and the Constitution of the Union of Burma.[28] But, "for the Defense Services simply to accept the National Ideology without giving thought to their role, or defining their attitude," the statement continues, "is to develop a strategy without devising the tactics." It also declares, "There is no obscure political meaning in the world 'role' and 'attitude.' What will the Defense Services do in the event of national crisis? What

---

[24] See further details in Everett E. Hagen, *On the Theory of Social Change* (Homewood: Darsey Press, 1962), p. 451.

[25] *Is Trust Vindicated?, op. cit.*

[26] Following the first take-over by General Ne Win.

[27] *Is Trust Vindicated?, op. cit.*, p. 534.

[28] See, for example, John S. Furnival, *The Government of Burma* (New York: Institute of Pacific Relations, 1960), pp. 28–29.

help will they render? What actions will they take? What attitude will they adopt? The answer to these questions will be determined by the role and attitude." The document goes on to declare that, "In view of the problems facing the nation, our national objectives should be: to restore peace and the rule of law—first; to implant democracy—second; to establish a socialist economy—third." And finally, "These three sections of the above program are interdependent. To establish a socialist economy, democracy is a prerequisite. For democracy to flourish, law and order is essential. Without peace and the rule of law, no country can be a democratic one. In an undemocratic country, a socialist economy can never be established—a totalitarian government will impose only a rigid economic system which will deny the right of private property."

There is a special interest in this applied definition of socialism as it is given in the National Ideology of the Defense Services. In addition to the general and classic definition—"to build up a society in which there will be no exploitation of man by man" or "a planned economy"—the statement refers to the ultimate problems of the Burmese economy. "The Union's economy is based on agriculture, but the methods of production are outmoded, and consequently our productive capacity is limited. Small industry is not sufficiently developed to provide adequate consumer goods for all citizens. Therefore, the main feature of the national economic policy should be to modernize the basic agricultural economy, and secondly, to develop local industries commensurate with the natural and human resources of the country. This will require deliberate and thoughtful planning. In the process of development this state-controlled economy may appear to differ from state capitalism. But it should be noted, at the same time, that the state will continue to encourage those private enterprises which contribute to increased national productivity."[29]

Ignoring for one moment the specific details of the above proclamation, we call attention to two important items that should be noted and remembered: first, that the military *as such* (before the coup) feels it necessary to formulate its own ideology which, although based on the National Ideology, is labeled the Ideology of the Defense Services; and secondly, that this ideology is all-embracing in character; it is an ideological setup which encompasses many areas of private and public activities of the nation.[30] This

[29] *Is Trust Vindicated?*, *op. cit.*, p. 540.

[30] It is interesting to note that the army issued a journal called *The Open Mind*, which "aims to disseminate modern thought in various subjects, and to stimulate discussions and diversified interest among the government servants and others of leadership standing." Quoted in Daniel Wolfstone, "The Burmese Army Experiment," *Far Eastern Economic Review* (February 12, 1960), 356. The journal consists of diversified international writings. Among the articles republished are Rostow's "Non-Communist Manifesto" and articles by such writers as Aldous Huxley, Viscount Montgomery, and Albert Einstein. The Army Director of Education and Psychological Warfare issued also a reading list recommended as essential reading for army officers. The list includes Marx, Engels,

phenomenon may, of course, have direct significance for the attitude of the military before and after the coup towards the basic problems of social and economic mobilization and its aims and instruments of action. Before turning to the problems of means and instruments of application of the ideology, however, one should ask whether this ideology, with its direct or indirect implications, is really a monopoly of the military. Or, to put it in another way, in what aspects does it resemble the ideologies of the previous ruling party and its opposition, and to what extent does it deviate from these? As this report is confined strictly to the description of the military establishment, no systematic comparison between the military ideology and the various civilian ideologies will be attempted. Instead, some typical examples will be cited which depict the main characteristics of a potential confrontation of the military and civilian ideologies. Most observers had no doubt even before the last coup as to the existence of serious cleavage between the military and important sections of the political community, and no doubt either about the impact of these cleavages on political developments in Burma. Butwell, for example, contended that "in the recent years the army seems to have been moving in different directions intellectually. Socialism continues to move the civilian politicians (as well as the army leadership), but the pragmatic army leaders have already given evidence that they understand better what socialism is and is not than most of the sloganizing politicians."[31] Very instructive in this context is a propaganda war which was held between the army and U Nu during the caretaker government. The army bought advertising space in all the leading newspapers and published a series of slogans. The main themes were:

> The Burmese Army resents fascism and imperialism. It has been in the forefront in the fight against the insurgents. It is giving the country correct leadership.
> The Burmese Army is not garrulous, it only works hard. The Army works for the country even at the risk of incurring unpopularity. The Army is not flattered by praise; neither is it afraid of intimidations.
> The Burmese Army is always willing to lay down its life for the country and the people. The Army does not accept obeisance—it will only give up its life.[32]

Behind these very general slogans lies the fact that the focuses of cleavage between the military and political sectors are quite numerous and include many intellectual and practical fields, including:

Lenin, Stalin, Bertrand Russell, Djilas, Grossman, Koestler, Cole, Howard Fast, Strachey, and Narayan.

[31] Butwell, "Civilians and Soldiers . . . ," *op. cit.*, p. 83. For one of the most recent declarations expressing the ideological orientation of the military, see a summary in the *Asian Recorder*, June 4–10, 1962.

[32] *The New York Times*, February 2, 1959.

(1) *The attitude towards tradition and religion.* In contrast to the well-known strongly religious orientation of U Nu, the military elite can almost be described as vigorously anti-traditional, although not to the same extent anti-religious. Ne Win did not hesitate to suspend, after the coup of 1962, the decree making Buddhism the state religion, despite the fact that this act was considered by U Nu as the most important development of the last decade in Burma; he also dissolved the Executive and General Council of the Buddha Sasana Council.[33] The second military government abolished as well the observance of the Buddhist Sabbath enacted by the previous government, which entailed the closing of all government offices on a different day each week, causing considerable confusion in the business community.[34] The military regime abolished also the ban on cattle slaughter, which is anathema for the Buddhist.

In spite of these extreme acts, the military elite can by no means be defined, or its acts interpreted, as reflecting a militant anti-religious attitude. It seems that the attitude of the military can be more properly characterized as being in favor of an institutional separation between state and church and in simultaneously encouraging a national culture based on a synthesis of the basic tenets of Buddhism and socialism.[35]

(2) *The concept of government.* Perhaps there is no other sphere in Burmese life with which the military leaders were more dissatisfied than the process and patterns of decision-making at every level of government. They felt that inefficiency, corruption, and political considerations—instead of rational and professional criteria—characterized the operations of the government, often with serious consequences for the nation. These charges were among the main issues in the military's opposition to the U Nu government. One might argue that these charges are not really ideological in character, but rather refer mainly to administrative practices which are the means of achieving ideological ends. Although this is essentially true, there is evidence that this extremely critical attitude is rooted in a basic disagreement about concepts and images of the ideal government. Lucien Pye, when referring to this problem, says, "The extraordinary fact was that the Burmese army in seeking to realize its ideal of government was in essence seeking to force

[33] *Asian Recorder*, June 25–July 1, 1962.

[34] One of most serious efforts made so far in Burma to synthesize Buddhism and Marxism was by the psychological warfare department of the Burmese army, which has published a booklet dealing with this issue.

The government announced as well in April 1962 the reconstitution of the Union Culture Council, with the aim "to strengthen traditional national culture and patriotism which are considered to be vital for the country's march towards the goal of socialism." See the *Asian Recorder*, May 14–20, 1962.

[35] Butwell, "The Four Failures . . . ," *op. cit.*, p. 4. See also *The New York Times*, March 15, 1962, and March 18, 1962.

upon Burmese society once again the basic structure and pattern of power of colonial Burmese government. Indeed, the ideals and the goals of the army seemed to be quite explicitly those of the old British Burma.[36] The government knows what's good for the country, and the masses should be educated and directed into agreement." For example, the army constantly tried to preserve and strengthen the authority of the central government apparatus against the local political leaders who used to interfere in the activities of government officials. The army favored a return to the power system of having village headmen and deputy commissioners, and in the process, it increasingly clashed with the AFPFL representatives.

(3) *Economic planning.* We have seen that the official ideological declaration of the defense services refers very seriously to the problems of economic planning and to specific priorities in capital investment. Some clear indications of basic differences between the attitudes of the military leaders in this field and the political leaders can be seen in the following statement made by Brigadier Aung Gyi after the coup d'etat in March 1962. "The economic program to be formulated gradually by the new regime will be cautious and more practical. We do not want to indulge in big dreams."[37] In more concrete terms, this means a return to the policies of the caretaker government, which placed greater emphasis on increasing agricultural production and less on industrial development.[38]

So far we have mentioned three crucial areas of disagreement of the armed forces with the daily policy of the civilian government, if not with its basic ideology. But the basic antagonisms are by no means confined to these areas alone. As a matter of fact, there is another area where the policy of the government was opposed, and ostensibly, at least, it provided the ultimate stimulus for the recent coup d'etat: the relationship between the constituent states and the central government. The last coup d'etat was justified by the contention that U Nu was inclined to give greater concessions to the constituent states, especially to the Shan state. In this respect, there is no doubt that "more than other groups in Burma, the army has subscribed to the Union idea and has forsaken particularism for loyalty to the country at large."[39]

It is unquestionably true that members of the armed forces, sharing as they do common interests and values, and perhaps more important, sharing a background of battlefield experience which develops a strong sense of com-

[36] Pye, *op. cit.*, p. 246.

[37] *The New York Times*, March 8, 1962.

[38] Butwell, "Civilians and Soldiers . . . ," *op. cit.*, p. 77. As to the policy of the second Ne Win government, see also *The New York Times*, March 18, 1962, and Butwell, "The Four Failures . . . ," *op. cit.*, pp. 3–4.

[39] Tinker, *op. cit.*, p. 329.

radeship and, frequently, enduring friendship, have a solid basis for developing into a status group with distinct status symbols, common frame of reference, and similar styles of life. Tinker put it this way: "To a striking extent the officer corps had developed a homogeneous professional character which is quite remarkable in view of the heterogeneous origin from which they have emerged. The officer's corps had come to regard itself as a 'band of Brothers.' "[40]

The Application of the National Ideology of Defense Services

The coup d'etat of March 1962 could be considered as proof that the military leaders believed it their duty to implement their ideology. However, it seems that even if the civilian authorities had been relatively more successful and efficient in performing their roles in greater accordance with the army's position, the army, in spite of its internal conflicts, would not have changed its insistence on assuming new roles and thus preparing the framework for realizing its ideology. What was the character of this framework?

In establishing the ideological basis the army directed its main efforts (not with equal endeavour and success) to three spheres of public activities: (1) economic enterprise; (2) political manipulation of support; and (3) educational and training functions.

The Military Economic Entrepreneur

The Burmese army, through the Defense Services Institute, has become the largest and most powerful business organization in Burma. The Institute was founded nine years ago to provide commissary services for the members of the armed forces and their families. During the first military regime, it began to flourish and to undertake large-scale enterprises. Its subsidiary concerns became the largest business organ-

[40] *Ibid.* This solidarity is by no means unshakable. The danger of internal ideological conflicts seemed to be, at least in part, a very real one. After the turnover of power to U Nu in April 1960, the army was divided into three groups. The first group, composed mostly of young officers, looked with reluctance to the withdrawal of the army to the barracks and considered it a mistake. The second group held the opposite position and argued that the army should not interfere in any way with politics. The third group saw "the army performing limited but still roles in national development." See Pye, *op. cit.*, pp. 249–50; Butwell, "Civilians and Soldiers . . . ," *op. cit.*, pp. 36–37; *The New York Times*, October 7, 1958. The resignation of some high-ranking officers in February 1961 is explained by Tinker and others to be the result of this internal conflict. See also *The New York Times*, February 19, 1961. After the coup of March 1962, there is no doubt that the first group has defeated the others or convinced them that their way should be adopted. However, the recent resignation of Brigadier Aung Gyi means a new split in the military elite.

izations in the vital fields of banking, shipping, construction, and fishing. Its other holdings included Rangoon's largest department store and the largest automobile service station, a bookstore, a bus line, a radio assembly plant, a motor workshop, and a factory turnout of shoes and boots for the army. It is also the nation's largest importer, controlling the trade in coal and coke, and holding the agencies for various automobile manufacturers. In addition, the DSI has entered into the tourist and hotel business.[41] Of course, these enterprises have enjoyed the advantages of such governmental favors as the refund of all duties like customs duty, port fees, and sales tax. The government also provided credit facilities and contracts for government business.

The legal status of the DSI was simply that of a public corporation. The institute as a non-profit organization received sizeable tax exemptions that its competitors did not enjoy.[42] Under the original memorandum of the associations of the company, all profits are to be used for the welfare of the members of the armed forces.[43] The main capital came from a government loan of K 600,000.[44] Between 1952 and 1958 the DSI department store alone was able to contribute over K 200,000 ($40,000) to the army welfare fund, and in 1959 it turned over to the command and brigade branches over K 7,200,-000 ($140,000).[45]

The pervasiveness of army activities and the speed of their development was justified by the army as its acceptance of the challenge to enter the battle on behalf of non-profit economic organizations. In this way, the army claimed, it contributed to the welfare of the people and to the economic progress of the country by creating more efficient competition in the private sector of the economy, which had been demoralized by the famous import license policy. After the 1960 elections and the reassuming of power by U Nu, the legal status of the DSI was changed, but not its subordinance to the military. Most of the DSI enterprises were taken over by the Burma Eco-

[41] The full list of the DSI lines of business was the following: (1) general stores —tinned provisions, foodstuffs, textiles, medicines, electrical goods, etc. (for defense services personnel only); (2) meat, fish, and poultry projects (for the public); (3) International Trade and Industries Division—general imports and exports; (4) Ava House—sale of books and stationery (to the public); (5) Five Star Line—shipping; (6) Ava Bank—banking; (7) Burma National Housing and Construction; (8) Burma International Inspection Co.—inspection of imports and exports; (9) City Transport—transportation services; (10) Rowe and Co.—department store (for the public); (11) Burma Hotels, Ltd.—hotels and tourist services; (12) Rangoon Electronic Works; (13) The United Coal and Coke Supplies (for government board and corporation); and (14) General Trading Co. See *Is Trust Vindicated?*, *op. cit.*, p. 229.

[42] *The New York Times*, September 25, 1960.

[43] *Is Trust Vindicated?*, *op. cit.*, pp. 224–25.

[44] Approximately $120,000. The regular military budget in 1957–58 was K 280,744,000 ($56,148,000); the national budget for this year, K 980,733,000 ($196,026,000).

[45] *Is Trust Vindicated?*, *op. cit.*, p. 230.

nomic Development Corporation. One-tenth of the profits from the BEDC went to armed services welfare (at least until the 1962 coup). Another tenth went to other government welfare organizations, and the remainder was invested back into the business. The corporation had seven members, with the general manager of the Union Bank and the ministerial secretaries included ex officio. The two other members and the chairman, however, were military men. The administration of the act establishing the BEDC was (until the recent coup) under the charge of the prime minister acting in cooperation with the chief of staff.[46]

The Military as Political Manipulator of Support

Along with the vast energy it devoted to building the "economic empire," the military elite by no means overlooked the importance of accumulation of popular support outside the traditional channels of the political parties. During the first Ne Win government, a countrywide movement called the National Solidarity Association was established. Its official purpose was to "inculcate the values of law and order, thus serving as a check against possible future excesses on the part of the politicians."[47] One of the undeclared aims of the NSA movement was, however, to encourage independent candidates to run for parliament and to generate popular support for them. The army leaders apparently hoped that such a body of independent professional men, of the sort who served the caretaker regime in various capacities, could be used to influence the results of the legislative process.[48] The NSA movement was not dissolved after the turnover of the government to U Nu in April 1960. It remained in the army's hands. Brigadier Aung Gyi, who was till recently the second man in the military regime, remained the central council's vice president, and Colonel Maung Maung its general secretary.[49] Brigadier Aung Gyi told a meeting in May 1960 "that the movement represents the foundation of democracy and that the NSA should help district administrative officers in the discharge of their duties."[50] The original intention of the army was that the NSA should be a mass movement, but after the return of U Nu it was apparently regarded by the army as "an elitist rather than a mass, an educational rather than an action organization."[51]

[46] Wolfstone, op. cit., pp. 296–99.
[47] Butwell, "Civilians and Soldiers . . . ," op. cit., p. 80.
[48] Ibid.
[49] See Butwell, "The New Political Outlook . . . ," op. cit., p. 24, n. 15, for a more detailed description of the composition of the Central Executive Council of the NSA.
[50] Butwell, "Civilians and Soldiers . . . ," op. cit., p. 85, n. 13.
[51] Tinker, op. cit. In 1961 U Nu ordered the central executive committee to disband on the grounds that the need for NSA was over. It is worthwhile to mention that the NSA was not the single instrument for indoctrination. In charge of the project of cleaning

The efforts to establish a broader political basis were renewed after the coup of March 1962. The Revolutionary Council formally committed itself on July 4, 1962, to the formation of a single political party. It is, however, interesting to note that the intention is to build this proposed political party gradually, rather than to base it on mass participation. In establishing the proposed party, the Revolutionary Council desires quality above quantity.[52] It seems that the revival of the Security Councils, which were abolished by U Nu and substituted by the Law and Order Committees, is also connected to the efforts of the military elite to establish a broader political basis which will be at the same time a more efficient and rational instrument of mobilization of resources of the Burmese society.

Educational and Training Activities

Up to the coup of March 1962, the activities towards the educational and ideological training of the Burmese army were limited in comparison with its roles in the economy and even with their indirect influence in political life. The army was mainly concerned with agricultural training and established for this purpose an agricultural vocational training school. The aim of this training center is to instruct soldiers in agriculture, animal husbandry, tractor driving, and maintenance.[53]

Another important service to the public in the educational field was given by the army through its training of civil service personnel. The director of the military training under Ne Win's first government was in charge of a special school for public administration. These two educational functions indicate the range of the non-military educational and training services which were given by the military to the wider Burmese society. Ideological indoctrination was apparently limited to the military itself and perhaps within the NSA movement, as well.

One of the most prominent results of these diversified activities was a considerable increase of the infiltration of officers into civilian posts. This fact was due less to a deliberate policy of planting officers and ex-officers in key positions within the civilian sector than to the expansion of the military roles previously described. The great opportunity for this was, of course, during the caretaker government. In this period, 74 officers were shifted to civilian posts. Even without knowing the exact number of officers in each

---

up the administration from corruption and strengthening its morale was the Burmese army psychological warfare department.

[52] See *Asian Recorder*, August 6–12, 1962; *The New York Times*, July 5, 1962; Badgley, "Burma Military Government . . . ," *op. cit.*, p. 9–11.

[53] The Burmese army pays special attention to resettlement of veterans on land when they go on pension. This project entails establishment of cooperative settlements with the cooperation of Israeli experts.

rank, it can be assumed that a very considerable number of these came from the senior ranks. It is known that some of the senior officers remained in civilian posts at the request of U Nu,[54] in addition to those officers who remained in civilian posts at their own request and subsequently resigned from military service. Quite a different source of ex-officers in civilian life were the purges. In the first year of independence, these purges were connected with the activities against the insurgents.[55] Unrest in the army after the resignation of Ne Win in 1960 was reflected in the fact that 12 high-ranking officers —two generals and ten colonels—had resigned from the service to take up careers as diplomats, businessmen, and politicians. Though no one dared to say so officially, it became clear that the announcement of Ne Win's decision to return his office to U Nu ended the struggle for power within the army.[56] Finally, it should be mentioned that, because of long-standing security problems, the army had also assumed many administrative functions, especially in border regions. Thus, in 1953–54, the army was in charge of vast administrative and social reforms in the Shan state.[57] Its main organs of administration were the security councils composed of army, police, and civil representatives established at the division, district, township, and village levels.[58]

IV. CONCLUSIONS

It was not our intention in this paper to deal with the historical and sociological background of the rule of the military in Burma. As well, no evaluation was made with regard to the degree of success or efficiency of the two military governments of General Ne Win.[59] Our aim was essentially to draw attention to the emergence of a relatively new type of military elite in underdeveloped countries, i.e., an entrepreneurial or production-oriented military elite.

There is no doubt that the role expansion described here of the military in Burma is, in a sense, a unique phenomenon.[60] Nevertheless, and perhaps

[54] *The New York Times*, May 1, 1960.

[55] Even as late as 1957 it was announced that Brigadier Kyaw Zaw, North Burma area commander, had been reduced in rank and retired because of inclinations toward the Communist Party. See the *Times* (London), May 9, 1957. This brigadier was one of the "Thirty Comrades" who went to Japan in 1940 with Aung San for underground training.

[56] *The New York Times*, February 19, 1961.

[57] See Josef Silverstein, "The Federal Dilemma in Burma," *Far Eastern Survey*, XVIII, No. 7 (July 1959), 100.

[58] Badgley, "Burma Military Government . . . ," *op. cit.*, p. 26.

[59] There is no consensus about the actual success of the military in the economic field. The general view is that the success can be scored in those fields in which the main trouble was a matter of corruption and discipline. As far as more basic economic problems are concerned, no exact evaluations can be made as yet.

[60] Thailand, and to some extent Pakistan and Israel, have some similar characteristics.

because of it, the Burmese case might be very challenging for the theoretical bases of the sociology of social change and political modernization in general and the sociology of revolutions and coups d'etat in particular. Successful and unsuccessful coups are occurring today in countries with very different social backgrounds. Moreover, they are carried out by very different types of armies, such as "ex-colonial armies" (Pakistan, Sudan), armies established during national liberation (Burma), "post-liberation armies" (Syria), and by armies in countries that were "traditionally independent" (Yemen, Ethiopia).[61]

In almost all of the new nations with developed armies, the assumption of unorthodox roles by the army, even *before* a coup, is an actual and relevant question for the military elites of these nations. Indeed, only a comparative study based on and oriented towards a broad theoretical framework is necessary in order to provide us with the relevant data concerning the problems involved in these cases; it will further help us to locate and depict the common patterns of these developments.

In this paper, an attempt has been made to spread some light on one of the ways to handle the sociological problem at stake, through a discussion which analyzes the growth of the political, economic, and ideological influence of the military in terms of the interaction and specific kind of exchange of services between a civilian society and its military establishment. The analysis has been of a one-way flowing of services, namely, from the military to the polity. These considerations, however, were made by referring to the economic, political, and psychological predicament[62] confronting the Burmese as they tried to mobilize manpower, material resources, and cultural assets for the modernization of their country. This troublesome task, details of which were not disclosed here, was involved with a specific pattern of uneven institutional changes. The weakness of this uneven institutional change lies in the gap between the ideology (which in a successful application might require revolutionary changes in the process of mobilization and the organization of rewards allocation) and the type of political organization, the character of national solidarity, and the psychological predisposition to change.

The military elite, considering itself from the beginning an "agent of mobilization," was particularly sensitive to this gap. Being unable to receive the appropriate services from the society at large—mainly by failure of the political elite to provide and establish a workable framework for mobilization —the military elite launched into productive entrepreneurial activities of its own, ending with the full take-over of political power.

We hope that the data given here might provide a basis for further com-

---

[61] For this typology, see Morris Janowitz, *The Military in the Political Development of New Nations*, prepared for the Fifth World Congress of Sociology, Washington, D.C., September 2–8, 1962.

[62] See Lucian W. Pye, *Politics, Personality, and Nation Building: Burma's Search for Identity* (New Haven: Yale University Press, 1962).

parative examination of the exchange of services between the military establishment and civilian society in the developing countries. Such an examination might yield considerable information about the problem which Janowitz called the process of "civilianization" of the military establishment and the accompanying "militarization" of eqivalent sectors of civilian society.[63] The data presented so far might also be used as basic evidence for a comparative analysis of the specific channels of power accumulation by the military elite before, during, and after their assumption of political power.

[63] Morris Janowitz, "Military Elites and the Study of War," *Conflict Resolution,* VII (March 1957), 13 (in the Bobbs-Merrill Reprint Series No. 134).

AGRICULTURAL IMPROVEMENT IN JAPAN: 1870-1900

Ronald P. Dore

Not the least remarkable feature of Japan's economic development in the nineteenth century is the way in which the growth of industry was matched by an increase in the productive capacity of agriculture. If industrial investment was largely financed out of the surplus produced by agriculture, this was not, at least, a process of mere spoliation. Agriculture was not entirely starved of capital, nor did the policy emphasis on industrial development mean that the task of increasing the productivity of agriculture was neglected. The purpose of this paper is to examine some of the mechanisms by which this improvement was achieved; the way in which new methods, tools and crop strains were evolved and diffused; the agents of, and the motives for, research and experiment; the channels of communication and the incentives for application. Following the general theme of these papers one concern will be to assess how far the improvement was self-generated within agriculture, and how far the stimulus came from the urban centers of commerce, industry and governmental authority.

From Ronald P. Dore, "Agricultural Improvement in Japan, 1870–1900," *Economic Development and Cultural Change*, 9:1:2:69–91 (October 1960). Reprinted by permission of The University of Chicago.

NOTES: In the footnotes to this article the major sources have been abbreviated as follows:

MZKJS: Nōrinshō, Nōmukyoku (*Meiji Zenki*) *Kannō Jiseki Shūroku*, 1939, 2 vols.
NT: Nōrinshō, *Nōmu Temmatsu*, 6 vols. 1952–57.
NNHS: Nogyo Hattatsu Shi Chosa Kai, *Nihon Nōgyō Hattatsu Shi*, 10 vols. 1953–58.

CONTINUITIES

The phrase "the greatest innovation is the idea of innovation itself" is a striking and in many ways a true one. It points up the contrast between a tradition-bound society in which antiquity is the greatest guarantor of both techniques and values, and, on the other hand, a society receptive to change, confident of the possibility of self-betterment, and instinctively tending to identify novelty with progress. Japan, with its sudden flowering of *bummei-kaika* enthusiasm after the Meiji Restoration, seems a typical case of sudden transition from the one to the other. In the realm of techniques, however, the picture of pre-Restoration Japan as a tradition-bound society requires qualification. As T. C. Smith has recently shown,[1] there was considerable innovation in agriculture—slow cumulative changes, evolved and actively preached by men who deliberately recorded and experimented in the conscious hope of making useful innovations. It was, moreover, a literate and articulate concern. Of the large number of works on agriculture written, and often printed, in the late Tokugawa period many, of course, were simply distillations of traditional lore copied from earlier works, many were simply exhortations to frugality and diligence; a large proportion were hints on edible fungi and herbs for use in famines. But a number were concerned with ways and means of improving production, by switching to new varieties and new crops, by adopting tools and fertilizers and methods discovered in other parts of the country, by introducing new subsidiary employments, and sometimes by applying the lessons of the writer's own experience and conscious experimentation.

This, then, is something to be borne in mind when considering developments after 1870. There was already a tradition of gradual improvement. There was a class of literate farmers, and some samurai, who were intelligently aware of the desirability and the possibility of change. The Meiji Restoration greatly intensified and diffused that awareness by opening up new sources of technical knowledge and by making the innovator one of the heroes of the new society. But some continuity there was nevertheless. One of the best illustrations, perhaps, is the publication in 1880, with a preface by the Minister of the Interior, of a proposal for land reclamation in Chiba written by Sato Shin'en in 1833.[2]

There was continuity in another sense. Tokugawa improvements in agricultural productivity had been actively promoted by the fief governments. Land reclamation schemes, in particular, had almost always been at the initiative of the fief. It was therefore natural that the new central government of the Meiji period should take a positive role in agricultural improvement.

[1] *The Agrarian Origins of Modern Japan* (Stanford, 1959).
[2] *Naiyō Kei-iki*, see *Nihon Sangyō Shiryō Taikei*, Vol. 1, 1926, p. 1010.

THE CENTRAL GOVERNMENT

It is with the role of the central government that our enquiry can best begin. Almost as soon as the Meiji Government was established, a section concerned with agriculture was created in the Ministry of the Interior. This, after several changes in location and organization, variously amalgamating with and separating from the section concerned with commerce and industry, eventually emerged, in 1881, as the agricultural half of the new Ministry of Agriculture and Commerce.[3] The main emphasis of the activities of this department varied with changing circumstances. In the first decade one predominant concern was, of course, fiscal. It is no accident that for a short period in 1872 and 1873 the Department was a sub-section of the Taxation Bureau of the Ministry of Finance.[4] Later, with the firm establishment of the land tax system and its reduction to a matter of routine, this preoccupation disappeared.

A second major concern in the first decade was land reclamation. The title of the Department when first established in February 1869 was the "Reclamation Bureau." Land reclamation in this period had, of course, a dual purpose—to find some work for the now displaced samurai, and to "increase the wealth of the country." Of these two aims the former was the most pressing. It was the starting point of Okubo's arguments when, as Minister of the Interior shortly before his death, he proposed to the Dajokan a grandiose scheme which would settle some 13,000 samurai families on new land at the cost of six million yen.[5] The *shizoku-jusan* scheme did do much on these lines, though not, with a total expenditure for all, including industrial, enterprises of only three million yen,[6] quite on the scale Okubo envisaged.

A third concern was with the promotion of exports and the reduction of imports by the substitution of home-grown products. The table of contents of the first half dozen farmers' bulletins published in 1874–6 show this early concern with foreign trade in the frequency of articles on silk production, on the reception of Japanese tea in foreign markets, and reports on successes in home-growing foreign cotton.[7]

Fourthly, the major continuing concern was with the general improvement of production wherever and however this could be done—with making two blades of grass grow where only one grew before. "Agriculture is the base of the country; if agriculture flourishes then the country prospers; if agriculture declines then the country is on the road to ruin." So spoke Shinagawa as head of the Agricultural Promotion Bureau at the first agri-

[3] A good summary of these administrative shifts is to be found in MZKJS. Vol. 1, pp. 5–10.

[4] *Ibid.*, p. 6.

[5] *Ibid.*, pp. 24–5.

[6] *Kyōto* Daigaku Kokushi Kenkyushitsu: *Nihonshi Jiten*, 1955.

[7] *Ibid.*, p. 204.

cultural congress in 1881,[8] and we may note in passing an important implication of his words. In thus enunciating one of the tenets of modern developmental economics, Shinagawa was, in fact, merely reiterating the views of orthodox Confucian conservatives of the Tokugawa period. For the Confucianist it was a fine and noble thing to sweat in the muddy bosom of nature (if not quite as fine and noble as fighting) whereas industry and commerce were ignoble occupations. One cannot overlook the importance of this tradition in ensuring that the Meiji government did not make the mistake of throwing agriculture overboard in a passionate pursuit of industrial modernity. (Later, of course, the tradition turned sour and in a defensively virulent form played a large part in the reactionary Japanism of the thirties.)

The Department pursued its goals by a variety of methods. The first decade was largely devoted to the assimilation of the new possibilities opened up by contact with the West, particularly after the emissaries returned from the Vienna Exposition of 1873 laden with plants and seeds and farm tools. The Shinjuku experimental station, established in 1872, was largely devoted to testing them. In 1876, for instance, it was growing 313 strains of foreign wheats and only 247 Japanese (though only Japanese rice). There were 398 foreign trees and grasses compared with 76 indigenous varieties.[9] By this time, too, the experimental station had got permission to use the remainder of its foreign tool purchasing budget to start its own factory and make farm tools on foreign models.[10] Already they had moved from the stage of adoption to the stage of domestication. (This factory remained a government enterprise longer than most and was not sold off until 1888.[11])

All this time Japanese officials and students were being sent abroad to study foreign agriculture, and foreigners were being hired as advisers in Japan. A total of 22 foreigners were employed by the Department before 1880 (including five Chinese experts in silk and egg incubation) and another dozen by the Kaitakushi which was concerned with the development of Hokkaido—the experimental grounds par excellence for foreign agriculture.[12]

Inevitably, this initial enthusiasm for things Western did not last indefinitely. The useful new crops were quickly assimilated; the new methods often proved unsuitable. After 1880 the emphasis turned back somewhat to more traditional concerns—improvement within the framework of Japanese agriculture, by developing new strains of traditional crops, and by diffusing more widely the best practices of particular regions. Shinagawa, in the speech quoted above at the agricultural congress in 1881, went on to talk of the danger "in leaping ahead to the new of neglecting what is good in the old,"

[8] *Nōdankai Nisshi* in NNHS, Vol. 1, p. 671.
[9] MZKJS, Vol. 1, p. 125.
[10] MZKJS, Vol. 1, p. 26.
[11] Nakayama Taishō, ed., *Shimbun Shūsei Meiji Hennen Shi*, Vol. 7, 1940, p. 14.
[12] MZKJS, Vol. 1, pp. 541–44, Vol. 2, p. 1804.

a danger just as great as conservative resistance to innovation. It is significant that the congress itself was a congress of "old farmers"—the heirs of the Tokugawa tradition of intelligent experimenting farmers—and they were called together expressly for the purpose of exchanging information about traditional practices in their regions.

More germane to the present discussion are the methods used to diffuse the knowledge thus accumulated. First, there was the exhibition method. Agriculture played an important part in the Promotion of Industries Exhibitions, five of which were held between 1877 and 1903.[13] In addition a number of national prize shows for various particular products were held, especially after 1880, and, from 1874 to 1885 a permanent Museum of Agriculture was maintained in Tokyo.[14] The experimental stations themselves were also designed as permanent exhibitions. One concern of the Government when it secured the Shinjuku site was that it should be in a well-frequented district.[15]

Secondly, the Department was charged with the promotion of agricultural schools and colleges. Directly under its own control was the Komaba college which later became the Faculty of Agriculture of Tokyo University. In addition the Kaitakushi had its own famous agricultural college at Sapporo, the home of the ambitious Mr. Clark. By 1883 the Komaba school had three departments—of agriculture proper, of chemistry, and of veterinary medicine. It then had a staff of thirteen, four of them foreigners, and 107 students, 46 of them supported by official scholarships.[16] A survey of their graduates in 1886 showed that almost without exception they had taken jobs with local prefectural governments.

Thirdly, the Department was charged with direct promotional and extension activity. Some of the relevant functions listed in the Department's charter of organization as drafted in 1874 were:[17]

1. To keep an eye open for all inventions and improvements which the Minister might reward with prizes and honors.

2. To make plans for the loaning of seeds and implements, or of cash to purchase them, to individuals and organizations.

3. To investigate all suggested schemes which could contribute to the national welfare, to test experimentally the principles involved, to make detailed estimates of costs and benefits and make suitable recommendations to the Minister.

The procedures followed were enterprising and *ad hoc*, most important in providing official encouragement for local initiative. In 1876, for instance, a farmer in Nara Prefecture forwarded to the Department a detailed record

13 MZKJS, Vol. 1, p. 463.
14 MZKJS, Vol. 1, p. 517.
15 MZKJS, Vol. 1, p. 517.
16 MZKJS, Vol. 1, p. 269.
17 MZKJS, Vol. 1, p. 22.

of experiments with rice strains which he had been carrying out since 1863, together with some samples of particularly successful varieties. Within a week a congratulatory letter had been written and he had been sent a number of fruit trees and asked to try them out. His own varieties were tried out in the Shinjuku testing grounds.[18]

The Department early set about the task of formalizing and expanding its channels of communication. In 1874 it began publication of a Bulletin and in 1877 prefectures were instructed to appoint regular correspondents who should report anything likely to be of value to the Department and receive the Department's Bulletin, as well as specific answers to specific queries, in exchange. At first it was envisaged that these should be prefectural officials, but from 1880 private individuals were appointed and allowed to correspond directly with the Department (by unstamped letter).[19] By 1885 there were nearly 2,000 farmers receiving the Department's Bulletins.[20]

The next step was the organization of local agricultural associations. Again these were the result of a mixture of local and central government initiative. It was in 1880 that the Department issued a circular to all prefectures urging the establishment of agricultural improvement associations. This was not an original idea; a number of Seed Exchange Societies and Agricultural Discussion Societies had already been formed, in some cases entirely on private initiative, in some cases with the assistance and encouragement of prefectural governments.[21] But again the Department played an important broker's role in diffusing and lending authority to the idea. The response in the prefectures seems to have been rapid, and the growth of local associations was further accelerated by the congress of "old farmers" (three from each prefecture) when it was held in Tokyo the following year. These became the founder members of the Japan Agricultural Association which developed out of the congress. At the same time they were key figures in the local associations. Thus began the organization which eventually grew into the Imperial Agricultural Association. By 1899, the year in which an Agricultural Association's Law gave legal backing, some government funds and model constitutions to the local associations and bound them into a tight pyramidical structure, the correspondent system could be abolished as superfluous. In 1905 membership in the Associations became compulsory for all farmers.[22] And eventually a solid and well-staffed organization emerged which was able to take over the semi-official functions of statistical reporting and, during the wartime period of total mobilization, of rationing, crop requisitioning, and planting controls as well.

18 NT, Vol. 1, pp. 11–12.
19 MZKJS, Vol. 1, p. 297.
20 MZKJS, Vol. 1, p. 285.
21 NNHS, Vol. 1, pp. 653–5.
22 NNHS, Vol. 5, p. 330.

It is difficult to assess the total effect of the central government's activity. The Department's staff was not large—a total of ninety ranking officials in 1877 and perhaps fewer ten years later.[23] Nor was it particularly well endowed with funds: in 1890 the total budget for the Ministry of Agriculture and Commerce was less than a million yen, a thirtieth of that of the Ministry of Finance, and less than a third of the allotment for the Imperial Household. Of that sum at least five-eighths was devoted to the administration of the national forests.[24]

It seems certain, though, that this small Department played an essential organizing role which greatly magnified the effect of local individual initiatives. In its early formative and improvising years, too, it seems to have shown a bold and apparently infectious reformist drive. But, in the very nature of things this enthusiasm could not last forever. Routinization set in, and with it complacency. Yanagita Kunio, reflecting on his official life in 1909 has some very pertinent things to say.[25] One great difference he perceives between his childhood days and the present is that people are less interested in argument and discussion.

> The fact that officials rarely issue memoranda and suggestions [for improvement] may be because the volume of business they have to deal with has increased, or because the boundaries of each person's authority have been fixed and no-one likes to take the risk of treading on another's territory. Anyhow, the fact is they have ceased.

The changing role of the government is matched by a change in the people.

> It seems a long time, too, since patriotic citizens, heedless of their own poverty, would journey long distances to the capital to present petitions and policy memorials. The establishment of the Diet was the turning point.

Now people only present petitions in their own interest. The patriotic league has become the pressure group; the farmer anxious to report an idea which might contribute to the national welfare has given place to the applicant for a subsidy.

PREFECTURAL GOVERNMENTS

The work of prefectural administrations in the development of agriculture in early Meiji was similar to that of the central government and at least as important. In many respects they played an intermediate role, working in obedience to the instructions of the central government, running tests of new varieties and reporting back to the Shinjuku experimental station and its successors, redistributing tools, live-

23 MZKJS, Vol. 2, pp. 1811–20.
24 Okura-sho, *Meiji Zaisei Shi,* Vol. 3, p. 549.
25 *Jidai to Nōmin,* 1910, repr. in *Yaanagita Kunio Sensei Chosaku Shū,* Vol. 4, p. 5.

stock and subsidies sent them from the central Department. But prefectural governments also took their own initiatives, subsidizing their own private schemes, importing their own seeds and making their own tests. At the 1881 congress of "old farmers" a number reported initiatives in livestock breeding which had been carried out by their prefectures. We have already seen that a few Agricultural Improvement Societies were already established before the central government sent out their instructions, some of them supported by prefectural or county funds. In the matter of education, too, by 1880 at least seven prefectures had independently established agricultural colleges—often combined with an experimental station—financed out of local funds.[26] Later the Ministry of Education took an active part in the matter of agricultural education, and its outline regulations for agricultural schools, promulgated in 1883, provided a further stimulus to local initiative. By 1886 the total number of provincial schools had grown to sixteen, including a number run by counties or groups of villages.[27] Ten years later the number was 46, about half being prefectural schools and half operated by lower government echelons.[28] Nine of the latter specialized exclusively in sericulture, and in 1886, at least, the average size seems to have been only about forty pupils. Nevertheless this was an important beginning.

It is not always easy to trace the source of initiative in these matters, but it is certain that a good deal depended on the energy of prefectural officials, even in the matter of implementing the suggestions and recommendations of the central government. In 1884, for instance, the central government issued model regulations for producers' unions,[29] the aim of which was to secure regular grading and quality controls over marketed rice. Not all prefectures took active steps to form such unions; some did nothing; some merely passed the model regulations on to village offices and left it at that.[30] Others actively urged and supervised the formation of such unions and some, such as Chiba, considerably amplified their sphere of competence and made them responsible for supervision of the whole process of rice cultivation and laid down specific rules to be followed from seed selection to the baling of threshed rice.[31]

The prefectural officials were, moreover, closer to the ground. They were in direct contact, if not with the mass of farmers, at least with the upper strata of village leaders. There was a difference between the central government mailing a circular recommending the selection of seed by salt water or the drying of sheaves on wooden racks, and the prefectural office issuing the same recommendations to village officials. In the latter face-to-face relation-

26 MZKJS, Vol. 2, p. 1585.
27 MZKJS, Vol. 2, pp. 1588–92.
28 NNHS, Vol. 3, pp. 590–4.
29 NNHS, Vol. 3, pp. 332–4.
30 NNHS, Vol. 5, p. 48.
31 NNHS, Vol. 3, pp. 336–7.

ship with its still strong *kanson-mimpi*—"the official is noble, the people base"
—overtones, a recommendation was likely to be taken as an order.

In some cases, indeed, the order was made explicit. Miyagi Prefecture,
for instance, issued in 1878 compulsory regulations concerning the threshing
and grading of rice, and penalties were prescribed for infringement.[32] This
offended against the liberal philosophy which Matsukata brought into economic policy, and in 1881 the Ministry ordered the regulation to be withdrawn. Things were different twenty years later, however. Beginning in 1896
with Miyazaki, a number of prefectures issued by-laws (*kenrei*) enforcing
practices which were considered beneficial to rice cultivation. Between 1896
and 1904, for instance, at least twenty-four prefectures ordered that rice
seedbeds should be oblong in shape and not more than four feet wide (to
facilitate weeding and the control of pests—especially the rice borer—from
the sides) and eight of these included penal provisions, ranging, in some
cases, up to ten days' imprisonment or a ten-yen fine.[33] Other prefectures forbade the use of lime fertilizer (and were somewhat discountenanced when a
few years later the Ministry announced that experiments had disproved the
current old wives' tales about the dreadful effects of using lime.)[34] Others
ordered the regular spacing of rice plants in rows to facilitate weeding, and
a number tried to impose rice grading regulations by fiat.[35] The inclusion of
penal provisions became more common during the Russo-Japanese War, but
many were abandoned not long thereafter. The "extension by the sabre
method" as Japanese historians call it in honor of Frederic the Great, was
not altogether popular. Clashes between police or agricultural officials and
the farmers were frequent. In one district the spaced planting method was
reputedly known as the wine-bottle method after a famous occasion on which
an inspector, having fortified himself on a *shō* of *sake*, charged into a field
brandishing the bottle over his head and began to uproot irregularly planted
rice. He was promptly set upon and beaten for his pains.[36] However, such
epic incidents go recorded while the doubtless far more common incidence of
compliant submission has to be inferred from the fact that the improvements
recommended did in fact become standard practice.

THE VILLAGE

In a country the
size of Japan it would seem unlikely on the face of it that the sort of governmental efforts we have been describing could have had much overall effect. A

32 NNHS, Vol. 5, p. 20.
33 NNHS, Vol. 2, p. 131.
34 NNHS, Vol. 4, p. 743.
35 NNHS, Vol. 4, pp. 751–94.
36 NNHS, Vol. 4, p. 108.

few prefectural by-laws, a few million yen's worth of tools and seeds distributed, the training of a few hundred graduates of agricultural colleges, the organization of a couple of thousand agricultural correspondents, would not seem to have much chance of leavening the conservatism of some five million farming households. And, if the nation's farmers had been individual, and individualist, entrepreneurs, the effect might indeed have been small. But they were not. The fact that farmers lived in small, tightly-packed hamlets, the fact that these hamlets displayed a great degree of community solidarity backed by numerous forms of cooperative activity and until recently by the collective legal responsibility for tax payments, and the fact that these communities were for the most part traditionally inclined to accept paternalistic, authoritarian leadership—all these had the effect of greatly magnifying the results achieved. The "old farmers" who gathered for the 1881 congress were working farmers of the traditional leadership stratum, men as conscious of their moral duty to guide their fellow villagers into better ways, and as confident of their right to do so, as they were devoted to good farming as an end in itself. Hear one of them, Hyogo prefecture, reporting to the congress:[37]

> The poor quality of rice in recent years is due in part to the ending of the old fief quality inspections and in part because people cut early and thresh roughly in order to get on with planting winter wheat. To counter-act this, about twenty-two or three villages got together, and we decided on a "stay-the-sickle" rule. People are not allowed to cut their rice until the reddish tinge appears. Farmers who are very hard up [and need money or food badly] can appeal to the village authorities and a section of their fields will be marked off which they are allowed to cut.

Another from Aichi says, during the discussion on rice bales:[38]

> I hear that there is a village in Mikawa where they have established a farmers' union which has got out a detailed list of rules for the yearly round of farm work that the farmers must abide by. One of these is that you must always use last year's [tougher] straw for the rice bales.

In this way a few energetic "old farmers" with traditionally supported authority could alter the farming practices of whole villages. The new rules were in an old tradition. It was no fresh and intolerable invasion of the farmer's independence that he could not cut his rice when he wanted to. He was used to village rules which prescribed the precise number of cups of *sake* which each guest could drink at his wedding, or which made it a community, rather than an individual, decision whether he could convert upland to paddy. This tradition greatly magnified the efficacy of the new Agricultural Associations which developed after 1880. They provided a new organizational framework in which the old pressures for conformity could be mobilized explicitly

---

37 NNHS, Vol. 1, p. 683.
38 NNHS, Vol. 1, p. 699.

for the control of cultivating methods. At the second "old farmers" congress in 1890 a Kyoto farmer reported:[39]

> We set up an inspection committee [in the Agricultural Association] whose job it was to tour the village [covering each farmer] three times in the process of ploughing and planting. Reports were written and when the harvest came we took sample cuts, and then awarded prizes on the basis of a combination of the earlier reports and the quality of the harvest. This is one way of encouraging lazy farmers to work. Count Shinagawa [former head of the Agricultural Department of the Ministry] praised this highly. His phrase was: "the landlord's footprints turn to dung," by which he meant, of course, that their walking round the owner-farmers' and tenants' land, and remonstrating with the indolent was worth a good dose of fertilizer."

The organization of prize shows—*himpyōkai* and *kyōshinkai*—became, in fact, one of the prime functions of the village Agricultural Associations in the decade or two following 1890. One strong impelling motive was to improve the quality, and so raise the price, of rice, particularly—since the Associations' leaders were generally landlords—of the rice paid to landlords in rent. But they soon, as in the example quoted, extended their concern to the whole productive process. A Niigata document outlining the prize system spells out in detail the method of judging, with prizes awarded for eight separate stages of cultivation, and—characteristically revealing the paternalistic tone of the whole affair—for the farmer's "general behaviour" as well.[40]

A charming caricature of the beehive nature of the Meiji village, though one written with serious prescriptive intent, is the novel, *The Model Village* (*Mohan-chōson*), published in 1907 by that fiery scholar and founding father of the modern *Nōhon-shugi* school of anti-urban back-to-nature thinkers, Yokoi Jikei.[41] The model nature of the village derives entirely from the energetic leadership of the dedicated mayor. As the visitor questions villagers concerning the recent innovations the constant preface to the replies is: "Yes, the mayor has paid particular attention to that problem." "Thanks to Chairman Mao and the Communist Party," one echoes, and indeed the village is like nothing more than a Chinese commune. There is a village hospital run by graduated taxation, there is a citizens' hall with a creche where the children play with model agricultural implements, and a communal restaurant which provides everyday meals in busy seasons and no-host party meals to eliminate competitive entertaining. The visitor is puzzled not to be offered tea at the houses he visits until he realizes that this is one of the rules of nationalized living, designed to eliminate useless conspicuous hospitality.

There are many communal farming activities, cooperative glass-houses, cooperative livestock breeding, cooperative incubators for the chickens.

---

[39] NNHS, Vol. 1, p. 657.

[40] Furushima Toshio and Morito Shirō, *Nihon Jinushi Sei Shi Ron*, 1957, p. 289.

[41] *Yokoi Hakase Shū*, Vol. 5, 1924.

Mostly, however, farming is still on a family basis, but with a great deal of communal direction overlaid. Holidays, for instance, are fixed for the whole village, and on every week day bells ring out to mark the hours at which farmers should go to their fields, the hours at which they may take a luncheon break, the hour to come home. And work and play are rigidly divided; "disorderliness was the mayor's chief dislike and even at rice-planting he forbade singing while at work. At first people felt deprived and upset and there were many who jeered at the mayor's prejudices, but now they are extremely grateful for the great results . . . The custom of girls dressing up at rice-planting and making it a time for choosing brides has automatically disappeared. One no longer sees the brash young men of the village teasing the girls while they are at work."[42] By way of compensation there are billiards at the citizens' hall, a "Morals Club" for the young men, dramatic clubs and choirs which sing pure, wholesome and improving songs to replace the deplorable bawdiness of traditional village ditties.

It is the Protestant ethic, all right; and yet Professor Yokoi's vision was not, after all, so far-fetched. At least one biographical account of a university graduate who returned to his native village, shows him working, with some success, on just these lines—with a temperance society and all.[43]

It is worth noting, however, that the mayor's influence in the model village, and the influence of the village leaders in the actual nineteenth century village, was not necessarily a mere matter of naked authority. The "old farmers" were able to secure their effect because the rules were not just their rules but "village rules." Their authority derived its legitimacy from the fact that in form, and to a varying degree in substance, the whole village gave its consent. Their rule was to guide the consensus rather than to issue orders. At the 1881 congress a Hyōgo man (and it is perhaps significant that it was a Hyōgo man and not someone from the mere authoritarian north) expressed his confidence that the matter of improving rice quality could soon be dealt with through the Agricultural Associations. In the associations which had just been formed in his prefecture[44]

> The officers were all elected from the farmers, and since the organization rests on a mutual contract (*meiyaku*) there is no doubt that its decisions will be rigidly observed.

Even when the authoritarianism of the landlord leaders was evident it was often made palatable to the villagers by the fact that the leaders were patently sincere in their efforts to improve their fellows. It was part of the Confucian virtue of benevolence that they should be.

42 Mohan Chōson, pp. 306–7.
43 Sōma Kokkō, Hotaka Kōgen, 195. I am indebted for this reference to Professor T. C. Smith.
44 NNHS, Vol. 1, p. 682.

It is also worth nothing that the growing commercialization of agriculture did not necessarily destroy the cooperative unity of the village. Unlike industrial enterpreneurs farmers were not in direct competition with each other—no single farmer's operations were big enough to affect the market. Hence there was no powerful economic incentive to keep the secret of successful improvements to oneself.[45]

LANDLORDS

In a sense the influence of landlords has already been discussed. The "old farmers," the village leaders who organized the Agricultural Associations were for the most part landlords. Particularly insofar as they used the constraint which could be exercised through the Association to improve the quality of rent rice and to forbid the use of lime fertilizer which was supposed to damage the fields, they were often as much concerned with raising the standard of their own tenants—to their own pecuniary profit—as they were with fulfilling a paternalistic duty towards their fellow-villagers, owner-farmers and the tenants of other landlords included. But this is not the sum total of the landlord's role; quite apart from their influence exerted through the village they also exercised a certain amount of direct control over the activities of their own tenants.

With few exceptions Japanese landlords were not, as in many share-cropping systems, joint entrepreneurs with the tenants, providing tools and seeds and sharing the proceeds. There was, however, considerable local variation in the extent to which the landlord-tenant relation was merely an impersonal contractual one or, on the other hand, was a personal relation in which protection and guidance were exchanged for service and submission over a whole range of life activities quite beyond the renting of land. The variation was reflected in the ease with which the fixed rental to be paid in kind could be adjusted for a poor harvest. When this was regularly done, even for moderate falls below average yields, not only was the landlord usually in a position to exercise a paternalistic authority over his tenants, he also had a strong economic incentive to exert that authority to improve his tenants' agricultural competence. It is probable that in the early Meiji period the vast majority of landlords fell into this paternalistic category, and moreover the vast majority still farmed directly themselves.

It is not surprising, then, that many landlords exercised close direction over their tenants' cultivation. In 1888 the Ministry held a long correspondence with Shizuoka prefecture concerning a certain farmer called Maruta who was reported to get a crop of six *koku* to the *tan*. Maruta provided a long

---

[45] A point made, apropos of American agricultural innovations in the nineteenth century by A. H. Cole, *Business Enterprise in Its Social Setting* (Harvard, 1959), p. 112. I am grateful to Professor T. C. Smith for drawing my attention to this interesting passage.

detailed exposé of his methods, but it appeared that the crop in question had been raised by a tenant on Maruta's land, though presumably under Maruta's close supervision.[46] Perhaps few landlords exercised such direct control, but a good number acted to pass on prefectural authorities' suggestions about the shape of seed-beds, spaced planting and the like as "orders" to their tenants. Some specified an interdiction on the use of lime in a written tenancy contract.[47] Others used the prize competition method. Furushima reports on a Niigata landlord who held prize competitions for his own tenants' rent rice for several years before they were replaced by village competitions organized by the Agricultural Association. Tenants who produced a superior product were rewarded with prizes of mattocks and sickles. At the subsequent feast, seating order was determined by standing in the competition, and it was a rule that those at the head of the list would be addressed by the landlord as *Mr. X (dono,* at least) the rest without such polite suffixes.[48] Other landlords used more tangible incentives. An Osaka farmer reported at the old farmers' congress that in his village landlords reduced rent by as much as a tenth of a *koku* per *tan* if it was paid in rice of the best quality.[49]

Tenants were not always, at any rate, responsive to instructions *not* backed by economic incentives. In at least one case, the landlords borrowed police authority. The *Chōya Shimbun* reported in 1888 that sericulture was spreading rapidly in the San-in district, thanks to the initiative of the prefectural and county officials. In one county in Tottori, officials had persuaded landlords to turn over as much as eight *chō* to mulberry. The landlords were agreed—provided their tenants did not object. The tenants were summoned to the county office, but they refused to go, complaining that they would starve —presumably in the interval before the mulberry began to produce. The county chief, accompanied by the police chief and secretaries, set out for the village. Police rounded up sixty or more tenants at the school and the county chief began his lecture. One woman fainted from excess of indignation, whereat a farmer seized a stick and began to lay about him. He was restrained, but, according to the newspaper account, "amity was not restored."[50]

The decline in landlord influence is quite clearly charted in the growing numbers of tenancy disputes from the time of the First World War. It was in part the result of a general loss of submissiveness on the part of the "lower orders" of Japanese society. In the particular case of the landlords its effect was intensified by what Japanese historians refer to as their growing "parasiticization." As the period wore on, fewer and fewer actually cultivated land themselves. Fewer and fewer knew or cared enough about farming to advise or instruct their tenants.

[46] NT, Vol. 1, pp. 19–30.
[47] NNHS, Vol. 2, p. 156.
[48] Furushima and Morita, *op. cit.,* p. 284.
[49] NNHS, Vol. 1, p. 686.
[50] *Shimbun Shusei Meiji Hennen Shi,* Vol. 7, p. 44.

THE ENTREPRENEUR

The Meiji period also saw the emergence of a new type of farmer—the capitalist entrepreneur. Typically he was an ex-samurai; he usually bought, or acquired as a gift, unreclaimed land; he usually started a new experimental type of Western farming; he usually had a government subsidy, and he usually did not last long. An example of a successful type of samurai entrepreneur was Karasawa Annin.[51] A samurai of Aizu, a fief scholar and official, he was imprisoned for anti-Imperialist activity at the time of the Restoration. Released, he set off, in 1873, to start a ranch in the northern tip of Honshu. He was given a government subsidy, employed two Englishmen for five years as advisors, and by 1876 was able to show the Emperor on a visit 180 head of cattle of mixed Western and indigenous breeds, and 24 horses. He also experimented with various new crops and carried out afforestation schemes. By 1889 he had created a village as an appendage to his ranch which he then left to his son. He himself moved to Tokyo to establish selling outlets for the ranch's products. He became founder of the Japan Livestock Association before he died a few years later.

Not all were as successful, by any means. Tsuda Sen, another ardent ex-samurai "Westernizer" who had been to the Vienna Exposition in 1873 started a mulberry and dairy farm on some 180 *cho* of land in Chiba. After a few years, however, he admitted defeat and let the land out of tenants.[52]

Another successful case—a cooperative village in the hills above Tsuruoba founded by a group of retainers of the local fief—perhaps gives a clue as to why Tsuda failed. These ex-samurai, too, were enterprising innovators; they rapidly developed high-quality silk-worm egg production and the village still supplies the bulk of the demand from Yamagata prefecture. But they started off on the traditional small-holding, family farm system.

In other words, the frequent failure of these innovators is probably ascribable to the same reason as prompted numbers of traditional large-scale farmers to cut down the size of their farms and let out land to tenants—the fact that the relative levels of rents and farm wages (somewhat raised by the opportunities for industrial employment) combined with the relative efficiency of hired and family-farm labor, made tenancy a more profitable proposition. Even the ranches often developed into a tenancy system, with breeding cows leased out to tenants. In thus falling into the traditional pattern of agricultural organization, however, the new ex-samurai entrepreneurs sometimes brought a new style of energetic management into their tenancy operations. An example is the Mitsubishi enterprise in Niigata which, early in the 1890s, instituted a system of *compulsory* interest-free loans for fertilizer to their tenants.[53]

[51] See *Dainihon Nōkō Den*, 1891, reprinted in *Nihon Sangyō Shiryo Taikei*, Vol. 3, pp. 1025–7.

[52] Sakurai Takeo, *Nihon Nōhonshugi*, 1935, p. 53.

[53] Furushima and Morita, *op. cit.*, p. 286–7.

The entrepreneurial function was, perhaps, more important in another field—in the food processing and distribution industries. The silk factories, the sweet potato processing plants, the tea export companies, and the sugar beet companies undoubtedly had a major effect in stimulating switches to more profitable crops. Very often these, too, had government subsidies. One of the major fights in the first Diet revolved around a subsidy to a tea export company which many members believed, and apparently with good reason, to be a facade.[54] A Hokkaido sugar-beet factory established by six Tokyo men in 1888 with a capital of 400,000 yen, was guaranteed by the Hokkaido government a straight 5 percent dividend on its capital from the month of subscription to the commencement of operations, and thereafter such subsidy as should be necessary to bring net profits (income less costs, less 5 percent depreciation) up to 5 percent of capital.[55]

There is a further point to be noted concerning this type of entrepreneurial activity. It was the more effective in that it was able to draw on established patterns of cooperation. It was reported in 1888, for example, that farmers in Shimane had succeeded in growing an improved type of local cotton, and fourteen of them had established a producers' cooperative (dōgyō kumiai on the model provided by the Ministry) to organize spinning and weaving on the putting-out system, and had sent representatives across the country to organize markets.[56]

Enterprise was thus the more effective in that it could be easily channelled into cooperative activity. But while cooperation was traditional, this was a new form. It was not just the cooperation based on ascribed status which prevailed within the solidary village community. It was a new functional and associational form deliberately created, and often cutting across hamlet and village boundaries. Again the State played an important role in providing models for the organization of such groups, model rules not only for the general producers' cooperatives mentioned above, but also for specific types, as, for instance, the model rules for tea-producers' unions circulated in 1883.[57]

Just how much capital investment there was in this type of processing and marketing activity it is difficult to estimate. In terms of the total scale of investments at this time it was probably small. In 1888, for instance, of the 549 new companies established with an average capital of something over 100,000 yen each, only 34, with an average capital of just over 10,000 yen, were designated agricultural.[58] This does not, however, include the small-time producers' union type of investment which was probably greater in its total effect on agricultural production.

[54] *Dai Nihon Toikoku Gikai Shi*, Vol. 1, 924 ff, 1524–31.
[55] *Shimbun Shūsei*, Vol. 7, p. 80.
[56] *Shimbun Shūsei*, Vol. 7, p. 39.
[57] *Shimbun Shūsei*, Vol. 7, p. 39.
[58] *Shimbun Shūsei*, Vol. 7, p. 87.

It is even more difficult to estimate how much of the total capital invested was urban in origin as in the example of the Hokkaido beet factory quoted above.

MOTIVES OF THE INNOVATOR

It is time to bring together the various channels of information and pressure towards improvement which have been discussed in a general consideration of the individual innovating farmer. Thousands of farmers in the Meiji period made new departures, did things they had never done before, or did old things in new ways. What were the motives that might have stimulated these innovations? Four are worth considering: a positive hospitality towards novelty as such, as part of a respect for the authority of science and a belief in the possibility and desirability of progress; patriotism; submission to authority; and the calculation of economic interest.

NOVELTY

That the first was important, particularly in early Meiji, cannot be doubted. It was in a spirit of adventure and experiment that Tsuda bought his farm in Chiba; it was from a missionary zeal for good farming that the ex-samurai, Hayashi Enri, experimented with his premature Lysenko methods of seed treatment and stumped the country giving lectures and distributing pamphlets at his own expense. It was from a desire to catch on to any good new thing that was going that farmers all over the country were stimulated by his pamphlets and his lectures to try his methods themselves. And perhaps when the mass of farmers who could not read pamphlets followed the lead of those who could and did, they too were prompted by something of the same sort of motive. Yanagita Kunio, for instance, had this to say about the farmers he met on lecture tours in 1909.[59]

> When we go to the provinces and talk to the farmers, unless we retail some Western theory we've got out of books or some examples drawn from distant parts of the country, our hearers lack interest and the speaker feels he has not done his job.

Already the "scientism" which is such a pervasive feature of the mood of modern Japan was apparently well established. It is an attitude which has something in common with American love of gadgetry, but with a difference. Whereas American gadgets are typically conceived as the product of the inventive entrepreneur, Japanese scientism, perhaps because it derives in part from the Confucian respect for learning, looks to the authority of the scholar;

[59] *Jidai to Nōmin*, p. 2.

there is nothing better than the theory "got out of books." Yanagita Kunio has a pertinent point again:[60]

> At the central level administrative authority is always backed by scholarly authority. The top officials are scholars in their own right. And the lower administrative organs feel that if they are retailing their superiors' scholarly opinions as well as their administrative authority they will be all right.

How strong this hospitality to new scientific ideas was among the mass of illiterate farmers in the early Meiji period, and how powerful it was to counter the innate tendency to conservatism of a traditional peasant society, must remain a matter of doubt. What is certain, though, is that the attiude became more powerful as the school system developed and as a new generation of farmers passed through the hands of school teachers who formed the lower ranks of an intellectual elite in which scientism and the belief in progress was well established. Today, the Japanese farmer is conservative in little more than his politics.

Where this attitude prevails, moreover, social prestige factors give it multiplier effects. The farmer who has a *new* tool acquires prestige thereby and others seek to emulate him. Keeping up with the Joneses has been important to the Japanese farmer not so much in the field of domestic consumption as in the field of ceremonial entertaining and productive equipment. Modern agricultural economists are frequently prone to deplore the abandon with which farmers buy hand-tractors which they can never make economically profitable on their small holdings.

PATRIOTISM

The strength of our second motive is even more difficult to assess. Repeatedly, in the directives of government authority, in the speeches of "old farmers" at their congresses, in the instructions of landlords to their tenants rings the refrain "we must increase production in order to advance the welfare of the nation." With a nice touch of egotism Yokoi Jikei has his model village mayor place on the wall of the citizens' hall the "Five Precepts for Farmers" composed by, and inscribed in the bold calligraphy of, Professor Yokoi Jikei. The first reads: "To increase the wealth of your family is to serve the nation; avoid luxury and always practice diligence" and the last: "Understand that farmers must be the nation's model class. Conduct yourself with dignity as befits the heirs of the Bushido tradition."[61]

Undoubtedly, patriotism, as the highest virtue in the calendar, often served as a respectable, if not hypocritical, cover for other less socially accepted motives. But we should beware of assuming that it was always a

[60] *Ibid.*, p. 10.
[61] *Mohen Chōson*, p. 308.

cover for economic interest. It could equally serve as a rationalization of the self-assertive adventurism of the samurai rancher, or the missionary egotism of the "old farmer" innovator. One should equally beware of assuming that it had no independent motivational force at all. Such as it had was probably most marked in the first two decades when there *was* a sense of national emergency. It may be significant that a newspaper writer remarks in 1888 that some time ago it was the fashion for everyone looking for a title for a new company or a new product to use the word *Kokueki:* match factories and beef butchers, all claimed to "profit the nation." Now, it was remarked, the word is out of fashion. The new cant-word is *Teikoku;* even the sewer man operates an Imperial Honey Bucket Service.[62] The magic of the national association is still there, but now reflecting a mood of complacency, latching on to the charisma of established authority, rather than a sense of participation in the striving of a nation trying to pull itself up by its own bootstraps.

SUBMISSIVENESS

Of our third possible motive enough illustration has already been given. Again we must note that the type of submissiveness that secured obedience to the orders of government, prefecture, mayor or landlord *solely* by virtue of the authority attaching to the latter's superior status became less common as the period went on. The principle that "the official is noble; the people base" became increasingly irksome as economic opportunity, universal conscription and universal education combined with subversive ideologies to spread egalitarian sentiments.

It was perhaps a reflection of the decline in the absolute authority of the administration that some prefectures resorted after 1890 to the promulgation of by-laws with penal provisions. The objective authority of the law was brought in to bolster declining *personal* authority. In other words, the period of "extension by the sabre" represented a weakening of authority rather than its intensification as Japanese historians have suggested. And even this did not last long. There was the beginning of articulate and informed opposition. According to one contemporary official reminiscing some fifty years later:[63]

> People argued that it was unconstitutional . . . If, they said, in order to sell what you have grown you have to submit it to inspection, have it graded and priced according to the grade, and are then forbidden to sell what does not come up to standard, this is a restriction of property rights and an infringement of liberty.

As the authority of officials declined, so, too, did that of landlords, as the increasing frequency of tenancy disputes after the First World War adequately testifies. But if officials and landlords lost their power to *coerce* by the

[62] *Shimbun Shūsei*, Vol. 7, p. 65.
[63] Ishiguro Tadaatsu, quoted in NNHS, Vol. 5, p. 361.

glare in their eye or by the use of punitive sanctions, they did not thereby lose their power to *influence* provided that they either (a) kept the authority relation a warmly paternalistic one or (b) utilized the mechanisms of the solidary village community. The official who came, not to give orders, but to suggest, advise and guide, "retailing the scholarly opinions as well as the administrative authority" of his superiors was still respected and welcomed. Indeed, Yanagita Kunio suggests in the same address that there was far too much reliance on the wisdom of authority.[64]

> In future the towns and villages must make greater efforts to study the agricultural economies of their region. The present "leave everything to those above" tendency to welcome the protection and interference of authority is hardly a desirable one.

By the beginning of the twentieth century paternal government benevolence took an increasingly concrete form—financial subsidies. These began to increase rapidly in amount after the establishment of a network of Agricultural Associations provided channels for their distribution to the cultivating farmer. In 1900 they amounted in total to approximately 1 percent of the budget of the Ministry of Agriculture and Commerce, about equal to the amount spent on experimental stations. Twelve years later they had quadrupled in amount and were double the size of the experimental budget.[65] And this amount was substantially augmented from prefectural funds.

Wisely used the subsidies were often a valuable spur to useful innovation. And it is worth noting that they were channelled, for the most part, through the Agricultural Associations, and served the secondary purpose of strengthening those organizations which fulfilled our second condition for successful authoritarian guidance.

The importance of this second condition is apparent if one considers the role of the post-war Agricultural Cooperatives, the successors of the old Agricultural Associations. They continue to be a powerful instrument for the execution of government policy and a powerful means whereby the exemplary effects of initiatives by go-ahead farmers can be intensified and accelerated. Their authority derives from the fact that their urgings represent, at least formally, a village consensus, not from the traditional authority of landlord leaders, whom in any case the land reform has removed from the scene.

ECONOMIC INTEREST

The economist, observing the increase in food production in Meiji Japan is apt to conclude that the market provided adequate incentives to encourage farmers to produce more —and by incentives is usually meant a well-sustained price.

[64] *Jidai to Nōmin*, p. 20.
[65] NNHS, Vol. 5, p. 311.

While it is true that the ability to find a selling outlet for increased production was a necessary condition for the farmer's willingness to produce
more, it is doubtful if price levels themselves had much effect on the volume
of production. It is unlikely, at any rate, that a typical Japanese farmer's
reaction to a fall in the price of his staple products—rice or silk—would be
that of the classical entrepreneur—to cut back his investment and the scale
of his operations. He was more likely to intensify his efforts to *increase* production—in order to maintain his income by selling more at the lower price.
His costs are (a) in fact inelastic and (b) not usually calculated by him in
precise terms in relation to the value of his product.

Generally speaking—though this will be qualified later—the Japanese
farmer was production-oriented rather than profit-oriented; or at least he
tended automatically to equate production maximization with profit maximization. "What was good for rice production and what was bad; what was
advantageous and what disadvantageous—this was what the farmers most
wanted to hear,"[66] remarks Sakawa Jōmei, one of the itinerant lecturers appointed by the Ministry in the 1880's. And whatever the price of rice it was
assumed that the more production the greater the profit.

There are, however, two important qualifications which must be entered
against this suggestion that the state of the market was irrelevant to the increase in production. The first concerns the matter of fertilizer. Most of the
innovations which formed the basis of government urgings did not cost anything. The five "essentials" enumerated in a central government guide to good
cultivation issued in 1903 were, for instance, the selection of seed by the salt-
water method; countermeasures for the wheat blight, the use of narrow oblong
seed beds, the use of the seed bed as an ordinary field after transplanting, and
the regular planting of rice in rows. No one will ever know just how much
these no-extra-cost improvements contributed to the total increase in agricultural production which took place. But it is certain that a great part of
the increase is attributable to increased use of commercial fertilizer, not, that
is to say, to innovation, but to farmers doing more of what most of them were
doing already. The cost of this extra investment *was* something of which the
farmer was acutely aware.

It still remains a question, however, how far the current prices for rice
directly affected the amount a farmer spent on fertilizer. One's impression
(derived from asking altogether over a hundred modern farmers about their
use of fertilizer and, as far as I remember, not getting a single answer which
related fertilizer cost to the price of rice) is that the use of fertilizer became
habitualized. Each increment was absorbed into the farmer's pattern of fixed
costs, and if at any time he bought less than the year before this was less
likely to be the result of an exact calculation—weighing the probable increment in crop and the probable price of that increment against the extra cost

[66] NNHS, Vol. 2, p. 629.

of fertilizer plus interest from spring to autumn—as because he had no cash to buy fertilizer or was so deeply in debt that he feared to extend his credit.

This is certainly the impression one gets from the discussion of the "old farmers" in 1881. In a long session on different types of fertilizer any number of farmers were prepared to give their views on what was the "proper" amount of this and that for use with various crops. But only two gave any suggestion of the exact increment in yield to be expected—without any calculation of cost, and only one gave a comparison of the relative costs of two types of fertilizer "which had the same effect"—without specifying in precise terms what that effect was.[67]

Rice prices did, of course, determine the amount spent on fertilizer, not by affecting incentives, but by affecting the farmer's financial ability to buy it. Even if next year's probable prices had little affect on how much the farmer wanted to spend on fertilizer, last year's prices determined how much he *could* spend.

To sum up, then, as far as rice cultivation is concerned; the economic incentive of increasing production was without doubt a major factor in securing the acceptance of innovations. On the other hand, year to year fluctuations in the market are unlikely to have had any great effect on the volume of production.

Where the market did have its effect was in inducing the substitution of one crop for another. This, however, was almost exclusively within the field of upland agriculture. There was something sacred about the rice field; it provided the staple of the family's diet, it represented security and it represented years of invested labor in irrigation and other facilities. Even though mulberry and sericulture generally offered a higher monetary yield per acre than rice,[68] it was rare for paddy fields to be turned into mulberry orchards. Crop substitution generally took the form of the replacement of cotton, flax, sugar-cane and millets by mulberry, barley, vegetables and other industrial crops.

The change in crop acreages was considerable. But it came slowly. Even the acreage under mulberry, for instance the prize example of an expanding profitable crop, never grew at a rate faster than 5 percent a year.[69] (On the other hand, the rate of *decline* of clearly unprofitable crops are somewhat faster.[70]) The farmer was cautious, and new ventures were risky. There was nothing comparable to the "agricultural crazes"—for merino sheep, mulberry trees or Berkshire pigs—which characterized the United States in the first half of the nineteenth century, or—to take a society more structurally similar to contemporary Japan—to the "tulipomania" of seventeenth century Holland.

[67] NNHS, Vol. 1, pp. 755–76.
[68] NNHS, Vol. 5, p. 179.
[69] NNHS, Vol. 5, p. 180.
[70] NNHS, Vol. 5, p. 174.

Perhaps the Japanese farmer's love of novelty was not, after all, as well developed as in these societies, perhaps non-official channels of communication were insufficient for these speculative crazes to "catch on" and develop momentum, or perhaps the Japanese farmer had a more sophisticated awareness of the instabilities of the agricultural market. Yanagita Kunio, again, comments in 1909 that there is no lack of bright and enterprising people who are tempted to try something new, to have a go at chicken farming, or start a fruit orchard. But individual decisions cannot take account of the risks of flooding the market. In the natural economy the question: "Why am I poor?" had a simple answer—"Because you did not work hard enough." In the commercial economy you can be tough and enterprising—and still lose money. Hence people turn to officials for advice—advice which the officials cannot give for, in all their wisdom, they cannot predict how the market will be in ten years' time.[71]

Even in responding to market inducements, in other words, farmers tended readily to seek official guidance. They also, frequently, sought psychological security and marketing convenience in a collective response. It was probably as common for a group of farmers to start something new as for one to start individually.

The way in which farmers' contacts were made with the market is a complex question, worth exploring in the context of urban-rural relations. Sometimes, again, officials were the mediators—as in the case of the conversion to mulberry in Shimane to which the tenants objected. In the early period the major role was doubtless played by individual merchants. But not all of these were urban-based merchants. The rural merchant-farmer, whose importance in the late Tokugawa period has recently been described by T. C. Smith, was doubtless of considerable importance. Later, as the Agricultural Associations became organized, they began to go half way to meet and even create opportunities—energetic leaders in the Association would seek arrangements with factories for the purchase of industrial crops. At a later stage came collective marketing operated by the Association itself or by cooperatives. Unfortunately, there is no way of making a quantitative assessment of the relative importance of merchant enterprise and farmer initiative in catalysing the crop substitutions which contributed an important part to the growth of agricultural productivity in the period.

THE OLD AND THE NEW: RURAL AND URBAN

In the foregoing discussion the main emphasis has been on the mixture of the old and the new in the factors which promoted the expansion of agriculture in nineteenth-century Japan. Important continuities with the Tokugawa period were pointed out; the Confucian tradition that

[71] *Jidai to Nōmin*, p. 10.

"agriculture is the base of the country" as a partial explanation of Government concern with agricultural policy; the—again originally Confucian—respect for learning which gave a traditional means whereby innovation could be legitimized as an application of scholarly theory, and whereby those who sought to induce improvements could invest themselves with authority; the tradition of the literate, carefully recording, sometimes consciously experimenting "old farmer"; the tradition of peasant submission to political authority which permitted improvement by fiat; the tradition of paternalistic patron-client relations between landlord and tenant which permitted the "old farmer" type of landlord to exert a guiding control; and finally the tradition of community solidarity and community homogeneity which required individual submission to the constraint of village rules and village opinion which it was open to innovators to manipulate.

These elements, with the exception of the first which was an attitude of the already "urban" samurai, were features of the rural tradition which facilitated agricultural improvement from within, sometimes operated even to initiate it, and in any case to magnify the effects of stimuli applied from without. Much of the stimuli did, of course, come from without—from the urban sector: the technology, flowing at first from the West and later increasingly from home experimental centers, channelled through the urban agricultural colleges and the urban centers of government; perhaps, in relatively small amounts, urban capital flowing into food processing industries; the new mass education system with its urban origin and—as men like Yokoi Jikei were apt to complain[72]—its excessively urban orientation, sharpening receptivity to change and providing new motivations; and finally the economic inducements presented to the farmer by the urban-based merchant. These elements of the urban new combined effectively with the rural old. New wine in old bottles is the cliché that comes immediately to mind, an inapt one since it cannot accommodate the fact that the bottles responded extraordinarily well.

[72] Shakai Solsaku Gakki: *Shakai Solsaku Ronsō*, No. 8, 1915, pp. 64–5.

PLANNING
AND IMPLEMENTATION:
PARADOXES
IN RURAL DEVELOPMENT

Gayl D. Ness

Although industrialization constitutes an important aspect of modern development, there is also recognition that development in the rural areas must be an integral part of the over-all process of development. In the new states the rural sector is the largest sector in terms of both population and productive capacity; it is also recognized as more backward and thus containing high potential for growth. Thus planning for economic development normally includes important goals for development in the rural areas.

For the most part the goal of rural development has been manifest in programs for community development. These programs begin with a recognition of the large size of the rural sector and the isolation and economic backwardness of traditional rural village communities. They also recognize that the colonial systems have often produced a more or less stagnant rural sector with powerful built-in obstacles to a process of modernization that will increase human productivity and integrate village communities into the emerging national life. The goals of community development have thus been couched in a laudable rhetoric that contains references to promoting local initiative and solidarity, increasing living standards, and bringing to rural peoples the benefits and amenities of modern life.

Unfortunately, community development programs normally can boast of little success. All too often the major products of such programs are public latrines and small fences produced and painted for the visits of government dignitaries from the towns, only to be left as unused and nonfunctional symbols of a program after the visitor leaves. Some of the most successful programs of rural development, on the other hand, have paradoxically either rejected community development symbols or violated the normal canons of community development programs. A closer examination of this paradox can help provide an understanding of the obstacles to development in the rural areas and the structural requirements of successful program planning and implementation.

Community development goals and programs have gained a distinctive identity that includes a set of norms for planning and action.[1] The norms specify general goals, units of organization, and mechanisms of implementation. The general goals emphasize changing values and attitudes of villagers, which will weaken their isolation and give them the initiative to improve themselves. High value is placed upon self-help rather than upon external government effort for the village. This also implies that the villagers' own felt needs must provide the basic substance of the goals toward which collective action is directed. The unit of organization is normally the village itself. It is assumed to be a community of interest with latent powers of mobilization for development. It is also normally assumed that the village once was a basically democratic and self-sufficient unit with capacities for mutual assistance and welfare, and that this functioning democratic community has been weakened and atrophied by the processes of colonial rule. Finally, a common mechanism for achieving the development of village communities is to provide them with a multipurpose village worker who can help villagers organize themselves for their own betterment, and can coordinate the actions of external technically specialized government agencies that have the special competence to assist villagers in bettering their own lives.

Three of the most successful rural development programs in Asia have been the Taiwan Joint Commission for Rural Reconstruction (JCRR), the East Pakistan Academy for Rural Development (EPARD), and the Malayan Ministry of Rural Development (MRD). These have been especially successful, respectively, in increasing rural incomes, mobilizing rural peoples into cooperatives that have increased incomes and greatly increased the potential for modern economic development, and in achieving a rapid build-up of the physical infrastructure that is needed for widespread economic development in the rural areas. These programs have all violated important community development norms in some respects. Both the JCRR and the EPARD have rejected the use of the village as the natural unit for development, the MRD rejected the village as the natural unit for its construction programs. All have rejected the norm of identifying a new position of a multipurpose village worker coming in from the outside to mobilize villagers and

[1] There is a large literature on community development. See, for example, United Nations, *Community Development and Economic Development*, E/CN.11/540 (Bangkok, 1960), and Ward H. Goodenough, *Cooperation in Change, An Anthropological Approach to Community Development* (New York, Russell Sage Foundation, 1963).

to coordinate external technical agencies. Finally, although all have emphasized goals and activities relevant to the villagers, they have made some relatively simple assumptions about villagers' needs. All have assumed that increased income is one of the most powerful needs and demands of the
villagers and that the specific requirements for increased income—such as a
new agricultural technology, new roads and markets, and a more rational and
economic organization of landholding—may not be easily articulated by
villagers, but are in any case relatively easy to determine.

A brief survey of these three programs will help to identify some of
the critical determinants of successful rural development. It will then be
possible to analyse more acutely how the implementation of the normal community development programs appears to have diverged considerably from
the types of actions most effective in achieving the goals of rural development.

JCRR[2]

The joint Commission for Rural Reconstruction in Taiwan was the
product of American legislation—PL 472, 80th Congress, "The China Aid
Act," April 3, 1948—and an agreement between the governments of the
United States and the National Republic of China. This specified that 10 percent of all American aid to China would be earmarked for rural reconstruction and would be administered by a five-man commission containing two
Americans appointed by the President of the United States and three Chinese
appointed by the President of the Republic of China. The joint commission
was to have wide latitude in deciding upon programs appropriate to promoting rural reconstruction in China. The initial formulation thus provided
two of the most important sources of JCRR's success. It gained long-term
financing independent of specific U.S. foreign aid missions in China, which
removed it from much of the vagaries of organizational instability in foreign
aid. Further, since it was a joint commission of high-status professionals in
agricultural development it had considerable insulation from both Chinese
and American political pressures in the field. The professional experience of
the commissioners allowed the JCRR to make decisions by playing officials of
the two governments against each other. Chinese commissioners could argue
to their government that the Americans alternately required or would not

2 This section draws especially on T. H. Shen, *Agricultural Development in Taiwan*
(Ithaca, 1965) ; John Montgomery, Rufus B. Hughes, and Raymond Davis, *Rural Develop-
ment and Political Development; The JCRR Model*, Papers in Comparative Administra-
tion, Special Series No. 7 (Washington, 1966) ; S. C. Hsieh and V. Ruttan, "Technological,
Institutional and Environmental Factors in the Growth of Rice Production: Philippines,
Thailand and Taiwan," *Food Research Institute Studies*, Vol. VII, No. 3 (1967); Chen
Cheng, *Land Reform in Taiwan* (Taipei, 1961) ; R. L. Hough and G. D. Ness, "The JCRR:
A Model for Internationally Induced Development," *International Development Review*,
Vol. X, No. 3 (September 1968).

accept certain programs, and the Americans could make the same argument to their government officers.

The JCRR first began its work on the mainland before the Communist victory, with work on land reform in Szechwan in 1948. With the Communist victory, the operation was moved to Taiwan where it immediately began intensive work on land reform and other rural development activities. The success of rural and agricultural development in Taiwan is well documented. During the decade of the 1950's Taiwan's agricultural sector grew at the rate of about 10 percent per year in real output. Every existing crop or product has shown steady and dramatic increases in both total output and both areal and human productivity. New crops have been introduced and a broad technology has been accepted. The technology, the pattern of organization and the standard of living of the rural areas have shared in and contributed significantly to the rapid over-all growth of the economy. Although it is impossible to measure precisely the relative role the JCRR played in this over-all development, it is widely recognized that its role has been a dominant one.

The major identifiable aim of the JCRR has been to increase rural incomes, to provide for rural welfare, and to promote social justice. The instrumental aspects of the aims—income and welfare—were supported in large part by the technical competence of the JCRR. The Commissioners were professional agriculturalists who had long experience in analysing and attempting to promote agricultural development. They created an organization and a staff that reflected and amplified their own technical competence. In this the JCRR had a great numerical advantage when it moved to Taiwan. The flight from the Communist victory meant that the physical magnitude of the rural development problem was reduced to about one-fiftieth of its previous size, without a proportionate reduction in the size of the technical staff. Taiwan was literally flooded with competent manpower as a result of the Communist victory on the mainland. Thus the JCRR had sufficient technical capacity to analyse the organization of rural production and to devise appropriate programs for increasing productivity.

The more expressive aspect of the aim—social justice—was supported by the political dynamics of the period. The Communist victory had provided a powerful negative demonstration of the political value of social justice. It gave urgent credence to those arguing for land reform, and was a central part of the success of these arguments in both Japan and Taiwan.[3] In addition, the political position of the Taiwanese landlords was untenable and powerless after the return of Taiwan from Japan to China. With powerful

---

[3] For the Japanese part of this argument, which was simply projected to the argument in Taiwan, see W. J. Ladejinsky, "Agrarian Revolution in Japan," *Foreign Affairs*, Vol. 38, No. 1 (October 1959), pp. 95–109; and W. M. Gilmartin and W. J. Ladejinsky, "The Promise of Agrarian Reform in Japan," *Foreign Affairs*, Vol. 26, No. 4 (January 1948), pp. 312–24.

arguments for land reform and social justice, and little or no counterargument from positions of political power, the JCRR found a friendly setting for the promotion of its value of social justice.

One of the first actions of the JCRR in Taiwan was to assist in the development of an effective land reform program. This required, first, attention to the political decision-making process, where the Commissioners could effectively use their autonomy and their alliance with reform orientations in the United States and China to propose and promote effective legislation. Next, it required intensive attention to the details of implementation. Land had to be surveyed and accurate records of utilization and ownership had to be prepared. Then farmers had to be made aware of their rights and assisted in acquiring them. Finally, farmers needed assistance with credit and other forms of financial resources to make the redistribution viable.

The land reform program moved from 1948 to 1952 through a variety of stages effectively programmed and integrated to produce widespread ownership of economically-sized holdings. Land reform began with a rent reduction and the prescription of tenant contracts, through the sale of government-owned land to the tillers, to a program of forced sale of lands above the maximum size and the resale of this land to small or landless farmers, with previous tenants gaining options on the land they had tilled. By all measures it was successful both economically and in terms of its social justice aim. From 1948 to 1956 owner-operators had grown from about 33 percent to about 57 percent of all farming families, as 200,000 families gained new land ownership. Pure tenants declined from 36 percent to 16 percent of all farm families. The widespread ownership brought powerful economic incentives for small farmers to increase their productivity, since the rewards of work would go directly to them.

Following the land reform program, which took a large share of JCRR's staff and energies in its early years, the Commission moved on to a variety of other activities. The Farmers' Associations that had been created by the Japanese were reorganized into multifunctional associations for credit, marketing, retailing, and extension work. They were democratically organized, using farmers in leadership positions and technically competent local managers for what became autonomous and individually responsible associations. JCRR promoted the reorganization and rationalization of agricultural credit for the entire island. It promoted a wide mange of new or improved techniques for increasing rural income and welfare. These ranged from animal husbandry and artificial insemination programs for hogs, the interplanting of papayas, the continued improvement of rice varieties, the provision of more fertilizer, a land consolidation program, the assistance in planning and implementing new large-scale irrigation systems, reforestation, and attention to home economics and welfare with instruction in hygiene, nutrition, construction of efficient stoves, and a close articulation with a well-organized rural health agency.

JCRR's work has been highly instrumental and pragmatic. With a concern for increased income and welfare, which are easily measured, it has been able to concentrate on effective programs and has been sufficiently flexible to discard activities that are demonstrably not effective. For example, early attention to building community halls and organizing village associations for solidarity was discarded when it was found that this was not effective in promoting increased productivity and welfare, and when the farmers themselves showed little interest in this type of activity. In most cases, the JCRR has worked with specific groups based on shared economic interests rather than with village-types of units. In addition, JCRR worked by providing technical assistance to groups that were willing and able to meet part of the cost themselves.

In summary, the JCRR has worked with economically defined groups, not villages as units of action. It worked in important ways to destroy the old village communities that were dominated by landlord interests. It has not been concerned with changing values and attitudes, but with increasing productivity, welfare and justice, all of which have received simple but effective operational definitions. Its rehtoric gave little emphasis to "felt needs" and "self-help" but its programmatic decisions carried it into activities judged successful only if they met the clear needs of the rural peoples, as measured by the willingness of those people to give their time, energy, and money to the activity.

EPARD[4]

The East Pakistan Academy for Rural Development at Comilla evolved a unique and successful program for dealing with the extremely backward economic structure of rural East Pakistan. Its antecedants lay in a normal community development type of program, the Village AID (Agricultural and Industrial Development) Program. Village AID had focused attention on villages as units of organization, used multipurpose village workers who were to help villagers identify their felt needs, and who were to help coordinate existing government technical services to meet these needs. It spoke of self-help and of helping villagers to break away from their established traditions of lethargy and impotence and to generate the initiative that

[4] This section draws on the published annual reports of the Academy, the author's personal interviews at the Academy, and the following publications: Elliott Tepper, "Changing Patterns of Administration in Rural East Pakistan," Asian Studies Center, Michigan State University, Occasional Paper, No. 5 (August 1966) ; "Rural Development in East Pakistan, Speeches by Akhter Hameed Kahn," Michigan State University, Asian Studies Center Occasional Paper, No. 2.

would make them a part of the modern world. Some of its major products were latrines and fences.

In the mid-1950s the Ford Foundation began active assistance to the Village AID program, especially through a plan to create two academies (one in East Pakistan and one in West Pakistan) to help train rural government officers in the business of development administration. Akhter Hameed Khan was selected to direct the East Pakistan Academy in Comilla. He developed a team, which then spent some months in study and training at Michigan State University. When it returned to East Pakistan, it established itself in an Ashram just outside of Comilla and began training government officers.

In its first training program the academy staff met a significant failure, from which it began to evolve its new program. The instruction was roundly criticized by the officers in attendance for being too textbookish and abstract. These officers could see the problems of low income and low productivity and wanted to know how to overcome them. Since the staff itself had had little contact with village life (with the important exception of the director), it began a program of study in the villages and discussions with village people to attempt to understand what were the local obstacles to increasing productivity. Two important things were discovered. One was that the villagers were well aware of their problems and their needs; these were primarily for water control to provide for cultivation in the dry season and for credit. Water for the dry season was as obvious and direct a need of the peasants in East Pakistan as was land reform for the peasants in Taiwan. The other discovery was that the village organization generally militated against the kind of rational organization of water control that was required.

The village itself contained a number of mutually conflicting groups: land-owning *rentiers*, owner-operator farmers, and landless laborers. The extent of cooperation among these groups was extremely low. The more traditional form of organization found family groups relatively closed and with little lateral cooperation and integration; each group was oriented upwards to individual government agencies or to superordinate landlord families. This meant that farmers with contiguous plots were unable to cooperate with one another sufficiently to make the acquisition of pumps economical and to make the distribution of water feasible. Government programs had previously made pumps available, but only to individual farmers, whose plots were too small to make them economical. Farmers had no real capacity to organize themselves into stable long-lasting units of like economic interest to make collective acquisition of pumps and distribution of water possible. The land was rich, but the social organization rendered the farmers poor.

The Academy offered pumps, but only on the condition that the farmers would organize into cooperatives of owner-operators, would save money regularly, and would make themselves collectively responsible for their individual actions. A series of agricultural failures in a few villages made groups of farmers from these villages sufficiently attuned to the necessity of reorganization so that they created the necessary cooperatives, pushed forward their own leaders, and organized the collective responsibility of water acquisition and distribution. The initial projects were highly successful and provided powerful demonstration effects for the other villages.

In the proliferation of village cooperatives that followed, the pattern of the Academy's action became distinctive. Academy staff provided technical and organizational support from the outside, but insisted on the formation of disciplined groups that elected their own leaders in the villages. The elected leaders spent one day a week in the Academy in discussion with other village leaders and with government officers. Common problems were identified and programs for their solution were formulated, always to be tested against performance in the field. The multi-purpose village level worker of the normal community development program was absent. And rather than use the entire village as the unit of organization, groups were formed on the basis of their common economic interests. Following the formation of cooperatives of owner-operators, other groups of tailors, trishaw drivers, and transportation workers and other like groups were formed.

The Academy continued its formal training of government officers, integrated with discussions with leaders of the various groups sponsored by the Academy. In addition, a small experimental plot was developed for the adaptation of a new agricultural technology to the local setting. The cooperatives became multi-purpose organizations, engaging in financing (through collective responsibility for credit), marketing and purchasing.

One of the major programs developed and promoted by the Academy was a rural construction program for the dry season. In what has become a widely known program, East Pakistan experimented with a project that used surplus U.S. wheat, provided under the PL 480 program, to finance rural construction. The wheat was sold at reduced prices on the rural market to provide funds to pay for labor in the construction of roads and drainage and irrigation projects. The program worked effectively without the inflationary pressures that many economists predicted and provided considerable additional income and higher living standards to rural Pakistanis.

The program of the Academy was developed through close attention to the local organization of production. It evolved a series of constraints, rewards, and punishments, and evaluating mechanisms specifically designed for the distinctive local setting. In this it demonstrated the same type of technical competence that JCRR had from its professional staff. The Academy resisted government pressures to extend its program widely and quickly. Rather it developed from its pilot experience, moving only gradually to encompass a larger and larger area, adjusting its control procedures to the specific problems it encountered with each successive step. Its external support from the Ford Foundation, and the political influence of the director, gave it the same critical insulation from economically nonrational pressures that JCRR had from its external financing and from its high-status staff.

MRD[5]

Malaya's Rural Development Program, developed by the newly created Ministry of Rural Development in 1959–60, emerged out of the specific political processes that brought the country to independence in 1957. It used the explosive situation provided by the delicate balance of Malay and Chinese populations to mobilize energies and direct them to a massive and very effective program of rural construction. The explosive situation that had powerful mobilizing potential was primarily a result of three sets of forces: economic, ethnic, and political.

In the first place, Malaya was a wealthy country. Under British colonial rule the territory had developed into the world's leading producer of tin and natural rubber. Its real output per capita was just below that of Singapore; the two are second only to Japan in all of Asia, and about two or three times the level of the other states in Southeast Asia. Along with its highly productive export economy came a highly developed communications structure and an efficient bureaucracy. The cases of Burma and Indonesia, however, indicate that a naturally wealthy economy is not sufficient for a successful development effort. Still, if that economy could be held together and directed to constructive ends, it could provide rich resources for a development program.

In addition to creating a productive export economy, British rule also produced a highly unbalanced socioeconomic structure. By the time of independence only about 50 percent of the population was indigenous Malay, about 40 percent was Chinese and about 10 percent Indian. For the most part the Chinese and Indians were concentrated in the modern export sector, living in urban areas or on the large rubber estates. Although many Malays had also moved into this sector, Malays were more concentrated in the traditional peasant village economy, growing rice and coconuts, engaging in fishing, and also in a form of smallholding rubber production that was fairly well integrated with traditional peasant agriculture. Malays and Chinese thus differed considerably in their location and economic activities. When to these differences are added the differences of language, religion (Malays are Muslim, Chinese are a mixture of Buddhist-Taoist-Confucianists), dress, and diet (pork, a delicacy for the Chinese, is repulsively unclean for Malays), the situation becomes one in which a series of significant social differences are crystallized along ethnic lines; the situation is an explosive one.

[5] I have dealt extensively with this issue in a larger study of the Ministry of Rural Development, in *Bureaucracy and Rural Development in Malaysia* (Berkeley, 1967).

Out of this considerable difference a unique type of politics developed, which can best be described as the politics of accommodation. From the end of the Japanese occupation in 1945, the process of political development saw a number of interrelated trends. The British began a withdrawal from power and increasingly, but gradually, passed self-rule to the emerging Malayan leadership. The process also required considerable popular mobilization, but given the ethnic differences this could only be accomplished along ethnic lines. That is, the major parties that demonstrated any viability in the national mobilization were essentially ethnic parties: Malay, Chinese, and Indian. In an early and quite fortuitous development in 1952, two of the ethnic parties, a Malay and a Chinese, formed an alliance to contest the first election—a small election for seats on the municipal council of the capital city, Kuala Lumpur. The alliance proved highly successful and the following year became a national Alliance Party, which went on to win all of the subsequent municipal council elections that were held throughout the country. The Alliance was joined by an Indian party and won an overwhelming victory in the first national election in 1955, which produced a Federal Legislative Council with an elected majority. In subsequent elections this Alliance has managed to maintain control over the government, though with varying success and appeal.

The Alliance presented a number of structural advantages, especially given the explosive situation of ethnic differences. It could mobilize individual voters on the basis of their highly particularistic ethnic identities, which were at once the most important and the most potentially destructive identities. Then in the relative seclusion of the executive committees it could arrange the distribution of seats and the mutual protection of interest that would effectively accommodate the diverse interests of the ethnic groups. Party leaders could argue forcefully for the interests of their own groups, without requiring that they take public stances from which compromise would be impossible. In this manner the Malays received certain guaranteed preferences in administrative positions in the civil service, while Chinese received guaranteed protection of their economic interests. Malay control in political and administrative matters was traded for Chinese control in economic matters. The structural advantages and the success of the Alliance also placed limits on the types of economic policies and development programs that could be pursued.

This entire process was strengthened by the Communist insurgency, which began in 1948 and was officially declared ended in 1960. The insurgents were primarily Chinese, who engaged in a terroristic movement that attempted to disrupt the economy and to drive the British out. Against this background the more constitutional development demonstrated to the masses that parliamentary processes were more effective in promoting their individual interests than was insurgency. It also hastened the process of independence, as the British moved quickly to undercut the Communist drive against foreign rule by passing power to indigenous leaders, in some cases moving more rapidly than indigenous leaders themselves.

Alongside the political development came a series of experimental attempts to change the character of the economy from a colonial export economy to a more nationally integrated and more highly productive economy. Among the experiments were a series of activities based on the model of community development programs. Under British direction these were essentially programs directed at changing the values and attitudes of the Malay community. They emphasized felt needs and self-help and organized a series of road-building and community hall building programs using village labor. In large part the attempt was to recreate the solidarity, self-sufficiency, and initiative that, supposedly, characterized the traditional village community.

With the creation of the Rural Development Program in 1959–60, the old community development programs were explicitly rejected. The new Ministry argued that the rural areas were poor not because they lacked initiative or the proper values, but because the government in the past had neglected them and turned its attention primarily to the urban areas and the export economy. The new program rejected the idea of self-help in the initial phase of the development program, arguing that the government could and would build up the physical and social infrastructure that modern development required. The rural people should turn their attention to their own forms of production and government would do the things it was explicitly capable of doing.

The Rural Development Program had a relatively limited set of goals. It was essentially concerned with increasing the output of goods and services that government agencies were technically competent to produce and to direct an increasing proportion of these to the rural areas. The success of this program has been quite outstanding. It has involved first a rapid increase in government allocations to rural social and economic development, especially evident in education, public works, and land development. Not only have allocations been increased rapidly, but there has also been a rapid increase in the ability of the bureaucracy to spend the amounts allocated. The physical impact of the program has been quite dramatic. In education the society has moved quickly from having a third of its primary-school-aged children in school to having practically all in school at the primary level, and a rapidly increasing proportion in school at the secondary and post-secondary level. The construction program has produced a wealth of activities with new schools, roads, bridges, health centers, village wells, communications networks, and other amenities being built especially in the rural areas, and a land development program that opens large new tracts of land and settles landless rural people on that land. Unlike most countries in the region, this frenetic activity goes on in the most remote rural areas as well as in and around the urban areas.

The distinctiveness of this approach is brought out clearly in the contrast with Indonesia and Burma, both of which had relatively rich export economies when they achieved independence following the Japanese occupation and the Allied victory. These countries were more concerned with achieving a rapid and radical change in the character of the economy, and were not constrained as was Malaya by the economic position of such a large minority. With much smaller Chinese populations in Indonesia (about 3 percent of the population) and Burma (Chinese were about 1 percent and Indians were less than 10 percent), nothing comparable to Malayan political accommodation emerged. Without this type of accommodation the Burmese and Indonesian governments could move with impunity against the economic interests of local Chinese, as well as those of other foreign owner powers. These moves have been relatively effective, but at the price of wholesale destruction of productive capacity.

The political and bureaucratic determinants of Malaya's success are relatively easy to perceive. In the first place the political situation placed constraints on government leaders that made certain types of activity completely unacceptable, but at the same time provided massive popular support for programs that were viable alternatives. That is, the community development approach was rejected largely because it was a chronic insult to the Malay population. It essentially said that Malays are lazy and improvident and need to change their values and attitudes in order to advance themselves in the modern world. In large measure the program had said that Malays must become like Chinese in order to stay alive in the modern world. This might be acceptable for a colonial district officer who had a paternal love for his rural peoples, but it was unacceptable to indigenous leaders who required popular votes to gain power. Other attempts to move with legal proscriptions against private urban economic interests, similar to those found in Burma and Indonesia, were unacceptable given the demands of political accommodation.

On the other hand, the program of physical and social construction in the rural areas provided advantages for everyone. It demonstrated to the Malays that their government was concerned for them and capable of providing services for them. In this way it drew them into the modern nation-state and gained their support. At the same time, Chinese economic interests, whether as contractors or simple retail merchants, benefited by the burst of economic activity. To the extent that government could show its effectiveness in promoting this type of activity, it could gain large-scale popular support, which gave it considerable power to act against what might be the conservative and obstructing character of the bureaucracy.

Although the bureaucracy that had emerged under the British was an efficient one, it was also relatively conservative. This was in part a product of the subculture that emerged in the colonial bureaucracy, emphasizing integrity, thoroughness and procedural purity. But it was also a product of the specific structure that had emerged under the British. This was a structure of increasing centralization in decision-making. A great deal of initiative could and did come from below, especially from the level of the district officer, but this had to be screened through successively higher and successively more conservative layers at the upper levels. The conservatism derived in part from the dominance of fiscal policy over economic policy. The Financial Secretariat, as usual, developed into one of the most powerful arms of government. Its major concern was with the balancing of revenues and expenditures. This produced a proclivity to overestimate expenditures and underestimate revenues, which in turn produced a procedural obstacle to initiative from lower levels of the bureaucracy.

The Ministry of Rural Development engaged in a series of reforms or reorganizations that removed many obstacles both to initiative and to lower level responses to demands for more output. In the first place the creation of the Ministry was a part of the process that shifted decision-making on economic development policy matters from the exclusive dominance of the Finance Ministry to the center of the nation's political power, the office of the Prime Minister. This set the stage for the active injection of political power into the immediate control over the planning and implementation of development policy. In the second place, the Ministry organized new coordinating bodies for government agencies at Federal, State, and District levels. These coordinating bodies, the Rural Development Committees, were composed of all heads of technical agencies at that level, plus elected members to state and federal legislatures at the respective levels. This had the double effect of concentrating political power and popular support on the development program, and of creating a new communications network within the bureaucracy. Under the Rural Development Plan, which created the coordinating bodies, officers were given instructions for planning and programming the new development effort. These contained the injunction to reduce correspondence and to use the telephone and the weekly meeting to effect the coordination of activities among agencies that was required to increase bureaucratic output.

The structure with its new coordinating procedures worked well, primarily because the Minister of Rural Development put a great deal of time and energy into activating and controlling the program. Through a series of frequent visits and briefing sessions at all levels, he was able to make a relatively clear assessment of the quality of performance of various offices and officers. Technical obstructions could be cleared with his intervention, and he had considerable powers to reward energetic officers and to punish the recalcitrant.

The success of this program was in some respects more limited than the successes in Taiwan or Pakistan. The success lay primarily in increasing the output of existing government services to the rural areas. It was primarily a building program, and although the importance of this cannot be minimized for the long-term promotion of economic development, the immediate and specific impact on productivity especially in the rural areas is more problematic.[6] In part the success is a function of the limited aims of the program. It is also, however, like the other two programs in its instrumental orientation and in its pragmatic adjustment of appropriate techniques to a given situation that is clearly understood by the program leaders. Like the other programs, it has rejected the model and the canons of community development for its own procedures, developed in and closely attuned to the conditions in which it exists.

LESSONS OF THE PARADOX

From these successes we can gain some understanding of the determinants of both success and the type of subversion indicated by the latrine and fence construction of many community development programs. Five points seem central to the analysis.

1. In the first place these three programs have all had considerable political power and influence behind them. The JCRR and the EPARD had some external financing and had either collective (JCRR) or individual (EPARD) leaders with considerable political influence. The MRD was directed by one of the two most powerful of the Malayan leaders. This allowed each to mobilize resources and to direct their utilization to rational and instrumental activities. The normal community development program is more often in a position of much lower priority relative to other activities. This means less resources, which is then reflected in lower quality of staff, higher staff turnover, and less insulation from external forces that are irrational from the point of view of developing rural areas.

2. The power issue is clearly reflected in the position of the multipurpose village worker who is charged with coordinating existing services at the village level in the normal community development program. Coordination requires power. Individual agencies must be subordinated to a common plan and a common program of action. The multipurpose village worker is normally

---

[6] In the area of rice production the construction program has clearly had a positive impact. This is easily seen in average yields per hectare for Malaysia, compared with the rest of Southeast Asia. The average for the region is about 1 ton per hectare. Malaysia has had a steadily increasing level of yields, reaching about 2.5 tons per hectare in the mid-1960s. This has largely been brought about by extensive national investment in irrigation and flood control. For raw data on rice in Malaysia see PEE Teck Yew, *A Statistical Source Book on Malayan Agriculture* 2 volumes (Kuala Lumpur, 1967).

placed in a position in which he has no power to direct other agents and thus must rely on persuasion to coordinate efforts. Unfortunately, because the community development programs are normally low-priority activities, their local workers often are less qualified technically than the agents whose activities they are charged to coordinate. This naturally weakens their persuasive power. With neither the power nor the technical capacity to coordinate, the village worker works exclusively with the villagers, attempting to induce them to perform some types of visible activity that will please the community development superiors. Fences and latrines emerge.

In the case of the MRD, the district officer was given the coordinating capacity at the lower levels. He had both considerable technical and administrative capacity, and had behind him the great power of the Ministry, which demanded cooperation from each of the individual technical services. In East Pakistan the EPARD was given technical directive authority over the individual agencies in the Thana, the local administrative level. In addition, the education and experience of the Academy director and his staff gave them the status and technical capacity to effect the coordination to which they were administratively entitled. JCRR had primarily its technical competence, plus financial power with which to effect a coordination. Their plans and proposals could be accepted by other agencies both because they were sound and because they could be financed. This put the JCRR in a position where it could assist the individual agencies in doing what they knew to be useful, without threatening the integrity of those agencies.

The use of the multipurpose village worker normally shows another type of weakness. It is a commonplace that bureaucrats in the new states have become separated from the village communities by their education, their experience, and by their mobility aspirations. Too often the village worker is a person with some education in the language of the ex-metropolitan power, large aspirations for the high-status bureaucratic positions and little interest in, knowledge of, or sympathy with the village community. His preferences would be to work for a higher status and higher priority agency, but his qualifications direct him to the lower positions in community development. Thus not only does he lack the power and the technical capacity to coordinate, he lacks the social-psychological characteristics that would make him an effective agent of change and coordination in the rural areas.

3. None of these successful programs used the village as the unit of development. It is probably one of the great mistakes of the normal community development program to see the village as a viable unit in which to mobilize initiative for self-sustained local development. The traditional village may well have been a community of interest with considerable solidarity, insulated by its isolation, and containing effective internal mechanisms for the resolution of the conflicts that normally exist in communities. The colonial experience, and even more the thrust for development in the independence

period, have broken much of that isolation. Market forces and political forces have entered to produce new types of conflicts and new groups of interests. Thus when the relatively powerless and somewhat ineffective village level worker attempts to mobilize some kind of collective village action, the only action he can generate is that on which there is little or no disagreement. This almost inevitably means projects that are of little real interest to any of the villagers—latrines and fences.

There is, however, another type of activity that shows another type of goal, subversion in community development programs. One of the highly perceptive Indian evaluations of Indian community development programs pointed out that village labor is often used in community development projects that help only the wealthy landowners of the village. Thus the projects have become tools by which the powerful villagers have mobilized poorer villagers to provide free labor for the benefit of the more powerful. Coercive labor mobilization and nonfunctional symbolic activity appear to be two major patterns of goal subversion that derive from the attempt to use the village as the unit for development.

4. The aims of community development programs, stated in terms of changing values and attitudes, contain a number of inherent weaknesses. The basic weakness for development programming is the inability to measure success and failure, or to measure performance more acutely. Group activity, for whatever purpose, often comes to represent in the official reports the emergence of a new and more appropriate set of attitudes. Without the ability to measure performance, there is no ability to control programs and to direct them toward their goals. One of the major advantages of the MRD program lay in its limited aims, infrastructure construction. The procedures for such construction were well understood and the output was clearly visible. It was possible to program stages in advance and to measure progress at any point against the planned stages. This gave the Ministry great capacities to evaluate rationally and effectively the performance of individual officers and agencies. The combination of accurate evaluation and power to apply rewards and punishments provided the program with a highly effective control procedure.

The JCRR and the EPARD defined their goals in the simple and pragmatic terms of income and productivity. The welfare and justice aims were similarly defined. This made it easy to determine which programs were more successful and which were less successful, giving both programs an effective capacity to direct their resources and energies in a rational manner.

5. Finally, each of the successful programs was locally developed and adjusted to local conditions. None resulted from the application of a model to a given situation. In each case the leadership came from people knowledgeable of the local political, economic and social conditions. Further, these were people highly involved and committed in the long run to the situation in which they found themselves. This is probably one of the most critical conditions of

success. It is also the most difficult to specify in any general terms. There will certainly be no disagreement with the argument that programs should be suited to local conditions; the problem is to organize programs so that they will have the organizational and personal capacity to analyze the local situation accurately and then develop specific lines of action that will have the most leverage on the local situation.

INDEX